Advanced ColdFusion 4.0 Application Development

Advanced ColdFusion 4.0 Application Development

Ben Forta
with Nate Weiss, Michael Dinowitz,
Ashley King, Gerry Libertelli, Jonathan Bellack

201 West 103rd Street, Indianapolis, Indiana 46290

Advanced ColdFusion 4.0 Application Development

Copyright © 1999 by Que

International Standard Book Number: 0-7897-1810-3

Library of Congress Catalog Card Number: 98-86973

Printed in the United States of America

First Printing: *December 1998*

00   99   4   3

Trademarks

Warning and Disclaimer

EXECUTIVE EDITOR
Bryan Gambrel

ACQUISITIONS EDITOR
Angela Kozlowski

MANAGING EDITOR
Patrick Kanouse

PROJECT EDITOR
Andrew Cupp

COPY EDITORS
Chuck Hutchinson
Tonya Maddox

INDEXER
Rebecca Hornyack

PROOFREADER
Wendy Ott

TECHNICAL EDITORS
Jason Wright
Emily Kim
Ken Fricklas
Truman H. Esmond III

SOFTWARE DEVELOPMENT SPECIALIST
Todd Pfeffer

INTERIOR DESIGN
Dan Armstrong

COVER DESIGN
Ruth Lewis

LAYOUT TECHNICIANS
Brandon Allen
Tim Osborn
Staci Somers
Mark Walchle

Contents at a Glance

V | Appendixes

Table of Contents

About the Author

Ben Forta is Allaire Corporation's product evangelist for the ColdFusion product line. Ben has over 15 years of experience in the computer industry and spent 6 years as part of the development team responsible for creating OnTime, one of the most successful calendar and group-scheduling products, with over one million users worldwide. Ben is the author of the popular *The ColdFusion 4.0 Web Application Construction Kit* (now in its third edition) and the more recent *Advanced ColdFusion 4.0 Application Development* (both published by Que). He coauthored the official Allaire ColdFusion training courses, writes a regular column on ColdFusion development, and now spends a considerable amount of time lecturing and speaking on ColdFusion and Internet application development worldwide. Born in London, England, and educated in London, New York, and Los Angeles, Ben now lives in Oak Park, Michigan, with his wife, Marcy, and their four children. Ben welcomes your email at ben@forta.com and invites you to visit his own ColdFusion Web site at http://www.forta.com/cf.

Nate Weiss is the technical director at International Commerce Exchange Systems (ICES), a direct-marketing service for buyers and sellers. Nate used ColdFusion to design the Web, fax, and email services at the core of the company's suite of services, as well as the back-end system that serves as the company's worldwide account management, data-entry, and reporting mechanism. Visit the ICES Web site at http://www.icesinc.com, or Nate's own Web site at http://www.nateweiss.com. Nate can be reached via email at eponymous@nateweiss.com.

Michael Dinowitz is head of House of Fusion, a consulting firm specializing in ColdFusion-, dynamic-, and database-driven applications. His work focuses on merging ColdFusion with other technologies/languages and using them to their maximum potential. He has been with ColdFusion almost since its start and hosts the New York ColdFusion User Group. Michael has worked on sites ranging from the Publisher's Clearing House commerce engine to the Individual Investor financial site, with many other works in between. Many of his CFX tags, modules, and applications are available to help ColdFusion programmers everywhere. As a collector of information, he hosts a site at http://www.houseoffusion.com with lots of ColdFusion-related information.

Ashley King is a software engineer at Allaire Corporation and is the former president and founder of Aspx Interactive Media (CreativeAspect, Inc.), where he developed the MrPost! Web Messaging Server for ColdFusion. Ashley began his fateful foray into the programming world 13 years ago when he developed games and graphics software for Timex Sinclair 1000 and Commodore VIC-20 computers. He continued his programming career at BDM Corporation and as a contractor. Ashley later worked as a graphic artist, radio DJ, and touring musician, releasing a CD and founding one of the first Web-based music stores with his consulting company. Ashley now lives in Lexington, Massachusetts, after wandering from his native Albuquerque, New Mexico. When he's not too far behind schedule, Ashley formulates theories on paranormal experiences and writes music. He can be reached via email on the Internet at ashley@aspx.com or via the World Wide Web at http://www.trey.com.

Gerry Libertelli has been the Managing Director of G. Triad Development Corporation since December of 1994. He is the driving force behind G. Triad's success in the network engineering and applications development marketplace. Mr. Libertelli was formerly the technical director at Smart Money Interactive, where he was responsible for all engineering and technical issues involving the production rollout of Smart Money Interactive, the World Wide Web site for *Smart Money* magazine. Prior to *Smart Money*, Gerry was a project manager at Charles Schwab and Company. He shared responsibility for several in-house projects building Schwab's electronic investment products, including Streetsmart (MS Windows) and Equalizer (DOS) software and the Telebroker system. Mr. Libertelli has held decision-making positions in systems maintenance and support, field marketing of interactive services, telecom management, and user interface testing for several corporations. Gerry has a B.A. in political science from Seton Hall University.

Jonathan Bellack has been developing Web sites on UNIX and Windows NT systems since 1994. He is currently the technical director at SmartMoney.com. He has developed Internet products as a consultant for publishing companies including Times Mirror Magazines and Consumers Union (the publishers of *Consumer Reports Magazine*). He also spent over a year at Wolff New Media, creators of the ill-fated NetBooks and Your Personal Net. Jonathan has a degree from Yale University. He can be reached via email at `jonathan@bellack.com`.

Acknowledgments

Ben Forta

This book was created in response to the requests of readers of my first ColdFusion book, *The ColdFusion 4.0 Web Application Construction Kit*—you know who you are. And so, first and foremost, I must thank you all for the inspiration. I hope this is what you were looking for.

Thanks to everyone at Macmillan Computer Publishing for making this book a reality. In particular, special thanks to my Acquisitions Editor, Angela Kozlowski, for all her time, patience, advice; for not letting things fall through the cracks; and for keeping us authors on some semblance of a schedule (no easy task at all). This book is my fourth collaboration with Angela, and the word *collaboration* is not an exaggeration. We could not have done it (neither this book, nor the previous ones) without her.

Thanks to my coauthors—Jonathan Bellack, Ashley King, Gerry Libertelli, Mike Dinowitz, and Nate Weiss—for their outstanding contributions. This book is as much theirs as it is mine.

Thanks to everyone at Allaire for all their hard work creating ColdFusion 4. The Internet application development community is indebted to you all. In particular, thanks to Jeremy Allaire, Tom Colutti, Seth Horan, Jack Lull, Patrick Muzila, Randy Nielsen, Steve Penella, and Sim Simeonov for the support they gave the authors and editors as this book evolved.

The accompanying CD-ROM contains a collection of some of the best ColdFusion add-on tags and utilities I have found. In addition to serving as examples of what ColdFusion can do, these tags will be of great value to all ColdFusion developers. A special thank you to all the developers who contributed tags. Unfortunately, there are too many of them to thank individually, but full credit is given in the documentation on the CD-ROM. If you find any of these tags or utilities useful, I urge you to email the developers directly to thank them.

A special thank you to my parents, Arye and Chana Forta, for all they have done for me over the years, including imparting values by example, encouraging my independence, teaching me to think, and imbuing me with a love for books. Me, an author...I guess the apple does not fall far from the tree after all.

And most importantly, even though she insists there is no need for me to thank her publicly again, I must thank my wonderful wife Marcy. Anything I am, anything I have become, and anything I will be, is thanks to her. Marcy, for all your encouragement, sacrifices, support, love, and so much more, thank you.

Tell Us What You Think!

As the reader of this book, *you* are our most important critic and commentator. We value your opinion and want to know what we're doing right, what we could do better, what areas you'd like to see us publish in, and any other words of wisdom you're willing to pass our way.

As the Executive Editor for the Client/Server Database team at Macmillan Computer Publishing, I welcome your comments. You can fax, email, or write me directly to let me know what you did or didn't like about this book—as well as what we can do to make our books stronger.

Please note that I cannot help you with technical problems related to the topic of this book, and that due to the high volume of mail I receive, I might not be able to reply to every message.

When you write, please be sure to include this book's title and author as well as your name and phone or fax number. I will carefully review your comments and share them with the author and editors who worked on the book.

Fax: 317-817-7070

Email: cs_db@mcp.com

Mail: Bryan Gambrel
          Client/Server Database
          Macmillan Computer Publishing
          201 West 103rd Street
          Indianapolis, IN 46290 USA

Introduction

Who Should Use This Book

ColdFusion is the world's leading cross-platform Web application development tool. While ColdFusion is an easy (and fun) product to learn, some of its more advanced concepts and technologies require ColdFusion experience.

This book is written for ColdFusion programmers. If you have yet to write ColdFusion code, this is not the only book you need. For starters, grab a copy of *The ColdFusion 4.0 Web Application Construction Kit* (Que Publishing, ISBN 0-7897-1809-X). That book will teach you everything you need to get up and running (including extensive coverage of prerequisite technologies such as Internet fundamentals, the basics of application and database design, and the SQL language). It will also teach you everything you need to write real-world Web-based applications.

The book you are holding in your hands is designed to pick up where that book leaves off. If you have ColdFusion programming experience (or are about to become an expert), this book will enhance your expertise with the knowledge you need to take your applications to the next level.

ColdFusion 4, the latest version of ColdFusion, introduces many new high-end technologies designed to let you create highly secure, scalable, and extensible applications. This book will teach you how these technologies work, how they are used, and how to incorporate them into your applications.

All this book's authors are programmers. Most develop or maintain massive Internet or intranet sites built entirely upon ColdFusion technology. The information in this book is based on the real-world experiences of these developers, allowing you to leverage years of hard-earned knowledge and experience within your own applications.

How to Use This Book

This book is not designed to be read sequentially from cover to cover, although you are more than welcome to do so. Rather, this book is organized into logical sections designed to address specific needs or problems. As such, each section stands on its own, allowing you to start at any section or chapter to obtain the information you need.

The books is divided into four sections:

Part I: Scalability   Part I of this book addresses application scalability. You learn what scalability actually is, how fault-tolerance and load-balancing technologies are used to guarantee application uptime, and how to use these technologies within your applications.

Chapter 1, "Monitoring Server Performance," introduces the basics of scalability by teaching you how to determine just how scalable your ColdFusion servers actually are. You learn how to use the built-in performance monitoring tools and how to pinpoint the source of scalability problems.

Chapter 2, "Different Ways to Scale," explains just what you can (and should) do to ensure that your applications and servers scale. You learn what works, what does not, and what to avoid at all costs.

Chapter 3, "Server Clustering Using Bright Tiger," teaches you how to use the bundled Bright Tiger ClusterCATS technology. ClusterCATS establishes server clusters that intelligently provide fault-tolerance and dynamic load balancing. (Note, however, that Bright Tiger ClusterCATS is only bundled with the Enterprise version of ColdFusion Application Server.)

Because session information is usually very server-specific, creating server clusters (or server farms) requires that you rethink how you manage session information. Chapter 4, "Managing Client State," teaches you how to manage sessions and session state across a cluster.

Part II: Security   In Part II you learn how to employ advanced security techniques and concepts in your applications.

Chapter 5, "Security Options," discusses the different techniques used to create and deploy secure Web-based applications. You learn what security features ColdFusion provides and how to determine which options are right for your application.

In Chapter 6, "The User Authentication Framework," you learn how to use ColdFusion's advanced security framework to build secure and robust applications with sophisticated access control. ColdFusion provides a series of tags and functions that are used within your application to interact with the framework; they are covered in detail as well.

Chapter 7, "Securing Specific Features and Components," covers securing specific parts of the ColdFusion development environment and the creation of server sandboxes. This includes securing your server so that developers only have access to the features they need. As such, this chapter will be of particular interest to ISPs, IT managers, or anyone who has to manage a server shared by multiple developers.

In Chapter 8, "Integration with NOS Security," you learn how to take advantage of security features built in to your underlying operating system.

Part III: Extending ColdFusion   ColdFusion is a highly extensible and flexible platform for application development and deployment. This section covers many of the new technologies that you can use to extend your applications.

Chapter 9, "Creating Custom Tags," teaches you how to write CFML language extensions in CFML. You learn how to pass attributes to tags, how to return data, and how to create complex tag sets made up of base and child tags.

In Chapter 10, "Writing CFX Tags in Visual C++," you learn how to extend ColdFusion using the CFAPI. You discover how to use the Microsoft Visual C++ ColdFusion tag wizards and how to write tags that can deliver a whole new level of flexibility and power to your ColdFusion applications.

While CFAPI is officially supported only in C and C++, it is possible to write CFX tags in other languages too. Chapter 11, "Writing CFX Tags in Delphi," teaches you how to use the CFAPI with Borland's popular Delphi development environment.

Chapter 12, "Extending ColdFusion with COM/DCOM," introduces COM and DCOM objects. These controls can be written in many languages, including C, C++, Visual Basic, Delphi, and Java. You can plug these objects into your ColdFusion code using the <CFOBJECT> tag.

Chapter 13, "Extending ColdFusion with CORBA," introduces CORBA technology. You learn about CORBA objects, how ORBs work, and how to take advantage of distributed processing using CORBA and the <CFOBJECT> tag.

Chapter 14, "Customizing ColdFusion Studio," teaches you to how to customize and extend the ColdFusion Studio development environment. You learn keyboard shortcuts, as well as how to change toolbars and how to build your own tag editor dialogs.

Chapter 15, "Scripting ColdFusion Studio," introduces another way to extend the ColdFusion Studio environment. ColdFusion Studio 4 includes a sophisticated object model that lets you programmatically manipulate the environment by writing scripts in JScript and VBScript. You learn how the object model works, what it can do, and how to take advantage of this powerful new feature.

Part IV: Advanced Application Development   Part IV covers some of the more advanced ColdFusion development technologies. Among other things, you learn how to distribute processing between servers, how to use regular expressions, and how to manage the system registry.

Chapter 16, "Using WDDX to Create Distributed Applications," introduces the Web Dynamic Data eXchange standard and teaches you how to use it to share data between different servers.

Chapter 17, "Advanced WDDX Integration," builds upon this knowledge by showing you how you can use WDDX to communicate with other development systems (such as ASP).

Chapter 18, "ColdFusion Scripting," introduces the ColdFusion <CFSCRIPT> tag. <CFSCRIPT> allows you to replace blocks of tag-based ColdFusion code with a more concise script-based interface. This technique will appeal primarily to developers who are comfortable working in other scripting languages, such as Perl and JavaScript.

In Chapter 19, "Structured Error and Retry Handling," you learn how to create try and catch blocks to give you total control over what happens when errors occur. You learn how to create custom error screens, how to intelligently handle database errors, and how to create a more professional and polished end-user interface.

Chapter 20, "Regular Expressions," introduces the powerful and flexible world of regular expression manipulation. Regular expressions allow you to perform incredible sophisticated and powerful string manipulations in simple one-line statements. ColdFusion supports the use of regular expressions in both find and replace functions, and this technology can greatly enhance these operations.

Chapter 21, "Intelligent Agents and Distributed Processing," teaches you how to use Internet protocols such as HTTP, FTP, and NNTP from within your code. With the help of these protocols, you can easily write applications that interact with other server and services anywhere on the public Internet or private intranets.

Chapter 22, "Interacting with the System Registry," shows you how the new <CFREGISTRY> tag can be used to manage your system registry. <CFREGISTRY> is a very powerful tag—and a potentially dangerous one. You learn how to use this tag, as well as how not to use it.

Appendixes   Appendix A, "ColdFusion Tag Reference," is the definitive reference for every ColdFusion tag, with descriptive explanations, syntax tables, and examples for each. Topics are cross-referenced extensively to related topics and appropriate tutorial chapters in the book.

Appendix B, "ColdFusion Function Reference," is a complete reference of every ColdFusion function organized by category. Thorough descriptions and examples are given for every function, and extensive cross-references are provided.

Appendix C, "VTML and WIZML Language Reference," provides an alphabetical listing of all the tags in the VTML and WIZML languages. These XML-based languages are used to manage and manipulate the ColdFusion Studio environment, and this appendix complements the information taught in Chapter 14, "Customizing ColdFusion Studio."

Appendix D, "The WDDX.DTD File," is a complete reprint of the XML Document Type Definition for the WDDX data-exchange format (with permission from Allaire). It describes what elements and attributes can legally appear in a WDDX Packet. It also lays down some ground rules about how certain special values—such as dates, null values, and carriage returns—should be treated. Think of it as the specification for WDDX itself.

The CD-ROM   The accompanying CD-ROM contains the following:

- Evaluation versions of ColdFusion 4 for Windows NT
- Evaluation version of ColdFusion 4 for Sun Solaris
- Evaluation version of ColdFusion Studio 4
- All the code listings in this book
- The Delphi CFAPI interface
- Lots of third-party add-ons and utilities that help you take your applications to the next level

Fire up your editor, pick the chapters that will help you most, and get to work. In no time you will be doing things with ColdFusion that you never thought possible.

Scalability

Monitoring Server Performance

Understanding Performance

This statement might sound ironic, but the biggest problem a Web developer can face is success. One day your site is getting 500 visitors and performing beautifully. The next, you have thousands of visitors, and they're all complaining that your site is too slow. You may even have trouble keeping your servers up and running under all that load. Because everything seemed fine at lower traffic levels, and your traffic increased so quickly, you're not sure what the problem is or even where to start looking for it.

Don't panic. The trick to solving your performance problem is to systematically analyze your site. Identify the individual components that make up your site, and examine them closely until you find the trouble spot—the bottleneck. After you find the bottleneck, you can either make that part of your site work better under load, or you can scale it—that is, add more server capacity to handle the extra stress caused by the traffic. This chapter will help you analyze your site for bottlenecks. The three chapters that follow will describe several ways you can scale your site, how ColdFusion can help you scale, and how to handle some of the challenges you'll face in building a ColdFusion site that has been scaled across multiple Web servers.

What We Talk About When We Talk About Performance

Apologies for the obscure Raymond Carver reference (*What We Talk About When We Talk About Love*), but to analyze your site effectively, you must understand exactly what factors affect performance.

The terms I'm about to use and the model I'm going to present of Web server performance are not gospel. The model I'm using reflects my experience solving performance problems on many different Web sites, some with ColdFusion and some without, and I'm confident that using this model will help you solve your own problems more quickly.

Your site's traffic is really just a series of requests. Answering a request uses some of your Web server's resources. This is true for even the simplest Web hit—say, for a plain, old GIF file. When a user's browser requests that GIF, it takes server resources to listen for the request, acknowledge the request, allocate a HyperText Transfer Protocol (HTTP) server thread to handle the request, find the GIF file on disk, read the file, and pass the contents of the GIF back to the user's browser. As it happens, none of the steps required for handling a request for a GIF file take many resources, so well-written Web servers can handle very high numbers of requests for plain files. A request for a ColdFusion page is very different, though, because it involves running ColdFusion Markup Language (CFML) code to produce a dynamic result. If your CFML is complex, or if you're using all the other capabilities that make ColdFusion great—database calls, CFX tags, COM and CORBA objects, even additional HTTP requests with CFHTTP—a single ColdFusion page can become extremely resource-intensive.

When traffic is low, your site might receive only one request for a resource-intensive ColdFusion page at a time. If your server can devote its full attention to that one request, the response to the request is usually pretty fast, even if a lot of resources were consumed in generating the response. You see a performance problem only when traffic increases; because each request takes a lot of resources, your server can handle fewer resource-intensive requests at one time. As a result, your server takes more time to handle each request, and your site seems slower. And it gets worse. If a few resource-intensive requests are hogging your Web server's processing power, even simpler ColdFusion pages are slower to process. Resource-intensive pages can drag down your overall site performance even if they are only a small percentage of your total requests. When you have a situation like this, the piece of your system that is holding back overall performance is called a *bottleneck*.

Resource bottlenecks are not the only kinds of bottlenecks, but they are the type of bottleneck that you'll encounter most often with a ColdFusion Web site. They also are the type of bottleneck that scaling to multiple Web servers helps most directly.

N O T E   Another major source of bottlenecks is system limitations. If you are using a slow hard drive, the time that your server takes to read files could become a big bottleneck. Moving to faster SCSI drives, or even a RAID array, can help solve this bottleneck. If your Web server has to read large amounts of data from another machine on your network, you might need to move from 10BaseT to 100BaseT Ethernet connections. Because these bottlenecks are not ColdFusion-specific, they're not addressed in this book, but you should examine all aspects of your site when analyzing a performance problem. If you don't, you could come to a very wrong conclusion. Jonathan once worked on a site that had a problem—users were constantly complaining that the site was too slow. After several weeks of poring over the source code to several dynamic parts of the site, the tech staff was at a loss. They hired a senior systems consultant to analyze the installation. The consultant quickly discovered that the system administrator hadn't installed several OS hotfixes related to networking. Installing the hotfixes increased the Web server's throughput by about 25 percent without changing any of the tech staff's code. ▨

The Middleware Problem

I want to share a slightly uncomfortable truth with you: *Middleware*, defined as the application layer that sits behind a Web server and communicates with back-end services such as file systems, databases, and so on, has some built-in performance limitations that frequently require you to add more hardware than you might expect.

This problem is the result of a few different factors. First, most middleware (such as ColdFusion and ASP) is interpreted: To run your code, you just have to put it up on the site. You don't have a compilation step, such as for CFX tags programmed in C++ or Java servlets. An interpreted language is always slower than a compiled language; the interpreter (in this case, the ColdFusion service) is more resource-intensive because it has to keep the script interpreter in memory and use it frequently. With a compiled language, the interpretation happens at compile time, so the resulting DLL or executable doesn't have to devote resources to converting the code to machine language. The advantage of using interpreted languages is rapid development; writing C/C++ or Java code is much more time-consuming and is more difficult to change because you have to go back to the source code and recompile every time you want to make a change.

continues

continued

Middleware is also slow because it has to bridge the gaps between so many disparate systems. Web servers, file servers, and even database servers are much more "single-function" systems: They can focus on solving one problem very well and don't have to worry about the other pieces of the puzzle. These systems have been optimized to perform their single task extremely well. Middleware tools such as ColdFusion have to know how to speak with a multitude of different servers and protocols. It's a great advantage, but it carries a lot of overhead with it.

Finally, middleware is a very new segment of the software market. Commercial database servers such as Oracle, Sybase, and Microsoft SQL Server have been in development for years, constantly being tuned and tweaked for efficiency and speed. Middleware didn't really exist until early Web developers took a UNIX report-generating language (Perl) and started to use it to write CGI programs. ColdFusion's performance has improved with almost every release, and moving from ColdFusion 3.1.1 to ColdFusion 4.0 will give you as much as a 30 to 40 percent performance enhancement. As the middleware market matures, products such as ColdFusion should improve until their performance characteristics are closer to that of database servers and other established server products.

Why does this matter? You need to attack your scalability problem with an understanding that your solution for a middleware product such as ColdFusion might seem less than elegant—buying more servers, changing functionality, even rewriting pieces of the site in CFX tags. If your boss gives you a problem, explain the middleware trade-offs reviewed here. If that approach doesn't work, sit with him or her for a few minutes and work out how much it would have cost if you wrote your entire ColdFusion application in raw C/C++ code. I'm sure the exorbitant cost of such an effort will help your boss understand that a few thousand dollars for another ColdFusion server is a small price to pay in the grand scheme of things.

Monitoring Your ColdFusion Server

Identifying bottlenecks takes information. Before you can start looking for performance bottle-necks, you have to know which pages on your site are receiving the most requests. A log analysis program is absolutely essential to this process. Because Web server log analysis isn't specific to ColdFusion, I'm mentioning it only in passing. You should know that, without a good log analysis tool, you'll be severely handicapped in all your other performance-analyzing ventures. If you don't have a log analysis tool right now, I recommend Analog, a good freeware log analy-sis tool written in Perl, and Microsoft Site Server, which among many other things includes an excellent (if slow) log analysis tool that stores its data in MS SQL Server. You can use Site Server's built-in reports or write SQL queries to build your own.

The best two places to find information about possible ColdFusion bottlenecks are the APPLICATION.LOG file and the Windows NT Performance Monitor. I'll talk briefly about the APPLICATION.LOG file and then focus on using the Performance Monitor (perfmon.exe) to watch your server's performance in real-time.

N O T E ColdFusion 4.0 uses different log files than ColdFusion 3.1.1 does. If you're using ColdFusion 3.1.1, look in the CFSERVER.LOG file instead of the APPLICATION.LOG file. ∎

The `APPLICATION.LOG` File

The `APPLICATION.LOG` file records every ColdFusion error on your site. Two types of errors are clear signs of a performance problem.

The first performance-problem error is a `Request timed out` message. This error is written if a ColdFusion page takes longer to process than the timeout value you set in the ColdFusion Administrator. If your server is experiencing performance problems, some pages take so long to process that they trigger this error. It's a pretty crude filter; if you set your timeout value to 20 seconds, you have no way to know if the pages that aren't timing out are taking 5 seconds or 15 seconds to process. If you're getting `Request timed out` errors for only a few specific ColdFusion pages, odds are that those pages are at least one cause for your performance problems. If your `Request timed out` errors are spread evenly across most or all of the pages on your site, you might have a single bottleneck that is affecting everything. Does every page on your site query the same database? If this isn't the case, then you're already a strong candidate for scaling.

You can set ColdFusion 4.0 to log information about requests that take longer than a certain time to run. This capability is a big step forward over ColdFusion 3.1.1 because you don't have to wait for a page to actually time out to see that it's running slow.

Another performance-problem error reports that your ColdFusion page is a "deadlock victim." This means that a collision occurred while trying to read data from your database. Because this error is very specific to the database you are running, I won't talk about it here other than to point out what it means.

You can analyze your `APPLICATION.LOG` files manually, just by reading them. I also recommend Ben Forta's handy `<CFX_VIEWCFLOG>` tag, which parses an `APPLICATION.LOG` file and writes the results into a ColdFusion query result set, suitable for further processing in a ColdFusion template. At SmartMoney Interactive, the staff used Ben's tag as the foundation for an automatic `APPLICATION.LOG` parser that lets developers request reports with the full text or summaries of ColdFusion errors matching specific text patterns.

The Windows NT Performance Monitor

The Performance Monitor (perfmon) is a tool that lets you watch your site's performance in real-time or record performance data for later analysis. Using it is an especially good way to watch utilization of server resources such as memory, processors, and drive space. With versions of ColdFusion before 4.0, not very many perfmon counters addressed ColdFusion specifically. (See the sidebar on using perfmon with ColdFusion 3.1.1 and earlier.) With ColdFusion 4.0, Allaire has added a special ColdFusion object that lets you monitor several ColdFusion-specific statistics.

perfmon Basics

If you've used perfmon before, you can skip this section and go straight to "The ColdFusion Object."

perfmon is located under Administrative Tools in your Start menu. When you open perfmon, you see an empty workspace, as shown in Figure 1.1.

FIGURE 1.1

This Windows NT Performance Monitor is not currently monitoring anything.

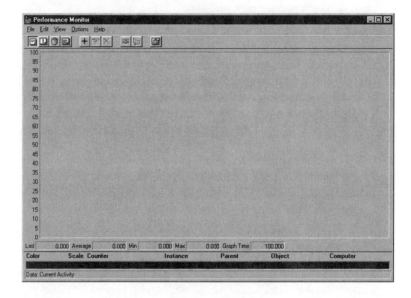

perfmon has four modes, which you can choose from the View menu:

- Chart—The Chart view shows you a moving graph of performance information, updated at a regular interval that you specify. Use Chart view to watch your server's current performance. By watching Chart view closely over a period of time, you can get a feel for how your server performs under "normal" conditions. Chart view also may show you symptoms of a performance problem—for example, an unusually large number of queued ColdFusion requests.

- Alert—In the Alert view, you can set perfmon to take action when your server's statistics pass thresholds you specify. Alerts can let you know when your server has performance problems, without requiring you to monitor your server manually. You can even set perfmon to perform system administration functions when alert criteria are met.

- Log—In the Log view, you can store perfmon data for later analysis. You can open a log file in perfmon and review the data at any time. This view is useful if you want to study your server's performance over a known time period—say, right after market close for a financial site.

- Report—Report view is like Chart view, except that it shows just a list of statistics instead of a dynamic chart.

The descriptions start by focusing on Chart view.

Chart View   You can add a statistic to perfmon by clicking the Plus button or by selecting Add to Chart from the Edit menu. The Add to Chart dialog box then appears, as shown in Figure 1.2. Here, you can choose statistics to watch for the current machine.

FIGURE 1.2

The Add to Chart dialog box.

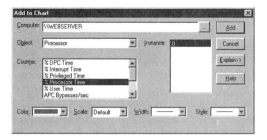

This dialog box contains a lot of information. At the top is the Uniform Naming Convention (UNC) name for the computer you want to see counters for; by default, this is the local machine. You can type a UNC to monitor another machine, or click on the ... (ellipsis) button to select a computer. Below the computer name is a pop-up menu listing the objects available to perfmon; each object is a collection of statistics, called *counters*, that can be viewed using perfmon. The list of counters is immediately below the Object pop-up menu.

On the right side of the screen is a list of instances of each object. Many objects have only one instance, so this box is blank. Other objects have many instances. For example, the Process object has as many instances as you have processes running on your server. If your server has multiple processors, each processor shows up as an instance of the Processor object.

At the bottom of the dialog box are display options for the current line. They are mostly self-explanatory. By assigning different scales to different counters, you can watch perfmon counters with different orders of magnitude on the same screen.

By default, perfmon reads counters once per second. (You can change this setting via Chart on the Options menu.) If you select the % Processor Time counter from the Processor object and let perfmon run for a minute or so, you should see a screen like the one shown in Figure 1.3.

FIGURE 1.3

A sample Performance Monitor chart, showing about one minute's worth of data.

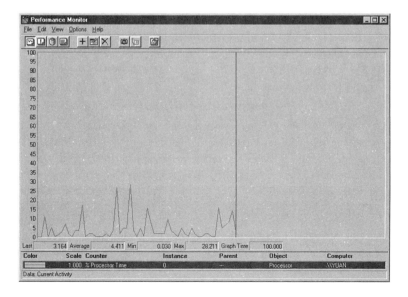

Take some time to explore the available objects, instances, and counters. If you haven't used perfmon before, you might be surprised at how many useful statistics are available. Because perfmon counters are generally not well-documented, if you want to get the most out of perfmon, you need to spend the time to learn about the objects provided by the applications you use.

Alert View   If you get to know your server's behavior well, you will probably be able to identify some warning signs—too many ColdFusion threads, an unusually high processor utilization, and so on. By setting up a perfmon that alerts you when a threshold is passed, you can go about your work confident that you'll be notified in case of a problem, in time to take preventive action. You can even tell perfmon to run an external program if a counter passes a threshold you specify.

When you are running perfmon in Alert view, you should keep it running 24 hours a day, seven days a week. Unfortunately, in NT 4.0, perfmon cannot be run as a service, so you need to remain logged in at the console while it is running. I strongly recommend that you run perfmon on a machine other than your Web server. If your Alert perfmon is running on your Web server, and your Web server has a problem or crashes, how do you get the alert?

To choose Alert view, click the exclamation-point button (second from the left), or select Alert from the View menu.

When you add a counter to Alert view, you see some different options from the other views, as shown in Figure 1.4. You can choose to receive an alert if your chosen statistic passes *over* or *under* your chosen threshold. You can select a program to run if an alert condition occurs. For example, you can have a command-line email program such as `blat.exe` send you an email message if ColdFusion's average request time counter goes over a certain value, which would indicate that your server is having a performance problem. See the following sections for descriptions of the ColdFusion Application Server (CFAS) object counters. (Thanks to Ian Brody for introducing the wonders of `blat`.)

FIGURE 1.4

The Add to Alert dialog box.

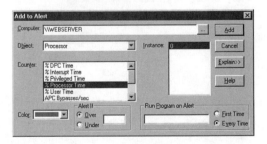

You can also have perfmon pop up a message box on your screen when an alert condition occurs. You do so by selecting Alert from the Options menu when you're in Alert view. Check the Send Network Message check box, and enter your computer name in the Net Name field. In the Alert dialog box, you also can write events into the machine's Application Event Log. This is a very good idea.

Log View   In addition to using perfmon for real-time monitoring, you can let a it run for hours or days and have it save its data in a file for later review and analysis. Perfmon can write data only at the Object level, though (it writes every instance and counter for a given object to disk), so perfmon log files can get very big very fast. If you intend to log perfmon data for any great length of time (more than a few hours at a pop), you probably need to reduce the sample frequency to once per minute or even once per 10 minutes. Although this data can be useful for averaging and detecting general trends, the spiky and fast-changing nature of ColdFusion load means that many of the useful details you can glean by watching perfmon directly in Chart view will be lost.

> **CAUTION**
>
> perfmon log files can become corrupted if a process or machine that you're running crashes or otherwise has problems. Corrupted files can seriously limit the usefulness of perfmon logging because getting a log file that shows both events leading to a crash and the crash itself is difficult.

You need to use perfmon to view a perfmon log file. You do so by selecting the Data From option from the Options menu. Click the Log File radio button, and enter the path to your log file in the field below. You can then view your stored data in Chart, Alert, or Report view. Realistically, only Chart view and Report view are useful for reviewing logged data.

If you want to set up perfmon to log, select Log from the View menu. You then see the dialog box shown in Figure 1.5. When you choose to add a counter, you get a dialog box that lists only the objects on your system (see Figure 1.6). You can select multiple objects, but remember that the more objects you choose to log, the faster your log file will grow in size.

FIGURE 1.5
The Log dialog box.

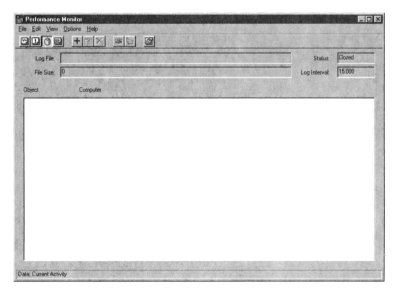

FIGURE 1.6

The Add to Log dialog box.

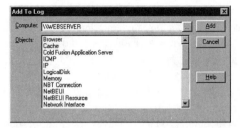

To choose a log file and begin to log, select Log from the Options menu. You then see a standard file dialog box. Choose the location for your log file, and enter a name. You can select the frequency of updates by entering a value in the Interval (Seconds) field. After you name your log file and choose an interval, click on the Start Log button to begin logging. The Log dialog box automatically closes.

To stop automatic logging, select Options, Log, and click the Stop Log button in the Log dialog box. Again, the dialog box automatically closes.

Report View   Report view is similar to Chart view in that it provides you with a view of current performance statistics. Instead of a chart, however, Report view simply displays a list of counters and their corresponding values. To use Report view, select Report from the View menu (see Figure 1.7). Otherwise, Report view functions almost identically to Chart view, minus the options for chart formatting.

FIGURE 1.7

The Add to Report dialog box.

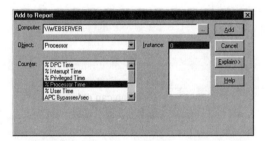

The ColdFusion Object

The new ColdFusion Application Server (CFAS) Performance Monitor object provides several useful new counters. To view the CFAS Performance Monitor object, go to Debugging in your ColdFusion Administrator, and check the Enable Use of Performance Monitor check box. You might need to restart your ColdFusion server after this step to register the object with your Performance Monitor.

The CFAS Performance Monitor object provides 10 counters:

- Avg DB Time (msec)—A running average of the amount of time, in milliseconds, an individual database operation, launched by ColdFusion, took to complete.

- Avg Queue Time (msec)—A running average of the amount of time, in milliseconds, requests spent waiting in the ColdFusion input queue before ColdFusion began to process that request.
- Avg Req Time (msec)—A running average of the total amount of time, in milliseconds, ColdFusion took to process a request. In addition to general page processing time, this value includes both queue time and database processing time.
- Bytes In/Sec—The number of bytes received by the ColdFusion Application Server per second.
- Bytes Out/Sec—The number of bytes returned by the ColdFusion Application Server per second.
- DB Hits/Sec—The number of database operations performed per second by the ColdFusion Application Server.
- Page Hits/Sec—The number of Web pages processed per second by the ColdFusion Application Server.
- Queued Requests—The number of requests currently waiting to be processed by the ColdFusion Application Server.
- Running Requests—The number of requests currently being actively processed by the ColdFusion Application Server.
- Timed Out Requests—The total number of requests that timed out waiting to be processed by the ColdFusion Application Server. These requests never got to run.

In addition to the counters associated with the CFAS object, you can monitor a few other aspects of ColdFusion performance via the Process object. Select the Process object, and then select the cfserver process from the Instance menu. Here are two particularly useful counters:

- % Processor Time—This counter reports ColdFusion's total processor utilization. This counter is a very important performance indicator. If you set ColdFusion's maximum simultaneous requests too high, ColdFusion can exhaust the server's processor resources trying to handle all the requests at once. This is an especially serious risk if your ColdFusion pages are heavy on CFML. If your ColdFusion pages are fairly simple (say, running a DB query without much subsequent CFML processing), you might be able to handle a much higher number of simultaneous requests without a problem. If you watch this counter as you adjust the number of simultaneous requests, you should be able to tune your ColdFusion server to use processor resources effectively, without overloading the machine.

Performance Monitor with Multiple Processors

By default, the Performance Monitor caps all "percentage" statistics at 100 percent. If you're monitoring % Processor Time, and you have only one processor in a machine, capping the statistics makes a lot of sense. If you have multiple processors in your Web server, however, how do you measure a single process's utilization? Does 100 percent mean the process is using 100 percent of

continues

continues

each processor? No. The Performance Monitor counts multiple-processor utilization cumulatively. If a process is using, say, 75 percent of each processor, the Performance Monitor reports that process's utilization as 150 percent. You can view processor utilizations over 100 percent by changing the Registry entry HKEY_CURRENT_USER\Software\Microsoft\PerfMon\CapPercentsAt100 from 1 to 0.

Thanks to Ian Brody, Network Manager at SmartMoney Interactive, for finding this extremely useful tidbit in the Microsoft knowledge base.

- Thread Count—This counter is mostly useful if you are running ColdFusion 3.1.1 or earlier and don't have access to the CFAS object. This counter reports the total number of threads in use by the cfserver.exe process. This number includes active request threads, queued request threads, and several utility threads that are always present. As such, it doesn't give you as much detail as the Queued Requests and Running Requests counters of the CFAS object, but it's better than nothing.

Other Useful Performance Monitor Statistics

You need to consider performance factors on a server besides ColdFusion itself, so monitoring some other statistics can round your picture of what's happening on your server. These useful stats include (but are not limited to) those discussed next.

Processor Utilization

OBJECT: Processor

INSTANCE: 0 (single processor); 1, 2, and/or 3 (2 to 4 processors)

COUNTER: % Processor time

This counter shows you what percent of your machine's processor(s) is in use. This information can be useful in a couple of ways. If this counter is higher than the counter for cfserver's % Processor Time, some other process on your server is stealing resources from ColdFusion. If you remove the other process, you might find that your ColdFusion performance radically improves. Your first step in optimizing and scaling a ColdFusion server should *always* be removal of all nonessential services and programs from your server. Anything your server does that isn't directly related to serving Web pages steals resources and limits your server's Web and ColdFusion performance.

The next few counters are specific to IIS. The data they monitor is useful for any Web server, however; if you're not using IIS, spending time with Performance Monitor to identify the analogous Performance Monitor counters is worthwhile.

OBJECT: HTTP Service

COUNTER: Connections/Sec

This counter gives you an idea of the total number of requests your server is getting at any one moment. This number includes requests for graphics, plain HTML pages, and other non-ColdFusion content on your site. Generally, IIS can handle a lot more traffic on its own than with ColdFusion because ColdFusion incurs the processing overhead inherent in all middleware. (See "The Middleware Problem" sidebar earlier in this chapter.) If the number of ColdFusion threads is climbing faster than the number of HTTP connections, that probably means some ColdFusion page is taking too long to process, and ColdFusion requests are "backing up" as each HTTP connection comes in.

> OBJECT: HTTP Service
>
> COUNTER: Current Connections

By default, IIS is set to "keep alive" HTTP connections for around 15 minutes. By monitoring the total number of current connections, you can get a "15 minute moving average" of how busy your site is. This stat changes more slowly than connections/sec, and as such gives you a better idea of traffic trends on your site over a given (brief) time period.

> OBJECT: HTTP Service
>
> COUNTER: Current ISAPI Extension Requests

This counter indicates the number of open ISAPI filter and extension requests on your IIS server. In a smoothly functioning Web site, an HTTP connection should generate an ISAPI extension request (the ColdFusion stub DLL) that generates a ColdFusion request (possibly an extra thread if needed), and all three should be resolved and closed in a timely fashion. If any one of the three becomes greatly different from the other two, you have some kind of server problem.

Configuration Options

Next you find a few tricks to make the Performance Monitor even more useful.

Monitoring Multiple and/or Remote Servers   By entering the UNC of a server that you have already touched over the network (via NET USE, drive mapping, or the like) into the Computer field of any Add dialog box, you can monitor the Performance Monitor counters for a remote machine from your desktop or from any designated monitoring station. If you enter one UNC and pick some parameters, and then enter another UNC and pick some more parameters, you can set up a single Performance Monitor workspace that monitors multiple computers. For example, at SmartMoney Interactive, the staff uses a single Performance Monitor workspace to show the Thread Count and % Processor Time for all the SmartMoney Web servers.

Saving Your Settings   By choosing Save Workspace from the File menu, you can preserve your hard-earned Performance Monitor settings to use again. You can even pass Performance Monitor configurations from machine to machine by copying the workspace files.

A Sample Performance Monitor Configuration

Consider this sample Chart view that I've found useful at SmartMoney Interactive. It includes a set of counters and some preference changes. Take this configuration as an example, but be sure to spend time customizing it for your own servers. Getting to know your server's performance (and getting to know the Performance Monitor tool) is like getting to know a race car and a track. The more times you take the car out for a spin on the same piece of road, the more of an intuitive feel you will begin to get for the vehicle and the road. You'll develop almost a "second sense" as to where the danger points are, what the server "feels like" when it's performing well, and what statistics you need to watch closely. In other words, your mileage may vary.

Performance Monitor Counters Used in the Sample Configuration

The following counters are used in the sample configuration:

- Processor object, % Processor Time—Included for each processor on your machine. Comparing this number with the % Processor Time for cfserver.exe lets you know if other processes are "stealing" processor time from ColdFusion.

- Process object, cfserver instance, % Processor Time—See above. Also, if ColdFusion's % processor time is at or near 100 percent (or 200 percent for multiple processors, and so on), you might need to reduce the number of simultaneous requests that ColdFusion tries to handle.

- CFAS object, Running Requests—(ColdFusion 4 only) This counter should never be larger than your simultaneous request limit in the ColdFusion Administrator.

- CFAS object, Queued Requests—(ColdFusion 4 only) If this counter is nonzero, the Running Requests counter should equal your simultaneous request limit in the ColdFusion Administrator. If this counter gets too high, you might find that some requests are timing out before being processed; in this case, add the Timed Out Requests counter.

- Process object, cfserver instance, Thread Count—If you're using ColdFusion 3.1.1 or earlier, this counter gives you a rough equivalent to Running Requests and Queued Requests combined.

- HTTP Service object, Current Connections, scale set to 0.1—(IIS only) With IIS's default "keep-alive" setting, this counter shows the total number of connection requests received in the past 15 minutes. This line gives you a general idea of the level of traffic on your site at any given time. You can use this counter to get an idea of what level of overall traffic begins to cause ColdFusion performance problems.

- HTTP Service object, Maximum Connections, scale set to 0.1—(IIS only) This "counter" is really just a number reflecting the highest value that the Current Connections counter has reached since the last time IIS was restarted. This counter gives you an easy way to see the highest traffic level your site has received recently and how your current traffic level compares.

Deciding What to Do Next

After you have a good grasp on the current performance of your site, you can start to analyze for bottlenecks. Every ColdFusion site is unique in one way or another, so making a generalization about specific symptoms and their relationship to specific bottlenecks can be hard. For example, SmartMoney Interactive uses a CFX tag to communicate with a proprietary stock quote database. Another site might have integrated ColdFusion with an Open Market transaction server. Many sites need to interface with a legacy mainframe database or with a credit card processor.

Some Things to Think About When Looking for Bottlenecks

A typical ColdFusion-driven site is fairly complex. Many factors, such as databases and network layout, contribute to performance. With the number of possible factors, your bottleneck is likely outside ColdFusion or only indirectly dependent on ColdFusion. If you are experiencing a performance problem, a good step is to closely examine what pages users were requesting at the time of the problem. What ColdFusion capabilities does this page use? If it makes a database call but doesn't do much else, pay close attention to the performance of your query using the ColdFusion debug information. Check the performance of your database server, and review your ODBC settings. If the page is heavy on CFML code, start by looking at the number of milliseconds the page takes to process with no traffic. Then eliminate sections of CFML and see what the effect is on total processing time. You might find a particular piece of code that is very resource-intensive. In the next section, you'll find a list of possible bottleneck points on a typical ColdFusion-based site. Make sure that you have examined all the likely possibilities before considering scaling.

Chart of Possible Bottlenecks

You should consider several possible bottlenecks:

- Bandwidth to your Web server.
- Web server performance, preset limits to simultaneous HTTP requests.
- Other processes running on the same server.
- Hard drive speed. This is not just for `<CFFILE>`; ColdFusion has to pull templates off the disk if they're not in cache. Remember `application.cfm` files and `<CFINCLUDE>` files, too. Even if you are caching templates, ColdFusion still checks the file on disk to see whether it has been modified, unless you specifically tell ColdFusion to trust cache files.
- Network latency (if you're communicating with other machines on the same network).
- Database server performance. (You can run ColdFusion on a four-processor workhorse, but what does it matter if ColdFusion has to wait for your database that's running on an old P133?)
- Time to run a query. (Think about clustered indices, table and record locking, and deadlock. Stored procedures are better than queries embedded in CFML.)
- ODBC configuration. (Think about connection pooling; tune your maximum simultaneous connections.)
- CFX tag performance.
- CORBA object performance.
- `<CFMAIL>`, `<CFFTP>`, `<CFHTTP>`, and so on; performance of the TCP/IP servers you're contacting (SMTP, FTP, HTTP, and so on); Internet latency to get there and back.

If you've examined all the non-ColdFusion bottleneck possibilities and are left with the question of how to improve your ColdFusion performance, you're left with two options: optimizing your code or adding more servers.

Optimizing Your Code Versus Adding More Servers

Identifying your bottleneck gives you a chance to rewrite your code so that the bottleneck isn't so resource-intensive. Often, though, you cannot fix a bottleneck simply by recoding. You might spend a week retooling a piece of CFML to use arrays instead of lists and get only a 5 or 10 percent improvement in performance. Not only is this time not very productive, but it's expensive; the time you spent recoding could have been spent creating something new for your site. Sometimes the cheapest way to solve a performance problem is to add more servers. Although this approach might seem like the "throwing hardware at it" approach to problem solving, if you've done your homework, you can clearly demonstrate that your site has a bottleneck and that the costs to recode the problem code just aren't worth it. If that's the decision you come to, you're ready to learn about scaling. Head for the next chapter for information about your options. ●

Different Ways to Scale

In this chapter

In the preceding chapter you learned about ways to monitor your site's performance and ana-lyze problems. This chapter focuses on one solution to a performance problem—scaling up your site by adding additional servers.

You can host a single Web site across multiple Web servers in two different ways. The first option, which is arguably the simplest, is to split your site's functionality across multiple ma-chines. If indexing your site and running full-text searches is slow, you can set up a separate Web server that just does searching and call it `search.`*`yourdomain`*`.com`. If e-commerce and credit card validation are your bottleneck, you can set up another machine called `store.`*`yourdomain`*`.com`. Many successful Web sites add additional machines in this manner. Some sites under particularly heavy traffic even put their images on a separate `images.`*`yourdomain`*`.com` server to segregate their HTTP traffic. This type of scaling is rela-tively easy because each machine can have a unique configuration. This way, you don't have to deal with many consistency or synchronization issues.

This strategy might work in some situations, but it has weaknesses. The first weakness is that this strategy doesn't provide any redundancy. If you move a search to a separate server, and your search machine crashes, you've just lost all search functionality, even though your main server is running fine. If you provide identical services on the two machines you own, the failure of one has an impact only on your ability to handle high traffic. It doesn't deactivate any features of your site.

The second problem you might encounter happens when you get so much traffic that one box isn't enough to handle your dedicated function. What happens when your search function becomes so popular that your single search box is running out of resources? Do you subdivide your search into, say, a site search and a news feed search, and set up `site.search`*`.yourdomain`*`.com` and `newsfeed.search.`*`yourdomain`*`.com`? Then you have to go into your exist-ing code and change all the old references to `search.`*`yourdomain`*`.com`. You have to deal with people who may have bookmarked your search machine. And that's assuming you can even subdivide your search function into two separate pieces. How do you split up an e-commerce application that just does credit card queries? `Visa.store.`*`yourmachine`*`.com` and `amex.store`*`.yourmachine`*`.com`? You can see that this solution isn't reasonable.

At some point, you're going to want to use two or more machines to provide a single service to your users, whether it's your entire site or just a subsection. You will want the users to have as seamless an experience as possible; ideally, your users shouldn't even know that the site they're visiting is a collection of machines. A group of machines serving identical content and services is generally known as a *cluster*, a name that nicely captures the homogenous nature of such an installation. You might also hear a cluster and its associated back-end machines re-ferred to as a *server farm*, presumably due to the natural tendency of server computers to proliferate like kudzu. This chapter will focus on the issues of running a single Web site across multiple Web servers.

Running one Web site on one server is relatively straightforward: You know that every Web request goes to the same Web server software and ColdFusion service, with the same settings and environment. But as soon as you add a second server, you are faced with a host of techni-cal challenges. This chapter will discuss the issues you'll face in moving to a multiple-server configuration and will then move to a review of some of the main technologies that enable you to distribute your traffic across multiple servers in a balanced way.

Part One: Understanding Scaling Issues

When you decide to add a second Web server, you need to address several issues that are essential to running in a scaled environment. You will face the following issues:

Part

I

Ch

2

- Determining optimal hardware configuration
- Configuring a network for multiple servers
- Keeping system and software configurations identical
- Balancing traffic among multiple servers
- Handling resource collisions
- Sharing data among multiple servers
- Keeping content synchronized across multiple servers
- Maintaining sessions among multiple servers

Determining Optimal Hardware Configuration

Adding hardware to a single server is not always the best solution for handling load. In Windows NT, you get diminishing returns for each additional CPU. Turning a one-CPU system to a two-CPU system improves performance by only around 70 percent, even if the two processors are identical. The third CPU adds only another 30 percent, and the fourth CPU gives you only another 15 percent boost. This is true because each additional CPU consumes operating system resources simply to keep each processor in sync with the others. Generally speaking, if a two-processor NT machine is running out of processor resources, you're better off adding a second two-processor machine than adding two processors to your existing machine. A rough mathematical proof of this problem is fairly simple:

- Four-processor box performance = $(((1 \times 170\%) \times 130\%) \times 115\%) = 2.5415$
- Two two-processor boxes = $(1 \times 170\%) + (1 \times 170\%) = 3.4$

You might ask why you would want a two-processor machine at all; why not use four one-processor machines instead? In an abstract measure of processor utilization, you might be right. But you also have to deal with problems of user experience. Even though you're not using 100 percent of the second processor, you are getting a strong performance boost. This performance boost might make a page that takes two seconds to process on a one-processor box take just over one second to process on a two-processor box. This amount can be the difference between a site that feels slow and a site with happy users. With the improved threading model of ColdFusion 4, your two-processor performance gain might be particularly strong. Another point in favor of two-processor machines: Many server-class machines, with configurations that support other advanced hardware features necessary for a robust server, support dual processors as part of their feature set. If you're investing in server-class machines, adding a second processor before adding a second server can be cost effective.

N O T E A *threading model* can refer to several characteristics of an NT program. One aspect of threading is thread management—how the program starts new threads, ends old threads, and keeps track of active threads. A poorly written program might use up a lot of server resources just managing threads, without actually doing meaningful work. ColdFusion 4's threading model is particularly improved in this respect. Another aspect of a threading model is whether a program has been written to distribute its threads across multiple processors in one machine. A program has to be specifically coded to use multiple processors. For example, SQL Server has been written to use as many as eight processors, so adding processors to a SQL server gives you a big performance boost. In contrast, the log reporting tool in Microsoft Site Server uses only one processor.

RAM is another hardware issue you have to consider. The bottom line is that RAM is cheap, so put as much RAM in each machine as you can afford. I recommend at least 256MB.

A third hardware issue is drive speed. Drive speed is an often-overlooked aspect of server performance. Make sure that you use fast SCSI drives for all your Web servers. Think about using a RAID (Redundant Arrays of Independent Disks) on a dedicated drive controller for fastest access. Most production-level RAID controllers allow you to add RAM to the controller itself. This is FIFO (First In First Out) cache allows recently accessed data to be stored and processed directly from the RAM on the controller. You get a pronounced speed increase from this type of system because data never has to be sought out and read from the drive.If you use a RAID controller with a lot of RAM on board, you also should invest in redundant power sup-plies and a good Uninterruptible Power System (UPS). This is due to the fact that the RAM on the RAID controller is only written back to the drive if the system is shut down in an orderly fashion. If your system loses power, all of the data in RAM on the controller would be lost. If you don't understand why this is bad, imagine that the record of your last 50 orders for your product were in the RAM cache, instead of on the disk, when the power failed. The more RAM you have on the controller, the larger the magnitude of your problem in the event of a power outage.

The type of load-balancing technology you use has a big impact on the way you build your boxes. If you are using load-balancing technology that distributes traffic equally to all boxes, you need each of your servers to be configured identically. Some dedicated load-balancing hardware can detect a failed server and stop sending traffic to it; if your system works this way, and you have some extra capacity in your cluster, each box can be somewhat less reliable, because if it goes down, the others can pick up the slack. But if you're using a simple load-balancing technology like round-robin DNS (RRDNS), which can't detect a down server, you need each box to be as reliable as possible because a single failure means some of your users cannot use your site.

Configuring a Network for Multiple Servers

Because scaling to multiple servers implies that you have a high volume of traffic to your Web site, your network configuration becomes especially important. You want your Web servers to seem to be as much "one machine" as possible, so you should separate their high traffic vol-ume from other traffic on your network. For this discussion, I'll assume that, in addition to your

Web servers, you have another set of servers providing critical "back-end" services such as databases, search engines, e-commerce applications, and so forth. If you have any services like this and haven't moved them to separate back-end machines, you shouldn't be scaling your Web servers yet anyway. Start by moving all possible services to back-end servers.

A multi-Web server network works best if it's divided into separate front-end and back-end segments (see Figure 2.1).

FIGURE 2.1

A sample network configuration for a Web cluster.

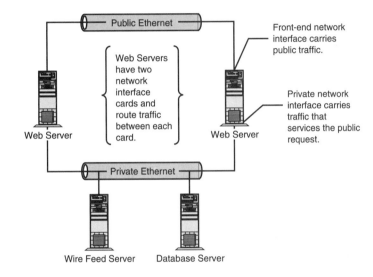

- Front end—The front end is the network segment between the public Internet and your Web cluster. The front end should be optimized for speed. I recommend that you make your front end a switched segment with lots of bandwidth. Your two primary goals on the front end are to avoid collisions and to minimize the number of *hops* (intervening network devices) between your Web servers and the public Internet.

- Back end—The back end is the network segment between your Web cluster and your supporting servers. Because your support servers need to talk only to your Web servers and your LAN, you don't need to make this segment directly accessible to the public Internet. In fact, you might do better to deliberately prevent any access to these machines from the public Internet. Doing so may allow you to take advantage of useful network protocols that would be a security risk if they were made available to the public Internet. Be sure to spend some time trying to minimize collisions on your back-end network as well.

- Dual-homed servers—One strategy used to protect your back-end servers is to put two network interface cards (NICs) into your Web servers—one that speaks to the front end, and one that speak to the back end. This strategy is known as *dual homing*. By following this approach, you can improve your Web server's network performance even more by preventing collisions between front-end and back-end packets.

In a Windows NT environment, you need to set up static routes to direct front-end and back-end traffic to the appropriate network interface card. This advanced topic is not ColdFusion-specific, so I won't get into the details here. If you're interested in learning more about advanced Windows NT networking, I recommend *Special Edition Using Windows NT Server* (Que Publishing).

CAUTION

If you choose to dual-home your Windows NT servers, you have to contend with a particularly nasty problem known as *Dead Gateway Detection*. Your server needs to detect whether a client across the Net has ended communications even though the request has not been fulfilled. This problem commonly occurs when a user hits the Stop button on a Web browser in the middle of a download and goes somewhere else. When WinNT goes to your front-end NIC, the client who aborted the request is nowhere to be found. Because your machine has two NICs, WinNT doesn't give up; instead, it tries to find the missing client on the back-end segment. Your WinNT machine starts routing all Web responses across your back-end segment. If (as I recommend) your back-end segment has no direct connection to the public Internet, these response packets are effectively "lost," and your site appears to stop responding. The solution to this problem is an advanced networking topic and beyond the scope of this book. You can find information on this subject at the Microsoft Web site at `http://www.microsoft.com/`.

 T I P In a dual-homed configuration, depending on what type of load balancing you are using, you can use private, nonroutable IP addresses to address machines on the back-end server farm. Using private nonroutables introduces another layer of complexity to your setup but can be a significant security advantage. To see how using private nonroutables works, see Figure 2.2.

FIGURE 2.2
Network address translations (NATs) across a front-end segment to private nonroutable IP addresses.

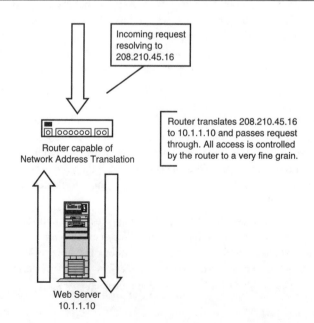

Incoming request resolving to 208.210.45.16

Router capable of Network Address Translation

Router translates 208.210.45.16 to 10.1.1.10 and passes request through. All access is controlled by the router to a very fine grain.

Web Server 10.1.1.10

Keeping System and ~~Software~~ Configurations Identical

Because you want ~~users to~~ have the same experience on your site, regardless of which server respon~~ds...~~ you need to keep your system configurations as close to identical as p~~ossible...~~ e to the advanced complexity of today's operating systems and app~~lications...~~ ~~ha~~rder than it sounds.

> **CAUTION**
>
> When you first built your s~~ite...~~ server somewhat haphazardly—adding a CFX tag here, an ODBC data source th~~at...~~ ~~w~~orked. Now, you're going to pay for your sins. When you set up your second se~~rver...~~ ~~comp~~rehensive, step-by-step list for what you need to do to set up a new and iden~~tical...~~ ~~th~~is point enough. If you don't figure this out early and write it down so that you ~~can...~~ ~~it down~~, you will never have full confidence that your servers are identical. If you think ~~that a single feature on one machine is hard, imagine having to test each feature exactly the same w~~ay on two diff~~erent machines and having to address separate problems on each machine. If you need ~~one new~~ machine, I promise you that you will need to add more in the near future. Don't wait until your ~~first two~~ machines are crashing out under the traffic, and you're up at 3 a.m. with the third trying to figure out wha~~t~~ Registry setting isn't correct. Figure it out the first time, and write it down.

You can speed up the process of setting up a new CF server by copying your existing server's ColdFusion settings directly via the Registry, instead of manually re-creating your settings with the HTML-based ColdFusion Administrator. Run `regedit` from the Run option of the Start menu, and look in the `\HKEY_LOCAL_MACHINE\SOFTWARE\ALLAIRE` key to see ColdFusion's Registry settings.

> **CAUTION**
>
> Changing the Registry can severely damage your NT system and require you to reinstall in order to recover functionality. My suggestion to copy Registry settings is just that—a suggestion. I've done it successfully, but I make no guarantees that you will have quick or easy results. If you're not comfortable with this technique, don't use it. And, if you blindly copy the whole key without examining it first and you have problems, don't blame me. For more information on working with the Registry and ColdFusion, see Chapter 22, "Interacting with the System Registry."

Balancing Traffic Among Multiple Servers

If all your machines have the same hardware resources and configuration, the way to get the most performance out of them is to use resources on each box equally. This suggestion might sound obvious, but you need to understand that this is not the same as sending the same number of sessions to each box or sending the same number of requests to each box. Consider these examples.

First, consider this statement: *Equal resources* are not the same as *equal sessions*. Say that you have two Web servers responding to your site requests. Two users come to your site. The first user is directed to your first server. He is just browsing and generates only three page views. This short session doesn't use many resources. The second user is directed to your second server. She is considering a purchase and wants to research your product in depth. This user generates 20 page views. Even though each machine has handled one session, the second session consumed many more resou·ces than the first. If, by coincidence, one machine had to handle several "type two" sessions, it could run out of resources even though server one, with a more balanced pattern of sessions, is still capable of handling more traffic. These *spot bottlenecks* can be a huge problem when load balancing because a user who is directed to the slower server will think your entire site is slow, even though it's a transitional situation that affects only one of your servers.

You can run into spot bottlenecks even if you go to a finer grain than sessions and you distribute your requests. Say you have two main features on your site. The first is a brochure that describes each of your company's products. It's mostly plain HTML, with only a few CFML tags for dynamic formatting. Each page takes under 100 milliseconds (ms) for ColdFusion to process.

The second feature is a store for your users to purchase your products. The store uses Secure Socket Layer (SSL) for security, which adds a layer of overhead. There is some intense CFML and database processing to record the user's contact information, check the availability of your products, and register the order. The final stage is a slow ColdFusion page that has to make an external TCP/IP call to a credit card validation service. Every page of the store takes at least 500ms for ColdFusion to process, and the final credit card step can take as long as five seconds.

Say two users come to your site and make 10 page requests each. The first user spends her time in the brochure, hitting 10 quick-loading pages for a total of one second of ColdFusion processing time. The second user hits the home page (100ms) and then heads right for the store. He generates seven requests to the ordering system (500ms each), one request to the credit card validator (2.5 seconds), and one final request to log the order (500ms). The second user has consumed 6.6 seconds of processing time, along with several ODBC database calls and one external TCP/IP connection. Even though both users made 10 requests, the second user consumed far more server resources. Your servers might be able to handle 100 brochure users at one time, but as few as 10 or 15 store users could generate the same amount of load. If you distribute requests randomly, at any one moment you could by coincidence send mostly catalog requests to one server and mostly brochure requests to another. Again, one server could end up with a spot bottleneck.

To some degree, spot bottlenecks can't be avoided. Engineering a system that avoids them entirely is almost impossible, so one facet of a multi-machine site is getting used to individual machines getting a bit bogged down from time to time, just based on the odds. In a perfect world, you would be able to invest in enough Web servers to make the odds of a spot bottleneck vanishingly thin. However, if you're living in the real world like the rest of us, your budget doesn't allow that luxury. Usually, the best you can do is avoid sending additional traffic to a server that is suffering from a spot bottleneck. Sophisticated load-balancing solutions, such as dedicated hardware, check the status of each Web server by testing performance statistics such as the time it takes your server to respond to an HTTP request. Some solutions even come with software agents that are installed on the servers and report resource utilization back to the load-balancing machine. These solutions reduce the number of requests that are routed to a machine under a temporarily high load. Therefore, the number of users exposed to a spot bottleneck is minimized, and the machine under load is allowed to clean up any hung requests quickly, making it ready to accept more traffic.

Handling Resource Collisions

If your Web servers need to talk to a back-end resource such as a database or a proprietary information source, make sure that the back-end server can accept multiple requests from the same user account. If it can't, you might need to set up each Web server to make a request with a different user ID and password. Some systems might not accept multiple users at all; in that case, you may need to engineer a bridge component that accepts multiple requests from your Web servers and feeds them to the back-end server one at a time. This type of bridge component is frequently known as a *request broker*. A request broker provides several advantages besides supporting multiple request sources. A request broker can also monitor the status of your back-end resource and quickly time out requests if the back-end resource gets bogged down or if it has a failure and ceases to operate. A more complex request broker could cache information from the back-end resource in RAM, allowing it to respond to requests even faster than the back-end resource could on its own. These sorts of strategies can alleviate the slow-down caused by inserting another software layer into your Web installation.

Whether or not you use a request broker model, be sure to test all back-end components in a two-server configuration before exposing them to the public. Make sure your databases are configured to handle an increased number of requests coming from two servers. Think about any data locking issues associated with multiple servers generating requests.

Sharing Data Among Multiple Servers

When you add your second server, any data that your initial Web server depended on now needs to be visible to all Web servers. Some material, such as HTML files, might best be handled by putting a copy on each Web server—a process known as *replication* (see the description later in this chapter). Other types of information or services might need to be unique for the whole site (say, a list of unique usernames).

> **CAUTION**
>
> If you have unique data on your current Web server, don't make it available by pointing your additional Web servers at the first. Doing so steals resources from your first Web server, making it less capable of handling Web requests. It also creates a single point of failure, where Web trouble could not only bring down your Web server, but also cut off other features of your site.

If you have a lot of unique data, think about putting it on a dedicated back-end file server. I've made this point before, but if you have services or other programs that run on the Web server itself, move them onto dedicated back-end machines. The classic example is moving your SQL Server or other database engine to a dedicated database machine. This move solves the multiple-Web-servers problem and improves performance of both the machine that doesn't have the database engine on it anymore and the database engine itself, which now has the resources of a dedicated machine. If you're on a limited budget, it's recommended that you move your database server to a separate machine before buying a second Web server.

Keeping Content Synchronized Across Multiple Servers

Your actual Web content—HTTP files, CFML templates, images, Java applets, and so on—is the most important content that needs to be available on every Web server. You can make it available in two ways.

The first method is to set up a dedicated file system on a back-end machine that contains all your Web content; you should point the roots of each machine's Web server at that shared volume. If you have a fast network, and the dedicated file system is highly optimized and reliable, this option can be efficient. You don't need to worry about sending copies of each file to each server. One risk is that the file system will receive a huge amount of load, and it will become a single point of failure. Don't even think about using a single file system that's not in a RAID 5 configuration with a hot spare always on hand. Think about setting up a redundant file system in case you suffer an extremely rare event like a controller card failure. The major disadvantage of this approach is that accessing files over the network is always slower than accessing a drive on the same machine ("on the bus"). You also have to worry about network collisions due to the high network traffic to this single file system.

The other option is to *replicate* your content across the drives of each Web server. You can replicate content several ways:

- Robocopy—If you are on a budget and own the *Windows NT Resource Kit* (as every good NT system administrator should), you can use a utility called Robocopy for file replication. Although you need a good understanding of scheduled system processes, Robocopy is a very powerful tool that you can use to synchronize content.

  Using Robocopy is as simple as invoking it from the command line, specifying a target and source directory, and pressing Enter. Robocopy also supplies several useful command-line attributes that allow you to customize your replication system as you see fit. Robocopy allows you to use UNCs (Uniform Naming Conventions) so that you can access content on NT servers across a network. After you figure out your content replication scheme, simply put your Robocopy command in a CMD file somewhere in the system path, and trigger it with the NT AT service on specified intervals.

- A content management system—Several commercially available software packages, such as Vignette StoryServer and NetObjects Fusion, allow you to deliver content to multiple systems via file copy or FTP. These systems tend to deal with content in a very static way, however, and their price point in some cases puts them firmly in the "very large site" range. They are designed to manage Web sites with thousands of documents that don't change frequently after they've been posted. Although these systems do more than replication (such as providing scripting functionality), the core replication routines simply make sure the files on all servers configured match each other. No ColdFusion-specific functionality is contained in these systems. (On the other hand, check out the Fusion2Fusion product for an attempt to make NetObjects Fusion work better with a ColdFusion-based site.)

■ Bright Tiger's Built-In Content Replication Cluster Cats—This, which is included with ColdFusion 4, contains a built-in system to replicate content across a Web server cluster that you define. This capability allows you to update one server and have Cluster Cats synchronize the content across all servers in the cluster.

Whichever replication method you choose, I recommend that you try to make the replication source be a machine other than your public Web servers. If one of your public Web servers has to do the work of replicating content, as well as serving Web requests, it will have fewer re-sources available to respond to Web requests. If your load-balancing solution cannot balance traffic according to server utilization, this can become a problem. Because a Web server/replication server is doing double duty, the higher level of stress could make the machine more failure-prone. If your dual-use server goes down, you haven't just lost a Web server, you've lost your only means of delivering content to your remaining servers. This statement is just a repetition of my current mantra—namely, don't put anything on your Web servers that isn't directly related to responding to a Web request.

Maintaining Sessions Among Multiple Servers

If you have built your site to use ColdFusion session variables, you might need to have each user use the same machine for the duration of his or her session. This situation can arise with other site features besides ColdFusion; for example, your e-commerce solution might require the user to go through a defined series of steps on a connection that is held open from a single computer. Simple load-balancing solutions do not allow you to dedicate sessions in this manner. More sophisticated solutions might allow you to do so, but you'll find that their support techni-cians will discourage you. Reread the earlier section about spot bottlenecks to see how keeping a user on the same machine for a session can lead to severe short-term performance problems. ColdFusion 4 alleviates much of this problem by allowing you to store session variables in a shared database instead of in RAM on an individual Web server. See Chapter 4, "Managing Client State," for more information about ColdFusion 4 and session variables.

Part Two: Choosing a Load-Balancing Solution

In this section, I will discuss some of the major solutions available for balancing load across multiple machines. Some of these options are extremely expensive, costing tens of thousands of dollars; others are as simple as changing a few lines in your DNS server. Predictably enough, you tend to get what you pay for.

■ Poor-man's load balancing—You can set up a crude form of server redirection using ColdFusion's application framework. You'll see this method as a coding example in Chapter 4.

Advantages
Inexpensive

Application-specific

Disadvantages
Home-made

Negates full proportional distribution of load

Does not provide for failover or email notification

■ Round-robin DNS (RRDNS)—This method of load balancing takes advantage of some capabilities of the way the Internet's Domain Name System handles multiple IP addresses with the same domain name. To configure round-robin DNS, you need to be comfortable with making changes to your DNS server.

CAUTION

Don't even think about making DNS changes unless you're certain you know what you're doing. Making an incorrect DNS change is roughly equivalent to sending out incorrect change of address and change of phone number forms to every one of your customers and vendors and having no way to tell the people at the incorrect postal destination or the incorrect phone number to forward the errant mail and calls back to you. If you broadcast incorrect DNS information, you could cut off all traffic to your site for days or weeks.

Simply put, RRDNS centers around the concept of giving your public domain name (www.*yourdomain*.com) more than one IP address. You should give each machine in your cluster two domain names: one for the public domain and one that lets you address each machine uniquely.

Public Address	Machine Name
www	web1
www	web2
www	web3

When a remote domain name server queries your domain name server for information about www.*yourdomain*.com (because a user has requested a Web page and needs to know the address of your server), your DNS returns one of the multiple IP addresses you've listed for www.*yourdomain*.com. The remote DNS then uses that IP address until its DNS cache expires, upon which it queries your DNS again, possibly getting a different IP address. Each sequential request from a remote DNS server receives a different IP address as a response.

CAUTION

Round-robin DNS is a very crude form of load balancing. When a remote DNS gets one of your IP addresses in its cache, it uses that same IP address until the cache expires, no matter how many requests originate from the remote domain and regardless of whether the target IP address is responding. This means that AOL's domain name servers read one of your many IP addresses and then direct all of AOL's traffic at that one IP address until AOL's cache expires. Similarly, if the machine at that IP address crashes, any user who tries to access your site from AOL is still directed to that IP address which is not responding. The user's experience will be that your site is *down*, even though you may have two or three other Web servers ready to respond to the request.

Because DNS caches generally take one to seven days to expire, any DNS change you make to a RRDNS cluster will take a long time to propagate. This means that in the preceding example of a server crash, removing the down server's IP address from your DNS server doesn't solve the AOL user's problem because the IP address of the down server is still in AOL's DNS cache. You can partially address this problem by setting your DNS record's TTLs (time to live) to a very low value so that remote DNSs are instructed to expire their record of your domain's IP address after a brief period of time. This solution can cause undue load on your DNS, however. And even worse, many remote DNS servers are not good Internet citizens and don't do what they're told. Even with low TTLs, an IP address you remove from the RRDNS cluster may still be in the cache of some remote DNSs for a week or more.

Advantages

Inexpensive

Probably the best solution if you can't make the investment in dedicated load-balancing hardware

Disadvantages

Negates full proportional distribution of load

Does not provide for failover or email notification

■ Bright Tiger and software-based load balancing—You can purchase software-based products such as Bright Tiger's Cluster Cats (included with ColdFusion 4) or Convoy Cluster to balance load across your Web cluster. A software product provides several key advantages over RRDNS. First, most load-balancing software includes some way to replicate content to all the servers involved in a cluster. Software can also make your cluster more aware of its own existence as a cluster, allowing individual Web servers to take action in case of a load imbalance or server failure.

In most methodologies, a service runs on each machine in a cluster. One machine is designated as the primary cluster server and distributes load to the other servers in the cluster. Should one server go down, the other machines in the cluster are notified by communication among each server's cluster service, and they act to absorb the extra load. One limitation of this approach is that it requires your Web servers to act as their own clustering agents, which goes against my aversion to making Web servers serve multiple purposes. Another limitation is the necessity for a primary cluster server, which undermines the key advantage of a cluster—redundancy. What happens if your primary cluster server goes down? However, server-based clustering can form a good middle ground between "dirt-cheap but dumb" RRDNS and expensive hardware-based solutions.

Advantages

Usually contains content replication system

Provides for failover

Can perform session-aware clustering

Can work with RRDNS as a two-layer approach

Disadvantages

Negates full proportional distribution of load

No intermediary between servers and load

Does not provide for network address translation for security

■ Dedicated load-balancing hardware—Using dedicated load-balancing hardware is the most sophisticated way to balance load across a cluster. This method is the only way to provide truly proportionate load balancing. Products such as HydraWeb, Cisco's Local Director, and F5 Labs BigIP lead the pack in this space.

In general, load-balancing hardware hides the true composition of your cluster from the public Internet. Requests come in to a single IP address for your domain. The load-balancing hardware answers the request and mediates with individual Web servers to provide a response that appears to have originated from your domain's single public IP address. This form of distribution relies on complex algorithms to determine which Web server is "most available" at the time the request is presented. This is usually done by server polling for HTTP response time and optionally by the use of agents residing on the Web servers that make up your cluster. These agents report back various aspects of your system's performance to the load-balancing hardware such as CPU utilization, process utilization, and other vital machine statistics. Based on this data, the device routes the request to the most available server. This method also provides graceful failover in case of a server outage because a server that is down fails any polling tests and doesn't return any usable performance data via its agent.

Setting up load-balancing hardware is fairly complex. Load-balancing hardware is generally *dual-homed* (see the discussion of dual homing earlier in this chapter). Configuration usually requires fairly robust knowledge of TCP/IP networking principles, as well as the ability to absorb new concepts associated with the load-balancing hardware itself. For example, one downside to load-balancing hardware is the old single-point-of-failure problem. To alleviate this issue, most load-balancing hardware manufacturers recommend that you purchase two boxes at once and set them up so that the second can seamlessly take over for the first in case of failure. This back-up box is known as a *hot spare*. You also need to address security and administration issues for your load-balancing hardware, just as you would for any other machine on your network.

CAUTION

Only qualified routing technicians should set up hardware-based load balancing. Because these machines actually translate addresses, you can affect the operation of other routers on your network with an incorrect installation or modification.

Part

I

Ch

2

On the plus side, load-balancing hardware can dramatically improve your site's availability to the public. Because the hardware handles slow servers and down servers quickly and seamlessly, and it masks the network characteristics of your cluster, your users will experience a single site that is rarely slow and almost never down. If you've been tied to a beeper because of server performance or stability problems, the cost of load-balancing software might be worthwhile just for the good night's sleep you'll get after it's installed. I believe that load-balancing hardware is a good investment if 24-hour-a-day, seven-days-a-week uptime is important for your site. Low-end hardware is available in the $20 to $25 thousand price range.

Hardware-based load balancing provides an enhanced level of security because most of this hardware uses NAT (network address translation). This way, an administrator can use private, nonroutable IP numbers to address Web servers and filter requests to those machines on specific ports at the NAT machine. For example, the NAT machine knows that 10.1.2.1 is a Web server behind it. An instruction is given to the NAT machine that says that a public address of 206.123.23.5 maps to 10.1.2.1 on port 80. Then, when a request comes to 206.123.23.5 on port 80, the NAT machine passes the request through to the back-end server. The user, however, never knows the true IP address of the server responding to the request, and a different server could be substituted for 10.1.2.1 by changing the mapping.

Advantages

Provides true distribution of load based on server resources

Acts as an added layer of security

Provides for automatic failover to standby machines

Disadvantages

Content replication must be handled separately

Requires advanced networking knowledge to set up and administer

Expensive

Server Clustering Using Bright Tiger

What Is Cluster Cats for ColdFusion Application Server 4?

Included with the Enterprise version of ColdFusion is Cluster Cats by Bright Tiger Software. A software-based load-balancing solution, Cluster Cats monitors your ColdFusion Application Server (CFAS) and can redirect requests away from a server that is beginning to enter a "busy" state. Note that Cluster Cats does not work on the network layer. When Cluster Cats redirects requests to another server, it does so by redirecting to the URL of another machine in the cluster. This means that if your server is completely out of commission (that is, not turned on), Cluster Cats cannot communicate with it and therefore cannot redirect requests away from it.

Perhaps the most attractive thing about using Cluster Cats for your load-balancing solution is its integration with the CFAS. Because Cluster Cats responds to elements of the CFAS, you get load balancing that is specific to your ColdFusion-based application. You get this benefit in addition to general failover and machine alerts.

An important point to note about Cluster Cats is that the version shipping with CFAS 4 does not include support for replication; however, the full version of Cluster Cats, available from Bright Tiger, does have replication built in. *Replication* is the ability to put your ColdFusion scripts on one machine in your cluster and have those scripts update on all machines in the cluster. Many administrators overlook replication when planning their load-balancing strategy. However, as code bases grow, and server architectures get more complex, replication plays a crucial role in content synchronization. Later this chapter outlines some simple strategies to include replication from the onset, and thus keep your job as server administrator manageable as your server cluster grows.

Understanding Cluster Cats

As you have learned in the preceding two chapters, many different methods for clustering servers are available. In particular, the methodologies employed in software-based clustering differ greatly. This fact will most definitely have an impact on how your server cluster serves your application. This section will give you a broad overview of the methodologies employed in Cluster Cats.

To begin, you need to note that Cluster Cats uses HTTP redirection to balance load across a cluster. Although, in general, this is a protocol-based redirection, it lacks certain network-level controls; therefore, I place it in the application layer of the networking hierarchy. In contrast, another popular software-based clustering strategy, Convoy Cluster (acquired by Microsoft in August 1998), attempts to use the network layer by advertising multicast MAC addresses to routing equipment. Because this discussion is about Cluster Cats, I will not go into the details of multicast MAC addressing. However, suffice it to say that Convoy makes your cluster look like one big IP address (see Figure 3.1), whereas Cluster Cats makes your cluster look like a lot of HTTP servers grouped together (see Figure 3.2). Depending on your situation, one approach may be better than the other, but they both do the same job.

FIGURE 3.1

Diagram of HTTP server redirection.

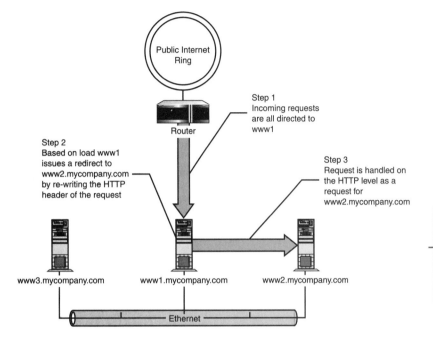

Step 1
Incoming requests are all directed to www1

Step 2
Based on load www1 issues a redirect to www2.mycompany.com by re-writing the HTTP header of the request

Step 3
Request is handled on the HTTP level as a request for www2.mycompany.com

www3.mycompany.com   www1.mycompany.com   www2.mycompany.com

Part
I

Ch
3

FIGURE 3.2

Diagram of multicast MAC addressing.

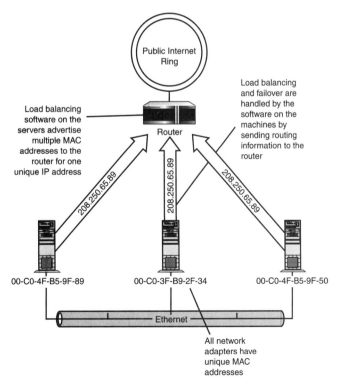

Load balancing software on the servers advertise multiple MAC addresses to the router for one unique IP address

Load balancing and failover are handled by the software on the machines by sending routing information to the router

208.250.65.89   208.250.65.89   208.250.65.89

00-C0-4F-B5-9F-89   00-C0-3F-B9-2F-34   00-C0-4F-B5-9F-50

All network adapters have unique MAC addresses

> **CAUTION**
>
> By extension of these differing methodologies, you must make concessions in the way you code your application to support the type of redirection being employed. In some cases, this solution may be as simple as not using absolute paths in your URL references; in other cases, you might need to make use of ColdFusion's advanced Client State management options (discussed in a later chapter) to mitigate these server redirections.

Now, take a look at the components of Cluster Cats. The software works with two primary components: the Server component and the Explorer component. Each plays a critical role in the configuration and support of your Cluster Cats clusters. Note that although you can have a cluster consisting of a mix of Sun Solaris and Windows NT-based servers running Cluster Cats, you must have at least one Windows NT server to run the Cluster Cats Explorer. You cannot configure your cluster without the Explorer component.

Cluster Cats Server

The Cluster Cats Server component runs on Windows NT 4.0 and Sun Solaris. This Server component is the heart of the cluster. It controls configuration of a machine's role in a particular cluster, handles redirection from the server in the event that load thresholds are breached, and controls access to the server based on restriction rules. The Server component must reside on all machines you are using for your cluster operations.

Cluster Cats Explorer

The Cluster Cats Explorer component runs only on Windows NT 4.0. It controls configuration of Cluster Cats clusters. I found that it was best to configure the server that the Explorer sits on as the primary server for all your incoming HTTP requests. I like to call it the "Controller Server." Its purpose is to handle all the incoming HTTP requests first and then redirect to other machines in the cluster as needed.

Tasks handled by the Cluster Cats Explorer include the following:

- Creating and removing clusters
- Adding and removing servers from a cluster and setting server load threshold levels
- Restricting or providing access to servers
- Registering cluster administrators
- Selecting events for alarms and specifying the recipients of alarm email distributions

How Cluster Cats Works

As mentioned previously, Cluster Cats uses HTTP redirection as its principal methodology for distributing load across a cluster. This means that the user's request is sent to another machine in the cluster and stays there until that machine needs to redirect the request to yet another machine.

For example, if a request comes to www.yourcompany.com, and www is too busy to handle new requests, it sends that request to www2 (or another machine based on availability of all machines in the cluster). The URL in the browser location box now reads www2.yourcompany.com (refer to Figure 3.1). Therefore, subsequent requests will go to www2 until that machine cannot accept more requests. At that point, www2 will attempt to redirect the request to another machine based on the information it has about other machine availability.

> **CAUTION**
>
> In the preceding example, the cluster essentially "cedes" control of redirections to the HTTP protocol. This means that there is no way to control what happens after that redirect is issued. If the target server crashes or otherwise does not respond to requests at all, a redirect fails with a `Server unavailable` response to the user. As of the writing of this book, the CFAS 4 implementation of Cluster Cats does not provide catastrophic server failover capabilities. This capability is expected in a later release of CFAS 4 and will mitigate this dilemma. With catastrophic server failover in place, the Cluster Cats HTTP redirection would know whether a server is available and thus not redirect a request to a failed server. This result is accomplished via each server listening for a heartbeat from other servers in the cluster. If a machine does not respond to the heartbeat within a specific period of time, another machine in the cluster assumes the IP address of the down machine (a process otherwise known as IP aliasing).

Part
I

Ch
3

Let me contrast this shortcoming of Cluster Cats in the CFAS 4 implementation: If your server is up and running, and you just want to take it out of the cluster for a while for maintenance, you can restrict that server. Restricting a server in a Cluster Cats cluster causes all requests to that server to be sent to other machines automatically.

Sample Application

Say that you have a ColdFusion application that needs to be clustered across two ColdFusion application servers. This application does not use session variables but instead employs a "cluster neutral" method of saving state: client cookies. The name of the Web site you are clustering is www.mycompany.com, and you will be using machines www1.mycompany.com and www2.mycompany.com in the configuration.

To provide two layers of load balancing, you can employ round-robin DNS in addition to Cluster Cats. By doing so, you can distribute general requests to both servers in the cluster. In this configuration, you can keep all load from initially being directed at one machine and better use resources. Although this result may seem inconsequential in the context of what's being described, it will have an impact on what you set in the load threshold level section of each cluster member.

Creating Your Application Cluster   Begin by installing the integrated Cluster Cats software included with ColdFusion 4 on both machines. If you are using Windows NT on both machines, the setup routine installs the Cluster Cats Explorer. In this example, you will use the Cluster Cats Explorer only on www1.mycompany.com.

After you install the software, you will see a new service (in addition to the ColdFusion 4 services) named Bright Tiger Server service in the Service Control Manager. It must be set to Automatic and should be running so that Cluster Cats can work properly. You should always check the Service Control Panel after a significant installation. Doing so helps you understand the components of your server application.

From the www1.mycompany.com console, open the Cluster Cats Explorer. Your screen should look like Figure 3.1.

Right-click the Cluster Manager icon in the left pane of the Cluster Cats Explorer. You then see a dialog box that looks like the one in Figure 3.3.

FIGURE 3.3

The Create New Cluster dialog box.

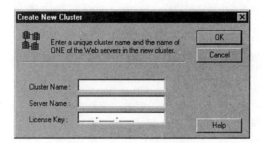

You need to enter the Cluster Name (see the following sidebar), the Server Name, which is the name of the primary server in your cluster, and the License Key included in your ColdFusion 4 Administrator Guide. Be sure to enter the Fully Qualified Host Name of the first machine in your cluster in the Server Name box. In the example, you would enter **www1.mycompany.com**.

Naming, and Why It Is Important

Note that the first name you enter in the Create New Cluster dialog box will become the default administrative manager for the cluster. The administrative manager is responsible for allowing other Web servers to be added and deleted from the SmartCluster. Apart from this, you also need to name your SmartCluster something that is specific to your task. For example, if you plan to host several ColdFusion applications responding to multiple IP addresses on your server, you might want to create clusters that have the same name that exists in your CFAPPLICATION tag. Doing so helps you balance load based on application and not just on the server. If you have a particular application that is CPU intensive, for example, you can give it more of a particular machine in your cluster and redirect other application requests away.

Creating Cluster Members After you create your initial cluster member from the Create New Cluster dialog box, you can add other cluster members by right-clicking on your cluster name, choosing New, and then selecting Cluster Member. In the resulting dialog box (see Figure 3.4), enter the Fully Qualified Host Name. In the example, you would enter www2.mycompany.com.

FIGURE 3.4
The Add New Server to
Cluster dialog box.

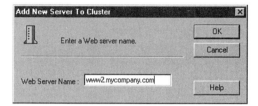

At this point, you should have two servers listed in the Cluster Cats for ColdFusion Explorer.
Cluster Cats might take a few seconds to connect to the servers in your cluster, depending on
the size of your cluster or network load. I found this process to be uneventful, and after the
cluster is synchronized, it does not have an impact on performance at all. Figure 3.5 shows an
example of a cluster in use at my company.

FIGURE 3.5
Cluster Cats Explorer
with two active servers.

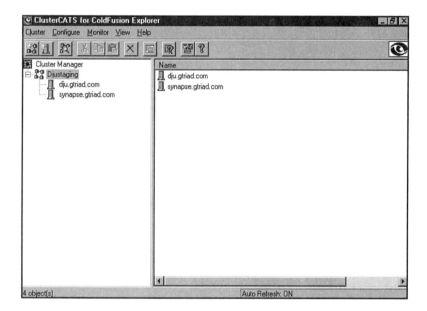

Setting Load Threshold Levels You can set each server in your cluster to respond to two load
thresholds:

- Load Threshold
- Gradual Redirection Threshold

Load Threshold is the top level you allow your server to accept before it enters a busy state.
When this situation occurs, Cluster Cats begins redirecting requests to other servers in the
cluster based on their availability. Cluster Cats continues redirecting requests until the actual
machine load dips beneath this line.

Gradual Redirection Threshold defines a secondary threshold at which user requests start being redirected. As the name implies, if the Gradual Redirection Threshold is reached, Cluster Cats redirects a portion of the load—but not all of the load—to available machines in the cluster. The Gradual Redirection Threshold and the Load Threshold work together to provide a smooth transition of load (see Figure 3.6).

N O T E   Be sure to remember the relationship of the Load Threshold to the Gradual Redirection Threshold. If the Gradual Redirection Threshold is set close to the Load Threshold, a greater number of requests is redirected from the server. Conversely, if the Gradual Redirection Threshold is set far from the Load Threshold, fewer requests are redirected from the server. ■

FIGURE 3.6
Cluster Cats Load Monitor with examples of both types of redirection set.

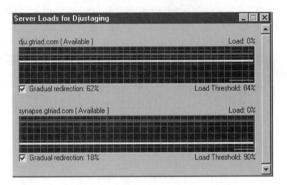

Replication: Keeping Your Content in Sync

Unfortunately, the replication features built into the Bright Tiger implementation of Cluster Cats are not included in the version shipping with CFAS 4. Replication is a mechanism employed to keep content on all your servers in sync with a central source. Anyone who runs multiple Web servers, grouped in a cluster, needs to be able to replicate content. Fortunately, many shareware and freeware utilities are available to help you synchronize your content. I like to use a utility named Robocopy from the Windows NT Resource Kit.

Sample Replication Strategy Using Robocopy   Robocopy and AT (the Windows NT Scheduler service) can combine to be a very effective replication strategy. Robocopy copies only changed files from a central source to target sources. It has an extremely large number of switches that allow you to customize your synchronization rules. Because Robocopy is a command-line utility, you can script fairly elaborate interactions with file systems using UNC names and the program's switches. To use Robocopy, you must have the Windows NT Resource Kit. The following is an example of a Robocopy script I use to replicate content to another Web server and backup RAID drive. Note that I also use the command-line utility called blat to send an email of the Robocopy log back to a central administration desk. If you are writing scripts like these, you would be wise to include some contact information at the top; this way, if your script fails, systems staff know whom they should contact.

```
cls
echo off
echo ***********************************************************
echo *****This is a G. Triad Automated Maintenance Script *****
echo *****Report Problems to gerryl@gtriad.com          *****
echo *****or 908-497-0510                     *****
echo ***********************************************************


del C:\temp\latest2Repl.txt
del C:\temp\latest3Repl.txt
echo Replication to Server 2 Initiated.....working....
robocopy D:\Inetpub\wwwroot\ \\Server2\90195 /E /PURGE >> C:\Temp\latest2Repl.txt
echo Replication to Server2 completed.
echo Replication to Server3 Initiated.... (BackingUp)....
robocopy D:\Inetpub\wwwroot\ \\Server3\90195 /E /PURGE >> C:\Temp\latest3Repl.txt
echo Replication to Server3 completed.
echo Notifying central administration.......
blat C:\temp\latest2Repl.txt -s "[MAINT] Server2 Replication Completed"
➥ -t gerryl@gtriad.com
blat C:\temp\latest3Repl.txt -s "[MAINT] Server3 Replication Completed"
➥ -t gerryl@gtriad.com
echo Notification Completed.
```

Strategies for Clustering with Cluster Cats

Because Cluster Cats works on the HTTP level, you can easily layer load-balancing strategies on top of the system. Combining hardware-based load balancing or round-robin DNS with Cluster Cats creates a two-tiered solution that can be configured in numerous detailed ways. Cluster Cats also provides a means for dealing with Web applications that require use of ColdFusion's session variables.

Dealing with Client State in Cluster Cats   CFAS 4 uses certain types of client state variables that are written into the memory of a Web server. They are known as *session* and *application* variables. These variables apply to a user's session or globally to an application defined with the CFAPPLICATION tag.

Obviously, if a user's session is reliant on persistent variables stored on a particular server in your cluster, you have to keep the user on the same server. If the ColdFusion application you are clustering requires that you not redirect users after they initially access a Web server, you can enable session-aware clustering. Do so by right-clicking the cluster you want to enable it for, selecting Configure, and selecting Administration (see Figure 3.7).

Selecting this option simply keeps users confined to the same server after they initially hit the server. No redirections are performed.

CAUTION

Using session-aware clustering has a direct impact on how you balance load between the servers in your cluster. I believe it is best to set a Load Threshold of approximately 60 percent. Adjust this setting according to the load that your ColdFusion application generates.

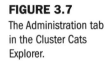

FIGURE 3.7

The Administration tab in the Cluster Cats Explorer.

Using Round-Robin DNS   Round-robin DNS (RRDNS), as you learned in Chapter 1, "Monitoring Server Performance," alternates requests from Web server to Web server based on entries found in your DNS server. In the example here, if you want to set up your cluster for RRDNS, you would enter two entries for the www machine: one pointing to www1.mycompany.com and another pointing to www2.mycompany.com. Thus, resolution requests for www.mycompany.com would alternate between the two servers in the cluster.

The big problem with RRDNS has been that if you have to take a server offline, every other new request to www.mycompany.com will hit a dead machine. With Cluster Cats, you can simply put that machine into a busy state and redirect requests. This type of general failover is included in the version of Cluster Cats shipping with CFAS 4.

Layering RRDNS on top of Cluster Cats provides a wider spread of load to your cluster. Whereas RRDNS never truly provides a true balance, Cluster Cats can help make that balance a little smoother by redirecting requests based on machine load. This load can then be controlled by the Load and Gradual Redirection Thresholds. ●

## CHAPTER 4

Managing Client State

What Is Client State?

The Web is a *stateless* environment. Every request that comes into your Web server looks like any other; it has no begin session or end session message that lets you know that a particular user will be making a series of related requests. To build an effective Web application, however, a Web developer needs to be able to track a user through a series of requests and ideally associate some variables with that user's session, as shown here:

```
<CFIF NOT(IsDefined("session.AuthLevel"))>
    <CFSET session.AuthLevel = 0>
</cfif>
```

Managing client state is the process of associating a series of HTTP requests with a unique user and keeping a set of variables for that session.

ColdFusion 4 gives you several powerful tools for managing client state. These tools range from flexible manipulation of browser-based cookies to a full set of application- and session-based variables. This chapter discusses these methods in the next section, but you should note that using each method of client state management poses some serious implications. When you manage state, you force the Web to do something it wasn't originally built for, so you have to be very careful. Managing client state becomes especially complex if you are planning on scaling your ColdFusion application across multiple ColdFusion servers.

In this chapter, I will discuss how to manage state using ColdFusion `Client` variables in a scaled environment. This task can be difficult and detail-oriented, depending on which option you choose. Choose carefully: If you are basing your application on saving state, scaled environments introduce a whole new set of methodologies.

Methods for Managing Client State

Consider a hypothetical Web-based application that requires the use of client state variables. As a reference point, you can deal with a login script that authenticates a user and sets some information about the user in `Client` variables. Instead of authenticating a user from scratch with every HTTP request, you can use sessions to perform an initial authentication once and then reference in-memory session variables for the rest of the user's requests. This way, you can reduce page build time and stress on the database. Although some people may consider this to be a security problem, session variables are stored on the server and are not transmitted over the public net. This approach is inherently more secure than setting something as sensitive as an account number in a cookie and transmitting it to the client browser. Figure 4.1 shows a login form for such a Web site. Listing 4.1 shows the code behind the form that responds to the data input.

The code in Listing 4.1 retrieves information from a data source and is ready to pass that information to some form of persistent variable. Remember that you want to optimize the functionality of the overall application by hitting the database once in a session and storing the user's data in some form of persistent variable.

FIGURE 4.1

A login form.

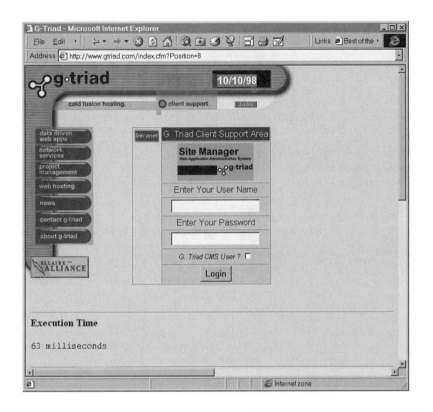

Listing 4.1 `validator.cfm`—**Code That Responds to** Form **Variables Submitted by the Login Form**

```
<!---
Name of file: Validator.cfm
Description of the script:  Authenticates user on login to the system.
Gerry Libertelli, G.Triad Development Corporation
Date created:  Saturday, March 14, 1998
Description of all dependent scripts
Change History:

   Date.......Name.......Description of Change.......

1.  3/14/98 GL  Initial Rev
--->

<cfquery name="getUser" datasource="#dsn#">
SELECT tblUserInfoInfo.*, tblSubsInfo.WorkshopID FROM tblUserInfo, tblSubsInfo
WHERE tblUserInfo.Username = '#Username#'
AND tblUserInfo.Password = '#Password#'
AND tblUserInfo.StudentID = tblSubsInfo.StudentID
</cfquery>
```

continues

Listing 4.1   Continued

```
<CFIF getUser.RecordCount IS 0>
        <CFLOCATION URL="/index.cfm">
        <CFABORT>
<CFELSEIF getUser.RecordCount GTE 2>
        <CFLOCATION URL="/index.cfm">
        <CFABORT>
<CFELSE>
<cfquery name="getWorkshopInfo" datasource="#dsn#">
SELECT StartDate, EndDate FROM tblWorkshop
WHERE WorkshopID = #getUser.WorkshopID#
</cfquery>

    <CFIF getUser.Status IS 0>
        <!--- User has had access revoked.  Initialize session vars for --->
        <!--- error handling and identify system account number for error --->
        <!--- shell. --->
            <CFSET client.theSystemNum = getUser.theSystemNum>
            <CFSET session.AuthLevel = 1>
            <CFSET session.StudentID = #getUser.StudentID#>
                <CFLOCATION URL="/
index.cfm?ShellStatus=LoginFailed&ReasonCode=1">
        <CFABORT>
    <CFELSEIF getWorkshopInfo.StartDate GT #Now()#>
            <CFSET client.theSystemNum = getUser.theSystemNum>
            <CFSET session.AuthLevel = 1>
            <CFSET session.StudentID = #getUser.StudentID#>
                <CFLOCATION URL="/
index.cfm?ShellStatus=LoginFailed&ReasonCode=3">
        <CFABORT>
    <CFELSEIF getWorkshopInfo.EndDate LTE #Now()#>
            <CFSET client.theSystemNum = getUser.theSystemNum>
            <CFSET session.AuthLevel = 1>
            <CFSET session.StudentID = #getUser.StudentID#>
                <CFLOCATION URL="/
index.cfm?ShellStatus=LoginFailed&ReasonCode=4">
        <CFABORT>
    <CFELSE>

                <CFSET session.AuthLevel = 1>
                <CFSET session.StudentID = #getUser.StudentID#>


                <cfquery name="updUser" datasource="#dsn#">
                    UPDATE tblUserInfo
                    SET LastAccess = #CreateODBCDateTime(Now())#
                    WHERE StudentID = #getUser.StudentID#
                </cfquery>


                <CFLOCATION URL="/index.cfm">
                <CFABORT>
    </cfif>
</cfif>
```

In the following sections, I'll describe three methods for storing and referencing persistent variables.

Information Embedded in the URL or in a FORM Post

In the early days of the Internet (way back in 1995), CGI programmers set up a roll-your-own method of maintaining client state. They used the HTTP protocol's built-in syntax for passing name/value pairs, either on the URL (with a GET request) or after the main body of the HTTP request (with a POST request, usually from a form). By being careful, a CGI programmer could hand the same name/value pairs from page to page of a site via URLs and forms. This method of managing client state created beautiful URL strings that look something like the Web site shown in Figure 4.2.

FIGURE 4.2
Notice the cryptic URL string on this Web site.

For obvious reasons, embedding information in URL strings is not the greatest idea. Aside from passing potentially sensitive information about the user (such as a password) in clear text in a URL or FORM post, appending and maintaining state information in a URL string is extremely difficult. You must expend painstaking effort in making sure that all FORM elements and URL strings are sending the correct information to the CGI or script.

In the core example, you would use a <CFLOCATION> tag to store name/value pairs containing information about the user. Refer back to Figure 4.1 for an example of a user getting error codes in the URL string to identify what type of failed login he or she received.

Cookies

Rather than force Web developers to remember to pass name/value pairs on every page, Netscape tried to help out by defining the *cookie* protocol, which stores name/value pairs on the user's machine and passes them automatically with every HTTP request to a specified Web site or subsection thereof.

Always the subject of heated debate, cookies soon became the persistent variable favorite of Web application developers. One key advantage is that cookies persist; they can be configured to stay on the user's machine from session to session, instead of expiring at the end of the current session. As a Web developer, you can give a user a permanent (and unique) identifier or even store important data on the user's machine. Because a user might access your site from more than one machine or browser (or could experience a system crash that wipes out his or her cookies), it's usually best to store a minimal user identifier in a cookie and store critical data on the server side.

Listing 4.2 stores cookies and provides a form button for the user to proceed to the next page.

Listing 4.2   `cookieValidator.cfm`—Validator Setting Cookies

```
<CFSET #Username# = #Form.Username#>
<CFSET #Password# = #Form.Password#>

<CFIF IsDefined("theSystemUser") IS "True">

    <cfquery name="validateUser" datasource="AccountingDb">
        SELECT * FROM tblSystemUser
        WHERE UserID = '#Username#'
        AND Password = '#Password#'
    </cfquery>

    <CFIF #ValidateUser.RecordCount# IS 1>
        <cfquery name="getInfo" datasource="AccountingDb">
            SELECT * FROM tblAccountInfo
            WHERE SubID = #ValidateUser.SubID#
        </cfquery>
    </cfif>
<cfelse>
    <cfquery name="validateUser" datasource="AccountingDb">
        SELECT * FROM Subscriptions
        WHERE Username = '#Username#'
        AND Password = '#Password#'
    </cfquery>
</cfif>

<cfif IsDefined("Cookie.FailedLogin") IS "True" >
```

```
    <CFSET FailedLogin = #Cookie.FailedLogin#>
</cfif>


<CFIF #validateUser.RecordCount# IS 0>

        <CFIF IsDefined("Cookie.FailedLogin") IS "True">
            <CFSET FailedLogin = Evaluate(#Cookie.FailedLogin# + 1)>
                <cfcookie name="FailedLogin" value="#FailedLogin#">
        <CFELSE>
            <cfcookie name="FailedLogin" value="1">
        </cfif>

        <html>
        <head>
        <title>Error</title>
        </head>
        <body bgcolor="White">



        <cfif #FailedLogin# IS 5 >

        <center>
        <table cellspacing="2" cellpadding="2">
        <tr>
            <td bgcolor="#0080C0"><font face="Arial, Helvetica" size="3"
➥ color="#FF0000"><b>Error!</b></font></td>
            <td bgcolor="#FFFFB7"><font face="Arial, Helvetica" size="1"
➥ color="#FF0000">Your client has been denied access to this system
➥ due to too many failed login attempts.  Please email <a
➥ href="mailto:sales@gtriad.com">sales@gtriad.com</a> for
➥ assistance.</font></td>
        </tr>
        </table>
        </center>
        <CFELSE>
        <center>
        <table cellspacing="2" cellpadding="2">
        <tr>
            <td bgcolor="#0080C0"><font face="Arial, Helvetica" size="3"
➥ color="#FF0000"><b>Error!</b></font></td>
            <td bgcolor="#FFFFB7"><font face="Arial, Helvetica" size="1"
➥ color="#FF0000">Username and Password Combination not Found!</font></td>
        </tr>
        <tr>
            <td colspan="2" align="center">
            <form action="/support/index.cfm" method="GET">
                <font face="Arial,Helvetica" size="1"><input type="Submit"
➥ name="" value="Try Again?"></font>
            </form>
            </td>

        </tr>
```

Part

I

Ch

4

continues

Listing 4.2   Continued

```
        </table>
        </center>
        </cfif>
        <CFINCLUDE template="/include/footer.cfm">
        </body>
        </html>
<cfelseif #validateUser.RecordCount# GT 1>

        <center>
        <table cellspacing="2" cellpadding="2">
        <tr>
            <td bgcolor="#0080C0"><font face="Arial, Helvetica" size="3"
➥ color="#FF0000"><b>Error!</b></font></td>
            <td bgcolor="#FFFFB7"><font face="Arial, Helvetica" size="1"
➥ color="#FF0000">There was an error in your login.  Please email
➥ <a href="mailto:sales@gtriad.com">sales@gtriad.com</a> referencing
➥ error code number 450 for assistance.</font></td>
        </tr>
        </table>
        </center>

<cfelse>
        <CFIF IsDefined("theSystemUser") IS "True">
            <cfquery name="getClient" datasource="AccountingDb">
            SELECT * FROM Clients
            WHERE SubRecord = #ValidateUser.SubID#
            </cfquery>
        <cfelse>
            <cfquery name="getClient" datasource="AccountingDb">
            SELECT * FROM Clients
            WHERE ID = #ValidateUser.ClientID#
            </cfquery>
        </cfif>
        <HTML>
        <HEAD>
        <TITLE>My Company</TITLE>
        </HEAD>
        <BODY BGCOLOR="D6D6D6" BACKGROUND="/images/back.gif" LiNK="006600"
➥ VLINK="CC6600">

        <!--- begin whole page table --->
        <CFINCLUDE template="/include/header.cfm">

        <center>
        <table border="0" cellspacing="0" cellpadding="0" width="140">
        <tr>
            <td>
                <table border="3" cellspacing="0" cellpadding="10">
                <tr>
                    <td bgcolor="#0080C0" align="center"><font face="Arial,
➥ Helvetica" size="3" color="#FF0000"><b>Login Successful!</b></font></td>
                </tr>
                <CFIF IsDefined("theSystemUser") IS "True">
```

```
                    <cfelse>
                    <Tr>
                        <td bgcolor="#FFFFB7" align="center"><font face="Arial,
➡ Helvetica" size="1" color="#FF0000">Welcome to the Client Support
➡ System <cfoutput>#getClient.ContactFirstName#</cfoutput></font></td>
                    </tr>
                    </cfif>
                    <tr>
                        <td align="center">
                        <CFIF IsDefined("theSystemUser") IS "True">
                        <form action="/support/private/ContentMgmt/index.cfm"
➡ method="GET">
                        <cfoutput>
                        <input type="Hidden" name="SubID" value=
➡"#ValidateUser.SubID#">
                        <input type="Hidden" name="Name" value=
➡"#ValidateUser.FirstName# #ValidateUser.LastName#">
                        <input type="Hidden" name="UserID" value=
➡"#ValidateUser.theSystemUserID#">
                        <input type="Hidden" name="Stage" value=
➡"#getInfo.StagingRoot#">
                        <input type="Hidden" name="Live" value="#getInfo.WebRoot#">
                        <input type="Hidden" name="RevDir" value=
➡"#Replace(getInfo.StagingRoot, 'Staging', 'Revs')#">
                        </cfoutput>
                            <font face="Arial,Helvetica" size="1">
➡<input type="Submit" name="" value="Enter System"></font>
                        </form>
                        <cfelse>
                        <form action="/support/private/index.cfm" method="GET">
                            <font face="Arial,Helvetica" size="1"><input type=
➡"Submit" name="" value="Enter System"></font>
                        </form>
                        </cfif>
                        </td>
                    </tr>
                    </table>
                </td>
        </tr>
        </table>
        </center>

        <CFIF IsDefined("theSystemUser") IS "True">

        <cfelse>
            <cfcookie name="SubID" value="#ValidateUser.ID#">
        </cfif>

        <CFINCLUDE template="/include/footer.cfm">
        </body>
        </html>

</cfif>
```

Scripts that need to reference this information need only call the variable by instantiating the cookie object.

N O T E You cannot use <CFLOCATION> in conjunction with <CFCOOKIE>. If you use <CFLOCATION>, <CFCOOKIE> does not set values. ■

Client, Application, and Session Variables

The old saying "What's past is prelude" is perhaps the best way to understand ColdFusion's implementation of session variables. ColdFusion 4 doesn't replace HTTP name/value pairs or cookies, but it does automate the process of identifying users and sessions; you therefore can concentrate on your session-dependent applications, instead of the mechanics of maintaining a session.

All server-side storage and retrieval are dependent on the existence of two variables: CFID and CFTOKEN. These two parameters define a unique "identity" for the user and reference variables being stored in one of several places on the ColdFusion server. CFID and CFTOKEN are most commonly implemented as cookies, but you can use ColdFusion sessions without cookies by relying on HTTP name/value pairs. Again, a fairly painstaking attention to detail is involved in making sure that these pairs are included in the URLs being passed between pages in your application.

Uniquely identifying the user is only half the value. To really leverage session management, you need to be able to store information about the user on the server. In ColdFusion 4, you have several methods for storing server-side variables. These various types, shown here, enable you to define layers of persistent variables:

■ Server—Server variables are global variables, stored in RAM, that are available to any ColdFusion page on the currently running server. Server variables are visible to all sessions.

■ Application—Application variables are similar to Server variables, but they are specific to the current ColdFusion application, as specified in the NAME parameter of the <CFAPPLICATION> tag. Application variables are visible to all sessions.

■ Client—Client variables are unique to the current user and persist across sessions. They can be stored in several locations, including a central database (you'll find more details on this subject later).

■ Session—Session variables act very much like Client variables, but they are stored in RAM and expire at the end of a user's session, based on a predetermined timeout.

In the core code example, you see an authentication query setting several Session variables. ColdFusion pages handling subsequent requests from this user can now reference a user's authentication parameters simply by calling the Session variable. Session variables are the best choice in this example because you want authentication to expire after the user is done using the site. In other words, you want the user to log in every time he or she begins a new session.

If you have only one ColdFusion server, it doesn't matter that `Server`, `Application`, and `Session` variables are stored in RAM or that `Client` variables are often stored on the server's hard drive. But what happens if you have two ColdFusion servers? A `Session` variable that's stored in RAM on server one isn't visible to a ColdFusion page on server two. You don't want the user to have to maintain a separate session for each physical server you have; you want the user to have a single session with your entire site. How can you take advantage of `Session` variables in a scaled environment?

Managing Client State in Scaled Environments   Load-balanced environments typically include multiple servers that are configured to appear identical to the users. Users are redirected from one server to the next based on available server resources. This setup creates a situation in which the Web developer cannot rely on users to always use the same machine.

The Scenario

Say that the aforementioned application resides in a cluster of ColdFusion servers. You want to provide the functionality of server-side variable storage, but you have to take into account that a client might not always be hitting the same machine.

I've outlined three options that deal with the problem of a client being redirected from one machine to another (see Figure 4.3):

Part

I

Ch

4

- Embed parameters in the URL string. This approach essentially allows the user to carry information about his or her session from one machine to the other using the same database residing behind the Web server.

- Keep the user on the same machine. This approach is employed by your load-balancing solution, and is seen in both hardware- and software-based environments.

- Use a central `Client` variable repository. This approach allows you to access the same client information from both machines in a central database.

Embed Parameters in the URL String

As long as all ColdFusion servers are pointing to the same database, a Web developer might opt to just embed status information in HTTP name/value pairs. As mentioned earlier in this chapter, this is a painstaking, difficult-to-maintain practice, and even the most intrepid Web developer should think twice before going down this road. The upside of this strategy is that it does not matter to the system if a user is redirected to another machine. All the information the script needs is contained in the URL referencing it. It is ultimately foolproof in a clustered server strategy—after tripling the amount of debugging and build time, that is.

Can you tell that I don't like this option? The only reason for using HTTP name/value pairs is to accommodate the fraction of your users who cannot or do not transmit cookies with their HTTP requests. Some users choose to turn off cookies because they feel they are an invasion of privacy; some corporate firewalls strip out cookie info for a similar reason. If you are unfortunate enough to have a significant cookie-less user base, you might need to consider the name/value pair approach. I wish you luck.

FIGURE 4.3
Diagram of client
redirecting from one
session to another.

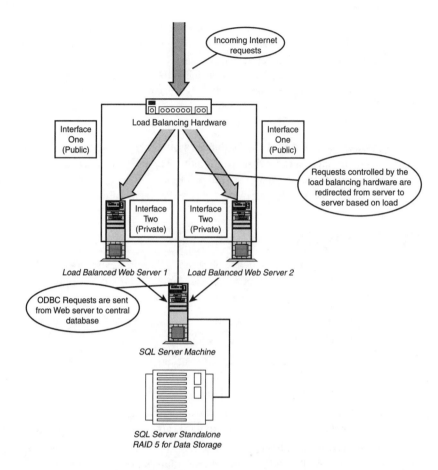

Keep the User on the Same Machine

The crudest method for managing client state in a scaled environment is to direct a user to the
server that's currently most available and to have the user continue to interact with the same
server for the duration of his or her session. This approach is accomplished via Cluster Cat's
session-aware clustering, or methods employed by third-party load-balancing hardware and
software. Although this method is certainly valid, obvious limitations exist when you're trying
to use your server resources to their fullest. For example, user one might make a quick stop to
your site, and only request three simple pages during her session. User two, who is a hardcore
user, requests 10 pages, including a complex database transaction, during his session. As a
result, server two is far busier than server one, even though both servers have handled one
session. Complete balance cannot be maintained. The advantage of session-aware clustering
is that it can be accomplished much more simply (and inexpensively) than truly session-
independent clustering. (See Chapter 2, "Different Ways to Scale.")

The Poor Coder's Cluster   If you are an experienced ColdFusion developer, you can implement session-aware clustering directly in your own ColdFusion code. I call this "the poor coder's cluster." I tried this approach on a few of my company's machines a while back and found the results to be marginally interesting.

The whole idea behind "the poor coder's cluster" is using your root's `application.cfm` file to test where a user was last.

Listing 4.3 contains some functionality that allows your application to test for the existence of a cookie variable named `GTCluster`. `Cookie.GTCluster` is the IP address of the first machine the user hit in a round-robin DNS setup. (See Chapter 2 for more information on round-robin DNS.) The first machine is also the place where the user established session variables for use in the Web application. This functionality was then incorporated into all the roots in the round-robin DNS setup. (When you're using this listing, be sure to include code to save the intended URL and redirect appropriately.)

Listing 4.3 `application.cfm`—File Testing and Sending a User to a Machine

```
<!--- Let Server 1 be 10.1.1.2 --->
<!--- Let Server 2 be 10.1.1.3 --->
<!--- Let the current server be Server 1 --->

<cfif IsDefined("cookie.appID")>
    <cfif cookie.appID IS "10.1.1.2">
        <!--- Do Nothing --->
    <cfelse>
        <cflocation url="#cookie.appID">
    </cfif>
<cfelse<
    <cfcookie name="appID" value="10.1.1.2">
    <!--- Set cookie, then do nothing. --->
</cfif>
```

If a user is redirected to another server, the `application.cfm` file senses that it is not the machine the user belongs on and redirects him or her back to the primary machine. The `application.cfm` file then aborts the rest of the page load.

Use a Central `Client` Variable Repository

A major enhancement in ColdFusion 4 is the capability to store client information in a central database. This new feature creates what I feel is the most effective way to save state across scaled Web servers. If you store `Client` variables in a central database, any of your ColdFusion servers with access to this database can access the same pool of `Client` variables. See Figure 4.3 for this type of configuration.

After you establish your central database, you can set parameters on clients from any of your front-end ColdFusion servers. They remain accessible even if a user switches from one machine to another. Because `Client` variables persist from session to session, you now have a collection of information for each user that can be accessed whenever the user visits your site. Given the simplicity of this type of a setup, I recommend this strategy to anyone who antici- pates needing to scale an application across multiple servers, even if you don't need to scale right away.

When you decide on this strategy, you need to configure your ColdFusion servers to take advantage of the database. I will assume that you have already set up a central database server, and you only need to configure your ColdFusion servers to use that database for client storage. Here's how to get started:

1. Create a blank database to store your client data.

2. On all your ColdFusion servers, create a data source in the ColdFusion 4 Administrator pointing to that central database (see Figure 4.4).

FIGURE 4.4

Setting up a data source in ColdFusion Administrator.

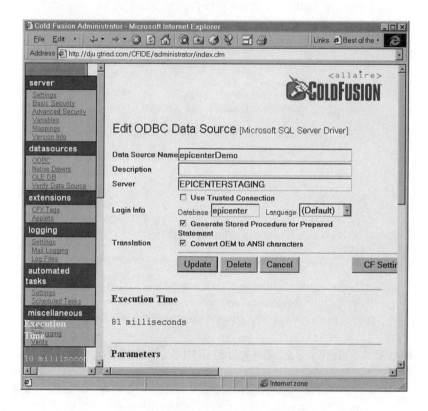

3. In the ColdFusion 4 Administrator, select Variables under the Server section, and choose that data source as a type of `Client` variable storage (see Figure 4.5). ColdFusion then creates data tables similar to those shown in Figure 4.6.

FIGURE 4.5

Setting up client storage management in ColdFusion Administrator.

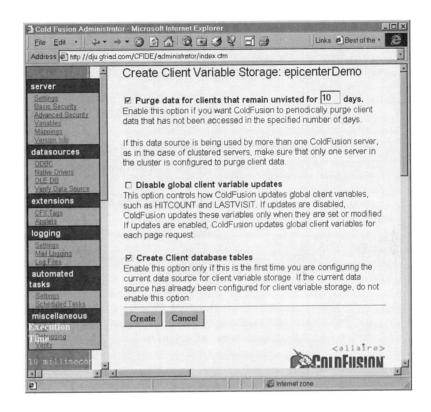

FIGURE 4.6

The tables ColdFusion creates in SQL Enterprise Manager.

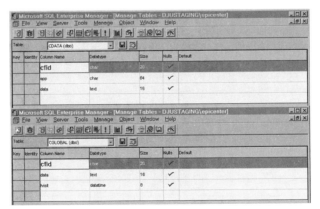

> **CAUTION**
>
> If this is the first time your database has been used for client storage, on the first ColdFusion server for which you configure `Client` variable storage, select Create Client Database. On subsequent ColdFusion servers, do not select this option when you configure `Client` variable storage. This option actually creates tables named CDATA and CGLOBAL in your database to physically store the `Client` variables.

4. Put the following code in the `application.cfm` files of your application:

```
<cfapplication name="epicenter" clientmanagement="Yes"
➥ clientstorage="epicenterDemo">
```

5. Use client-scoped variables in your application to reference persistent data:

```
<cfif IsDefined("client.LastAccess")>
    <cflocation url="/index.cfm">
<cfelse>
    <cfset client.LastAccess = DateFormat(Now())>
    <cflocation url="/index.cfm">
</cfif>
```

After you complete these steps, all `Client` variables are stored in the data source. As long as all your Web servers are configured to use the central database, you don't need to worry about which server a given user's request goes to. ●

Security

Security Options

Every ColdFusion developer needs or will eventually have a need for a security framework in an application. Whether it is for a simple administration page that needs to be secured or a complex secured content site, most of us have built a security system using ColdFusion. Using persistent Client or Session variables, cookies, or URL parameters, building integrated security in ColdFusion has been relatively easy, but granular control over elements of application pages remains a difficult and time-consuming endeavor.

Internet service providers and Internet presence providers need to secure specific elements of the ColdFusion Application Server (CFAS) to provide a stable and secure Web hosting environment. Granular control over each tag and data source is key to maintaining a high service level. ColdFusion 4 Security Services addresses all these issues, providing granular control over tags, data sources, and other system and user-defined resources in a highly intuitive manner. Optional integration with NetTegrity's SiteMinder product provides extensive and robust security options for your Web applications.

How Security Works with ColdFusion

ColdFusion Security Services consist of combinations of rules, user directories, policies, and code that "enforces" the security policies created. ColdFusion also implements a Security Sandbox, which can contain an application and restrict resources available to that application based on the user who owns the application. For developer-controlled granular control over user access to items on a page, authentication and authorization functions are provided. In this chapter you take a look at the big picture and see what these elements really are and how they all fit together.

Rules, Rules, Rules

The basic element of Advanced ColdFusion security is the *rule*. A rule defines a specific resource and optionally an attribute of that resource. A rule is actually a resource, so the name is a bit misleading. A rule by itself does not decide what can or cannot be done with a particular resource. A rule simply says, "We are defining this item as a resource."

An example of a rule could be a data source. This rule could also have an attribute of insert. This rule would mean that you could enable or disable INSERT queries to this data source. Nothing in the rule itself could do this, but after it is defined, this resource can be secured. You create rules in the ColdFusion Administrator.

User Directories

Another basic element of ColdFusion security is *user directories*. ColdFusion allows the definition of a group of users from an LDAP server or a Windows NT domain. User groups themselves do not have any privileges; they simply define who is in a group and who is not.

An example of a user directory could be the employee group Accounting from an LDAP directory. Another example could be the Domain Users group from a Windows NT domain, \\CONTINUUM. User directories are also defined in the ColdFusion Administrator, as you'll see in the next chapter.

Policies

As bureaucratic as it may sound, a *policy* is simply a grouping of rules and user directories. By creating a policy, you are in effect saying, "These users are allowed access to these resources." A policy can contain one or more rules, so many resources can be secured at once. Whether the resources covered in a policy are secured upon creation of the policy depends on the type of security environment the policy will be used in, as you'll soon see.

An example of a policy could be that the group Administrators in the Windows NT domain `\\CONTINUUM` is allowed to use `CFFILE` to write to the file system as well as `CFREGISTRY`. After a policy is defined, ColdFusion becomes aware that the resource is to be secured and checks for authentication when a request is made for access to that resource. In other words, when ColdFusion knows you want the resource to be secured, it asks for authentication before allowing access. This process can be automatic, depending on the security mode.

Security Levels

After you decide what resources you want to secure and whom you would like to access them, you can decide how ColdFusion will secure them. ColdFusion provides two runtime modes for security: the *Security Sandbox* and *User Security*. The difference between the two is who has control over the actual implementation of the security—the administrator or the developer. The Security Sandbox is closely related to *Remote Development Security,* which allows restrictions to be placed on remote developers connecting to your ColdFusion Application Server using ColdFusion Studio. All these security levels are managed by *Administrator Security*, which provides control over the administration of the server.

The Security Sandbox   For administrative control over resources on a server, ColdFusion provides a Security Sandbox for applications to run in. The name is appropriate: Imagine a sandbox that contains all the toys you would like your developer to play with. If you place the developer in the sandbox, he or she cannot step out of that sandbox to play with your chain saw and nail gun. The Security Sandbox maps a policy to a particular user by applying this policy to a directory and its subdirectories. Any ColdFusion template that executes within those directories is automatically run within the context of the assigned policy. If a data source that is not allowed by the assigned policy is called, an error is returned by the template. Using the Security Sandbox, you can truly lock up your server in a hosting environment.

Several types of resources are available for Security Sandbox mode. Shown in Table 5.1, each applies to a different type of ColdFusion resource. These settings automatically apply across the entire sandbox, lessening administration workload and increasing transparency.

Part

II

Ch

5

Table 5.1   Advanced Security Resource Types

Name	Description
Application	Name of an application
CFML	ColdFusion tag name

continues

Table 5.1   Continued

Name	Description
Collection	Verity collection name
Component	CFOBJECT class name, CFX tag name, or CFApplet name
Custom Tag	Fully qualified Custom Tag name
DataSource	Data source name
File	Full path to file
UserObject	User-defined object (not associated with any ColdFusion resource)

Remote Development Security   ColdFusion version 3.1 introduced the capability to remotely edit and manage applications on a ColdFusion server. Managing individual access control was problematic because access was all or nothing. In ColdFusion 4, you now can manage what resources each remote developer can access. This capability is very important for Internet service providers and IS managers who need to segment developer access for security and integrity.

Remote Development Security (RDS) binds developer access to a security context. All rules, policies, and user directories within the context apply to each developer using RDS. Each user can access only the data sources and files that are assigned to him or her. RDS access and Security Sandbox access are controlled simultaneously, making it easy for administrators to keep their systems secure.

User Security   One of the most powerful features of the ColdFusion Security Framework is the capability to secure individual sections of code at runtime. This control is completely in the hands of the programmer, allowing complex and very granular security to be implemented with significantly less development time than a customized security scheme. ColdFusion relies on the developer to mark sections of code to be secured. This increases the efficiency of the application by minimizing the security overhead. You'll build an extranet application in the next chapter to see how User Security works.

User Security allows you to control the resource types shown in Table 5.1 on a user-by-user basis. You can allow one user to see only the description of an item, whereas a privileged user can see the full text of an item. ColdFusion provides authentication tags and functions that allow you to programmatically determine the authentication status and the authority of each user.

Administrator Security   Users who are allowed to access portions of the ColdFusion Administrator are designated using Administrator Security. Just as in the case of Remote Development Security, Administrator Security provides more granular control over administration access. Access to the administrator can now be delegated to other users as necessary, allowing teams to work more efficiently and administration workloads to decrease proportionately.

Security Administration

For administrators who do not require these features, ColdFusion provides basic security for the ColdFusion Administrator, ColdFusion RDS, and a subset of CFML tags. The administration page shown in Figure 5.1 allows you to set a username and password combination for both the administrator and RDS. You can also check which tags you want to enable across the entire installation.

FIGURE 5.1

Basic security options.

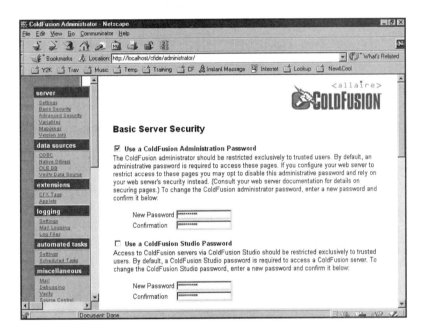

General Settings   For advanced security options, the administration page shown in Figure 5.2 allows you to modify global security server settings. To enable Advanced Security, check Use Advanced Server Security. By checking this box, you override any settings that may be present on the Basic Security page in Figure 5.1. The Security Server field determines where ColdFusion will look for its security permissions. This field is usually set to 127.0.0.1, but it can be any ColdFusion or NetTegrity server. This subject is covered in Chapter 6, "The User Authentication Framework."

The next field is Shared Secret. It is an encryption key that is shared by all transactions made by this security server. By default, it is the same for all ColdFusion servers, so changing it is a good idea. A Shared Secret can be any string of characters and should be similar in structure to a password.

The Authentication and Authorization Ports are the ports the security server listens on for any requests. They should remain as they are set unless they conflict with another port on your system. In this case, make sure any other ColdFusion servers that use this server as a security provider also reflect the changes to these values that you have made. By default, the timeout is set to 20 seconds, which is a good setting to keep.

FIGURE 5.2

Advanced security options.

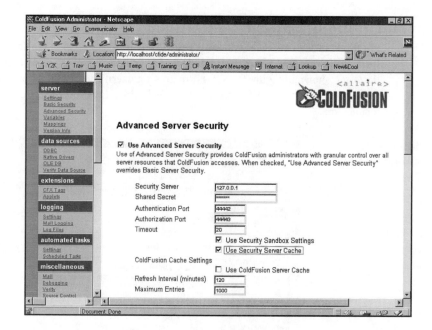

If you plan to use Security Sandboxes, select the Use Security Sandbox Settings check box to enable this feature. I'll cover configuring a Security Sandbox in depth in Chapter 7, "Securing Specific Features and Components." If you do not plan to implement Security Sandboxes, leave this box unselected.

Cache Settings   The ColdFusion Security Server can cache access information to improve performance. Likewise, the ColdFusion server can cache user authentication data for increased performance. The trade-off is that data is not refreshed as it is changed, so caching is not a good idea for sites that frequently update user directories and require immediate access to changes.

You can configure the refresh interval for the cache as well as the maximum size. Set the interval to a high number for sites with static security data, and set a low interval for sites that change access data throughout the course of a day.

These and other configuration options are covered in more detail in Chapters 6, 7, and 8. User Security, Security Sandboxes, integrating security with Windows NT domains, and LDAP user directories are covered in these chapters. ●

The User Authentication Framework

In Chapter 5, "Security Options," you learned the security options available in ColdFusion 4. In this chapter you examine each element in detail and put them all together in an extranet application. Many extranets have several different levels of access. Suppliers might have access to data that you may not want distributors to see, and administration areas need to be secured from outside users. You'll build a simple extranet application to see how to exercise granular access control over your applications.

Defining the Security Context

The first step in securing an application is the creation of a *security context*. The security context encompasses the rules, policies, and user groups that are used to control access to an application. A security context can contain several policies, with each policy applying to a different set of users. Security contexts can span multiple applications, and an application can use more than one security context. Many ColdFusion servers can share a security server; security can be handled by a single provider in clustered environments.

The Security Context dialog box is part of the Security section of the ColdFusion Administrator. Security contexts are contained by a security server, so create a security server now. To access the Advanced Server Security dialog box, open the ColdFusion Administrator and choose Advanced Security. You then see the dialog box shown in Figure 6.1.

FIGURE 6.1

The advanced security options.

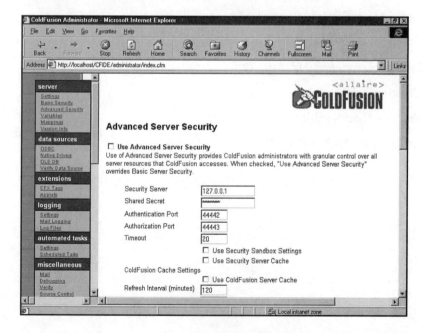

To activate the security server, you must first enable Advanced Server Security by checking the Use Advanced Server Security check box. By checking this check box, you override any settings contained in the Basic Security section of the Administrator, so you need to secure any server resources you want to restrict using the Security Sandbox. I'll cover this topic in the next chapter.

Enter **127.0.0.1** in the Security Server text field, and click Apply. You've just created a security server that can contain your security contexts. To create a security context, click the Security Contexts button. You then see the form in Figure 6.2. Type **Extranet** in the text field and click Add. The New Security Context form shown in Figure 6.3 then asks you to add a description for your security context. Type **Permissions for extranet access** and click Add. Your security context is now active. To use it, you need to add rules, policies, and users.

FIGURE 6.2
The Security Contexts form.

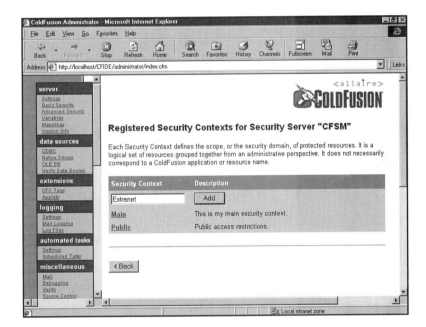

Creating Rules

From the list of security contexts that is now visible, click on your new context, Extranet. The New Security Context form shown in Figure 6.3 allows you to create rules and assign policies. Click the Rules button to view the Resource Rules list for this security context. Notice the Resource Type list. You want to restrict access to certain areas of the extranet that display parts information, so you need to use the Application type. Enter **Parts** in the Rule Name field, choose UserObject from the Resource Type list, and click Add.

Part
II
Ch
6

The New Resource Rule form shown in Figure 6.4 requests a description of your rule as well as an application name. You should be as detailed as possible when entering text in the Description field so that you will remember exactly what the rule is for later. In the Description field, enter **This rule restricts parts data access to suppliers only. Read only access is granted..** Enter **Parts list** in the UserObject Name field so that you know the list of parts is to be secured. Enter **view** in the Action field so that you know you are granting read permission for this resource. Then click Add. You then should see the Resource Rules list (refer to Figure 6.3), and you should see your new rule in the list.

N O T E   If you don't add a rule to a policy, no one has access to the resource assigned to the
rule. ■

FIGURE 6.3

The New Security
Context form.

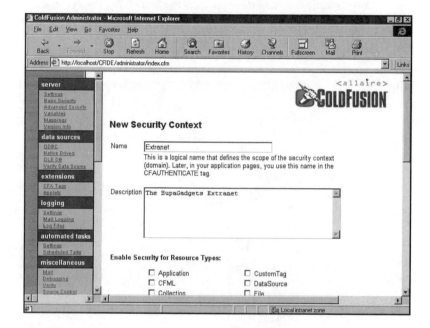

FIGURE 6.4

The New Resource Rule
form.

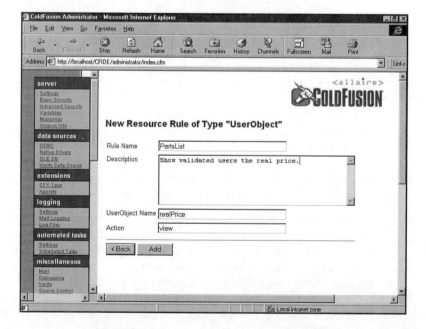

User Directories and LDAP

Now thatyou've defined a rule for your security context, you can define some groups of users to associate these rules with. Click the Advanced Security section of the ColdFusion Administrator to return to the Security Server dialog box (refer to Figure 6.1). Click the User Directories button to display the Registered User Directories list shown in Figure 6.5. For this extranet application, use an LDAP server to contain the user directories. You need to tell ColdFusion where the user directories are and how to access them.

FIGURE 6.5

The Registered User Directories list.

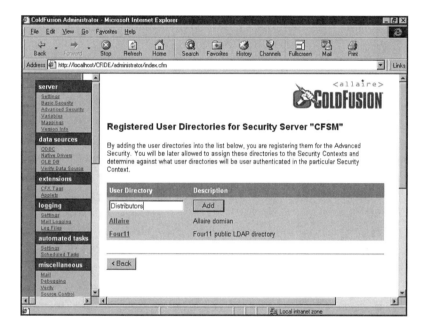

To define the first user directory, enter **Distributors** in the User Directory field, and click Add. The New User Directory form shown in Figure 6.6 contains all the fields necessary to create a new directory. The directory name is already entered, so enter a description. Again, being very descriptive is a good idea. Enter **Active SuperGadgets distributors in good standing** in the Description field. In the Namespace list, you can choose to retrieve the directory from an LDAP server or from a Windows NT domain (Windows NT only). Choose LDAP for this directory. I'll discuss Windows NT domains in Chapter 8, "Integration with NOS Security."

Part

II

Ch

6

For the LDAP directory, you need to add some information that is unique for each LDAP server. For this chapter, the SuperGadgets extranet requires you to have access to an LDAP server with a directory of users on it. For the dialog box in Figure 6.6, you need the domain name or IP where the LDAP server is hosted and authentication information if necessary. You also need to know information about the schema of the directory. Specify the search root, the lookup start, and the lookup end. The timeout values are usually okay, unless you have a slow network connection between your ColdFusion server and the LDAP server.

FIGURE 6.6

The New User Directory form.

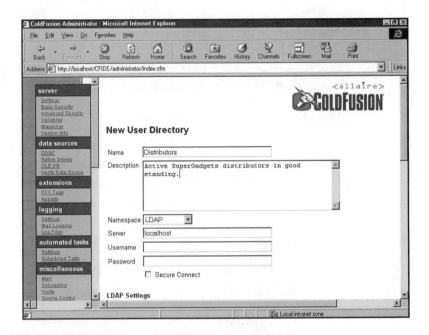

N O T E   The Netscape Directory Server has a very useful schema built in.

Click Add, and you then should see your new user directory in the Registered Directories list (refer to Figure 6.5).

Creating Policies

You now can combine your rules and user directories to create a set of policies that will govern access to sensitive data in your application. To decide what policies you need to create, you need to decide how many levels of access you need in your application. SuperGadgets has a default level and a higher level for distributors. You need only one policy because the default level of access can be defined as users who have not been authenticated.

Now add a new policy. Click the Back button to go back to the Advanced Security administration page. Click on Security Contexts, and then click on the extranet security context in the list (refer to Figure 6.2). The New Security Context form then appears (see Figure 6.3). Click on Policies at the bottom of the page to go to the Resource Policies page, as shown in Figure 6.7. Here, you name your new policy. Type `LetThemIn` in the dialog box, and click Add. You then move to the Policy Form page. In the Description field, type `Allow access to sensitive data`, and then click Apply.

Now you have several choices at the bottom of the Policy Form page. The Map button shows you a map of all defined rules in this policy, but because you haven't added any rules to this policy, click on the Rules button. On the Rules page, click Add/Remove. You then see a

PartsList rule in the list on the right. Select it and click on the left arrow button to add it to the new policy. Click the Back button to return to the Policy Form page.

FIGURE 6.7
The Resource Policies page.

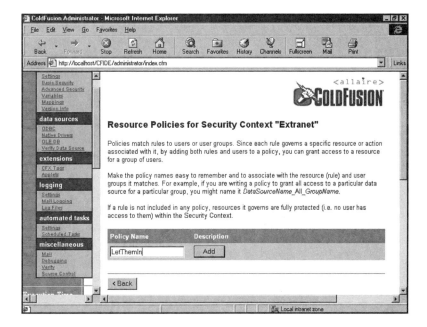

A rule is associated with this security level, so now you need some users from the user directory. Click Back again to get to the Policy Form page. Click the Users button to go to the Users form. Make sure the user directory Distributors is selected, and click Add/Remove. Select a user from the list of available users on the right, click the left arrow to move it to the list of users associated with this policy on the left, and click Back. You've now successfully created a policy.

Runtime User Security

At this point, you've created a security server, a security context, rules, user directories, and policies. Now you're ready to put them together with an application to see how User Security is implemented at runtime. ColdFusion provides a tag, CFAUTHENTICATE, and two related functions, IsAuthenticated() and IsAuthorized(), to bind security contexts and policies to actual applications.

Using the CFAUTHENTICATE Tag

The CFAUTHENTICATE tag authenticates a user against a defined user directory in a security context. CFAUTHENTICATE requires three attributes, as shown in Table 6.1. This tag should be executed once per session for a user. An effective way to use this tag is to test to see whether a username and password have been passed, and if so, run the authentication tag. Listing 6.1 shows an example of this test.

Table 6.1 CFAUTHENTICATE **Attributes**

Name	Description	Required
SECURITYCONTEXT	The name of a preset security context as defined in the Administrator	Yes
USERNAME	The username to use for authentication	Yes
PASSWORD	The password to use for authentication	Yes

Listing 6.1 AUTHENTICATE_USER.CFM—**Testing for a Username and Password Before Using** CFAUTHENTICATE

```
<!--- Set defaults --->
<cfparam name="username" default="">
<cfparam name="password" default="">

<!--- Check the values --->
<cfif trim(username) is not ""
 and trim(password) is not "">

    <!--- Authenticate user --->
    <cfauthenticate securitycontext="Extranet"
     username="#username#"
     password="#password#">

<cfelse>

    <!--- Throw exception --->
    <cfthrow message="No username or password specified">

</cfif>

<!--- Check the success of the authentication --->
<cfif not isAuthenticated(username,"Extranet")>

    <!--- Throw exception --->
    <cfthrow message="Invalid user">

</cfif>
```

Now that the user has been authenticated, you can use IsAuthenticated() to determine the success of the authentication. If CFAUTHENTICATE can find no user matching the username and password, an exception is thrown. You can catch this exception in your application. For more information on handling exceptions, see Chapter 19, "Structured Error and Retry Handling."

The IsAuthenticated() Function

The IsAuthenticated() function checks the result of the CFAUTHENTICATE tag and returns a result of True or False. Its syntax, shown in Table 6.2, is simple to understand. If the username is allowed in a specified security context, and the CFAUTHENTICATE tag is successful, IsAuthenticated() returns True. If any of these conditions are not met, IsAuthenticated() returns False. If the user is valid but is not a part of the specified security context, IsAuthenticated() again returns False. In Listing 6.1 an exception is thrown if the authentication test fails.

Table 6.2 IsAuthenticated **Parameters**

Name	Description	Required
UserName	The username used for authentication	Yes
SecurityContext	The predefined security context	Yes

The IsAuthorized() Function

Unless you specifically check to see whether a user is authorized to access a resource, the ColdFusion Application Server does not do this job for you. For every resource you want to secure in a runtime User Security environment, you must use the IsAuthorized() function to validate permissions granted by your policies. Server Sandbox security, discussed in the next chapter, checks all resources by default. When you're using User Security, you must determine how much (or how little) security is required for an application.

IsAuthorized() requires three parameters, as shown in Table 6.3. Descriptive names for rules come in handy here. This function asks, "For the current authenticated user, can this ResourceAction be performed on this ResourceName of ResourceType?" The function returns True or False.

Table 6.3 IsAuthorized() **Parameters**

Name	Description	Required
ResourceType	The resource type set in the rule	Yes
ResourceName	The name of the rule	Yes
ResourceAction	The action requested	Yes

Part

II

Ch

6

An Extranet Application

Now you're ready to build an application using what you've learned about ColdFusion security. One of the main reasons security is used in a Web application is to segment access to data. In most situations, segmenting access involves writing an entire application to manage users and determine authentication status. In the SuperGadgets extranet, you're going to use the same application pages to display limited and full data sets depending on user status.

For this application, use an LDAP server as your user directory. The Netscape Directory Server works well with ColdFusion, so for this chapter, examples refer to this server. You can download it from the Netscape Web site at `http://www.netscape.com`. In Chapter 8 you see how to use your application with Windows NT domains.

N O T E The ColdFusion Web Application Construction Kit has more information on using LDAP and ColdFusion together. ■

You've already set up the LDAP user directory (refer to Figure 6.6), and you've defined the rules and policies within the extranet security context. Now, you can use this security context in your application.

User Authentication

After all the configuration you've done, the implementation is straightforward. The main function of User Security is authenticating users, so I'll cover this topic first. Because user authentication must occur for every application page, put it in the `application.cfm` page, as shown in Listing 6.2.

Listing 6.2 `APPLICATION.CFM`—User Authentication in the SuperGadgets Extranet

```
<!--- SuperGadgets! application.cfm --->

<!--- Set defaults for username and password --->
<CFIF ISDEFINED("COOKIE.USERNAME")>

    <CFSET USERNAME=COOKIE.USERNAME>

<CFELSE>

    <CFSET USERNAME="">

    <!--- User is attempting to login --->
    <CFIF ISDEFINED("form.username")>

        <!--- set username variable and cookie --->
        <CFSET USERNAME=FORM.USERNAME>
        <CFCOOKIE NAME="username" VALUE="#form.username#">

    </CFIF>

</CFIF>

<CFIF ISDEFINED("COOKIE.PASSWORD")>

    <CFSET PASSWORD=COOKIE.PASSWORD>

<CFELSE>
```

```
<CFSET PASSWORD="">

<!--- User is attempting to login --->
<CFIF ISDEFINED("form.password")>

    <!--- set password and cookie --->
    <CFSET PASSWORD=FORM.PASSWORD>
    <CFCOOKIE NAME="password" VALUE="#form.password#">

</CFIF>

</CFIF>

<!--- Check to see if user has been authenticated --->
<CFIF NOT ISAUTHENTICATED()>

    <!--- We'll enclose this in a CFRTY block.  CFAUTHENTICATE throws
an exception if the user does not exist in this mode. --->
    <CFTRY>

        <CFAUTHENTICATE SETCOOKIE="No" SECURITYCONTEXT="Extranet"
➥ USERNAME="#username#" PASSWORD="#password#">

        <!--- If an exception is thrown --->
        <CFCATCH TYPE="Security">

        <!--- Kill cookies --->
        <CFCOOKIE NAME="username" VALUE="" EXPIRES="NOW">
        <CFCOOKIE NAME="password" VALUE="" EXPIRES="NOW">

        </CFCATCH>

    </CFTRY>

</CFIF>

<!--- Define the application --->
<CFAPPLICATION NAME="SuperGadgets" CLIENTMANAGEMENT="Yes" SESSIONMANAGEMENT=
➥"Yes" SETCLIENTCOOKIES="Yes">
```

Part
II
Ch
6

Notice the first section in Listing 6.2. Here, you check to see whether the username and password cookies have been set. If not, you set the local username and password variables to null. This setting forces the user to authenticate because you've set CFAUTHENTICATE to throw an exception if the user is not found in the user directory you set. In the CFCATCH block, you can handle this exception any way you want. You will not do anything special here, but you can give users the opportunity to log in using the form shown in Figure 6.8. Upon submission, this login form sets the password and username cookies and sets the local variables appropriately, as you can see in Listing 6.3.

Also, if a user tries to log in with the wrong data, you have to expire his or her cookies so that they aren't detected and the default section runs. Remember that the application.cfm application page runs before each page in the application, so the entire application is protected. Now, you have two authentication states: authenticated and not authenticated.

FIGURE 6.8

The SuperGadgets Login page.

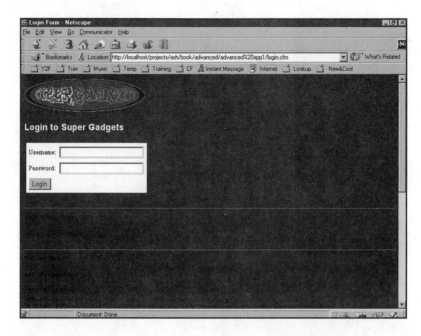

Listing 6.3 APPLICATION.CFM—Login Form in the SuperGadgets Extranet

```
<!--- SuperGadgets login.cfm--->

<!DOCTYPE HTML PUBLIC "-//W3C//DTD HTML 4.0 Transitional//EN">

<HTML>
<HEAD>
    <TITLE>Login Form</TITLE>
</HEAD>

<BODY BGCOLOR="#400000" LINK="#800000" VLINK="#800000" ALINK="#FFFF00">

<IMG SRC="supergadgets.GIF" WIDTH=250 HEIGHT=69 BORDER=0 ALT="SuperGadgets"><P>

        <B><FONT FACE="Arial" SIZE="+1" COLOR="#FFFF00">Login to Super Gadgets
➥</FONT></B><BR>

        <!--- Display login form --->
        <CFFORM ACTION="index.cfm">
        <TABLE BGCOLOR="#ffffff">
            <TR>
                <TD>
        <TABLE>
            <TR>
                <TD><FONT SIZE="-1">Username:</FONT></TD>
                <TD><CFINPUT TYPE="text" NAME="username"></TD>
            </TR>
            <TR>
                <TD><FONT SIZE="-1">Password:</FONT></TD>
                <TD><CFINPUT TYPE="text" NAME="password"></TD>
```

```
        </TR>
        <TR>
            <TD COLSPAN="2"><INPUT TYPE="submit" VALUE="Login"></TD>
        </TR>
    </TABLE>
    </TD>
        </TR>
    </TABLE>
    </CFFORM>


</BODY>
</HTML>
```

Securing Sections of an Application Page

Now that you have the basic pages for authentication and logins, you can use them to identify what the user should see. You now have two authentication states, but you also have as many access levels as you have policies. For now, you've defined only the LetThemIn policy. You can use it to decide whether the prices should be displayed.

Listing 6.4 shows the code to use in the index.cfm page. At first, it looks like any other application page, but it adds a security function to see whether the user is part of a policy. The IsAuthorized() function you learned about earlier now checks to see whether the resource type, rule, and action specified are valid for the user. If both the rule and the user are joined in a policy, then this function returns True, and the prices appear as shown in Figure 6.9. If not, only a partial list of products is shown, as in Figure 6.10.

FIGURE 6.9
The SuperGadgets authorized page.

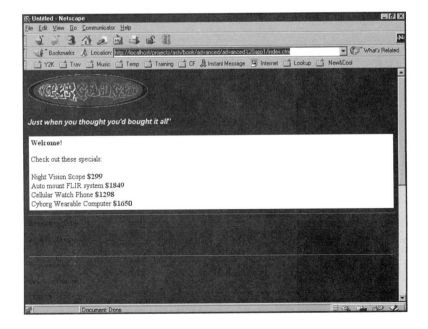

Part

II

Ch

6

FIGURE 6.10

The SuperGadgets default page.

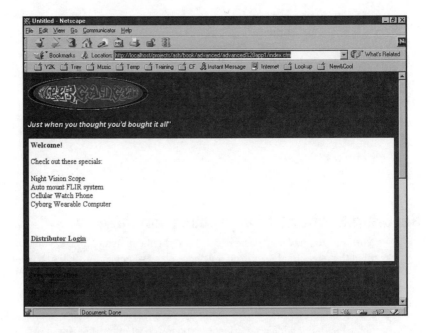

Listing 6.4 `APPLICATION.CFM`—**The Display Page in the SuperGadgets Extranet**

```
<!DOCTYPE HTML PUBLIC "-//W3C//DTD HTML 4.0 Transitional//EN">

<HTML>
<HEAD>
    <TITLE>SuperGadgets!</TITLE>
</HEAD>


<BODY BGCOLOR="#400000" LINK="#800000" VLINK="#800000" ALINK="#FFFF00">

<IMG SRC="supergadgets.GIF" WIDTH=250 HEIGHT=69 BORDER=0 ALT="SuperGadgets"><P>

        <B><FONT FACE="Arial" COLOR="#FFFF00"><I>Just when you thought you'd
➥ bought it all</I>"</FONT></B><BR>

        <P>

        <TABLE BORDER="0" WIDTH="100%" ALIGN="right" BGCOLOR="#ffffff">
        <TR><TD>

        <TABLE BORDER="0">
        <TR><TD>

        <B>Welcome!</B><P>
        Check out these specials:
        <P>
```

```
<!--- Check to see the authorization level of the user --->
<CFIF NOT ISAUTHORIZED("userObject", "PartsList", "view")>
    Night Vision Scope<BR>
    Auto mount FLIR system<BR>
    Cellular Watch Phone<BR>
    Cyborg Wearable Computer<BR>
<CFELSE>
    Night Vision Scope  <B>$299</B><BR>
    Auto mount FLIR system <B>$1849</B><BR>
    Cellular Watch Phone <B>$1298</B><BR>
    Cyborg Wearable Computer <B>$1650</B><BR>
    Bioluminescent Kevlar Jacket <B>$2299</B><BR>
</CFIF>

<BR><BR><BR>

<!--- Show the login link if necessary --->
<CFIF NOT ISAUTHENTICATED()>
<B><A HREF="login.cfm">Distributor Login</A></B>
</CFIF>

<BR><BR><BR>
</TD></TR>
</TABLE>

</TD></TR>
</TABLE>

<BR CLEAR="right">


</BODY>
</HTML>
```

Adding Multiple Rules and Policies

You can create even more access levels by adding a rule for each resource you want to secure and joining each rule to a group of users in a policy. You can have all the rules in one policy, as in the SuperGadgets extranet, or you can create a policy for each access level and have different sets of users in each policy. You could, for example, have another policy called Internal that would allow users to view sensitive internal data. The flexibility of the ColdFusion Security framework allows you to create complex applications with much less code than ever before.

You can also create multiple security contexts for separate applications. You can even use them for sections of the same application. As long as a CFAUTHENTICATE tag executes prior to the use of any IsAuthorized() functions, you can place this tag wherever you need it. I recommend that you put it in application.cfm or at least a shared include file. ●

Part

II

Ch

6

Securing Specific Features and Components

The power of ColdFusion Markup Language and ColdFusion Studio can be a double-edged sword. While developers can create sophisticated Web applications and access required resources remotely, administrators must be able to balance this access with the needs of other users on a system as well as the needs of the system itself. It is not a good idea to allow users full control over the file system and registry of a server. Bad things will happen. By creating Security Sandboxes for developers and matching Remote Development Security (RDS) to these sandboxes, administrators can rest easy knowing critical system resources and other users applications are safe.

Chapter 5, "Security Options," discusses the concept of Security Sandboxes and RDS. In this chapter you restrict access to critical resources on your ColdFusion Application Server and establish access restrictions for remote developers using ColdFusion Studio. Data source access, file system access, Registry access, and Administration Security using the supplied resource types are all covered. At the end of this unit, your system will have a good level of security in place, and you'll be able to enhance your security as needed.

Creating a Security Sandbox

The first step in creating a Security Sandbox is similar to the runtime user security: You create a security context, assign user directories, create rules, and bind them to policies. The difference is that you use all of the resource types except UserObject to secure your resources.

N O T E   When utilizing user security and Security Sandboxes in the same applications, the Security Sandbox settings take precedence. ■

Procedures covered in Chapter 6 are referred to frequently, so if you haven't yet read that chapter, you might want to do that now. First you must have defined a security server. To define a security server, click Advanced Security in the ColdFusion Administrator; enter **127.0.0.1** in the Security Server field shown in Figure 7.1 and click Apply.

Now you need to define a security context. Click the Security Contexts button at the bottom of the page; you will see the Security Context list shown in Figure 7.2. Enter **TestSandbox** in the dialog box and click Add. This takes you to the New Security Context form shown in Figure 7.3. Enter a description for the context: **Basic Sandbox Security**. Select the resource types you plan to secure in this context. Select all of the resource types except UserObject. You use the resource types later. Make sure you've created a user directory for your Windows NT domain. If you haven't done this yet, see Chapter 8, "Integration with NOS Security," for instructions. Leave Add Existing User Directories checked so you can utilize any user directories already installed. Click Add; you are now back on the Security Sandbox Form page. From here, you can create rules and policies.

 T I P   When selecting resource types for a security context, choose only those you will use. This enhances the performance of the ColdFusion Application Server.

FIGURE 7.1

Advanced security options.

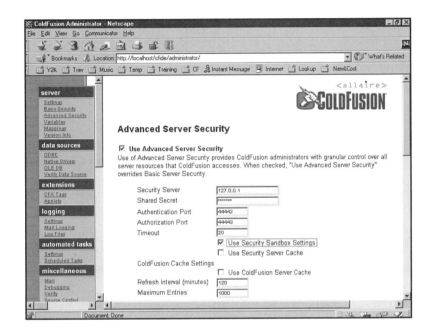

FIGURE 7.2

Security Context list.

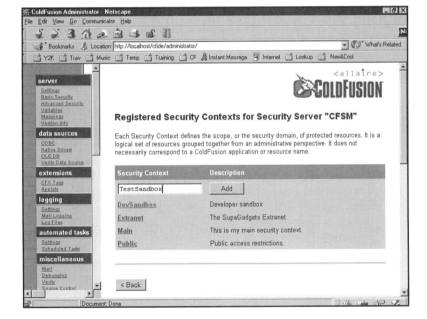

FIGURE 7.3

New Security Context list.

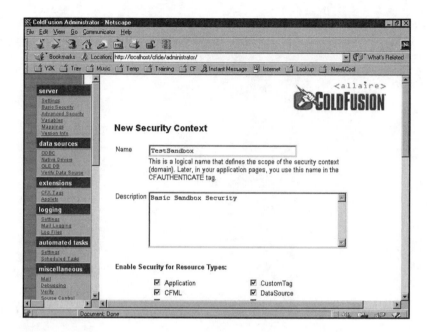

Securing the File System

The file system is a good starting point in securing your server. You want to segment each user's access to the file system. By defining rules for the file resource type, you can create a restricted access area for the developer.

The Rules button is at the bottom of the screen in Figure 7.3. Click this button to go to the Resource Rule list. Enter **UserDirectory_Read** in the Rule Name field. Select File from the Resource type drop-down list and click Add. You're now seeing the Resource Rule form, shown in Figure 7.4. Here, you enter the description **Read access directories** and enter a path in your Web root. Select the Read radio button. Any users assigned to a policy that contains this rule can read the path and directories under it. Click Add to create this rule. Follow these steps again, creating a rule called **UserDirectory_Write**, with the same path. Select the Write radio button and click Add. You now have defined read and write access for your sandbox. You can also add read access to the shared Custom Tags directory if you'd like your users to have access to this.

Now add some rules to restrict the use of CFFILE. You can also do this for CFCONTENT and CFDIRECTORY. These tags only work within the paths you set earlier, but you can also enable or disable certain (or all) actions for these tags.

You should now be back on the New Resource Rule list page that's shown in Figure 7.4. Let's create a rule for the CFFILE tag—action=delete. Type **CFFILE_Delete** in the Rule Name field and choose CFML from the drop-down list. Click Add to go to the New Resource Rule form shown in Figure 7.4. In the description field, type **Security sandbox restrictions for**

CFFILE - delete. Select CFFILE from the Tag Name drop-down list. The Action drop-down list is now populated with all available actions for CFFILE. Choose Delete and click Add. The CFFILE_Delete rule is now active. You can also either add rules for each of the actions for CFFILE or create one rule for all actions. Remember, this rule now restricts all access to CFFILE action=delete until you assign it to a policy.

FIGURE 7.4
New Resource Rule form.

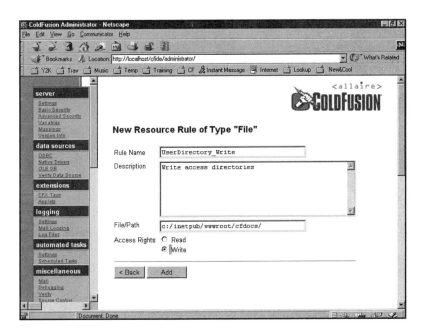

Securing the Registry

Developers have absolute system power with the CFREGISTRY tag. This is a tag you definitely want to restrict within a hosting environment. By restricting this tag, you control what developers, if any, have access to the system registry. You do this in much the same way you secured CFFILE.

Click the Rules button at the bottom of the New Security Context form in Figure 7.3. This again takes you to the New Resource Rule list in Figure 7.4. Create a rule for the CFREGISTRY tag by typing **CFREGISTRY_All** in the Rule Name field, while choosing CFML from the drop-down list. Click Add to go to the New Resource Rule form shown in Figure 7.4. Type **Security sandbox restrictions for all CFREGISTRY actions** in the Description field. Select CFREGISTRY from the Tag Name drop-down list. The Action drop-down list is again populated with all available actions for CFREGISTRY. Choose All Actions and then click Add. The CFREGISTRY_All rule is now active. You add this to a policy, along with CFFILE_Delete and the UserDirectory rules, later.

Part
II

Ch
7

Securing Data Sources

There are many cases when data source access on a ColdFusion server should be restricted. Data integrity can be compromised if unauthorized access from other applications or users is allowed. It is critical that users in an ISP environment be precluded from accessing data sources that they do not own. Now secure a data source using Advanced Security.

Click the Rules button at the bottom of the Security Context form in Figure 7.3. This takes you to the Resource Rules list once again. Type **MyDatasource** in the Rule Name field and choose Datasource from the drop-down list. Click Add to go to the New Resource Rule form shown in Figure 7.4. Type **Secured datasource example** in the Description field. Enter **CFExamples** in the Datasource Name field. (This data source is already configured for use with ColdFusion.) Select All from the Restrict SQL radio buttons. Notice that you can exercise more granular control over data sources by adding a rule for each restriction. Click Add. You're ready to secure a Custom Tag for your security context.

Securing Other Resources

Other resources can also be secured using Security Sandboxes. Let's secure a Custom Tag so that only designated users can access it in an application. The procedure for this is nearly identical to the procedure you used earlier, but a little repetition won't hurt.

Click the Rules button at the bottom of the New Security Context form in Figure 7.3. This takes you to the New Resource Rule list in Figure 7.4. Create a rule for the CF_WebSearch tag by typing **CF_WebSearch** in the Rule Name field and choosing Custom Tag from the drop-down list. Click Add to go to the New Resource Rule form shown in Figure 7.4. Type **Restricted access rule for CF_WebSearch** in the Description field. Enter the full path to the CF_WebSearch tag, which could be c:/cfusion/customtags/Websearch.cfm. You might remember from Chapter 6 that you use forward slashes for paths in the Advanced Security Administrator. For now, you can enter this path even if you haven't installed this tag. Click Add to activate the CF_WebSearch rule. Now you need to combine all of these rules with users in a policy.

Creating a Policy

You'll create a policy and associate users with these rules by clicking the Back button to go to the Security Context form shown in Figure 7.3. Click Policies to go to the Resource Policies list shown in Figure 7.5. Enter **AdminAccess** in the Policy Name field and click Add. You're now on the New Security Policy page shown in Figure 7.6. Enter the description for this policy: **All access pass!**. Click Add to return to the Resource Policies list.

Now add rules to your policy. Click the AdminAccess policy to return to the Resource Policies form; click Rules at the bottom of the page. This takes you to the Resource Rules page shown in Figure 7.7. Click Add/Remove to go to the Add/Remove Rules page in Figure 7.8. Select all of the rules in the right list and click the left arrow to move them into your policy. Your rules are now associated with a policy. Any users associated with this policy will have access to the resources you've defined in your rules. Click Back to return to the Resource Policy form.

FIGURE 7.5
Resource Policies list.

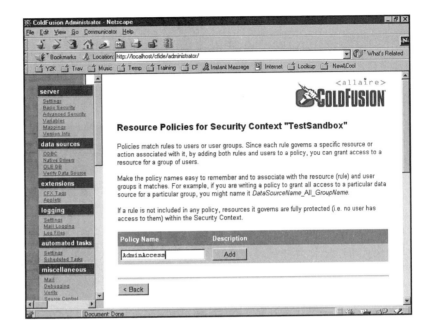

FIGURE 7.6
New Security Policy
form.

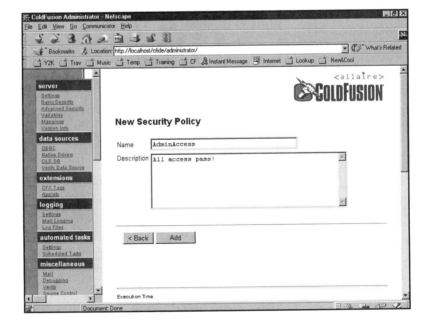

FIGURE 7.7
Resource Rules list.

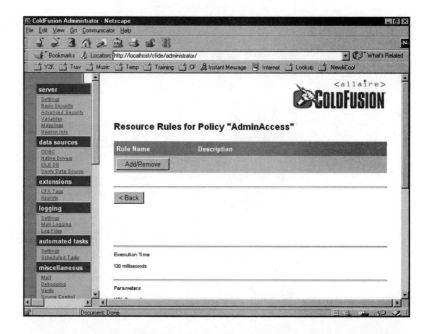

FIGURE 7.8
Add/Remove Rules.

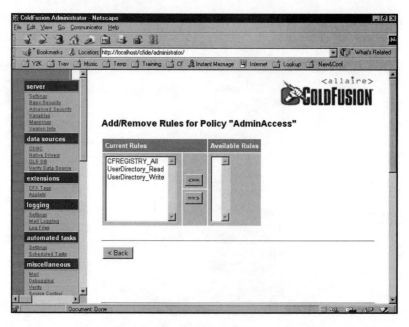

To complete the policy, select a user who will have access to all of these resources. Click Users to go to the Users list shown in Figure 7.9. Select the User Directory created for your Windows NT domain (see Chapter 8) and click Add/Remove to go to the Add/Remove Users Form in

Figure 7.10. In the Enter User field, enter your username from your Windows NT domain; click Add. The security context is now configured; assign this to a Security Sandbox.

FIGURE 7.9
User list.

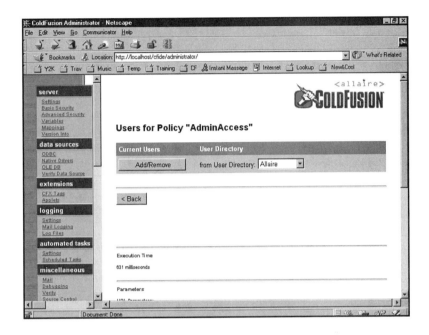

FIGURE 7.10
Add/Remove Users form.

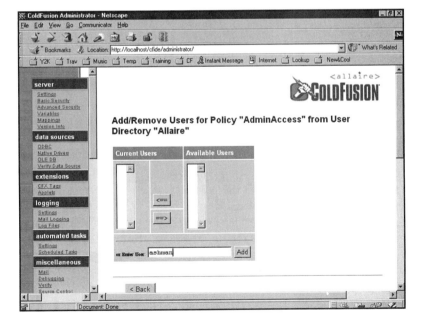

Part

II

Ch

7

Creating the Sandbox

In the Cold Fusion Administrator, click Advanced Security to go to the main security form shown in Figure 7.1. To make sure Security Sandboxes are enabled, see that the Use Security Sandbox Settings check box is selected. If it is not, check it and click Apply. Click the Security Sandbox button at the bottom of the page; you're now on the Registered Security Sandboxes list shown in Figure 7.11. Enter the path to your CF Examples directory, which may be `c:/inetpub/wwwroot/cfdocs/`, depending on your server and configuration. (You'll probably want to remove this after testing.) Click Add.

You're now on the Security Sandbox form shown in Figure 7.12. Select your TestSandbox security context and enter your Windows NT domain username and password. Make sure this user matches the user you added to your policy earlier; click Add. Your sandbox is configured!

To create multiple sandboxes with separate resource rules for each, create separate sets of resource rules and a unique policy for each user. In the policy, associate only the user you want to have access to the associated resource rules. Now you can create multiple Security Sandboxes, one for each user. Enter the directory path for each user's application as the location for his or her sandbox and add the username and password in the Security Sandbox dialog box. Each user will now have separate areas for development and a security buffer between applications.

FIGURE 7.11
Registered Security
Sandboxes.

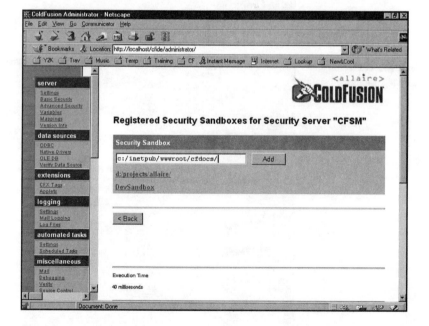

FIGURE 7.12
Security Sandbox form.

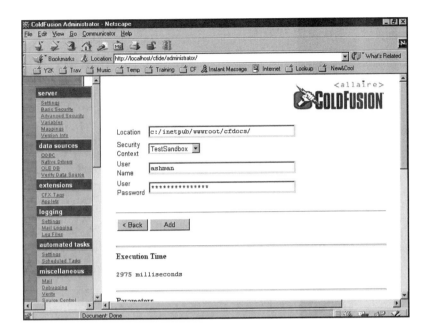

Remote Development Security

ColdFusion Studio's powerful development environment allows developers to access application pages and data sources from a remote ColdFusion server. Developers can also debug applications remotely using the Debugger within ColdFusion Studio. It is just as important to secure resources from unauthorized remote access as it is local access, so let's see how you can do this with Advanced Security.

Remote Development Security can be bound to a security context in the ColdFusion administrator. This allows you to define a security context once and use it for both your Security Sandboxes and your Remote Development Security. Since you've already defined a security context for your Security Sandboxes, bind it to Remote Development Security.

Choose Advanced Security from the ColdFusion Administrator to go to the Advanced Server Security page in Figure 7.1. The ColdFusion Studio Security section is near the bottom of the page. In the Security Context drop-down list, choose TestSandbox (the Security Context you just created); click Apply. Now all of the rules and policies you've defined apply also to all remote developers on your server.

File System Access

You've already defined file access rules for your security context. These rules also apply to any users within an associated policy when accessing the ColdFusion server remotely. Any directories you assign to a rule and a policy will be accessible by any users associated with that policy.

Part

II

Ch

7

Data Source Access

Data sources also are secured within your security context. Any data sources that are assigned to a user with rules and policies are also viewable remotely in ColdFusion Studio. Sensitive data sources are now protected from unauthorized access.

Debugger Access

The same permissions allowed for file access apply to debugging access. When ColdFusion Studio is debugging an application, it needs to have access to all files that are a part of the application. If the user does not have read access to these files, the debugging session cannot load them. Application pages are secured from unauthorized debugger access this way. ●

## CHAPTER 8

Integration with NOS Security

Heretofore, the security discussions have dealt mostly with LDAP directories. ColdFusion's security services also tightly integrate with Windows NT network operating system security, making it easy to match permissions already granted to users in your domain to ColdFusion security contexts. In this chapter you work with a user domain and give security access permissions to members of this domain. You also modify your SuperGadgets application created in Chapter 6, "The User Authentication Framework," to use Windows NT domain user lists.

It is assumed that you already know the basics of managing a Windows NT domain and that you have configured your own domains for your network. For a detailed discussion on managing Windows NT domains, try *Special Edition Using Windows NT Server 4, Second Edition*, by Roger Jennings, available from Que.

Adding User Directories

As you've seen in Chapter 6 and Chapter 7, "Securing Specific Features and Components," you must first add user directories and rules to build a security context. Adding a user directory from a Windows NT server is a straightforward process. Select Advanced Security in the ColdFusion Administrator. The Advanced Server Security form shown in Figure 8.1 is displayed. For more detailed information on this form, see Chapter 6. Click the User Directories button to access the Registered User Directories list shown in Figure 8.2. Enter **DomainUsers** in the User Directory field and click Add.

FIGURE 8.1

The Advanced Server Security form.

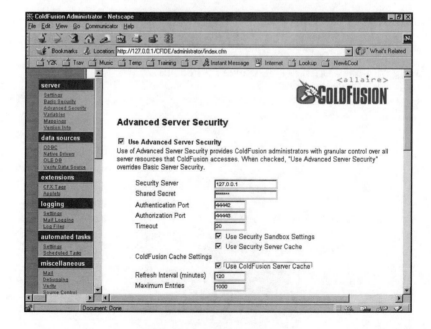

The New User Directory form shown in Figure 8.3 should look familiar to you; it's from Chapter 6. Enter **All Domain Users** in the Description field. This time choose Windows NT for the Namespace field. Enter your domain in the Server field without backslashes, so that \\CONTINUUM becomes CONTINUUM. Click Add; the new User Directory appears in the list.

Part

II

Ch

8

FIGURE 8.2

The Registered User Directories list.

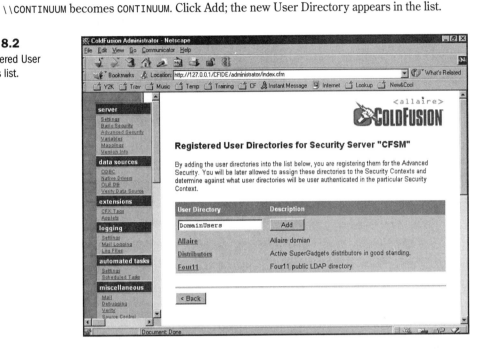

FIGURE 8.3

New User Directory form.

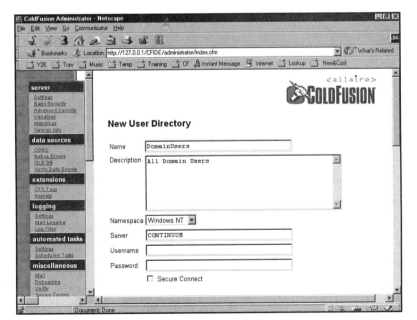

Adding a User Directory to an Existing Security Context

In Chapter 6 you created a security context for your SuperGadgets extranet. Now that you've added a new user directory to your Security Server, add this to your extranet security context and use it in our policy.

Navigate to the Advanced Security section of the ColdFusion Administrator and then click the Security Contexts button. The familiar dialog box from Chapter 6 is displayed, as shown in Figure 8.4. Select the Extranet Security Context. The Edit Security Context dialog box appears; it is shown in Figure 8.5. The next step in your integration is adding the user directory to the security context.

FIGURE 8.4

Security contexts.

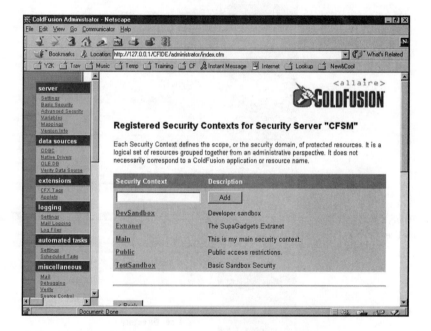

Click the User Directories button to go to the Add/Remove User Directories form shown in Figure 8.6. You already have the Distributors directory listed under Current Directories. It must also be in the Current Directories list in order for your policies to access users from the Domain Users directory. Select Domain Users from the Available Directories list on the right and click the left arrow button. Domain Users is now in the Current Directories list. Click Back to return to the Security Context form. Now you can modify your policy to have users from your new directory.

FIGURE 8.5
The Edit Security
Context form.

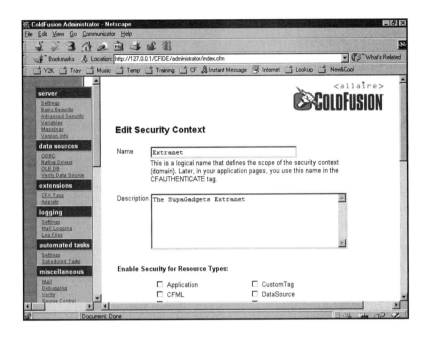

FIGURE 8.6
The Add/Remove User
Directories form.

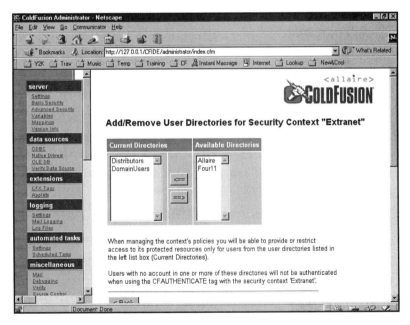

Modifying a Policy

Once again, you're in familiar territory. Chapter 7 covers creating resource rules and policies, and here you modify the policy you created for the SuperGadgets extranet. You're now on the Resource Policies list page shown in Figure 8.7. Click LetThemIn to go to the Edit Security Policy form in Figure 8.8.

FIGURE 8.7

The Resource Policies list.

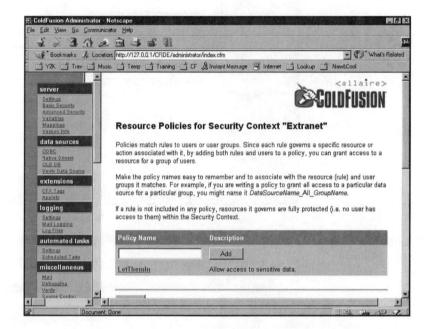

Click the Users button on the Resource Policies form to go to the Add/Remove Users form. Select the Domain Users User Directory from the drop-down list and then click Add/Remove. You are now on the Resource Policy Users form shown in Figure 8.9. In the Add User field, enter a valid username from the Windows NT domain assigned to the Domain Users User Directory. Click Add to make this user a member of the LetThemIn Policy.

Now test your results. Point your browser to the SuperGadgets application. From the home page, click the Login link. Enter the username and password for the user you've just added. You can see in Figure 8.10 that the Login link disappears, and we can view all of the items and their associated prices.

Using Multiple Domains and Managing Policies

As you can see, using multiple user directories within the same security context and even within policies is possible. You can also share user directories across security contexts and policies. In most cases, only one user directory is active within a security context.

FIGURE 8.8
The Edit Security Policy form.

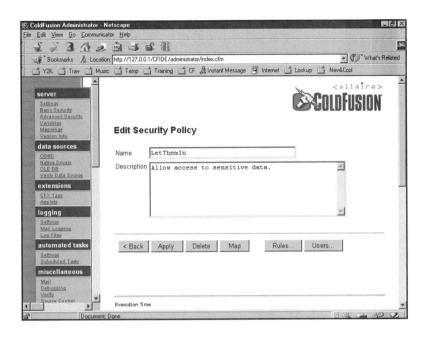

FIGURE 8.9
The Add/Remove Users form.

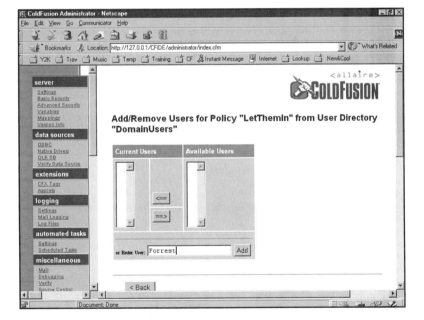

FIGURE 8.10

The SuperGadgets extranet.

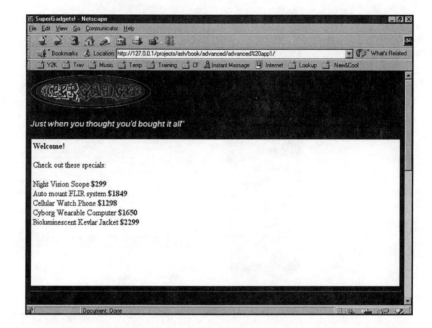

By creating separate policies for different groups of users in a domain you can create access levels within applications that mirror the access levels in your Windows NT domain. For instance, you can create a policy called Administrator_Access and assign the group Administrators to this policy. A separate policy, User_Access, can be assigned the group Domain Users in your Windows NT domain. This policy can be associated with a more restrictive set of resource rules, mirroring the access levels you've already created for your domain. ●

Extending ColdFusion

Creating Custom Tags

Understanding Custom Tags

The ColdFusion Markup Language, known as CFML, is a tag-based language, similar to HTML itself. The tag orientation has enabled ColdFusion creators to provide sophisticated functionality (database integration, POP and SMTP support, and LDAP integration, for example) without having to expose developers to any of the low-level details. These tags, however, are an integral part of ColdFusion, and originally developers had no way of enhancing the language with their own tags.

This situation changed with the release of ColdFusion version 2. Allaire published an API that would allow C and C++ programmers to write add-on tags as DLLs that could be called directly from within ColdFusion templates. In subsequent releases of ColdFusion, Allaire has taken this openness even further by adding support for COM and DCOM objects, CORBA, and by allowing programmers to write Custom Tags in CFML.

Table 9.1 lists the various forms of language extensions supported by ColdFusion 4.

Table 9.1   Extending the ColdFusion Language

Interface	Description
CFAPI	The ColdFusion API (also called CFX); tags are written in C or C++; see Chapter 10, " Writing CFX Tags in Visual C++," for more information. Using third-party software libraries, you also can write these extensions in Delphi; see Chapter 11, "Writing CFX Tags in Delphi," for more information.
COM Objects	Written in C, C++, Java, Visual Basic, Delphi, and other languages; supported via the CFOBJECT tag; see Chapter 12, "Extending ColdFusion with COM/DCOM," for more information.
CORBA	Written in C, C++, Java, Visual Basic, Delphi, and many other languages; supported via the CFOBJECT tag; see Chapter 13, "Extending ColdFusion with CORBA," for more information.
Custom Tags	Written in CFML; explained in this chapter.

Unlike CFAPI (and the COM/DCOM and CORBA interfaces), Custom Tags are written in CFML, the same language you are already using to write your ColdFusion applications. If you can write a ColdFusion template, you already know most of what you need to be able to write Custom Tags.

On the CD

You can find all the Custom Tags introduced in this chapter on the accompanying CD-ROM, along with a collection of other Custom Tags that you might find useful.

Defining Custom Tags

A ColdFusion Custom Tag is a ColdFusion template, just like any other template in your ColdFusion application. The template is written in CFML just like any other template. It might make ODBC calls via `<CFQUERY>`, set variables with `<CFSET>`, access local files using `<CFFILE>`, and even call other tags. In fact, Custom Tags can do *anything* that regular ColdFusion templates can do because Custom Tags are ColdFusion templates themselves.

What makes Custom Tags different, however, is how they interact with the rest of your application. To understand this concept, look at a simple example. Suppose you have a standard format for displaying the current date and time on your page. You can use the CFML `Now()` function to return the current date and time and then use `DateFormat()` and `TimeFormat()` to display the information as desired. The code might be as simple as

```
<CFOUTPUT>#DateFormat(Now())# #TimeFormat(Now())#</CFOUTPUT>
```

Rather than copy this code into every template, you can encapsulate it into a tag called `CF_DateTime` (or any other name you want) and just call `<CF_DateTime>` wherever you want to display the data and time information. This way, if you want to change the formatting, you can just change the code in the Custom Tag knowing that the new format will be displayed correctly wherever the tag is used.

Of course, you can accomplish the same thing by using a `<CFINCLUDE>` statement, and for code as simple as this, that would be a very workable solution. For more complex tags—tags that take attributes as parameters or tags that return values—Custom Tags are a far more elegant solution. In fact, you need to understand two very important differences between Custom Tags and included templates:

■ Templates included with `<CFINCLUDE>` are actually included right into the calling template at the location of the `<CFINCLUDE>` statement. Any variables or queries defined above the `<CFINCLUDE>` are visible to the included code. Similarly, any variables set within the included template are visible to any code in the calling template that comes after the `<CFINCLUDE>` statement. Custom Tags, on the other hand, have their own scope and are treated as entirely separate templates. Any variables set in the calling template are not visible within the Custom Tag, and vice versa.

■ You cannot pass parameters to an included template. To pass values, you must set them as local variables and then refer to the variables explicitly within the included template. Custom Tags are true tags. That is, they can take attributes just like any other HTML or CFML tag. As a result, you can formalize the interface between a Custom Tag and any calling code, which in turn enables you to *black box* (or encapsulate) code.

N O T E   Only read-write variables are hidden from the Custom Tag's scope. They are hidden to prevent them from being overwritten accidentally. Read-only variables—such as CGI variables, form fields, and URL parameters—are visible within Custom Tags because they cannot be overwritten anyway. ▪

Using Custom Tags

Before you actually introduce any tags, and to appropriately whet your appetite, look at this list of some of the things you might want to use Custom Tags for:

Part
III

Ch
9

- Creating standard menus and toolbars.
- Writing agents that communicate with other HTTP or FTP servers.
- Black boxing code, hiding complex sets of functionality from novice or inexperienced developers. You can instruct them to call a tag and give them any necessary attributes, if appropriate, without requiring them to know what is happening under the hood.
- Wrapping Java and ActiveX controls into easy-to-use tag interfaces.
- Securing code or processes from prying eyes or careless misuse.

In fact, the reasons to use Custom Tags almost always fall into one of the following three categories:

- Hiding complex functionality behind a simple interface
- Facilitating code reuse
- Securing code so that it can be executed but not modified (or even seen)

Any code that falls into one or more of these categories is a candidate for turning into a Custom Tag.

TIP

If you are looking for Custom Tags, the best place to start is the Allaire Tag Gallery at `http://www.allaire.com/taggallery`. The Tag Gallery is an online Custom Tag exchange containing hundreds of freeware, shareware, and commercial Custom Tags for you to download. The Tag Gallery is also a great place to publish any Custom Tags you write that you would like to share with the rest of the ColdFusion development community.

Locating Custom Tags

As noted previously, a Custom Tag is simply a ColdFusion template. So, what makes it a Custom Tag? The answer is simply, "Where it is located."

Go back to the example used before. If you were to include the code `<CF_DateTime>` in your template, ColdFusion would attempt to locate a tag named `CF_DateTime`. The actual filename for this tag would be `DATETIME.CFM`. (The `CF_` is what tells ColdFusion that this is a Custom Tag; the rest of the tag name is the tag filename.)

ColdFusion would first try to find a file named `DATETIME.CFM` in the current directory—the same directory as the calling template. If the file did not exist there, ColdFusion would look in a directory named `CustomTags` beneath the ColdFusion directory (usually `C:\CFUSION`) or any directory beneath it. As soon as the first filename `DATETIME.CFM` was found, ColdFusion would execute it.

CAUTION

Make sure to uniquely name each Custom Tag you write. If you have more than one file with the same name, ColdFusion will execute the first one it locates, and that might not be the one you expect.

You therefore can write *global* tags and *local* tags. Global tags are visible to all templates in all applications. Local tags are visible only to templates in the same directory.

TIP Global Custom Tags are stored in the ColdFusion CustomTags directory or any directory beneath it. You would be wise not to store all your tags in this directory, but rather to create subdirectories beneath it, and group tags in some logical structure. This way, you can make managing your tags much easier.

Creating a Simple Example

To understand Custom Tags, look at a simple example. The code shown in Listing 9.1 is the complete code for a Custom Tag called CF_DateTime. Save this code as DATETIME.CFM in the directory called CustomTags beneath the ColdFusion directory on your Web server (it is usually C:\CFUSION\CustomTags) or in any directory beneath that.

On the CD

Listing 9.1 DATETIME.CFM—**Code for** CF_DateTime **Tag**

```
<!--- Display date and time --->
<CFOUTPUT>
#DateFormat(Now())# #TimeFormat(Now())#
</CFOUTPUT>
```

To test the tag, create a CFM file in any directory beneath your Web server root, and add the code <CF_DateTime> to it. Then point to that CFM file with your browser. You should see a display similar to the one shown in Figure 9.1.

FIGURE 9.1
Custom Tags can be used to encapsulate user interface elements.

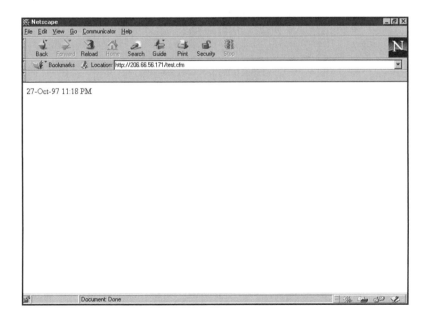

Now look at the code in Listing 9.1 again. It contains the same simple CFML that you looked at earlier. In fact, nothing about it is special at all. What is special is the fact that the file was stored in the CustomTags directory structure.

And that's all there is to writing Custom Tags.

Creating the CF_EmbedFields Example

The <CF_DateTime> example is extremely simple but not entirely useful. So, look at another example. As HTML forms are extremely limiting, HTML authors often create multipart forms. They are simply HTML forms whose values are passed to another form. That second form passes the values it receives to a third form, and so on, until an operation is completed. As each part of the multipart form is processed individually (each part is a separate page or template), the form can be changed or customized on-the-fly based on prior field submissions.

A popular way to pass values that are submitted by one form to another form is to embed the passed values as hidden form fields within the second form. The ColdFusion syntax for this would look something like

```
<CFOUTPUT><INPUT TYPE="hidden" NAME="dob" VALUE="#dob#"></CFOUTPUT>
```

Hidden HTML form fields are submitted along with all other form fields when the user clicks the Submit button, but they are not displayed on the screen, nor can they be edited or changed.

Passing values between forms as hidden fields also means that the application is *back button safe*. Because no processing or database interaction occurs until the final form is submitted, the users can safely use the browser's back and forward buttons (as users expect to be able to do).

The only complexity with passing form fields as hidden fields is that each form is required to hard-code the values that were passed to it so as to be able to embed them correctly. Of course, the result is that if the first form changes, all subsequent forms would have to change accordingly.

A better solution is to use a ColdFusion tag that *automatically* embeds any submitted form fields if any are present.

Listing 9.2 is the complete code listing for a Custom Tag called CF_EmbedFields. To use it in your own multipart forms, just add the code <CF_EmbedFields> between your <FORM> and </FORM> (or <CFFORM> and </CFFORM>) tags. Any and all passed form fields then are automatically embedded into your form as hidden fields.

On the CD

Listing 9.2 EMBEDFIELDS.CFM—Code for CF_EmbedFields **Custom Tag**

```
<!---
NAME:
CF_EmbedFields

DESCRIPTION:
ColdFusion custom tag to embed all submitted form fields as hidden
fields in another form. Designed to be used within multipart forms.
```

To use just call this module between the <FORM> and </FORM> tags.

ATTRIBUTES:
None.

NOTES:
Tag processes the comma delimited list of field names available as
FORM.fieldnames (this variable is automatically available if any
form fields were submitted). Each field is checked to see that
it has not already been processed (if there were multiple fields
with the same name then they'd appear multiple times in the
FORM.fieldnames list), and then it is written out as a hidden
FORM field (INPUT TYPE="hidden").

USAGE:
To use, just include <CF_EmbedFields> anywhere between the <FORM>
and </FORM> tags (or <CFFORM> and </CFFORM>). Any passed form
fields will automatically be embedded. If no form fields are
present then nothing is embedded, and processing continues.

AUTHOR:
Ben Forta (ben@forta.com) 7/15/97
--->

```
<!--- Check that fieldnames exist --->
<CFIF IsDefined("FORM.fieldnames")>

 <!--- Create empty list of processed variables --->
 <CFSET fieldnames_processed = "">

 <!--- Loop through fieldnames --->
 <CFLOOP INDEX="form_element" LIST="#FORM.fieldnames#">

  <!--- Try to find current element in list --->
  <CFIF ListFind(fieldnames_processed, form_element) IS 0>

   <!--- Make fully qualified copy of it (to prevent accessing the wrong
➥field type) --->
   <CFSET form_element_qualified = "FORM." & form_element>

   <!--- Output it as a hidden field --->
   <CFOUTPUT>
   <INPUT TYPE="hidden" NAME="#form_element#"
➥ VALUE="#Evaluate(form_element_qualified)#">
   </CFOUTPUT>

   <!--- And add it to the processed list --->
   <CFSET fieldnames_processed = ListAppend(fieldnames_processed, form
element)>
  </CFIF>

 </CFLOOP>

</CFIF>
```

Now look at the code in Listing 9.2. Custom Tags should always be as crash-proof as possible. You should never make assumptions about what users will or will not pass to you, and what environment you are running under. For this reason, the entire code portion of the `<CF_EmbedFields>` tag is enclosed in a `<CFIF>` statement that tests for the existence of `FORM.fieldnames`. This field is present only if the calling template receives any form fields, so by testing for its existence and executing the actual processing code only if it does indeed exist, you can ensure that errors will not be generated if the tag is misused.

The actual processing code uses a `<CFLOOP>` to loop through `FORM.fieldnames`, which is a comma-delimited list of all submitted form fields. Each field is then written as a hidden form field only if it has not already been written. (`FORM.fieldnames` can contain multiple occurrences of the same field name if more than one field has the same name.)

The CFML `Evaluate()` function is used to dynamically determine the value of the form field being processed within each loop iteration.

Commenting Custom Tags   The code in Listing 9.2 starts with detailed comments describing the tag and what it does; in fact, the comments take up more room than the tag code itself. This is not a bad thing at all. Actually, commenting the code is a habit you should get into immediately. Custom Tags are often written and put away, and not looked at again for quite a while. The next time you need to modify the tag, you'll greatly appreciate the comments. This is even more true if you write tags for others to use. If your code contains all the documentation needed to use the tag, you'll find yourself having to provide less user support and hand-holding.

Commenting tags requires no fixed format, but as a rule your comments should include a description, usage notes, author information (so users can contact you if needed), and usage examples if appropriate.

Testing `CF_EmbedFields`   To test `<CF_EmbedFields>`, create any form with any form controls in it, and set the form `ACTION` attribute to another template containing a form. Add the code `<CF_EmbedFields>` anywhere between the `<FORM>` and `</FORM>` tags on the second template.

When you submit the first form, all the submitted form fields are embedded into the second form. To verify this fact, use your browser to view the source of the second form.

Passing Data To and From Custom Tags

The examples you have looked at so far have all worked with local data (`<CF_DateTime>`) or data that was visible to them (`<CF_EmbedFields>`). To really harness the power of Custom Tags, you need to be able to pass values to them and retrieve data from them.

As mentioned earlier, the code in a Custom Tag is hidden from the calling template, and vice versa. The visibility of data is known as its *scope*, and Custom Tags and the templates that call them each have their own scopes.

Because of this scope, you cannot simply set a variable using `<CFSET>` or `<CFPARAM>` and expect to use it within your Custom Tag. If you want data exposed to your Custom Tag, you must specifically expose it. And just like HTML and CFML tags, the way data is exposed to Custom Tags is via tag *attributes*.

Working with Attributes

Many tags take attributes. The HTML <BODY> tag takes many *optional* attributes that let you specify factors such as text color and background file. Other tags have *required* attributes—for example, the DATASOURCE attribute in the CFML <CFQUERY> tag.

Some attributes are single words without values, and other attributes are passed in pairs of ATTRIBUTE=VALUE, with each attribute separated by a whitespace character (space, tab, newline character). The following <BODY> tag is being passed three attributes:

```
<BODY BGCOLOR="white" ALINK="blue" VLINK="blue" LINK="blue">
```

Attributes can be passed in any order, so the preceding code accomplishes the exact same thing as this next example:

```
<BODY ALINK="blue" LINK="blue" VLINK="blue" BGCOLOR="white">
```

Attributes are not case sensitive, so BGCOLOR="white" is the same as bgcolor="white". In addition, the values passed to attributes may or may not be enclosed within double quotation marks. Quotation marks are required only if the value has spaces in it, in which case the quotation marks tell the browser that the entire text (including the spaces and text after them) is part of the value.

 Enclosing all attribute values within double quotation marks is generally good practice. You'll find no downside to using them, and if you do end up with spaces in a value at a later date, your code won't break.

Referring to Passed Attributes Within a Custom Tag

To refer to a passed attribute within a Custom Tag, you must use the ATTRIBUTES type specifier. So, to refer to a passed attribute called NAME, you refer to ATTRIBUTES.NAME. If you omit the specifier, ColdFusion assumes that you are referring to a local variable (or some other visible variable), and if it does not exist, an error is thrown.

To see how passed attributes are used, update your <CF_DateTime> tag. The new and improved version (call this one <CF_DispDateTime> to distinguish them) allows the caller to specify whether to display the individual date and time elements. For example, the following call displays just the time:

```
<CF_DispDateTime SHOWDATE="No" SHOWTIME="Yes">
```

The code for this new Custom Tag is shown in Listing 9.3. The tag accepts two optional parameters: SHOWDATE (value of YES to show the date, or NO to not) and SHOWTIME (same possible values). You can pass both, either, or none of these attributes. Modify the test CFM page you wrote earlier so that it calls <CF_DispDateTime> instead of <CF_DateTime>, and experiment with the different attribute combinations.

Listing 9.3 `DISPDATETIME.CFM`—**Code for** `CF_DispDateTime` **Custom Tag**

```
<!--- Initialize values --->
<CFSET display_date = "Yes">
<CFSET display_time = "Yes">

<!--- Should date be displayed? --->
<CFIF IsDefined("ATTRIBUTES.showdate")>
 <CFSET display_date = ATTRIBUTES.showdate>
</CFIF>

<!--- Should time be displayed? --->
<CFIF IsDefined("ATTRIBUTES.showtime")>
 <CFSET display_time = ATTRIBUTES.showtime>
</CFIF>

<!--- Display date and time as requested --->
<CFOUTPUT>
<CFIF display_date>#DateFormat(Now())#</CFIF>
<CFIF display_time>#TimeFormat(Now())#</CFIF>
</CFOUTPUT>
```

Now take a closer look at Listing 9.3. The code starts by initializing two local variables `display_date` and `display_time`, both of which are set to default values of `Yes`.

Next, the code checks to see if `ATTRIBUTES.showdate` or `ATTRIBUTES.showtime` is passed by using the `IsDefined()` function. If either of them is present, then the `display_date` and `display_time` variables are updated with the passed values. So, the following code causes `display_date` to retain its `Yes` value, while `display_time` is updated with a `No` value:

```
<CF_DispDateTime SHOWTIME="No">
```

Finally, the tag displays the actual date and time elements if they were requested.

Figure 9.2 is an example of what the preceding call might display.

Using Optional and Required Attributes

Custom Tags have no built-in mechanism to automatically flag attributes as required. If your Custom Tag requires that certain attributes be present, you are responsible for verifying that they exist, and you must also handle any error reporting or processing as desired. This next example demonstrates one technique you can use to accomplish this feat.

`CF_MailForm` is a very useful tag; it simply sends the contents of any submitted form to a specified email address. Basically, this tag has two functions: form field processing and mail generation. The form field processing is very similar to the `<CF_EmbedFields>` example you looked at earlier. The mail generation is accomplished using the standard ColdFusion `<CFMAIL>` tag.

The code for `<CF_MailForm>` is shown in Listing 9.4. Once again, the tag starts with detailed comments, usage notes, and code examples.

FIGURE 9.2

Custom Tags can take one or more attributes that might change the tags' behavior.

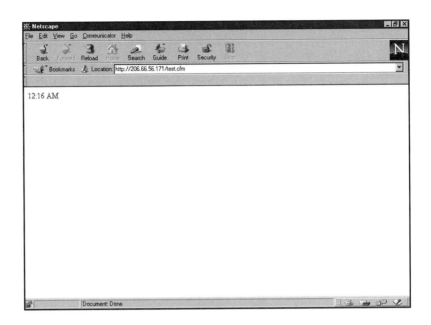

Listing 9.4 MAILFORM.CFM—Code for CF_MailForm **Custom Tag**

```
<!---
DESCRIPTION:
ColdFusion custom tag to automatically E-Mail the contents of
any form to a specified E-Mail address.

ATTRIBUTES:
FROM    - (required) Sender's E-Mail address.
SUBJECT - (optional) Message subject, defaults to
          "Form submission" if not specified.
TO      - (required) Recipient's E-Mail address.

NOTES:
Tag processes the comma delimited list of field names available
as FORM.fieldnames. Each field is checked to see that it has not
already been processed (if there were multiple fields with the
same name then they'd appear multiple times in the FORM.fieldnames
list). The finished list of fields is then sent via E-Mail to
the specified recipient. The message is formatted with each field
on its own line, in "FIELD: value" format. The message is also
automatically date and time stamped.

USAGE:
To use, just enter <CF_MailForm> on any form action page, making
sure you specify TO and FROM addresses. An optional SUBJECT may be
specified too if desired.

EXAMPLES:
  Send form results to a fixed address:
  <CF_MailForm TO="webmaster@forta.com" FROM="#FORM.email#">
```

continues

Listing 9.4 Continued

```
Specifying the message subject:
  <CF_MailForm TO="webmaster@forta.com" FROM="#FORM.email#" SUBJECT=
➥"#FORM.subject#">

AUTHOR:
Ben Forta (ben@forta.com) 9/25/97
--->

<!--- Initialize variables --->
<CFSET proceed = "Yes">
<CFSET error_message = "">
<CFSET CRLF = Chr(13) & Chr(10)>

<!--- Check that fieldnames exist --->
<CFIF IsDefined("FORM.fieldnames") IS "No">
 <CFSET proceed = "No">
 <CFSET error_message = "No form fields present!">
</CFIF>

<!--- Check that TO and FROM were specified --->
<CFIF proceed>
 <CFIF (IsDefined("ATTRIBUTES.to") IS "No") OR (IsDefined("ATTRIBUTES.from")
➥ IS "No")>
  <CFSET proceed = "No">
  <CFSET error_message = "TO and FROM attributes are required!">
 </CFIF>
</CFIF>

<!--- Check that TO and FROM are not empty --->
<CFIF proceed>
 <CFIF (Trim(ATTRIBUTES.to) IS "") OR (Trim(ATTRIBUTES.from) IS "")>
  <CFSET proceed = "No">
  <CFSET error_message = "TO and FROM may not be left blank!">
 </CFIF>
</CFIF>

<!--- If okay to go, process it --->
<CFIF proceed>

 <!--- Create variable for message body --->
 <CFSET message_body = "">

 <!--- Create empty list of processed variables --->
 <CFSET fieldnames_processed = "">

 <!--- Loop through fieldnames --->
 <CFLOOP INDEX="form_element" LIST="#FORM.fieldnames#">

  <!--- Try to find current element in list --->
  <CFIF ListFind(fieldnames_processed, form_element) IS 0>

   <!--- Make fully qualified copy of it (to prevent accessing the wrong
➥field type) --->
   <CFSET form_element_qualified = "FORM." & form_element>
```

```
   <!--- Append it to message body --->
   <CFSET message_body = message_body & form_element & ": "
➥ & Evaluate(form_element_qualified) & CRLF>

   <!--- And add it to the processed list --->
   <CFSET fieldnames_processed = ListAppend(fieldnames_processed, form_
➥element)>

  </CFIF>

 </CFLOOP> <!--- End of loop through fields --->

 <!--- Build subject --->
 <CFIF IsDefined("ATTRIBUTES.subject")>
  <CFSET subject = ATTRIBUTES.subject>
 <CFELSE>
  <CFSET subject = "Form submission">
 </CFIF>

 <!--- Send mail message --->
 <CFMAIL FROM="#ATTRIBUTES.from#" TO="#ATTRIBUTES.to#" SUBJECT="#subject#">
 The following is the contents of a form submitted on
➥#DateFormat(Now())# at #TimeFormat(Now())#:

 #message_body#
 </CFMAIL>

<CFELSE>

 <!--- Error occurred --->
 <CFOUTPUT><H1>#error_message#</H1></CFOUTPUT>
 <CFABORT>

</CFIF>
```

Take a close look at Listing 9.4. It starts by initializing a set of variables, one of which is called proceed. This variable is initialized to Yes. The proceed variable is used here as a flag indicating that it is safe to proceed with the actual processing, and every operation in this Custom Tag first checks to see whether it is safe to proceed by calling <CFIF proceed>.

If any operation fails, proceed is set to No. This setting prevents any other operations from being executed. In addition, a variable named error_message is set with a description of the failure that can be displayed later.

<CF_MailForm> has two required attributes: FROM and TO. The Custom Tag first checks to see that both are defined (that is, if they are passed to the tag). If either is not present, then the proceed flag is set to No. If, however, both are present, the tag checks to ensure that they are not empty, and once again, if this test fails, the proceed tag is set to No.

After all the testing is complete, the actual processing occurs. The Custom Tag loops through FORM.fieldnames to extract each field and its value, and appends the field to an ever-growing text field named message_body. By the time all the form fields have been processed, message_body contains the entire form contents as they are to be mailed. The last step is to actually send the mail using <CFMAIL>.

The following is generally a good layout to follow when you're writing Custom Tags:

- Display comments and a description.
- Initialize variables and set any default values.
- Check for the existence of required attributes or the lack thereof.
- Perform the actual tag processing.

N O T E Using <CFABORT> in a Custom Tag aborts *all* processing, even calling template processing. The ColdFusion <CFEXIT> tag can be used to exit a Custom Tag (essentially aborting Custom Tag processing) while continuing to process the calling template. ■

Using Caller Variables

Custom Tags often need to return data back to the calling template, and although tags can receive parameters in the form of attributes, they have no way to return data. To work around this limitation, ColdFusion allows Custom Tags to explicitly access the scope of the calling template. If you precede a variable name with the CALLER specifier, Custom Tags can both read and write to variables within the calling template's scope. So, to refer to a variable named *company* in the calling template, code in the Custom Tag would refer to CALLER.*company*.

The CALLER specifier is *required* to access the calling template's scope. If it is not specified, ColdFusion assumes you are referring to a local variable.

To demonstrate the use of the CALLER specifier, take a look at another Custom Tag. CF_CapFirst, shown in Listing 9.5, takes a string of text in a required attribute named text and converts the text so that each word is capitalized.

On the CD

Listing 9.5 CAPFIRST.CFM—Code for CF_CapFirst Custom Tag

```
<!---
DESCRIPTION:
ColdFusion custom tag to capitalize the first letter of each
word in a string, and lowercase the rest.

ATTRIBUTES:
TEXT - (required) the text to be converted.

NOTES:
Tag processes the passed string (passed to TEXT attribute)
as a space-delimited list, this allows the loop to process
one word at a time. The code within the loop gradually builds
a new string by appending one word at a time, and capitalizing
the first letter of each word.

LIMITATIONS:
The tag only treats a space as a delimiter.
```

```
Multiple spaces in a string will be converted to a single space.
--->

<!--- Check TEXT attribute was passed --->
<CFIF IsDefined("ATTRIBUTES.text")>

 <!--- Create empty string to store converted text --->
 <CFSET converted_text = "">

 <!--- Loop through words, one word at a time --->
 <CFLOOP INDEX="word" LIST="#ATTRIBUTES.text#" DELIMITERS=" ">

  <!--- Append converted first character to converted string --->
  <CFSET converted_text = converted_text & " " & UCase(Left(word, 1))>

  <!--- If the word to be converted is more than 1 char long,
       append rest of word --->
  <CFIF Len(word) GT 1>
   <CFSET converted_text = converted_text & LCase(Right(word, Len(word)-1))>
  </CFIF>

 </CFLOOP>

 <!--- And write converted string to caller template as "text" --->
 <CFSET CALLER.text = converted_text>

<CFELSE>

 <!--- If TEXT not passed, display an error message, and halt processing --->
 <H1>Error!</H1>TEXT attribute not specified!
 <CFABORT>

</CFIF>
```

Part

III

Ch

9

By now, most of the code here should be familiar to you. The tag first checks to see that the
text attribute is passed and then loops through the text using CFLOOP to extract one word at a
time. Using the UCase() and LCase() functions, each word is converted so that only the first
letter is capitalized. After the processing is complete, the following code is executed:

```
<CFSET CALLER.text = converted_text>
```

This code creates (or overwrites) a variable called text in the calling template's scope and
saves the converted text into it.

Putting It All Together

To wrap up this discussion, look at one last example. <CF_SpiderSubmit> is a powerful Custom
Tag that demonstrates many techniques you'll find useful when writing tags of your own.
<CF_SpiderSubmit> submits URLs to Internet search engines and spiders. You pass it the URL
to submit, and it contacts each of the supported search engines and submits an add URL request. This feat is accomplished using the <CFHTTP> tag that lets you make HTTP requests
from within your ColdFusion templates.

The code for `<CF_SpiderSubmit>`, shown in Listing 9.6, is extensively commented, as it is designed to be updated by users if needed.

On the CD

Listing 9.6   **SPIDERSUBMIT.CFM—Code for** `CF_SpiderSubmit` **Custom Tag**

```
<!---
NAME:
CF_SpiderSubmit

DESCRIPTION:
ColdFusion custom tag to submit URLs to Internet search
engines and spiders.

ATTRIBUTES:
EMAIL    - (required) E-Mail address of the person responsible for
           search engine submissions, many search engines will refuse
           entries without a valid E-Mail address. Typically this
           is set to the webmaster address.
ENGINES  - (optional) Comma delimited list of the engines to submit
           the URL to; if omitted, then URL will be sent to ALL
           listed engines. Valid engines are:
              * ALTAVISTA
              * EXCITE
              * HOTBOT
              * INFOSEEK
              * LYCOS
              * WEBCRAWLER
NAME     - (optional) Name of the query to be returned containing
           the submission status information. If specified, then
           a query will be returned with the following columns:
              * NAME    - The search engine or spider name
              * SUCCESS - YES if submission was successful,
                                   NO if not
              * RESULTS - The complete HTML results page as
                                   returned from the search engine
URL      - (required) The URL to submit, must be a fully qualified
           URL beginning with HTTP.

NOTES:
This tag submits URLs to Internet search engines and spiders,
and optionally returns a query containing status information for
each submission. URL submissions can be time consuming, particularly
if submitting to multiple engines. Make sure you specify a
RequestTimeout high enough so that the process does not time out
prematurely. For more information on the RequestTimeout parameter
see the ColdFusion documentation.

USAGE:
To use just call <CF_SpiderSubmit URL="url" EMAIL="email"> from
within your ColdFusion template, obviously replacing "url" with
the URL to be submitted, and email with a valid E-Mail address.
All other attributes are optional.

EXAMPLES:
 Submit URL to all engines:
```

```
  <CF_SpiderSubmit
   EMAIL="webmaster@allaire.com"
   URL="http://www.allaire.com">

 Submit dynamic URL to a single engine:
  <CF_SpiderSubmit
   EMAIL="#email#"
   URL="#url#"
   ENGINES="ALTAVISTA">

 Checking submission status:
  <CF_SpiderSubmit
   EMAIL="webmaster@allaire.com"
   URL="http://www.allaire.com"
   NAME="submissions">
  <CFOUTPUT QUERY="submissions">
   #name# - #success#<BR>
  </CFOUTPUT>

AUTHOR:
Ben Forta (ben@forta.com) 9/23/97
--->

<!---
====================================================================
This first section lists all the search engines and spiders
supported by this tag. To add a spider, add a record to the
"engines" query, copying a block of code from those below.
NAME should be set to a UNIQUE name that identifies the search
engine, URL is the URL where requests should be sent, and SUCCESS
is a string of text that can be used to identify a completed
submission. When specifying the URL, enter the text *URL* where
the URL should go, and #EMAIL# where the E-Mail address should go,
and the tag will replace those tokens with the actual values prior
to submission.
====================================================================
--->

<!--- Create query to contain search engine info  --->
<CFSET engines = QueryNew("name, url, success")>

<!--- AltaVista --->
<CFSET LastRow = QueryAddRow(engines)>
<CFSET temp = QuerySetCell(engines, "name", "ALTAVISTA")>
<CFSET temp = QuerySetCell(engines, "url", "http://add-url.altavista.
➥digital.com/cgi-bin/newurl?ad=1&q=*URL*")>
<CFSET temp = QuerySetCell(engines, "success", "This URL has been recorded
➥ by our robot")>

<!--- Excite --->
<CFSET LastRow = QueryAddRow(engines)>
<CFSET temp = QuerySetCell(engines, "name", "EXCITE")>
<CFSET temp = QuerySetCell(engines, "url",
➥"http://www.excite.com/cgi/add_url.cgi?url=*URL*&email=*EMAIL*")>
<CFSET temp = QuerySetCell(engines, "success", "Thank you")>
```

continues

Listing 9.6   Continued

```
<!--- HotBot --->
<CFSET LastRow = QueryAddRow(engines)>
<CFSET temp = QuerySetCell(engines, "name", "HOTBOT")>
<CFSET temp = QuerySetCell(engines, "url",
➥"http://www.hotbot.com/addurl.html?newurl=*URL*&email=*EMAIL*")>
<CFSET temp = QuerySetCell(engines, "success", "Got it")>

<!--- Infoseek --->
<CFSET LastRow = QueryAddRow(engines)>
<CFSET temp = QuerySetCell(engines, "name", "INFOSEEK")>
<CFSET temp = QuerySetCell(engines, "url",
➥"http://www.infoseek.com/AddURL/addurl?url=*URL*&pg=URL.html&ud5=
➥Add%2FUpdate+URL")>
<CFSET temp = QuerySetCell(engines, "success", "has been submitted")>

<!--- Lycos --->
<CFSET LastRow = QueryAddRow(engines)>
<CFSET temp = QuerySetCell(engines, "name", "LYCOS")>
<CFSET temp = QuerySetCell(engines, "url", "http://www.lycos.com/
➥cgi-bin/spider_now.pl?query=*URL*&email=*EMAIL*")>
<CFSET temp = QuerySetCell(engines, "success", "We successfully spidered
➥ your page")>

<!--- WebCrawler --->
<CFSET LastRow = QueryAddRow(engines)>
<CFSET temp = QuerySetCell(engines, "name", "WEBCRAWLER")>
<CFSET temp = QuerySetCell(engines, "url", "http://info.webcrawler.com/
➥cgi-bin/addURL.cgi?action=add&url=*URL*")>
<CFSET temp = QuerySetCell(engines, "success", "has been scheduled for
➥ indexing")>

<!---
=================================================================
This next section initializes variables, and checks that required
attributes are present.
=================================================================
--->

<!--- Initialize variables --->
<CFSET proceed = "Yes">
<CFSET error_message = "">
<CFSET feedback = "">

<!--- Check required attributes present --->
<CFIF (IsDefined("ATTRIBUTES.url") IS "No") OR (IsDefined("ATTRIBUTES.
➥email") IS "No")>
 <CFSET error_message = "ERROR! URL and EMAIL attributes are required!">
 <CFSET proceed = "No">
</CFIF>

<!--- Check required attributes not empty --->
<CFIF (Trim(ATTRIBUTES.url) IS "") OR (Trim(ATTRIBUTES.email) IS "")>
 <CFSET error_message = "ERROR! URL and EMAIL attributes may not be empty!">
```

```
  <CFSET proceed = "No">
</CFIF>

<!--- Get list of search engines to submit to --->
<CFSET engine_list = ""> <!--- Initialize variables --->
<CFIF IsDefined("ATTRIBUTES.engines")> <!--- If specified, use instead
of default --->
 <CFSET engine_list = ATTRIBUTES.engines>
</CFIF>
<CFIF Trim(engine_list) IS ""> <!--- Verify didn't get set to "" --->
 <CFSET engine_list = ValueList(engines.name)> <!--- Default to all --->
</CFIF>

<!--- Check that feedback query is not empty if specified --->
<CFIF IsDefined("ATTRIBUTES.name")>
 <CFIF Trim(ATTRIBUTES.name) IS "">
  <CFSET error_message = "ERROR! NAME must not be empty if specified!">
  <CFSET proceed = "No">
 <CFELSE>
  <!--- Feedback required, set feedback variable to query name --->
  <CFSET feedback = "CALLER." & ATTRIBUTES.name>
 </CFIF>
</CFIF>


<!---
==================================================================
If okay to proceed, this next section performs the actual
submissions, and provides any user feedback.
==================================================================
--->

<!--- Okay to proceed? --->
<CFIF proceed IS "Yes">

 <!--- If providing feedback, create feedback query --->
 <CFIF feedback IS NOT "">
  <CFSET "#feedback#" = QueryNew("name, success, results")>
 </CFIF>

 <!--- Loop through engines --->
 <CFLOOP QUERY="engines">

  <!--- Is this one on the list? --->
  <CFIF ListFind(engine_list, engines.name)>

   <!--- Build URL to submit, replace tokens with actual values --->
   <CFSET submit_url = #ReplaceList(engines.url, "*URL*,*EMAIL*",
➥ "#URLEncodedFormat(ATTRIBUTES.url)#,#ATTRIBUTES.email#")#>

   <!--- Submit it --->
   <CFHTTP METHOD="GET" RESOLVEURL="Yes" URL="#submit_url#">
   </CFHTTP>

   <!--- Provide feedback if required --->
```

continues

Listing 9.6 Continued

```
    <CFIF feedback IS NOT "">

    <!--- Add a row --->
    <CFSET LastRow = QueryAddRow(Evaluate(feedback))>

    <!--- Set name column --->
    <CFSET temp = QuerySetCell(Evaluate(feedback), "name", "#engines.name#")>

    <!--- Set SUCCESS column to either YES or NO --->
    <CFSET temp = QuerySetCell(Evaluate(feedback), "success",
➥"#IIf(Find(engines.success, CFHTTP.FileContent)
➥ IS 0, DE("No"), DE("Yes"))#")>

    <!--- Save results from CFHTTP call --->
    <CFSET temp = QuerySetCell(Evaluate(feedback), "results", "#CFHTTP.
➥FileContent#")>

    </CFIF>

  </CFIF>

  </CFLOOP>

<CFELSE>

<!--- Failed, display error and abort --->
<CFOUTPUT><H1>#error_message#</H1></CFOUTPUT>
<CFABORT>

</CFIF>
```

<CF_SpiderSubmit> starts by manually creating a query in which to store the properties of the supported spiders and search engines. It is the same type of query that is returned by the <CFQUERY> tag, except that it is created using calls to QueryNew() (to create the query), QueryAddRow() (to add rows to the query), and QuerySetCell() (to set query cell values).

The advantage in using a query here instead of just setting variables (or even an array) is that ColdFusion queries are easy to work with, and important tags, such as <CFLOOP>, support them automatically. Simulating query results in this fashion allows you to break your code into clean, distinct parts and lets you use standard tags and procedures just as if you were deriving data from a database lookup. In addition, because the list is stored as a query, adding another spider to the list is simply a matter of modifying one section of the code, and everything else falls into place automatically.

The next section initializes variables and verifies that the required attributes are passed.

Next comes the actual submission. The tag loops through the list of engines (or the passed list if only a subset is wanted) and submits the request to each one of them using the <CFHTTP> tag.

▶ **See** Chapter 21, "Intelligent Agents and Distributed Processing," **p. 483**

In addition, if the user requested feedback, another query is built, this time in the calling template's scope. This query is again constructed using the previously mentioned query manipulation functions, and it allows the caller to check the status of each submission to each spider or search engine.

Unlike in the `<CF_CapFirst>` example, the data returned to the caller template (in this example, the query) is not hard-coded to a specific name; rather, the user passes the desired query name, and the Custom Tag creates it. This use is consistent with how CFML tags such as `<CFQUERY>` and `<CFPOP>` work and provides a safer and more scalable interface.

Part
III

Ch
9

Creating Tag Pairs

All the tags you have looked at until this point use a simple tag syntax—just one tag with possible attributes. ColdFusion also allows you to create more complex Custom Tags that are made up of starting and ending tag sets.

To understand this kind of tag, take a look at a simple example. Text in an HTML page should not contain certain characters (for example, <, >, &, "). Instead, you are supposed to use special references (called *entity references*). So, instead of <, you must specify `&lt;`, and instead of &, you must specify `&amp;`.

If you are hard-coding static pages, you can easily search and replace all invalid characters with their correct entity references. (Because hundreds of them are in use, manually searching and replacing can get quite tedious.) But when data is served dynamically (perhaps from a database), making all these replacements on-the-fly is very difficult.

This job of searching and replacing is ideal for a Custom Tag. The following syntax converts all the text in between the tags:

```
<CF_SafeText>
... text goes here ...
</CF_SafeText>
```

The text in between the tags can be fixed text, variables, database output, or anything else. The `<CF_SafeText>` tag processes the text and makes the needed replacements.

Listing 9.7 contains the source code for `<CF_SafeText>`.

Listing 9.7 SAFTETEXT.CFM—Code for CF_SafeText **Custom Tag**

```
<CFSETTING ENABLECFOUTPUTONLY="Yes">
<!---
NAME:
 CF_SafeText

DESCRIPTION:
 Converts specified text into "HTML safe" text, replacing any potential
 problem characters with their appropriate HTML entity references.
```

continues

Listing 9.7   Continued

```
ATTRIBUTES:
 NONE

NOTES:
 This tag requires ColdFusion 4 or later.

USAGE:
 To use CF_SafeText, just pass the text to be processed between the
 <CF_SafeText> and </CF_SafeText> tags.

EXAMPLES:
 Output a database field converted to HTML safe text:
  <CF_SafeText>
  #query.column#
  </CF_SafeText>

AUTHOR:
 Ben Forta (ben@forta.com) 10/1/98
--->

<!--- Define list of "bad" characters --->
<CFSET bad_chars="&,<,>,"",Æ,Á,Â,À,Å,Ã,Ä,Ç,Ð,É,Ê,È,Ë,Í,Î,Ì,
Ï,Ñ,Ó,Ô,Ò,Ø,Õ,Ö,Þ,¶,Ú,Û,Ù,Ü,Ý,á,â,æ,à,å,ã,
ä,ç,é,ê,è,á,ë,í,î,ì,ï,ñ,
ó,ô,ò,ø,õ,ö,ß,Þ,ú,û,ù,ü,
ý,ÿ,¡,£,¤,¥,¦,§,¨,©,ª,«,¬,-,®,¯,°,±,
²,³,´,µ,¶,·,¸,¹,»,¼,½,¾,¿,×,÷,¢">

<!--- Define list of "good" (entity) characters --->
<CFSET good_chars="&amp;,&lt;,&gt;,&quot;,&AElig;,&Aacute;,&Acirc;,&Agrave;,,
➥&Aring;,&Atilde;,&Auml;,&Ccedil;,&ETH;,&Eacute;,&Ecirc;,&Egrave;,&Euml;,,
➥&Iacute;,&Icirc;,&Igrave;,&Iuml;,&Ntilde;,&Oacute;,&Ocirc;,&Ograve;,,
➥&Oslash;,&Otilde;,&Ouml;,&THORN;,&Uacute;,&Ucirc;,&Ugrave;,&Uuml;,,
➥&Yacute;,&aacute;,&acirc;,&aelig;,&agrave;,&aring;,&atilde;,&auml;,,
➥&ccedil;,&eacute;,&ecirc;,&egrave;,&eth;,&euml;,&iacute;,&icirc;,,
➥&igrave;,&iuml;,&ntilde;,&oacute;,&ocirc;,&ograve;,&oslash;,&otilde;,,
➥&ouml;,&szlig;,&thorn;,&uacute;,&ucirc;,&ugrave;,&uuml;,&yacute;,&yuml;,,
➥&iexcl;,&pound;,&curren;,&yen;,&brvbar;,&sect;,&uml;,&copy;,&ordf;,,
➥&laquo;,&not;,&shy;,&reg;,&macr;,&deg;,&plusmn;,&sup2;,&sup3;,&acute;,,
➥&micro;,&para;,&middot;,&cedil;,&sup1;,&ordm;,&raquo;,&frac14;,&frac12;,,
➥&frac34;,&iquest;,&times;,&divide;,&cent;">

<!--- Only process this if in END ExecutionMode --->
<CFIF ThisTag.ExecutionMode is "END">

 <!--- Replace GeneratedContent with updated GeneratedContent --->
 <CFSET ThisTag.GeneratedContent=ReplaceList(ThisTag.GeneratedContent,
➥ bad_chars, good_chars)>

</CFIF>

<CFSETTING ENABLECFOUTPUTONLY="No">
```

As should all Custom Tags, the listing starts with a descriptive comment block. This block explains what the tag does and provides attribute and usage information.

The tag itself starts by creating two ColdFusion lists. The first list, bad_chars, is a list of characters that should not be used in an HTML page. The second list, good_chars, is a list of entity references for each of the characters in the bad_chars list. The lists each have the same number of items in them, and each item in the good_chars list corresponds to the item in the same position in the bad_chars list. The first element in the good_chars list, &, thus corresponds to the first element in the bad_chars list, &.

Part
III
Ch
9

The actual replacement is done with the ColdFusion ReplaceList() function. ReplaceList() takes three parameters, the text to be processed, the list of characters to look for, and the list of characters to replace them with. ReplaceList() replaces all the items in the first list with the matching elements in the second list.

The text being replaced is ThisTag.GeneratedContent. ThisTag is a special structure that is automatically available in every Custom Tag. It contains several different members, as listed in Table 9.2, all of which pertain to the Custom Tag being processed. GeneratedContent contains the body text that is in between the start and end tags in the calling page. You can read and write this variable as needed, changing it if necessary. The following syntax replaces the text in ThisTag.GeneratedContent with the text output from the ReplaceList() function:

```
<CFSET ThisTag.GeneratedContent=ReplaceList(ThisTag.GeneratedContent, bad_chars,
➡ good_chars)>
```

Table 9.2 ThisTag Structure Members

Variable	Description
AssocAttribs	Array of structures with associated attributes, present only if <CFASSOCIATE> is used; discussed later in this chapter.
ExecutionMode	Current execution mode; possible values are START (when the open tag is called), END (when the close tag is called), and INACTIVE (when not processing the tag itself).
GeneratedContent	The body text in between the start and end tags; may be written to and updated.
HasEndTag	TRUE if this tag has an end tag; FALSE if not.

The actual replacement occurs within a <CFIF> statement that looks like this:

```
<CFIF ThisTag.ExecutionMode is "END">
```

ExecutionMode is another member of the ThisTag structure. Complex Custom Tags, ones that have start and end tags (and possibly child tags), are called multiple times by ColdFusion. The code called on the end tag is the same code that is called on the open tag. The ExecutionMode variable tells your code which call is being processed. ExecutionMode is START when the tag code is called on the open tag and is END when the close tag is called. You therefore can write code that differs based on which call is being processed. Checking to see that ThisTag.ExecutionMode is END ensures that you process the replacement only after the body text (the text in between the tags) is read.

> **CAUTION**
>
> If you do not use a <CFIF> statement here, the code is executed twice and possibly throws error messages because you could be referring to variables that do not exist yet.

N O T E As a rule, most Custom Tag processing should be done when ThisTag.ExecutionMode is END. The BEGIN mode is primarily used for initializing variables and similar activities. ■

Using Child Tags

ColdFusion also allows you to create tag families, which are sets of tags with child tags (similar to ColdFusion's own <CFTREE> and <CFTREEITEM> tag, or <CFHTTP> and <CFHTTPPARAM>). Using child tags is a little more complex than writing Custom Tag pairs and requires a little more care in attribute passing, as you will see.

Creating tag sets involves creating multiple CFM files, one for each tag. The tags are associated with each other using the ColdFusion <CFASSOCIATE> tag in the child tag. <CFASSOCIATE> serves two purposes:

- Relating a child tag to its parent, thereby publishing any attributes passed to the child tag up to the parent tag
- Allowing the child tag to use the GetBaseTagList() and GetBaseTagData() functions to access data and variables within the parent tag

N O T E Child tags can be nested, so a child tag can be a parent to another tag. Every child tag must contain a <CFASSOCIATE> call. <CFASSOCIATE> is used only in child tags, never in the top-level parent tag. ■

To see how to use child tags and the <CFASSOCIATE> tag, look at an example. Dynamic HTML, or DHTML, is a powerful technology that you can use to create sophisticated user interfaces. The problem with DHTML is that you typically must write your code in JavaScript (or VBScript), and you then must invoke your code with complex statements embedded into your HTML.

ColdFusion Custom Tags are well suited for encapsulating DHTML into a simple tag-based interface. As an example, look at a DHTML menu tree library. The DHTML menus allow you to create pop-up menus within your Web page. These highly configurable menus can contain selections and submenus, which point to URLs that are selected when a menu selection is made.

N O T E The example used here is built on top of DHTML code written by Jeremie Miller; it is used with his permission. This code works with Microsoft Internet Explorer 4 or later; it does not work with Netscape browsers. Be sure to visit Jeremie's Web site at `http://www.jeremie.com`. ■

The code to embed a simple menu looks like this:

```
<A HREF="" MENU="top:100;left:100;src:menusrc2;">Browsers</A>
<DIV ID="menusrc2" STYLE="display:none">
Microsoft IE!http://www.microsoft.com/ie!Download Microsoft Internet Explorer!
➥216;Netscape Navigator!http://www.netscape.com/computing/download/
➥!Download Netscape Navigator!216;
</DIV>
```

Although the preceding code is not impossibly complicated, you can create the same menu using ColdFusion Custom Tags as a wrapper around the DHTML libraries like this:

```
<CF_DHTMLMenu CAPTION="Browsers" TOP="100" LEFT="100" SCRIPTDIR="/js">
  <CF_DHTMLMenuItem CAPTION="Microsoft IE" URL="http://www.microsoft.com/ie"
➥ DESCRIPTION="Download Microsoft Internet Explorer" ICON="216">
  <CF_DHTMLMenuItem CAPTION="Netscape Navigator" URL="http://www.netscape.com/
computing/download/" DESCRIPTION=
➥"Download Netscape Navigator" ICON="216">
 </CF_DHTMLMenu>
```

Obviously, the ColdFusion syntax is easier to work with and simpler to implement.

Writing the `<CF_DHTMLMenu>` tag actually involves creating three CFM files. `DHTMLMenu.CFM` (shown in Listing 9.8) is the actual menu creation code, the parent tag. `DHTMLMenuItem.CFM` (shown in Listing 9.9) is the menu item code; this tag is a child tag associated with the parent tag, `DHTMLMenu.CFM`. `DHTMLMenuSubMenu.CFM` (shown in Listing 9.10) is the code used to create submenus, and it too is a child tag associated with the parent tag, `DHTMLMenu.CFM`.

Listing 9.8 `DHTMLMENU.CFM`—**Code for** `CF_DHTMLMenu` **Custom Tag**

```
<CFSETTING ENABLECFOUTPUTONLY="Yes">

<!---
NAME: <CF_DHTMLMenu>

DESCRIPTION: <CF_DHTMLMenu> is a set of ColdFusion tags that create
             DHTML based pop-up menus. Menus may contain text,
             descriptions, icons, URLs, and even submenus.
             <CF_DHTMLMenu> uses a wonderful DHTML menuing
             script written by Jeremie Miller, and is being used
             with his permission.

ATTRIBUTES: CF_DHTMLMenu is made up of three tags, each with its own
            set of attributes. Several attributes are colors used to
            control menu appearance. Colors may be specified as
            text strings or RGB values.
  CF_DHTMLMenu
  ============
```

continues

Listing 9.8 Continued

ARROW	(Optional)	Should arrows be shown indicating submenus? Valid values are TRUE and FALSE, defaults to TRUE.
ARROWOFFSET	(Optional)	Position of arrow in pixels, relative to the left edge of the menu, defaults to 135.
BACKGROUND	(Optional)	Menu background color, defaults to white.
BORDERWIDTH	(Optional)	Menu border width, defaults to 1.
BORDERCOLOR	(Optional)	Menu border color, defaults to black.
CAPTION	(Required)	Menu caption text (or HTML e.g. an IMG tag).
FONTCOLOR	(Optional)	Text font color, defaults to black.
FONTFAMILY	(Optional)	Title text font face or family.
FONTSIZE	(Optional)	Item text (and arrow) size, valid values are the 9 CSS size specifiers (SMALL, LARGE, etc).
HEIGHT	(Optional)	Height of each row (in pixels), defaults to 22.
HIGHLIGHT	(Optional)	Color of menu item when mouse passes over it, defaults to #DCDCDC.
ICONCOLOR	(Optional)	Icon and arrow color, defaults to black.
LEFT	(Required)	Menu position, number of pixels from left of browser window.
MENUOFFSET	(Optional)	Distance (in pixels) from the right edge of the menu where submenu should be displayed, defaults to 1, negative values are allowed.
MENUTOPOFFSET	(Optional)	Distance (in pixels) from the top of the row where submenu should be displayed, defaults to 1, negative values are allowed.
SCRIPTDIR	(Required)	Location of MENUS.JS file, this should be a relative path beneath your Web server document root, so if you save the file in a directory name "JS" under your Web server root, you'd specify "/js" in this attribute.
SHOWROW	(Optional)	Should lines be displayed between menu items? Valid values are TRUE and FALSE, defaults to TRUE.
TOP	(Required)	Menu position, number of pixels from top of browser window.
WAIT	(Optional)	Milliseconds to display menu after it loses focus, default is 500.
WIDTH	(Optional)	Width of rows (in pixels), defaults to 150.

```
CF_DHTMLMenuItem
================
```

CAPTION	(Required)	Menu item caption text.
DESCRIPTION	(Optional)	Description text, pop-up displayed when mouse is over the item.
ICON	(Optional)	ASCII character number of a wingding font character as an item icon, the icon is displayed to the left of the CAPTION text.
URL	(Optional)	URL to go to when menu selection is made, if no URL is specified the current page

URL will be assumed (as a rule you should
always specify a URL).

```
CF_DHTMLMenuSubMenu
===================
 CAPTION          (Required) Submenu caption text.
```

NOTES:
The DHTML code used in this tag was created by Jeremie Miller, and is
being used with his permission. Check out Jeremie's homepage at
http://www.jeremie.com.
The DHTML code only supports Microsoft Internet Explorer 4 or later;
This code will not work with Netscape browsers.
This tag requires ColdFusion 4 or later.

USAGE:
<CF_DHTMLMenu> is a wrapper around Jeremie Miller's excellent DHTML
menuing code. To use this tag, you must first save the MENUS.JS
file into a directory beneath your Web server root. You will need to
specify the path to this file in the SCRIPTDIR attribute.
Each menu must begin with a <CF_DHTMLMenu> tag and end with a
</CF_DHTMLMenu> tag. Between these tags you specify the menu items.
Menu items may be menu selections (specified with the <CF_DHTMLMenuItem>
tag), or submenus (specified with the <CF_DHTMLMenuSubMenu> and
</CF_DHTMLMenuSubMenu> tags). There is no programmatic limit to the
number of menu items and submenus that a menu can contain, nor is there
a limit to the number of menus that you may place on a single page.

EXAMPLES:
This example is a simple two-item menu using only the required attributes:
```
 <CF_DHTMLMenu CAPTION="Browsers" TOP="10" LEFT="100" SCRIPTDIR="/js">
  <CF_DHTMLMenuItem CAPTION="Microsoft IE" URL="http://www.microsoft.com/ie">
  <CF_DHTMLMenuItem CAPTION="Netscape Navigator" URL=
➡"http://www.netscape.com/computing/download/">
 </CF_DHTMLMenu>
```

This next example sets specific colors:
```
 <CF_DHTMLMenu CAPTION="Browsers" TOP="10" LEFT="100" SCRIPTDIR="/js"
  BORDERCOLOR="red" BACKGROUND="black" HIGHLIGHT="navy" FONTCOLOR="white">
  <CF_DHTMLMenuItem CAPTION="Microsoft IE" URL="http://www.microsoft.com/ie">
  <CF_DHTMLMenuItem CAPTION="Netscape Navigator" URL=
➡"http://www.netscape.com/computing/download/">
 </CF_DHTMLMenu>
```

This next example provides optional description text and icons:
```
 <CF_DHTMLMenu CAPTION="Browsers" TOP="10" LEFT="100" SCRIPTDIR="/js">
  <CF_DHTMLMenuItem CAPTION="Microsoft IE" URL="http://www.microsoft.com/ie"
➡ DESCRIPTION="Download Microsoft Internet Explorer" ICON="216">
  <CF_DHTMLMenuItem CAPTION="Netscape Navigator" URL=
➡"http://www.netscape.com/computing/download/"
➡ DESCRIPTION="Download Netscape Navigator" ICON="216">
 </CF_DHTMLMenu>
```

This next example creates a menu with options and two submenus:
```
 <CF_DHTMLMenu CAPTION="Browsers" TOP="10" LEFT="100" SCRIPTDIR="/js">
```

continues

Listing 9.8 Continued

```
  <CF_DHTMLMenuItem CAPTION="Option1" URL="">
  <CF_DHTMLMenuItem CAPTION="Option2" URL="">
  <CF_DHTMLMenuSubMenu CAPTION="Submenu1">
   <CF_DHTMLMenuItem CAPTION="Submenu1 Option1" URL="">
   <CF_DHTMLMenuItem CAPTION="Submenu1 Option2" URL="">
  </CF_DHTMLMenuSubMenu>
  <CF_DHTMLMenuSubMenu CAPTION="Submenu2">
   <CF_DHTMLMenuItem CAPTION="Submenu2 Option1" URL="">
   <CF_DHTMLMenuItem CAPTION="Submenu2 Option2" URL="">
  </CF_DHTMLMenuSubMenu>
 </CF_DHTMLMenu>
```

This next example creates a menu with two levels of subnesting:

```
 <CF_DHTMLMenu CAPTION="Browsers" TOP="10" LEFT="100" SCRIPTDIR="/js">
  <CF_DHTMLMenuItem CAPTION="Option1" URL="">
  <CF_DHTMLMenuItem CAPTION="Option2" URL="">
  <CF_DHTMLMenuSubMenu CAPTION="Submenu1">
   <CF_DHTMLMenuItem CAPTION="Submenu1 Option1" URL="">
   <CF_DHTMLMenuItem CAPTION="Submenu1 Option2" URL="">
   <CF_DHTMLMenuSubMenu CAPTION="Submenu2">
    <CF_DHTMLMenuItem CAPTION="Submenu2 Option1" URL="">
    <CF_DHTMLMenuItem CAPTION="Submenu2 Option2" URL="">
   </CF_DHTMLMenuSubMenu>
  </CF_DHTMLMenuSubMenu>
 </CF_DHTMLMenu>

AUTHOR:
 Ben Forta (ben@forta.com) 10/1/98
--->

<!--- Only process in END execution mode --->
<CFIF ThisTag.ExecutionMode IS "START">

 <!--- Create submenu lists --->
 <CFSET ThisTag.submenu_start_list="">
 <CFSET ThisTag.submenu_end_list="">

<CFELSEIF ThisTag.ExecutionMode IS "END">

 <!--- Erase any tag content (if there is any) --->
 <CFSET ThisTag.GeneratedContent="">

 <!--- Create counter in caller space if not present --->
 <CFPARAM NAME="CALLER.DHTMLMenu" DEFAULT="0">
 <CFSET CALLER.DHTMLMenu=CALLER.DHTMLMenu+1>

 <!--- Embed script location into HEAD block (only for first menu) --->
 <CFIF CALLER.DHTMLMenu IS 1>
 <CFHTMLHEAD TEXT="#Chr(60)#SCRIPT SRC=#Chr(34)##ATTRIBUTES.scriptdir#/
➥menus.js#Chr(34)##Chr(62)##Chr(60)#/SCRIPT#Chr(62)#">
 </CFIF>

 <!--- Create menu text (required attributes) --->
```

```
<CFSET menu_text="">
<CFSET menu_text=menu_text&"top:#ATTRIBUTES.top#;">
<CFSET menu_text=menu_text&"left:#ATTRIBUTES.left#;">
<CFSET menu_text=menu_text&"src:menusrc#CALLER.DHTMLMenu#;">

<!--- Create menu text (optional attributes) --->
<CFIF IsDefined("ATTRIBUTES.arrow")>
 <CFSET menu_text=menu_text&"arrow:#ATTRIBUTES.arrow#;">
</CFIF>
<CFIF IsDefined("ATTRIBUTES.arrowoffset")>
 <CFSET menu_text=menu_text&"arrow-offset:#ATTRIBUTES.arrowoffset#;">
</CFIF>
<CFIF IsDefined("ATTRIBUTES.background")>
 <CFSET menu_text=menu_text&"background:#ATTRIBUTES.background#;">
</CFIF>
<CFIF IsDefined("ATTRIBUTES.bordercolor")>
 <CFSET menu_text=menu_text&"border-color:#ATTRIBUTES.bordercolor#;">
</CFIF>
<CFIF IsDefined("ATTRIBUTES.borderwidth")>
 <CFSET menu_text=menu_text&"border-width:#ATTRIBUTES.borderwidth#;">
</CFIF>
<CFIF IsDefined("ATTRIBUTES.fontcolor")>
 <CFSET menu_text=menu_text&"font-color:#ATTRIBUTES.fontcolor#;">
</CFIF>
<CFIF IsDefined("ATTRIBUTES.fontfamily")>
 <CFSET menu_text=menu_text&"font-family:#ATTRIBUTES.fontfamily#;">
</CFIF>
<CFIF IsDefined("ATTRIBUTES.fontsize")>
 <CFSET menu_text=menu_text&"font-size:#ATTRIBUTES.fontsize#;">
</CFIF>
<CFIF IsDefined("ATTRIBUTES.height")>
 <CFSET menu_text=menu_text&"height:#ATTRIBUTES.height#;">
</CFIF>
<CFIF IsDefined("ATTRIBUTES.highlight")>
 <CFSET menu_text=menu_text&"highlight:#ATTRIBUTES.highlight#;">
</CFIF>
<CFIF IsDefined("ATTRIBUTES.iconcolor")>
 <CFSET menu_text=menu_text&"icon-color:#ATTRIBUTES.iconcolor#;">
</CFIF>
<CFIF IsDefined("ATTRIBUTES.menuoffset")>
 <CFSET menu_text=menu_text&"menu-offset:#ATTRIBUTES.menuoffset#;">
</CFIF>
<CFIF IsDefined("ATTRIBUTES.menutopoffset")>
 <CFSET menu_text=menu_text&"menu-topoffset:#ATTRIBUTES.menutopoffset#;">
</CFIF>
<CFIF IsDefined("ATTRIBUTES.showrow")>
 <CFSET menu_text=menu_text&"showrow:#ATTRIBUTES.showrow#;">
</CFIF>
<CFIF IsDefined("ATTRIBUTES.wait")>
 <CFSET menu_text=menu_text&"wait:#ATTRIBUTES.wait#;">
</CFIF>
<CFIF IsDefined("ATTRIBUTES.width")>
 <CFSET menu_text=menu_text&"width:#ATTRIBUTES.width#;">
</CFIF>
```

Part
III

Ch
9

continues

Listing 9.8 Continued

```
<!--- Embed menu call --->
<CFOUTPUT><A HREF="" MENU="#menu_text#">#ATTRIBUTES.caption#</A></CFOUTPUT>

<!--- Create menu definition --->
<CFOUTPUT><DIV ID="menusrc#CALLER.DHTMLMenu#" STYLE="display:none"></CFOUTPUT>

<!--- Loop through items --->
<CFLOOP INDEX="i" FROM="1" TO="#ArrayLen(ThisTag.AssocAttribs)#">

 <!--- Initialize item --->
 <CFSET item="">

 <!--- Check if this is an end submenu specifier --->
 <CFIF StructKeyExists(ThisTag.AssocAttribs[i], "submenu")
  AND ListFind(ThisTag.submenu_end_list, i)>

   <!--- Terminate a submenu --->
   <CFSET item="]">

 <CFELSE>

  <!--- Add caption --->
  <CFSET item=item&ThisTag.AssocAttribs[i].caption>
  <CFSET item=item&"!">

  <!--- Add URL if it exists --->
  <CFIF StructKeyExists(ThisTag.AssocAttribs[i], "url")>
   <CFSET item=item&ThisTag.AssocAttribs[i].url>
  </CFIF>

  <!--- Check if either "description" or "icon" were specified --->
  <CFIF StructKeyExists(ThisTag.AssocAttribs[i], "description")
   OR StructKeyExists(ThisTag.AssocAttribs[i], "icon")>

   <!--- Add description if one exists --->
   <CFSET item=item&"!">
   <CFIF StructKeyExists(ThisTag.AssocAttribs[i], "description")>
    <CFSET item=item&ThisTag.AssocAttribs[i].description>
   </CFIF>

   <!--- Add icon if one exists --->
   <CFSET item=item&"!">
   <CFIF StructKeyExists(ThisTag.AssocAttribs[i], "icon")>
    <CFSET item=item&ThisTag.AssocAttribs[i].icon>
   </CFIF>
  </CFIF>

  <!--- Close item --->
  <CFSET item=item&";">

  <!--- Check if this is an end submenu specifier --->
  <CFIF StructKeyExists(ThisTag.AssocAttribs[i], "submenu")
   AND ListFind(ThisTag.submenu_start_list, i)>
```

```
    <!--- Start a submenu --->
    <CFSET item=item&"[">

  </CFIF>

  </CFIF>

  <!--- Write item --->
  <CFOUTPUT>#item#</CFOUTPUT>

</CFLOOP>

<!--- End menu definition --->
<CFOUTPUT></DIV></CFOUTPUT>

</CFIF>

<CFSETTING ENABLECFOUTPUTONLY="No">
```

Listing 9.9   DHTMLMENUITEM.CFM—Code for CF_DHTMLMenuItem **Custom Tag**

```
<!---
NAME: <CF_DHTMLMenuItem>

NOTES:
 Part of the <CF_DHTMLMenu> tag, see DHTMLMenu.CFM for details.

AUTHOR:
 Ben Forta (ben@forta.com) 10/1/98
--->

<!--- Associate this tag with <CF_DHTMLMenu> --->
<CFASSOCIATE BASETAG="CF_DHTMLMenu">
```

Listing 9.10   DHTMLMENUSUBMENU.CFM—Code for CF_DHTMLMenuSubMenu
Custom Tag

```
<!---
NAME: <CF_DHTMLMenuItem>

NOTES:
 Part of the <CF_DHTMLMenu> tag, see DHTMLMenu.CFM for details.

AUTHOR:
 Ben Forta (ben@forta.com) 10/1/98
--->

<!--- Associate this tag with <CF_DHTMLMenu> --->
<CFASSOCIATE BASETAG="CF_DHTMLMenu">

<!--- Get the parent tag data --->
```

continues

Listing 9.10 Continued

```
<CFSET Base=GetBaseTagData("CF_DHTMLMENU")>
<CFSET BaseData=Base.ThisTag>

<!--- Add a "submenu" element to the structure to tell parent
➥ this is a submenu --->
<CFSET temp=StructInsert(BaseData.AssocAttribs[ArrayLen(BaseData.AssocAttribs)],
➥ "submenu", "", "TRUE")>

<!--- Tell parent where to put START and END submenu indicators --->
<CFIF ThisTag.ExecutionMode IS "START">
 <CFSET BaseData.submenu_start_list=ListAppend(BaseData.submenu_start_list,
➥ ArrayLen(BaseData.AssocAttribs))>
<CFELSEIF ThisTag.ExecutionMode IS "END">
 <CFSET BaseData.submenu_end_list=ListAppend(BaseData.submenu_end_list,
➥ ArrayLen(BaseData.AssocAttribs))>
</CFIF>
```

First, take a look at Listing 9.9, which contains the code to associate menu items to the parent tag. Listing 9.9 contains this single line of code:

```
<CFASSOCIATE BASETAG="CF_DHTMLMenu">
```

This code associates this child tag to CF_DHTMLMenu. Any attributes passed to this tag (four attributes are possible in this example) automatically are passed up to the parent tag and stored in the ThisTag.AssocAttribs array. AssocAttribs contains an element for each child tag. If <CF_DHTMLMenuItem> were to be called twice, the array would have two items. Each item is a structure, and the members of the structure are the attributes passed to the child tag. Thus, to access the CAPTION attribute for the second call to <CF_DHTMLMenuItem>, you refer to ThisTag.AssocAttribs[2].Caption.

The bulk of the work happens in the DHTMLMenu.CFM file, shown in Listing 9.8. Once again, the tag starts with detailed comments. As this is the parent of a tag set, details about those child tags are presented here as well.

The code in Listing 9.8 starts with a <CFIF> statement that checks the ExecutionMode. Two variables, submenu_start_list and submenu_end_list, are needed within the child tags, so they are created in START ExecutionMode. The core code itself is all processed *after* all child tags have been processed, so that code is in the END ExecutionMode block.

The core processing code first deletes the contents of ThisTag.GeneratedContent. As you are about to generate content of your own, you should remove any content that might have already been placed in between the tags (although none should have been there, removing it is an extra precaution).

To use the menus, you need to add an HTML <SCRIPT> tag to the page header block. You should add this tag only once, so you need a way of counting the number of menus embedded in a page. The following code creates a variable in the caller space that counts the number of menus embedded in the page. You use <CFPARAM> so that you do not overwrite the variable if it already exists:

```
<CFPARAM NAME="CALLER.DHTMLMenu" DEFAULT="0">
```

The next line of code increments this value. The first time a menu is called in a page, CALLER.DHTMLMenu will be 1; the next time, 2; and so on.

The next piece of code, shown here, checks to see whether this is the first menu in this page. If it is, the ColdFusion <CFHTMLHEAD> tag is used to embed the <SCRIPT> tag into the page's HTML head block.

```
<CFIF CALLER.DHTMLMenu IS 1>
 <CFHTMLHEAD TEXT="#Chr(60)#SCRIPT SRC=#Chr(34)##ATTRIBUTES.scriptdir#/
➥menus.js#Chr(34)##Chr(62)##Chr(60)#/SCRIPT#Chr(62)#">
 </CFIF>
```

The generated output looks something like this:

```
<SCRIPT SRC="/js/menus.js"></SCRIPT>
```

Now you have to start constructing the code to create the menu. To do so, you use the following code:

```
<!--- Create menu text (required attributes) --->
<CFSET menu_text="">
<CFSET menu_text=menu_text&"top:#ATTRIBUTES.top#;">
<CFSET menu_text=menu_text&"left:#ATTRIBUTES.left#;">
<CFSET menu_text=menu_text&"src:menusrc#CALLER.DHTMLMenu#;">
```

menu_text contains the text to be embedded in the <A> tag's MENU attribute. It starts as an empty string, and then the TOP and LEFT attributes are added to it (they are required attributes). Each menu needs a unique name too, so the CALLER.DHTMLMenu variable is used to construct a dynamic name on-the-fly.

Next comes a whole series of <CFIF> statements. They append the optional attributes to menu_text if they have been specified. By the time the last <CFIF> is processed, the menu_text variable is complete, and it can be embedded into the <A> tag, as follows:

```
<CFOUTPUT><A HREF="" MENU="#menu_text#">#ATTRIBUTES.caption#</A></CFOUTPUT>
```

Next, the individual menu selections are embedded. A <CFLOOP> is used to loop through the AssocAttribs array. It contains all the attributes specified in the child tags (<CF_DHTMLMenuItem> and <CF_DHTMLMenuSubMenu>). They are appended to a variable named item, which is reset at the top of each loop. Depending on what attributes are set, item is constructed as a menu item or a submenu. If the calling code is <CF_DHTMLMenuItem CAPTION="Option1" URL="">, item is Option1!;. After each item is constructed, it is written to the output with a simple <CFOUTPUT> call:

```
<CFOUTPUT>#item#</CFOUTPUT>
```

The last file to look at is the code for creating submenus, shown in Listing 9.10. This page is a little more complicated than the code for adding menu items. It starts with a simple <CFASSOCIATE>, which publishes any parameters passed to <CF_DHTMLMenuSubMenu> to the parent tag.

Then a member is manually added to the parent's `AssocAttrib` array. To do so, it uses the `GetBaseTagData()` function. This function exposes the variable scope of the parent tag to the associated tag. The following code creates a variable called `BaseData`, which can be used to access variables within the parent's `ThisTag` scope:

```
<!--- Get the parent tag data --->
<CFSET Base=GetBaseTagData("CF_DHTMLMENU")>
<CFSET BaseData=Base.ThisTag>
```

Next, a member is added to the current child's structure in the parent's `AssocAttribs` array. The member `submenu` tells the parent that this is a submenu call, not another item. Without this code, `DHTMLMenu.CFM` could not distinguish between rows and submenus, unless the user manually specified this difference. The following code solves this problem:

```
<CFSET temp=StructInsert(BaseData.AssocAttribs[ArrayLen(BaseData.AssocAttribs)],
➡ "submenu", "", "TRUE")>
```

The last thing the code does is add the current row number either to the `submenu_start_list` list or the `submenu_end_list` list in the parent's scope. These lists are used in the `<CFLOOP>` in `DHTMLMenu.CFM` to embed the submenu specifiers needed by the DHTML code.

```
<!--- Tell parent where to put START and END submenu indicators --->
<CFIF ThisTag.ExecutionMode IS "START">
 <CFSET BaseData.submenu_start_list=ListAppend(BaseData.submenu_start_list,
➡ ArrayLen(BaseData.AssocAttribs))>
<CFELSEIF ThisTag.ExecutionMode IS "END">
 <CFSET BaseData.submenu_end_list=ListAppend(BaseData.submenu_end_list,
➡ ArrayLen(BaseData.AssocAttribs))>
</CFIF>
```

The end result is that you can write ColdFusion code that looks like this:

```
<CF_DHTMLMenu CAPTION="Browsers" TOP="10" LEFT="100" SCRIPTDIR="/js">
 <CF_DHTMLMenuItem CAPTION="Option1" URL="">
 <CF_DHTMLMenuItem CAPTION="Option2" URL="">
 <CF_DHTMLMenuSubMenu CAPTION="Submenu1">
  <CF_DHTMLMenuItem CAPTION="Submenu1 Option1" URL="">
  <CF_DHTMLMenuItem CAPTION="Submenu1 Option2" URL="">
  <CF_DHTMLMenuSubMenu CAPTION="Submenu2">
   <CF_DHTMLMenuItem CAPTION="Submenu2 Option1" URL="">
   <CF_DHTMLMenuItem CAPTION="Submenu2 Option2" URL="">
  </CF_DHTMLMenuSubMenu>
 </CF_DHTMLMenuSubMenu>
</CF_DHTMLMenu>
```

`<CF_DHTMLMenu>` generates the following result for you:

```
<A HREF="" MENU="top:10;left:100;src:menusrc1;">Browsers</A>
<DIV ID="menusrc1" STYLE="display:none">
Option1!;Option2!;Submenu1!;[Submenu1 Option1!;Submenu1 Option2!;Submenu2!;
➡[Submenu2 Option1!;Submenu2 Option2!;]]
</DIV>
```

And that's all there is to it. Using these techniques, you can write tags that are as complex and sophisticated as you like. As long as you write your tags with a simple and easy-to-use interface, you'll never have to think about the underlying complexities again.

Securing Your Tags

By now, you should be convinced that ColdFusion's Custom Tags are powerful, scalable, and very usable. You are probably already coming up with ideas for tags of your own. Before you run off, though, you need to examine one last topic: securing your tags.

ColdFusion Custom Tags are written in CFML, and CFML is readable code. If you give users a copy of your Custom Tag, they can both read the code and make changes to it.

So, how do you protect your code, both from prying eyes and from careless users?

Using CFCRYPT

ColdFusion comes with a utility called CFCRYPT that lets you *encrypt* your ColdFusion templates. Encrypted templates have the same .CFM extension as regular templates, but their contents are not readable by anything other than ColdFusion itself.

CFCRYPT is in your ColdFusion executable directory (usually C:\CFUSION\BIN). To use it, simply execute CFCRYPT and pass the name of the file to encrypt and an optional file to be created. If you omit the destination file, the file you specify is overwritten with an encrypted version.

> **CAUTION**
>
> You cannot *decrypt* encrypted templates. Make sure that you always keep a copy of your unencrypted templates for future use.

You also can use CFCRYPT to encrypt entire directory structures. To encrypt the contents of a directory and all subdirectories, use the /r parameter.

 Execute CFCRYPT.EXE without any parameters to display the usage instructions.

Distributed Processing

Another form of code security is distributed processing. With this processing, you break up the code into two (or more) parts. One part makes processing requests, and the other part fulfills the requests and returns the results to the first part.

For example, suppose you publish a Custom Tag that returns confidential sales figures. You want the users of the Custom Tag to have access to the results returned by the tag but not to the underlying logic that interacts with your databases.

To safely accomplish this feat, you can create two Custom Tags, one that actually interacts with your databases and one that submits HTTP requests (using <CFHTTP>) to the former. You distribute only the second tag, and when users execute it, it submits a request to your own tag, which in turn processes the request and returns the results.

▶ **See** Chapter 21, "Intelligent Agents and Distributed Processing," **p. 483**

Writing CFX Tags in Visual C++

As you learned in the previous chapter, it's possible to write your own custom tags using ColdFusion's native language, CFML. In this chapter you look at creating CFX tags, which are a different kind of tag that you can add to ColdFusion.

The big difference between writing CFML Custom Tags and writing CFX tags is that you don't use ColdFusion's own functions and tags to put the tag together. Instead, you use an external development environment—such as Microsoft Visual C++ or Borland Delphi—to create the tags.

N O T E You need to use Microsoft Visual C++ in order to follow along with this chapter. Microsoft Visual C++ is a separate product that is not included with ColdFusion. The figures in this chapter show Visual C++ 5.0, but you should be able to use different versions of the product—such as Visual C++ 6.0, which was brand new at the time of this writing—as well. ■

T I P If you don't have Microsoft Visual C++ but plan on buying it now so you can create CFX tags with it, you might want to consider buying Microsoft Visual Studio rather than buying Visual C++ alone. Visual Studio is a bundle that includes Visual C++ as well as Visual Basic (which you could use to create COM objects for use with the CFOBJECT tag), Visual InterDev (which is especially handy to have around if you're using Microsoft SQL Server 6.5), Visual FoxPro (which you can use to build FoxPro database tables to use with ColdFusion), and more. At the time of this writing, the latest version of the bundle is called Visual Studio 6.0 and is priced right if you have a need for two or more of the tools.

What Are CFX Tags?

In your travels as a ColdFusion developer, you've probably seen tags that start with CF_, and you know that those are Custom Tags written in CFML. In the preceding chapter you learned that the actual programming for each CF_ tag sits in a .cfm file. You may also have seen CFX tags used in ColdFusion templates somewhere. They start with CFX_ instead of CF_, and the actual code is contained in a .dll (dynamic link library) file instead of in a .cfm file. Table 10.1 illustrates the differences between CF_ and CFX_ tags.

Table 10.1 Quick Comparison: CFML Custom Tags Versus CFX Tags

CFML Custom Tags	CFX Tags
Start with CF_.	Start with CFX_.
Written using normal CF tags and functions.	Written in C++ (or Delphi).
Actual code is in a .cfm file.	Actual code is in a .dll file.
Are not compiled programs; can only do the kinds of things normally possible in ColdFusion.	Are compiled programs that can do just about anything, such as call native Windows functions or work with another program by calling functions that the other program provides.

CFML Custom Tags	CFX Tags
To be able to use a Custom Tag, you place the .cfm file into your server's CustomTags folder or into the folder where you use the tag.	To be able to use a CFX tag, you register the .dll using the ColdFusion Administrator, a step that's like creating a new ODBC data source.

When to Write (and Avoid Writing) a CFX Tag

The concept of CFX tags was introduced in ColdFusion 2.0. At that time, ColdFusion did not include many of the integration tags that it includes today—CFOBJECT, CFLDAP, and CFSEARCH. The concept of CML Custom Tags—which was discussed in the preceding chapter—was not introduced until ColdFusion 3.0. Between ColdFusion 2.0 and 3.0, the only way to extend ColdFusion's base capabilities was by writing a CFX tag (as discussed in this chapter). In practice, this meant you needed to know something about C++ programming.

Today, it's not always necessary to write a CFX tag in order to extend ColdFusion. It's now possible to write Custom Tags in CFML, and support for third-party COM and CORBA objects is available via the CFOBJECT tag. When you start thinking about adding your own tag to ColdFusion, think first about doing it as a CFML Custom Tag. Generally, you only need to write a CFX tag if what you're doing isn't normally possible with ColdFusion.

 TIP Another time to consider writing a CFX tag is if you already wrote your tag in CFML but it turned out too slow; for instance, if your project requires nested loops that execute hundreds or thousands of times. Since CFX tags are native executables, they are generally faster than the CFML equivalent. Consider your own time as a developer as well. CFML tags are much easier to write and faster to put together, are easier to troubleshoot, and are much less likely to cause any serious problems on your machines.

Figure 10.1 shows how you might proceed.

FIGURE 10.1
Deciding whether you should write a CFX tag.

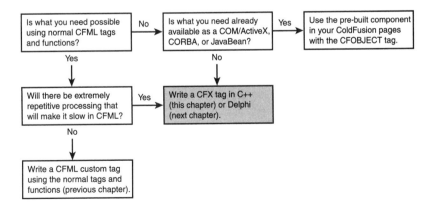

Part III

Ch 10

Choosing Between C++ and Delphi

This chapter covers writing CFX tags via Microsoft Visual C++, which is the method of creating CFX tags Allaire had in mind when it created the CFX interface; it is the only method Allaire officially supports. In theory, you should also be able to use other C++ compilers—such as Turbo C++ or Borland C++ Builder—to create CFX tags, but that isn't covered in this book.

It is also possible to create CFX tags using Delphi instead of Visual C++. Many people consider Delphi programming easier and faster than C++ programming, without giving up power and flexibility. If you are interested in creating CFX tags with Delphi, read Chapter 11, "Writing CFX Tags in Delphi," after reading this one.

N O T E Since the programming for each CFX tag sits inside a compiled .dll file, you should be able to create CFX tags with any development tool that allows you to create 32-bit DLLs. It would be a good deal of work, however, since you would need to port the essential classes (which is discussed in this chapter) to your other tool's language on your own. In fact, that's why it's possible to create CFX tags in Delphi—someone did such a port. ■

The Three Classes That Make Up the CFXAPI

Allaire has defined a number of functions for ColdFusion developers to use when creating CFX tags. These are the functions that you use in your CFX code to actually talk to the template that is using the CFX tag. These functions are referred to collectively as the *ColdFusion Extension API*, or the *CFXAPI* for short.

In C++ it's customary to talk about functions in little groups called *classes*. Each class covers a specific topic, like a chapter in a book. For instance, there is a CFX class for manipulating queries, another for manipulating lists, and so on. Each of the functions in a class is often called a *member function*. Using that terminology, then, you can see that there are three *classes* that make up the CFXAPI, made up of a total of 27 *member functions*.

N O T E If you're not familiar with the term, *API* stands for Application Programming Interface. It's a general term that's commonly used to describe a set of functions, supporting files, or libraries that give developers a way to hook into a piece of software in order to extend or control it programmatically. ■

Interacting with the Calling Template: CCFXRequest

The functions in the CCFXRequest class are about sending information back and forth between the ColdFusion template that is using the CFX tag. Table 10.2 lists each of the functions in the class and provides a brief summary of what each function does. You see most of these functions in action throughout the examples in this chapter.

N O T E For many of the functions in the CFXAPI, there are equivalent CFML functions or tags; they can be used to do about the same thing if you were doing your coding in a normal

ColdFusion template. These equivalents are listed in the third column of Tables 10.2, 10.3, and 10.4. You may find that the comparisons allow you to get a quick handle on what each function will be used for in real-world situations. ▪

Table 10.2 Functions Provided By Allaire's `CCFXRequest` Class

Function	What It Does	Similar to (in CFML)
AddQuery	Creates a new query result set, which can then be manipulated by the `CCFXQuery` functions	The `QueryNew` function
AttributeExists	Checks if a parameter were passed to the tag by the calling template	The `IsDefined` function
CreateStringSet	Creates a new StringSet, which can then be manipulated by the `CCFXStringSet` functions	The `ArrayNew` function
Debug	Indicates whether Debug information was requested by the calling template	N/A
GetAttribute	Gets the value of a parameter passed to the tag by the calling template	The `Evaluate` function
GetAttributeList	Gets a list of parameters passed to the tag by the calling template	N/A
GetCustomData	Gets a value previously set with the `SetCustomData` function	N/A
GetQuery	Gets a query result set from the calling template, which can then be manipulated by the `CCFXQuery` functions listed in Table 10.4	The `CFSET` tag
GetSetting	Reads a value from a special part of the machine's system Registry	The `CFREGISTRY` tag
ReThrowException	Causes something that caused an error to be tried again	The `CFTHROW` tag
SetCustomData	Creates a new typeless variable to be used within the `CFX` tag	The `CFSET` tag
SetVariable	Sets a variable in the calling template	The `SetVariable` function
ThrowException	Stops all template execution	The `CFABORT` tag
Write	Sends output to the browser	The `CFOUTPUT` tag
WriteDebug	Sends debug output to the browser	The `CFOUTPUT` tag

Part
III

Ch
10

Manipulating Lists of Data: CCFXStringSet

The functions in the CCFXStringSet class are about dealing with sets of strings. These sets are similar in many ways to the lists that are frequently dealt with in normal ColdFusion templates. They are also a lot like one-dimensional arrays.

Table 10.3 describes each of the member functions for the CCFXStringSet class. For more information about StringSets and to see these functions in action, see "Holding the List's Values in a StringSet" later in this chapter.

Table 10.3 Functions Provided by Allaire's CCFXStringSet Class

Function	What It Does	Similar to (in CFML)
AddString	Appends a new value to the list	The ListAppend function
GetCount	Counts the number of items in the list	The ListLen function
GetString	Gets the value that is sitting at a particular position in the list	The ListGetAt function
GetIndexForString	Finds what position in the list a particular value is sitting in	The ListFindNoCase function

Working with Query Result Sets: CCFXQuery

The functions in the CCFXQuery class are about creating and manipulating query result sets. These query result sets can then be used by name in the calling template, just as if the results came from a database via the CFQUERY tag.

Table 10.4 lists each of the functions in the CCFXQuery class. To see these functions in action, see "Dealing with Query Result Sets" later in this chapter.

Table 10.4 Functions Provided by Allaire's CCFXQuery Class

Function	What It Does	Similar to (in CFML)
AddRow	Adds a new, blank row to the results	The QueryAddRow function
GetColumns	Gets the list of column names	The ColumnList variable
GetData	Gets the value in a particular row and column of a query result set	#Queryname.ColumnName#
GetName	Gets the name of the query passed to the tag by the calling template	N/A
GetRowCount	Counts the number of rows in a query result set	#Queryname.RecordCount#
SetData	Places a new value in a particular row row and column of a query result	The QuerySetCell function

Function	What It Does	Similar to (in CFML)
SetQueryString	Specifies what text to show as the SQL for the query in debug output	N/A
SetTotalTime	Sets the elapsed time to show up for the query in debug output	N/A

N O T E   Actually, there is a fourth class in the CFXAPI—CCFXException. It defines the exception object that you're interacting with internally when you use the ThrowException and ReThrowException functions listed earlier. Since the CCFXException class doesn't have any member functions of its own, it's not being discussed as a separate topic in this book.

Part III
Ch 10

Building Your First CFX Tag: CFX_ListRemoveDuplicates

This chapter walks through the process of creating three CFX tags for ColdFusion. The first example you build is a tag that removes duplicate values from a comma-separated list. It's called, appropriately, CFX_ListRemoveDuplicates.

T I P   As you create a CFX tag, try to make the name of the tag as descriptive as possible. For instance, the name CFX_ListRemoveDuplicates is more descriptive (though less titillating) than the name CFX_Strip is. The more descriptive the name, the more self-documenting your code becomes when you (or other people) actually use the CFX tag in ColdFusion templates.

How It Would Look as a CFML Custom Tag

This ListRemoveDuplicates project is an example of a tag that could be written as a CFML Custom Tag (CF_ListRemoveDuplicates) or as a CFX tag (CFX_ListRemoveDuplicates). Let's build it both ways.

What the Tag Needs to Do   The internal logic of the removing-duplicates process will be about the same in the CFML and CFX versions of the tag. Basically, you create an empty variable that represents the new list, and then loop through the old list. You check to see if each item in the old list already exists in the new list. If it exists in the new list already, it's a duplicate and can be ignored. If it does not exist in the new list yet, you append it to the end of the (new) list.

CFML Code Listing   The code for the CFML version of your tag is provided in Listing 10.1. It is assumed that you are already familiar with the basic ColdFusion tags and functions that are being used here, including CFPARAM, CFLOOP, ListFindNoCase, and so on. If you need to brush up on them, consult the *ColdFusion Language Reference* that came with ColdFusion.

N O T E Unfortunately, there isn't enough space in this chapter to explain the following code in detail. Read the comments—the code is largely self explanatory. ◼

Listing 10.1 `ListRemoveDuplicates.cfm`—**The CFML Version of the Tag**

```
<!--- 1)  Get tag parameters --->
<!--- 1a) Parameter LIST          :the list to make distinct --->
<CFPARAM NAME="Attributes.List">

<!--- 1b) Parameter VARIABLE      :new variable name         --->
<CFPARAM NAME="Attributes.Variable">

<!--- 1c) Parameter DELIMITER     :what LIST is delimited by --->
<CFPARAM NAME="Attributes.Delimiter" DEFAULT=",">


<!--- 2) Create ssList, an empty "list". This is what we   --->
<!---    will pass out to the calling template at the end --->
<CFSET ssList = "">


<!--- 3) Loop through the original list, item by item. --->
<CFLOOP LIST="#Attributes.List#" INDEX="ThisItem"
DELIMITERS="#Attributes.Delimiter#">

  <!--- 3a) If ThisItem is not in ssList yet, then append it --->
  <!---     to ssList, followed by the delimiter character    --->
  <CFIF ListFindNoCase(ssList, ThisItem, Attributes.Delimiter) is "No">
    <CFSET ssList = ssList & ThisItem & Attributes.Delimiter>
  </CFIF>

</CFLOOP>


<!--- 4) There's an extra delimiter at end of ssList, so remove it --->
<CFSET ssList = Left(ssList, Len(ssList) - 1)>


<!--- 5) Pass the completed ssList out to the calling template --->
<CFSET Temp = SetVariable("Caller.#Attributes.Variable#", ssList)>
```

Using the Tag in a ColdFusion Template   To make sure that our CFML Custom Tag works correctly, we can make a test template for it. That includes making up a test list that has some duplicates, then using your Custom Tag to remove the duplicates and display the results. Listing 10.2 provides the test template's simple code.

Listing 10.2 `ListTestCFML.cfm`—**Testing the CFML Version**

```
<HTML>
<HEAD><TITLE>ListRemoveDuplicates (CFML Version)</TITLE></HEAD>
<BODY>
```

```
<!--- Make up a list of values for testing --->
<CFSET OldList = "Red,Blue,Blue,Green,Red,Red">

<!--- Ask our tag to remove the duplicates --->
<CF_ListRemoveDuplicates
  LIST="#OldList#"
  VARIABLE="NewList"
  DELIMITER=",">

<!--- Display the before-and-after results! --->
<CFOUTPUT>
  Old List: #OldList# <BR>
  New List: #NewList# <BR>
</CFOUTPUT>


</BODY>
</HTML>
```

When you bring the code in Listing 10.2 up in a Web browser, you find that the duplicate values were indeed removed from the list and stored in the NewList variable, just as you wanted. Figure 10.2 shows the before-and-after results, demonstrating that the tag behaves as intended.

FIGURE 10.2

Testing the CFML version of the tag.

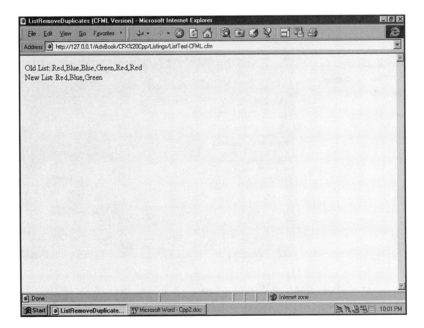

Getting Started Quickly with the ColdFusion Tag Wizard

Now that you've successfully created the tag as a CFML Custom Tag, all you need to do is re-create it in C++. Using the CFML version as a model makes things easier as you explore the CFXAPI for the first time. For the most part, the C++ code is similar in its structure.

TIP The ColdFusion Tag Wizard is probably already installed on your system if Visual C++ were present on your computer when you installed ColdFusion itself. If Visual C++ was not on your system when you installed ColdFusion, or if you don't have ColdFusion installed on the machine that you will be using Visual C++ on, you need to run the ColdFusion setup program on your Visual C++ machine in order to proceed. When you run the setup program, make sure to check the box for the CFXAPI Tag Development Kit. This installs all the files needed to run the wizard and compiles the skeletal tag that it writes for you.

Starting the Wizard in Microsoft Visual C++   Allaire provides a ColdFusion Tag Wizard that helps you get started quickly and easily. The wizard builds a skeleton of a CFX tag for you. Follow these simple steps to start the wizard:

1. Start Microsoft Visual C++.
2. Choose File, New from the menu. The New dialog box appears.
3. Click the Projects tab.
4. Select ColdFusion Tag Wizard from the list of projects.
5. Type **CFX_ListRemoveDuplicates** in the blank for Project Name.
6. Make a note of the folder name in the Location blank. The actual .dll file for your new CFX tag will be placed within this folder. You need to know this later.
7. Confirm that your screen looks something like Figure 10.3 and then click OK.

FIGURE 10.3
Starting the ColdFusion
Tag Wizard.

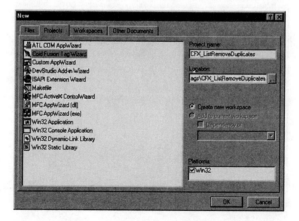

The ColdFusion Tag Wizard appears when you click OK in the New dialog box. Follow these simple steps to give the wizard the information it needs:

1. To name the new tag, type **CFX_ListRemoveDuplicates** in the first blank.
2. Type a short description of the tag in the second blank. This description is included as comments in the source code for your tag.
3. For the choice about using the MFC library, leave the default As a Statically-Linked Library option selected. MFC stands for Microsoft Foundation Classes, a topic that is

beyond the scope of this chapter. Unless you are an experienced C++ developer and have worked with the MFC before, leave this option alone.

4. Verify that the Wizard looks something like Figure 10.4.

5. When you're done, click Finish. A confirmation dialog box appears, summarizing the choices you just made. Go ahead and click OK.

FIGURE 10.4

Completing the ColdFusion Tag Wizard.

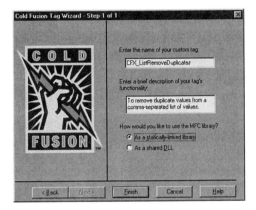

Part

III

Ch

10

Compiling the Default "Hello, World" Functionality   You now should have a working chunk of C++ code that can be compiled as is into an actual CFX tag. Of course, it's not going to actually know how to remove duplicates from a list yet, since you haven't added any actual programming. Instead, all the tag does currently is display a "Hello, World"-type message when it is used in a ColdFusion template (.cfm).

It's a good idea at this point to make sure that the "Hello, World" functionality works correctly, so you can be assured that everything has been set up successfully on your system. To compile the current version of the tag, choose Build, Build CFX_ListRemoveDuplicates from the menu. Visual C++ whirs around for a minute or so as it compiles various files and eventually creates your new .dll file. You should see a Build Status window that indicates the compiler's progress. This will seem slow the first time around, but is much faster the next time you build the tag.

 As a shortcut, you can press the F7 key to build your tag, instead of using the Build menu.

Registering the New Tag in the CF Administrator   Before you can actually use a CFX tag for the first time, you make sure it is registered in the ColdFusion Administrator. This step tells ColdFusion what the name of the tag is and where the .dll file can be found on your system. Perform the following steps to register the tag:

1. If you're running ColdFusion and Visual C++ on different machines, copy the CFX_ListRemoveDuplicates.dll file that you just built to a folder on your ColdFusion machine. You can place it anywhere you like; the CFUSION\CustomTags folder is probably a good spot.

2. Bring the ColdFusion Administrator up in your browser and click the CFX Tags link in the left margin. The Registered CFX Tags page appears.

3. Check to see if a link for the CFX_ListRemoveDuplicates tag is already in the list. If it is, click the link. If not, add the new tag by typing **CFX_ListRemoveDuplicates** in the blank at the top of the page; click the Add button.

4. The Edit CFX Tag page appears. CFX_ListRemoveDuplicates should already be entered for the Tag Name.

5. Provide the location of the .dll file that you just created by using the Browse Server button next to the Server Library (DLL) blank. Alternatively, you can type the location of the .dll file manually. If ColdFusion and Visual C++ are on the same machine, this is probably already filled in for you.

6. Leave the Procedure blank unchanged. This defines ColdFusion's entry point into the .dll and should always be left at the default value: ProcessTagRequest.

7. Uncheck the Keep Library Loaded check box. This tells ColdFusion not to keep the .dll file loaded into its memory space between page requests. Always keep this check box unselected when you are developing your CFX tags. If you leave it selected, you will need to stop and restart ColdFusion each time you want to try out a newly-compiled version of your tag. Only when your tag is complete should you check this box, which puts your tag into production and improves performance somewhat.

8. Optionally, you can type a short description for your tag. If ColdFusion and Visual C++ are on the same machine, this is probably already filled in for you, based on the description you provided to the wizard.

Testing the New Tag   To test your new CFX tag, use the same test template code that you used to test the tag's CFML version. Notice that the code in Listing 10.3 is exactly the same as the code in Listing 10.1, except for one letter: the X in the tag name.

Listing 10.3   ListTestCFX.cfm—Testing the CFX Version

```
<HTML>
<HEAD><TITLE>ListRemoveDuplicates (CFX Version)</TITLE></HEAD>
<BODY>


<!--- Make up a list of values for testing --->
<CFSET OldList = "Red,Blue,Blue,Green,Red,Red">

<!--- Ask our tag to remove the duplicates --->
<CFX_ListRemoveDuplicates
  LIST="#OldList#"
  VARIABLE="NewList"
  DELIMITER=",">

<!--- Display the before-and-after results! --->
<P>
<CFOUTPUT>
  Old List: #OldList# <BR>
```

```
    New List: #NewList# <BR>
  </CFOUTPUT>


  </BODY>
  </HTML>
```

If you bring the code in Listing 10.3 up in a browser, you see that the tag does something—although obviously not what you want it to do in the end (see Figure 10.5).

FIGURE 10.5

The CFX tag's "Hello World" message.

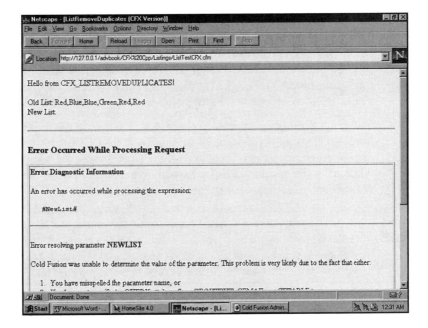

As you can see, when the CFX tag is executed, it includes the message Hello from CFX_LISTREMOVEDUPLICATES! onto the Web page. The CFX tag itself is running fine, without any errors. However, as soon as the code in the test template tries to refer to the #NewList# variable (which you know eventually holds the duplicates-removed version of the list when you're done with our tag), ColdFusion stops with an error message. This makes a lot of sense, since you haven't added any code to your CFX tag that would set the #NewList# variable.

You're probably curious where that hello message came from—and how you can get rid of it as quickly as possible! To find the spot in the C++ code that included the message onto the Web page, look at the Request.cpp file in the tag's C++ source code. To find this spot in the code, follow these simple steps:

1. Make sure the Workspace is showing. (The Workspace looks a lot like the Resource tab in ColdFusion Studio, an Explorer-like interface with icon tabs at the bottom.) If it's not showing, choose View, Workspace from the menu.

2. Click the FileView tab at the bottom of the Workspace pane.

3. Expand the CFX_ListRemoveDuplicates files branch and then expand the Source Files branch.

4. Double-click Request.cpp. (The cpp stands for C Plus Plus, or C++.)

You can delete the line that reads //Write output back to the user here... and the pRequest line directly underneath it. If you want, you can recompile the tag now and retest it by reloading the ListTestCFX.cfm page in your Web browser. You will see that the Hello message is gone, but the error message about the missing variable remains.

Establishing the Tag's Parameters

Before your CFX_ListRemoveDuplicates tag can do anything useful, it must be able to accept parameters from the ColdFusion template that's using it. Just like the CFML version of the tag, this CFX tag needs to require a LIST parameter and a VARIABLE parameter, and it also should be able to accept an optional DELIMITER parameter.

To find out whether a parameter has been passed to the tag, use the AttributeExists function from the CCFXRequest class that Allaire supplies in the CFXAPI; then, to stop execution and display an error message if a required parameter is not supplied, use the ThrowException function. Finally, to get the actual value of the parameter and store it in a local variable that the CFX tag can use internally, use the GetAttribute function.

TIP As you read the syntax for each of these functions, note that in general all of Allaire's functions deal with LPCSTR-type values, which is a type that you can use in C++ to work with string values. See your C++ documentation to learn more about LPCSTR values. In particular, you might want to read about the various differences between the LPCSTR, LPTSTR, CString, and char types of values.

Introducing New CFXAPI Function

CCFXRequest::AttributeExists (attribute_name as a LPCSTR value or variable)

Returns: Whether the requested attribute exists as a Boolean TRUE or FALSE value

Introducing New CFXAPI Function

CCFXRequest::GetAttribute (attribute_name as a LPCSTR)

Returns: The value of the requested attribute as a LPCSTR

Introducing New CFXAPI Function

CCFXRequest::ThrowException (error_message as a LPCSTR, explanation as a LPCSTR)

Returns: Nothing; displays error_message and explanation and then halts all template execution

How to Establish a Required Parameter To make the tag accept and require the LIST parameter, add the following code to the Request.cpp file. Put it right where the two lines of code for the Hello message were.

```
// Parameter LIST: list to make distinct
if ( pRequest->AttributeExists("LIST")==FALSE ) {
    pRequest->ThrowException("CFX_ListRemoveDuplicates", "LIST is required.");
}
LPCSTR lpszList = pRequest->GetAttribute("LIST");
```

If you ignore all the braces, arrows, and other symbols for a moment, this snippet of code is fairly easy to read as plain English: "If there is no attribute by the name of LIST passed to the tag, stop and display an error message. Otherwise, create a LPCSTR variable called lpszList and set its value to whatever was passed to the LIST parameter by the calling template."

TIP If this is your first glimpse at a piece of C++ code, you are probably noticing how similar the general syntax is to JavaScript. There's a semicolon at the end of each line of code. The == operator is used to see if two values are equal. The condition for an `if` statement is enclosed in parentheses, and then whatever the `if` is meant to carry out is enclosed in curly braces. The lesson here is that JavaScript and C++ evolved from similar roots. For that reason, you can use your knowledge of JavaScript to grasp many of the C++ syntax basics.

N O T E Check out the `->` (arrow) syntax needed to use the Allaire-supplied functions. This notation is needed because pRequest is a pointer to the ColdFusion page request that you're currently processing. Specifically, pRequest is a pointer to a `CCFXRequest` structure. The arrow syntax is needed because the `AttributeExists` and other functions used are all members of the `CCFXRequest` class. A full explanation of the C++ concepts at work here is beyond the scope of this chapter, but the point is that you should use the `->` operator to use all of the Allaire-supplied functions in the CFX classes. For more information, consult either your Visual C++ documentation or a general text on C++. ■

How to Establish an Optional Parameter You used the `GetAttribute` function earlier to create the variable lpszList, giving it the value from the required LIST parameter passed to the tag. If you want to make a parameter optional, the easiest thing to do is declare the variable first, assigning it whatever default value you want. Check to see if the parameter was passed to the tag; if it was, give the variable the passed value.

To create the optional DELIMITER variable, add the following code immediately after the required parameter LIST that you just added:

```
// 1c) Parameter DELIMITER      :what LIST is delimited by
LPCSTR lpszDelimiter = ",";
if (pRequest->AttributeExists("DELIMITER")==TRUE) {
    lpszDelimiter = pRequest->GetAttribute("DELIMITER");
}
```

As you can see, the lpszDelimiter variable is created with a default value of a comma. If the tag is being provided with a DELIMITER parameter by the calling ColdFusion template, the variable is reset with that value. Otherwise, execution of the CFX tag code skips the GetAttribute code altogether, using the comma as the delimiter.

Part

III

Ch

10

Sending Information Back to the Calling Template

As a CFX tag does its processing, often it needs to output text onto the current Web page or set variables that the calling template can use in CFML tags and functions after the CFX tag. To output text onto the current Web page, use Allaire's Write function from the CFXAPI. Use the SetVariable function to set a variable in the calling template.

Introducing New CFXAPI Function

CCFXRequest::**Write** (*text* as LPCSTR)

Returns: Nothing; outputs the text you provide, verbatim, to the current Web page; the text can include any HTML tags that you want the browser to interpret

Introducing New CFXAPI Function

CCFXRequest::**SetVariable** (*variable_name* as LPCSTR, *new_value* as LPCSTR)

Returns: Nothing; sets a variable with the value you specify

For instance, the preliminary version of the CFX_ListRemoveDuplicates tag shown in Listing 10.4 receives the tag's required and optional parameters as discussed in the preceding section, displays the values of the parameters, and sets the #NewList# variable that will eventually hold the no-duplicates version of the list.

N O T E   If you want, you can copy and paste the code in Listing 10.4 from the Listing04.cpp file on this book's CD. You should replace all of the wizard-produced code that you already have with the code from the listing.

Listing 10.4   Sending Values Back to the Calling Template

```
//////////////////////////////////////////////////////////////////////
//
// CFX_LISTREMOVEDUPLICATES - ColdFusion custom tag
//
// Copyright 98. All Rights Reserved.
//


#include "stdafx.h"       // Standard MFC libraries
#include "cfx.h"        // CFX Custom Tag API


void ProcessTagRequest( CCFXRequest* pRequest )
{
    try
    {
        // 1) ***** GET TAG PARAMETERS *****

        // 1a) Parameter LIST            :the list to make distinct
        if (pRequest->AttributeExists("LIST")==FALSE) {
            pRequest->ThrowException("CFX_QueryAddData: Missing LIST
➥Parameter.", "");
```

```
        }
        LPCSTR lpszList = pRequest->GetAttribute("LIST");

        // 1b) Parameter VARIABLE           :new variable name
        if (pRequest->AttributeExists("VARIABLE")==FALSE) {
            pRequest->ThrowException
➥("CFX_QueryAddData: Missing VARIABLE Parameter.", "");
        }
        LPCSTR lpszVariable = pRequest->GetAttribute("VARIABLE");

        // 1c) Parameter DELIMITER          :what LIST is delimited by
        LPCSTR lpszDelimiter = ",";
        if (pRequest->AttributeExists("DELIMITER")==TRUE) {
            lpszDelimiter = pRequest->GetAttribute("DELIMITER");
        }


        // As a test, output values in current web page
        pRequest->Write("<P>The value of LIST is: ");
        pRequest->Write(lpszList);
        pRequest->Write("<P>The value of VARIABLE is: ");
        pRequest->Write(lpszVariable);
        pRequest->Write("<P>The value of DELIMITER is: ");
        pRequest->Write(lpszDelimiter);


        // set the requested variable with the value of LIST.
        pRequest->SetVariable(lpszVariable, lpszList);



        // Output optional debug info
        if ( pRequest->Debug() )
        {
            pRequest->WriteDebug( "Debug info..." ) ;
        }
    }

    // Catch ColdFusion exceptions & re-raise them
    catch( CCFXException* e )
    {
        pRequest->ReThrowException( e ) ;
    }

    // Catch ALL other exceptions and throw them as
    // ColdFusion exceptions (DO NOT REMOVE! --
    // this prevents the server from crashing in
    // case of an unexpected exception)
    catch( ... )
    {
        pRequest->ThrowException(
            "Error occurred in tag CFX_LISTREMOVEDUPLICATES",
            "Unexpected error occurred while processing tag." ) ;
    }
}
```

This preliminary version of the CFX tag can now be compiled (using the Build menu in Visual C++, just like the first time) and tested with the ListTextCFX.cfm template from Listing 10.3. Figure 10.6 shows the Web page that results when this current version of the CFX tag is used in the test template.

FIGURE 10.6

Variables set by CFX tags can be used just like native variables.

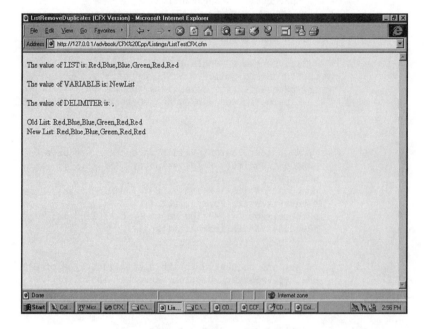

As you can see in the figure, much about what the tag is supposed to do is now working properly. It knows how to read parameters and set the value of the correct variable in the calling template. Of course, there's not much point to the tag yet, since it doesn't remove the duplicates from the list. That's the next step.

N O T E The CFX SetVariable function (like the normal CFML SetVariable function) can also set variables in ColdFusion's client, session, application, or server scopes. This means that it is fine to use VARIABLE="Session.NewList" with this tag in a template, as long as ColdFusion's session management feature has been enabled with the CFAPPLICATION tag.

However, the CFX SetVariable function cannot set array or structure values. This means that if the tag were passed a parameter of VARIABLE="NewList[1]", the SetVariable function would throw an exception, all execution would stop, and an "Unexpected error occurred while processing tag" message would appear. ▧

Holding the List's Values in a StringSet

The only task left is to add the code that makes the CFX_ListRemoveDuplicates tag actually remove the duplicates from the list it receives. This means that it needs to make use of some kind of mechanism that treats lists of strings as a group. Using the Allaire-defined concept of a StringSet is one way to approach the problem, and is demonstrated here.

N O T E There are certainly other ways to approach the task. For instance, you could explore using structures and functions from C++'s Standard Template Library (STL), but that's beyond the scope of this chapter. ▪

What Is a StringSet?   A *StringSet* is kind of a hybrid between CFML-style arrays and the CFML concept of a list. Basically, a StringSet is an array of strings that you can load one at a time with individual string values. Once the StringSet is populated, Allaire provides some basic functions for finding and extracting specific StringSet values.

StringSets are used to do many of the same things that lists are used to do in CFML. However, they are very different from CFML lists in one important way: There is no concept of a delimiter when dealing with StringSets. Whereas each value in a CFML List is separated from the next by a delimiter (usually a comma), each value in a StringSet lives in its own little cell that you can refer to by number. StringSets are like lists in what they are used for, but are more like one-dimensional arrays in how they are stored.

Part
III

Ch
10

Creating the StringSet   Use the `CreateStringSet` function from Allaire's `CCFXRequest` class to create a new, empty StringSet.

Introducing New CFXAPI Function

`CCFXRequest::`**`CreateStringSet`**`()`

Returns: A new, empty StringSet

To use the `CreateStringSet` function, you declare a variable of type `CCFXStringSet` and immediately set it to the StingSet that the function generates. For instance, the following code snippet creates a new StringSet called `ssList`.

```
// 2) ***** CREATE ssList, AN EMPTY"STRING SET" *****
CCFXStringSet* ssList = pRequest->CreateStringSet();
```

Adding Individual Values to the StringSet   In order to carry out its mission to remove duplicates from the list, the `CFX` tag loops through the elements of `LIST`, using whatever delimiter has been called for by the calling template. For each value in the list, the tag checks to see if the value is already in the StringSet, by calling the `GetIndexForString` function from Allaire's `CCFXStringSet` class. If the value is not in the StringSet yet, it is added to the end of the StringSet with the `AddString` function. If, on the other hand, the value is already in the list, it must be a duplicate value and is not added to the StringSet.

The `strtok` function—one of the C++ string-manipulation functions—carries out the actual looping through the list according to the desired delimiter.

Introducing New CFXAPI Function

`CCFXStringSet::`**`GetIndexForString`** (*string_to_find* as LPCSTR)

Returns: The position of the first matching value in the StringSet, as an Int. If there are no strings in the StringSet that match *string_to_find*, the constant CFX_STRING_NOT_FOUND is returned. The search ignores case.

Introducing New CFXAPI Function

CCFXStringSet::**AddString** (*string_to_add* as LPCSTR)

Returns: The position in the StringSet that the just-added string now occupies, as an Integer. In other words, the function returns the new length of the StringSet.

Introducing New C++ Function

strtok (*string* as char, *delimiters* as const char)

Returns: The first time the function is called, it returns the first token in the string, as a char value. The second call to the function returns the second token, and so on. After the last token is found, subsequent calls to the function return NULL.

The following code snippet shows how to use these three functions together to get the needed effect. It's actually quite simple, and is easily compared to the equivalent section in the CFML version of the tag that was shown back in Listing 10.1.

The only tricky concept is the way that the strtok function works. The first time it is called, it is given a copy of the lpszList variable. After that, it must be given the value NULL. That value is a signal to the strtok function that it is still working on the same project, and so should return the next token rather than the first token. If for some reason you want it to start over at the beginning, you supply it with the lpszList variable again, rather than NULL. In other words, NULL informs the function that there's nothing new about the list, and that it should therefore maintain state between calls. See your C++ documentation for more details about the strtok function.

```
// 2) ***** CREATE ssList, AN EMPTY "STRING SET" *****
CCFXStringSet* ssList = pRequest->CreateStringSet();

// Establish "ThisItem" variable and put 1st "token" in it
char *ThisItem = strtok( (LPTSTR)lpszList, lpszDelimiter );

// While there are still tokens left in the list
while( ThisItem != NULL )    {
    if (ssList->GetIndexForString(ThisItem) == CFX_STRING_NOT_FOUND) {
ssList->AddString(ThisItem);
    }
    // Fetch the next token.  If there are no more tokens,
    // ThisItem will get set to NULL, which will end the loop.
    ThisItem = strtok( NULL, lpszDelimiter );
}
```

N O T E   The strtok function requires that its first parameter be a non-constant string. Because the lpszList variable is of type LPCSTR, which is a constant string type, it is necessary to cast the lpszList variable to type LPTSTR, which can be thought of as the non-constant equivalent to LPCSTR. That's why the word LPTSTR appears in parentheses before lpszList in the preceding code's second line. The parentheses tell C++ to cast the value right after the parentheses into the type specified in the parentheses. ■

TIP To get help and example syntax for the `strtok` function—or just about any C++ function or keyword—just highlight the word `strtok` with your mouse and press F1. Visual C++ will show the appropriate page from the online C++ documentation. The explanations, while formal, are quite good and often include helpful, real-world examples.

Converting the StringSet Back into a CF-Style Delimited List   Now that the StringSet has been populated with the distinct values from the original list, all that's left to do is to send the contents of the StringSet back to the calling template. Since the StringSet is an array of strings rather than a delimited list of strings, it is necessary to loop through the StringSet, building a simple delimited list with each StringSet value.

To accomplish this, the CFX tag uses the `GetCount` function from Allaire's `CCFXStringSet` class to figure out how many times it needs to perform the loop. For each iteration of the loop, the `GetString` function is used to get the appropriate value from the StringSet.

Introducing New CFXAPI Function

`CCFXStringSet::GetCount()`

Returns: The number of individual strings in the StringSet, as an `Integer`

Introducing New CFXAPI Function

`CCFXStringSet::GetString (position as an Integer)`

Returns: The string at the requested position number returned as a `LPCSTR`

The following code snippet uses these two functions in a simple `for` loop that builds a delimited list out of the contents of the StringSet. Note that the variable for the new list is defined as a `CString` variable, which allows the use of the + operator for string concatenation. It also allows the use of the `Left` and `GetLength` functions to remove the trailing delimiter character from the end of the new list. See your C++ documentation (or the Visual C++ online help) for more information about these functions.

```
// Initialize a CString variable with an empty string
CString csNewList = "";

// For each string in the StringSet
for (int Counter = 1; Counter <= ssList->GetCount(); Counter++) {
   // Add the string to new list, followed by a delimiter
   csNewList = csNewList + ssList->GetString(Counter) + lpszDelimiter;
}

// There's an extra delimiter left at the end, so delete it
csNewList = csNewList.Left(csNewList.GetLength() - 1);
```

The Final Code

Listing 10.5 shows the completed `Request.cpp` file for the `CFX_ListRemoveDuplicates` tag. If you want, you can copy and paste the code from the `Listing05.cpp` file on this book's CD. You should replace all of the wizard-produced code that you already have with the code from the listing.

Listing 10.5 The Completed CFX_ListRemoveDuplicates Code

```cpp
///////////////////////////////////////////////////////////////////////
//
// CFX_LISTREMOVEDUPLICATES - ColdFusion custom tag
//
// Copyright 98. All Rights Reserved.
//


#include "stdafx.h"        // Standard MFC libraries
#include "cfx.h"           // CFX Custom Tag API


void ProcessTagRequest( CCFXRequest* pRequest )
{
    try
    {
        // 1) ***** GET TAG PARAMETERS *****

        // 1a) Parameter LIST             :the list to make distinct
        if (pRequest->AttributeExists("LIST")==FALSE) {
            pRequest->ThrowException("CFX_QueryAddData: Missing LIST
➥Parameter.", "");
        }
        LPCSTR lpszList = pRequest->GetAttribute("LIST");

        // 1b) Parameter VARIABLE         :new variable name
        if (pRequest->AttributeExists("VARIABLE")==FALSE) {
            pRequest->ThrowException("CFX_QueryAddData: Missing VARIABLE
➥Parameter.", "");
        }
        LPCSTR lpszVariable = pRequest->GetAttribute("VARIABLE");

        // 1c) Parameter DELIMITER        :what LIST is delimited by
        LPCSTR lpszDelimiter = ",";
        if (pRequest->AttributeExists("DELIMITER")==TRUE) {
            lpszDelimiter = pRequest->GetAttribute("DELIMITER");
        }


        // 2) ***** CREATE ssList, AN EMPTY "STRING SET" *****
        CCFXStringSet* ssList = pRequest->CreateStringSet();

        // Establish "ThisItem" variable and put 1st "token" in it
        char *ThisItem = strtok( (LPTSTR)lpszList, lpszDelimiter );

        // While there are still tokens left in the list
        while( ThisItem != NULL )   {
            if (ssList->GetIndexForString(ThisItem) == CFX_STRING_NOT_FOUND) {
                ssList->AddString(ThisItem);
            }
            // Fetch the next token.  If there are no more tokens,
            // ThisToken will get set to NULL, which will end the loop.
            ThisItem = strtok( NULL, lpszDelimiter );
        }
```

```
/* Build CF-Style list from StringList */

// Initialize a CString variable with an empty string
CString csNewList = "";

// For each string in the StringSet
for (int Counter = 1; Counter <= ssList->GetCount(); Counter++) {
    // Add the string to new list, followed by a delimiter
    csNewList = csNewList + ssList->GetString(Counter) + lpszDelimiter;
}

// There's an extra delimiter left at the end, so delete it
csNewList = csNewList.Left(csNewList.GetLength() - 1);



// Pass completed CF List out to calling template
pRequest -> SetVariable(lpszVariable, csNewList);


// Output optional debug info
if ( pRequest->Debug() )
{
    pRequest->WriteDebug( "Debug info..." ) ;
}
}

// Catch ColdFusion exceptions & re-raise them
catch( CCFXException* e )
{
    pRequest->ReThrowException( e ) ;
}

// Catch ALL other exceptions and throw them as
// ColdFusion exceptions (DO NOT REMOVE! --
// this prevents the server from crashing in
// case of an unexpected exception)
catch( ... )
{
    pRequest->ThrowException(
        "Error occurred in tag CFX_LISTREMOVEDUPLICATES",
        "Unexpected error occurred while processing tag." ) ;
}
}
```

The code can now be compiled using the Build menu, and tested with the ListTestCFX.cfm test template from Listing 10.3. When the test template is run, all duplicate values should be successfully removed from the list. Figure 10.7 demonstrates that the CFX tag indeed does what it is supposed to do.

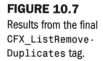

FIGURE 10.7
Results from the final
`CFX_ListRemove-`
`Duplicates` tag.

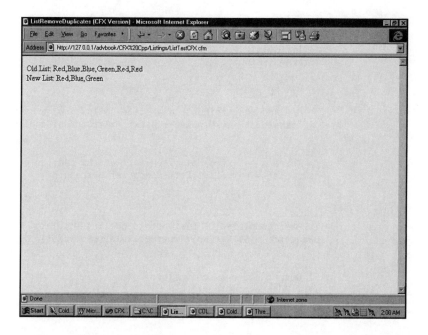

Shortening Your Source Code with the "Macros" on the CD-ROM

In C++, there is a concept of a *preprocessor directive*, which provides instructions for the compiler (here, Microsoft Visual C++) to carry out before it compiles a program. These directives all start with the # symbol, and together compose a sort of macro language that can help you simplify certain repetitive aspects of C++ coding. For instance, the Tag Wizard puts the `#include` directive at the very top of the `CFX_ListRemoveDuplicates` tag, to include all of the code from the `cfx.h` file on disk. This keeps all of that code from having to appear in the actual tag source code itself. It's a lot like the `CFINCLUDE` tag in CFML.

N O T E Just because these directives start with the # sign doesn't mean that they are in any way related to ColdFusion variables. It's just a coincidence that the # sign happens to have special meaning in the C++ and CFML languages. ■

`#define` is another helpful directive; it allows certain words to be "defined" as special user-defined keywords. For instance, if you look in the `cfx.h` file that is included in each CFX project, you can see that the `CFX_STRING_NOT_FOUND` constant used earlier in this chapter was set up using the `#define` directive:

```
#define CFX_STRING_NOT_FOUND     -1
```

This causes the sting `CFX_STRING_NOT_FOUND` to be replaced with -1 when Visual C++ compiles your code. As a programmer, you don't necessarily need to understand that `CFX_STRING_NOT_FOUND` is just a fancy word for -1. The goal of these directives is generally to make code more readable.

You will find a modified version of the `cfx.h` file on the CD included with this book. This modified version includes several additional `#define` directives that make it much easier to do certain common operations, such as establishing tag parameters. If you replace the `cfx.h` file now on your system with the modified version from the CD, you can then use the following macros in your CFX code. Each of them is established with its own `#define` directive, which you can view directly, by opening the modified `cfx.h` file in a text editor.

RequiredParam(ParamName, *VariableName*)

Establishes a required parameter for the CFX tag and stores its value as a LPCSTR variable with the name you supply in *VariableName*. There is no need to declare the variable beforehand.

OptionalParam(ParamName, *VariableName*, *DefaultValue*)

Establishes an optional parameter for the CFX tag—with the default value you supply in *DefaultValue*—and stores its value as a LPCSTR variable with the name you supply in *VariableName*. There is no need to declare the variable beforehand.

StringSetToList(StringSet, *VariableName*, Delimiter)

Converts a StringSet to a CF-style delimited list. The new list is stored in the LPCSTR variable with the name you supply in *VariableName*. There is no need to declare the variable beforehand.

ListToStringSet(List, *StringSetName*, Delimiter)

Converts a CF-style delimited list to a StringSet object. The new StringSet has the name you supply in *StringSetName*. There is no need to create the StringSet beforehand.

After replacing the `cfx.h` file, it is possible to crunch the completed CFX tag code from Listing 10.5 down to its bare essentials. Listing 10.6 shows the results. Note that the tedious-to-write code about the tag's parameters has been pared down to almost nothing. The resulting code is faster to write, less error-prone, and easier to read. You can copy and paste the code from the `Listing06.cpp` file on this book's CD.

Part III

Ch 10

Listing 10.6   The Same CFX Tag Code, Shortened with the Macros from the CD

```
////////////////////////////////////////////////////////////////////////
//
// CFX_LISTREMOVEDUPLICATES - ColdFusion custom tag
//
// Copyright 98. All Rights Reserved.
//
#include "stdafx.h"        // Standard MFC libraries
#include "cfx.h"        // CFX Custom Tag API


void ProcessTagRequest( CCFXRequest* pRequest )
{
    try
```

continues

Listing 10.6   Continued

```
{
    // 1) ***** GET TAG PARAMETERS *****
    RequiredParam(LIST, lpszList);
    RequiredParam(VARIABLE, lpszVariable);
    OptionalParam(DELIMITER, lpszDelimiter, ",");


    // 2) ***** CREATE ssList, AN EMPTY "STRING SET" *****
    CCFXStringSet* ssList = pRequest->CreateStringSet();

    // Establish "ThisItem" variable and put 1st "token" in it
    CString csList = lpszList;
    char *ThisItem = strtok( csList.GetBuffer(0), lpszDelimiter );

    // While there are still tokens left in the list
    while( ThisItem != NULL )   {
        if (ssList->GetIndexForString(ThisItem) == CFX_STRING_NOT_FOUND) {
            ssList->AddString(ThisItem);
        }
        // Fetch the next token.  If there are no more tokens,
        // ThisToken will get set to NULL, which will end the loop.
        ThisItem = strtok( NULL, lpszDelimiter );
    }


    /* Build CF-Style list from StringList */
    StringSetToList(ssList, csNewList, lpszDelimiter);


    // Pass completed CF List out to calling template
    pRequest -> SetVariable(lpszVariable, csNewList);


    // Output optional debug info
    if ( pRequest->Debug() )
    {
        pRequest->WriteDebug( "Debug info..." ) ;
    }
}

// Catch ColdFusion exceptions & re-raise them
catch( CCFXException* e )
{
    pRequest->ReThrowException( e ) ;
}

// Catch ALL other exceptions (DO NOT REMOVE!)
catch( ... )
{
    pRequest->ThrowException(
        "Error occurred in tag CFX_LISTREMOVEDUPLICATES",
        "Unexpected error occurred while processing tag." ) ;
}
}
```

Distributing the New Tag

When a CFX tag has been completed, it should be tested to make sure it actually does what it was designed to do. You may want to consider allowing someone else to do the testing, especially if the tag is relatively complicated. Often someone else can identify problems or bugs in your tag that you might never catch. If you intend for the CFX tag to be used by others, this is a good time to write some documentation for the tag. If another person can understand what the tag is supposed to do, how to use it in their own ColdFusion templates, and can successfully put it into use, your work is probably done.

TIP If you are creating a CFX tag for other ColdFusion developers to use, consider creating a Tag Editor (.vtm file) for ColdFusion Studio, so that your CFX tag becomes integrated into the Studio interface. See Chapter 14, "Customizing ColdFusion Studio," for information about creating .vtm files for Studio.

After the tag has been tested to your satisfaction, it should be recompiled one last time in Visual C++'s Win32 release configuration. Until this point, all of the work has been done in the Win32 Debug configuration. Recompiling it as release code decreases the file size of the compiled .dll and allows the tag to run properly on any ColdFusion server.

TIP If you or someone else gets a message that says something like "Could not load the tag library DLL" when the tag is installed on another ColdFusion server, make sure that you provided a version of the .dll that was compiled for the Win32 release.

Perform the following steps to recompile the tag in the Win32 release configuration:

1. Choose Build, Set Active Configuration from the Visual C++ menu.
2. Select the Win32 Release option and click OK.
3. Recompile the CFX tag. Note that the location of the newly compiled .dll is now placed into the Release subdirectory, rather than the Debug subdirectory. This means that you need to alter the tag's entry in the ColdFusion Administrator if you want to test the release version of the tag yourself.
4. Now that the tag has been recompiled, you can move the .dll to the desired location on your production ColdFusion server. If necessary, be sure to update the CFX tag's entry in the ColdFusion Administrator to reflect the .dll's new location.
5. Finally, select the Keep Library Loaded check box for your tag in the ColdFusion Administrator. This should improve performance somewhat, especially for more complicated tags.

Building Your Second CFX Tag: CFX_QueryAddColumn

One of the important things the CFX classes allow you to do is manipulate query result sets. Each CFX tag can have a QUERY parameter that receives any query's results from the calling template so the tag can work with the results somehow. Each CFX tag can also create new

Part
III

Ch
10

query result sets in the calling template, which can then be used by the calling template just like the results of a CFQUERY tag. You build a tag called CFX_QueryAddColumn to experience the query-manipulation capabilities of the CFX classes.

This idea for this tag came from a need to provide a solution to a specific problem for Chapter 26, "Full-Text Searching with Verity" of *ColdFusion Web Application Construction Kit* (Que, 1998), which is this book's beginning-to-intermediate companion. That chapter discusses running a Verity search with the CFSEARCH tag and then running a database query that retrieves the record from the database table that corresponds to each record that the Verity search found. The database query fetches the actual data to display to the user, based on those primary keys. The one problem with this technique is that the relevancy score of the Verity search is essentially lost because the database query does not provide this information; ColdFusion provides no direct means to merge data from one query result set (in this case, the Verity search) with the data from the other result set (the database search).

The goal is for CFX_QueryAddColumn to take three main parameters: QUERY, KEYS, and VALUES. QUERY is any query that a ColdFusion developer wants to add a column to (in the example discussed earlier, that is the results of the database search). KEYS is a comma-separated list of values that match the values in one of the query's columns. VALUES is the information that should actually be added to the query in the form of a comma-separated list of values that correspond with the KEYS list. For instance, if the first value in the KEYS list is 10 and the first value in the VALUES list is Blue, then the word Blue is placed in the added column for each row that had a value of 10 in a certain column of the query. In this way, it becomes possible to do simple joins between different types of data providers.

Dealing with Query Result Sets

Allaire provides a number of functions for creating and manipulating query result sets, and passing them back and forth between a CFX tag and the calling template. In your CFX source code, each query result set is represented by a variable of the type CCFXQuery, which is a special type of structure that knows how to store data in the same way that ColdFusion stores its queries. A CCFXQuery variable is created in one of two ways: either it's created from scratch or it's fetched from the calling template. The CFX_QueryAddColumn tag built in this section needs to do both.

> **N O T E** *Query result set* refers to a set of data that can be used in a ColdFusion template as if it were the results of a CFQUERY tag. CFPOP, CFLDAP, CFDIRECTORY, and CFSEARCH are all examples of tags that generate query result sets to expose to you the data they find. In the ColdFusion documentation and elsewhere, the word *query* is often used as shorthand for the phrase *query result set*. You'll see the terms used interchangeably. ▪

Retrieving the Query from the Calling Template

A ColdFusion template can execute a CFQUERY tag (or any other tag that returns a query result set) and then pass the results to a CFX tag by providing a QUERY parameter. For instance, take a look at Listing 10.7, which serves as your test template as you build this tag. It runs a simple query using the CFQUERY tag and then passes the results of the query to the CFX tag by specifying the query's name as the tag's QUERY parameter.

Listing 10.7 `QueryTestCFX.cfm`—**Test Template for the `CFX_QueryAddColumn` Tag**

```
<HTML>
<HEAD><TITLE>CFX_QueryAddColumn Test</TITLE></HEAD>
<BODY>

<!--- Retrieve names and favorite colors (as hex values) --->
<CFQUERY NAME="GetPrefs" DATASOURCE="AdvBook">
  SELECT PersonID, Name, FavoriteColor
  FROM Preferences
</CFQUERY>

<!--- Ask our tag to add descriptive color names by hex value--->
<CFX_QueryAddColumn
  QUERY="GetPrefs"
  ADDCOLUMN="ColorText"
  KEYCOLUMN="FavoriteColor"
  KEYS="FFFFFF,000000,0000FF,00FF00,FF0000,FFA500,800080"
  VALUES="White,Black,Blue,Green,Red,Orange,Purple"
  NAME="ColorTextAdded">

<!--- Display the results! --->
<CFOUTPUT QUERY="ColorTextAdded">
  #Name#'s favorite color is #ColorText# (#FavoriteColor#) <BR>
</CFOUTPUT>

</BODY>
</HTML>
```

Part

III

Ch

10

N O T E A CFX tag can only access one query from the calling template, and the query must be supplied as a parameter called QUERY. It is impossible for a CFX tag to access or manipulate the contents of more than one query result set from the calling template. It is possible, however, for a CFX tag to return more than one query to the calling template. In other words, the AddQuery function (discussed in a moment) can be used several times in a CFX tag, but the GetQuery function can be used only once. ▪

Fetching the Query from the Calling Template   Use the GetQuery function from Allaire's CCFXRequest class to access the query passed into the tag's QUERY parameter by the calling template.

Introducing New CFXAPI Function

CCFXRequest::**GetQuery**()

Returns: Returns a pointer to a query result set structure. Returns NULL if no QUERY parameter is provided for the CFX tag.

For instance, the following code snippet conceptually grabs the query results from the calling template and sticks them into a CCFXQuery variable called pQuery. If the person using the CFX tag did not provide a QUERY parameter, the tag throws an exception and an error message is shown.

```
// Get the query as passed to us by the calling template
CCFXQuery* pQuery = pRequest->GetQuery();
if (pQuery == NULL) {
    pRequest->ThrowException("Error in CFX tag.", "No QUERY parameter given.");
}
```

N O T E   The GetQuery function returns a pointer—pQuery in the preceding snippet—to the query result set in the calling template, rather than making a local copy of the query results. This means that if you change any of the data in the query in your CFX tag, those changes are reflected in the calling template after the CFX tag executes. ▪

Getting the Column Names   Once the pQuery variable has been initialized with the GetQuery function, you can learn what the query's column names are via the GetColumns function from the CCFXQuery class. You are given a StringSet that contains the column names. This is similar conceptually to the built-in ColumnList variable that you can use in normal CFML code.

Introducing New CFXAPI Function

CCFXQuery::**GetColumns**()

Returns: A StringSet that contains the query's column names

For instance, the following code snippet obtains the column names from the result set associated with the pQuery variable that was initialized in the previous snippet:

```
// Get the column names from the original query
CCFXStringSet* ssColumns = pQuery->GetColumns();
```

The first part of the CFX_QueryAddColumns tag can be written at this point. Listing 10.8 establishes the tag's parameters and uses one of the previously discussed macros to convert load the KEYS and VALUES parameters into StringSets for later processing. It then receives a query from the calling template, finds out what the query's column names are, and makes sure that the value specified for KEYCOLUMN is one of those columns. It adds the new column name specified in the tag's ADDCOLUMN parameter to the StringSet of column names.

Along the way, this code populates a few variables that are needed later. For instance, for the next part of the tag, it is handy to have an integer variable that contains the number of columns in the query passed to the tag. Since the list of column names is contained in a StringSet, it's quite simple to get this number. All that's needed is to use the GetCount function—which was also used in the last tag example—to count the number of strings in the StringSet.

If you want, you can copy and paste the code in Listing 10.8 from the Listing08.cpp file on this book's CD.

On the CD

Listing 10.8 The First Part of the CFX_QueryAddColumn Tag

```
/////////////////////////////////////////////////////////////////////
//
// CFX_QUERYADDCOLUMN - ColdFusion custom tag
//
// Copyright 98. All Rights Reserved.
//

#include "stdafx.h"        // Standard MFC libraries
#include "cfx.h"           // CFX Custom Tag API


void ProcessTagRequest( CCFXRequest* pRequest )
{
    try
    {

        // ***** ESTABLISH TAG PARAMETERS *****
        RequiredParam(NAME, lpszNewQueryName);
        RequiredParam(KEYCOLUMN, lpszKeyColumn);
        RequiredParam(ADDCOLUMN, lpszAddColumn);
        RequiredParam(KEYS, lpszKeys);
        RequiredParam(VALUES, lpszValues);
        OptionalParam(KEYS_DELIMITER, lpszKeysDelimiter, ",");
        OptionalParam(VALUES_DELIMITER, lpszValuesDelimiter, ",");


        // ****** CONVERT THE TWO LISTS OF DATA TO STRINGSETS *****
        // Populate a StringSet with the "KEYS" parameter
        ListToStringSet(lpszKeys, ssKeys, lpszKeysDelimiter);

        // Populate a StringSet with the "VALUES" parameter
        ListToStringSet(lpszValues, ssValues, lpszValuesDelimiter);

        // Make sure the two StringSets have the same number of elements
        if ( (ssKeys->GetCount() != ssValues->GetCount()) ) {
            pRequest->ThrowException(
                "KEYS and VALUES do not match up!",
                "The KEYS and VALUES lists must be the same length.");
    }



        // ****** CREATING THE NEW, EMPTY QUERY *******
        // Get the query as passed to us by the calling template
        CCFXQuery* pQuery = pRequest->GetQuery();
        if (pQuery == NULL) {
            pRequest->ThrowException(
                "Error in CFX tag.",
                "No QUERY parameter given.");
        }

        // Get the column names from the original query
        CCFXStringSet* ssColumns = pQuery->GetColumns();
```

Part
III

Ch
10

continues

Listing 10.8 Continued

```
            // Which column number is KEYCOLUMN?
            int intKeyColumn = ssColumns->GetIndexForString(lpszKeyColumn);
            // Stop if the user specified a KEYCOLUMN that doesn't exist in QUERY.
            if (intKeyColumn == CFX_STRING_NOT_FOUND ) {
                pRequest->ThrowException(
                    "Invalid KEYCOLUMN parameter.",
                    "Column doesn't exist in QUERY.");
            };

            // How many columns were in the old query?
            int intOldQueryColumnsCount = ssColumns->GetCount();
            // The new column number will be that number, plus one
            int intAddedColumn = intOldQueryColumnsCount + 1;

            // Add NEWCOLUMN to the column list
            ssColumns->AddString(lpszAddColumn);


            // Output optional debug info
            if ( pRequest->Debug() )
            {
                pRequest->WriteDebug( "Debug info..." ) ;
            }
    }

    // Catch ColdFusion exceptions & re-raise them
    catch( CCFXException* e )
    {
        pRequest->ReThrowException( e ) ;
    }

    // Catch ALL other exceptions and throw them as
    // ColdFusion exceptions (DO NOT REMOVE! --
    // this prevents the server from crashing in
    // case of an unexpected exception)
    catch( ... )
    {
        pRequest->ThrowException(
            "Error occurred in tag CFX_QUERYADDDATA",
            "Unexpected error occurred while processing tag." ) ;
    }
}
```

Creating a New Query

To create a new query, you first need to create a StringSet that holds the column names for the new query. This was accomplished in Listing 10.8—the ssColumns StringSet has the column names for the new query that the CFX tag will ultimately pass back out to the referring template; pass the StringSet to the AddQuery function from Allaire's CCFXQuery class.

Introducing New CFXAPI Function

`CCFXQuery::`**`AddQuery`**`(`*`new_query_name`* as a `LPCSTR`, *`columns`* as a StringSet)

Returns: A new, empty query result set structure

For instance, the following code snippet creates the new query structure. By specifying the `lpszNewQueryName` variable for the first parameter of the `AddQuery` function, the new query will be visible to the calling template by the name provided to the tag's `NAME` parameter.

```
// Create New Query, using new column list
CCFXQuery* NewQuery = pRequest-> AddQuery(lpszNewQueryName, ssColumns);
```

> **N O T E** If this code were added to the first part of the tag code (shown Listing 10.8), it is possible to start using the CFX tag in our `QueryTestCFX.cfm` template without errors. It wouldn't be particularly useful because the new query doesn't have any rows of data in it yet, but at least the test template would execute without errors. There would indeed be a new query with the column names that the template is expecting. ◼

Adding Rows to the New Query   After the query result set has been created with the `AddQuery` function, rows can be added to it with Allaire's `AddRow` function. This adds an empty row to the query results. The new row appears after any rows that already exist in the result set.

Once a new row has been added, the individual cells of the new row can be filled in using Allaire's `SetData` function. Each column of the new row needs to be filled in one at a time, using its own `SetData` function. There is also a corresponding `GetData` function that does the opposite of what `SetData` does. It gets the current value of a particular column from a particular row of a query. The `CFX_QueryAddColumn` tag uses these functions together to copy data from the original query to the newly-created query.

Introducing New CFXAPI Function

`CCFXRequest::`**`AddRow`**`( )`

Returns: The number of the row that was just added to the query. In other words, the function returns the number of rows now in the query result set.

Introducing New CFXAPI Function

`CCFXRequest::`**`SetData`** `(`*`row`* as an `Integer`, *`column`* as an `Integer`, *`new_data`* as a `LPCSTR`)

Returns: Nothing; sticks the new data into the row and column specified

Introducing New CFXAPI Function

`CCFXRequest::`**`GetData`** `(`*`row`* as an `Integer`, *`column`* as an `Integer`)

Returns: The data that's currently sitting in the specified row and column of the query as a `LPCSTR` value

Introducing New CFXAPI Function

`CCFXRequest::`**`GetRowCount`**`( )`

Returns: The number of rows currently in the query, as an `Integer`

For instance, the following code snippet copies the values from all the rows and columns of the old query to the new query:

■ The outer for loop moves through each row in the query by gradually incrementing the value of the Row variable until it is equal to the number of rows in the query.

■ The inner for loop moves through each column in the current row of the query by incrementing the value of the Col variable; then, inside the loop, the Row and Col variables (which together identify the current cell in the query) are used by the GetData function to get the appropriate value from the original query. The Row and Col variables are then used again by the SetData function to save that value in a corresponding cell of the new query.

```
// ...copy in existing data from old query....
for ( int Row = 1; Row <= pQuery->GetRowCount(); Row++) {
    for (int Col = 1; Col <= intOldQueryColumnsCount; Col++) {
        NewQuery->SetData(NewRow, Col, pQuery->GetData(Row, Col));
    }
}
```

TIP So far, the code snippet leaves the last column—the added column, the one named by the CFX tag's ADDCOLUMN parameter—of the new query uninitialized. That is, the cells in the last column have not been set to any values at all—not even to empty strings (" "). An error message generally results if the calling template attempts to refer to any of these uninitialized cells. If errors are occurring when a template tries to display a query generated by one of your tags, consider whether some of the query's cells are uninitialized. If so, use the SetData function to set those cells to blank (to an empty string) and try again.

Giving the Tag Its Actual Functionality

It is now possible to construct the code that actually gets the CFX tag to do what it is supposed to do. Remember that there are two result sets that the tag is dealing with: the original query passed to the tag with the QUERY parameter and a new query, the name for which was specified with the NAME parameter. The new query has all of the same column names as the original query, plus one extra column that was named with the ADDCOLUMN parameter.

Basically, the tag needs to move through each row of the original query. For each row, it should add a row to the new query and copy the data from the current row of the original query and put it into the current row of the new query. It should then look at the key value for the current row of the original query and see if it exists in the KEYS list. If the value is in the KEYS list, it should place that value into the new query's additional column. If, on the other hand, the key value is not in the KEYS list, the new query's additional column should be set to an empty string to indicate that there is no corresponding value.

Listing 10.9 shows the C++ code that will get the job done. Note that the now-familiar GetIndexForString and GetString functions do much of the searching and matching work for you. You can copy and paste the code in Listing 10.9 from the Listing09.cpp file on this book's CD.

On the CD

Listing 10.9 Working Code for the `CFX_QueryAddColumn` Tag

```
//////////////////////////////////////////////////////////////////////
//
// CFX_QUERYADDCOLUMN - ColdFusion custom tag
//
// Copyright 98. All Rights Reserved.
//

#include "stdafx.h"        // Standard MFC libraries
#include "cfx.h"           // CFX Custom Tag API


void ProcessTagRequest( CCFXRequest* pRequest )
{
    try
    {
        // ***** ESTABLISH TAG PARAMETERS *****
        RequiredParam(NAME, lpszNewQueryName);
        RequiredParam(KEYCOLUMN, lpszKeyColumn);
        RequiredParam(ADDCOLUMN, lpszAddColumn);
        RequiredParam(KEYS, lpszKeys);
        RequiredParam(VALUES, lpszValues);
        OptionalParam(KEYS_DELIMITER, lpszKeysDelimiter, ",");
        OptionalParam(VALUES_DELIMITER, lpszValuesDelimiter, ",");


        // ****** CONVERT THE TWO LISTS OF DATA TO STRINGSETS *****
        // Populate a StringSet with the "KEYS" parameter
        ListToStringSet(lpszKeys, ssKeys, lpszKeysDelimiter);

        // Populate a StringSet with the "VALUES" parameter
        ListToStringSet(lpszValues, ssValues, lpszValuesDelimiter);

        // Make sure the two StringSets have the same number of elements
        if ( (ssKeys->GetCount() != ssValues->GetCount()) ) {
            pRequest->ThrowException(
                "KEYS and VALUES do not match up!",
                "The KEYS and VALUES lists must be the same length.");
        }


        // ****** CREATING THE NEW, EMPTY QUERY *******
        // Get the query as passed to us by the calling template
        CCFXQuery* pQuery = pRequest->GetQuery();
        if (pQuery == NULL) {
            pRequest->ThrowException(
                "Error in CFX tag.",
                "No QUERY parameter given.");
        }


        // Get the column names from the original query
        CCFXStringSet* ssColumns = pQuery->GetColumns();
```

continues

Part
III

Ch

10

Listing 10.9   Continued

```
// Which column number is KEYCOLUMN?
int intKeyColumn = ssColumns->GetIndexForString(lpszKeyColumn);
// Stop if the user specified a KEYCOLUMN that doesn't exist in QUERY.
if (intKeyColumn == CFX_STRING_NOT_FOUND ) {
    pRequest->ThrowException(
        "Invalid KEYCOLUMN parameter.",
        "Column doesn't exist in QUERY.");
};

// How many columns were in the old query?
int intOldQueryColumnsCount = ssColumns->GetCount();
// The new column number will be that number, plus one
int intAddedColumn = intOldQueryColumnsCount + 1;

// Add NEWCOLUMN to the column list
ssColumns->AddString(lpszAddColumn);

// Create New Query, using new column list
CCFXQuery* NewQuery = pRequest-> AddQuery(lpszNewQueryName, ssColumns);


// ***** FILL NEW QUERY WITH ACTUAL DATA *****
int NewRow;          // row number of current row in new query
LPCSTR LookingFor;   // current value of KEYCOLUMN in old query
int FoundAt;         // position of LookingFor in KEYS list


// For each row in the old query...
for ( int OldRow = 1; OldRow <= pQuery->GetRowCount(); OldRow++) {

    // ...add a row to the new query ...
    NewRow = NewQuery->AddRow();

    // ...copy in existing data from old query....
    for (int Col = 1; Col <= intOldQueryColumnsCount; Col++) {
        NewQuery->SetData( NewRow, Col, pQuery->GetData(OldRow, Col) );
    }

    // What is the key value of the current row of the old query?
    LookingFor = pQuery->GetData(OldRow, intKeyColumn);

    // ... does the key value in this row match up with a value in KEYS?
    FoundAt = ssKeys->GetIndexForString(LookingFor);

    // if the query's key value is not in the key list at all, add a row
➥with a blank cell
    if (FoundAt == CFX_STRING_NOT_FOUND) {

        // then set the new column to blank
        NewQuery->SetData(NewRow, intAddedColumn, "");

    } else {
```

```
                // copy matching value for this key in the list
                NewQuery->SetData(NewRow, intAddedColumn, ssValues->
➥GetString(FoundAt));

            }

        }


        // Output optional debug info
        if ( pRequest->Debug() )
        {
            pRequest->WriteDebug( "Debug info..." ) ;
        }
    }
    // Catch ColdFusion exceptions & re-raise them
    catch( CCFXException* e )
    {
        pRequest->ReThrowException( e ) ;
    }

    // Catch ALL other exceptions and throw them as
    // ColdFusion exceptions (DO NOT REMOVE! --
    // this prevents the server from crashing in
    // case of an unexpected exception)
    catch( ... )
    {
        pRequest->ThrowException(
            "Error occurred in tag CFX_QUERYADDDATA",
            "Unexpected error occurred while processing tag." ) ;
    }
}
```

The code can now be compiled, and the tag can be tested by running the QueryTestCFX.cfm template from Listing 10.7. The results are shown in Figure 10.8. The completed CFX tag is fairly simple, but it has accomplished something pretty interesting. It has effectively joined information from two different data sources.

Displaying Debug Information

You can have your CFX tag produce debugging output, which will be displayed on the calling template if DEBUG="Yes" (or DEBUG) is included as one the tag's parameters. This allows you to include secret status messages that indicate information about the tag's progress, or perhaps just to output your name and email address so that another ColdFusion developer can get in touch with you if she encounters problems with your tag. To add debug information, use the Debug and WriteDebug functions from Allaire's CCFXRequest class.

Introducing New CFXAPI Function

CCFXRequest::**Debug**()

Returns: A BOOL value (TRUE or FALSE) indicating whether a DEBUG parameter was supplied to the CFX tag by the calling template.

FIGURE 10.8

The CFX_QueryAddColumn tag joins query data and list data.

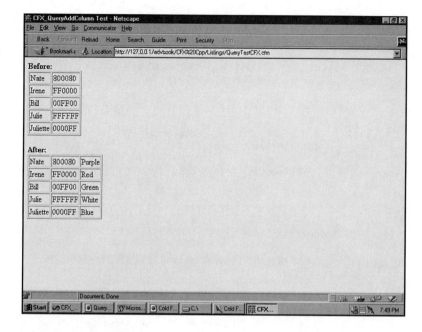

Introducing New CFXAPI Function

CCFXRequest::**WriteDebug** (*debug_message* as a LPCSTR)

Returns: Nothing; outputs the message onto the current Web page if a DEBUG parameter is supplied to the CFX tag by the calling template.

Introducing New CFXAPI Function

CCFXQuery::**GetName**()

Returns: The name of the query as a LPCSTR.

For instance, the code shown in Listing 10.10 can be added to the final CFX_QueryAddColumn code shown in Listing 10.9 in order to display the name of the original query, as well as the names and values of all the other parameters that were passed to the tag. Place it at the end of the existing code, replacing the three Output optional debug info lines that are there now.

Listing 10.10   Code Snippet to Output Debugging Information

```
// Output optional debug info
if ( pRequest->Debug() )
{
    // Output name of QUERY to calling template
    LPCSTR lpszQueryName = pQuery->GetName();
    pRequest->WriteDebug("Name of Query passed to CFX_QueryAddColumn: ") ;
    pRequest->WriteDebug(lpszQueryName);

    // Get list of parameters ("Attributes") passed to tag
    CCFXStringSet* ssAttribs = pRequest->GetAttributeList();
```

```
        // Output a HTML table of Attribute names and values
        pRequest->WriteDebug("<TABLE BORDER>");
        for (int Count = 1; Count<=ssAttribs->GetCount(); Count++) {
            LPCSTR ThisAttrib = ssAttribs->GetString(Count);
            pRequest->WriteDebug("<TR><TD>");
            pRequest->WriteDebug(ThisAttrib);
            pRequest->WriteDebug("</TD><TD>");
            pRequest->WriteDebug(pRequest->GetAttribute(ThisAttrib));
            pRequest->WriteDebug("</TD></TR>");
        }
        pRequest->WriteDebug("</TABLE>");
    }
```

If you add this code snippet to the CFX_QueryAddColumn tag, recompile it and then add DEBUG="Yes" to the tag in the QueryTestCFX.cfm test template. The debug output shown in Figure 10.9 is output to the browser when the template is executed.

Part

III

Ch

10

FIGURE 10.9
Providing debug output can be useful for troubleshooting.

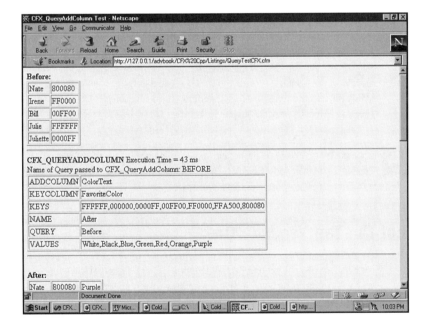

N O T E   When ColdFusion 2.0 was released, two more functions were documented as being part of the CCFXQuery class: SetTotalTime and SetQueryString. These functions were never actually implemented in any version of ColdFusion, and are no longer listed as being part of the CFXAPI. Ignore any reference to these functions that you find in earlier documentation. ■

Building Your Third CFX Tag: CFX_GetDiskSpace

The tags created in this chapter thus far have used the Allaire-supplied functions almost exclusively. The first tag dealt with manipulating StringSets, and the second tag dealt with manipulating queries. Of course, what makes CFX development interesting is the fact that the tags are not limited to the functions that Allaire supplies. CFX tags can do anything that is possible to do with C++ on the platform that you are working with.

On the Windows platform, that means you take advantage of any of the functions and classes provided by Windows itself, including the Windows Messaging API (MAPI), the Telephony API (TAPI), and so on. You also can hook into any third-party libraries that you have access to.

In other words, you're writing a real piece of native code, which means that your CFX tags can do just about anything you can dream up. For instance, you might need to get information from some kind of external data store that doesn't understand SQL or support ODBC. If there is some kind of C++ API available for that data store—or if there is a .dll available that exports some functions that you can use to interact with the data store—you can probably construct a CFX tag by surrounding the appropriate C++ code with some of the Allaire-supplied functions to get the information back to the calling template. In other words, the Allaire functions become a shell for interacting with ColdFusion. You're free to do whatever you want inside the shell.

N O T E   This example uses the GetFreeDiskSpaceEx function originally provided by Microsoft as part of the core Windows NT kernel. This function can report drive information on all Windows NT and Windows 98 machines, but only on Windows 95 machines that have OEM Service Release 2. You will not be able to run the tag created in this section if you are using an earlier version, unless you rework it to use the GetFreeDiskSpace function instead of GetFreeDiskSpaceEx. (See your Visual C++ documentation for details.) ■

T I P   If you are running Windows 95 but are unsure whether you have OEM Service Release 2, right-click My Computer and then click Properties. On the General tab, look at the Windows 95 version number. If it's 4.00.950 B (or later), you have Service Release 2.

What This Tag Needs to Do

As you probably know, the normal ColdFusion CFDIRECTORY tag can be used to obtain a directory listing of a folder on you ColdFusion server's drive. However, in normal CFML there is no way to find out how large a drive is or how much space is left free on a drive. It's easy to think of a situation where this might be a useful piece of information. For instance, you might want to make sure that there is plenty of disk space available on the target drive before accepting a file upload from a browser with the CFFILE tag.

This tag's purpose is to provide this basic drive information functionality. To do so, it calls the GetFreeDiskSpaceEx function that Microsoft provides as a part of Windows itself.

The tag accepts one required parameter, DRIVE, which is the drive letter that the tag should get disk space information for. The simple CFML code in Listing 10.11 demonstrates the functionality that the tag should have when finished.

Listing 10.11 `DriveTestCFM.cfm`—**A Template for Testing the**
`CFX_GetDiskSpace` **Tag**

```
<HTML>
<HEAD><TITLE>CFX_GetDiskSpace Test</TITLE></HEAD>
<BODY>

<!--- Get disk space info for the CF server's C drive --->
<CFX_GetDiskSpace
  DRIVE="c:">

<!--- Display the returned information to the user --->
<CFOUTPUT>
  <BR> Drive Size: #NumberFormat(Drive_TotalBytes)# bytes
  <BR> Space Free: #NumberFormat(Drive_FreeBytes)# bytes
<CFOUTPUT>

</BODY>
</HTML>
```

 TIP If you're curious about where the `GetFreeDiskSpaceEx` function actually resides, it is made
available (exported) by the `kernel32.dll` file, which is found in your Windows system folder.

Part

III

Ch

10

Calling the Function

The first thing you need to do before calling any native Windows function is to figure out what
function you need to use and what parameters that function requires to work. In general, you
can find this information easily by searching through the Developer Studio InfoViewer (that is,
the Visual C++ online help).

According to the InfoViewer topic on `GetFreeDiskSpaceEx`, the function requires four parameters. The function and its parameters are documented for you there, as shown in Figure 10.10.

TIP To get to this spot in the Visual C++ 5.0 online documentation, just type the word
`GetFreeDiskSpace`, highlight it with your mouse, and then press the F1 key.

Take a look at the function syntax shown at the bottom of Figure 10.10. It tells you that the
function accepts four parameters. The first is the drive letter that the `GetDiskFreeSpaceEx`
function should return information about. Fortunately, the function wants this parameter as a
simple string type, which is exactly what the tag will have after retrieving the `DRIVE` parameter
passed to the tag by the calling template.

The remaining three parameters are described as pointers to variables that hold the various
pieces of information found by the function. Note that the parameters are documented as type
`PULARGE_INTEGER`; think of the `P` as standing for pointer. This means that three variables of type
`ULARGE_INTEGER` should be declared in order to use the function. Their memory addresses—
rather than the variables themselves—then should be passed to the function so that the

function knows where to store the values it finds. This type of operation is common for functions that need to return more than one value.

FIGURE 10.10

Online help is available
for Windows functions
and their parameters.

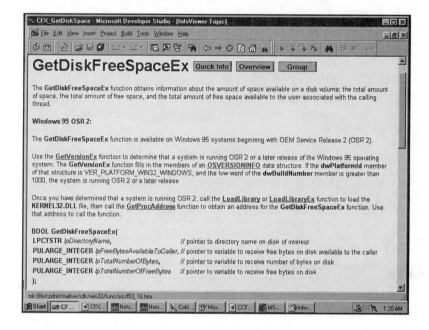

Finally, the word BOOL before the function name tells you that the function returns TRUE when it succeeds, FALSE if it fails.

N O T E   A full explanation of the concept of pointers is well beyond the scope of this chapter. Actually, you have been using them all along in this chapter—each LPCSTR value you've used is a type of pointer and each time you've referred to pRequest in your code, you've been using a pointer to the tag request itself. Pointers are an important aspect of C++ programming, so you should learn about them if you plan to do anything involved. Consult your Visual C++ documentation or a general text on C++ for a more complete exploration of the topic.

The Completed CFX_GetDiskSpace Tag Code

Listing 10.12 shows the complete C++ code needed to create the CFX_GetDiskSpace tag. As you can see, the code is actually quite simple—quite a bit more simple than the other two tags created earlier in this chapter. In fact, the CFX tag is really little more than a thin wrapper for the GetFreeDiskSpace function.

Listing 10.12   Source Code for CFX_GetDiskSpace

```
//////////////////////////////////////////////////////////////////////
//
// CFX_GETDISKSPACE - ColdFusion custom tag
//
// Copyright 98. All Rights Reserved.
//

#include "stdafx.h"        // Standard MFC libraries
#include "cfx.h"           // CFX Custom Tag API

void ProcessTagRequest( CCFXRequest* pRequest )
{
    try
    {
        // Establish Tag Parameters
        RequiredParam(DRIVE, lpszDrive);


        // Set up variables to receive drive information
        ULARGE_INTEGER lpFreeBytesAvailableToCaller;
        ULARGE_INTEGER lpTotalNumberOfBytes;
        ULARGE_INTEGER lpTotalNumberOfFreeBytes;

        // Establish a char variable for use with the sprintf function
        char outstr[50];


        // Ask Windows for information about the drive
        if ( GetDiskFreeSpaceEx(
                lpszDrive,
                &lpFreeBytesAvailableToCaller,
                &lpTotalNumberOfBytes,
                &lpTotalNumberOfFreeBytes)
            )
        {
            // (this code executes if the function succeeds)

            // Place "total bytes" into variable in calling template
            //sprintf( outstr, "%d", lpTotalNumberOfBytes);
            pRequest->SetVariable("Drive_TotalBytes", outstr);

            // Place "free bytes" into variable in calling template
            sprintf( outstr, "%d", lpTotalNumberOfFreeBytes);
            pRequest->SetVariable("Drive_FreeBytes", outstr);

        } else {
            // (this code executes if the function fails)

            // Ask Windows what the last error was (probably error 3)
            INT intLastError = GetLastError();
            sprintf( outstr, "Could not obtain drive information.
➥    Windows error %d occurred.", intLastError);
```

continues

Listing 10.12   Continued

```
                // Display error message and halt all processing
                pRequest->ThrowException("Error in CFX_GetDiskSpace tag", outstr);

        }

    }

    // Catch ColdFusion exceptions & re-raise them
    catch( CCFXException* e )
    {
        pRequest->ReThrowException( e ) ;
    }

    // Catch ALL other exceptions and throw as CF Exceptions
    catch( ... )
    {
        pRequest->ThrowException(
            "Error occurred in tag CFX_GETDISKSPACE",
            "Unexpected error occurred while processing tag." ) ;
    }
}
```

Aside from the function call, the rest of this tag covers familiar territory. At the very top, the RequiredParam macro discussed earlier in this chapter is used to get the value of the DRIVE parameter. The GetFreeDiskSpaceEx function is then called, using the value just obtained from the calling template as the first parameter. Finally, the sprintf function is used to convert the numeric values returned by the functions into character-type values that can be used with the SetVariable function to pass the values back to the calling template.

Note that the Windows GetLastError function provides some troubleshooting information for the person using this tag if the GetFreeDiskSpaceEx function fails for some reason. The GetLastError function simply returns the standard Windows error code (as an integer) for the last error that occurred. If used directly after an error condition is encountered—as is done here—it can be very helpful in figuring out what went wrong.

 It's easy to find the meaning of a particular Windows error code. On a Windows NT machine, open a MS-DOS Prompt window and type **net helpmsg** and the error code on the command line. For instance, net helpmsg 3 shows a message similar to "Error 3: The specified path does not exist on that drive." The procedure is the same on a Windows 95 or Windows 98 machine, except that you should use **net help** instead of net helpmsg.

In the GetFreeDiskSpaceEx function call itself, note the & signs used before the names of each variable that is accepting a value from the function. Conceptually, the & sign stands for "address of." Supplying the variable names without the & signs provides the values of the variables to the function. That's not what is needed here because this function is not interested in the values of those variables. What it is interested in is a spot in the computer's memory where it can stick the drive space information. Of course, you also need to be able to refer to the value later on in your code. That's what the use of pointers here is all about. You set aside the little spot in the computer's memory and give the spot a name when you first declare a variable. Then, by using the & sign, you are asking C++ to let the function know where exactly that little spot in the computer's memory is. The function faithfully deposits its information into that little spot, which is why, after the function executes, referring to the variable by name returns the information you need.

T I P In practice, one way to think of the & sign is this: Parameters without an & generally can be considered input parameters, whereas parameters with an & could generally be considered output parameters. That explanation is somewhat of an oversimplification of what's really going on, but it's helpful keep in mind when you're learning about a new function and are trying to figure out how to call it correctly.

N O T E Don't confuse C++'s use of the & with use of the & sign in normal ColdFusion templates. As noted earlier, the & in C++ is about memory addresses. In CFML, however, the & is used for something much more basic: concatenating two strings into one.

It is now possible to compile the `CFX_GetDiskSpace` tag with the code shown in Listing 10.10 and test it with the `DriveTestCFX.cfm` template shown in Listing 10.9. The test template is brought up in the browser, as shown in Figure 10.11. (As you can see, this author could use a new hard drive!)

FIGURE 10.11
The `CFX_GetDiskSpace` tag in action.

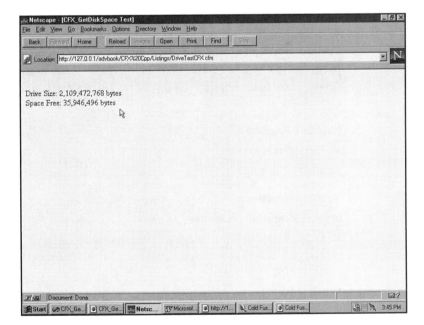

Reading Tag Settings from the Registry

Allaire's `CCFXRequest` class provides a `GetSetting` function that allows a `CFX` tag to read a value from a special branch of the Windows Registry. Typically, some kind of startup settings for the tag are placed into the appropriate position of the Registry, either by the person who is administering the ColdFusion server or, if the CFX tag is being developed for sale to other ColdFusion developers, by some kind of install program.

Please note that the Registry support Allaire provides via the CFXAPI is fairly minimal. The GetSetting function cannot read just any old value from the Registry that it pleases. It can only read values from its own Key (folder) in the Registry, and it cannot write new values to the Registry at all. The intention of the function is to provide limited access to the Registry—just enough for the tag to learn about how it is supposed to behave on a particular machine.

TIP

Note that beginning with ColdFusion 4, it is possible to read and write any value to and from any position in the Registry, using the new CFREGISTRY tag in normal ColdFusion template code. If you need your CFX tag to be aware of a Registry value that the GetSetting function cannot obtain, you might consider obtaining the value in the calling template with CFREGISTRY and then passing the value to the CFX tag as one of its parameters.

As an example, a version of the CFX_GetDiskSpace tag that allows the tag to be restricted to only one particular drive can be created. For instance, if you placed a new value in the Registry called RestrictTo, and specified c: as that value's data, it would be quite simple to read that c: from the Registry, compare it to the DRIVE parameter passed to the tag, and refuse to process the request if the parameter and the Registry setting did not match.

New CFX Function

CCFXRequest::**GetSetting** (*setting_name* as a LPCSTR)

Returns: The value of the specified value in the Windows Registry. If the specified value does not exist in the Registry Key for the CFX tag, the function returns an empty string ("").

New C++ Function

CString.**GetLength**()

Returns: The number of characters in a CString as an Integer

New C++ Function

CString.**CompareNoCase**(*other_string*)

Returns: Returns 0 if the strings are the same (ignoring case). Returns –1 if the CString is less than *other_string*; returns 1 if the CString is greater than *other_string*.

For instance, if the following code snippet were added to Listing 10.12 immediately following the RequiredParam line at the top of the code, the tag would halt with an error message if the CFX tag were executed with a DRIVE parameter that was different from the RestrictTo value stored in the Registry. The net effect is that the CFX tag only proceeds if DRIVE is what has been "permitted" by the Registry value.

```
// Get the setting, if any, from the Registry
CString lpszRestrictTo = pRequest->GetSetting("RestrictTo");

// If the setting existed in the Registry
if ( lpszRestrictTo.GetLength() > 0 ) {

// If the DRIVE parameter does not match the Registry value
if ( lpszRestrictTo.CompareNoCase(lpszDrive) != 0 ) {
        pRequest->ThrowException("Access Denied", "Tag may not access that
drive.");
    }
}
```

Adding the Initial Setting Value to the Registry   To add a value to the Registry that the GetSetting function can access, follow these steps:

1. Open the Registry Editor. To Open the Registry Editor on a Windows NT 4.0 or Windows 95/98 machine, click the Windows Start menu, choose Run, and then type **regedit** in the Run dialog box.

2. Expand the folder for HKEY_LOCAL_MACHINE, SOFTWARE, Allaire, ColdFusion, CurrentVersion, and then CustomTags.

3. Right-click the tag name (in this case, CFX_GETDISKSPACE). Then, from the pop-up menu, choose New, String Value, as shown in Figure 10.12. A new item should appear in the right pane, called New Value #1 (or something similar).

4. Right-click the value you just added and choose Rename. Type **RestrictTo** for the new name of the value.

5. Double-click the value you just renamed. Enter **c:** for the value's data; click OK. If you recompiled the tag with the GetSetting code added, this Registry setting causes the CFX tag to be restricted to the c: drive only.

FIGURE 10.12

Adding a value to the Registry for the CFX tag's use.

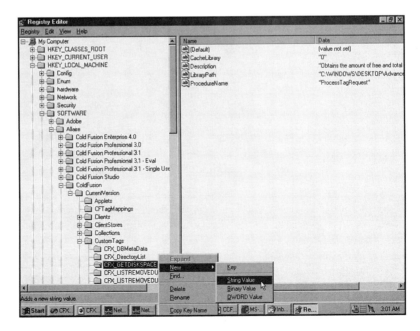

CAUTION

Remember that ColdFusion 4 supports the new CFREGISTRY tag in normal CFML templates. This means that the Registry setting shown earlier could be changed or deleted by any ColdFusion developer that has access to the CFREGISTRY tag. Keep this in mind if you are using the GetSetting functionality to provide a security feature (such as the RestrictTo setting of the CFX_GetDiskSpace tag) on a server that is being used by many different developers. You may need to restrict access to the CFREGISTRY tag for the other developers. See Chapter 7, "Securing Specific Features and Components," for information on restricting access to certain ColdFusion tags like CFREGISTRY.

Editing a Tag Setting in the ColdFusion Administrator   Once the setting has been added to the Registry with the Registry Editor, with the CFREGISTRY tag, or with some kind of tag installation script of your own design, its value can be changed at any time using the ColdFusion Administrator. Just click CFX Tags in the left margin and then click the link for the appropriate tag. At the bottom of the tag's page, any additional settings that have been added to the tag's folder in the Registry will be displayed, with convenient entry blanks to change the values. Figure 10.13 shows how the RestrictTo setting can be edited for the CFX_GetDiskSpace tag.

FIGURE 10.13

Changing a CFX tag's setting in the ColdFusion Administrator.

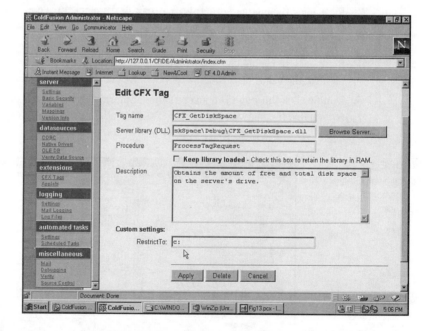

   On Windows NT, the CFX_GetDriveSpace tag should support UNC-style paths as well as mapped drives, provided that the ColdFusion service is running under a Windows NT domain account that has appropriate permissions. UNC paths are written in the general form of \\ServerName\ShareName\ FolderName\Filename, where ServerName is (in theory) the name of another Windows, Novell, or UNIX-based server accessible to your local network.

Writing CFX Tags in Delphi

About Delphi and CFX Tags

In Chapter 10, "Writing CFX Tags in Visual C++," you learned that you can extend ColdFusion's functionality by writing your own CFX tags with Microsoft's Visual C++. You also can write your own CFX tags by using Borland's Delphi product instead of Visual C++. In this chapter, you will learn how to write each CFX tag that was written in Chapter 10, except using Delphi.

> **N O T E** I highly recommend that you look at Chapter 10—which explains how to write CFX tags using Visual C++—before you start looking at the examples in this chapter. There, you will find an explanation of each function in the *CFXAPI*—that is, the special functions that you need to use to allow your CFX tags to interact with ColdFusion. So even if you plan to write CFX tags in Delphi only, skimming through Chapter 10 is still a good idea. At the very least, read the section titled "The Three Classes That Make Up the CFXAPI" before you continue reading here. ▪

Delphi is a development environment for creating 32-bit Windows applications. In many respects, Delphi and ColdFusion are kindred spirits. Both products are about rapid application development, both products are developer-friendly and encourage code reuse, and both products have extremely loyal followings because they can be lots of fun to use.

If you haven't worked with Delphi before, think about it at first as a kind of hybrid between Visual C++ and Visual Basic (although die-hard Delphi enthusiasts might cringe at the comparison). You have the power and direct control that C++ gives you, coupled with the ease of use and heavy component availability of something like Visual Basic.

> **N O T E** The company that makes Delphi recently changed its name from Borland International to Imprise. This change means simply that versions of Delphi from here on—beginning with Delphi 4—will have the Imprise logo on the box. The product is still being developed and sold by the same company. ▪

A Note About Writing CFX Tags in Delphi

You should understand that writing CFX tags in Delphi isn't directly supported by Allaire. As you learned in Chapter 10, Allaire has defined a set of functions collectively referred to as the *CFXAPI*. Allaire ships a wizard and C++ include files that make it easy to use these API functions with Visual C++.

It's not the development tool that a CFX tag is written in that makes ColdFusion able to interact with it. Rather, it's because the tag is compiled as a Windows DLL that behaves in a certain way. Because Delphi can produce these DLLs just as well as C++ can, you can use Delphi to write CFX tags.

> **N O T E** You must use a 32-bit version of Delphi to create CFX tags, which as of this writing means Delphi 2, Delphi 3, or the brand-new Delphi 4. You cannot use the first version of Delphi (now referred to as Delphi 1.0). ▪

Installing the Delphi Libraries on the CD-ROM

The CD-ROM that accompanies this book includes the tools you need to create CFX tags with Delphi. Together, they provide the same functionality as what Allaire provides for programming in C++. You can find two separate items on the CD-ROM:

- Several Delphi Compiled Unit (DCU) files that allow Delphi to "understand" the various functions that make up the CFXAPI. These unit files are the Delphi equivalent of the cfx.h file used with Visual C++. These unit files are provided by an independent developer and have been included on this book's CD for your convenience. The unit files are *shareware*, which means that you can develop CFX tags with them for free on a trial basis, but when you have a finished tag that you want to put into production, you are meant to buy the full version of the unit files for a nominal fee. See the Readme.txt file included in the DelphiCFX folder on the CD-ROM for information about purchasing the full version of the unit files.

- The ColdFusion CFX Tag Wizard for Delphi, which helps you get started quickly with your Delphi CFX tags. It is the equivalent of the Allaire-supplied ColdFusion Tag Wizard used with Visual C++. The wizard is provided by Nate Weiss (the author of this chapter) at no charge.

N O T E Delphi itself should already be installed on your computer before you install the Delphi libraries from this book's CD-ROM. ▪

Part
III

Ch
11

To install the unit files, look in the DelphiCFX folder on the CD-ROM for this chapter. That folder contains three subfolders, named Delphi2, Delphi3, and Delphi4. Copy the three DCU files from the folder that matches your version of Delphi, placing them with the other DCU files in your Delphi installation. For instance, you might place them in the c:\Program Files\Borland\Delphi\Lib folder, depending on how your copy of Delphi is installed and configured.

To install the CFX Wizard, simply copy the DelphiWiz.exe file from the Wizard folder to this chapter on the CD-ROM, placing it anywhere you want on your computer's hard drive. For instance, you might want to place it on your desktop. Then you can simply double-click the DelphiWiz.exe file to run the wizard.

Building the CFX_ListRemoveDuplicates Tag with Delphi

The first example of writing a CFX tag with Delphi will be to re-create the CFX_ListRemoveDuplicates tag created in Chapter 10 with Visual C++. The goal is for the Delphi-produced version of the tag to behave just like the C++ version. It will take the same parameters and produce the same results when used in a ColdFusion template (CFM) file.

Getting Started with the CFX Tag Wizard for Delphi

Starting a new CFX tag project with Delphi is quite similar to starting a new CFX tag using Visual C++. The wizard builds skeletal code for you based on a few questions. Then you add the actual functionality you need by adding Delphi code—also called *Object Pascal code*—to the skeleton.

Specifying the Project Details   The wizard's first step is about naming the tag and specifying where the wizard should store the skeletal Delphi code that it generates. Follow these steps:

1. For the Tag Name, type **CFX_ListRemoveDuplicates**.

2. For the tag's Brief Description, type something like **To remove duplicates from a comma-separated list of values**.

3. Use the Browse button to choose a folder on your computer where you want the wizard to create your new Delphi project. I recommend that you create a new folder for each CFX tag that you start with the wizard. For instance, you might create a folder named something like **c:\Delphi Projects\CFX Tags\ListRemoveDuplicates** and tell the wizard to use that folder.

4. If you want the wizard to register your new CFX tag with ColdFusion for you automatically, leave the Register Tag in CF Administrator check box checked. If you uncheck the box, remember that you'll need to register the CFX tag manually by using the ColdFusion Administrator. Refer to the section titled "Registering the New Tag in the CF Administrator" in Chapter 10 for instructions on how to register the CFX tag with the administrator.

> **N O T E**   The Register Tag in CF Administrator check box is unavailable if ColdFusion isn't running on your computer. You'll have to register the CFX tag by using the ColdFusion Administrator for the machine that you intend to use your new tag on. ■

The wizard should now look something like Figure 11.1.

FIGURE 11.1
Name and describe your new CFX tag during the wizard's first step.

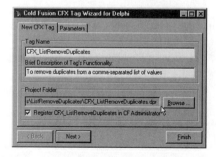

Specifying the New CFX Tag's Parameters   The Delphi wizard actually goes a bit further than the Visual C++ wizard because it helps you write the code for accepting and requiring your CFX tag parameters. Just click the Next button at the bottom of the wizard, or click the Parameters tab at the top of the wizard. You then see the Parameters page.

The Delphi-built CFX_ListRemoveDuplicates tag needs to take the same parameters as the C++ version of the tag did. Follow these steps to specify those parameters:

1. For Parameter 1, type **LIST**. Because the LIST parameter should be required for the new CFX tag, leave the Default for Parameter 1 blank.

2. For Parameter 2, type **VARIABLE**. This parameter is also required for the new CFX tag, so leave the Default for Parameter 2 blank.

3. For Parameter 3, type **DELIMITER**. Because this parameter will be optional for the new CFX tag, type a comma for the Default for Parameter 3. The wizard will build code that uses the comma as the DELIMITER parameter by default.

The wizard should now look something like Figure 11.2.

FIGURE 11.2

Specify the CFX tag's parameters during the wizard's second step.

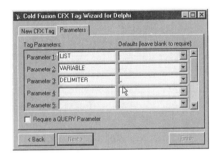

 TIP Remember, the wizard is just here to get you started quickly. You can always add or change the parameters that your new CFX tag accepts or requires later.

Now click Finish. After a moment, the wizard will display a message indicating that it has completed setting up your new tag. Click OK when the message appears. Now you can open the new project in Delphi.

Compiling and Testing the Default "Hello World" Functionality

You now should have a working CFX tag, ready to be compiled and tested with a simple test template. To compile the new tag, follow these steps:

1. Start Delphi.

2. Choose Open from Delphi's File menu.

3. Navigate to the folder you specified as the project folder to the wizard, highlight the DPR file that the wizard created in that folder, and then click Open. Your screen should look something like Figure 11.3.

Part
III

Ch
11

FIGURE 11.3

The wizard creates a basic skeleton for you to add code to.

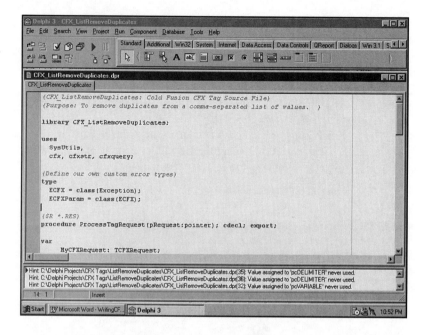

4. Compile the tag by choosing Compile from the Project menu. Hints appear at the bottom of the screen (in Figure 11.3) as helpful reminders that your code has declared variables that it doesn't use (which makes sense because the tag hasn't been programmed to actually do anything useful yet). Other than the hints, though, the code should compile without problems. Notice how quickly the code gets compiled—much more quickly than with Visual C++. This speed is a nice perk when you're working with Delphi.

The completed DLL for the CFX tag should now be sitting in the project folder with the DPR file that you're working on. Assuming that you allowed the wizard to register the tag in the ColdFusion Administrator for you, you should be able to use the new CFX tag in actual ColdFusion templates right away. If the wizard didn't register the tag for you, you need to register it manually by using the ColdFusion Administrator before attempting to use it in a template. Refer to the section titled "Registering the New Tag in the CF Administrator" in Chapter 10 for instructions on how to register the CFX tag with the administrator.

 Because you generally won't use any of Delphi's visual application-building facilities when writing CFX tags, close Delphi's Object Inspector by choosing Object Inspector from the View menu or by pressing F11. Now you can expand the actual code window to take up the entire width of your screen.

You can now test the tag by executing it from within a simple test template. Listing 11.1 shows a simple ColdFusion template that you can use for testing purposes. It is the same code used to test the C++ version of the tag in Chapter 10.

Listing 11.1 `ListTextCFX.cfm`—**Testing the** `CFX_ListRemoveDuplicates` **Tag**

```
<HTML>
<HEAD><TITLE>ListRemoveDuplicates (CFX Version)</TITLE></HEAD>
<BODY>

<!--- Make up a list of values for testing --->
<CFSET OldList = "Red,Blue,Blue,Green,Red,Red">

<!--- Ask our tag to remove the duplicates --->
<CFX_ListRemoveDuplicates
  LIST="#OldList#"
  VARIABLE="NewList"
  DELIMITER=",">

<CFSET MyQuery = QueryNew("Hello")>
<CFSET Hello = QueryAddRow(MyQuery, 5)>

<!--- Display the before-and-after results! --->
<P>
<CFOUTPUT>
  Old List: #OldList# <BR>
  New List: #NewList# <BR>
</CFOUTPUT>

</BODY>
</HTML>
```

Part
III

Ch
11

When you run the test template at this point, the CFX tag should be able to run without problems; however, the template itself displays an error message when it attempts to display the #NewList# variable. This makes sense because no code has been added to the CFX tag that would set the #NewList# variable yet. Figure 11.4 shows the results. Notice that this figure is almost exactly the same as Figure 10.5 in the preceding chapter, when the C++ version of the tag was in the equivalent stage of its infancy.

Establishing the Tag's Parameters

You now can go ahead and add the functionality that makes the tag actually remove the duplicates from the list in the way that it's supposed to. The basic structure and logic of the tag is the same as the C++ version discussed in Chapter 10. The only task at hand is to come up with the Delphi syntax (that is, the Object Pascal syntax) needed to do the same thing as Chapter 10's C++ syntax.

Before this tag can do anything useful, it needs to be able to accept parameters from the ColdFusion template that's using it. Just like the C++ version of the tag, this CFX tag needs to require LIST and VARIABLE parameters, and it also should be able to accept an optional DELIMITER parameter.

FIGURE 11.4

The tag compiles without errors but doesn't accomplish anything yet.

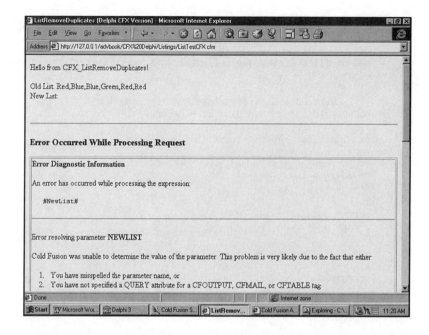

To find out whether a parameter has been passed to the tag, use the AttributeExists function from the cfx unit (included in the project for you by the uses keyword at the top of the wizard-created code). Then, to get the actual value of the parameter and store it in a local variable that the CFX tag can use internally, use the GetAttribute function, as demonstrated next.

Establishing a Required Parameter

When you specify a required parameter in the second page of the Delphi wizard (refer to Figure 11.2), code is automatically generated to cause the CFX tag to ensure that the required parameter exists. If the parameter doesn't exist—that is, if the parameter isn't supplied by the calling template—all template execution stops and an error message is displayed.

For instance, the following code snippet is included by the wizard for this tag's LIST parameter, near the top of the code:

```
if AttributeExists('LIST') then pcLIST := GetAttribute('LIST')
  else raise ECFXParamRequired.Create('LIST');
```

This code snippet is fairly easy to read as plain English: "If no attribute by the name of LIST is passed to the tag, stop and display an error message. Otherwise, just populate the PChar variable called pcLIST with whatever value was actually passed to the LIST parameter by the calling template."

Handling Errors with Delphi's Raise Statement

Note that error handling works a little differently when you're creating CFX tags in Delphi than when you're creating CFX tags in C++ because Delphi encourages programmers to use a structured error-handling mechanism. A complete explanation of the way exceptions are handled in

Delphi is beyond the scope of this chapter, but the basic idea is that all your actual Delphi code will be placed between the words `try` and `except` in your project. Whenever anything goes wrong in the `try` part, the `except` part immediately kicks in to attempt to clean up any problems.

So, when a required parameter is missing, Delphi's `raise` statement is used to create an exception of a special type. All code execution then jumps to the `except` part of the Delphi project. In the `except` part, each type of exception is taken care of by calling the CFX `ThrowException` function. At that moment, ColdFusion template execution halts, and the appropriate error message is displayed to the user.

For instance, the wizard adds the following code snippet near the bottom of the code it generates. Notice that whenever an exception of type `ECFXParamRequired` is encountered, the `ThrowException` function from the Allaire CFXAPI is used to display a special message to users to explain that the parameter is required. You'll see this process in action when the completed code is assembled in a moment.

```
except
  on E: ECFXParamRequired do
    ThrowException(
      'Could not execute CFX_ListRemoveDuplicates tag',
      PChar('A required Parameter, '+E.Message+', was not provided.'));
```

Establishing an Optional Parameter

When you specify an optional parameter in the second page of the Delphi wizard by providing a default for the parameter (see Figure 11.2), code is automatically generated for you to cause the CFX tag to use the default if the parameter isn't supplied by the calling template. For instance, the wizard includes the following code snippet for this tag's optional `DELIMITER` parameter:

```
if AttributeExists('DELIMITER') then pcDELIMITER := GetAttribute('DELIMITER')
  else pcDELIMITER := ',';
```

The Finished `CFX_ListRemoveDuplicates` Code

Listing 11.2 shows working code for the `CFX_ListRemoveDuplicates` tag. You can compile and successfully run this code in the `ListTestCFX.cfm` template from Listing 11.1. Each part of the code is similar conceptually to the equivalent C++ code from Listing 10.5 in the preceding chapter.

> **Listing 11.2** `CFX_ListRemoveDuplicates.dpr`—**The Delphi Version of**
> `CFX_ListRemoveDuplicates`

```
{CFX_ListRemoveDuplicates: ColdFusion CFX Tag Source File}
{Purpose: To remove duplicates from a comma-separated list of values.  }

library CFX_ListRemoveDuplicates;
```

Part
III

Ch
11

continues

Listing 11.2 Continued

```
uses
  SysUtils,
  cfx, cfxstr, cfxquery;

{Define our own custom error types}
type
  ECFX = class(Exception);
  ECFXParamRequired = class(ECFX);

{$R *.RES}
procedure ProcessTagRequest(pRequest:pointer); cdecl; export;

var
    MyCFXRequest: TCFXRequest;
    pcLIST: PChar;
    pcVARIABLE: PChar;
    pcDELIMITER: PChar;

    ssList: TCFXStringSet;
    NewList, OldList: String;
    token: PChar;
    TokenAt, Counter : Integer;

begin
    MyCFXRequest := TCFXRequest.Create(pRequest);
    with MyCFXRequest do begin
      try
        {Retrieve attributes from calling template}
        if AttributeExists('LIST') then pcLIST := GetAttribute('LIST')
          else raise ECFXParamRequired.Create('LIST');

        if AttributeExists('VARIABLE') then pcVARIABLE :=
        ➥GetAttribute('VARIABLE')
          else raise ECFXParamRequired.Create('VARIABLE');

        if AttributeExists('DELIMITER') then pcDELIMITER :=
        ➥GetAttribute('DELIMITER')
          else pcDELIMITER := ',';

        {Create String-type variable from PChar-type pcList variable}
        OldList := pcList;

        {Create ssList, an empty StringSet}
        ssList := TCFXStringSet.Create(CreateStringSet);

        repeat
          {Find the next delimiter in the list}
          TokenAt := Pos(pcDELIMITER, OldList);
          Token := PChar(Copy(OldList, 0, TokenAt-1));

          {If this Token is not in the StringSet yet, add it}
          if ssList.GetIndexForString(Token) = -1 then
            ssList.AddString(Token);

          {Remove this token from the beginning of the list}
```

```
            OldList := Copy(OldList, TokenAt+1, Length(OldList));
        until
          Pos(pcDELIMITER, OldList) = 0;

        {Check the remaining single value in OldList }
        if ssList.GetIndexForString(PChar(OldList)) = -1 then
          ssList.AddString(PChar(OldList));

        {For each string in the StringSet}
        for Counter := 1 to ssList.GetCount do begin
            {Add the string to the new list, followed by a delimiter}
            NewList := NewList + ssList.GetString(Counter) + pcDELIMITER;
        end;
        {There's an extra delimiter left at the end, so delete it}
        NewList := Copy(NewList, 0, Length(NewList) -1);

        {Finished with the ssList StringSet object}
        ssList.Free;

        {Send completed list out to calling template}
        SetVariable(pcVARIABLE, PChar(NewList));

    except
        on E: ECFXParamRequired do
          ThrowException(
            'Could not execute CFX_ListRemoveDuplicates tag',
            PChar('A required Parameter, '+E.Message+', was not provided.'));
        on E: ECFX do
          ThrowException(
            'Error Occurred in tag CFX_ListRemoveDuplicates',
            PChar(E.Message));
    else
        ThrowException(
          'Error occurred in CFX tag CFX_ListRemoveDuplicates',
          'Unexpected error occurred while processing tag.');

    end;
    Free;
  end
end;

exports
ProcessTagRequest;
begin
end.
```

If you just want to use the CFX tag but don't have Delphi, you can find the compiled CFX_ListRemoveDuplicates.dll file in the "source code" folder on this book's CD-ROM.

The Parts of the Code Explained

Unfortunately, explaining Delphi programming completely in these few pages is not possible; however, this fairly simple code can be explained step-by-step. When you understand what's happening in this code, you can use it as a model for how to structure your own CFX tags in Delphi.

Here's what each part of the code does, one step at a time:

1. The library keyword at the top is the project's library initialization code. Basically, it tells Delphi to assemble the code into a DLL file named CFX_ListRemoveDuplicates.

2. The uses clause tells Delphi which Object Pascal units to make available to the project. By default, the general-purpose SysUtils unit is included, as well as the three units that make up the Delphi port of the CFXAPI. If these units weren't included, Delphi couldn't "understand" what the various CFX functions (such as GetAttribute and AddString) meant. Conceptually, this clause accomplishes the same thing as the #include cfx.h directive at the top of each C++ CFX tag.

3. In the type declaration part, any custom types for the Delphi project are established. The wizard establishes two custom types here:

   - ECFX, defined from Delphi's built-in Exception class. In other words, ECFX is a type of Exception.

   - ECFXParamRequired, defined from the ECFX type. In other words, a little hierarchy of Exception types has been set up. ECFX is a type of Exception, and ECFXParamRequired is a type of ECFX exception.

   Each type is handled in the except part of the code, near the end of the project's code.

4. The procedure declaration defines the entry point that ColdFusion will use to actually interact with the compiled DLL that this code creates. In general, you should never change or alter this line.

5. The var keyword indicates the beginning of the Delphi project's *variable declaration block*, which simply means that all variables must be defined here. This includes any variables that you add to the code, such as String or Integer-type variables. Also, the wizard places code that defines a PChar-type variable to correspond with each of the tag's parameters. To use any CFX StringSet functions in your Delphi code, a variable must be declared of the type TCFXStringSet. Similarly, to use any of the various query-manipulating functions in your code, a variable of type TCFXQuery must be defined in this block for each query that you need to manipulate.

6. The begin keyword indicates the end of the variable declaration block and the start of the code that should be executed each time the CFX tag is used in a ColdFusion template.

7. The next line uses the Create constructor to create a new pointer that represents the request coming into the tag from ColdFusion. This abstract object provides the other CFX functions a context in which to work.

8. The with MyCFXRequest line says that everything between the word begin and the corresponding end near the end of the code should be considered within the context of the MyCFXRequest pointer. This is just for ease of coding. For instance, it allows the AttributeExists function to be called alone rather than as MyCFXRequest.AttributeExists. If you include with, Delphi assumes that you're calling a function that belongs to the MyCFXRequest object unless you specify otherwise. See your Delphi documentation for more information about the with statement.

9. The next few lines deal with accepting and requiring the various attributes of the tag, as discussed in the preceding section.

10. The `OldList := pcList` line sets the `OldList` variable, which has been declared as type `String`, to the value of the `pcList` variable (from the tag's `LIST` parameter), which is of type `PChar`. You will sometimes find it handy to convert your `PChar` variables to `String` variables so that you can make use of Delphi's Pascal-style string-handling routines, such as the `Copy` and `Pos` functions (used in a moment). You can think of the `PChar` and `String` types as the Delphi equivalents of the `LPCSTR` and `CString` types, respectively, in C++.

11. The next line uses the `TCFXStringSet.Create` constructor to create a new StringSet object. This line is equivalent to the `pRequest->CreateStringSet()` line in the C++ version of the tag.

12. The next part of the code sets up a Delphi `repeat..until` block, which is similar to the equivalent `while` block used in the C++ version of the tag. This portion of the code is responsible for looking at the individual items in the list, picking them apart by commas (or whatever the user-specified delimiter is). Basically, the `repeat..until` structure says that everything after the word `repeat` will be repeated until the condition after the word `until` is met.

13. The line beginning with `TokenAt` uses Delphi's `Pos` procedure to set the `TokenAt` variable to get the position of the first delimiter character in the list passed to the tag by the calling template. The next line uses that position and Delphi's `Copy` procedure to set the `Token` variable to the current item in the list. The `Pos` and `Copy` procedures are like the `Find` and `Mid` functions, respectively, in normal CFML.

14. The CFX function `GetIndexForString` is then used to determine whether the current `Token` is already in the StringSet called `ssList`. If it is, the current `Token` must be a duplicate and shouldn't itself be added. If the `Token` isn't currently in the StringSet, the `GetIndexForString` function returns `-1`, which causes the code to use the `AddString` CFX function to add the value of the `Token` variable to the StringSet.

15. Right before the word `until`, the `Copy` procedure is used again to remove the current `Token` from the `OldList` variable. Thus, the next pass through the `repeat` loop will cause the `Token` to be the second item in the original list, and so on.

16. Because of the way this code is structured, the `repeat..until` loop will never test the last item in the list (as soon as no more delimiters appear in the `OldList` variable, the loop stops). You therefore need to test the last element of the list (which is held in the `OldList` variable after the loop finishes) separately. Now the StringSet holds the unique items from the original list.

17. You now use a simple Delphi `for..do` loop to iterate through each item in the StringSet and build the final `NewList` variable, which will be passed out to the calling template. The `Counter` variable is increased by one for each pass through the loop, and the `GetString` CFX function is used to get the current item in the StringSet, stick it onto the end of the `NewList` variable, and then add a delimiter character at the end. This step leaves an extra delimiter at the end of the list when the `for..do` loop finishes executing, which is easily removed right after the loop ends. See your Delphi documentation for more information about `for..do` loops.

Part
III

Ch
11

18. Because the `ssList` StringSet variable is no longer needed, the `Free` procedure is used to release the memory used by the variable. As a rule of thumb, every `Create` procedure in your code should have a corresponding `Free` procedure, to prevent problems such as memory leaks. See your documentation for more information about the `Create` and `Free` procedures.

19. The `SetVariable` line takes care of the last order of business that the tag needs to take care of to complete its task: passing the final version of the list (with all duplicates eliminated) to the calling template.

20. The `except` part of the code sets up an exception block that will kick in if any exceptions are encountered as the preceding code executes. An exception could be an operating system error (such as a disk being full or memory not being available), for example, or it could be an exception that your code throws on purpose, using the `raise` keyword.

    In any case, the code that the wizard built first tests to see whether the exception was of type `ECFXParamRequired`. If so, the `ThrowException` CFX function is used to halt all ColdFusion processing and display a message on the calling Web page. If the exception wasn't of type `ECFXParamRequired`, the code checks to see whether it was of type `ECFX`. If so, the error message passed to the exception by the `Create` function that raised the error is displayed to the calling template, by using the `E.Message` variable that Delphi makes available in `except` blocks. If the exception isn't of type `ECFXParamRequired` or `ECFX`, the `else` keyword kicks in and displays a general `Unexpected error occurred while processing request` message.

21. The final `Free` keyword frees the `MyCFXRequest` object, thus releasing the pointer to the abstract object that represents this particular tag request. Finally, the `exports` clause exposes the procedure to ColdFusion.

The preceding information may seem like a lot to learn at first, but remember that everything except for points 11 through 20 were written for you by the wizard and really aren't any more complicated than the equivalent parts of the C++ version of the tag. For a more detailed discussion about the general logic of the tag and what StringSets are, look at the section titled "Holding the List's Values in a StringSet" in Chapter 10.

When the finished code is compiled and run in the `CFXListTest.cfm` test template, it should prove to be functionally equivalent to the C++ version of the tag.

Building the `CFX_QueryAddColumn` Tag with Delphi

The second sample tag from Chapter 10 about creating CFX tags in C++ was the `CFX_QueryAddColumn` tag. You can port this tag to Delphi just as easily as you can the `CFX_ListRemoveDuplicates` tag.

To get started, run the Delphi CFX Tag Wizard again, this time specifying **`CFX_QueryAddColumn`** for the tag name (refer to Figure 11.1). The Delphi version of the tag should take the same parameters as the C++ version did, so on the wizard's second page, specify the following required parameters: **NAME**, **KEYCOLUMN**, **ADDCOLUMN**, **KEYS**, and **VALUES**. Also, specify **KEYS_DELIMITER** and **VALUES_DELIMITER** as optional parameters that default to a comma (just like the DELIMITER parameter for the CFX_ListRemoveDuplicates tag, as shown in Figure 11.2).

Creating Your Own Delphi Procedures to Use Internally

If you believe that you will use a particular routine or chunk of code again when working on another project, or that you need to use it more than once in the code for a single CFX tag, you might want to consider putting the chunk of code into its own procedure. A complete discussion about creating your own Delphi procedures (or functions) is well beyond the scope of this chapter, but I can demonstrate the basic idea for you by adapting the CFX_ListRemoveDuplicates code a bit.

The code snippet in Listing 11.3 creates a ListToStringSet procedure that parses a comma-delimited list into a corresponding StringSet. The procedure accepts three parameters: List, StringSet, and Delimiter. The procedure then uses the same basic repeat..until structure used earlier to move through the list one element at a time, adding each element to the StringSet as it goes.

Listing 11.3 Creating the ListToStringSet Function

```
procedure ListToStringSet(List:String; StringSet:TCFXStringSet;
Delimiter:PChar);
var
     TokenAt : Integer;
     Token : PChar;
begin

repeat
  {Find the next delimiter in the list}
  TokenAt := Pos(Delimiter, List);
  Token := PChar(Copy(List, 0, TokenAt-1));

  {Add the token to the StringSet}
  StringSet.AddString(Token);

  {Remove this token from the beginning of List}
  List := Copy(List, TokenAt+1, Length(List));
until
  Pos(Delimiter, List) = 0;

  {Add the remaining single value in List}
StringSet.AddString(PChar(List));

end;
```

You should place this procedure near the top of the project's code, before the ProcessTagRequest procedure. You can then use it quite simply in your code. For instance, if your code has defined an ssKeys variable of type TCFXStringSet, you can use code similar to the following snippet to use the ListToStringSet procedure. Doing so causes the ssKeys StringSet to be populated with the three strings in the list ("One", "Two", and "Three"):

```
ssKeys := TCFXStringSet.Create(CreateStringSet);
ListToStringSet('One,Two,Three', ssKeys, ',');
```

You can now use the ListToStringSet procedure in the CFX_QueryAddColumn tag to convert the passed-in KEYS and VALUES lists into StringSets.

TIP   Delphi also provides a built-in TStringList object that you can use to traverse the comma-separated elements in the list. See your Delphi documentation for more information about TStringList, particularly its CommaText property.

The Delphi Code

Listing 11.4 shows the final working code for the CFX_QueryAddColumn tag. The general logic of this code is the same as the C++ version of the tag, as discussed in the preceding chapter. For a detailed explanation about what this tag accomplishes and how to create new query result sets with the AddQuery function and the like, refer to the corresponding section in Chapter 10.

Listing 11.4   CFX_QueryAddColumn.dpr—Completed Delphi Code for the CFX_QueryAddColumn Tag

```
{CFX_QueryAddColumn: ColdFusion CFX Tag Source File}
{Purpose: Adds correlated data to an existing query result set.}

library CFX_QueryAddColumn;

uses
  SysUtils,
  cfx, cfxstr, cfxquery;

{Define our own custom error types}
type
  ECFX = class(Exception);
  ECFXParamRequired = class(ECFX);

{$R *.RES}
procedure ListToStringSet(List:String; StringSet:TCFXStringSet;
Delimiter:PChar);
var
    TokenAt : Integer;
    Token : PChar;
begin

repeat
  {Find the next delimiter in the list}
  TokenAt := Pos(Delimiter, List);
  Token := PChar(Copy(List, 0, TokenAt-1));
```

```
  {Add the token to the StringSet}
  StringSet.AddString(Token);

  {Remove this token from the beginning of List}
  List := Copy(List, TokenAt+1, Length(List));
until
  Pos(Delimiter, List) = 0;

  {Add the remaining single value in List}
  StringSet.AddString(PChar(List));

end;

procedure ProcessTagRequest(pRequest:pointer); cdecl; export;

var
    MyCFXRequest: TCFXRequest;
    pQuery, NewQuery: TCFXQuery;
    pcNAME: PChar;
    pcKEYCOLUMN: PChar;
    pcADDCOLUMN: PChar;
    pcKEYS: PChar;
    pcVALUES: PChar;
    pcKEYS_DELIMITER: PChar;
    pcVALUES_DELIMITER: PChar;

    ssKeys, ssValues, ssColumns: TCFXStringSet;
    intKeyColumn, intOldQueryColumnsCount, intAddedColumn : Integer;
    FoundAt, NewRow, OldRow, Col : Integer;
    LookingFor : PChar;

begin
    MyCFXRequest := TCFXRequest.Create(pRequest);
    with MyCFXRequest do begin
      try
        {Retrieve attributes from calling template}
        if AttributeExists('NAME') then pcNAME := GetAttribute('NAME')
          else raise ECFXParamRequired.Create('CFX_QueryAddColumns');

        if AttributeExists('KEYCOLUMN') then pcKEYCOLUMN :=
        ➥GetAttribute('KEYCOLUMN')
          else raise ECFXParamRequired.Create('CFX_QueryAddColumns');

        if AttributeExists('ADDCOLUMN') then pcADDCOLUMN :=
        ➥GetAttribute('ADDCOLUMN')
          else raise ECFXParamRequired.Create('CFX_QueryAddColumns');

        if AttributeExists('KEYS') then pcKEYS := GetAttribute('KEYS')
          else raise ECFXParamRequired.Create('CFX_QueryAddColumns');

        if AttributeExists('VALUES') then pcVALUES := GetAttribute('VALUES')
          else raise ECFXParamRequired.Create('CFX_QueryAddColumns');

        if AttributeExists('KEYS_DELIMITER') then pcKEYS_DELIMITER :=
        ➥GetAttribute('KEYS_DELIMITER')
```

Part

III

Ch

11

continues

Listing 11.4   Continued

```
      else pcKEYS_DELIMITER := ',';

  if AttributeExists('VALUES_DELIMITER') then pcVALUES_DELIMITER :=
➥GetAttribute('VALUES_DELIMITER')
    else pcVALUES_DELIMITER := ',';

  {Obtain QUERY result set from calling template}
  pQuery := TCFXQuery.Create(GetQuery);
    if pQuery.pCFXQuery = nil then
      raise ECFX.Create('Invalid QUERY parameter provided.');

  {Populate a StringSet with the "KEYS" parameter}
  ssKeys := TCFXStringSet.Create(CreateStringSet);
  ListToStringSet(pcKEYS, ssKeys, pcKEYS_DELIMITER);

  {Populate a StringSet with the "VALUES" parameter}
  ssValues := TCFXStringSet.Create(CreateStringSet);
  ListToStringSet(pcVALUES, ssValues, pcVALUES_DELIMITER);

  {Get the column names from the original query}
  ssColumns := TCFXStringSet.Create(pQuery.GetColumns);

  {Which column number is KEYCOLUMN?}
  intKeyColumn := ssColumns.GetIndexForString(pcKEYCOLUMN);
  {Stop if user specified a KEYCOLUMN that isn't in QUERY}
  if intKeyColumn = -1 then
    raise ECFX.Create('Invalid KEYCOLUMN parameter.');

  {How many columns were in the old query?}
  intOldQueryColumnsCount := ssColumns.GetCount;
  {The new column number will be that number, plus one}
  intAddedColumn := intOldQueryColumnsCount + 1;
  {Add NEWCOLUMN to the column list}
  ssColumns.AddString(pcADDCOLUMN);

  {Create new query, using revised column list}
  NewQuery := TCFXQuery.Create(AddQuery(pcName, ssColumns.pCFXStr));

  {For each row in the old query....}
  for OldRow := 1 to pQuery.GetRowCount do begin

    {Add a row to the new query...}
    NewRow := NewQuery.AddRow;

    {Copy in existing data from old query...}
    for Col := 1 to intOldQueryColumnsCount do
      NewQuery.SetData(NewRow, Col, pQuery.GetData(OldRow, Col));

    {What is the key value of the current row of the old query?}
    LookingFor := pQuery.GetData(OldRow, intKeyColumn);

    {Does key value in this row match up with a value in KEYS?}
    FoundAt := ssKeys.GetIndexForString(LookingFor);
```

```
        {if query's key value is not in KEYS list, add a row with a blank cell}
          if FoundAt = -1 then NewQuery.SetData(NewRow, intAddedColumn, '')
            {otherwise, add the corresponding element from the VALUES list}
            else NewQuery.SetData(NewRow, intAddedColumn,
              ⮕ssValues.GetString(FoundAt));

      end;

    except
        on E: ECFXParamRequired do
          ThrowException(
            'Could not execute CFX_QueryAddColumns tag',
            PChar('A required Parameter, '+E.Message+', was not provided.'));
        on E: ECFX do
          ThrowException(
            'Error Occurred in tag CFX_QueryAddColumns',
            PChar(E.Message));
      else
          ThrowException(
            'Error occurred in CFX tag CFX_QueryAddColumns',
            'Unexpected error occurred while processing tag.');

      end;

      Free;
    end
  end;

exports
ProcessTagRequest;
begin
end.
```

Part

III

Ch

11

If you just want to use the CFX tag but don't have Delphi, you can find the compiled `CFX_QueryAddColumn.dll` file in the "source code" folder on this book's CD-ROM.

Building the `CFX_GetDiskSpace` Tag in Delphi

The third sample tag from Chapter 10 was `CFX_GetDiskSpace`. To get started with writing this tag in Delphi, run the Delphi CFX Tag Wizard again, this time specifying **CFX_GetDiskSpace** for the tag name. The Delphi version of the tag should take the same parameter as the C++ version did, so on the second page of the wizard, specify **DRIVE** as a required parameter.

Listing 11.5 shows how you can code the tag in Delphi 4. Structurally, the code is extremely similar to the C++ version of the tag that was provided in Chapter 10. First, the GetSetting function is used to populate the RestrictTo variable with the corresponding value from the Registry (if any). Delphi's StrIComp function, which is not case sensitive, is then used to determine whether the tag is authorized to provide the information about the specified drive. For a detailed explanation of the GetSetting function and the general logic of the tag, refer to the corresponding section in Chapter 10.

Then, just as in the C++ version of the tag, the Windows GetDiskFreeSpaceEx function is used to get the actual data about the drive in question. Assuming that the function succeeds, variables are set in the calling template. If the function fails (for instance, if the DRIVE parameter does not represent a valid path), the Windows GetLastError function is used to get the number of the error that caused the problem, and an exception is raised providing the error number to the calling template.

 TIP Whenever you refer to Windows functions in your code, make sure that you include the Windows unit in the project's uses clause.

NOTE Listing 11.5 works only with Delphi 4 and up because it makes use of the Int64 (very large integer) data type, which is not available in previous versions of Delphi. If you are using Delphi 2 or Delphi 3, you need to adjust the code so that the ULARGE_INTEGER data type is used instead of Int64; doing so may require some extra steps. As an alternative, you can use the GetDiskFreeSpace Windows function instead of GetDiskFreeSpaceEx, or you can use Delphi's native DiskFree and DiskSize functions instead of using Windows functions at all. ■

Listing 11.5 CFX_GetDiskSpace.dpr—**The Delphi Version of**
CFX_GetDiskSpace

```
{CFX_GetDiskSpace: ColdFusion CFX Tag Source File}
{Purpose: Determines the amount of free space on the server's drive.}

library CFX_GetDiskSpace;

uses
  SysUtils, Windows,
  cfx, cfxstr, cfxquery;

{Define our own custom error types}
type
  ECFX = class(Exception);
  ECFXParamRequired = class(ECFX);
  ECFXWindowsNumber = class(ECFX);

{$R *.RES}
procedure ProcessTagRequest(pRequest:pointer); cdecl; export;

var
    MyCFXRequest: TCFXRequest;
    pcDRIVE: PChar;

    TotalBytes, FreeBytes, AvailToCaller: Int64;
    intLastError: Integer;
    RestrictTo: PChar;

begin
    MyCFXRequest := TCFXRequest.Create(pRequest);
```

```
with MyCFXRequest do begin
  try
      {Retrieve attributes from calling template}
      if AttributeExists('DRIVE') then pcDRIVE := GetAttribute('DRIVE')
        else raise ECFXParamRequired.Create('DRIVE');


      {Get the "Restriction" setting, if any, from the Registry}
      RestrictTo := GetSetting('RestrictTo');

      {If the setting existed in the Registry, and the DRIVE}
      {parameter does not match Registry value, raise exception}
      if Length(RestrictTo) > 0 then
        if StrIComp(RestrictTo, pcDrive) <> 0 then
          raise ECFX.Create('Access Denied.');


      {Get info about drive, using Windows GetDiskFreeSpaceEx function}
      {The info will be placed into the three Int64 variables}
      if GetDiskFreeSpaceEx(
          pcDRIVE,
          AvailToCaller,
          TotalBytes,
          @FreeBytes)

      {If the GetDiskFreeSpaceEx function was successful...}
      then begin
        {Set variables in calling template, using SetVariable from CFXAPI}
        {The IntToStr function is used to convert numbers to strings}
        SetVariable('Drive_FreeBytes', PChar(IntToStr(FreeBytes)));
        SetVariable('Drive_TotalBytes', PChar(IntToStr(TotalBytes)));

      {If the function was not successful...}
      end else begin
        {Get error number from Windows, stop CF, and display error message}
        intLastError := GetLastError();
        raise ECFXWindowsNumber.Create(IntToStr(intLastError));

      end;

  {Handle exceptions...}
  except
      {...if a required parameter was not supplied to the tag}
      on E: ECFXParamRequired do
        ThrowException(
          'Could not execute CFX_GetDiskSpace tag.',
          PChar('A required parameter, '+E.Message+', was not provided.'));
      {...if a numbered Windows error occurred}
      on E: ECFXWindowsNumber do
        ThrowException(
          'Error Occurred in tag CFX_GetDiskSpace',
          PChar('Windows Error Number '+E.Message+' occurred.'));
      {...if any other "we know what happened" error occurred}
      on E: ECFX do
        ThrowException(
```

continues

Part

III

Ch

11

Listing 11.5 Continued

```
                    'Error Occurred in tag CFX_GetDiskSpace',
                    PChar(E.Message));
         else
            {catch all other exceptions and raise them as CF errors}
            ThrowException(
              'Error occurred in CFX tag CFX_GetDiskSpace',
              'Unexpected error occurred while processing tag.');

         end;

         Free;
      end
  end;

  exports
  ProcessTagRequest;
  begin
  end.
```

If you just want to use the CFX tag but don't have Delphi, you can find the compiled CFX_GetDiskSpace.dll file in the "source code" folder on this book's CD-ROM.

You can now compile and use the code in the same way that you used the C++ version of the tag. For instance, you can test it with the DiskTestCFX.cfm template provided in Chapter 10.

TIP To get more control over the Registry, you can use Delphi's built-in TRegistry object instead of using the GetSetting CFX function. See your Delphi documentation for details.

Extending ColdFusion with COM/DCOM

Understanding the CFOBJECT Tag

The CFOBJECT tag is basically a remote call to an external program extension called a COM object. The *call* itself initializes the object and makes it accessible to the ColdFusion page that's calling it:

```
<CFOBJECT Action="Connect" Name="NTAccess" Class="NTUser.Group">
```

This says that you're connecting to an object on your machine with an identity of ntuser.groups. This object allows you to play around with the groups a person belongs to in the Windows NT user database. The object has been initialized with a name of ntaccess. In previous chapters you learned about the scope of variables; this is now the scope of any variable going to and coming from the object.

CFOBJECT allows you to use almost any COM object on your machine, another machine on the network, and in special cases, on machines on other networks. At the time of this writing CFOBJECT only supports COM, but in time CORBA and JavaBeans will be added in (according to Studio). COM is currently only supported by Windows NT 4.0 and Windows 95. A UNIX port is being worked on, and will probably be public by the time you read this. In order to use COM with Windows 95, you have to download DCOM for Windows Version 1.1 from http://www.microsoft.com/msdn.

What You Need to Use an Object

To use an object, you need to know its program ID or filename, the methods and properties available for it, and the arguments and return types of its methods. In most cases this information is provided to you in the object's documentation. If it's not, you have to hunt it down yourself using the OLEView utility. (See "Understanding the OLEView Program," later in this chapter.)

Now that you have the object's program ID, you have to say how you want to connect to it. There are two ways you connect, which fits the two types of objects. The standard connect method is Create, which takes a COM object (usually a .dll file) and instantiates it, which means the CFOBJECT tag wakes it up for use. The other connection type is Connect, which links to an object (usually an .exe file) that is already running on the server. All you need now is a scope name.

Of course, there are a few other attributes and options for the tag. These are listed in Table 12.1.

Table 12.1 CFOBJECT **Attributes**

Name	Status	Description
ACTION	Required	Create or Connect. Use Create to instantiate a COM object (typically a .dll) prior to invoking methods or properties. Use Connect to connect to a COM object (typically an .exe) that is already running on the server specified in SERVER.
CLASS	Required	Enter the component ProgID for the object you want to invoke.

Name	Status	Description
NAME	Optional	Enter a name for the object. This is the scope for all operations with the object later in the template.
TYPE	Optional	This specifies the type of object connecting to. This is not currently supported by CFOBJECT but may be put in soon. Values can be COM, CORBA, or JavaBeans. COM is default.
SERVER	Required	Required when CONTEXT="Remote". Enter a valid server name using UNC (universal naming convention) or DNS (Domain Name Server) conventions, in one of the following forms: SERVER="\\lanserver" SERVER="lanserver" SERVER="http://www.servername.com" SERVER="www.servername.com" SERVER="127.0.0.1"

Using an Object

Now that Table 12.1 showed how to connect to an object, you have to actually use it. This is done by making use of the CFSET tag. Using this tag, you set a variable to the return value of one of the object's operations. Use CFOBJECT in Listing 12.1, which connects to the object called NTAccess.Groups and allows you to view and manipulate user and group information on a Windows NT server. This example returns the full name of a user (#username#) on a server named HOME. The object used can be found at this link: http://www.zaks.demon.co.uk/code/.

Listing 12.1 CFOBJECT Example: Getting Username from Group

```
<!-- Create object -->
<CFOBJECT CLASS="ntaccess.groups"
    ACTION="Create"
    NAME="GetName">

<!-- Set a couple of properties -->
<!--- Set the servername of the machine that holds the information we want-->
<CFSET GetName.Server="\\HOME">
<!--- Set the username we want the information for -->
<CFSET GetName.User="#username#">

<!--- Call a method with a property --->
<CFSET GetName.User = GetName.StripDomain(GetName.User)>
<CFSET NAME = GetName.GetUsersFullName()>

<!-- Output result -->
<CFOUTPUT>
    #name#
</CFOUTPUT>
```

Once you connect to the object, you have to set some of its properties.

Part
III

Ch

12

Setting Object Properties

A *property* is a variable setting within the object itself. You can read from it and write to it. Setting properties consists of passing information into the object for later use. A property value is saved for the life of the template on which it is called. Properties can be used alone as variables or combined with methods, which are the COM object's actual workers. A *method* is a function that performs some operation. Methods can use pre-set properties as arguments or can have arguments added into their operation. When an argument is used in a method, it must be contained within double quotation marks. The example calls the geterrorinfo method and passes it three attributes:

```
<cfset temp = ftp.geterrorinfo("ErrorCode", "WinErrorCode", "ErrorText")>
```

The first property set is the server. While in these examples the object scope is set on the left side, normally it can be set on either. One note with this specific program is that the getname.user property holds both the username and the domain it's attached to. For this reason, the first method used is stripdomain. This method takes a username that has already been set and removes the domain information from it. This has to be done because the second method, GetUsersFullName, needs just the username. You'll notice that this method doesn't send any arguments. This is because it uses the current username set as a property. All methods must have open and close parentheses at the end even if no arguments are being passed. You might be thinking this all looks rather easy—it is. Now look at what properties and methods actually exist for this object.

Existing Object Properties and Methods

An object's properties often return information or store information about a component. The properties of the ntaccess.groups object are listed in Table 12.2.

Table 12.2 Properties for ntaccess.groups Object

Property	Description
User	The username to be queried, either "DOMAIN\USERNAME" or "USERNAME". If calling a domain controller, it appears that the domain name part must be removed; the function StripDomain exists to do this.
Server	This holds the server name (in the "\\servername" format), or can be left blank to reference the local machine.
Global	This specifies whether local groups or global groups are queried, global groups are only available using domain controllers, and should be set to TRUE for global groups.

Methods (also called *functions*) perform actions and have return values you can use. They are always set with a place for arguments, even if no arguments are present. Some of the methods used by the ntaccess.groups object are listed in Table 12.3.

Table 12.3 Methods for `ntaccess.groups` Object

Method	Description
GetGroups	This queries the specified server and fetches the relevant list of groups; 0 is returned for success, other numbers indicate failure.
CheckGroups("GroupName")	This searches the previously retrieved list of groups for the specified group; this is not case sensitive, and returns true if the specified group is found.
StripDomain("domain\username")	This takes a string and removes the domain part. The string is returned.
GetUsersFullName	This returns the user's full name as set in the user manager; the server and user properties must be set first.

Examine a method in a bit more detail. Assume you're using the OLEViewer to look at an object's method (more on the OLEViewer later). The Execute method for this object has three arguments:

```
Recordset* Execute(
[in] BSTR CommandText,
[out, optional] VARIANT* RecordsAffected,
[in, optional, defaultvalue(-1)] long Options);
```

The first is expecting a variable and is required. The second is expecting to return the number of records affected to a variable name you select. This variable name must be in quotation marks. According to the method information, this is optional. The final attribute, which is also optional, can be set with an option and has a default value of -1.

Example 1:

```
<CFSET INSQL="select country from countries where country LIKE 'b%'" >
<CFSET RecordCount=0>
<CFSET #rsGrid#=dataConn.Execute(INSQL,"RecordCount",1) >
```

Example 2:

```
<CFSET #rsGrid#=dataConn.ExecuteINSQL,"RecordCount") >
```

Example 3:

```
<CFSET #rsGrid#=dataConn.Execute(INSQL) >
```

Example 4:

```
<CFSET #rsGrid#=dataConn.Execute("select country
➥from countries where country LIKE 'b%'") >
```

Notice that Example 1 is the most comprehensive. It takes into account all of the method's arguments, sets a default value on the variable being returned, and sets the query as a variable for neatness and ease of alteration.

Threading Problems

While COM is a nice technique, it is still a growing technology. This means that a module will not work as normally expected in some cases. You may have a threading problem if ColdFusion seems to hang after executing a template that contains a CFOBJECT tag. This may be because the object does not have a threading model, and potentially has not been made thread-safe. This may be due to older versions of Delphi or Visual Basic being used. To work around these, you should change the threading model to Free by using the OLEView program.

Changing the Threading Model

To change the threading model to Free, run the OLEView program and find the object as follows:

1. Select the object and click the Implementation tab in the right window.
2. Check the Threading Model for the entry marked Inproc Server.
3. If it is set to None, you must change it to Apartment.

Threading is explored in more detail later, when you build an object from scratch. (See "Creating COM Objects" later in this chapter.)

Looping Over a COM Collection

Besides the standard character, integer, and string data types, CFOBJECT supports arrays both as input arguments and return values. Returned arrays are called *collections*. A collection is referred to as a group rather than individually, which means that a single variable can contain multiple pieces of returned data. You can normally access the first piece of data from the collection, but not the others. To solve this problem, the CFLOOP tag has been modified to add a collection attribute to it. This setting allows you to go over each element in a collection returned from an object.

In Listing 12.2 ITEM is assigned a variable called file2, so that each item in the collection is referenced with each cycle in the CFLOOP. In the CFOUTPUT section, the file2 item's name property is referenced for display.

The example employs a COM object to output a list of files. In this example, FFUNC is a collection of file2 objects.

Listing 12.2   Item Assigned a Variable Called file2

```
<CFOBJECT CLASS=FileFunctions.files
   NAME=FFunc
   ACTION=Create>

<CFSET FFunc.Path = "c:\">
<CFSET FFunc.Mask = "*.*" >
<CFSET FFunc.attributes = 16 >
<CFSET x=FFunc.GetFileList()>
```

```
<CFLOOP COLLECTION=#FFUNC# ITEM=file2>
    <CFOUTPUT>
        #file2.name# <BR>
    </CFOUTPUT>
</CFLOOP>
```

N O T E The CFOBJECT tag can be disabled from the ColdFusion Administrator for security reasons.
It can also be disabled from the Registry by setting the value EnableCFOBJECT to 0 in
the Software/Allaire/Coldfusion/Currentversion/Server subkey of the
HKEY_LOCAL_MACHINE hive. Touching the Registry is not suggested unless you know what you're
doing and have a very recent backup. ▤

With the release of ColdFusion Studio, the inclusion of tags such as CFOBJECT has gotten a lot
easier. A CFOBJECT button has been added to the control bar's Advanced ColdFusion Tags
section. By pressing this button, you get a small wizard that prompts you for the values you
want for your object (see Figure 12.1). This is simply the CFOBJECT tag itself, not the setting of
variables or a view of the objects that exist (which are covered next). One word of warning,
though: The TYPE setting is not implemented in the current version of CFOBJECT. Only COM is
currently supported. The type setting makes it look like CORBA and JavaBeans are supported
as well. You have to wait for 4.0 to see if this is true.

FIGURE 12.1

The CFOBJECT tag
wizard.

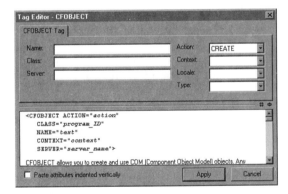

Understanding the OLEView Program

The OLEView program is probably the single most important tool you will use when dealing with
COM objects. To use a COM object, you must know its program ID, methods, and properties.
This information usually comes in the documentation bundled with a distributed object. When
this information is not given, it must still be found. That's where the OLEView program comes in.

Part
III

Ch
12

The OLEView program retrieves all OLE objects and controls from the registry, then presents the information in an easy-to-use format that can be viewed. Figure 12.2 shows the components sorted into groups for easy viewing.

FIGURE 12.2

Objects are retrieved and sorted into categories.

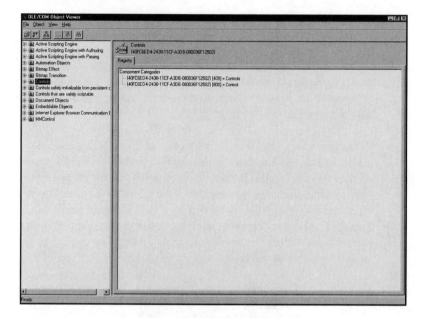

You can see the program ID by selecting the category and then the component you want to use (see Figure 12.3); in this case it's ColdFusion.CFFtp.3. This also gives you access to options for the object's operation. Threading (which is discussed later) is one of the options that can be controlled at this point.

The selected object can now be expanded to show all of the interfaces supported (see Figure 12.4). In most cases, the interface on top has the information needed. By right-clicking the object, an option to view it comes up. This accesses the TypeInfo view, which contains the object's methods and properties. Some objects will not have any access to the TypeInfo area. This is determined when an object is built and the language used.

An object's *properties* are information that can be read from or written to the object.

They can be seen as storage variables that hold information in the object (see Figure 12.5) and become more important when combined with methods.

Methods are functions that are used to execute an operation. These operations are the core of the COM object. A method passes information to this core code and, in many cases, returns a result (see Figure 12.6).

This program is now a standard item included with the distribution of Visual C++ 5. The latest version can always be downloaded from the Microsoft site at http://www.microsoft.com/oledev/olecom/oleview.htm. The current version hasn't changed in the last year.

FIGURE 12.3

A component's ID is shown when you select that component.

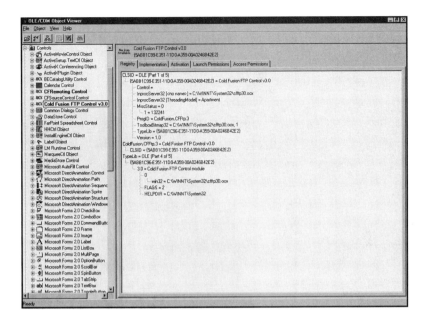

FIGURE 12.4

All interfaces supported for an object.

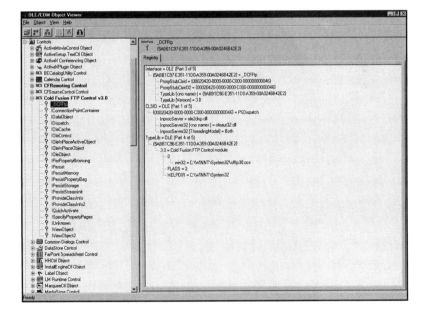

FIGURE 12.5

The properties available.

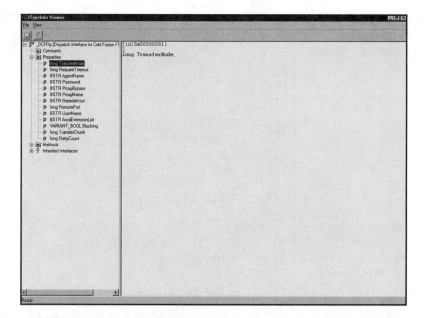

FIGURE 12.6

The methods available.

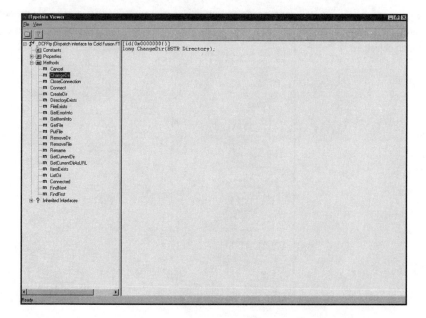

Once you've acquired the object you want to use, you may need to register it with Windows NT in order for ColdFusion (or anything else) to find it. Some objects may be deployed with their own setup programs that register objects automatically, while others may require the use of the Windows NT regsvr32 utility. You can invoke `regsvr32.exe` either from a command prompt (also known as a DOS box) or using the Windows NT Run command, in the following form:

```
regsvr32 c:\path\filename.dll
```

This is the standard registration for VC++ and VB COM objects. Java-based objects have to be placed in the Java path. Other objects written in other languages may have different registration needs. These should be in the documentation that comes with the object.

Understanding COM

This is the point in the chapter where everyone is tempted to roll their eyes and move on. Everyone wants to use COM, but few really care what it is. This section is short and to the point.

COM is the Component Object Model set forth as a software specification from Microsoft. It is an evolving software technique that includes such things as Active Server/ActiveX components, Active Data Objects (ADO), OCX, Normandy server components, Windows NT BackOffice server components, and third-party controls. One of COM's biggest problems is that the name keeps changing; that makes it hard to know what you're really dealing with.

COM objects, as used by ColdFusion, are dynamically linked (late binding) components. *Late binding* means that the component is not linked into ColdFusion until it's actually needed. If you want to change a component on a live site, you must make sure no one is using it; if it's not in use, it's free to be swapped out.

Objects can be distributed either as dynamic link libraries (DLLs) or as executables (EXEs). COM components are fully language-independent and can be written using almost any procedural language, from modern VC++ and Java down to Ada and Pascal. Almost any language can be modified to use COM components. Later in the chapter you write a simple object in VC++.

COM works by taking chunks of code and giving specific access to them via interfaces. An *interface* is an abstraction layer between two software components. On one side is the service calling the COM object (in this case, ColdFusion) and on the other is the object itself. The calling service doesn't have to know anything about the object it's calling, only what interface is supported and what methods and properties are exposed.

To represent an interface graphically, you use a floating box with plug-in jacks extending to one side for each interface (see Figure 12.7).

The COM objects used by ColdFusion must be server-side, non-visual objects rather than those with a user interface. If an object with a user interface is used, the interface pops up on the Web server each time it is called. This can use up the machine's memory, pulling the site to a halt.

Part
III

Ch
12

FIGURE 12.7

A graphical representation of a COM object.

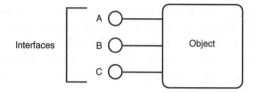

COM components can be transparently relocated on a network. A component on a different machine on a network is treated the same as a component on the local system. Components can also be referenced on machines outside of the local network via DCOM.

DCOM (Distributed Component Object Model) is an extension of COM and was created to allow transparent access to components residing on other machines. This is greater than the standard COM capability to be used by any machine on a network. DCOM can be accessed across the Internet. This is a big push for Microsoft when dealing with big businesses that have Wide Area Networks (WANs). The CFOBJECT tag deals with this just by setting the location and then treating it like any other COM object. One thing to note is that DCOM is also known as COM+.

Creating COM Objects

You use Microsoft Visual C++ version 5.0 for your example on a COM framework. This release has a built-in wizard to help generate a COM object's structure. Because COM is both an extension of an old idea for Microsoft (OLE) and the core of a new one (ASP), most of the Microsoft visual languages (Visual Basic, Visual C++, Visual Java) have COM wizards built into them. The wizard exists to make the writing of an object quick and easy. Older methods of object writing took a long time with lots of code. This is still needed when using languages without a COM wizard.

Once you start your Visual C++, select File and choose the New File selector (Ctrl+N also works). Because this is a COM object, you're going to choose the ATL COM AppWizard and then enter a project name (see Figure 12.8). You really don't have to worry about a location because it's generated based on the name you give. The only reason the option is given is if you want the files stored somewhere else.

You're only going to write a small object, so you want only a .dll file (see Figure 12.9). You'll rarely ever write any form of COM executable or service, so you should not worry about those. The merging of proxy and stub code is really used when you're writing an executable object. It cuts down on size by lumping all the files into a single package. Because you're not dealing with executables, ignore that. The support Microsoft Foundation Classes (MFC) allow you to program. The good thing is that MFC has a lot of easy commands that can enhance your code. The bad thing is that you have to distribute the MFC runtime DLL with any code you write using it. If you don't need MFC, don't check this box.

At this point you're finished with the basics and can choose Finish. Once you do so, the program generates all of the basic code you need for your object.

FIGURE 12.8

Start building a COM
object with the ATL
COM AppWizard.

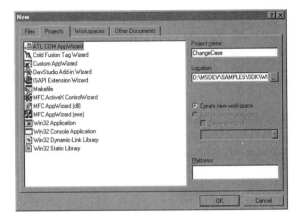

FIGURE 12.9

Setting server types.

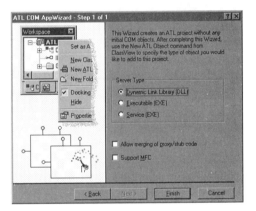

You now have a skeleton to hold the real pieces of the object (see Figure 12.10). To add these
pieces, you have to go to the Insert menu and select New ATL Object.

Remember that you're just writing a basic, non-graphical object. This means that you are limited at this point about what you can choose. Select the Object category and then select the
Simple Object icon (see Figure 12.11). This is nearly all you need for the generation of your
object (this and the code that goes behind it).

Here you can control all of your object's naming conventions (see Figure 12.12). A simple,
descriptive name is usually best. Once you write in a short name, it is copied over to all of the
fields with slight variations. You wouldn't usually touch any of these except for the program ID.
This is how the CFOBJECT tag communicates with the object, and many developers like to alter
it with easier-to-read variables. You have to go to the Attributes tab to finish this part of the
process.

Remember that threading issue mentioned earlier? This is where it comes from (in some
cases). Without going deeply into threading, just assume that Both is the option you want. This
allows multiple users to use the object and makes sure the object can be used with both older
and newer COM applications.

Part
III

Ch
12

FIGURE 12.10

All of the skeleton code is generated.

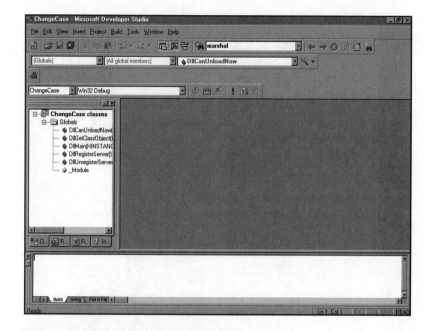

FIGURE 12.11

Selecting the object type.

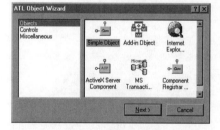

FIGURE 12.12

Adding the object information.

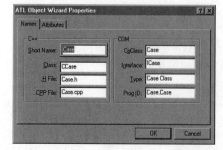

The next point is the interface method used. You want your object to be late binding, while early binding is the default. Choose Duel, so you can use what you need. Aggregation is used when one object is actually a front end to another object. It's unlikely you'll ever do that, but you should know where to set it. For now, set it to No (see Figure 12.13). You're not going to deal with the final options at all and they can be ignored.

FIGURE 12.13

Setting object attributes.

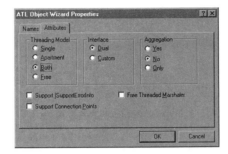

You now have your object. It's totally legal and will compile at this point. The only thing it is missing is something to do and a way to communicate outside. You need to create a method in order to give an object something to do (see Figure 12.14).

FIGURE 12.14

Add a method to the object.

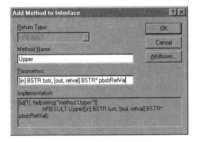

This is the point where you really have to know some VC++ (or whatever language you're using). You must give the method a name, which is used to call it. The method's parameters are set as what is expected in and what is expected out (if anything). In this case, you're setting a single parameter in what will be a string value. The return value is of the same value. You can also set attributes for the method, but in this case it has no effect.

You're not using any properties with this example, but they can be set using the same basic instructions as the method. Properties consist of a few simple settings—a type, which is the value it expects to store; a name to access the property with; and a location for parameters, if you want to add any custom information to the property. Look at Figure 12.15 to see what property is set for this example. Finally, there is a section that defines the property's access status. While it doesn't actually use these words, the idea of read-only, write-only, and full access is here.

Now that the method is defined, you have only to set some code to go with it. The following example is a modified sample given out by Microsoft for teaching COM. The first method takes in a string and changes it to uppercase.

```
CComBSTR bstrTemp(bstr);
wcsupr(bstrTemp);
*pbstrRetVal = bstrTemp.Detach();
return S_OK;
```

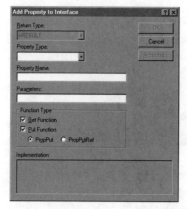

FIGURE 12.15

Add a property to the object.

The second method does the same thing, but returns lowercase:

```
CComBSTR bstrTemp(bstr);
wcslwr(bstrTemp);
*pbstrRetVal = bstrTemp.Detach();
return S_OK;
```

As you can see, a COM object is relatively easy to write. ●

Extending ColdFusion with CORBA

Introduction to CORBA

ColdFusion has been around for over three years. It has been used on some major sites in the field of e-commerce, finance, and even government, but for all its accomplishments the majority of the business world hasn't adopted it. That is, until now.

For a product to be accepted as an enterprise-level applications server for many in the business world, it must support certain technologies. One of these technologies is a distributed object system called CORBA (Common Object Request Broker Architecture).

CORBA is basically a specification for a system of cross-platform distributed software objects created by the Object Management Group (OMG). Because it is an object specification, all access to objects' functions are encapsulated and are accessible through well-defined interfaces. The location and implementation of each object are hidden from the client requesting the services. Remember that we're talking about a software object specification, not an object-oriented language (though you can write CORBA objects in an OO language).

CORBA objects are distributed by nature and can be located anywhere on a machine or network. CORBA objects can interact with objects written for and working on other operating systems. CORBA objects can be written in any programming language for which there is a mapping from OMG IDL to that language.

CORBA is only a specification, and various vendors and research organizations have provided implementations for the ORB (Object Request Broker). The most popular of the commercial ORBs are VisiBroker from Borland (http://www.inprise.com/visibroker), Orbix from IONA (http://www.orbix.com), and CorbaPlus from Expersoft (http://www.expersoft.com).

ColdFusion supports CORBA on both Windows and Solaris through the CFOBJECT tag. As you've seen in the previous chapter, this tag is used to connect to distributed objects outside the core ColdFusion. Much of the description and usage carries over from that section. CORBA is currently only supported in the Enterprise edition of ColdFusion 4 and the level of CORBA functionality supported is 2.0.

What Is the OMG?

The Object Management Group (OMG) is an organization that was created in 1989 by a number of computer technology companies with the purpose of "promoting theory and practice of object technology in distributed computing systems." Originally formed by 13 companies, the OMG now has over 800 software vendors, developers, and end users. Their primary goal is to create and promote a common framework for object-oriented applications.

The OMG hosts a Web site at http://www.omg.org that always contains the most up-to-date documentation on CORBA as well as other related material. From here you can find links to other sites using CORBA, offering products related to it as well as advanced training materials.

How CORBA Works

In order to understand how CORBA works, you're going to walk through it step by step and use a number of pictures. CORBA follows a very simple flow of operations. Figure 13.1 shows the basic steps used by CORBA to perform an operation. Basically, a client makes a request that is accepted by the ORB. The ORB takes this request, performs various operations (which is discussed in a moment), and hands the request to an object service. Any return values are passed back through the ORB to the client for use. This is the simplest, most basic level of how CORBA works. You take each of the three pieces of the CORBA operation, examine each one in step, and see where ColdFusion fits in.

FIGURE 13.1
CORBA's flow of operation.

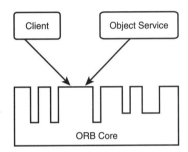

The Client: ColdFusion

The CFObject tag has been enhanced to handle not only its standard COM/DCOM, but all interactions with CORBA objects. The only difference is minor changes in the CFObject tag itself. The setting of parameters and use of functions remain exactly the same.

The basic structure (as seen in Figure 13.2) is the ColdFusion engine using the CFObject tag—the CFObject tag now interfacing with a layer that allows it to communicate with objects. This layer is VisiBroker 3.2 for C++. On the whole, the details of how ColdFusion communicates with an ORB are unnecessary at this point. The ORB section discusses how the client talks to the ORB. Knowledge of the communication layer (VisiBroker 3.2) may help in creation of ORBs later on.

FIGURE 13.2
ColdFusion's basic communication structure with the ORB.

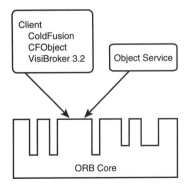

Part

III

Ch

13

CFOBJECT Attributes for CORBA   When using the CFOBJECT tag for CORBA, the attributes required and used differ from those used for COM. The two major differences are in type and location. In COM, there are two types of objects; services that are running and objects that need to be initiated to be used. Both of these are treated the same way under the hood, but ColdFusion needs to be told by using the Action attribute. CORBA doesn't make any distinction and doesn't need an action. Additionally, CORBA is distributed by its very nature, much like DCOM is. Therefore, the server attribute is also unnecessary. Other than those attributes, all the others are required. The following code is an example of the CFOBJECT syntax used to call a CORBA object. See Table 13.1 for a listing of all the attributes used by CFOBJECT when dealing with CORBA.

```
<CFOBJECT TYPE="CORBA"
   CONTEXT="context"
   CLASS="file or naming service"
   NAME="text">
```

Table 13.1   Attributes for CFOBJECT When Dealing with CORBA

Name	Status	Description
Type	Required	Specifies the object type to be accessed. May be COM or CORBA. This must be set to CORBA in order for ColdFusion to run CORBA applications.
CONTEXT	Required	Specifies one of the following:
		IOR—ColdFusion uses the Interoperable Object Reference (IOR) to access the CORBA server.
		NameService—ColdFusion uses the naming service to access server.
Class	Required	Specifies different information, depending on the CONTEXT specification:
		If CONTEXT is IOR—Specifies the name of a file that contains the stringified version of the IOR. ColdFusion must be able to read this file at all times; it should be local to ColdFusion server or on the network in an open, accessible location.
		If CONTEXT is NameService—Specifies a period-delimited naming context for the naming service, such as Allaire.Department.Doc.empobject.
NAME	Required	Enter a name for the object. Your application uses this to reference the CORBA object's methods and attributes.

How ColdFusion Connects

ColdFusion uses runtime libraries from VisiBroker (C++ 3.2 runtime libraries) to locate and invoke objects. You need an appropriate compiler or development package to actually write or compile a service object. Three such packages are VisiBroker for C++ on Windows NT/95 that requires Visual C++ 4.2 (or higher) or an equivalent compiler; Borland's JBuilder, which uses its own runtime libraries; and Java 1.2 beta 4 has a number of CORBA-related modules that should help in the creation of ORBs and object services.

ColdFusion supports CORBA through the Dynamic Invocation Interface (DII). To use CFOBJECT with CORBA objects, you need to know either the name of the file containing the information about the IOR or the object's naming context in the naming service. This is covered within the context and class attributes of the CFOBJECT tag. One major difference from COM/DCOM is that there is no ObjectViewer that can be used to view object capabilities. This means you need to know the object's attributes, method names, and method signatures. Additionally, ColdFusion does not support user-defined types like structures. This is a minor limitation and may change in the future, but shouldn't hold anyone back.

When connecting, the client has no knowledge of the CORBA object's location or implementation details, nor which ORB is used to access the object. A client may only invoke methods that are specified in the CORBA object's interface. A CORBA object's interface is defined using the OMG Interface Definition Language (IDL). An *interface* defines an object type and specifies a set of named methods and parameters, as well as the exception types that these methods may return. An IDL compiler translates the CORBA object definitions into a specific programming language according to the appropriate OMG language mapping. All of this is dealt with in more detail later. In order for this process to start, you have to examine how ColdFusion calls the ORB and makes use of the information.

The ORB: Communications

The purpose of the ORB is to facilitate communication between a client and an object service. A request comes from the client and is intercepted (through methods that this book deals with later), translated into a binary format, sent to the ORB associated with the service, translated back into a request, and given to the object service. The object service does whatever it has to do at this point and sends the results down to its ORB to have the process reversed. The process of encoding and decoding is called *marshalling/unmarshalling*.

As you can see in Figure 13.3, an ORB actually has many different types of interfaces. Two interfaces are used for direct communication with the client: the Dynamic Invocation Interface (DII) and the IDL stubs. ColdFusion operates through the DII, so you concentrate your attention on its use.

Part

III

Ch

13

The way the ORB talks to the object service is on the other side of the communication. This is done either through the IDL skeleton or the Dynamic Skeleton Interface.

The Dynamic Invocation Interface (DII)   You are constrained to using the Dynamic Invocation Interface (DII) approach because of the way ColdFusion processes information. This is basically the same thing as using *automation* for COM/DCOM servers and has the same performance penalties associated with late binding.

The DII interface allows a client to directly access the underlying request mechanisms provided by an ORB. Applications use the DII to dynamically issue requests to objects without requiring IDL interface-specific stubs to be linked in. It is used when at compile time a client does not have knowledge about an object that it wants to invoke. Once an object is discovered, the client program can obtain a definition of it, issue a parameterized call to it, and receive a reply from it—all without having a type-specific client stub for the remote object.

FIGURE 13.3

The architecture of an ORB core.

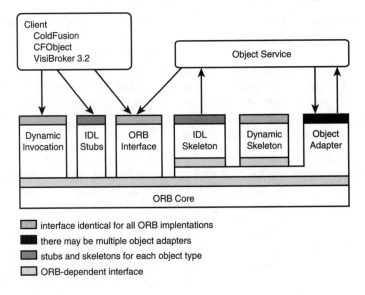

interface identical for all ORB implentations

there may be multiple object adapters

stubs and skeletons for each object type

ORB-dependent interface

Object Request Broker (ORB)

An ORB is the middleware that establishes the client-server relationships between objects. Using an ORB, a client can transparently invoke a method on a server object, which can be on the same machine or across a network. The ORB intercepts the call and is responsible for finding an object that can implement the request, pass it the parameters, invoke its method, and return the results. The client does not have to be aware of where the object is located, its programming language, its operating system, or any other system aspects that are not part of an object's interface. In so doing, the ORB provides interoperability between applications on different machines in heterogeneous distributed environments and seamlessly interconnects multiple object systems.

To put it simpler, this means that the ORB takes a request from ColdFusion, finds the object that ColdFusion is trying to communicate with, and sends the request to it. The object service can reside on the same or another machine. The system views client requests as local procedure calls. Any response from the object service is then returned through the ORB to ColdFusion.

The ORB hides the object location, implementation, execution state, and communication mechanisms. An object reference is created whenever a CORBA object is created. Clients use the object references to make requests on the object. These object references can be obtained via object creation, directory service, or converting stringified IORs.

OMG Interface Definition Language (OMG IDL)

An object's *interface* specifies the methods and properties that an object supports. Interfaces for objects are defined in the *OMG Interface Definition Language* (OMG IDL). Interfaces are similar to classes in C++ and interfaces in Java.

An important feature of OMG IDL is its *language independence*. OMG IDL is a declarative language, not a programming language; as such, it does not provide features such as control constructs, nor is it directly used to implement distributed applications. Instead, *language mappings* determine how OMG IDL features are mapped to the facilities of a given programming language. Language mappings force interfaces to be defined separately from object implementations. This allows objects to be constructed using different programming languages and yet still communicate with one another. Language-independent interfaces are important within large networks, since not all programming languages are supported or available on all platforms. Language mappings for C, C++, Java, Smalltalk, and Ada have been specified at this time.

Logging

A directory for logging output from VisiBroker is created when you start ColdFusion Enterprise 4. This directory is called `vbroker\log` and its location is determined as follows:

1. If VisiBroker is already installed on the server, the log directory is the directory pointed to by the `VBROKER_ADM` environment variable in the registry.

2. If this is a new VisiBroker installation, the log directory is created on the root of the drive from which ColdFusion 4 is started. For example, if ColdFusion 4 is installed on `c:\cfusion`, the log directory is `c:\vbroker\log`.

3. If the creation of the log directory on the root fails, the directory is created in the ColdFusion 4 directory.

Who Supports COM/DCOM, CORBA, and JavaBeans at Allaire?

Bushan Byragani is Allaire's Component languages guru. He's responsible for COM/DCOM, CORBA and JavaBeans support in ColdFusion. ●

Customizing ColdFusion Studio

Many of us who developed early HTML and ColdFusion applications searched for a development tool that would work the way we do and accelerate our development pace. For most of us, this was much like the search for the Holy Grail, and we settled for Notepad. The problem with most of the tools on the market was not their features, but their interfaces. They just got in the way of the development process.

ColdFusion Studio 3.0, built on the popular HomeSite development tool, lightened the load for development teams everywhere by allowing a great deal of customization, as well as access to data sources and remote ColdFusion server resources. In version 4, ColdFusion Studio's customization features have become so powerful that virtually any development style can be accommodated. In this chapter you'll learn to customize ColdFusion Studio to make development easier and faster.

Customization Features in ColdFusion Studio 4

ColdFusion Studio 4 allows you to suit the development environment to your needs by allowing you to assign your own keyboard shortcuts, organize and build your own menus, create code templates to reduce type time, build your own advanced tag dialog boxes, and set the look and feel of your environment. The majority of the customization features are menu driven, but using Visual Tools Markup Language (VTML) and its counterpart, Wizard Markup Language (WIZML), you can create powerful tools that extend the capabilities of your development environment.

Two of the most welcome customization features in ColdFusion Studio are keyboard shortcuts and code templates. Every time your hand leaves your keyboard to move the mouse and click on a menu, you waste seconds that can add up to hours during the lifetime of a project. Keyboard shortcuts allow you to use predefined key combinations to access almost any function of the development environment. You can define your own keyboard shortcuts quickly and easily for simple functions such as saving a document to more complex operations—for example, converting a selection to lowercase or stepping through an application using the ColdFusion Studio debugger. You can even define keyboard shortcuts to insert ColdFusion Markup Language (CFML) tags. In addition, there's an even cooler way to add frequently used code to your application pages.

Code templates allow you to define a series of characters that ColdFusion Studio expands into a predefined set of code. Using this feature, if you type dt2, ColdFusion Studio automatically converts it to `<!DOCTYPE HTML PUBLIC "-//IETF//DTD// HTML 2.0//EN>`. For frequently used sections of code, this feature can save you many minutes per session. But wait—there's more!

You can also build snippets of code that can have beginning and ending sections, just as you could in earlier versions. Now you can assign these snippets their own keyboard shortcuts. You could, for instance, type Home, hold down Ctrl+Shift and press the back arrow to select this text, and then press Ctrl+Shift+A to add the proper link code around it so that it reads `<A HREF="/">Home</a>`, all without touching your mouse.

When the mouse is more efficient, having icons and menus organized in a logical manner is helpful so that features are easy to find. Unfortunately, everyone has a different idea of what "logical" means, and my ideal layout probably would seem awkward to any other developer. ColdFusion Studio accommodates this difference by allowing you to organize existing menus and create your own. You also can move menus, allowing you to float menus anywhere on your desktop or dock them in any order inside ColdFusion Studio. You can even choose the icons for each menu item.

Tag editors, Tag Insight, and the Tag Inspector allow you to access the attributes of any tag quickly and easily. Tag editors are dialog boxes that accept input and generate the correct code for a tag. Tag Insight watches as you type and shows the attributes and values available for the tag you are typing. The Tag Inspector shows all the current attributes for the selected tag in an organized manner. All these features can be extended using VTML, so you can define your own templates for custom tags. You can also easily modify the settings for existing tags using the Tag Definition Editor.

ColdFusion Studio's color-coding feature lets you quickly see the different components of your application templates. HTML, CFML, JavaScript, Cascading Style Sheets (CSS), and more are all distinguishable by color, and attributes of tags and different types of tags are all assigned their own colors. You can customize the colors used to display these components, as well as the background of your document window.

Each of these customization features can save great amounts of development time, allowing you to make more money or get more sleep. The more time you invest initially to set up your environment, the more time you'll save in the long run. So, I won't waste any more of your time describing the features; now you can start to customize your ColdFusion Studio environment.

Keyboard Shortcuts

ColdFusion Studio comes with many predefined shortcuts, most of which you probably would not want to modify. Ctrl+B is common as the keyboard shortcut for Bold in many text editors and word processors, and it also comes predefined in ColdFusion Studio. Many shortcuts are not defined, and they are the ones you'll look at now.

To access the Keyboard Shortcuts dialog box, from ColdFusion Studio, choose Options and then Customize. The Customize dialog box shown in Figure 14.1 then appears. You can also access this dialog box by pressing Shift+F8 (which you can also customize!). Remember where this dialog box is because you'll come back to it throughout this chapter. Choose the Keyboard Shortcuts tab to list all the available shortcuts and their associated key combinations. As you see, many of the most often used shortcuts are predefined. For this example, choose a shortcut that has no definition, and assign a key combination to it.

The SQL Builder in ColdFusion Studio is used often by many developers, so it's a good place to start. Scroll down the list of items in the Keyboard Shortcuts window until you see SQL Builder in the Description column, and select it. Notice that in the text field at the bottom left of the dialog box, the word None appears. This window normally contains the key combination assigned to the selected shortcut. Click or tab to that text field, and then press Shift+Ctrl+Q. The selection then moves up into the list of assigned shortcuts, and the key combination you entered appears in the Shortcut column. Test your shortcut now. Click Close and then press Shift+Ctrl+Q. The SQL Builder should open, as shown in Figure 14.2.

Part
III

Ch
14

FIGURE 14.1

The Customize dialog box.

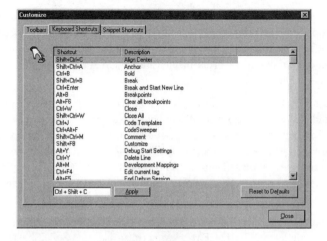

FIGURE 14.2

The SQL Builder.

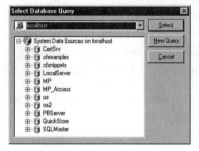

As you can tell now, Shift+Ctrl+Q can be a bit awkward because all the keys are almost in a vertical alignment using one hand. So, edit this shortcut and make it a bit more usable, but do so without using the mouse this time. Press Shift+F8 to open the Customize dialog box, and select the Keyboard Shortcuts tab once again. Press Tab to move focus to the shortcut list, and press Page Down and the down arrow until the SQL Builder shortcut is highlighted. Now press Tab twice to move focus to the text field that contains the key combinations, and press Shift+Alt+Q. The text field reflects the change. Press Enter to close the dialog box, and then try the new key combination by pressing Shift+Alt+Q. The SQL Builder opens once again. Using these techniques, you can modify any of the shortcuts available to fit your needs.

Snippet Shortcuts

ColdFusion Studio Snippets allow you to easily reuse pieces of commonly used code by defining start text and, optionally, end text to be placed around the current selection in your document. Now you're ready to build a snippet and assign a shortcut to it so that you can see how powerful this feature can be.

Build the snippet to create the link back to the home page. Choose the Snippets tab of the Resource Tab, and then right-click in the window. Choose Create Folder from the context menu, and name the new menu **Web**. Now right-click on Web and choose Add Snippet from the context menu. The Snippet dialog box shown in Figure 14.3 then appears. In the Description field, enter **Home Link**. Enter **<A HREF="/">** in the Start Text box and **</A>** in the End Text box. Click OK.

FIGURE 14.3

The Snippet dialog box.

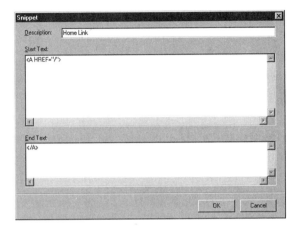

Now you can apply a key combination to this snippet. Press Shift+F8 to open the now-familiar Customize dialog box, and choose the Snippet Shortcuts tab. Notice that the view is similar to that of the Snippets tab on the Resource Tab, but the key combination text field also appears at the bottom left, as shown in Figure 14.4. Drill down into the Web folder, and select the Home Link snippet. Tab over to the key combination field, and press Ctrl+Shift+H. Press Enter to assign this key combination to the Home Link snippet.

FIGURE 14.4

The Snippet Shortcuts tab of the Customize dialog box.

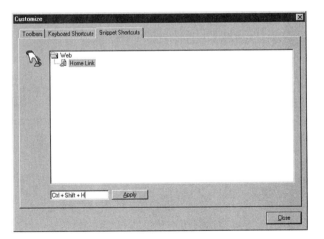

Part
III

Ch
14

In a new document, type **Return to the homepage**. Press Shift+Home to select the entire line of text, and then press Ctrl+Shift+H. The snippet is applied to the text, and your hands never leave your keyboard.

You must be thinking at this point, "What happens if I assign a key combination that is already in use?" If you try to assign a key combination that either ColdFusion Studio or Windows uses, it is not accepted. If the shortcut is in use by ColdFusion Studio, the name of the snippet or function is displayed below the key combination field. If you click Apply, a dialog box appears to confirm the overwrite, as shown in Figure 14.5. Unless you click OK to overwrite the shortcut, you can't overwrite another shortcut without first editing it.

FIGURE 14.5

A confirm overwrite confirmation.

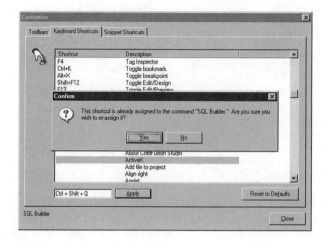

Code Templates

Key combinations are useful, but only so many combinations are available for you to assign. Also, key combinations can be hard to remember, especially if you plan to assign a lot of them. ColdFusion Studio includes a powerful feature called *code templates* that allows you to define a more meaningful abbreviation, which is then replaced on-the-fly with the assigned text.

Try an example. Defining the DTD for all documents as the first line of the document is good practice. Many programmers and designers do not do so because they forget the syntax, or it is just extra typing that they know they can get away with not doing. Code templates make it easy to add the proper DTD to your documents. Type **dt3** in a new blank document. Activate the code template by pressing Ctrl+J. The dt3 is then replaced with <DOCTYPE HTML PUBLIC "-//W3C//DTD HTML 3.2//EN">. As you can see, the excuses for not including these elements are fading fast.

The real power in this feature is that you can add your own code templates for code you frequently use. Now you can add another tag to your code templates that you probably should use in your documents. To open the Code Templates dialog box, select Settings from the Options menu or press F8. You should remember this dialog box also, because I'll refer to it later in the chapter. Choose the Code Templates tab to see the dialog box shown in Figure 14.6.

Notice that several keywords are defined for META tags. For this example, you'll add another META tag to the list. To get started, click on the Add button to reveal the Code Template dialog box shown in Figure 14.7. Type `metaauth` in the Keyword field. Type `META Author` in the Description field. Then type `<META NAME="Author" CONTENT="¦">` in the Value field. Notice the pipe character (¦) in between the quotation marks after `CONTENT`. It tells ColdFusion Studio where to place the cursor when this code is applied to a page so that you can easily fill in values. Next, click OK to add the code template to the list, and then click OK to return to your document.

FIGURE 14.6

The Code Templates tab is in the Settings dialog box.

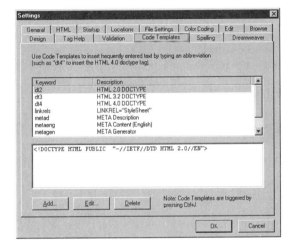

FIGURE 14.7

The Code Template dialog box.

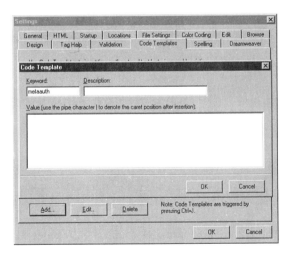

In your document, type `metaauth` and then press Ctrl+J. The code you entered in the dialog box then appears, with the cursor in the correct position for entering data. The flexibility of code templates can save you a lot of time and effort.

Toolbars and Toolbuttons

The first thing that users of previous versions of ColdFusion Studio notice is the change in the toolbars in ColdFusion Studio 4. The toolbars can now be docked and undocked, allowing you to place them anywhere on your screen. You can also edit the toolbuttons, changing the order of the toolbuttons on a toolbar, adding and removing toolbuttons from toolbars, and even creating your own toolbuttons with custom icons.

Try moving the File toolbar around. Look to the left of the New Document icon in the File toolbar (to find it, look for the image of a document with a star on it; it says New on mouse over), and you will see two vertical lines called *grippers*. Click and drag the gripper to the center of the screen, and notice how the toolbar follows, as shown in Figure 14.8. The toolbar now has its own window that can be positioned anywhere on the screen. To dock the toolbar, double-click in its title bar. The menu returns to its position. You can also change the order of the menus by dragging them to the position you want them to occupy. Try dragging the File toolbar to the end of itself. The toolbar then switches places with the Edit toolbar.

FIGURE 14.8

Moving a toolbar.

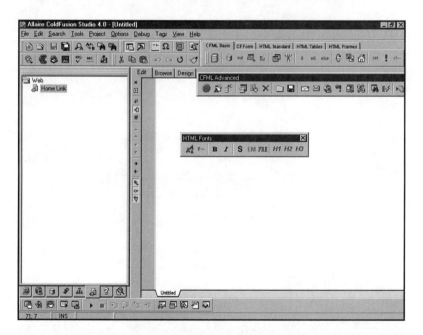

You also can organize toolbars in a more compact manner by using the Quick Bar. To activate the Quick Bar, choose Quick Bar from the View menu or press Ctrl+H. A tabbed set of toolbars appears above the Resource Tab and document window, as shown in Figure 14.9. You can now drag toolbars to and from the Quick Bar to organize your workspace.

Not all available toolbuttons are included in the toolbars. You can add or remove toolbuttons to create toolbars that suit your needs. To edit your toolbars, select Options and then choose Customize, or press Shift+F8 to open the Customize dialog box. Choose the Toolbars tab to display the dialog box shown in Figure 14.10. From the Toolbars list, choose the Debug toolbar. The check box to the left, when selected, makes the toolbar visible. Make sure the check box is selected.

FIGURE 14.9

A tabbed set of toolbars.

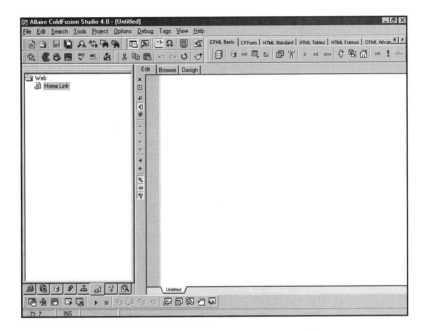

FIGURE 14.10

Toolbar settings.

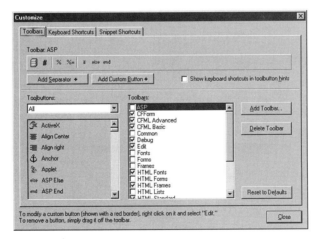

Notice that the toolbar appears at the top of the dialog box. Click on the Clear All Breakpoints toolbutton (the hand with the *x*), and drag it to the right of the Enable/Disable Breakpoint toolbutton (the hand with diagonal shading behind it). The toolbutton moves to the place that you've dragged it. Now add a toolbutton to the toolbar. From the drop-down list in the

Part
III

Ch
14

Toolbuttons list, choose Debug. Look for the Break toolbutton, and drag it to the Debug toolbar in the dialog box. Drop it to the right of the Start toolbutton (the play icon). You've now added an item to the Debug toolbar.

Creating your own toolbar is easy. To do so, click on the Add Toolbar button. ColdFusion Studio then asks for a name for the new toolbar, as shown in Figure 14.11. For this example, call it **My Code** and click OK. You now have a blank toolbar in your dialog box. Click Add Custom Button to reveal the dialog box shown in Figure 14.12. You can use a toolbutton to display a dialog box created in VTML, which I'll discuss later. You can also use the toolbutton to launch an external application or execute an ActiveScript file. These options are covered in Chapter 15, "Scripting ColdFusion Studio." Right now, choose the first option, Insert Custom Start and End Tags into the Current Document. This is another, less detailed version of a snippet. In the Start Tag field, enter **<CF_MyTag>**. In the End Tag field, enter **</CF_MyTag>**. You can choose a custom icon in the Button Image field. (One is provided in the code section of the CD. You can copy it to the `UserData\Toolbars` directory under the ColdFusion Studio root directory and select it by using the Button Image dialog box.) Next, enter **My Tag** in the Caption field. Type **My Custom Tag** in the Hint field. Click OK; your new button is added to the toolbar.

FIGURE 14.11
The Add Toolbar dialog box.

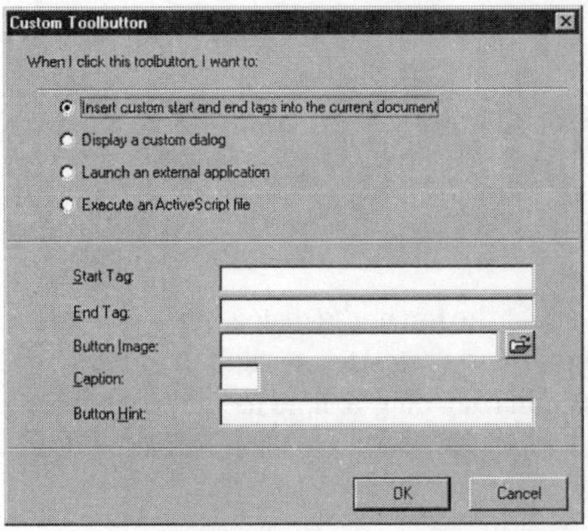

FIGURE 14.12
The Custom Toolbutton dialog box.

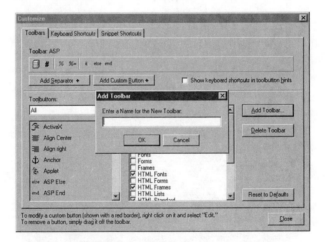

Using the toolbar in this method is a neat feature, but you can use toolbuttons in more powerful ways. You can create your own custom tag editors and add them to your toolbars to make them even more powerful.

Tag Definitions and VTML

Now that you've created your own toolbars and toolbuttons, you're ready to create a tag definition. ColdFusion Studio uses the Visual Tools Markup Language to create tag definitions and tag editors. Using VTML, you can create your own tag definitions or extend existing definitions, allowing you to seamlessly integrate your Custom Tags into the ColdFusion Studio IDE.

VTML is an extensive definition language, and all the tags are covered in Appendix C. The language is similar to CFML, so there is not a difficult learning curve in using VTML. You can also extend the tag definitions in ColdFusion Studio without using VTML. Build a tag definition now using the Tag Definition Editor, and then view the resulting VTML file to see how it looks behind the scenes.

To access the Tag Definition Editor, go to the Tag Inspector on the Resource Tab by choosing the last tab. The icon for the Tag Definition Editor is a gear. When you click on this icon, you'll see the Tag Definitions Library dialog box shown in Figure 14.13. Click on Add Tag, and the New Tag Definition dialog box shown in Figure 14.14 appears. Enter `CF_MYTAG` and click OK. Notice that the tag already appears in the list of known tags on the left of the Tag Definition Editor. Also, a default attribute has been added. Next to the Attributes list, click Add. Enter the name of the attribute, `Value`, and click OK. The Value attribute then appears in the list. You can decide what kind of attribute it is by selecting a type from the Attribute Settings box. Choose Text from the list.

FIGURE 14.13
The Tag Definitions Library dialog box.

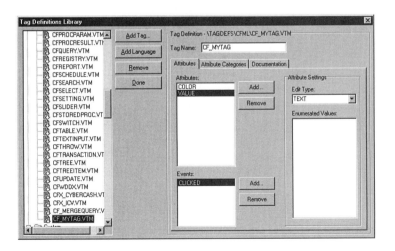

Part
III

Ch
14

Now add another attribute by clicking Add next to the Attributes list. Name it `Color` and click OK. In the Edit Type list, choose Color as the attribute type. ColdFusion Studio automatically creates categories for the attributes you enter. Click on the Attribute Categories tab to see the categories you've already created (see Figure 14.15). You can add new categories here and assign existing attributes to new categories. For your purposes, the Misc category will work well.

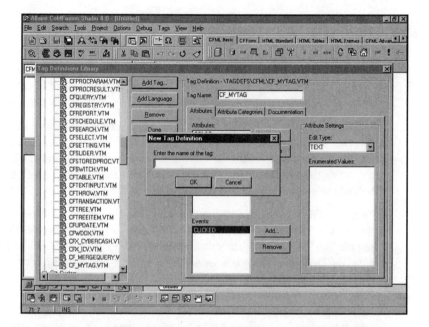

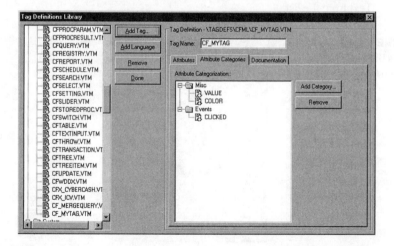

If you had an HTML help file to add for your tag, you could add it by clicking the Documentation tab in the Tag Definition Editor. Here, you can set the help file to load when tag help for this tag is selected. Back at the top of the Tag Definition Editor, enter **CF_MYTAG** in the Tag

Name field. Because you're now finished with your creation, you can click Done. Notice that you can even add new languages and assign tags to them by clicking Add Language. For now, just look at the tag definition.

Listing 14.1 shows the VTML created automatically by the Tag Definition Editor. Using the information from Appendix C, you can edit this file within ColdFusion Studio, or you can open the Tag Definition Editor to edit it further. Put your cursor in the document window, and try typing <cf_mytag without completing it. The Tag Insight will show the options you entered. You can even right-click your tag and choose Edit Tag to open a Tag Edit dialog box. The Tag Definition Editor is both powerful and easy to use.

Listing 14.1 MYTAG.VTM—**The Actual VTML Code for the New Tag**

```
<TAG>

    <EDITORLAYOUT HEIGHT=225>
        <CONTAINER   NAME="MainTabDialog"    TYPE="TabDialog" MAXWIDTHPADDING=0
➥ MAXHEIGHTPADDING=0 WIDTH=MAXIMUM HEIGHT=MAXIMUM>

            <CONTAINER  NAME="TabPage1" TYPE="TabPage" CAPTION="MYTAG Tag">

                <CONTAINER   NAME="Panel1" TYPE="Panel" DOWN=5 RIGHT=10
➥ WIDTH="MAXIMUM" HEIGHT=125>

                    <CONTROL NAME="lblSource" TYPE="Label" CAPTION="Source:"
➥ DOWN=17 RIGHT=10 WIDTH=50>
                    <CONTROL NAME="txtSource" TYPE="TextBox" ANCHOR="lblSource"
➥ CORNER="NE" WIDTH="MAXIMUM">

                    <CONTROL NAME="lblAlign"    TYPE="Label" CAPTION="Align:"
➥  ANCHOR="lblSource" CORNER="SW" DOWN=11 WIDTH=50>
                    <CONTROL NAME="dropAlign"    TYPE="DropDown"
➥ ANCHOR="lblAlign" CORNER="NE" WIDTH=100>
                        <ITEM VALUE="TOP"          CAPTION="TOP" >
                        <ITEM VALUE="MIDDLE"       CAPTION="MIDDLE" SELECTED>
                        <ITEM VALUE="BOTTOM"       CAPTION="BOTTOM" >
                    </CONTROL>

                </CONTAINER>

                <CONTAINER   NAME="Panel2"    TYPE="Panel" CAPTION=" Panel 2 "
                        ANCHOR="Panel1"  CORNER="SW"    DOWN=5
➥ WIDTH="MAXIMUM" HEIGHT=MAXIMUM>
                </CONTAINER>

            </CONTAINER>

            <CONTAINER   NAME="Advanced" TYPE="TabPage" CAPTION="Advanced">
            </CONTAINER>

        </CONTAINER>

    </EDITORLAYOUT>
```

Part

III

Ch

14

continues

Listing 14.1 Continued

```
<ATTRIBUTES>
     <ATTRIB NAME="SRC"          CONTROL="txtSource">
     <ATTRIB NAME="ALIGN"     CONTROL="dropAlign">
</ATTRIBUTES>



<TAGDESCRIPTION>
     <FONT FACE="Arial" SIZE="1">Insert tag description here.
➥ Use HTML !!!</FONT>
</TAGDESCRIPTION>



<TAGLAYOUT>
     <WIZIF OPTIONLowerCaseTags EQ 'true'>
          <WIZSET MYTAG     = 'mytag'>
          <WIZSET SRC       = 'src'>
          <WIZSET ALIGN     = 'align'>
     <WIZELSE>
          <WIZSET MYTAG     = 'MYTAG'>
          <WIZSET SRC       = 'SRC'>
          <WIZSET ALIGN     = 'ALIGN'>
     </WIZIF>

     <WIZIF OPTIONLinearLayout EQ 'true'>
          <WIZSET SpacingGap =  ' ' >
     <WIZELSE>
          <WIZSET SpacingGap =  Chr(13) & Chr(10) & '        ' >
     </WIZIF>

<$${MYTAG} $${SRC}="$${txtSource}"<WIZIF dropAlign NEQ ''     >$${SpacingGap}
➥$${ALIGN}="$${dropAlign}"</WIZIF><WIZIF TAGDATAUnknownAttributes NEQ ''>
➥$${SpacingGap}$${TAGDATAUnknownAttributes}</WIZIF>>
     </TAGLAYOUT>



</TAG>
```

Color Coding and Fonts

Now that you've created your own tag definitions, the finishing touch on your customized ColdFusion Studio environment is the color combinations used to display your documents. As you tested the various customization features, you probably noticed that the text entered in the document window has been color-coded according to its type and attributes. All the colors used to display text in the document window are customizable. Color coding can make your development environment singular and very personal.

Select Settings from the Options menu or press F8 to open the Settings dialog box; then choose the Color Coding tab. Notice the drop-down list of Color-Coding Schemes. You can have an entirely different set of color-coding settings for each document type you work with. You can also select one scheme as the default. Choose HTML from the list and click Edit Scheme. You then see the dialog box shown in Figure 14.16. Each element in the list can be assigned a custom color, as well as a bold, italic, or underline treatment. If you get a bit carried away as you change the color settings, you can always click the Reset to Defaults button to return to the predefined color-coding scheme.

FIGURE 14.16
Color scheme settings.

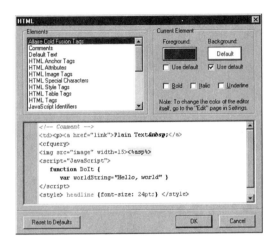

Even More Customization

ColdFusion Studio does more than allow you to modify the development environment. Until now only static modifications to the environment have been covered. The story does not end here. ColdFusion Studio also allows you to build automation, scripting, and ActiveX controls into your toolbars and dialog boxes. These powerful features are covered in the next chapter. ●

Part
III

Ch
14

Scripting ColdFusion Studio

Your ability to customize ColdFusion Studio does not end with keyboard shortcuts and VTML. One of the most impressive features of ColdFusion Studio is the capability to script or automate its behavior. Not only can you build macros that automate tasks such as opening sets of documents and deploying toolbars, but you also can add new functionality to ColdFusion Studio itself. If you need it, you can build it.

To take advantage of this functionality, you must meet a few requirements. Because ColdFusion Studio understands only scripts written in JavaScript or VBScript, you need to be familiar with working in one or both of these languages. This chapter assumes you understand the basics of working in these environments. Even if you do not work with these languages, however, you can still install helpful scripts. Also, to use VBScript, you need Microsoft's ActiveScripting engine installed on your system. You can download it from http://www.microsoft.com, but you already have it installed if you have Internet Explorer 4.0 or higher on your system.

The Visual Tools Object Model

ColdFusion Studio 4 exposes control of the application in the Visual Tools Object Model, or VTOM. Using the VTOM objects, properties, and methods, you have full control over the application itself, the documents loaded in the application, toolbars, panes, and even code within the documents themselves. In this chapter, you'll take a tour through the VTOM and then use it to add functionality to ColdFusion Studio.

The Application Object

The application object in the VTOM contains many read-only properties that allow your scripts to detect their environment. This capability is important not only for compatibility with future versions of ColdFusion Studio, but also because scripts that use the VTOM can be used in HomeSite. The application object also allows access to global settings and functions. The properties of this object are listed in Table 15.1.

Table 15.1 Application Object Properties

Function	Description
`ActiveDocument [object, read-only]`	This property returns the active document. You'll see more information about it in the description of the `ActiveDocument` object.
`AppPath [OLEString, read-only]`	This property returns the full path to the ColdFusion Studio program.
`CurrentFolder [OleString]`	This property returns the path that is currently shown in the resource window. This property is writeable, so you can also set the path using this property.

Function	Description
CurrentView [ITCurrentViewType]	The current view can be read or set using this property. You can use only the following values: 1 - vwEditSource (Edit mode) 2 - vwPreview (Browse mode) 3 - vwDesign (Design mode)
DocumentCache [array of objects, read-only]	This read-only property returns an array of objects that represent the currently cached documents. You'll find more details on this property in the description of the DocumentCache object.
DocumentIndex [Integer]	This property returns the tab position of the current document in the document tabs. You can also change the position of the current document using this property.
DocumentCount [Integer, read-only]	This property tells you how many documents are currently open in ColdFusion Studio.
ExeName [OleString, read-only]	This read-only property tells you the name of the ColdFusion Studio executable (cfstudio.exe), as well as the full path to it.
Height [integer]	You can resize the height of the ColdFusion Studio window or get the current height using this property.
HInstance [integer, read-only]	This property returns the instance handle of the application.
hWnd [integer, read-only]	This property returns the handle to the main window.
IsColdFusionStudio [WordBool, read-only]	This property always returns True if you are using ColdFusion Studio. Because VTOM scripts are compatible with both HomeSite and ColdFusion Studio, checking this property before using Studio-specific features proves to be useful. False is returned if the script is executed within HomeSite.

continues

Table 15.1 Continued

Function	Description
Left [Integer]	Using this property, the left, or x, position of the window is set or returned. You can use this property in conjunction with the Top property to move the window on the desktop or find its current position.
ResourceTabShowing [WordBool]	This property toggles the display of the resource tab and returns its current state.
ResultsShowing [WordBool]	You can use this property to determine whether the results pane is visible or to change its visibility.
Top [Integer]	This property sets and returns the top, or y, position of the ColdFusion Studio window. Use it in conjunction with the Left property described previously.
VersionText [OleString, read-only]	This property is used for version checking. It returns a string that contains the name of the application (ColdFusion Studio) and version.
WindowState [Integer]	You can determine the current state of the application window using this property. The methods for this property are listed in Table 15.2. You can also set this state within the following values: 1 - Normal 2 - Minimized 3 - Maximized

Table 15.2 WindowState Methods

Name	Syntax	Description
BringToFront	procedure BringToFront;	Brings the ColdFusion Studio window to the front of the windows on the desktop.
BrowseText	procedure BrowseText(sText, BaseHREF: OleVariant);	Displays text in the Browse window. You can pass text to this method or use the BaseHREF parameter to specify a path to the text. Use a relative path in BaseHREF if the file is local.

Name	Syntax	Description
CloseAll	function CloseAll (wbPromptToSave: WordBool): WordBool;	Closes all open documents in ColdFusion Studio. If this process is successful, this method returns True. To allow the user to confirm this action before it executes, set wbPromptToSave to True. If the user cancels the operation, the method returns False.
GetImageSize	function GetImageSize(const wsImageFile: WideString; var nHeight, nWidth: Integer): WordBool;	Determines the size of any image. Pass the path to the image in the parameter wsImageFile. If an error occurs in determining the image size, the method returns False.
GetTabIndexForFile	function GetTabIndexForFile (const wsFile: WideString): Integer;	Determines whether a file is open and determines the tab index of the file if it is open. You can pass the path to the file using the parameter wsFile. If the file is not open, the method returns –1.
GetURL	function GetURL (const wsURL: WideString): widestring;	Retrieves the contents of a URL. You can pass a valid URL in the wsURL parameter.
GetURLStatus	function GetURLStatus(const wsURL: WideString; var vResponse: OleVariant): Integer;	Used in conjunction with GetURL. The response code of the URL is returned by this method, as well as the text of the response. The response text is returned using the vResponse parameter.
HideProgress	procedure HideProgress;	Hides the progress bar. The ShowProgress method (described later) brings the progress bar back.
InputBox	InputBox(const wsCaption, wsPrompt, wsDefault: WideString): WideString;	Allows you to display a prompt and get user input.
IsFileOpen	function IsFileOpen(sFile: OleVariant): WordBool;	Determines whether the file that passes in the parameter sFile is open.

continues

Table 15.2 Continued

Name	Syntax	Description
IsFileModified	function IsFileModified (sFile: OleVariant): WordBool;	Determines whether the file passed in the parameter sFile is open and whether it has been modified.
MessageBox	MessageBox(const wsText, wsCaption: WideString; nType: Integer): Integer;	Displays a box for user confirmation or information.
NewDocument	procedure NewDocument (wbUseDefaultTemplate: WordBool);	Creates a new document, optionally from the default template.
OpenFile	function OpenFile (const wsFile: WideString): WordBool;	Opens the passed file, returning True if successful. Note that this method returns True if the file is already open. Passing an empty string to OpenFile displays the Open File dialog box, enabling the user to select the file(s) to open.
NextDoc	procedure NextDoc;	Moves to the next document in the document tab. If the last document is showing, it wraps to the first.
PreviousDoc	procedure PreviousDoc;	Moves to the previous document in the document tab. If the first document is showing, it wraps to the last.
SaveAll	function SaveAll: WordBool;	Saves all open documents, returning True if successful.
SendToBack	procedure SendToBack;	Sends the main window to the back of other applications.
SetActiveResults	procedure SetActiveResults (resType: TCurrentResultsType);	Sets the active page in the results tab. Allowed values are as follows: resSearch resValidator resLinks resThumbnails.
SetProgress	procedure SetProgress (nProgress: Integer);	Sets the position of the progress bar in the status area. Allowed values are 1 to 100.

Name	Syntax	Description
SetStatusText	procedure SetStatusText (sMessage: OleString);	Sets the text to be displayed in the status area.
StatusWarning	procedure StatusWarning(const wsMsg: WideString);	Displays a warning message in the status bar. The message appears on a blue background for at least 5 seconds.
StatusError	procedure StatusError(const wsMsg: WideString);	Displays an error message in the status bar. The message appears on a red background for at least 5 seconds.
ShowThumbnails	procedure ShowThumbnails (sFolder: OleString);	Shows thumbnails for all images in the passed folder.
ShowProgress	procedure ShowProgress;	Shows the progress bar.
Wait	procedure Wait(nMilliseconds: Integer);	Pauses for given number of milliseconds. You can use Wait to enable scripts to execute loops and still allow access to the user interface.

The following properties apply to toolbars. Toolbars are stored in a directory that you can retrieve by using the `ToolbarDir` property.

ToolbarDir (widestring, read-only property)		Returns the path where toolbar files are located.
CreateToolbar	function CreateToolbar (wsToolbarName: WideString): WordBool;	Creates a new, undocked toolbar of the passed name. Fails if a toolbar of the same name already exists.
HideToolbar	function HideToolbar (wsToolbarName: WideString): WordBool;	Hides a toolbar. Fails if the toolbar doesn't exist.
DeleteToolbar	function DeleteToolbar (wsToolbarName: WideString): WordBool;	Physically deletes the toolbar. Fails if the toolbar doesn't exist or if the toolbar is one of the built-in toolbars. (Works only on custom toolbars; built-in toolbars can be hidden but not deleted.)

continues

Table 15.2 Continued

Name	Syntax	Description
ShowToolbar	function ShowToolbar (wsToolbarName: WideString): WordBool;	Displays a toolbar if it's not already showing. Fails if the toolbar doesn't exist.
AddAppToolbutton	AddAppToolbutton (wsToolbarName, wsExeFile, wsCmdLine, wsHint: WideString): WordBool;	Adds a toolbutton for an external application to the passed toolbar. Fails if the toolbar doesn't exist or if the toolbutton cannot be added. Returns True if the same toolbutton (based on wsExeFile and wsCmdLine) already exists on the toolbar, but doesn't add a duplicate button.
AddTagToolbutton	function AddTagToolbutton (wsToolbarName, wsTagStart, wsTagEnd, wsHint, wsCaption, wsImageFile: WideString): WordBool;	Adds a tag toolbutton (inserts tag pair when clicked) to the passed toolbar. It fails if the toolbar doesn't exist. It returns True if the toolbutton already exists, but doesn't add a duplicate button.
AddScriptToolbutton	function AddScriptToolbutton (wsToolbarName, wsScriptFile, wsHint, wsCaption, wsImageFile: WideString): WordBool;	Adds a script toolbutton (executes passed JavaScript or VBScript file when clicked) to the passed toolbar. Fails if the toolbar doesn't exist. Returns True if the toolbutton already exists, but doesn't add a duplicate button.
AddVTMToolbutton	function AddVTMToolbutton (wsToolbarName, wsScriptFile, wsHint, wsCaption, wsImageFile: WideString): WordBool;	Adds a VTM tool button (displays passed VTM dialog box when clicked) to the passed toolbar. Fails if the toolbar doesn't exist. Returns True if the toolbutton already exists, but doesn't add a duplicate button.
ToolbarExists	function ToolbarExists (wsToolbarName: WideString): WordBool;	Returns True if the passed toolbar exists.

Name	Syntax	Description
SetToolbarDockPos	function SetToolbarDockPos (wsToolbarName: WideString; nDockPos: Integer): WordBool;	Sets the docking position of the toolbar. Allowed values for nDockPos are as follows: 1 = Top 2 = Bottom 3 = Left 4 = Right Fails if the toolbar doesn't exist.

You can use the nType *parameter to determine the type of box shown using a combination of these values:* MB_ICONINFORMATION = 64, MB_ICONWARNING = 48, MB_ICONQUESTION = 32, MB_ICONSTOP = 16, MB_ABORTRETRYIGNORE = 2, MB_OK = 0 (*Default*), MB_OKCANCEL = 1, MB_RETRYCANCEL = 5, MB_YESNO = 4, MB_YESNOCANCEL = 3. *The result returned is the ID of the button the user pressed. It is one of these values:* IDOK = 1, IDCANCEL = 2, IDABORT = 3, IDRETRY = 4, IDIGNORE = 5, IDYES = 6, IDNO = 7, *or* IDCLOSE = 8.

The DocumentCache Object

The DocumentCache object gives you access to a document currently in the cache. Any document that is present in the document tabs is in the document cache. The application object property DocumentCache returns an array of the documents currently in the cache. All properties for this object shown in Table 15.3 are read-only.

Table 15.3 DocumentCache Object Properties

Name	Description
Text (OleString)	Returns the text (file contents) of the cached document
CanUndo (WordBool)	Returns True if changes can be undone
CanRedo (WordBool)	Returns True if changes can be redone
Modified (WordBool)	Returns True if the cached document has been modified since it was last saved
Filename (OleString)	Returns the filename of the cached document
ReadOnly (WordBool)	Returns True if the cached document is read-only

The ActiveDocument Object

With the ActiveDocument object, some real magic can happen. This object gives you access to the active document or the currently selected document. Using this object and the properties in Table 15.4, you can manipulate the contents of a document and create behavior based on that content.

Table 15.4 `ActiveDocument` **Object Properties**

Name	Description
CanUndo (WordBool, read-only)	Returns True if changes can be undone.
CanRedo (WordBool, read-only)	Returns True if changes can be redone.
Filename (OleString, read-only)	Returns the filename of the active document.
Lines[Index: integer] (OleString)	Gets or sets the text of the line at the passed index.
LineCount (integer, read-only)	Returns the number of lines in the active document.
Modified (WordBool, read-only)	Returns True if the document has been changed since it was last saved.
ReadOnly (WordBool, read-only)	Returns True if the active document is read-only.
SelStart (integer)	Gets or sets the start of the current selection.
SelLength (integer)	Gets or sets the length of the current selection.
SelText (OleString)	Gets or sets the text in the current selection.
TabIndex	Gets or sets the tab index of the document tab.
Text (OleString)	Gets or sets the complete document text. This property is very useful when used with the methods in Table 15.5.

Table 15.5 Text Methods

Name	Syntax	Description
BeginUpdate	procedure BeginUpdate	Turns on screen updating for the active document.
EndUpdate	procedure EndUpdate;	Turns off screen updating for the active document.
Clear	procedure Clear;	Clears all text from the active document.
Close	function Close (wbPromptToSave: WordBool): WordBool;	Closes the active document. If wbPromptToSave is True, the user is prompted to save any changes. Returns True if the document was closed (that is, the user didn't cancel saving changes).

Name	Syntax	Description
GetCaretPos	procedure GetCaretPos(var x, y: integer);	Returns the caret position (x=column, y=line).
GetNextChar	function GetNextChar: OleVariant;	Returns the next character. Note that that this function (along with GetPreviousChar) can be slow when used in long loops.
GetPreviousChar	function GetPreviousChar: OleVariant;	Returns the previous character.
GotoNextStartTag	function GotoNextStartTag (wbSelect: WordBool): WordBool;	Moves to the next starting tag, selecting it if wbSelect is True. Returns False if no tag is found.
GotoPreviousStartTag	function GotoPreviousStartTag (wbSelect: WordBool): WordBool;	Moves to the previous starting tag, selecting it if wbSelect is True. Returns False if no tag is found.
GotoNextEndTag	function GotoNextEndTag (wbSelect: WordBool): WordBool;	Moves to the next end tag, selecting it if wbSelect is True. Returns False if no tag is found.
GotoPreviousEndTag	function GotoPreviousEndTag (wbSelect: WordBool): WordBool;	Moves to the previous end tag, selecting it if wbSelect is True. Returns False if no tag is found.
Indent	procedure Indent;	Indents the current selection.
InsertTag	procedure InsertTag (sStartTag, sEndTag: OleVariant; wbOverwriteSelection: WordBool);	Inserts the passed tag pair at the current cursor position, overwriting the selection if wbOverwriteSelection is True. The cursor is positioned between the start and end tags after this operation, and if wbOverwriteSelection is False, the current selection is surrounded by the tags.
InsertText	procedure InsertText (InsertStr: OleVariant; wbOverwriteSelection: WordBool);	Inserts the passed string at the current cursor position, overwriting the selection if wbOverwriteSelection is True.

continues

Table 15.5   Continued

Name	Syntax	Description
Print	procedure Print (wbNoPrompt: WordBool);	Prints the active document. Prompts the user for print settings unless wbNoPrompt is True.
ReplaceAll	function ReplaceAll (strSearch, strReplace: OleVariant; bMatchCase: WordBool): Integer;	Replaces all occurrences of strSearch with strReplace, matching case if bMatchCase is True. Returns the number of replacements made.
Redo	procedure Redo;	Performs a single redo operation.
Reload	procedure Reload (wbPromptToSave: WordBool);	Reloads the active document, prompting to save changes if wbPromptToSave is True.
Save	function Save: WordBool;	Saves changes to the active document, returning True if successful.
SaveAs	function SaveAs (wsFileName: widestring): WordBool;	Saves changes to the active document to the file specified in the wsFileName parameter, returning True if successful. If wsFileName is empty, the standard Save As dialog box is displayed to the user. Note that existing files are overwritten by this function, so use it with caution.
SelectAll	procedure SelectAll;	Selects all the text in the active document.
SetCaretPos	procedure SetCaretPos (x, y: Integer);	Sets the current column/line.
SelectLine	procedure SelectLine (Index: Integer);	Highlights the passed line.
SelectCurrentLine	procedure SelectCurrentLine;	Highlights the current line.
Undo	procedure Undo;	Performs a single undo operation.
Unindent	procedure Unindent;	Unindents the current selection.

Cursor Movement Procedures

To position the cursor, use the methods (all of which are procedures) listed in Table 15.6. You can extend the current selection to the new cursor position by setting wbSelect to True.

Table 15.6   Cursor Movement Procedures

Name

```
CursorLeft(wbSelect: WordBool);

CursorRight(wbSelect: WordBool);

CursorWordLeft(wbSelect: WordBool);

CursorWordRight(wbSelect: WordBool);

CursorDown(wbSelect: WordBool);

CursorUp(wbSelect: WordBool);

CursorPageDown(wbSelect: WordBool);

CursorPageUp(wbSelect: WordBool);

CursorDocStart(wbSelect: WordBool);

CursorDocEnd(wbSelect: WordBool);

CursorLineStart(wbSelect: WordBool);

CursorLineEnd(wbSelect: WordBool);
```

Building VTOM Scripts

When you're building a VTOM script, you need to include some basic structure. Each script must have a function that contains the main section of code, and the initialization of the script must contain an application reference. In the following sections, you'll see how these requirements work for JavaScript and VBScript.

JavaScript Version

In JavaScript, the main section of the script is contained in the function Main(). Listing 15.1 shows the basic structure elements of a JavaScript VTOM script. In the initialization, notice that an application reference is created. This script simply displays a message box.

Listing 15.1   JavaScriptExample.js—Basic Structure of a VTOM Script Using JavaScript

```
// ====================================================================
//       VTOM Script (JavaScript)
// ====================================================================
// Basic structure for a VTOM script
// ====================================================================
function Main() {

    // Do Initialization here
```

continues

Listing 15.1 Continued

```
    // Create an application reference
    var app = Application;

// store the index of the current document for future reference
    var nCurrentIdx = app.DocumentIndex;


    alert('Script Has Run!');
}
```

VBScript Version

In VBScript, the Sub Main contains the main section of code. In this example, an application reference is created in the initialization section, and the reference is cleaned up at the end of Sub Main. This example in Listing 15.2 opens a message dialog box.

Listing 15.2 VBScriptExample.bas—Basic Structure of a VTOM Script Using VBScript

```
' =====================================================================
'       VTOM Script using VBScript
' =====================================================================
'       Basic structure for a VTOM script
' =====================================================================
Sub Main
    dim theApp


    ' Create an application reference

    set theApp = Application

    ' store the index of the current document for future reference
    nCurrentIdx = app.DocumentIndex


    ' display a message
    MsgBox "Script has run!"

    ' at the end of our code, we should free the references
    set theApp = nothing
End Sub

' an example of calling a function
function GetDisplayName(fname)
    if fname = "" then
        GetDisplayName = "(untitled)"
    else
        GetDisplayName = fname
    end if
end function
```

Importing and Executing Scripts

By no means are you limited to the scripts you create yourself in ColdFusion Studio. You can use any compatible scripts by simply saving them on your system and creating a button on a toolbar to point to the script. In this way, you can add new functions and automation features to your development environment without reinventing the wheel. You can also share your cool scripts with others. You can find new scripts in several places, but the best resource by far is the Allaire Developer center at `http://www.allaire.com/developer/`. Check the Gallery often, as new scripts are frequently uploaded by dedicated ColdFusion Studio users. ●

Advanced Application Development

Using WDDX to Create Distributed Applications

When developing Web applications with ColdFusion, you are often dealing with complex chunks of data, such as recordsets returned from database queries or arrays that you fill with various pieces of information. Often, you need to get that data from one place to another. Sometimes you even need to pass these chunks of data between environments. For instance, you might want to move information from ColdFusion to JavaScript or from a COM-enabled environment such as Visual Basic to ColdFusion.

At the same time, your Web applications generally need to be able to talk in terms of plain text. For instance, you might need to pass data between two servers over the Internet. Various strategies for getting the data from place to place might already be springing into your mind. You might start thinking about passing the data around in email messages or making it available on special back-end Web pages from which another system could collect the data. Because email and Web pages are basically plain-text media, you need some way to turn your recordsets, arrays, and structures into blocks of ordinary ASCII text and back again.

Introducing WDDX

The Web Dynamic Data Exchange (WDDX) format was created to address these kinds of challenges. The idea is to be able to take any kind of data—whether it be a single number or a complex structure of arrays within other arrays—and turn it into a chunk of text. That chunk of text is kept in the WDDX format and can be passed around from place to place with reckless abandon. When it's time to actually use the data again, the data can be read from the WDDX format back to the way it was before the whole process began.

Perhaps the coolest thing about exchanging data with WDDX is that it takes care of preserving data types for you. So, if part of the data started as a date variable on the way into the WDDX format, it ends up as a date variable when it comes back out. This result holds true even if the data gets passed between two different programming environments.

For instance, consider a ColdFusion array that holds a number, a date, and an ordinary string. This array can be converted to WDDX and provided to a JavaScript routine on a Web browser. The JavaScript routine can refer to the array just like any other JavaScript-style array, and the date stored in the array is a true JavaScript Date object, and the number is a true JavaScript Number object. The array is successfully "passed" from CFML to an entirely different kind of language (JavaScript).

Of course, you can achieve this result yourself, by writing your own ColdFusion code that dynamically creates the appropriate JavaScript code. But doing so would be pretty complicated, especially when you start thinking about the work it takes to preserve data types, such as dates and Boolean values. By using WDDX, the whole process is done for you, nearly transparently.

Some WDDX Terminology

Because WDDX is a new technology, it introduces some new concepts and new terminology. As you read this chapter and start working with WDDX, you'll come across some words that you might not have seen used in this kind of context before. Next, you'll find the basic terms and ideas to keep in mind as you start thinking about WDDX.

WDDX Packet   A *WDDX Packet* is any chunk of data stored in the WDDX format. As you will soon see, a WDDX Packet looks somewhat like a snippet of HTML or CFML. Because it's tag-based like HTML, a WDDX Packet is simple, easy to read, and practically describes itself. Each piece of information is surrounded by opening and closing tags (similar to opening and closing BODY or TITLE tags in an HTML document), which allows complex data types to be stored in the packet. That's something which is pretty hard to accomplish with other text-based formats—for example, comma-separated or space-delimited text.

Serializing   *Serializing* is the process of taking some piece of data and converting it into a WDDX Packet. To serialize data, you need to use a language or environment that has access to some kind of function or procedure that knows about the WDXX format and how to serialize data properly. For instance, in a ColdFusion template, the serialization process is performed by the CFWDDX tag. In other languages and environments, the functions or methods that you use to serialize a particular chunk of data are different, but the resulting WDDX Packet should be the same and can be understood by any program that supports WDDX properly.

Consider this example. Serializing the string "Hello, World!" creates a WDDX Packet that includes the string itself, surrounded by a pair of string tags, like this:

```
<string>Hello, World!</string>
```

As you can see, this structure allows the WDDX Packet to hold descriptions of your data right along with the data itself. That's one of the neatest things about the WDDX format: The packet can describe itself to whatever application needs to read it.

Deserializing   *Deserializing* is the opposite of serializing. It's the process of taking an existing WDDX Packet and pulling the actual data out of it. For instance, if an application needs to "un-pack" the "Hello, World" snippet shown in the preceding section, it first looks at the tags to learn what kind of data is in the packet. Because WDDX says that this packet contains string data, the application knows that it should store the value sitting between the tags as a string. For "typed" development environments, such as Visual Basic, C++, or Delphi, the data type is often very important.

Tools and Languages Supported by WDDX

WDDX support is available for a number of languages and development tools. Of course, it's supported by CFML, which just means that Allaire has built WDDX right into the ColdFusion Application Server (CFAS). In classic Allaire style, all the WDDX functionality is exposed to ColdFusion developers as a single, easy-to-use package: the CFWDDX tag. You'll find the CFWDDX tag in nearly all the code listings in this chapter.

Allaire also provides WDDX support for JavaScript, which allows you to make ColdFusion variables "visible" to JavaScript. You therefore can make your pages and forms "dynamic" with much less scripting than ever before—without locking you into proprietary code from any one browser vendor.

Allaire also provides a COM object that brings WDDX functionality to any COM-enabled development tool or application. This means that you can use WDDX to share information among

ColdFusion, Active Server Pages (ASP), Visual Basic, and applications built with COM-enabled development tools such as Visual Basic, Delphi, Visual C++, or PowerBuilder. This COM object is capable of performing all the WDDX-related tasks that ColdFusion templates can do natively.

This chapter covers using WDDX with ColdFusion and JavaScript. The next chapter, "Advanced WDDX Integration," discusses how to use WDDX with Allaire's COM object. Examples are provided for Active Server Pages and Visual Basic. Chapter 17 also discusses how to use WDDX with Perl.

The WDDX Format: It's XML!

You've already learned that a simple string value is placed between `<string>` tags. The WDDX specification says that a few additional tags must appear at the beginning and end of every WDDX Packet for it to be considered valid or well-formed.

Listing 16.1 shows a complete WDDX Packet that contains the `"Hello, World"` string value described previously. The entire packet is enclosed between a pair of `<wddxPacket>` tags. As of this writing, the version attribute will always be 0.9. If the WDDX specification changes at some point in the future, the version number will be updated accordingly. This way, before an application attempts to deserialize a packet, it can check the version number to make sure that it knows how to read all the tags in the packet before it actually starts.

A `<header>` tag appears next. The `<header>` tag doesn't really serve any purpose in WDDX at this time but may come to hold significant information in a future version of WDDX. After the `<header>` tag, a pair of `<data>` tags appears, and all the tags that contain the actual serialized information are placed between them. For instance, in Listing 16.1, a single pair of `<string>` tags is placed between the `<data>` tags. If the data in the packet were a date value instead of a string, a pair of `<dateTime>` tags would appear there instead.

Listing 16.1   `StringPacket.txt`—A Simple WDDX Packet

```
<wddxPacket version='0.9'>
  <header/>
  <data>

    <string>Hello, World!</string>

  </data>
</wddxPacket>
```

You'll find more complicated examples of WDDX Packets later in this chapter. For instance, to see what a ColdFusion structure looks like when serialized into a WDDX Packet, skip ahead to Listing 16.6. To see what a query recordset looks like after being converted to WDDX, skip ahead to Listing 16.10. As you can see, the `<wddxPacket>`, `<header>`, and `<data>` parts always remain the same.

N O T E Whitespace is ignored between the pairs of tags in a WDDX Packet. The blank lines, hard returns, and indenting that appear in Listing 16.1 can be removed without affecting anything. For instance, Figure 16.1 shows the same WDDX Packet without any added whitespace. In general, the packets produced by ColdFusion and other systems do not have any whitespace added, which keeps the packet size smaller. However, you can add whitespace if you want, to make the packet more readable. ■

As you'll see in this chapter and the next chapter, WDDX can do a lot for you. As an added bonus, the WDDX format is compliant with the EXtensible Markup Language (XML) specification, which means that the packet shown in this section—and every WDDX Packet generated by your applications{md}will be "well-formed" XML.

Of course, the fact that WDDX was conceived as an XML-compliant technology is nice; open standards are a good thing. But the XML-ness of it all doesn't really have much of an impact on your day-to-day life as a ColdFusion developer because Allaire's support for WDDX successfully hides all the details about XML parsing from you. In particular, you don't have to worry about "real" XML concepts such as entities, attributes, and Document Type Definitions (DTDs). In other words, the fact that WDDX is actually XML "under the hood" is so transparent that it hardly even matters.

If you're a stickler for XML technicalities and want to look at the DTD for the WDDX format, it's included on the CD for this chapter. The filename is `wddx_0090.dtd`, and should be understood by any XML editor or validation tool.

WDDX and ColdFusion

As you've already learned, WDDX is not something that exists only for ColdFusion. It can also be used to pass information between other types of applications; in fact, that may be the most interesting thing about it. But because you're already developing ColdFusion applications, and because WDDX can be helpful in ColdFusion-only situations in a number of ways, learning about using WDDX in ColdFusion first makes sense. In the following sections, you'll see what an actual WDDX Packet looks like and how to serialize and deserialize the packet in a ColdFusion template.

The CFWDDX Tag

Each of the environments that support WDDX has some way to serialize and deserialize WDDX Packets. In a ColdFusion template, you use the CFWDDX tag to serialize and deserialize data from native ColdFusion variables to the WDDX Packet format. You can also use the CFWDDX tag to deserialize the data from the WDDX Packet format back into native ColdFusion variables.

Serializing Data into WDDX Packets Using the CFWDDX tag, you can easily serialize a ColdFusion variable into the WDDX format. For instance, take a look at Listing 16.2. This template defines a ColdFusion variable called Message that holds a simple string value. It then passes the variable to a CFWDDX tag as the tag's INPUT parameter.

The most important item in this template is the CFWDDX tag's ACTION parameter, which is set to CFML2WDDX. This parameter tells the tag that you are interested in taking a value from CFML and converting it to WDDX (the "2" in the parameter name stands for "to"). After the CFWDDX tag serializes the message, it stores the resulting WDDX Packet in the variable specified in the OUTPUT parameter of the tag. So, in this template, the converted message gets stored in a variable called MyWDDXPacket.

The template then outputs the packet to the browser so that you can see what the serialized version of the message looks like. Figure 16.1 shows the results.

Listing 16.2   Serialize.cfm—Serializing a Simple String into the WDDX Format

```
<!DOCTYPE HTML PUBLIC "-//W3C//DTD HTML 4.0 Transitional//EN">

<HTML>
<HEAD>
  <TITLE>Message Serializer</TITLE>
</HEAD>

<BODY>
<H2>Message Serializer</H2>

<!-- Set the #Message# variable to a simple string value -->
<CFSET Message = "Hello, World!">

<!-- Serialize the #Message# variable into a WDDX Packet -->
<CFWDDX
  INPUT="#Message#"
  OUTPUT="MyWDDXPacket"
  ACTION="CFML2WDDX">

<!-- Output WDDX Packet so we can see what it looks like -->
<!-- (HTMLEditFormat function lets us see tags properly) -->
<CFOUTPUT>
  <P><B>Original Message:</B> #Message#</P>
  <P><B>The message was serialized into the following WDDX Packet:</B></P>

  #HTMLEditFormat(MyWDDXPacket)#

</CFOUTPUT>

</BODY>
</HTML>
```

N O T E   Because the MyWDDXPacket variable contains tags that look like HTML tags, a Web browser generally does not display the packet's contents unless each < and > sign is converted to a < or > symbol. ColdFusion's HTMLEditFormat function escapes these kinds of special characters automatically, which is the reason that it's used in Listing 16.2. You can leave out the HTMLEditFormat function if you want, but in that case you need to use the browser's View Source command to actually see the packet's contents. ∎

TIP You can use ColdFusion's `HTMLCodeFormat` function instead of the `HTMLEditFormat` function to output the `MyWDDXPacket` variable. Doing so causes the browser to display the packet's contents using a fixed-width font, all on one long line.

FIGURE 16.1

Simple strings get placed between `<string>` tags in the WDDX format.

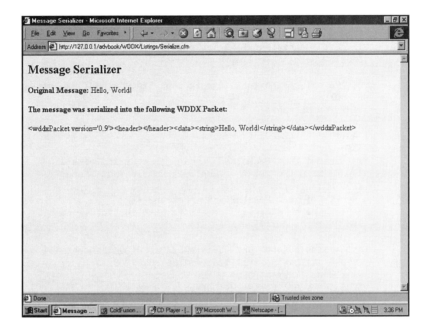

Deserializing Data from WDDX Packets You can just as easily perform the WDDX conversion in the opposite direction—that is, take an existing WDDX Packet and parse it into the appropriate ColdFusion variable. For instance, a template can take a WDDX Packet posted by a form, deserialize it, and place the deserialized value into a variable. The variable then contains the original message string (`"Hello, World!"`) and can be used in the rest of the template just like any other variable.

To demonstrate this idea, you can modify the template from Listing 16.2 so that it includes a simple form that posts the WDDX Packet to another template. All that's needed in the form is a single hidden field to hold the packet itself and a submit button. Listing 16.3 shows the code to produce this simple form, which is shown in Figure 16.2.

Listing 16.3 `Serialize2.cfm`—**Posting a WDDX Packet to Another ColdFusion Template**

```
<!DOCTYPE HTML PUBLIC "-//W3C//DTD HTML 4.0 Transitional//EN">

<HTML>
<HEAD>
```

continues

Listing 16.3   Continued

```
  <TITLE>Message Serializer</TITLE>
</HEAD>

<BODY>
<H2>Message Serializer</H2>

<!-- Set the #Message# variable to a simple string value -->
<CFSET Message = "Hello, World!">

<!-- Serialize the #Message# variable into a WDDX Packet -->
<CFWDDX
  INPUT="#Message#"
  OUTPUT="MyWDDXPacket"
  ACTION="CFML2WDDX">

<!-- Output WDDX Packet so we can see what it looks like -->
<!-- (HTMLEditFormat function lets us see tags properly) -->
<CFOUTPUT>
  <P><B>Original Message:</B> #Message#</P>
  <P><B>The message was serialized into the following WDDX Packet:</B></P>
  #HTMLEditFormat(MyWDDXPacket)#

  <!-- Simple form that posts WDDX Packet as hidden field -->
  <FORM ACTION="Deserialize.cfm" METHOD="POST">
    <INPUT TYPE="HIDDEN" NAME="WDDXContent"
VALUE="#HTMLEditFormat(MyWDDXPacket)#">
    <INPUT TYPE="SUBMIT" VALUE="Post WDDX Packet to Next Page">
  </FORM>

</CFOUTPUT>

</BODY>
</HTML>
```

N O T E   Because WDDX Packets often contain double quotation marks, you should use the HTMLEditFormat function when supplying a packet's contents to the VALUE parameter of an INPUT or OPTION tag on a form. For instance, if the Message variable contains a double quotation mark, the browser thinks that the VALUE parameter of the hidden field ends at that quotation mark (instead of the ending quotation mark that's in the CFM template itself, after the #MyWDDXPacket# variable). In this case, the form page probably does not display properly, and when the form is posted, the packet's contents are chopped off at the embedded quotation mark, making it unusable. ■

The form in Listing 16.3 posts its data to a template called Deserialize.cfm, so putting that template together is the next task at hand. The template needs to take the posted WDDX Packet—which is available in the #Form.WDDXContent# variable—and deserialize it into a native ColdFusion variable.

FIGURE 16.2

A WDDX Packet can be "hidden" in a form and posted to another Web page.

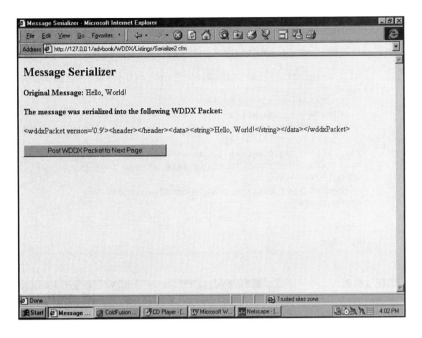

The code in Listing 16.4 does just that. Just like the serialization templates you've seen so far, this template uses the CFWDDX tag to do all the WDDX conversion work. Because it is interested in getting data from WDDX to CFML, this template uses WDDX2CFML for the tag's ACTION parameter (instead of CFML2WDDX, which was used previously). The #Form.WDDXContent# variable—which holds the WDDX Packet from the preceding form—is fed to the tag's INPUT parameter.

Working with the data extracted from the packet is simple and straightforward. The CFWDDX tag's OUTPUT parameter tells ColdFusion to extract the actual value from the packet and place it into the #PostedMessage# variable. You are then free to work with the variable just as you would work with any other variable. This simple example just displays the variable's value on the current Web page to prove that the packet was deserialized successfully. Figure 16.3 shows the results.

Listing 16.4 `Deserialize.cfm`—**Deserializing a WDDX Packet into a Normal ColdFusion Variable**

```
<!DOCTYPE HTML PUBLIC "-//W3C//DTD HTML 4.0 Transitional//EN">

<HTML>
<HEAD>
  <TITLE>Message De-serializer</TITLE>
</HEAD>

<BODY>
```

continues

Listing 16.4 Continued

```
<H2>Message De-serializer</H2>

<!-- Deserialize the WDDX Packet posted by form field -->
<CFWDDX
  INPUT="#Form.WDDXContent#"
  OUTPUT="PostedMessage"
  ACTION="WDDX2CFML">

<!-- Output WDDX Packet so we can see what it looks like -->
<!-- (HTMLEditFormat function lets us see tags properly) -->
<CFOUTPUT>
  <P><B>Posted Message:</B> #PostedMessage#</P>
</CFOUTPUT>

</BODY>
</HTML>
```

FIGURE 16.3

You can easily deserialize an incoming WDDX Packet from another page.

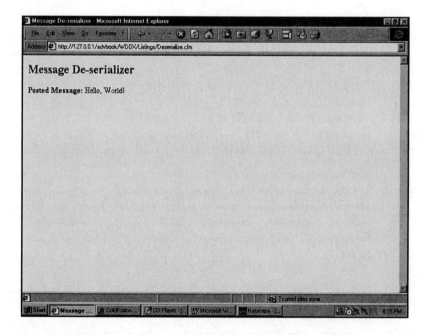

Serializing Structures and Arrays You've seen that a string can be serialized, passed to another page, and then deserialized back to its original form. Although the process appears to work just fine, you might be thinking that it's not exactly ground breaking. For instance, why not just pass the #Message# variable itself in the form's hidden field and skip all this serialization and deserialization business altogether?

Well, things get a whole lot more interesting when you consider that the INPUT parameter of the serialization template (see Listing 16.3) can accept any ColdFusion variable, not just a simple string value. It can be an array, a structure, an array within a structure, and so on.

 TIP

The code in this section makes use of ColdFusion *structures*, which are new for ColdFusion 4. Structures are similar to arrays but are indexed by "key" rather than by number. Structures are basically the same as what other languages call "associative arrays." See the "Working with Structures" chapter in your ColdFusion documentation if you want to learn more about structures.

Suppose that you need to build a "book finder" Web page that submits a request for information from another server or application. The request will include a few parameters about the books for which information is needed, such as author names, number of pages, and publication date. These parameters need to be submitted with the request, and the other server or application will presumably respond by sending back information about books that match those parameters.

A good way to get these parameters to the other application is to create a ColdFusion Structure that holds each of the parameters. Then you need only modify the code in Listing 16.3 so that it serializes the structure instead of the simple #Message# variable that you've been serializing up to now.

The code in Listing 16.5 does just that. It creates a structure called #Request# that holds a date value, a numeric value, and an array of author names. The whole structure is serialized into a WDDX Packet, and the packet is placed into a hidden field just as in Listing 16.3. Figure 16.4 shows the results.

Listing 16.5 Serialize3.cfm—Serializing Complex Data Types Requires No Additional Work

```
<!DOCTYPE HTML PUBLIC "-//W3C//DTD HTML 4.0 Transitional//EN">

<HTML>
<HEAD>
  <TITLE>Remote Book Finder</TITLE>
</HEAD>

<BODY>
<H2>Remote Book Finder</H2>


<!-- Create an array of Author names -->
<CFSET Authors = ArrayNew(2)>
<CFSET Authors[1][1] = "Ben">
<CFSET Authors[1][2] = "Forta">
```

continues

Listing 16.5 Continued

```
<CFSET Authors[2][1] = "Douglas">
<CFSET Authors[2][2] = "Adams">

<!-- #Request# structure to hold the array and other info -->
<CFSET Request = StructNew()>
<CFSET Request["Author"] = Authors>
<CFSET Request["PubDateFrom"] = ParseDateTime("3/18/1997")>
<CFSET Request["PagesAtLeast"] = Val(200)>


<!-- Serialize the #Request# variable into a WDDX Packet -->
<CFWDDX
  INPUT="#Request#"
  OUTPUT="MyWDDXPacket"
  ACTION="CFML2WDDX">

<!-- Output WDDX Packet so we can see what it looks like -->
<!-- (HTMLEditFormat function lets us see tags properly) -->
<CFOUTPUT>
  <P><B>The structure was serialized into the following WDDX Packet:</B></P>
  #HTMLEditFormat(MyWDDXPacket)#

  <!-- Simple form that posts WDDX Packet as hidden field -->
  <FORM ACTION="Deserialize3.cfm" METHOD="POST">
    <INPUT TYPE="HIDDEN" NAME="WDDXContent" VALUE=
➥"#HTMLEditFormat(MyWDDXPacket)#">
    <INPUT TYPE="SUBMIT" VALUE="Post WDDX Packet to Next Page">
  </FORM>

</CFOUTPUT>

</BODY>
</HTML>
```

 If you need to ensure that ColdFusion knows to serialize a particular value as a number (rather than as a string), use the Val function when setting the variable—as Listing 16.5 does for the PagesAtLeast element. Otherwise, ColdFusion's "typeless" nature causes it to put <string> tags instead of <number> tags around the value. These tags could be a problem if you're passing the serialized packet to an application that isn't as forgiving about data types.

 Similarly, if you need to ensure that a date gets serialized as a dateTime "object" in the WDDX Packet (rather than as a simple string value), use the ParseDateTime function, as shown in Listing 16.5. Alternatively, you can use the CreateDate function (handy if you have the year, month, and day as separate values). Either function returns a ColdFusion date/time value, which CFWDDX serializes properly to WDDX's dateTime data type.

FIGURE 16.4

Structures and arrays can also be serialized and deserialized with ease.

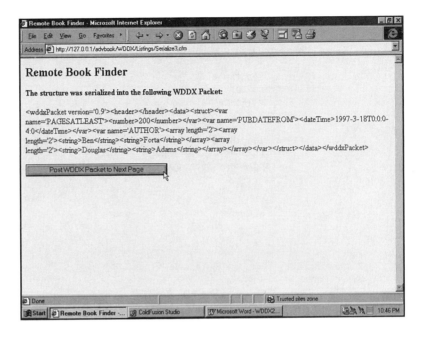

Taking a moment to examine the structure of the WDDX Packet shown in Figure 16.4 is worthwhile. It looks a bit cryptic when the tags are all mashed together, but the format of the packet is really quite simple. If some indenting is added to the packet to make it easier to read, you can clearly see how sensibly WDDX deals with structures and arrays. Listing 16.6 shows what you might end up with if you copy and paste the packet into a text editor and add some indenting.

Listing 16.6 `StructPacket.txt`—The WDDX Packet Shown in Figure 16.4, Indented for Clarity

```
<wddxPacket version='0.9'>
  <header/>
  <data>

    <struct>

      <var name='PAGESATLEAST'>
        <number>200</number>
      </var>

      <var name='PUBDATEFROM'>
        <dateTime>1997-3-18T0:0:0-4:0</dateTime>
      </var>

      <var name='AUTHOR'>
```

continues

Listing 16.6 Continued

```
        <array length='2'>

          <array length='2'>
            <string>Ben</string>
            <string>Forta</string>
          </array>

          <array length='2'>
            <string>Douglas</string>
            <string>Adams</string>
          </array>

        </array>
      </var>

    </struct>

  </data>
</wddxPacket>
```

You already know that the <wddxPacket>, <header>, and <data> tags are always the same, so just concentrate on the stuff between the <data> tags. Next in the chain is the pair of <struct> tags that enclose the entire structure. Then each element of the structure is described by a pair of <var> tags that specify the element's "key" in its name attribute. Then, inside the <var> tags, you can describe the simple values (the number and the date) by enclosing the value within <number> or <dateTime> tags.

Because the third element in the structure is an array, its individual values (the names of the two authors) are surrounded by two levels of <array> tags. The outer level indicates the first dimension of the two-dimensional array. (A two-dimensional array is technically an array of arrays.) The inner level represents the second dimension of the array, which is made up of one array for first names and a second array for last names. Inside the <array> tags, the actual data is treated in the same way as the simple number and date values were. Pretty simple stuff, really, but well-thought out and quietly powerful.

Even though indentation and blank lines have been added to Listing 16.6, it's still a perfectly valid WDDX Packet. It will be deserialized in exactly the same way as the packet shown in Figure 16.4 will be. So, if you want to make your application WDDX Packets more readable for human beings by adding lines, spaces, and tabs between the tags, go right ahead. All that extra whitespace is ignored by the WDDX deserialization process.

Deserializing Structures and Arrays   To receive and work with the "request" packet shown in Listing 16.6, the deserialization code from Listing 16.4 must be adapted only slightly to prove that the structure can be successfully extracted from the WDDX Packet without losing any-thing. Actually, nothing about the CFWDDX tag needs to change, which is one of the great things about WDDX. The conversion process—in both directions—is completely transparent to ColdFusion developers. Complex data types and simple data types are dealt with in exactly the same way.

The only thing that you need to change is the code to display the data. You would have to write this code anyway to display the data on the browser. Listing 16.7 provides code that will deserialize the structure, display its simple number and dateTime elements, and iterate through the array of authors, displaying the value of each item in the array. Figure 16.5 shows the results.

Listing 16.7 `Deserialize3.cfm`**—Deserializing the Structure and the Embedded Array**

```
<!DOCTYPE HTML PUBLIC "-//W3C//DTD HTML 4.0 Transitional//EN">

<HTML>
<HEAD>
  <TITLE>Request De-serializer</TITLE>
</HEAD>

<BODY>
<H2>Request De-serializer</H2>

<!-- Deserialize the WDDX Packet posted by form field -->
<!-- Original structure values now in #PostedRequest# -->
<CFWDDX
  INPUT="#Form.WDDXContent#"
  OUTPUT="PostedRequest"
  ACTION="WDDX2CFML">


<!-- Display info in structure (from the WDDX packet)  -->
<CFOUTPUT>
  <!-- Output simple-value elements from the structure -->
  <P><B>Only books over:</B><BR>
  #PostedRequest["PagesAtLeast"]# pages

  <P><B>Published After:</B><BR>
  #DateFormat(PostedRequest["PubDateFrom"], "mmmm d, yyyy")#

  <!-- We know "Author" element of structure is an array -->
  <!-- Set it to a local array variable for simplicity  -->
  <CFSET PostedAuthors = PostedRequest["Author"]>

  <!-- Loop thru PostedAuthors array to output each name -->
  <P><B>Authors:</B><BR>
  <CFLOOP FROM="1" TO="#ArrayLen(PostedAuthors)#" INDEX="Counter">
    Author #Counter#:
      #PostedAuthors[Counter][2]#,     <!-- Last Name  -->
```

continues

Listing 16.7 Continued

```
        #PostedAuthors[Counter][1]#<BR> <!-- First Name -->
    </CFLOOP>

</CFOUTPUT>

</BODY>
</HTML>
```

FIGURE 16.5

The WDDX deserialization process preserves complex data types, too.

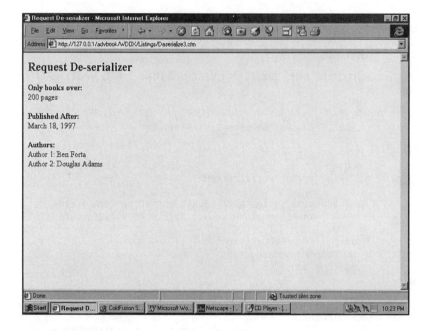

WDDX's real strength is that it can exchange complex data types such as structures and arrays without a problem. As you'll see in the next section, it can also be used to exchange entire query-style recordsets, like the results returned by a CFQUERY tag.

Exchanging WDDX Packets via Special Web Pages

If you've done any work with ColdFusion's CFHTTP tag, you know that you can use it to fetch Web pages from any Web server on the Internet. Basically, the CFHTTP tag pretends to be a Web browser, supplying any parameters that would normally be supplied by form input, cookies, or CGI variables. ColdFusion developers already use this tag to have their applications automatically visit other Web pages programmatically.

For instance, a ColdFusion application might need to know the current temperature. By using CFHTTP to fetch a page that includes the current temperature—perhaps the "current conditions" page of the local airport's Web site—the application can obtain a document that has the needed information in it. Then, using ColdFusion's string manipulation functions or some regular expressions, the application can parse through the page's source code and extract the few characters that represent the temperature.

N O T E Refer to Chapter 21, "Intelligent Agents and Distributed Processing," for a complete discussion of how you can use the CFHTTP tag to fetch Web pages from other Web servers on the Internet or from servers on your intranet or extranet. ▨

Part
IV

Ch
16

The Concept of a Back-End Web Page   Okay, now imagine taking things a step further. What if the airport's Web site has a special page that isn't meant to be looked at, but rather is meant only to supply information to other systems? That is, instead of including pictures, links, table and font tags, explanatory text, and so on, what if all the page contains is a WDDX Packet with the temperature? Maybe the packet includes other information as well, such as the barometric pressure, runway conditions, and so on.

In that case, any ColdFusion application could use the CFHTTP tag to pick up this packet and then use CFWDDX to extract all the information from the packet into local variables. Just two lines of CFML code later, the application has the information it needs. You can easily imagine that other airports around the world might set up the same kind of back-end Web pages to report the current conditions. The airports might even use these pages to get information about each other's current conditions to be able to tell customers what the weather is like at their destinations.

Suddenly, the airport's Web site is no longer just supplying information to people who happen to visit the Web site and click on the "current conditions" page. It's now a part of an ambitious information and automation network. No expensive communications channels were set up, and no complicated "integration" work was done. By using the infrastructures already in place—namely, the airport's Web server and Internet connection—the airport can transform itself into a source of raw data for any application that knows how to fetch a Web page and how to deserialize a WDDX Packet.

N O T E Of course, ColdFusion knows how to perform both of these tasks, and fetching the WDDX Packet and deserializing it with ColdFusion are what you'll learn to do next. But as you'll see later in this chapter and in the next chapter, you also can use Perl and JavaScript to fetch and deserialize the information. And so can any COM-enabled application such as Visual Basic, Delphi, or Visual C++. ▨

Creating a Back-End Web Page   The Deserialize3.cfm template shown in Listing 16.7 demonstrated how a ColdFusion structure could be easily collected from form input and deserialized, making the structure's various elements available for display. Now, instead of just displaying the information from the structure, turn the code from Listing 16.7 into a kind of automated "robot" that waits for incoming requests and responds to them.

Take a look at the BookRobot.cfm template shown in Listing 16.8. This robot will run a database query based on the parameters contained within the incoming Request structure and send back the query results as a WDDX Packet. Don't worry; the robot template may appear to be complicated at first glance, but as soon as you take a closer look, you'll see that it's actually very simple.

Really, only three ColdFusion tags are of any consequence here, each taking care of a specific logical step. The first CFWDDX tag—unchanged from Listing 16.7—deserializes the incoming WDDX Packet and places it in the PostedRequest structure.

Next, the CFQUERY tag builds a database query on-the-fly, based on the various elements contained within the structure. Finally, the second CFWDDX tag converts the entire recordset returned by the CFQUERY into a WDDX Packet, outputting it to the current page.

> **N O T E** The first CFWDDX tag is placed inside a CFIF block that makes sure that a variable named WDDXContent has been passed to the template. If the variable was not passed, the CFSET tag in the CFELSE part of the block kicks in and creates a new, empty structure named PostedRequest. This means that a structure named PostedRequest will always exist, which allows the rest of the code to execute without errors if the template is called without any parameters at all. The net result is that the template "assumes" that it should return all records if no specific criteria are provided. ▪

Listing 16.8 `BookRobot.cfm`—A Book Robot That Answers Queries via WDDX

```
<!-- Deserialize the WDDX Packet posted by form field -->
<!-- Original structure values now in #PostedRequest# -->
<!-- If no WDDXContent variable provided in form/url, -->
<!-- Then create an "empty" PostedRequest structure   -->
<CFIF ParameterExists(WDDXContent)>
  <CFWDDX
    INPUT="#WDDXContent#"
    OUTPUT="PostedRequest"
    ACTION="WDDX2CFML">
<CFELSE>
  <CFSET PostedRequest = StructNew()>
</CFIF>

<!- The PostedRequest Structure may contain these elements:
  "Columns"     - the database columns to fetch from table
  "ISBN"        - the ISBN number for a specific book
  "PagesAtLeast" - only books with this many pages or more
  "PubDateFrom" - only books published on/after this date
  "Author"      - a 2D array of author first/last names
  "Sort"        - order in which to return the results
-->


<!-- Fetch the information from the database -->
<CFQUERY NAME="GetBooks" DATASOURCE="A2Z">

  <!-- If request structure has a "Columns" element, -->
  <!-- SELECT those. Otherwise default to ISBN/Title -->
```

```
<CFIF StructKeyExists(PostedRequest, "Columns")>
  SELECT #PostedRequest["Columns"]#
<CFELSE>
  SELECT ISBN, Title
</CFIF>

FROM Inventory
WHERE 0=0

<!-- If "ISBN" element in request structure -->
<CFIF StructKeyExists(PostedRequest, "ISBN")>
  AND ISBN = '#PostedRequest["ISBN"]#'
</CFIF>

<!-- If "PagesAtLeast" element in request structure -->
<CFIF StructKeyExists(PostedRequest, "PagesAtLeast")>
  AND Pages > #PostedRequest["PagesAtLeast"]#
</CFIF>

<!-- If "PubDateFrom" element in request structure -->
<CFIF StructKeyExists(PostedRequest, "PubDateFrom")>
  AND PublicationDate >= #CreateODBCDate(PostedRequest["PubDateFrom"])#
</CFIF>

<!-- If "Author" element (array) in request structure -->
<CFIF StructKeyExists(PostedRequest, "Author")>

  <!-- Set local array variable for simplicity -->
  <CFSET PostedAuthors = PostedRequest["Author"]>
  AND (0=1

  <!-- Loop through each author in the array -->
  <CFLOOP FROM="1" TO="#ArrayLen(PostedAuthors)#" INDEX="ThisAuth">
    OR (AuthorFirstName = '#PostedAuthors[ThisAuth][1]#'
    AND AuthorLastName  = '#PostedAuthors[ThisAuth][2]#')
  </CFLOOP>

  )
</CFIF>

  <!-- If request structure has a "Sort" element, -->
  <!-- ORDER BY that.  Otherwise default to Title -->
  <CFIF StructKeyExists(PostedRequest, "Sort")>
    ORDER BY #PostedRequest["Sort"]#
  <CFELSE>
    ORDER BY Title
  </CFIF>

</CFQUERY>


<!-- Convert the query results (recordset) to WDDX -->
<CFWDDX
  INPUT="#GetBooks#"
  ACTION="CFML2WDDX">
```

The second part of the template—the dynamically created query statement—makes the template look complicated. If you imagine that the "Author" part of the CFQUERY code were taken out, for instance, or handled in a simpler manner, the template would really be short and sweet. Considering what it does—you'll see it in action in a moment—its brevity and simplicity are pretty amazing.

TIP When you want a Web page to return only a WDDX Packet, remember not to include the various HTML tags that you would normally include in a ColdFusion template or static Web page. For instance, Listing 16.8 has no HEAD, TITLE, or BODY tags because it is not intended to ever be rendered visually by a Web browser.

N O T E The second CFWDDX tag shown in Listing 16.8 does not have an OUTPUT parameter. As a result, the tag simply outputs the WDDX Packet it creates onto the current page, instead of placing the packet's contents into a variable. If you want, you can add an OUTPUT parameter that specifies a variable name and then output the variable's contents by placing it between a pair of CFOUTPUT tags (after the CFWDDX tag). The results are exactly the same. Omitting the OUTPUT parameter is just a shortcut. ■

Testing the Robot with an Ordinary Form   Because the robot is going to respond to queries with a WDDX Packet rather than by displaying a normal Web page, it's not really designed to be accessed by humans. It can be tested with an ordinary HTML form and a Web browser, however, to make sure that the robot actually works correctly.

You can use the simple "tester" code shown in Listing 16.9 to test the robot. It just creates a simple form that a WDDX Packet can be pasted into. When the form is submitted, the robot examines the packet, runs the appropriate database query, and returns the results as a new WDDX Packet.

Listing 16.9   **BookRobotTester.cfm—A Simple Form That Invokes the Book Robot**

```
<!DOCTYPE HTML PUBLIC "-//W3C//DTD HTML 4.0 Transitional//EN">

<HTML>
<HEAD>
    <TITLE>Robot Tester</TITLE>
</HEAD>

<BODY>

<FORM ACTION="BookRobot.cfm" METHOD="POST">
  To test the robot, paste a WDDX Packet in here and submit:<BR>

  <TEXTAREA NAME="WDDXContent" ROWS="10" COLS="60" WRAP="VIRTUAL"></TEXTAREA>
```

```
    <P><INPUT TYPE="Submit">
  </FORM>

  </BODY>
  </HTML>
```

You already have a WDDX Packet that you can use with the tester—the packet from Listing 16.6. Just bring up the `Serialize3.cfm` template in your browser (see Figure 16.4); then cut and paste the packet into the tester form's text area and submit it. Figure 16.6 shows what the form looks like after the packet has been pasted into it.

FIGURE 16.6

The Book Robot can be tested with an ordinary HTML form.

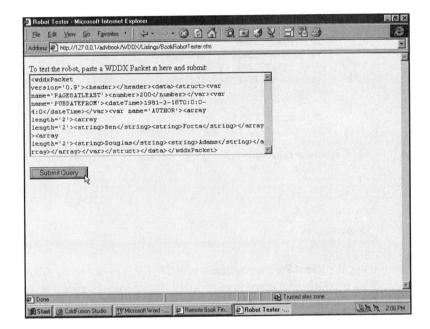

The robot's response to the form submission doesn't look like much. Depending on the browser, you might see some book titles run together into one long paragraph, or you may just get a blank page. If you use your browser's View Source command, you'll see that the robot indeed responds with a WDDX Packet that contains the ISBN number and Title for each book that matches the parameters from the test packet you submitted.

Listing 16.10 shows the WDDX Packet returned by the robot, with extra lines and indenting added. This is the first time you're seeing how WDDX serializes a recordset. As you can see, the result is very similar to the way that WDDX treats structures (see Listing 16.6). First, the entire recordset is wrapped in a pair of `<recordset>` tags. The opening `<recordset>` tag specifies the number of rows in its `rowCount` attribute and the column names from the database in the `fieldNames` attribute. Inside the `<recordset>` tags, the actual contents of each column are provided, with each column enclosed in a pair of `<field>` tags. Within each `<field>` tag, the data from each row from the column appears between a pair of `<string>`, `<number>`, or `<dateTime>` tags, as appropriate.

Listing 16.10   `RecordsetPacket.txt`—The Robot's Response to the Test, with Whitespace Added for Clarity

```
<wddxPacket version='0.9'>
  <header/>
  <data>

    <recordset rowCount='3' fieldNames='ISBN,TITLE'>

      <field name='ISBN'>
        <string>0345391829</string>
        <string>0789709708</string>
        <string>0517545357</string>
      </field>

      <field name='TITLE'>
        <string>Life, the Universe and Everything</string>
        <string>The Cold Fusion Web Database Construction Kit</string>
<string>The Restaurant at the End of the Universe</string>
      </field>

    </recordset>

  </data>
</wddxPacket>
```

Using the Robot Programmatically with CFHTTP   Now that the robot has been proven to work correctly, all that you need to do is come up with the code that will actually submit requests to the robot. Instead of using an onscreen form as the tester template does, you can use the CFHTTP tag to mimic a form submission. Then the robot's response—which is structured like the packet shown in Listing 16.10—can be deserialized and shown to the users.

The CFFORM-based code in Listing 16.11 creates a simple onscreen form that people can use to get information about books in the A2Z database's Inventory table (see Figure 16.7). Users might not realize it, but when they use the form, they aren't directly interacting with a copy of the database on the server. Instead, the form is posted to the BookFinder.cfm template (discussed in a moment), which sends the request on to the Book Robot. So, the Book Robot handles the actual database queries; the template that this form posts to merely acts as a sort of proxy for the Book Robot.

Listing 16.11   `FinderForm.cfm`—A Search Form for Users to Interact with the Book Robot

```
<!DOCTYPE HTML PUBLIC "-//W3C//DTD HTML 4.0 Transitional//EN">

<HTML>
```

```
<HEAD>
  <TITLE>Book Finder</TITLE>
</HEAD>

<BODY>
<H2>Book Finder</H2>


<!-- Simple form where the user can enter parameters -->
<CFFORM ACTION="BookFinder.cfm" METHOD="POST">

  <!-- Blank to enter publication date "filter" -->
  <P><B>Only books published after:</B><BR>
  <CFINPUT
    NAME="PubDateFrom"
    SIZE="10"
    VALIDATE="DATE"><BR>

  <!-- Blank to enter min. number of pages -->
  <P><B>Only books with at least:</B><BR>
  <CFINPUT
    NAME="PagesAtLeast"
    SIZE=5
    VALIDATE="integer"> pages<BR>


  <!-- Drop-down menu to choose RobotServer -->
  <P><B>Location:</B><BR>
  <SELECT NAME="RobotServer">
    <OPTION VALUE="http://127.0.0.1">This store
    <OPTION VALUE="http://nyc.a2zbooks.com">New York store
    <OPTION VALUE="http://tokyo.a2zbooks.com">Tokyo store
  </SELECT><BR>


  <!-- Blanks to enter up to 5 author names -->
  <P><B>Authors:</B> (LastName, FirstName)<BR>
  <CFLOOP FROM="1" TO="5" INDEX="Counter">
    <CFOUTPUT>
      <INPUT NAME="LastName#Counter#">,
      <INPUT NAME="FirstName#Counter#"><BR>
    </CFOUTPUT>
  </CFLOOP>


  <!-- Submit button -->
  <HR><CENTER><INPUT TYPE="Submit" VALUE="Find Books Now"></CENTER>


</CFFORM>

</BODY>
</HTML>
```

FIGURE 16.7

Users can query a Book Robot operating at any store location worldwide.

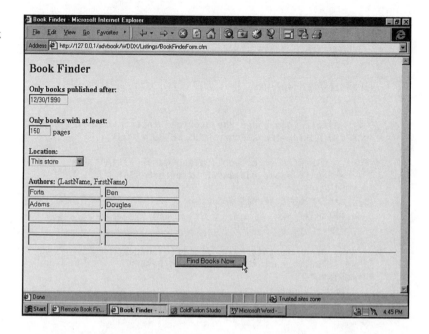

Now take a look at Listing 16.12, which receives the input posted by the form in Listing 16.11, serializes the form input into a WDDX Packet, and posts the packet to the Book Robot template. Again, this template looks a bit more complicated than it actually is. If you look at its component parts, you can see that it is made up of just a few ColdFusion tags, each of which represents a discreet logical step. As you look it over, note that except for the CFHTTP part at the end, the basic idea of this template is similar to the code found in Listing 16.5.

TIP

This template makes use of ColdFusion scripting, which is new for ColdFusion 4. If the syntax in the CFSCRIPT block looks unfamiliar to you, take a quick look at Chapter 18, "ColdFusion Scripting," for a discussion about the if, for, and assignment statements used in this template.

Listing 16.12 `BookFinder.cfm`—**Interacting with the Book Robot via CFHTTP**

```
<!DOCTYPE HTML PUBLIC "-//W3C//DTD HTML 4.0 Transitional//EN">

<HTML>
<HEAD>
  <TITLE>Book Finder</TITLE>
</HEAD>

<BODY>
<H2>Book Finder - Results</H2>
```

```
<!-- Assemble the user's input into structure -->
<CFSCRIPT>
  // New request structure to pass to robot
  Request = StructNew();

  // If user entered a date, include in structure
  if (IsDate(Form.PubDateFrom)) {
    Request["PubDateFrom"] = Form.PubDateFrom;
  }

  // If user entered minimum number of pages
  if (IsNumeric(Form.PagesAtLeast)) {
    Request["PagesAtLeast"] = Form.PagesAtLeast;
  }

  // Create 2D array for Authors entered on form
  Authors = ArrayNew(2);

  // For each of the 5 blanks, check if name was entered
  for (Counter = 1; Counter LT 5; Counter = Counter + 1) {
    First = Evaluate("Form.FirstName#Counter#");
    Last = Evaluate("Form.LastName#Counter#");

    // if a name was entered, add to Authors array
    if ( (First is not "") AND (Last is not "") ) {
      Authors[Counter][1] = First;
      Authors[Counter][2] = Last;
    }
  }

  // if names in Authors array, add to Request structure
  if (ArrayLen(Authors) GT 0) {
    Request["Author"] = Authors;
  }
</CFSCRIPT>

<!-- Convert the structure to WDDX Packet -->
<CFWDDX
  INPUT="#Request#"
  OUTPUT="RequestAsWDDX"
  ACTION="CFML2WDDX">

<!-- Post the WDDX Packet to the "robot" page as a form field -->
<CFHTTP URL="#Form.RobotServer#/Robots/BookRobot.cfm" METHOD="POST">
  <CFHTTPPARAM
    NAME="WDDXContent"
    VALUE="#RequestAsWDDX#"
    TYPE="FORMFIELD">
</CFHTTP>

<!-- Extract recordset from WDDX Packet in robot's response -->
<CFWDDX
  INPUT="#CFHTTP.FileContent#"
```

continues

Part

IV

Ch

16

Listing 16.12   Continued

```
      OUTPUT="FetchedBooks"
      ACTION="WDDX2CFML">

   <!-- Output the "fetched" books to browser -->
   <UL>
   <CFOUTPUT QUERY="FetchedBooks">
     <LI>#Title#
   </CFOUTPUT>
   </UL>

 </BODY>
 </HTML>
```

The first thing the template in Listing 16.12 needs to do is to put together a request structure to pass to the Book Robot. This takes place in the CFSCRIPT block at the top of the template. It looks long and complicated, but it's really not; all it does is check to see whether a user entered anything in each of the form fields and, if so, adds a corresponding element to the request structure. Next, the structure is serialized into a WDDX Packet called WDDXContent, which will look more or less like the WDDX Packet generated by Listing 16.5 and shown in Listing 16.6.

Then the template uses the CFHTTP tag to post the request to the Book Robot template. The robot processes the request and responds, just as it did when the request was coming from the test form (refer to Figure 16.6). ColdFusion stores the robot's response in the #CFHTTP.FileContent# variable, which should contain a WDDX Packet that looks a lot like Listing 16.10. That variable is fed to the second CFWDDX tag, which deserializes the robot's response back into a recordset called FetchedBooks.

Finally, the template can display the title of each book returned by the robot by referring to the #Title# variable inside a CFOUTPUT block that specifies FetchedBooks as its QUERY parameter. In other words, the FetchedBooks query recordset can be used just as if the CFQUERY had taken place earlier in the same template.

N O T E   The URL parameter of the CFHTTP tag is looking for the BookRobot.cfm template to be located in a directory called Robots. In other words, after the #Form.RobotServer# variable is evaluated, ColdFusion goes to http://127.0.0.1/Robots/RobotServer.cfm to post the request. So, if you are trying to follow along with these examples, you need to configure your Web server to have a virtual directory that maps /Robots to the folder where the RobotServer.cfm file actually is located. ∎

At this point, the whole thing should actually work. Type some search criteria into the form and submit it. The BookFinder.cfm template will receive the form input, interact with the Book Robot, and display the titles of the matching books. Figure 16.8 shows the results.

FIGURE 16.8

The Book Robot's response is deserialized and displayed to the users.

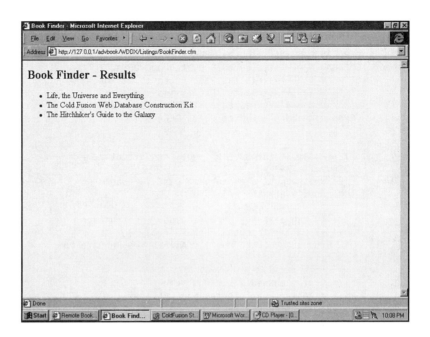

Simplifying the Use of the Robot with a Custom Tag   The bulk of the code in Listing 16.12—that is, the parts that put together the request, interact with the robot, and deserialize the robot's response—might need to be reused in other templates. Therefore, wrapping up the functionality into a CFML Custom Tag makes a lot of sense.

The code in Listing 16.13 creates a `CF_UseBookRobot` tag that can be used in any template that needs to request information from the Book Robot. It's practically the same as Listing 16.12, except that most of the variables are in the Attributes scope (typical for CFML Custom Tags). In addition, a few extra lines of code are added to the `CFSCRIPT` block to allow the Custom Tag to add `ISBN` and `Sort` elements to the request structure when appropriate. Finally, the last line of the Custom Tag makes the fetched result set visible to the calling template with the name specified in the tag's `NAME` parameter.

 TIP   The code in Listing 16.13 will make more sense to you if you know the basics about creating CFML Custom Tags. Refer to Chapter 9, "Creating Custom Tags," for a complete discussion on the subject.

Listing 16.13   `UseBookRobot.cfm`—A Custom Tag That Does Most of What Listing 16.12 Does

```
<!-- Tag parameters -->
<CFPARAM NAME="Attributes.Name">
<CFPARAM NAME="Attributes.RobotServer" DEFAULT="#CGI.SERVER_NAME#">
<CFPARAM NAME="Attributes.Columns" DEFAULT="">
```

continues

Listing 16.13   Continued

```
<CFPARAM NAME="Attributes.ISBN" DEFAULT="">
<CFPARAM NAME="Attributes.PubDateFrom" DEFAULT="">
<CFPARAM NAME="Attributes.PagesAtLeast" DEFAULT="">
<CFPARAM NAME="Attributes.FirstNames" DEFAULT="">
<CFPARAM NAME="Attributes.LastNames" DEFAULT="">
<CFPARAM NAME="Attributes.Sort" DEFAULT="">


  <!-- Assemble the user's input into structure -->
  <CFSCRIPT>
    // New request structure to pass to robot
    Request = StructNew();

    // If tag passed a date, include in structure
    if (IsDate(Attributes.PubDateFrom)) {
      Request["PubDateFrom"] = Attributes.PubDateFrom;
    }

    // If tag passed a minimum number of pages
    if (IsNumeric(Attributes.PagesAtLeast)) {
      Request["PagesAtLeast"] = Attributes.PagesAtLeast;
    }

    // If tag passed a specific ISBN number
    if (Attributes.ISBN is not "") {
      Request["ISBN"] = Attributes.ISBN;
    }

    // If tag passed what columns to fetch
    if (Attributes.Columns is not "") {
      Request["Columns"] = Attributes.Columns;
    }

    // If tag passed a specific sort order
    if (Attributes.Sort is not "") {
      Request["Sort"] = Attributes.Sort;
    }

    // Handle any author names passed to tag
    Authors = ArrayNew(2);
    for (Counter = 1; Counter LTE ListLen(Attributes.FirstNames);
➥ Counter = Counter + 1) {
      Authors[Counter][1] = ListGetAt(Attributes.FirstNames, Counter);
      Authors[Counter][2] = ListGetAt(Attributes.LastNames, Counter);
    }
    if (ArrayLen(Authors) GT 0) {
      Request["Author"] = Authors;
    }
  </CFSCRIPT>

  <!-- Convert the structure to WDDX Packet -->
  <CFWDDX
    INPUT="#Request#"
```

```
  OUTPUT="RequestAsWDDX"
  ACTION="CFML2WDDX">

<!-- Post the WDDX Packet to the "robot" page as a form field -->
<CFHTTP URL="#Attributes.RobotServer#/Robots/BookRobot.cfm" METHOD="POST">
  <CFHTTPPARAM
    NAME="WDDXContent"
    VALUE="#RequestAsWDDX#"
    TYPE="FORMFIELD">
</CFHTTP>

<!-- Show an error message if CFHTTP tag didn't get anything -->
<CFIF CFHTTP.FileContent is "">
  <CFABORT SHOWERROR="Error - No data retrieved from RobotServer">
</CFIF>

<!-- Extract recordset from WDDX Packet in robot's response -->
<CFWDDX
  INPUT="#CFHTTP.FileContent#"
  OUTPUT="FetchedBooks"
  ACTION="WDDX2CFML">

<!-- Send fetched recordset to calling template -->
<CFSET "Caller.#Attributes.Name#" = FetchedBooks>
```

Now you can trim down the `BookFinder.cfm` template from Listing 16.12 to a simple template that contains only a few ColdFusion tags. The `BookFinder2.cfm` template in Listing 16.14 shows the new version of the code, which makes use of the new `CF_UseBookRobot` tag to do most of the actual work. The results look exactly the same as the results from Listing 16.12 did (see Figure 16.8), except that each book title now is a link that can be clicked on for more detail.

Listing 16.14 `BookFinder2.cfm`—**The Custom Tag Keeps Everything Simple and Abstract**

```
<!DOCTYPE HTML PUBLIC "-//W3C//DTD HTML 4.0 Transitional//EN">

<HTML>
<HEAD>
  <TITLE>Book Finder</TITLE>
</HEAD>

<BODY>
<H2>Book Finder - Results</H2>

  <!-- Custom Tag that interacts w/ Robot via HTTP & WDDX -->
  <CF_UseBookRobot
    ROBOTSERVER="#RobotServer#"
    PAGESATLEAST="#PagesAtLeast#"
    PUBDATEFROM="#PubDateFrom#"
```

continues

Listing 16.14 Continued

```
    FIRSTNAMES="#FirstName1#,#FirstName2#,#FirstName3#,#FirstName4#,#FirstName5#"
    LASTNAMES="#LastName1#,#LastName2#,#LastName3#,#LastName4#,#LastName5#"
    NAME="FetchedBooks">

  <!-- Output the "fetched" books to browser -->
  <CFOUTPUT QUERY="FetchedBooks">
    <LI><A HREF="BookFinderDetail.cfm?ISBN=#URLEncodedFormat(ISBN)#&RobotServer=
➥#URLEncodedFormat(RobotServer)#">#Title#</A>
  </CFOUTPUT>

</BODY>
</HTML>
```

Reusing the Robot for a Details Page   Creating the detail template is now very simple because most of the work is already encapsulated in the CF_UseBookRobot Custom Tag. The Custom Tag lets you reuse all the serialization, CFHTTP, and deserialization code that's already been written. Creating the details page, shown in Listing 16.15, is extremely simple and requires just a few lines of code.

Here, the Custom Tag is used to get the details about a particular book. Because the ROBOTSERVER parameter is set to #URL.RobotServer#, the users communicate with the same Book Robot that the search results came from. Because the COLUMNS attribute is set to "*", the Rook Robot does a SELECT * type of query from the database, so all the information from the table (the Title column, the Description column, and so on) is available for display in the CFOUTPUT block. The results are shown in Figure 16.9.

Listing 16.15 BookFinderDetail.cfm—Reusing the Book Robot and Custom Tag for a Details Page

```
<!DOCTYPE HTML PUBLIC "-//W3C//DTD HTML 4.0 Transitional//EN">

<HTML>
<HEAD>
  <TITLE>Book Finder</TITLE>
</HEAD>
<H2>Book Finder - Detail</H2>

<BODY>

  <!-- Use our Custom Tag to get all data for this ISBN -->
  <CF_UseBookRobot
    ROBOTSERVER="#URL.RobotServer#"
    ISBN="#URL.ISBN#"
    NAME="BookDetail"
    COLUMNS="*">

  <!-- Output the information to the browser -->
  <CFOUTPUT QUERY="BookDetail">
```

```
<!-- Make TH table headers gray (in 4.0+ browsers) -->
<STYLE>
  TH {background=silver};
</STYLE>

<TABLE BORDER="1">
  <TR>
    <TH>ISBN</TH><TD>#ISBN#</TD>
    <TH>Author</TH><TD>#AuthorLastName#, #AuthorFirstName#</TD>
  </TR>
  <TR>
    <TH COLSPAN="2">Title</TH><TD COLSPAN="2">#Title#</TD>
  </TR>
  <TR>
    <TH COLSPAN="2">Description</TH><TD COLSPAN="2">#Description#</TD>
  </TR>
</TABLE>
</CFOUTPUT>

</BODY>
</HTML>
```

FIGURE 16.9

This details page appears when a user clicks a title in the search results.

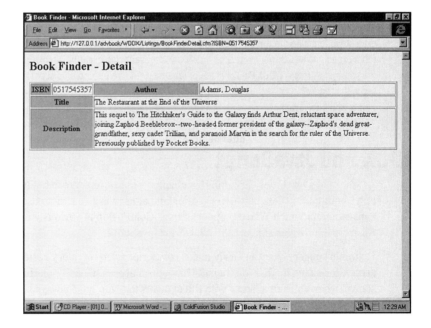

What It All Means   In the preceding sections, you created a Book Robot and learned how its use can be wrapped up into a Custom Tag, to the point where accessing data via the Book Robot becomes no more complicated than accessing a conventional data source (with a normal CFQUERY tag in the actual searching or details templates).

A little work was required to get to this point. But now that it's done, just think of what you've accomplished. When a new A2Z store opens anywhere in the world, all the staff needs to do to allow its inventory to be searched by the other stores is to make the BookRobot.cfm template available on its Web server. The other stores need only add that store's server to the Location drop-down list on the search form. Instant, inexpensive access!

The Book Robot—and the pages that fetch data from it—is really a distributed or three-tier application. This kind of thinking—that Web pages can act as "data slaves" to other Web pages, applications, or development tools—has the potential to become more prevalent in the near future. WDDX makes the development of such systems much easier.

And the benefits keep getting better because not only ColdFusion applications can interact with the BookFinder; any application that can fetch a Web page and interpret WDDX Packets can use its services as well. You'll see it in action with JavaScript later in this chapter and with other applications in the next chapter.

N O T E   The Book Robot and the templates that use it were designed to demonstrate how to use WDDX with structures and arrays and to demonstrate how to use WDDX in two directions (both to and from the robot). In practice, you could simplify the process somewhat. First, the fact that the author names to search for are expected to be passed as an array (rather than as a simple list, or only allowing the users to search for one author at a time) makes it necessary to go through some extra steps to create the two-dimensional array from the various blanks on the form. Also, having the robot expect the search parameters as individual form variables might be simpler than wrapping up all the parameters into a WDDX Packet. Each parameter would be passed as a separate CFHTTPPARAM tag in the "finder" template, and only the resulting recordset would need to be converted to the WDDX format and back again. ▪

WDDX and JavaScript

As you read a few times earlier in this chapter—but have yet to actually see—WDDX is not only about getting data between ColdFusion pages; it is also about passing data between any application for which WDDX support exists. ColdFusion is obviously one such application, but Allaire also provides support for WDDX for JavaScript.

With this support, you can easily make JavaScript aware of query result sets, structures, and arrays, for example, that traditionally have been accessible only "on the server side." For instance, when you run a query with the CFQUERY tag, you have always been able to send the information to the browser as a dynamically produced Web page. That's what ColdFusion has always been all about. WDDX lets you go a step further by letting you make the recordset itself a scriptable object. This capability really makes your Web interfaces "come alive" in a way that would have required a lot of very clever coding in the past.

N O T E This section assumes that you have at least a bit of familiarity with JavaScript. You certainly don't need to know the language inside and out to follow along, but if you have never dealt with JavaScript at all before, you might want to at least skim some sort of primer document about the basics. Documentation about JavaScript is available online at `http://developer.netscape.com`. ■

T I P Don't get confused between *JavaScript*—which is what this section deals with—and *Java*. The names are similar because they were originally conceived to be used together, but they are very different things. JavaScript is a simple interface-scripting language with support for WDDX today. Java is more complicated and does not have WDDX support at the time of this writing.

Part

IV

Ch

16

Passing ColdFusion Variables to JavaScript

If you use the CFWDDX tag, ColdFusion can automatically write JavaScript code for you that translates whatever data you have in a WDDX Packet into native JavaScript variables. For instance, if you have set a ColdFusion variable to hold a simple string, you already know how to convert that variable into a WDDX Packet. You can then run the packet through the CFWDDX tag again, this time to convert the WDDX Packet into JavaScript code. That JavaScript code, when interpreted by the browser, will set a JavaScript variable to the string value that was contained within the WDDX Packet.

Letting CFWDDX Write JavaScript Code for You   Take a look at Listing 16.16. It takes the `Serialize.cfm` template from the beginning of this chapter (refer to Listing 16.2) and adds a few lines of code at the end to make JavaScript aware of the #Message# variable. You've already seen the top part of the template; it converts the contents of the #Message# variable to a WDDX Packet named MyWDDXPacket.

The new part of the code uses the CFWDDX tag to convert the packet from the WDDX format to JavaScript code, by supplying the MyWDDXPacket variable to the tag's INPUT parameter. The TOPLEVELVARIABLE parameter tells the CFWDDX tag to write the JavaScript code such that it creates a JavaScript variable named MyJSVariable. Later, you can use your browser's View Source command to see the JavaScript code generated by the CFWDDX tag.

The JavaScript code is placed in the variable called DynamicJSCode because that's what is specified in the tag's OUTPUT parameter. The variable is then output between a pair of SCRIPT tags, which tell the browser to interpret everything between them as JavaScript code. When the browser interprets the JavaScript code, the JavaScript variable called MyJSVariable is set to the original WDDX Packet's contents.

Finally, this template uses JavaScript's alert method to display the JavaScript variable's contents in a pop-up dialog box, proving that the variable was passed successfully. The resulting Web page is exactly the same as before, except for the pop-up message. Figure 16.10 shows the results.

Listing 16.16 `JSSerialize.cfm`—**Making JavaScript Aware of a ColdFusion Variable**

```
<!DOCTYPE HTML PUBLIC "-//W3C//DTD HTML 4.0 Transitional//EN">

<HTML>
<HEAD>
  <TITLE>Message Serializer</TITLE>
</HEAD>

<BODY>
<H2>Message Serializer</H2>

<!-- Set the #Message# variable to a simple string value -->
<CFSET Message = "Hello, World!">

<!-- Serialize the #Message# variable into a WDDX Packet -->
<CFWDDX
  INPUT="#Message#"
  OUTPUT="MyWDDXPacket"
  ACTION="CFML2WDDX">

<!-- Output WDDX Packet so we can see what it looks like -->
<!-- (HTMLEditFormat function lets us see tags properly) -->
<CFOUTPUT>
  <P><B>Original Message:</B> #Message#</P>
  <P><B>The message was serialized into the following WDDX Packet:</B></P>

  #HTMLEditFormat(MyWDDXPacket)#
</CFOUTPUT>


<!-- **** new Code starts here **** -->


<!-- Ask CFWDDX tag to convert packet from WDDX to JavaScript -->
<!-- Resulting JavaScript code gets placed in #DynamicJSCode# -->
<CFWDDX
  INPUT="#MyWDDXPacket#"
  OUTPUT="DynamicJSCode"
  ACTION="WDDX2JS"
  TOPLEVELVARIABLE="MyJSVariable">


<!-- Output dynamically-produced JavaScript code from CFWDDX -->
<!-- Must be between SCRIPT tags so JS knows to interpret it -->
<SCRIPT LANGUAGE="JavaScript">
  // The following code was produced by the CFWDDX tag.
  // It will set a variable named "MyJSVariable" to the
  // Contents of the WDDX Packet supplied to 2nd CFWDDX
  <CFOUTPUT>#DynamicJSCode#</CFOUTPUT>
```

```
    // Now display the variable in a pop-up dialog box
    alert(MyJSVariable);
</SCRIPT>


</BODY>
</HTML>
```

T I P Always remember to use CFOUTPUT tags around a variable that contains dynamic JavaScript code—
such as the DyanamicJSCode variable in this example—between SCRIPT tags. Otherwise, the actual
name of the variable (with the # signs around it and all) is sent to the browser. Because the variable
name is not valid JavaScript code (only its contents are), this action causes the browser to "choke" and
display a JavaScript error message.

FIGURE 16.10

The Web page itself is
now aware of the
"message" variable.

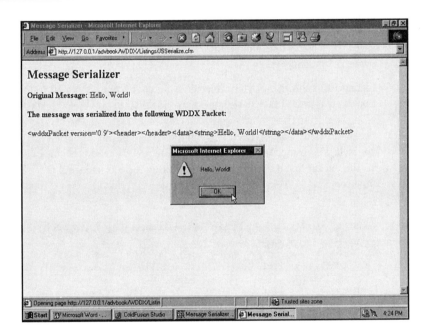

If you use your browser's View Source command so that you can see the final page code that
was sent to the browser, you can see the JavaScript that the CFWDDX added to the page. Listing
16.17 shows the SCRIPT portion of the page's source code. Notice that the generated JavaScript
code is very simple, and is exactly what you would probably have written if you had wanted to
assign the string "Hello, World!" to a variable named MyJSVariable.

> **Listing 16.17** `JSSerialize-SourceSnippet.html`—**The JavaScript Code That Listing 16.16 Produces**

```
<SCRIPT LANGUAGE="JavaScript">
  // The following code was produced by the CFWDDX tag.
  // It will set a variable named "MyJSVariable" to the
  // Contents of the WDDX Packet supplied to 2nd CFWDDX
  MyJSVariable="Hello, World!";

  // Now display the variable in a pop-up dialog box
  alert(MyJSVariable);
</SCRIPT>
```

Eliminating the Intermediate WDDX Step   The code in Listing 16.16 used two CFWDDX tags—one to convert from CFML to WDDX, and a second to convert from WDDX to JavaScript. The CFWDDX tag allows you to use ACTION="CFML2JS", which converts a ColdFusion value directly to JavaScript without needing to include the WDDX conversion as a separate step. This shortcut saves you a step while coding. Internally, the CFWDDX tag behaves just as if you had used it twice, as in Listing 16.16.

Listing 16.18 shows how you can reduce the code from Listing 16.16 to just a few tags. Notice that the two CFWDDX tags have been consolidated into one. Also, the OUTPUT parameter has been eliminated from the CFWDDX tag, which causes it to spit out the JavaScript code right then, between the SCRIPT tags. This saves you the step of having to output the DynamicJSCode variable yourself. This template will behave the same way that the previous one did (refer to Figure 16.10), except that it doesn't bother outputting the message and the original WDDX Packet to the users.

> **Listing 16.18** `JSSerialize2.cfm`—**Simplifying Matters by Going Straight from CFML to JavaScript**

```
<!DOCTYPE HTML PUBLIC "-//W3C//DTD HTML 4.0 Transitional//EN">

<HTML>
<HEAD>
  <TITLE>Message Serializer</TITLE>
</HEAD>

<BODY>
<H2>Message Serializer</H2>

<!-- Set the #Message# variable to a simple string value -->
<CFSET Message = "Hello, World!">

<!-- Ask CFWDDX tag to convert packet from CFML to JavaScript -->
<SCRIPT LANGUAGE="JavaScript">
  // The following code was produced by the CFWDDX tag.
  // It will set a variable named "MyJSVariable" to the
  // Contents of the ColdFusion #Message# variable
```

```
<CFWDDX
   INPUT="#Message#"
   ACTION="CFML2JS"
   TOPLEVELVARIABLE="MyJSVariable">

   // Now display the variable in a pop-up dialog box
   alert(MyJSVariable);
</SCRIPT>


</BODY>
</HTML>
```

 TIP When you leave out the CFWDDX tag's OUTPUT parameter as shown in Listing 16.18 (so the tag inserts its JavaScript code at the current spot in the template), always make sure to place the CFWDDX tag between SCRIPT tags. Otherwise, the browser doesn't know to interpret the code as JavaScript; instead, it will just display the code on the page as if it were ordinary text.

Building an Offline Data-Browsing App

You've seen how you can use the CFWDDX tag to transport a variable from ColdFusion to JavaScript. This process is certainly interesting but not exactly exciting. For instance, you probably have realized that you could have used a simple CFOUTPUT tag to create that same JavaScript code that the CFWDDX tag created. What's the big deal?

Well, again, as you saw earlier in this chapter, although WDDX can pass simple variables—such as numbers, strings, and dates—around just fine, it gets really interesting only when you start using it to pass complex data types around, such as arrays, structures, and especially recordsets.

Sending a Recordset from ColdFusion to JavaScript ColdFusion allows you to take the contents of any query—such as the results of a CFQUERY tag—and make it available to JavaScript. This process is really no more complicated than passing a simple value, such as a number or a string. ColdFusion generates JavaScript code that creates a special kind of JavaScript variable. Rather than a variable of type string or type number, the variable is of type WddxRecordset, which is a type of "custom" object that has been defined by Allaire.

Take a look at Listing 16.19. It creates a Web page with a simple form on it. This code runs a query to get the ISBN number for each book in the A2Z database's Inventory table. It then uses the CFWDDX tag to convert the query's results to a JavaScript WddxRecordset object named Books. A WddxRecordset object contains a separate array for each query column, indexed by row number. For example, if you need to get the Title from the fifth row of the recordset, you can refer to Books.title[5] in your JavaScript code. Similarly, Books.isbn[1] returns the ISBN number of the first row returned by the query.

The scripting part of the template then goes on to create a user-defined function called InitControls(), which is responsible for populating the SELECT box in the simple form at the bottom of the template. This function is pretty simple, but if you're not familiar with JavaScript, it might be confusing. First, BookID.options.length is set to zero. The options property of the BookID object represents the available choices in the SELECT box. Setting it to zero simply clears any choices that may currently be sitting in the SELECT box.

Next, the SELECT box is populated by the code inside the for loop. Basically, the for statement says to execute the loop once for each row in the query recordset, incrementing the RowNum variable by one each time through the loop. When the RowNum variable reaches the length of the Books.bookid array (which is the number of rows in the query), the loop stops. Inside the loop, a new Option object called NewOpt is created; it is a special type of object that represents a choice in a SELECT box. The "value" of the new option (the value that is submitted by the form) is given the BookID from the current row of the recordset, and the "text" of the new option (the value that the users see) is given the Title of the current row of the recordset. Finally, the new option is added to the array of options in the BookID object (the SELECT box itself).

When you first open this page in a browser, the SELECT box does not have any book choices in it. When you click the Populate Drop-Down button, the InitControls() function is executed, which fills the SELECT box with the information about the books fetched by the original CFQUERY. Figure 16.11 shows what the form looks like after the button is clicked.

TIP Always consider using with statements to make your JavaScript code simpler and easier to read. For instance, the template in Listing 16.19 uses the with(document.dataForm) statement to say that every object referred to within the curly braces should be assumed to be an element of the DataForm object. Without the with statement, each reference to the BookID object would need to be typed in its "fully qualified" form: document.DataForm.BookID.

TIP Always remember that JavaScript is case sensitive. Because the function is defined (near the top of the SCRIPT block) as InitControls(), you must use that spelling exactly to invoke the function when you refer to it elsewhere. For instance, if you use different capitalization in the onLoad parameter of the document's BODY tag, you get a JavaScript error, complaining that the function does not exist.

N O T E When you refer to a column of a recordset in JavaScript code, you must always type the column's name in lowercase. Because ColdFusion is not case sensitive (and thus does not necessarily know the exact capitalization of your database's column names), but JavaScript is case sensitive, the folks at Allaire needed to make a decision about whether column names would be implemented as all uppercase or all lowercase. They chose all lowercase, presumably because other JavaScript stuff (like the names of all the functions and methods) is generally in lowercase as well. ■

Listing 16.19 `JSBrowser1.cfm`—**Making an Entire Query Recordset Available to JavaScript**

```
<!-- Get data about books from database -->
<CFQUERY NAME="GetBooks" DATASOURCE="A2Z">
  SELECT BookID, Title, ISBN
  FROM Inventory
  ORDER BY Title
</CFQUERY>


<HTML><HEAD>
<TITLE>Book Browser</TITLE>

<!- Include Allaire's WDDX / JavaScript support -->
<SCRIPT SRC="/cfide/scripts/wddx.js" LANGUAGE="JavaScript"></SCRIPT>

<SCRIPT LANGUAGE="JavaScript">

   <!-- Convert query to JavaScript object named "Books" -->
   <CFWDDX
     ACTION="CFML2JS"
     INPUT="#GetBooks#"
     TOPLEVELVARIABLE="Books">


  function InitControls() {

    // Everything in this "with" block pertains to the form
    with (document.DataForm) {

      // Clear any current OPTIONS from the SELECT
      BookID.options.length = 0;

      // For each book record...
      for (var RowNum = 1; RowNum < Books.bookid.length; RowNum++) {

        // Create a new OPTION object
        NewOpt = new Option;
        NewOpt.value = Books.bookid[RowNum];
        NewOpt.text = Books.title[RowNum];

        // Add the new object to the SELECT list
        BookID.options[BookID.options.length] = NewOpt;

      }
    }
  }
</SCRIPT>

<HEAD>
```

continues

Listing 16.19 Continued

```
<BODY BGCOLOR="SILVER">
<H2>Offline Book Browser</H2>


<!-- Start building a JavaScript-enabled form -->
<FORM NAME="DataForm">

  <!-- Gets populated by InitControls() function -->
  <SELECT NAME="BookID" SIZE="10">
    <OPTION>=========================================
  </SELECT>

  <!-- Button to execute the InitControls() function -->
  <P><INPUT TYPE="BUTTON" VALUE="Populate Drop-Down" onClick="InitControls()">

</FORM>


</BODY>
</HTML>
```

TIP Always include LANGUAGE="JavaScript" in your SCRIPT tags, even though it's technically optional as far as HTML is concerned. Because Microsoft Internet Explorer understands both JavaScript and VBScript, you don't want it to try to guess which of the two languages your script code is written in. So, always specifying the LANGUAGE in any SCRIPT tag is good practice.

TIP If you ever get a JavaScript message that says something like WddxRecordset is undefined, you probably forgot to include a reference to the wddx.js script file—like the SCRIPT SRC tag near the top of Listing 16.19. Make sure that the tag comes before any ColdFusion-generated JavaScript code that talks about query recordsets—which probably means putting it before a CFWDDX tag.

Working with Recordsets on the Client Because JavaScript is now aware of the results re-turned by the GetBooks query, you can easily add some client-side scripting to make the form "dynamic." Because JavaScript knows which Author, Title, and so on go with each BookID, you can let your users browse through data—displaying related information as they do so—with a minimum of coding.

Take a look at Listing 16.20. It takes the code from Listing 16.19 and adds text input boxes for the ISBN, Title, and Author name for each book (see Figure 16.12). Two user-defined JavaScript functions have also been added to make the form "come alive." The functions are astonishingly simple, mainly because Allaire's WddxRecordset object makes it so simple to access a recordset's values.

FIGURE 16.11

The SELECT box in this form is populated by JavaScript when the page loads.

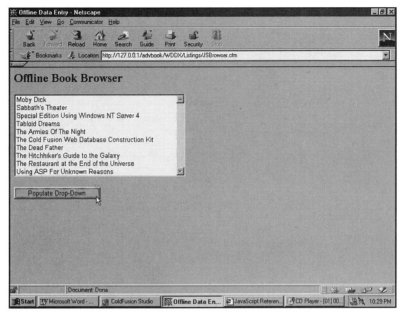

The `FillControls()` function fills the four text boxes with the Title, Author, and so on for the currently selected book in the SELECT list. Because the `FillControls()` function is referred to in the SELECT tag's onChange handler, the function executes whenever a user chooses a different book from the list. The function itself is extremely simple; it just sets a variable called RowNum that represents the currently selected book. Then the function assigns the appropriate element of the Books recordset object to the Value property of the appropriate text box. For instance, to fill the text box named Title, the script simply sets `Title.value` to whatever data is in `Books.title[RowNum]`.

The `KeepChanges()` function does just the opposite. It reads the values from the four text boxes and places their values into the appropriate spots in the Books WddxRecordset object. Next, it executes the `InitControls()` function (to redraw the items in the SELECT box, causing the new record to appear as the last choice in the SELECT box). Then it sets the SELECT box's selectedIndex property to -1 (which causes none of the choices to be selected for a split second) and immediately sets selectedIndex back to the choice that was selected before the function was called. The function is assigned to the Keep These Edits button by referring to the function's name in the INPUT tag's onClick handler.

Listing 16.20 `JSBrowser2.cfm`—**Populating Related Controls at Runtime from a Recordset**

```
<!-- Get data about books from database -->
<CFQUERY NAME="GetBooks" DATASOURCE="A2Z">
  SELECT BookID, Title, ISBN, AuthorFirstName, AuthorLastName
```

continues

Listing 16.20 Continued

```
  FROM Inventory
  ORDER BY Title
</CFQUERY>

<HTML><HEAD>
<TITLE>Book Browser</TITLE>


<!-- Include Allaire's WDDX / JavaScript support -->
<SCRIPT SRC="/cfide/scripts/wddx.js" LANGUAGE="JavaScript"></SCRIPT>

<SCRIPT LANGUAGE="JavaScript">

  <!-- Convert query to JavaScript object named "Books" -->
  <CFWDDX
    ACTION="CFML2JS"
    INPUT="#GetBooks#"
    TOPLEVELVARIABLE="Books">

  /////////////////////////////////////////////////////
  // This function fills the SELECT list with books
  function InitControls() {    with (document.DataForm) {

      // Clear any current OPTIONS from the SELECT
      BookID.options.length = 0;

      // For each book record...
      for (var i = 1; i < Books.getRowCount(); i++) {

        // Create a new OPTION object
        NewOpt = new Option;
        NewOpt.value = Books.bookid[i];
        NewOpt.text = Books.title[i];

        // Add the new object to the SELECT list
        BookID.options[BookID.options.length] = NewOpt;

      }
    }
  }


  /////////////////////////////////////////////////
  // This function populates other INPUT elements
  // when an option in the SELECT box is clicked
  function FillControls() {
    with (document.DataForm) {
      // Add one to the OPTION number to get the data row number
      var RowNum = BookID.selectedIndex+1;

      // Populate textboxes with data in that row
      ISBN.value = Books.isbn[RowNum];
      Title.value = Books.title[RowNum];
```

```
      AuthorF.value = Books.authorfirstname[RowNum];
      AuthorL.value = Books.authorlastname[RowNum];
    }
  }


  ///////////////////////////////////////////////////
  // This function "saves" data from the various
  // text boxes into the WddxRecordset object
  function KeepChanges() {
    with (document.DataForm) {
      // Add one to the OPTION number to get the data row number
      var SelectedBook = BookID.selectedIndex;
      var RowNum = SelectedBook + 1;

      // Populate javascript data array with info from textboxes
      Books.isbn[RowNum] = ISBN.value;
      Books.title[RowNum] = Title.value;
      Books.authorfirstname[RowNum] = AuthorF.value;
      Books.authorlastname[RowNum] = AuthorL.value;

      // Re-initialize the SELECT list
      InitControls();

      // Re-select the book that was selected before
      BookID.selectedIndex = SelectedBook;
    }
  }

</SCRIPT>
<HEAD>


<!-- After document loads, run InitControls() function -->
<BODY onLoad="InitControls();">
<H2>Offline Book Browser</H2>


<FORM ACTION="Client2.cfm" METHOD="POST" NAME="DataForm">


<TABLE BORDER CELLPADDING="10">
<TR VALIGN="TOP">
<TD>
  <!-- SELECT populated by InitControls() function -->
  <!-- When clicked, calls FillControls() function -->
  <SELECT NAME="BookID" SIZE="10" onChange="FillControls()">
    <OPTION>============= (loading) =================
  </SELECT>
</TD>


<TD>
  <!-- These controls get populated by FillControls() -->
```

continues

Listing 16.20   Continued

```
    <B>ISBN:</B><BR>
    <INPUT NAME="ISBN" SIZE="20" MAXLENGTH="13"><BR>

    <B>Author (first, last):</B><BR>
    <INPUT NAME="AuthorF" SIZE="18" MAXLENGTH="13">
    <INPUT NAME="AuthorL" SIZE="20" MAXLENGTH="13"><BR>

    <B>Title:</B><BR>
    <INPUT NAME="Title" SIZE="40" MAXLENGTH="50"><BR>

    <P>
    <!-- Button to "keep" edits with KeepChanges() function -->
    <INPUT TYPE="BUTTON" VALUE="Keep These Edits" onClick="KeepChanges()">
    <!-- Button to cancel edits with FillControls() function -->
    <INPUT TYPE="BUTTON" VALUE="Cancel" onClick="FillControls()"><BR>
  </TD>

  </TR>
  </TABLE>

  </FORM>


  </BODY>
  </HTML>
```

N O T E   In the FillControls() function, you need to add one to the selectedIndex property of the BookID object so that the RowNum variable represents the correct row in the recordset. You add one because the options in a SELECT box are numbered beginning with zero, but the rows in a recordset are numbered beginning with one. So, if the user clicks the fourth item in the SELECT box, the selectedIndex property is 3, but the appropriate row in the recordset is 4. ■

The users can browse through the records and make changes to the data, all without any inter-action at all with the server. In the past, this kind of effect would generally have taken a lot more work to create. In fact, many ColdFusion developers don't even try to put together this kind of form because the kind of JavaScript code that the CFWDDX tag generated can take awhile to come up with from scratch. Instead, they generally put together some kind of solution—often using "invisible" frames—that makes a round-trip to the server to get the detail informa-tion for each data record that the users want to look at.

So, by leveraging CFWDDX and JavaScript, you might be able to cut down or eliminate frequent trips to the server. Doing so reduces the load on your server, makes the application run faster, and provides zippier performance for your users.

N O T E   At this point, when users use the Keep These Edits button, they are changing the data only in the Books WddxRecordset. That is, they are changing only the "local copy" of the recordset that's in the browser's little brain. The actual database on the server is not updated. The next code listing does that job. ■

FIGURE 16.12

When a user clicks an item in the list, the other inputs are filled with the corresponding information.

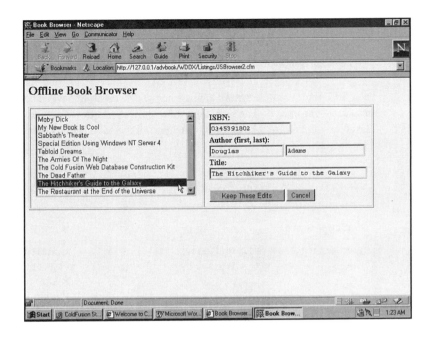

Getting Data from JavaScript Back to ColdFusion

Of course, the Book Browser application would not be complete without a way to actually commit the users' changes to the database on the server. Additionally, it would be nice if the users could enter data for new books using the same screen. These new records would also need to be inserted into the database on the server.

Allaire's WDDX and Recordset-Manipulation Functions   Allaire provides a number of JavaScript functions for working with WDDX from JavaScript code. All the functions are defined in the wddx.js JavaScript source file. Each of the Book Browser examples in this chapter includes these functions with the SCRIPT tag that appears near the top of the templates.

The wddx.js file defines two custom JavaScript objects. The first object that it defines is the WddxSerializer object, which is used to serialize data into WDDX Packets. This object has only one function available for your use, the serialize function. This function takes any JavaScript variable or object as its argument and returns the appropriate WDDX Packet as a JavaScript string value.

The second object defined in wddx.js is the WddxRecordset object, which represents a data recordset structure. A recordset is the JavaScript equivalent of a ColdFusion query result set. In other words, when you use CFWDDX to convert a CFQUERY tag's results to JavaScript, you are creating a WddxRecordset object that contains the same columns and rows returned by the original query. Allaire provides a number of functions that you can use to manipulate the data in WddxRecordset objects.

TIP You can find more information about the recordset-manipulation functions in the "WDDX JavaScript Objects" section of the *CFML Language Reference*, which is part of the documentation that Allaire ships with ColdFusion Application Server.

Table 16.1 shows sample syntax to use when you're creating new `WddxSerializer` and `WddxRecordset` objects. The table also shows how to use the various Allaire-defined functions. The code snippets are taken almost exactly from the code listings that follow during the rest of this chapter.

Table 16.1   JavaScript Functions for WDDX Serialization and Recordset Manipulation

JavaScript Syntax	What It Does
`MySerializer = new WddxSerializer`	Creates a new `WddxSerializer` object named `MySerializer`. Required before you can use the `serialize` function (see the description later in this chapter).
`MyPacket = MySerializer.serialize(MyJSVariable)`	Serializes the JavaScript variable or object named `MyJSVariable` and places the resulting WDDX Packet into the string variable named `MyPacket`.
`Books = new WddxRecordset`	Creates a new, empty `wddxRecordset` object named `Books`. In general, you do not need to create a recordset object from scratch like this because the `CFWDDX` tag creates the recordset for you if you use it to convert a ColdFusion query to JavaScript.
`Books.setField(3, "title", "Moby Dick")` or `Books.title[3] = "Moby Dick"`	Sets the third row of the title column to `"Moby Dick"`. You can use any simple value in place of `"Moby Dick"`, such as a JavaScript number or date variable.
`MyTitle = Books.getField(3, "title")` or `MyTitle = Books.title[3]`	Sets the `MyTitle` variable to whatever value is currently in the third row of the `Books` recordset's title column.

JavaScript Syntax	What It Does
`Books.addRows(1)`	Adds one row to the recordset object named `Books`. The new row is added to the end of the recordset. All the columns in the row are blank unless you set values to them.
`Books.addColumn("wasedited")`	Adds a column named `wasedited` to the `Books` recordset. All the rows in the column are blank unless you set values to them.
`NumRows = Books.getRowCount()`	Sets the `NumRows` variable to the number of rows currently in the `Books` recordset.

Part
IV
Ch
16

N O T E The `wddx.js` file is placed into the `CFIDE/Scripts` subfolder in your Web server's document root for you when you install ColdFusion. The examples in this chapter assume that the file has not been moved and can be accessed by a browser at the absolute URL `/CFIDE/Scripts/wddx.js` on your Web server. If you have moved or deleted the `CFIDE` folder, or if you are in some kind of virtual domain or hosted server situation such that the file is not available at that URL, you can just place a copy of the `wddx.js` file in the same folder as your actual ColdFusion templates (CFM files). Then remove the path information from the `SCRIPT` tag's `SRC` parameter so that it reads `SRC="wddx.js"`, indicating to the browser that the file can be found in the current directory. ■

 If you're curious about how the various functions are defined, open the `wddx.js` file in a text editor. You'll notice that a number of other functions defined for the `WddxSerializer` object are not discussed in this chapter. For instance, you'll find a `WddxSerializer_serializeValue` function and a `WddxSerializer_serializeString` function. Just ignore all the serializing functions except for the actual `serialize` function, which is the only function that's intended for use by ColdFusion developers. The other functions are used internally by the `serialize` function.

Editing Records and Sending the Changes to the Server   Take a look at Listing 16.21, the results of which are shown in Figure 16.13. This listing adds two additional JavaScript functions in the `SCRIPT` portion of the template, with a button to invoke each function. Specifically, a New Record button has been added to the form, which executes the `NewRecord()` function when clicked. Also, a Commit Changes To Server button has been added under the editing portion of the page, which executes the `CommitToServer()` function when clicked. Take a closer look at these two functions now.

The template's `NewRecord()` function uses three of the functions that Allaire supplies for use with `WddxRecordset` objects (like the Books object in this example). First, it uses the `addRows` function to add one new row to the Books recordset. The new row is added to the bottom of the recordset. Next, it uses the getRowCount function to set a variable named NewRow, which holds the row number of the just-added row. Then it uses the setField function to set each column of the new row to some initial values. Note that the BookID column is set to the string "new". This string indicates to the next template that the record is a new record and thus should be inserted (rather than updated) to the database. Finally, the function redraws the SELECT list with the InitControls() function, sets its selectedIndex so that the new record appears "selected" in the form, and calls the FillControls() function so that the data entry inputs are filled with the new (mostly blank) values.

The template's CommitToServer() function is in charge of serializing the recordset into a new WDDX Packet and then placing the packet in a hidden field and submitting the form. Thanks to the wddx.js file that Allaire provides, the serializing part requires only two lines of JavaScript code. First, a new WDDX Serializer object called MySerializer is created, with the help of JavaScript's new keyword. This step is necessary whenever you want to serialize a value from JavaScript. Next, the serialize function of the MySerializer object is used to serialize the Books recordset into a WDDX Packet, placing the packet into a JavaScript variable called BooksAsWDDX. Then the function sets the new variable to place the packet's contents into a hidden form field called WDDXContent. Finally, the function submits the form.

The end result is that the ColdFusion template that this form submits to (JSBrowserCommit.cfm) can refer to a variable called #Form.WDDXContent#. The variable can hold the WDDX Packet that contains the edited version of the recordset.

Listing 16.21 JSBrowser3.cfm—**Allowing the Users to Insert New Records and Commit to Database**

```
<!-- Get data about books from database -->
 <CFQUERY NAME="GetBooks" DATASOURCE="A2Z">
   SELECT BookID, Title, ISBN, AuthorFirstName, AuthorLastName
   FROM Inventory
   ORDER BY Title
 </CFQUERY>

<HTML><HEAD>
<TITLE>Book Browser</TITLE>


<!-- Include Allaire's WDDX / JavaScript support -->
<SCRIPT SRC="/cfide/scripts/wddx.js" LANGUAGE="JavaScript"></SCRIPT>

<SCRIPT LANGUAGE="JavaScript">

   <!-- Convert query to JavaScript object named "Books" -->
   <CFWDDX
     ACTION="CFML2JS"
```

```
    INPUT="#GetBooks#"
    TOPLEVELVARIABLE="Books">

// Add a column called "wasedited" to the recordset
// A "Yes" in this column means the row was "touched"
Books.addColumn("wasedited");

///////////////////////////////////////////////////
// This function fills the SELECT list with books
function InitControls() {
  with (document.DataForm) {

    // Clear any current OPTIONS from the SELECT
    BookID.options.length = 0;

    // For each book record...
    for (var i = 1; i < Books.getRowCount(); i++) {

      // Create a new OPTION object
      NewOpt = new Option;
      NewOpt.value = Books.bookid[i];
      NewOpt.text = Books.title[i];

      // Add the new object to the SELECT list
      BookID.options[BookID.options.length] = NewOpt;

    }
  }
}


///////////////////////////////////////////////////
// This function populates other INPUT elements
// when an option in the SELECT box is clicked
function FillControls() {
  with (document.DataForm) {
    // Add one to the OPTION number to get the data row number
    var RowNum = BookID.selectedIndex+1;

    // Populate textboxes with data in that row
    ISBN.value = Books.isbn[RowNum];
    Title.value = Books.title[RowNum];
    AuthorF.value = Books.authorfirstname[RowNum];
    AuthorL.value = Books.authorlastname[RowNum];
  }
}


///////////////////////////////////////////////////
// This function "saves" data from the various
// text boxes into the WddxRecordset object
function KeepChanges() {
  with (document.DataForm) {
```

continues

Listing 16.21 Continued

```
        // Add one to the OPTION number to get the data row number
        var SelectedBook = BookID.selectedIndex;
        var RowNum = SelectedBook + 1;

        // Populate javascript data array with info from textboxes
        Books.isbn[RowNum] = ISBN.value;
        Books.title[RowNum] = Title.value;
        Books.authorfirstname[RowNum] = AuthorF.value;
        Books.authorlastname[RowNum] = AuthorL.value;
        Books.wasedited[RowNum] = 'Yes';

        // Re-initialize the SELECT list
        InitControls();

        // Re-select the book that was selected before
        BookID.selectedIndex = -1;
        BookID.selectedIndex = SelectedBook;
    }
}


//////////////////////////////////////////////////
// This function inserts a new row in the
// WddxRecordset object, ready for editing
function NewRecord() {
  with (document.DataForm) {
    // Add a new row to the recordset
    Books.addRows(1);
    NewRow = Books.getRowCount()-1;

    Books.setField(NewRow, "bookid", "new");
    Books.setField(NewRow, "title", "(new)");
    Books.setField(NewRow, "isbn", "");
    Books.setField(NewRow, "authorfirstname", "");
    Books.setField(NewRow, "authorlastname", "");

    // Re-initialize the SELECT list
    InitControls();

    // Re-select the book that was selected before
    BookID.selectedIndex = NewRow-1;
    FillControls();
  }
}


//////////////////////////////////////////////////
// This function inserts a new row in the
// WddxRecordset object, ready for editing
function CommitToServer() {
  with (document.DataForm) {
```

```
        // Create new WDDX Serializer object (supplied by Allaire)
        MySerializer = new WddxSerializer();

        // Serialize the "Books" recordset into a WDDX packet
        BooksAsWDDX = MySerializer.serialize(Books);

        // Place the packet into the "WDDXContent" hidden field
        WDDXContent.value = BooksAsWDDX;

        // Submit the form
        submit();
    }
  }

</SCRIPT>
<HEAD>


<!-- After document loads, run InitControls() function -->
<BODY onLoad="InitControls();">
<H2>Offline Book Browser</H2>


<FORM ACTION="JSBrowserCommit.cfm" METHOD="POST" NAME="DataForm">
  <!-- CommitToServer() function gives this a value -->
  <INPUT TYPE="HIDDEN" NAME="WDDXContent">

<TABLE BORDER CELLPADDING="10">
<TR VALIGN="TOP">
<TD>
  <!-- SELECT populated by InitControls() function -->
  <!-- When clicked, calls FillControls() function -->
  <SELECT NAME="BookID" SIZE="12" onChange="FillControls()">
    <OPTION>============= (loading) =================
  </SELECT>
</TD>


<TD>
  <!-- These controls get populated by FillControls() -->
  <B>ISBN:</B><BR>
  <INPUT NAME="ISBN" SIZE="20" MAXLENGTH="13"><BR>

  <B>Author (first, last):</B><BR>
  <INPUT NAME="AuthorF" SIZE="18" MAXLENGTH="13">
  <INPUT NAME="AuthorL" SIZE="20" MAXLENGTH="13"><BR>

  <B>Title:</B><BR>
  <INPUT NAME="Title" SIZE="40" MAXLENGTH="50"><BR>

  <P>
  <!-- Button to "keep" edits with KeepChanges() function -->
```

Part

IV

Ch

16

continues

Listing 16.21   Continued

```
<INPUT TYPE="BUTTON" VALUE="Keep These Edits" onClick="KeepChanges()">
<!-- Button to cancel edits with FillControls() function -->
<INPUT TYPE="BUTTON" VALUE="Cancel" onClick="FillControls()">
<!-- Button to insert new book with NewRecord() function -->
<INPUT TYPE="BUTTON" VALUE="New Record" onClick="NewRecord()"><BR>
</TD>

</TR>
</TABLE>

<!-- Button to save to server w/ CommitChanges() function -->
<P><CENTER>
 <INPUT TYPE="BUTTON" VALUE="Commit Changes To Server" onClick=
➥"CommitToServer()"><BR>
</CENTER>

</FORM>


</BODY>
</HTML>
```

FIGURE 16.13

This version of the page allows the users to insert records and update the actual database.

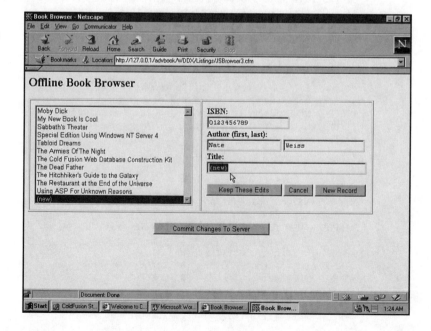

Receiving the Edited Records on the Server Side   The JSBrowserCommit.cfm template that receives the WDDX Packet from the Book Browser is actually quite simple (see Listing 16.22). Because the packet's contents were stored in the hidden field named WDDXContent just before the form was submitted, the packet is available to this template in the #Form.WDDXContent# variable. All the template needs to do is use CFWDDX to deserialize the packet into a query recordset named EditedBooks. Then it can use a CFLOOP over the query to quickly examine each data row to see whether it is a new or changed record.

If the BookID column of the current record is set to the string "new", then the template knows that the record was inserted by the Book Browser's NewRecord() function. Therefore, it runs a simple INSERT query to insert the new row into the Inventory table.

If the BookID column of the current record is not set to "new", the template checks to see whether the WasEdited column has been set to "Yes". If it has, then the template knows that the record was edited by the Book Browser's KeepChanges() function. Therefore, it runs a simple UPDATE query to update the corresponding row in the Inventory table, using the BookID column as the primary key.

Finally, the template displays a simple message to let the users know that the records were inserted or updated successfully. A summary is provided to show the number of inserted records and the number of updated records. Figure 16.14 shows the results.

Listing 16.22 JSBrowserCommit.cfm—Receiving the Edited Recordset and Updating the Database

```
<!DOCTYPE HTML PUBLIC "-//W3C//DTD HTML 4.0 Transitional//EN">

<HTML>
<HEAD>
  <TITLE>Untitled</TITLE>
</HEAD>

<BODY>
<H2>Committing Changes to Database</H2>


<!-- Convert the incoming WDDX Packet to "EditedBooks" query -->
<CFWDDX
  INPUT="#Form.WDDXContent#"
  OUTPUT="EditedBooks"
  ACTION="WDDX2CFML">

<!-- We'll increment these counters in the loop -->
<CFSET InsertCount = 0>
<CFSET UpdateCount = 0>

<!-- Loop over each of the records in the query -->
<CFLOOP QUERY="EditedBooks">

  <!-- If it's a new book (the user inserted it) -->
  <CFIF EditedBooks.BookID is "new">
    <CFQUERY DATASOURCE="A2Z">
      INSERT INTO Inventory (ISBN, Title, AuthorFirstName, AuthorLastName)
      VALUES ('#ISBN#', '#Title#', '#AuthorFirstName#', '#AuthorLastName#')
```

continues

Listing 16.22   Continued

```
      </CFQUERY>
      <CFSET InsertCount = InsertCount + 1>

    <!-- It's an existing book (user may have edited) -->
    <CFELSEIF EditedBooks.WasEdited is "Yes">
      <CFQUERY DATASOURCE="A2Z">
        UPDATE Inventory SET
          ISBN = '#ISBN#',
          Title = '#Title#',
          AuthorFirstName = '#AuthorFirstName#',
          AuthorLastName = '#AuthorLastName#'
        WHERE BookID = #BookID#
      </CFQUERY>
      <CFSET UpdateCount = UpdateCount + 1>

    </CFIF>
</CFLOOP>


<!-- Display message about what exactly happened -->
<CFOUTPUT>
<P><B>Changes Committed!</B>
<UL>
  <LI>Records Updated: #UpdateCount#
  <LI>Records Inserted: #InsertCount#
</UL>
</CFOUTPUT>


</BODY>
</HTML>
```

More About JavaScript and WDDX

Currently, Allaire's JavaScript support for WDDX does not provide a way to deserialize a WDDX Packet. That is, when you use the CFWDDX tag to convert a ColdFusion variable to JavaScript, you are not passing a WDDX Packet to JavaScript, which JavaScript then deserializes into native JavaScript objects. Instead, JavaScript code is written for you on-the-fly to create the native JavaScript objects from scratch. The effect is the same and puts much less stress on the browser. It's a good thing.

Deserializing WDDX Packets with JavaScript   Still, you might come across a few situations in which your JavaScript application has a WDDX Packet that it needs to deserialize. Using the hidden-form-field technique from Listing 16.21, you can have the application post the packet to an intermediate ColdFusion template. The template can then use the CFWDDX tag to send the deserialized values back to JavaScript.

FIGURE 16.14
New records get
inserted into the
database and changed
records get updated.

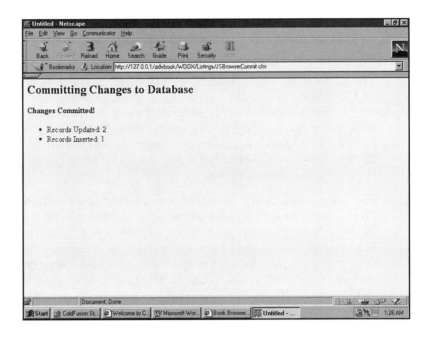

This approach is simple enough, but if something about your application makes that intermediate step undesirable, you can execute a `wddxDeserialize` function from JavaScript code. This function is not distributed with ColdFusion and was not created by Allaire. It was written by Nate Weiss, the author of this chapter. You'll find the `wddxDeserialize` function in the `wddxDes.js` file, which is included on the book's CD for your convenience. The next code listing shows this function in action.

N O T E The `wddxDeserialize` function depends on Xparse, an excellent, lightweight XML parser written entirely in JavaScript. Xparse is made freely available by Jeremie for noncommercial use and is found in the `XPARSE.JS` file, which is included on this book's CD for your convenience. Whenever you include `wddxDes.js` with the `SRC` attribute of a `SCRIPT` tag, you must also include `XPARSE.JS` in a separate `SCRIPT` tag. If you do not, the `wddxDeserialize` function will not work correctly. ▨

N O T E When this book went to press, the `wddxDeserialize` function was still a work in progress. The version of the function included on this book's CD—the latest version available at press time—does not work properly with most versions of Microsoft Internet Explorer 3.0x. Check `http://www.allaire/com/developer/wddx` or `http://www.nateweiss.com/cf/wddx` for the latest version of the JavaScript deserializer. ▨

Saving WDDX Packets on the Browser's Local Drive If you don't mind using some browser-dependant functionality, you might even consider allowing the users to save the contents of the

Part
IV

Ch
16

Books recordset to a file on their local machine. This way, people can save their work while they add and edit records, without affecting the database on the server until they are totally done with everything.

This approach might be ideal for situations in which laptop users want to be able to bring a page up in their browsers and then disconnect from the Internet to do their data entry. They can save their work as they see fit, perhaps spending several hours or days offline as they enter all the information they need to. They are free to close their browsers or turn off their computers. When they open the page again, they just reload the records from disk and continue working. When they are finished with all editing, they can reconnect to the Internet and click the Commit Changes To Server button.

The code in Listing 16.23 provides this functionality for Internet Explorer 4.0 and later. It gets the job done by adding two additional JavaScript functions called LocalFileSave() and LocalFileOpen(). The functions are executed by the new Save To File and Load from File buttons, respectively. Both functions refer to the MyLocalFS object, which is defined by the OBJECT tag that appears at the top of the template. The MyLocalFS object is an instance of Microsoft's Scripting.FileSystemObject COM object, which is available from Microsoft's Web site at the URL provided in the CODEBASE attribute of the OBJECT tag.

TIP

A complete discussion of the Scripting.FileSystemObject and the objects and methods it provides (such as TextStream, SaveTextFile, ReadAll, and Write) is beyond the scope of this chapter. You can get more information about these methods in Microsoft's *Internet Client SDK*, which is highly recommended if you want to get deeper into Internet Explorer's more proprietary features. The SDK is available for purchase (cheap!) or free download from http://msdn.microsoft.com.

The LocalFileSave() function first uses Allaire's serialize function to serialize the recordset into the WDDX Packet named BooksAsWDDX (see the explanation for Listing 16.21 for details). It then uses Microsoft's CreateTextFile function to create a file named BooksAsWDDX.txt. The function returns a TextStream object that facilitates access to the new file. Next, the TextStream object's Write method is used to "stream" the contents of the BooksAsWDDX variable into the file. Then the TextStream object's Close method is used to release the browser's "handle" on the file. Finally, the function displays a message on the browser's status bar so that users can see how many records were actually saved to disk.

The LocalFileOpen() function uses Microsoft's OpenTextFile function to open the text file and associate a TextStream object with it, to facilitate reading from the file. The TextStream object's ReadAll function is then used to load the file's entire contents into the BooksAsWDDX variable. The browser's handle on the file is then released with the Close method. Now the function needs to deserialize the WDDX Packet back into the recordset of book information. To do so, it simply uses the wddxDeserialize function from Nate Weiss's wddxDes.js file. This function returns the deserialized recordset, which immediately replaces the Books recordset with which the rest of the functions interact. Finally, the InitControls() function is executed to "repaint" the book titles in the SELECT box with the information that was loaded from disk (see Figure 16.15).

For Netscape Communicator (version 4.0 and later), you should be able to use Java, LiveConnect, and "Signed Scripts" to get similar access to the browser's file system. Because this use is somewhat more complicated, it is not covered in this chapter. To find information on getting this kind of access to the local file system with a Netscape browser, visit http://developer.netscape.com/.

Listing 16.23 `JSBrowser4.cfm`—**This Version Allows the Users to Save and Open Packet Files Locally**

```
<!-- Get data about books from database -->
<CFQUERY NAME="GetBooks" DATASOURCE="A2Z">
  SELECT BookID, Title, ISBN, AuthorFirstName, AuthorLastName
  FROM Inventory
  ORDER BY Title
</CFQUERY>

<HTML><HEAD>
<TITLE>Book Browser</TITLE>

<!-- Include Microsoft's "Scripting Run-time Library" -->
<!-- Creates FileSystemObject object called MyLocalFS -->
<OBJECT ID="MyLocalFS" WIDTH=0 HEIGHT=0
    CLASSID="CLSID:0D43FE01-F093-11CF-8940-00A0C9054228"
    CODEBASE="http://msdn.microsoft.com/scripting/scrrun/x86/
➥srt31en.cab#version=3,1,0,2230">
</OBJECT>

<!-- Include Allaire's WDDX / Javascript support -->
<SCRIPT SRC="/cfide/scripts/wddx.js" LANGUAGE="JAVASCRIPT"></SCRIPT>
<!-- Include Nate Weiss's wddxDeserializer function -->
<SCRIPT SRC="wddxDes.js" LANGUAGE="JAVASCRIPT"></SCRIPT>
<!-- Include the Xparse XML Parser, required by wddxDes.js -->
<SCRIPT SRC="XParse.js" LANGUAGE="JAVASCRIPT"></SCRIPT>


<SCRIPT LANGUAGE="JAVASCRIPT">

  <!-- Convert query to Javascript object named "Books" -->
  <CFWDDX
    ACTION="CFML2JS"
    INPUT="#GetBooks#"
    TOPLEVELVARIABLE="Books">

  Books.addColumn("wasedited");

  //////////////////////////////////////////////////
  // This function fills the SELECT list with books
  function InitControls() {
    with (document.DataForm) {

      // Clear any current OPTIONS from the SELECT
      BookID.options.length = 0;
```

continues

Listing 16.23 Continued

```
    // For each book record...
    for (var i = 1; i < Books.getRowCount(); i++) {

      // Create a new OPTION object
      NewOpt = new Option;
      NewOpt.value = Books.bookid[i];
      NewOpt.text = Books.title[i];

      // Add the new object to the SELECT list
      BookID.options[BookID.options.length] = NewOpt;

    }
  }
}


//////////////////////////////////////////////////
// This function populates other INPUT elements
// when an option in the SELECT box is clicked
function FillControls() {
  with (document.DataForm) {
    // Add one to the OPTION number to get the data row number
    var RowNum = BookID.selectedIndex+1;

    // Populate textboxes with data in that row
    ISBN.value = Books.isbn[RowNum];
    Title.value = Books.title[RowNum];
    AuthorF.value = Books.authorfirstname[RowNum];
    AuthorL.value = Books.authorlastname[RowNum];
  }
}


//////////////////////////////////////////////////
// This function "saves" data from the various
// text boxes into the WddxRecordset object
function KeepChanges() {
  with (document.DataForm) {
    // Add one to the OPTION number to get the data row number
    var SelectedBook = BookID.selectedIndex;
    var RowNum = SelectedBook + 1;

    // Populate javascript data array with info from textboxes
    Books.isbn[RowNum] = ISBN.value;
    Books.title[RowNum] = Title.value;
    Books.authorfirstname[RowNum] = AuthorF.value;
    Books.authorlastname[RowNum] = AuthorL.value;
    Books.wasedited[RowNum] = 'Yes';

    // Re-initialize the SELECT list
    InitControls();

    // Re-select the book that was selected before
    BookID.selectedIndex = -1;
```

```
      BookID.selectedIndex = SelectedBook;
   }
}


///////////////////////////////////////////////
// This function inserts a new row in the
// WddxRecordset object, ready for editing
function NewRecord() {
  with (document.DataForm) {
    // Add a new row to the recordset      Books.addRows(1);
    NewRow = Books.getRowCount()-1;

    Books.setField(NewRow, "bookid", "new");
    Books.setField(NewRow, "title", "(new)");
    Books.setField(NewRow, "isbn", "");
    Books.setField(NewRow, "authorfirstname", "");
    Books.setField(NewRow, "authorlastname", "");

    // Re-initialize the SELECT list
    InitControls();

    // Re-select the book that was selected before
    BookID.selectedIndex = NewRow-1;
    FillControls();
  }
}


///////////////////////////////////////////////
// This function inserts a new row in the
// WddxRecordset object, ready for editing
function CommitToServer() {
  with (document.DataForm) {
    // Create new WDDX Serializer object (supplied by Allaire)
    MySerializer = new WddxSerializer();

    // Serialize the "Books" recordset into a WDDX packet
    BooksAsWDDX = MySerializer.serialize(Books);

    // Place the packet into the "WDDXContent" hidden field
    WDDXContent.value = BooksAsWDDX;

    // Submit the form
    submit();
  }
}


///////////////////////////////////////////////
// This function saves the Books recordset to
// disk as a WDDX Packet
function LocalFileSave(){
```

continues

Listing 16.23   Continued

```
  // Serialize the Books recordset into WDDX Packet
  WddxSerializer = new WddxSerializer();
   BooksAsWDDX = WddxSerializer.serialize(Books);

  // Save the WDDX Packet to disk as c:\BooksAsWDDX.txt
  textstream = MyLocalFS.CreateTextFile("c:\\BooksAsWDDX.txt", true);
  textstream.Write(BooksAsWDDX);
  textstream.Close();

  // Show a message to the user
  window.defaultStatus = Books.getRowCount() + ' Records Saved';
}

//////////////////////////////////////////////////
// This function loads the Books recordset from
// disk (as a WDDX Packet) and deserializes it
function LocalFileOpen(){
  // Load the WDDX Packet from BooksAsWDDX.txt file
  textstream = MyLocalFS.OpenTextFile("c:\\BooksAsWDDX.txt");
  BooksAsWDDX = textstream.ReadAll();
  textstream.Close()

  // Deserialize the packet into the Books recordset
  Books = wddxDeserialize(BooksAsWDDX);
  InitControls();

  // Show a message to the user
  window.defaultStatus = Books.getRowCount() + ' Records Loaded';
}

</SCRIPT>
</HEAD>


<!-- After document loads, run InitControls() function -->
<BODY onLoad="InitControls();">
<H2>Offline Book Browser</H2>


<FORM ACTION="JSBrowserCommit.cfm" METHOD="POST" NAME="DataForm">
  <!-- CommitToServer() function gives this a value -->
  <INPUT TYPE="HIDDEN" NAME="WDDXContent">

<TABLE BORDER CELLPADDING="10">
<TR VALIGN="TOP">
<TD>
  <!-- SELECT populated by InitControls() function -->
  <!-- When clicked, calls FillControls() function -->
  <SELECT NAME="BookID" SIZE="12" onChange="FillControls()">
    <OPTION>============= (loading) ==================
```

```
  </SELECT>
</TD>


<TD>
  <!-- These controls get populated by FillControls() -->
  <B>ISBN:</B><BR>
  <INPUT NAME="ISBN" SIZE="20" MAXLENGTH="13"><BR>

  <B>Author (first, last):</B><BR>
  <INPUT NAME="AuthorF" SIZE="18" MAXLENGTH="13">
  <INPUT NAME="AuthorL" SIZE="20" MAXLENGTH="13"><BR>

  <B>Title:</B><BR>
  <INPUT NAME="Title" SIZE="40" MAXLENGTH="50"><BR>

  <P>
  <!-- Button to "keep" edits with KeepChanges() function -->
  <INPUT TYPE="BUTTON" VALUE="Keep These Edits" onClick="KeepChanges()">
  <!-- Button to cancel edits with FillChanges() function -->
  <INPUT TYPE="BUTTON" VALUE="Cancel" onClick="FillControls()">
  <!-- Button to insert new book with NewRecord() function -->
  <INPUT TYPE="BUTTON" VALUE="New Record" onClick="NewRecord()"><BR>
</TD>

</TR>
</TABLE>

<!-- Button to save to server w/ CommitChanges() function -->
<P><CENTER>
 <INPUT TYPE="BUTTON" VALUE="Commit Changes To Server" onClick=
➥"CommitToServer()"><BR>
 <INPUT TYPE="BUTTON" VALUE="Save To File" onClick="LocalFileSave()">
 <INPUT TYPE="BUTTON" VALUE="Load from File" onClick="LocalFileOpen()"><BR>
 </CENTER>

</FORM>


</BODY>
</HTML>
```

N O T E This example only works with Microsoft Internet Explorer—version 4.0 and later—on Windows 95, Windows 98, and Windows NT. It requires that the `Scripting.FileSystemObject` object be present on a user's machine. This COM object does not ship with Internet Explorer for security reasons but may already be present on the user's machine anyway (for instance, if the user has the Windows Scripting Host installed). At any rate, the `OBJECT` tag at the top of the template should automatically download and install the object if it is not already installed (prompting the user for permission before doing so, of course). For more information on Microsoft's `FileSystemObject` and the other objects in Microsoft's Scripting Runtime Library, or to download the `srt31en.cab` file referred to in the `OBJECT` tag to your own Web server (so that the client machine goes to your Web server instead of Microsoft's Web server to install the object), visit `http://msdn.microsoft.com/scripting/`. ▧

FIGURE 16.15

When JavaScript deserialization and file access is possible, pages can stand on their own.

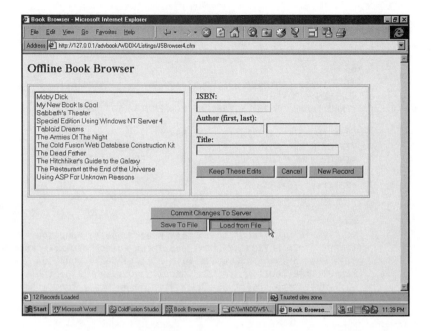

Using WDDX to Help Script Dynamic HTML Pages   The Book Browser examples that you've seen in this chapter all use form elements like SELECT lists and TEXT input boxes to allow the users to scroll through records and see correlated information about each record. You also can use Dynamic HTML (DHTML) and Cascading Style Sheets (CSS) to get a similar effect without using form controls. This way, you can give your application a slicker, more visually sophisticated look without much additional coding.

N O T E   This section assumes that you have some familiarity with CSS and DHTML. A complete discussion of tags such as STYLE and DIV—and how to script them with innerText, className, and so on—is well beyond the scope of this chapter. Complete reference materials on Microsoft's implementation of CSS and DHTML are available in the *Internet Client SDK*. You can also refer to the HTML 4.0 specification, which is available for viewing at http://www.w3.org. ∎

The code in Listing 16.24 creates an interface somewhat like the interface shown back in Figure 16.12, except that it cannot be edited and it doesn't place any form elements on the page. The interface is shown in Figure 16.16. Instead of putting a SELECT list on the page, this template uses a traditional CFOUTPUT block to output a separate DIV tag for each book's title along the left-hand side of the page. Because each DIV tag has a CLASS="choice" attribute, it inherits the font and color specifications that are defined for the choice class in the template's STYLE block.

Each of the DIV tags contains an onMouseOver and onMouseOut event handler that changes the class of each DIV as the users hover their mouse pointer over the titles, giving the page a slick, interactive feel. Each DIV tag also defines an onClick handler, which changes the tag's class to choiceSel—bold white text on a white background—when the users click on a book title. The onClick handler also fires the FillControls() function, which changes the innerText property of the related DIV tags to the appropriate Author name, Title, and so on.

Part
IV
Ch
16

Listing 16.24 `JSBrowserDHTML.cfm`—**Scripting with Dynamic HTML Instead of Form Elements**

```
<!-- Get data about books from database -->
<CFQUERY NAME="GetBooks" DATASOURCE="A2Z">
  SELECT *
  FROM Inventory
  ORDER BY Title
</CFQUERY>

<HTML><HEAD>
<TITLE>Book Browser</TITLE>


<!-- Include Allaire's WDDX / JavaScript support -->
<SCRIPT SRC="/cfide/scripts/wddx.js" LANGUAGE="JavaScript"></SCRIPT>

<SCRIPT LANGUAGE="JavaScript">

  <!-- Convert query to JavaScript object named "Books" -->
  <CFWDDX
    ACTION="CFML2JS"
    INPUT="#GetBooks#"
    TOPLEVELVARIABLE="Books">



  /////////////////////////////////////////////////
  // This function populates other INPUT elements  // when an option in the
SELECT box is clicked
  function FillControls(RowNum) {
    with (document.DataForm) {
      RowNum = RowNum - 1;

      // Populate textboxes with data in that row
      ISBN.innerText = Books.isbn[RowNum];
      Title.innerText = Books.title[RowNum];
      Pages.innerText = Books.pages[RowNum];
      Description.innerText = Books.description[RowNum];
      Author.innerText = Books.authorlastname[RowNum]
                    + ', ' + Books.authorfirstname[RowNum];
```

continues

Listing 16.24 Continued

```
    }
  }


</SCRIPT>
<HEAD>


<BODY>

<!-- Define CSS styles to control the "look" of the DIV tags-->
<STYLE TYPE="text/css">
  Div             {width:350px; padding-left:3px; font:smaller Arial}
  Div.choice      {background:wheat};
  Div.choiceSel   {background:black; color:white; font-weight:bold};
  Div.choiceOver  {background:beige; color:brown};

  Div.bar         {background:brown; color:white; font:bold small Arial};
  H2              {background:black; color:white}
</STYLE>


<H2>Offline Book Browser</H2>


<FORM NAME="DataForm">

<TABLE CELLPADDING="10">
<TR VALIGN="TOP">

<!-- Books to choose from.  User can click on each Title -->
<TD>
  <DIV CLASS="bar">Books</DIV>
  <CFOUTPUT QUERY="GetBooks">
    <DIV CLASS="choice"
      onClick="this.className = 'choiceSel'; FillControls(#CurrentRow#)"
      onMouseOver="this.className = 'choiceOver'"
      onMouseOut="this.className = 'choice'">#Title#</DIV>
  </CFOUTPUT>
</TD>

<!-- This info gets updated when user clicks on a Title -->
<TD>
  <DIV CLASS="bar">ISBN</DIV>
  <DIV CLASS="choice" ID="ISBN"></DIV><BR>

  <DIV CLASS="bar">Author</DIV>
  <DIV CLASS="choice" ID="Author"></DIV><BR>

  <DIV CLASS="bar">Title</DIV>
  <DIV CLASS="choice" ID="Title"></DIV><BR>
```

```
    <DIV CLASS="bar">Pages</DIV>
    <DIV CLASS="choice" ID="Pages"></DIV><BR>

</TD>
</TR>

<!-- So does the description, underneath -->
<TR><TD COLSPAN="2">
    <DIV CLASS="bar">Description</DIV>
    <DIV CLASS="choice" ID="Description" STYLE="height:100px;width=auto">
➥ </DIV><BR>
</TD></TR>

</TABLE>


</FORM>


</BODY>
</HTML>
```

FIGURE 16.16

This version of the Book Browser adds DHTML and CSS formatting for a sophisticated look.

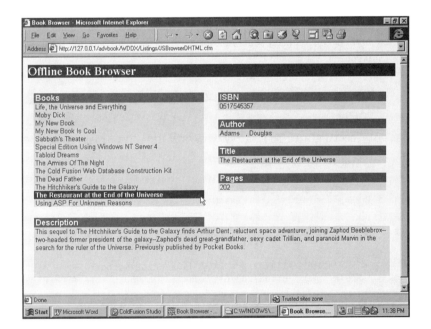

Using WDDX with Custom JavaScript Objects   You've learned that you can use Allaire's WddxSerializer to serialize simple JavaScript variables into WDDX Packets. You've also seen that you can serialize arrays and recordsets in the same way.

Note that the serializer is also perfectly capable of serializing just about any object that JavaScript is aware of. That means that if you create custom objects in your JavaScript code programmatically, you can easily wrap them into WDDX Packets by calling the same `serialize` function that you call to serialize a simple variable, array, or recordset.

> **N O T E** This topic is rather advanced. What it really means to define your own types of objects (and instances of those objects) in JavaScript can't be explained fully here. So it's assumed that you have at least some understanding of this "object-oriented" aspect of JavaScript. Consult a book about JavaScript or the online JavaScript documentation at `http://developer.netscape.com/` for a complete discussion of the topic. ■

For instance, consider the ColdFusion template shown in Listing 16.25. It includes a JavaScript function called `Car()`, which you can use to create new objects of type `Car`. Each `Car` object created with this function has four properties: `make`, `model`, `year`, and `doors`.

Each `Car` object also has a `register()` function, which can be used to attach the owner's name and state to the car. This feat is accomplished by attaching the separate `Car_register()` function to the `Car` object as a property called `register`. Subsequent code can create a `Car` object with JavaScript's `new` keyword and then call the object's `register()` function to provide the various ownership details. Again, I can't fully explain what's going on here in these pages; you might need to consult some further JavaScript documentation if this technique is unfamiliar to you.

Listing 16.25   `Object.cfm`—Creating and Serializing a Custom JavaScript Object

```
<!DOCTYPE HTML PUBLIC "-//W3C//DTD HTML 4.0 Transitional//EN">

<HTML>
<HEAD>
  <TITLE>Serializing a Custom JavaScript Object</TITLE>
</HEAD>

<BODY>
<H2>Serializing a Custom JavaScript Object</H2>

<!-- Include Allaire's WDDX / Javascript support -->
<SCRIPT SRC="/cfide/scripts/wddx.js" LANGUAGE="JAVASCRIPT"></SCRIPT>

<!-- JavaScript code to create objects of type "Car" -->
<SCRIPT LANGUAGE="JavaScript">
  /////////////////////////////////////////////////////
  // This function creates a new Car object
  /////////////////////////////////////////////////////
  function Car(NewMake, NewModel, NewYear, NewDoors) {
```

```
    this.make = NewMake;
    this.model = NewModel;
    this.year = NewYear;
    this.doors = NewDoors;

    // Attach registration function (below) to each Car
    this.register = Car_register;
  }

  /////////////////////////////////////////////////////
  // This function "registers" an existing Car object
  /////////////////////////////////////////////////////
  function Car_register(FirstName, LastName, State) {
    this.ownerFirstName = FirstName;
    this.ownerLastName = LastName;
    this.plateState = State;
  }
</SCRIPT>


<!-- Our demonstration code -->
<SCRIPT LANGUAGE="JavaScript">
  function CarDemo() {

    // Create a new car, called (unfortunately) MyCar
    MyCar = new Car('Chevrolet', 'Nova', '1985', 5);
    MyCar.register('Nate', 'Weiss', 'TX');

    // Another car
    JeanmariesCar = new Car('Ford', 'Mustang', '1965', 2);
    JeanmariesCar.register('Jeanmarie', 'Williams', 'VA');

    // Another car
    JedsCar = new Car('Honda', 'Prelude', '1984', 2);
    JedsCar.register('Jed', 'Freeman', 'NJ');
    JedsCar.condition = 'pristine';

    // Place cars into an array of Cars
    CarArray = new Array;
    CarArray[0] = MyCar;
    CarArray[1] = JeanmariesCar;
    CarArray[2] = JedsCar;

    // Create an instance of Allaire's WddxSerializer
    // and use it to serialize MyCar into MyPacket
    MySer = new WddxSerializer();
    MyPacket = MySer.serialize(CarArray);

    // Place packet in form's HIDDEN field and display it
    document.DataForm.WDDXContent.value = MyPacket;
    alert(MyPacket);
```

continues

Listing 16.25   Continued

```
    }
</SCRIPT>


<!-- Simple form -->
<FORM NAME="DataForm" ACTION="ObjectShow.cfm" METHOD="POST">
  <INPUT TYPE="HIDDEN" NAME="WDDXContent">

  <INPUT TYPE="BUTTON" VALUE="Serialize The Car Object" onClick="CarDemo()">
  <INPUT TYPE="SUBMIT" VALUE="Post the packet to ColdFusion">
</FORM>


</BODY>
</HTML>
```

As you can see, the template also creates a simple form with a hidden field and two buttons. The first button calls a `CarDemo()` function, which creates a few `Car` objects with the `new` keyword and serializes them into a WDDX Packet. The second button is just an ordinary submit button that submits the form.

Clearly, most of the action is in the `CarDemo()` function itself. First, JavaScript's `new` keyword is used along with the `Car()` function to create a new `Car` object named `MyCar`. The `MyCar.register()` function is then used to specify that the car has been registered to some strange person named Nate Weiss who lives in Texas. If you were now to display the value of the `MyCar.model` property, for instance, it would be `"Nova"`, and the `MyCar.ownerLastName` property would be `"Weiss"`.

The same steps are taken to create two more `Car` objects named `JeanmariesCar` and `JedsCar`. All three cars are then placed into an array of `Car` objects named `CarArray`. So, you could at this point refer to `CarArray[2].year` in your JavaScript code, and you would get back the value `"1984"`. Allaire's `serializer` object is then used to serialize the entire array into a WDDX Packet called `MyPacket`.

The packet is placed into the form's hidden field so that it will be available to the `ObjectShow.cfm` template when the form is submitted. The packet is also displayed in a pop-up message box, using JavaScript's `alert` function. Figure 16.17 shows the pop-up message that appears when the button is clicked. As you can see, the WDDX Packet is rather long, but it's easy enough to understand if some indenting is added for clarity.

Listing 16.26 shows an indented version of the the WDDX Packet. As you can see, the array of `Car` objects is represented by the pair of `<array>` tags. Each individual `Car` object has been translated into a pair of `<struct>` tags, and each car's properties are listed as elements of the structure by pairs of `<var>` tags. All custom JavaScript objects get translated into structures like this when serialized into WDDX. (The exception to this rule is Allaire's own custom `WddxRecordset` object, which, of course, gets translated into `<recordset>` tags rather than `<struct>` tags, as you saw earlier in this chapter.)

FIGURE 16.17

The array of custom Car objects is serialized into a WDDX Packet in one step.

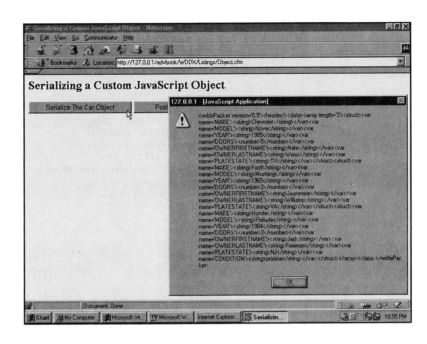

Listing 16.26 `ObjectPacket.txt`—The WDDX Packet Shown in Figure 16.17, with Indenting Added for Clarity

```
<wddxPacket version='0.9'>
  <header/>
  <data>
    <array length='3'>

      <struct>
        <var name='MAKE'><string>Chevrolet</string></var>
        <var name='MODEL'><string>Nova</string></var>
        <var name='YEAR'><string>1985</string></var>
        <var name='DOORS'><number>5</number></var>
        <var name='OWNERFIRSTNAME'><string>Nate</string></var>
        <var name='OWNERLASTNAME'><string>Weiss</string></var>
        <var name='PLATESTATE'><string>TX</string></var>
      </struct>

      <struct>
        <var name='MAKE'><string>Ford</string></var>
        <var name='MODEL'><string>Mustang</string></var>
        <var name='YEAR'><string>1965</string></var>
        <var name='DOORS'><number>2</number></var>
        <var name='OWNERFIRSTNAME'><string>Jeanmarie</string></var>
        <var name='OWNERLASTNAME'><string>Williams</string></var>
```

continues

Listing 16.26   Continued

```
        <var name='PLATESTATE'><string>VA</string></var>
      </struct>

      <struct>
        <var name='MAKE'><string>Honda</string></var>
        <var name='MODEL'><string>Prelude</string></var>
        <var name='YEAR'><string>1984</string></var>
        <var name='DOORS'><number>2</number></var>
        <var name='OWNERFIRSTNAME'><string>Jed</string></var>
        <var name='OWNERLASTNAME'><string>Freeman</string></var>
        <var name='PLATESTATE'><string>NJ</string></var>
        <var name='CONDITION'><string>pristine</string></var>
      </struct>

    </array>
  </data>
</wddxPacket>
```

When the form is submitted, it posts the WDDX Packet to the ColdFusion template shown in Listing 16.27. This template simply deserializes the WDDX Packet posted by the form's hidden field, placing the data into a ColdFusion array called CarInfo. The rest of the template simply displays the model of each car to prove that all three cars were successfully serialized and deserialized; it then uses a CFLOOP tag to "dump" all the properties of the first car object onto the current Web page. Figure 16.18 shows the results.

N O T E   You can use the CFLOOP technique shown at the bottom of Listing 16.27 to iterate through the name/value pairs of any ColdFusion structure. Within the loop, the ThisProperty variable holds the pair's name ("key"), which allows you to output or manipulate each value without necessarily knowing what keys exist in the structure beforehand. ■

Listing 16.27   ObjectShow.cfm—A Simple Template to Display Data from the Packet Shown in Listing 16.26

```
<!DOCTYPE HTML PUBLIC "-//W3C//DTD HTML 4.0 Transitional//EN">

<HTML>
<HEAD>
  <TITLE>Deserializing the Custom JavaScript Object</TITLE>
</HEAD>

<BODY>
<H2>Deserializing the Custom JavaScript Object</H2>

<!-- Deserialize the WDDX Packet posted by the form -->
<!-- Results are placed into Array called #CarInfo# -->
<CFWDDX
  ACTION="WDDX2CFML"
```

```
   INPUT="#Form.WDDXContent#"
   OUTPUT="CarInfo">


<!-- Loop through the array, outputting the Model for each -->
<CFLOOP FROM="1" TO="#ArrayLen(CarInfo)#" INDEX="LoopCount">
  <CFOUTPUT>
    Car number #LoopCount# is a
    #CarInfo[LoopCount]["Model"]# <BR>
  </CFOUTPUT>
</CFLOOP>


<!-- Each car is represented in CFML as a ColdFusion Structure. -->
<!-- Loop through the #CarInfo[1]# Structure and output each -->
<!-- of its elements onto the current Web page.     -->
<P><B>Here is all the information about the first car:</B><BR>
<CFLOOP COLLECTION="#CarInfo[1]#" ITEM="ThisProperty">
  <CFOUTPUT>
    #ThisProperty#:
    #CarInfo[1][ThisProperty]# <BR>
  </CFOUTPUT>
</CFLOOP>

</BODY>
</HTML>
```

Part

IV

Ch

16

FIGURE 16.18

The three JavaScript Car objects are successfully translated into native CFML stuctures.

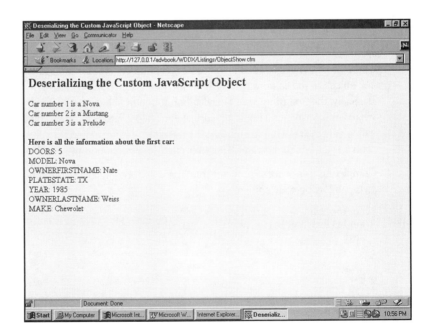

CAUTION

You also can use Allaire's `serialize` function to serialize the various built-in objects in your browser's Document Object Model (DOM), although doing so generally is not helpful. For instance, you can serialize the `document.links` object to generate a WDDX Packet full of the HTML links on the current page. Do not, however, attempt to use Allaire's `serialize` function to serialize an object that contains "recursive" references. The built-in `window` object is a good example. If you attempt to serialize this object, you will most likely get—after a long wait—some kind of `too much recursion` error message. You might even crash the browser.

Allowing Your JavaScript Objects to Serialize Themselves   Allaire's `WddxSerializer` serializes all properties of a custom JavaScript object by default. You saw this in action a moment ago; every property of each `Car` object was included in the WDDX Packet shown in Listing 16.26.

In certain rare instances, you might want to have a finer level of control over how your custom JavaScript objects get serialized. For instance, you might not want certain properties of the car to be included in the resulting WDDX Packet. Or you might want to reformat or consolidate some of the object's properties before it gets serialized.

To address these kinds of issues, Allaire allows you to create your own serialization functions for your custom JavaScript objects. Before it serializes each object, Allaire's serializer checks to see whether the object has a function with the special name `wddxSerialize`. If the object has such a function, the serializer calls that function instead of merely serializing each of the object's properties as it normally does.

Therefore, all that's needed is to create a custom car-serialization function and attach it to the `Car` object, in the same way that the registration function was attached to the `Car` object earlier. Basically, the first thing your serialization function needs to do is to obtain or assemble whatever information should be serialized. Then it needs to use a special function from Allaire called `serializeValue` to serialize the assembled information. Finally, your function needs to return `True`, which indicates that your custom serialization process has completed successfully.

Completing this process is easier than it sounds. For instance, the function could be as simple as the following code snippet:

```
function Car_serializer(serializer) {
  serializer.serializeValue('A Car Object');
  return true;
}
```

N O T E   The `serializeValue` function is a method of Allaire's `WddxSerializer` object. This means that any custom serialization function that you write needs to accept a single parameter, as shown here. When your function is executed, this parameter holds a reference to the `WddxSerializer` that is calling the function. You can name the parameter anything you want, but I suggest that you call it `serializer`. Regardless of what you name the parameter, you need the object reference that it provides so that you can call the `serializeValue` function. ■

If you attach the preceding snippet to the Car object's definition, it causes every Car object to be serialized in exactly the same way: as the simple string value "A Car Object". In this case, each Car object is no longer represented by a pair of <struct> tags with the object's actual properties inside; instead, each car is simply represented as a pair of <string> tags. That is, instead of what you saw between the <data> tags in Listing 16.26, the array of Car objects is serialized like this:

```
<array length='3'>
  <string>A Car Object</string>
  <string>A Car Object</string>
  <string>A Car Object</string>
</array>
```

Clearly, this result would not be terribly helpful in most situations. But it does illustrate the point that you get to decide exactly how your custom objects "present themselves" to the serialization process. This opens up the possibility of having JavaScript objects that have certain "private" properties that don't get exposed to the WDDX-enabled world. Only the properties that you decide should be "public" are passed to ColdFusion (or whatever application is receiving the WDDX Packets that your JavaScript code generates).

Listing 16.28 provides a more realistic serialization function for the Car object. Note that except for the addition of the serialization function, this listing is the same as the Object.cfm template shown in Listing 16.25.

Listing 16.28 Object2.cfm—Providing Your Own Serialization Function for a Custom JavaScript Object Type

```
<!DOCTYPE HTML PUBLIC "-//W3C//DTD HTML 4.0 Transitional//EN">

<HTML>
<HEAD>
  <TITLE>Serializing a Custom JavaScript Object</TITLE>
</HEAD>

<BODY>
<H2>Serializing a Custom JavaScript Object</H2>

<!-- Include Allaire's WDDX / Javascript support -->
<SCRIPT SRC="/cfide/scripts/wddx.js" LANGUAGE="JAVASCRIPT"></SCRIPT>

<!-- JavaScript code to create objects of type "Car" -->
<SCRIPT LANGUAGE="JavaScript">
  ///////////////////////////////////////////////////
  // This function creates a new Car object
  ///////////////////////////////////////////////////
  function Car(NewMake, NewModel, NewYear, NewDoors) {
    this.make = NewMake;
    this.model = NewModel;
```

continues

Part
IV

Ch
16

Listing 16.28   Continued

```
        this.year = NewYear;
        this.doors = NewDoors;

        // Attach registration function (below) to each Car
        this.register = Car_register;

        // Attach serialization function (below) to each Car,
        // with the property name of wddxSerialize.  Allaire's
        // WddxSerialize() function will see this function and call it
        // instead of merely serializing every property of each Car
        this.wddxSerialize = Car_serializer;
    }

    /////////////////////////////////////////////////////
    // This function "registers" an existing Car object
    /////////////////////////////////////////////////////
    function Car_register(FirstName, LastName, State) {
        this.ownerFirstName = FirstName;
        this.ownerLastName = LastName;
        this.plateState = State;
    }

    /////////////////////////////////////////////////////
    // This function knows how to serialize a Car object
    /////////////////////////////////////////////////////
    function Car_serializer(serializer) {
        // Create a new JavaScript object to actually serialize.
        // The object will include only certain data about the car
        var TempObject = new Object;

        // Put together a simple string that describes the car
        var DescString = this.year +' '+ this.make +' '+ this.model;

        // Attach the string and certain other info to the new object
        TempObject.model = DescString;
        TempObject.owner = this.ownerFirstName +' '+ this.ownerLastName;
        TempObject.numberOfDoors = this.doors;

        // Have the serializer serialize the object
        //serializer.serializeValue(TempObject);
        serializer.serializeValue(TempObject);

        // Tell serializer that we finished serializing ourselves ok
        return true;
    }
</SCRIPT>


<!-- Our demonstration code -->
<SCRIPT LANGUAGE="JavaScript">
    function CarDemo() {

        // Create a new car, called (unfortunately) MyCar
        MyCar = new Car('Chevrolet', 'Nova', '1985', 5);
```

```
        MyCar.register('Nate', 'Weiss', 'TX');
        MyCar.condition = 'unknown';

        // Another car
        JeanmariesCar = new Car('Ford', 'Mustang', '1965', 2);
        JeanmariesCar.register('Jeanmarie', 'Williams', 'VA');

        // Another car
        JedsCar = new Car('Honda', 'Prelude', '1984', 2);
        JedsCar.register('Jed', 'Freeman', 'NJ');
        JedsCar.condition = 'pristine';

        // Place cars into an array of Cars
        CarArray = new Array;
        CarArray[0] = MyCar;
        CarArray[1] = JeanmariesCar;
        CarArray[2] = JedsCar;

        // Create an instance of Allaire's WddxSerializer
        // and use it to serialize MyCar into MyPacket
        MySer = new WddxSerializer();
        MyPacket = MySer.serialize(CarArray);

        // Place packet in form's HIDDEN field and display it
        document.DataForm.WDDXContent.value = MyPacket;
        alert(MyPacket);
    }
</SCRIPT>


<!-- Simple form -->
<FORM NAME="DataForm" ACTION="ObjectShow.cfm" METHOD="POST">
  <INPUT TYPE="HIDDEN" NAME="WDDXContent">

  <INPUT TYPE="BUTTON" VALUE="Serialize The Car Object" onClick="CarDemo()">
  <INPUT TYPE="SUBMIT" VALUE="Post the packet to ColdFusion">
</FORM>


</BODY>
</HTML>
```

Take a look at the Car_serializer() function in Listing 16.28. It first creates a new object called TempObject, which serves as a sort of abbreviated version or proxy for the Car object that has been asked to serialize itself. This temporary object—rather than the underlying Car object itself—actually gets exposed to WDDX.

The next few lines add several properties to the TempObject. Note that the function can refer to JavaScript's this keyword to obtain properties of the underlying Car object. For instance, the year, make, and model properties of the car are concatenated into a string value called DescString. This string is attached to the TempObject as its model property. In other words, when the MyCar object gets serialized, its model property is not serialized as "Nova", as it would be normally, but rather as "1985 Chevrolet Nova". Similarly, the ownerFirstName and ownerLastName properties of the Car object are concatenated into a single property called owner. And the doors property of the underlying Car object is renamed numberOfDoors when serialized.

Finally, the TempObject is serialized with the serializeValue function, and True is returned to the calling serializer process to indicate "success." When the revised template is used in a browser, it generates the WDDX Packet shown in Listing 16.29. Compare this code to the previous version of the packet that was shown back in Listing 16.26.

Listing 16.29 ObjectPacket2.txt—The Custom-Serialized WDDX Packet with Indentation Added for Clarity

```
<wddxPacket version='0.9'>
    <header/>
    <data>
      <array length='3'>

        <struct>
          <var name='MODEL'><string>1985 Chevrolet Nova</string></var>
          <var name='OWNER'><string>Nate Weiss</string></var>
          <var name='NUMBEROFDOORS'><number>5</number></var>
        </struct>

        <struct>
          <var name='MODEL'><string>1965 Ford Mustang</string></var>
          <var name='OWNER'><string>Jeanmarie Williams</string></var>
          <var name='NUMBEROFDOORS'><number>2</number></var>
        </struct>

        <struct>
          <var name='MODEL'><string>1984 Honda Prelude</string></var>
          <var name='OWNER'><string>Jed Freeman</string></var>
          <var name='NUMBEROFDOORS'><number>2</number></var>
        </struct>

      </array>
    </data>
</wddxPacket>
```

As you can see, each Car object has successfully decided which of its properties is exposed to the serialization process and in what form. When the packet is submitted to the Object.cfm template, ColdFusion is aware only of the modified versions of each car's properties. Notably, the plateState and condition properties that are available for the Car objects within JavaScript are not exposed to WDDX. You can imagine that this information might be considered confidential or otherwise irrelevant to the WDDX-enabled world. Figure 16.19 shows the results.

FIGURE 16.19

Only selected information about each JavaScript Car object is available to ColdFusion.

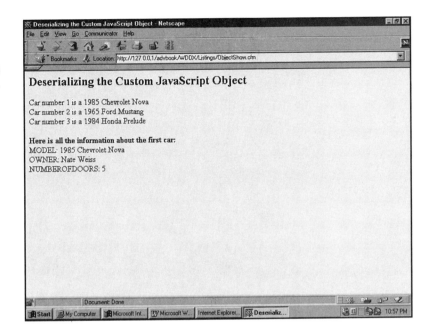

Advanced WDDX Integration

Allaire's WDDX Interface for COM

In Chapter 16, "Using WDDX to Create Distributed Applications," you saw that WDDX can be used to pass data between two different ColdFusion servers, or between a browser and server via JavaScript serialization/deserialization. In this chapter you learn how WDDX can be used to integrate ColdFusion with other types of applications that are built with a variety of development tools, including Active Server Pages, Visual Basic, and Perl.

Most of the integration work done in this chapter depends on a COM object that Allaire ships with ColdFusion. The object provides the same kind of functionality that the CFWDDX tag provides ColdFusion templates. For instance, it provides a function to serialize variables and record sets into WDDX Packets, and a function to deserialize WDDX Packets back into native variables and data types that can be used in whatever development tool you happen to be working with. All that's required is that the development tool supports COM—and most serious Windows-based development tools do.

N O T E   Allaire considers the version of the COM object that shipped with ColdFusion 4 a pre-
release version. This means that while the object works fine for the ways ColdFusion and
ColdFusion Studio interact with it internally, it has not been thoroughly tested with all other COM-
enabled applications (Active Server Pages, Visual Basic, Delphi, and so on). Allaire is releasing the final
"for public use" version of the COM object as part of the WDDX Software Development Kit (SDK), which
should be released by the end of 1998. Please check http://www.allaire.com/developer/
wddx to obtain the latest news about the availability of the SDK and the updated COM object.   ■

N O T E   This chapter assumes that you have at least a basic understanding of what a COM object
is. If you need to refresh your memory, please refer to Chapter 12, "Extending ColdFusion
with COM/DCOM," for an explanation.   ■

Installation of Allaire's COM Object

Any application that you develop via Allaire's COM object for WDDX needs to have the object available to it at runtime. This means that if you use the object in a script for Active Server Pages (ASP), the COM object needs to be available on the ASP server. If you are developing an application with Visual Basic, the COM object needs to be available on your development machine and on every machine that you want the application to run on.

The good news is that the COM object is installed automatically when you install ColdFusion Application Server 4, ColdFusion Studio 4, or HomeSite 4. This makes it likely that the object is already available to both your ColdFusion server and your development machine; you can probably go straight to work.

T I P If you don't know whether the object is installed on a particular machine, you can use Microsoft's OLE-COM Object Viewer (OleView.exe) to see if the WDDX Serializer class appears in the Automation Controls category. If it does, you should be set. See Chapter 12 for instructions on how to use the Object Viewer.

If you have a machine that does not have the COM object already installed, you can get it set up automatically by installing either ColdFusion Application Server, ColdFusion Studio, or HomeSite on the machine in question. Alternatively, you can install it manually copying the file onto the server and registering it with the regsvr32 utility that ships with Windows.

Follow these steps to register the COM object:

1. Find a copy of wddx_com.dll on a machine that has the COM object properly installed. It is probably in the Windows System folder. On Windows NT machines, the System folder is usually located at c:\WinNT\System32. On Windows 95 or Windows 98 machines, it is usually located at c:\Windows\System. You can alternatively copy the file from this book's CD-ROM.

2. Copy the file to the server that needs the object, placing it into the new machine's System folder.

3. Type the following command at an MS-DOS prompt: **regsvr32 wddx_com.dll**.

4. Repeat steps 1–3 for the xmltok.dll and the xmlparse.dll files.

After a moment you should get a message explaining that the object was registered successfully. If you do not, verify that you indeed placed the wddx_com.dll file into the Windows System directory. See your Windows documentation for more information on the System directory and the regsvr32 utility.

WDDX Classes and Functions Provided by the COM Object

When Allaire's COM object is installed on your machine, five new component classes are made available to your system. You are free to develop with these classes using any development tool that supports COM.

The Five Component Classes   Together, they provide a way to serialize and deserialize WDDX Packets, including complex data types like record sets and arrays that your development environment may not support natively. Table 17.1 lists the five component classes and explains what each of them can do for you.

Part

IV

Ch

17

Table 17.1   The Five WDDX-Related Classes Provided by Allaire

Component Class	What It Does
WDDX Serializer	Provides a way to serialize a value into a WDDX Packet. The value could be a simple value (a string or number), or could be a complex data structure (an array or record set).
WDDX Deserializer	Provides a way to take a WDDX Packet and deserialize it into the proper simple value, array, structure, or record set. The record set's data type.
WDDX Recordset	Provides a way to create new record sets, add columns and rows to the record sets, and receive record sets from other environments. Since the record set is maintained by the COM object, WDDX Recordset classes can be utilized even by programs that don't include a concept of a record set as part of their native language.
WDDX Struct	Provides a way to create new structure objects, which are based on ColdFusion's Structure data type. Similar conceptually to what some programming languages call *associative arrays*. Again, since the structure is maintained by the COM object, even languages that don't have such a concept natively can work with WDDX-style structure objects.
WDDX JSConverter	Provides a way to convert a simple value, record set, array, structure, or WDDX Packet into dynamically-produced JavaScript code that re-creates the appropriate value or object when executed in a browser. Helpful for setting up communications between a browser and server.

Using the Component Classes in Your Code   To use the component classes, you must create an instance of the object you want to use in your development environment. The syntax to use or the steps you need to take to create an instance of a component class vary, depending on the development tool you're working with. You may need to add a reference to the wddx_com.dll file using some kind of References, Objects, or Components menu or dialog box. You may then need to use some kind of special object-related statements or keywords, such as Set, New, or CreateObject. In any case, the basic syntax should be available in the documentation for the tool you're using, under something like "Using COM Objects" or "Working with Server-Side ActiveX Controls."

Functions Provided by Each of the Component Classes   Once an instance of a component class has been created, each of the component classes listed earlier provides at least one function that gives you a way to interact with the object. Again, the syntax that you use to invoke these functions varies from development tool to development tool. The actual functionality provided—what the functions actually do when used—is the same, regardless of the environment you're in. That's the magic of COM, and that's why it's so exciting that Allaire is providing support for WDDX via this new COM object.

Tables 17.2 through 17.6 show the functions that each of Allaire's component classes provides.

Table 17.2 Functions Available for the WDDX Serializer Class

Function	Example Syntax	What It Does
serialize	MySer = CreateObject("WDDX.Serializer.1") MyPacket = MySer.serialize(MyVar)	Serializes the value into a WDDX Packet. The packet is placed into a new variable called MyPacket.

Table 17.3 Functions Available for the WDDX Deserializer Class

Function	Example Syntax	What It Does
deserialize	MyDeser = CreateObject("WDDX.Deserializer.1") MyVar = MyDeser.deserialize(MyPacket)	Extracts the value stored in the WDDX Packet called MyPacket. The value is placed into a new variable called MyVar.

Table 17.4 Functions Available for the WDDX Recordset Class

Function	Example Syntax	What It Does
addColumn	MyRS = CreateObject("WDDX.Recordset.1") MyRS.addColumn("Company")	Adds a new, empty column named Company to the MyRS record set. Each of the data cells in the new column will be empty. Returns the column number of the just-added column.

continues

Part

IV

Ch

17

Table 17.4 Continued

Function	Example Syntax	What It Does
addRows	MyRS.addRows(5)	Adds five new rows to the record set. Each of the data cells in the new rows will be empty.
setField	MyRS.setField(3, "Company", "Allaire")	Places the word Allaire in the Company column of the third row of the record set. The value can then be retrieved with the getField function.
getField	MyVar = MyRS.getField(5, "Company")	Retrieves the value stored in the Company column of the fifth row of the record set. Here, the value is placed in the new variable called MyVar.
GetRowCount	NumRows = MyRS.getRowCount()	Returns the number of rows currently in the record set. Here, the number is placed into the variable called NumRows.

Function	Example Syntax	What It Does
GetColumnCount	NumCols = MyRS.getColumnCount ( )	Returns the number of columns currently in the record set. Here, the number is placed into the variable called NumCols.
GetColumnNames	arNames = MyRS.getColumnNames ( )	Returns an array that holds the names of the record set's column names. Here, the array is stored with the name of arNames.
GetIdOfColumn	ColNum = MyRS.getIdOfColumn ("Company")	Returns the column number of the Company column. Here, the number is stored in the ColNum variable. You can use this column number in the getField or setField functions, instead of the column name.

Table 17.5   Functions Available for the WDDX struct Class

Function	Example Syntax	What It Does
setProp	MyStruct = CreateObject("WDDX.Struct.1") MyStruct.setProp("White", "FFFFFF")	Stores the value FFFFFF in the structure, with the key name of White. Comparable to the following in CFML: MyStruct["White"] = "FFFFFF".
getProp	MyVar = MyStruct.getProp("White")	Retrieves the value stored in the structure under the key name of White. Here, the value is placed in the variable named MyVar.
GetPropNames	arProps = MyStruct.getPropNames()	Returns an array of all the keys in the structure. Each item in the array would be a valid name to supply to the getProp function.
clone	MyNewStruct = MyStruct.clone()	Returns an exact copy of the structure. Here, the new copy of the structure is stored under the name of MyNewStruct.

Table 17.6 Functions Available for the WDDX JSConverter Class

Function	Example Syntax	What It Does
ConvertData	`MyConv = CreateObject("WDDX.JSConverter.1")` `MyJS = MyConv.convertData(MyVar, "MyJSVar")`	Creates dynamically produced JavaScript statements that will re-create the value of MyVar if included in a script. When the script runs, the value will be available as the JavaScript variable called MyJSVar.
ConvertWddx	`MyJS = MyConv.convertWddx(MyPacket, "MyJSVar")`	Creates dynamically produced JavaScript statements that will re-create the value stored in the WDDX Packet called MyPacket. When the script runs, the value will be available as the JavaScript variable called MyJSVar.

Integrating with Active Server Pages

As you see in this chapter, there are a lot of places where you can use the WDDX support that Allaire provides through its COM object. One of the most exciting places to use the COM object is within scripts written for Microsoft's ASP.

It's an interesting topic, since Active Server Pages and ColdFusion are often thought of as competing products. They are similar in many respects, and people often find themselves choosing one over the other. Indeed, most of what you can do with ColdFusion you can also do with ASP, and vice versa. You could argue about which tool is better until the day you die, but the reality is that both tools have become widely accepted and are here to stay. The sooner you can get them working together, the better!

Creating the Store Robot Back-End Page

Chapter 16 spent time putting together a Book Robot, which is a ColdFusion template that waits for requests and responds by sending back WDDX Packets full of book information (see Listing 16.8). A JavaScript Book Browser application was then put together; it uses the Book Robot to display and edit the inventory of the fictional A2Z bookstore (see Listing 16.21).

An interesting feature of the Book Browser is its capability to query Book Robots anywhere on the Internet. If A2Z Books had locations in various cities worldwide, the user could easily switch between them by selecting the store of his choice from a drop-down list. This works well enough, but there's one problem. What happens when a new A2Z bookstore opens in a new city? As it stands, the available stores are hard-coded into the ColdFusion template itself. Of course, the code could be changed so that the store locations are kept in a database table called Stores instead of being hard-coded into the template. That doesn't really solve the problem, however, since it would still be necessary to update the Stores table at each store worldwide.

What's needed is a single server that acts as the authority on the list of bookstore locations worldwide. The ColdFusion servers at each location can ask this server for the current list of stores at any time and use the answer to populate the drop-down list the user interacts with. Of course, ColdFusion could be used to create a Store Robot that does exactly that. What if, for some reason, the Book Robot needs to be created using Active Server Pages instead of ColdFusion?

The first thing to do is create a table named Stores, with three columns: StoreID, Name, and Host. The Store Robot will query this table to supply the current list of store locations to whatever application needs access over the Internet. This table is provided in the A2Z example database that's included on this book's CD-ROM. It's been populated with some sample data about the bookstore's locations worldwide, as shown in Figure 17.1.

FIGURE 17.1

The columns and sample data for the Stores table.

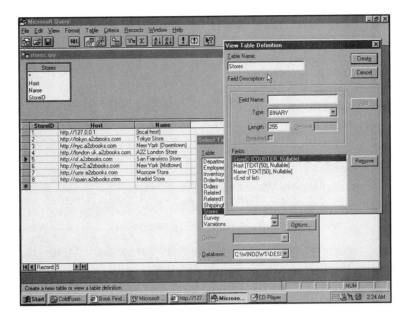

Creating the Store Robot with ASP   It's not hard to deliver such a back-end Web page using Active Server Pages. Listing 17.1 is an ASP script that creates the Store Robot with a little help from Allaire's WDDX COM object. It publishes the current list of stores as a WDDX Packet, which means that any application that knows how to pick up WDDX Packets can come to it for the authoritative list at any time.

N O T E   At this point it's assumed that you are somewhat familiar with Active Server Pages and have some idea of how to write .asp scripts. If not, the basic concepts are explained a little later in this chapter; if you start getting confused, you may want to consult a book about ASP or go to Microsoft's Web site to take a quick look through the ASP documentation online.

Listing 17.1   `StoreRobot.asp`—**Creating the Store Robot with Active Server Pages**

```
<%@ LANGUAGE=JScript %>

<%
   // Run a query against the Stores table in A2Z database
   DBConn = Server.CreateObject("ADODB.Connection")
   DBConn.Open("A2Z")
   SQLQuery = "SELECT StoreID, Name, Host FROM Stores ORDER BY Name"
   rs_Stores = DBConn.Execute(SQLQuery)

   // Create instance of Allaire's WDDX Serializer object
   MyRS = Server.CreateObject("WDDX.Recordset.1")
```

continues

Listing 17.1 Continued

```
MyRS.AddColumn("STOREID")
MyRS.AddColumn("NAME")
MyRS.AddColumn("HOST")

// For each row in the ADO Recordset...
RowNum = 0
while (!rs_Stores.EOF) {
  // Add a row to the MyRS Recordset
  MyRS.addRows(1)
  RowNum++

  // Copy the row from ADO Recordset to MyRS Recordset
  MyRS.setField(RowNum, "STOREID", rs_Stores("STOREID").Value)
  MyRS.setField(RowNum, "NAME", rs_Stores("NAME").Value)
  MyRS.setField(RowNum, "HOST", rs_Stores("HOST").Value)

  // Move on to the next row in ADO Recordset, if any
  rs_Stores.moveNext()
}

// Create instance of Allaire's WDDX Serializer object
MySer = Server.CreateObject("WDDX.Serializer.1")

// Serialize the MyRS recordset into packet called MyPacket
MyPacket = MySer.serialize(MyRS)

Response.Write(MyPacket)
%>
```

N O T E Active Server Pages allows you to script your pages in either VBScript or JScript. At the time this book went to press, the pre-release version of Allaire's COM object was not working correctly with VBScript. Therefore, the code in Listing 17.1 uses JScript, but could easily be re-coded in VBScript when the final version of the COM object is released. The main changes would be to add the Set keyword to each line that uses CreateObject, and to use single quotation marks instead of slashes for comments. ▪

The first line of code in Listing 17.1 is very important. It uses the CreateObject function to create an instance of Allaire's WDDX Recordset component. In other words, an empty record set—analogous to a query's result set in ColdFusion—has been created and given the name MyRS. At the moment, the record set doesn't have any rows or columns in it; it's just an empty data structure waiting to hold information. Any of the functions that Allaire provides for the WDDX Recordset component can be used with the MyRS object.

TIP This type of CreateObject syntax is routine in ASP development. You'll see it being used whenever an ASP script needs to use a COM object. Think of it as the ASP equivalent of the CFOBJECT tag. You can find out more about CreateObject in your ASP documentation.

Next, Allaire's `addColumn` function (see Table 17.4) is used to add three columns to the `MyRS` record set: `STOREID`, `NAME`, and `HOST`. The record set now has three columns, but no rows of data. It's as if you ran a query against a table that contained no data. The next task at hand is to get the actual rows from the database.

If you've worked with ASP before, the next few lines of code will look familiar. They simply create an instance of Microsoft's ADO Recordset object and use its `Open` method to run a simple query that fetches all the rows of the Stores table from the A2Z database. The fetched rows are stored in `rs_Stores`, which is an instance of Microsoft's ADO Recordset object. If you're not familiar with ASP, just think of these four lines of code as being the ASP equivalent to the following ColdFusion code snippet:

```
<CFQUERY NAME="rs_Stores" DATASOURCE="A2Z">
  SELECT StoreID, Name, Host
  FROM Stores
  ORDER BY Name
</CFQUERY>
```

N O T E The 3 provided to the third parameter of the `rs_Stores.Open` method is important because it tells ASP to fetch the records from the database as a static record set. Without the 3, the record set would be opened in Forward Only mode, which would be a problem for this code because the `RecordCount` property of an ADO record set is not available in this mode. That's not necessarily a problem; it just means that you would have to code the loop slightly differently, based on the record set's `EOF` property instead of `RecordCount`. See your ASP documentation for details. ▪

Now the script needs to copy the data from the `rs_Stores` record set into the `MyRS` record set. This is because the script's ultimate goal is to serialize the data into a WDDX Packet, and there is no easy way to serialize an ADO Recordset object. It is, on the other hand, very easy to serialize a `WDDXRecordset` object. That's what the next block of code is all about.

A simple `for` loop moves through the records in the ADO Recordset. The code inside the loop is executed once for every row in the record set, advancing the `RowNum` variable by one as it goes. Inside the loop, Allaire's `setField` function is used to take the `Value` of each column of the ADO Recordset and store it in the corresponding column of the `MyRS` record set. Then the `moveNext` function is used to move the ADO Recordset to the next row. When the `RowNum` variable reaches the `RecordCount` property of the `rs_Stores` record set, the loop has finished its work and script execution continues after the curly braces. The result is that the `MyRS` record set now holds the same data as the `rs_Stores` record set.

Now the `MyRS` record set can be serialized into a WDDX Packet. To do so, `CreateObject` is used to create an instance of Allaire's WDDX Serializer component called `MySer`. Note that this line is practically the same as the line that created the `MyRS` record set object. Next, the code uses `serialize` function to serialize the `MyRS` record set into a WDDX Packet; the function is part of the Serializer component. The function returns the packet as a string, which gets set to the variable named `MyPacket`.

Now all that needs to be done is to output the value of the `MyPacket` variable onto the current Web page, so that it can be picked up by whatever application requested the information. This is accomplished by using the `Response.write` method, which is a lot like a pair of `CFOUTPUT` tags in a ColdFusion template—it simply outputs whatever you include inside the parentheses onto the current Web page.

 TIP

ASP's built-in `Response` object and the methods it provides—such as the `write` method used here—is pretty important when coding for Active Server Pages. You might want to learn more about it by consulting your ASP documentation.

The Store Robot should now be operational. You can test it by bringing the .asp page up in a browser. Since a WDDX Packet is what the ASP script outputs, you have to use your browser's View Source command to see the packet and make sure that it contains the store data it should.

Using the Store Robot in a ColdFusion Template Connecting to the Store Robot from a ColdFusion template is really very simple. Listing 17.2 shows a version of the Book Finder form that is discussed in Chapter 16 (see Listing 16.11). This form looks exactly the same to the user; indeed, hardly any of the original code has been changed. The only major addition is the short block at the top of the template, which is in charge of interacting with the Store Robot.

Listing 17.2 `BookFinderForm2.cfm`—**Communicating with the ASP Store Robot from ColdFusion**

```
<!--- Fetch WDDX Packet of store names from Store Robot --->
<CFHTTP
  METHOD="GET"
  URL="http://127.0.0.1/Robots/StoreRobot.asp">

<!--- Place the WDDX Packet into StoresAsWDDX variable --->
<CFSET StoresAsWDDX = CFHTTP.FileContent>

<!--- Extract WDDX recordse from ASP page and store as qStores --->
<CFWDDX
  ACTION="WDDX2CFML"
  INPUT="#StoresAsWDDX#"
  OUTPUT="qStores">



<!DOCTYPE HTML PUBLIC "-//W3C//DTD HTML 4.0 Transitional//EN">

<HTML>
<HEAD>
  <TITLE>Book Finder</TITLE>
</HEAD>
```

```
<BODY>
<H2>Book Finder</H2>


<!--- Simple form where the user can enter parameters --->
<CFFORM ACTION="BookFinder2.cfm" METHOD="POST">

  <!--- Blank to enter publication date "filter" --->
  <P><B>Only books published after:</B><BR>
  <CFINPUT
    NAME="PubDateFrom"
    SIZE="10"
    VALIDATE="DATE"><BR>

  <!--- Blank to enter min. number of pages --->
  <P><B>Only books with at least:</B><BR>
  <CFINPUT
    NAME="PagesAtLeast"
    SIZE=5
    VALIDATE="integer"> pages<BR>

   <!--- Drop-down menu to choose RobotServer --->
  <P><B>Location:</B><BR>
  <CFSELECT NAME="RobotServer"
     SIZE="1"
     QUERY="qStores"
     VALUE="Host"
     DISPLAY="Name">
  </CFSELECT><BR>

  <!--- Blanks to enter up to 5 author names --->
  <P><B>Authors:</B> (LastName, FirstName)<BR>
  <CFLOOP FROM="1" TO="5" INDEX="Counter">
    <CFOUTPUT>
      <INPUT NAME="LastName#Counter#">,
      <INPUT NAME="FirstName#Counter#"><BR>
    </CFOUTPUT>
  </CFLOOP>


  <!--- Submit button --->
  <HR><CENTER><INPUT TYPE="Submit" VALUE="Find Books Now"></CENTER>


</CFFORM>

</BODY>
</HTML>
```

Part

IV

Ch

17

This template first uses the CFHTTP tag to fetch the WDDX Packet full of store information from the Store Robot that was just completed. The Store Robot's response is placed into the StoresAsWDDX variable. The variable is immediately passed to the CFWDDX tag, which deserializes the packet into a ColdFusion-style record set named qStores. This record set can now be used as if it were the result of an ordinary CFQUERY tag.

This allows for the only other change in the template to be made, which is to use the CFSELECT tag to populate the Location drop-down list in the form. By specifying qStores for the CFSELECT tag's QUERY parameter, and by specifying Host and Name for the tag's VALUE and DISPLAY parameters, you end up with a drop-down list that shows each store's name to the user (see Figure 17.2). When the form is submitted, the store's hostname is available to the next template as the #Form.RobotServer# variable.

 TIP   See Appendix A, "ColdFusion Tag Reference," for more information about the CFSELECT tag and how it can be used to dynamically populate a drop-down list with no coding or looping.

FIGURE 17.2

The current list of stores is fetched from the Store Robot and presented as choices to the user.

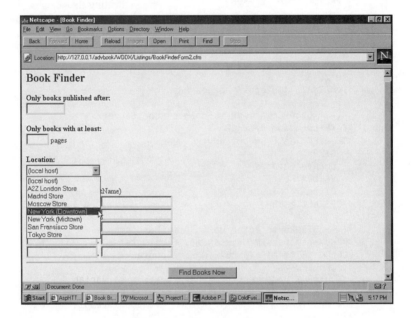

Caching the Store Robot's Response in RAM   You've seen that the Store Robot has been successfully integrated into the Book Finder application, melding the worlds of ASP and ColdFusion. However, you realize that the Store Robot probably doesn't need to be contacted every time the form page is viewed; it's unlikely that the list of stores is going to change that often. By adding a few more lines of ColdFusion code, you can get the template to cache the list of stores for up to an hour—or whatever period of time you choose. This should reduce network traffic and cause the application as a whole to work more quickly, especially if the Store Robot is far away from the ColdFusion server.

Take a look at the BookFinderForm3.cfm template shown in Listing 17.3. It makes two changes to create the desired caching effect. First, the name of the fetched record set has been changed from qStores to Application.qStores. This causes the record set to remain in the server's memory after the template executes, rather than being discarded immediately after the page is sent to the browser. It also allows the record set to be accessible (*shared*) by any other ColdFusion templates on the same server.

The second change is the CFIF logic around the actual packet-processing code. The idea is that a variable called Application.qStoresRefreshAt should be maintained to indicate the time that a refresh of the store list is due. The first time the template runs, the CFPARAM tag at the top of the template sets the variable to the current time, indicating that the list of stores is due to be refreshed immediately. When the DateCompare function compares the variable to the current time, the function returns 0 (since the two dates are the same). Thus, code execution continues inside the CFIF block, which contains the code that interacts with the Store Robot.

At the end of the CFIF block, the DateAdd function is used to set the Refresh At variable to an hour from the current time. Therefore, if the template is used again after just a few minutes, the DateCompare function returns a value of 1 (indicating that the refresh time is still in the future) and the CFIF code is skipped; this causes the template to use the copy of the record set in the server's memory. After the hour has passed, the DateCompare function returns a value of –1 (indicating that the refresh time has passed), which causes the Store Server to be contacted again.

Part
IV
Ch
17

 T I P See Appendix B, "ColdFusion Function Reference," for more information about the DateCompare and DateAdd functions used in Listing 17.3.

N O T E Listing 17.3 uses CFLOCK tags to ensure that the code inside the CFIF block does not get executed by more than one page request at the same time. It's generally a good idea to use CFLOCK tags around any code that manipulates objects in the Application scope. See Appendix A for more information about CFLOCK. ▪

Listing 17.3 `BookFinderForm3.cfm`—**Caching the Store Robot's Response**

```
<!--- Enable ColdFusion's Application-level variables --->
<!--- This tag is usually placed in Application.cfm,   --->
<!--- But it's fine to use in it individual templates --->
<CFAPPLICATION NAME="Bookstore">


<!--- If no "Refresh At" time is defined, we should refresh right now --->
<CFPARAM NAME="Application.qStoresRefreshAt" DEFAULT="#Now()#">

<!--- So, if the refresh time is right now, or has already passed --->
<CFIF DateCompare(Application.qStoresRefreshAt, Now()) is not 1>

  <CFLOCK TIMEOUT="30">

    <!--- Fetch WDDX Packet of store names from Store Robot --->
    <CFHTTP
      METHOD="GET"
      URL="http://127.0.0.1/Robots/StoreRobot.asp">

    <!--- Place the WDDX Packet into StoresAsWDDX variable --->
    <CFSET StoresAsWDDX = CFHTTP.FileContent>
```

continues

Listing 17.3 Continued

```
    <!--- Extract WDDX recordset from ASP page and store as qStores --->
    <CFWDDX
      ACTION="WDDX2CFML"
      INPUT="#StoresAsWDDX#"
      OUTPUT="Application.qStores">

    <!--- Set next "Refresh At" time to an hour from now --->
    <CFSET Application.qStoresRefreshAt = DateAdd("h", 1, Now())>

  </CFLOCK>

</CFIF>


<!--- *********************************************************** --->
<!--- If you wanted all templates in the current directory tree --->
<!--- To be able to use the store list in Application.qStores,   --->
<!--- Just place all of the above in your Application.cfm file!  --->
<!--- *********************************************************** --->


<!DOCTYPE HTML PUBLIC "-//W3C//DTD HTML 4.0 Transitional//EN">

<HTML>
<HEAD>
  <TITLE>Book Finder</TITLE>
</HEAD>

<BODY>
<H2>Book Finder</H2>


<!--- Simple form where the user can enter parameters --->
<CFFORM ACTION="BookFinder2.cfm" METHOD="POST">

  <!--- Blank to enter publication date "filter" --->
  <P><B>Only books published after:</B><BR>
  <CFINPUT
    NAME="PubDateFrom"
    SIZE="10"
    VALIDATE="DATE"><BR>

  <!--- Blank to enter min. number of pages --->
  <P><B>Only books with at least:</B><BR>
  <CFINPUT
    NAME="PagesAtLeast"
    SIZE=5
    VALIDATE="integer"> pages<BR>

  <!--- Drop-down menu to choose RobotServer --->
  <P><B>Location:</B><BR>
  <CFSELECT NAME="RobotServer"
    SIZE="1"
```

```
        QUERY="Application.qStores"
        VALUE="Host"
        DISPLAY="Name">
    </CFSELECT><BR>

    <!--- Blanks to enter up to 5 author names --->
    <P><B>Authors:</B> (LastName, FirstName)<BR>
    <CFLOOP FROM="1" TO="5" INDEX="Counter">
      <CFOUTPUT>
        <INPUT NAME="LastName#Counter#">,
        <INPUT NAME="FirstName#Counter#"><BR>
      </CFOUTPUT>
    </CFLOOP>


    <!--- Submit button --->
    <HR><CENTER><INPUT TYPE="Submit" VALUE="Find Books Now"></CENTER>


  </CFFORM>

</BODY>
</HTML>
```

T I P This is a simple but effective technique that can be used to cache any variable in the Application scope for a certain period of time. For database record sets fetched directly with the CFQUERY or CFSTOREDPROC tags, however, you should use ColdFusion 4's built-in query-caching mechanism instead. Look up the CFQUERY tag's CACHEDAFTER and CACHEDWITHIN attributes in your ColdFusion documentation for more information about this powerful new feature.

N O T E If you want other templates in the same directory (or subdirectories of the current directory) to be able to access the Application.qStores query result set, you could move the top portion of Listing 17.3 into an Application.cfm file; there's a comment in the listing itself that indicates which part to move. All templates in the directory tree would then be able to refer to the query in CFSELECT, CFOUPUT, and other tags, and they would all be sharing the same refreshed hourly copy of the list of store locations.

The Big Picture Take a moment to consider the big picture here. The user is now able to search the inventory at any of A2Z's bookstores worldwide. The list of available stores is coming from one WDDX-enabled robot that's operating at one server, and the list of books is coming from a different robot that could be at an entirely different server. All communications between the servers is being done over simple, low-cost HTTP connections, without introducing any of the complexity that comes with attempting to replicate databases over the Internet.

What's more, the two robots were created with entirely different development tools—ASP and ColdFusion, who most people think of as feuding competitors rather than symbiotic partners. The robots may have been developed by different development teams in different parts of the world, employing developers with entirely different programming backgrounds and preferences. WDDX is providing a simple, open means to integrate the two environments and get them to behave as one. There's even some reasonably intelligent caching going on.

What's more, as you soon see in the Visual Basic section of this chapter, either robot can be used to provide information to non–browser-based applications as well. Remember also that either robot could have been built with just about any other type of Web development tool out there. As long as it supports COM and HTTP, it can probably be used to create WDDX-enabled applications that can successfully talk to each other over the Internet.

Interacting with ColdFusion and JavaScript at Once

You've seen that it's very possible to use Allaire's COM object in an ASP script to supply data to a ColdFusion server. What if you want to integrate with ColdFusion in the other direction? That is, what if you want to get data from a ColdFusion server to an ASP-based page? It's actually pretty simple—again, WDDX can be used as general-purpose "integration glue" that allows the two environments to communicate fairly easily over HTTP.

Listing 17.4 re-creates the DHTML Book Browser created in the last chapter, using an ASP script instead of a ColdFusion template. Just like the ColdFusion version of the page, this listing displays a list of book titles that react when the mouse is moved over them and allows the user to see a book's details by clicking the title (see Figure 17.3). See Listing 16.24 in Chapter 16 for an explanation of the JavaScript and DHTML code—such as the DIV and STYLE tags—used in this example.

FIGURE 17.3

The DHTML interface created with ASP looks just like the ColdFusion version from Chapter 16.

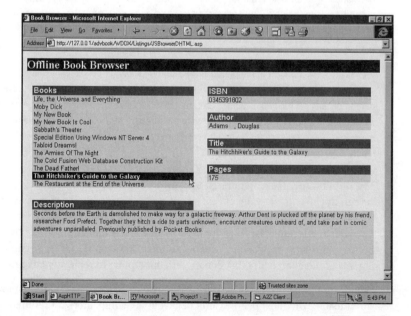

In addition to re-creating the DHTML functionality of the original, this listing adds a new twist. Instead of getting its data straight from the database table, as the ColdFusion version of the page did, this ASP page gets its data from the Book Robot that was created in the last chapter. By the time the page gets to the browser, the book information has been sent from the ColdFusion server (where the Book Robot is) to the ASP server, and is then converted to native JavaScript objects for the DHTML scripting to refer to on the client side.

N O T E Because ASP does not provide the equivalent of ColdFusion's CFHTTP tag as part of the product, this example uses a third-party COM object called AspHTTP to communicate with the Book Robot. The component is available from a company called ServerObjects, and is commonly used in ASP scripts that need to fetch pages from or post form data to other Web servers. It's available on a try-before-you-buy basis from http://www.serverobjects.com. ∎

Listing 17.4 JSBrowserDHTML.asp—The DHTML Version of the Book Browser, as an Active Server Page

```
<%@ LANGUAGE=JScript %>

<%
  // Create instance of ServerObjects's ASPHttp Control
  HttpObj = Server.CreateObject("AspHTTP.Conn")

  // Create instances of Allaire's WDDX components
  MySer = Server.CreateObject("WDDX.Serializer.1")
  MyDeser = Server.CreateObject("WDDX.Deserializer.1")
  MyConv = Server.CreateObject("WDDX.JSConverter.1")

  // Create Structure object, set its Columns property to "*"
  // (to ask Book Robot for all columns), then serialize it.
  MyRequest = Server.CreateObject("WDDX.Struct.1")
  MyRequest.setProp("Columns", "*")
  RequestAsWDDX = MySer.serialize(MyRequest)

  // Post the Structure to the Book Robot as form parameter
  // ColdFusion will recieve packet as #Form.WDDXContent#
  HttpObj.Url = "http://127.0.0.1/Robots/BookRobot.cfm"
  HttpObj.PostData = "WDDXContent=" + RequestAsWDDX
  HttpObj.RequestMethod = "Post"
  MyPacket = HttpObj.GetURL()

  // We know the ColdFusion server's response is a WDDX Packet
  // Deserialize it into Allaire recordset object named MyRS
  MyRS = MyDeser.deserialize(MyPacket)

  // Also, convert the same packet into JavaScript code, which
  // will create JavaScript wddxRecordset object named Books.
  MyJS = MyConv.convertWddx(MyPacket, "Books")
%>

<HTML><HEAD>
```

continues

Listing 17.4 Continued

```
<TITLE>Book Browser</TITLE>


<!--- Include Allaire's WDDX / JavaScript support --->
<SCRIPT SRC="/cfide/scripts/wddx.js" LANGUAGE="JAVASCRIPT"></SCRIPT>

<SCRIPT LANGUAGE="JAVASCRIPT">

    // The following JavaScript was created by the WDDX JSConverter
    <%= MyJS %>


    //////////////////////////////////////////////////
    // This function populates other INPUT elements
    // when an option in the SELECT box is clicked
    function FillControls(RowNum) {
      with (document.DataForm) {
        RowNum = RowNum - 1;

        // Populate textboxes with data in that row
        ISBN.innerText = Books.isbn[RowNum];
        Title.innerText = Books.title[RowNum];
        Pages.innerText = Books.pages[RowNum];
        Description.innerText = Books.description[RowNum];
        Author.innerText = Books.authorlastname[RowNum]
                          + ', ' + Books.authorfirstname[RowNum];
      }
    }


</SCRIPT>
</HEAD>


<BODY>

<!--- Define CSS styles to control the "look" of the DIV tags--->
<STYLE TYPE="text/css">
  Div            {width:350px; padding-left:3px; font:smaller Arial}
  Div.choice     {background:wheat};
  Div.choiceSel  {background:black; color:white; font-weight:bold};
  Div.choiceOver {background:beige; color:brown};
  Div.bar        {background:brown; color:white; font:bold small Arial};
  H2             {background:black; color:white}
</STYLE>


<H2>Offline Book Browser</H2>


<FORM NAME="DataForm">
```

```
<TABLE CELLPADDING="10">
<TR VALIGN="TOP">

<!--- Books to choose from.  User can click on each Title --->
<TD>
  <DIV CLASS="bar">Books</DIV>

  <!--- This is like a CFOUTPUT QUERY="MyRS" block in ColdFusion --->
  <% for (Count = 1; Count < MyRS.getRowCount(); Count++) { %>
    <% ThisTitle = MyRS.getField(Count, "TITLE") %>

    <DIV CLASS="choice"
      onClick="this.className = 'choiceSel'; FillControls(<%= Count %>)"
      onMouseOver="this.className = 'choiceOver'"
      onMouseOut="this.className = 'choice'"><%= ThisTitle %></DIV>

  <% } %>

</TD>

<!--- This info gets updated when user clicks on a Title --->
<TD>
  <DIV CLASS="bar">ISBN</DIV>
  <DIV CLASS="choice" ID="ISBN"></DIV><BR>

  <DIV CLASS="bar">Author</DIV>
  <DIV CLASS="choice" ID="Author"></DIV><BR>

  <DIV CLASS="bar">Title</DIV>
  <DIV CLASS="choice" ID="Title"></DIV><BR>

  <DIV CLASS="bar">Pages</DIV>
  <DIV CLASS="choice" ID="Pages"></DIV><BR>

</TD>
</TR>

<!--- So does the description, underneath --->
<TR><TD COLSPAN="2">
  <DIV CLASS="bar">Description</DIV>
  <DIV CLASS="choice" ID="Description" STYLE="height:100px;width=auto"> 
➥</DIV><BR>
</TD></TR>

</TABLE>


</FORM>


</BODY>
</HTML>
```

This ASP page first creates instances of the various COM objects that it will need to use. An instance of the AspHTTP component (called HttpObj) is created. The script uses this object to communicate with the Web server where the Book Robot is located. Similar CreateObject syntax is used to create instances of Allaire's Serializer, Deserializer, and JavaScript Converter components.

Next, an Allaire-style Structure object named MyRequest is created. This Structure object is used to pass a request structure to the Book Robot, telling the Book Robot which columns you want it to retrieve from the database. Once the MyRequest object has been created, Allaire's setProp function adds a new key/value pair to the structure. The name of the pair is Columns, and its value is set to *; this indicates that you want the Book Robot to run a SELECT * type of query (see Listing 16.8). Allaire's serialize function is then used to serialize the structure into a WDDX Packet called RequestAsWDDX.

Now the script is ready to communicate with the Book Robot. The Book Robot needs the request structure to be posted as a form parameter called WDDXContent, so the AspHTTP control's RequestMethod parameter is set to Post. The control's PostData property is set to a simple key-value pair that specifies WDDXContent as the name of the form parameter and the value of the RequestAsWDDX variable as the value of the form parameter. Finally, the control's GetURL method is called to actually post the request to the ColdFusion server. The Book Robot's response is stored in the variable called MyPacket.

N O T E See the online documentation for the AspHTTP component at http://
www.serverobjects.com for more information about Postdata, GetURL, and the
other properties and methods that the object provides. ▪

At this point the script knows that the MyPacket variable holds a WDDX Packet full of the book information that it requested from the Book Robot. All that needs to be done now is to convert the data from WDDX format to an actual record set object. That's what the next line of code does. It uses Allaire's deserialize function to deserialize the data in MyPacket. Since MyPacket contains a record set, the function returns a WDDX Recordset object. The object is stored with the name MyRS. Any of the functions provided by Allaire's WDDX Recordset component class can now be used with the MyRS object.

Finally, the script needs to convert the record set to a native JavaScript object so that the DHTML scripting in the rest of the page can function correctly. This is accomplished by using Allaire's convertWddx function, which takes the same WDDX Packet and creates a series of dynamically created JavaScript statements that create the needed record set object on the client side. When the code is executed in the browser, the record set will be available as the JavaScript object named Books.

N O T E The convertWddx function accomplishes the same thing that the CFWDDX ACTION=
"CFMLTOJS" tag did in Listing 16.24 in Chapter 16. You might want to look back at that
listing to refresh your memory about how that template worked. ▪

When the `JSBrowserDHTML.asp` page is viewed in a browser, it looks just like the ColdFusion version of the page (see Figure 17.3). Active Server Pages, ColdFusion, and JavaScript are all working together successfully, thanks to the WDDX data format.

Integrating with Visual Basic

One of the easiest and most interesting places to use COM objects is within applications created with Microsoft's Visual Basic development environment. Even though more and more business applications are being created with Web-based interfaces on company intranets, there are many times when a native Windows application makes more sense than a Web interface based on HTML forms and JavaScript. By providing support for WDDX via COM, Allaire has opened the possibility of creating native Windows executables that communicate with WDDX-based Web pages over the Internet.

> **N O T E**   You are not limited to Visual Basic for creating native Windows applications like the example in this section. You could do very similar things with other visual development tools, such as Delphi or C++ Builder from Borland, Visual C++ from Microsoft, or PowerBuilder from PowerSoft. (With Delphi, for instance, much of the code would be nearly identical to the code discussed in the following pages.) All that's required is that the development tool know how to create native Windows applications and how to use COM objects. ▪

Part
IV
Ch
17

Creating the A2Z Client Application

This section shows how to use Visual Basic to create a native Windows application (called A2Z Client) that mimics the functionality of the JavaScript-based Book Browser created in the previous chapter. By the time the application is finished, it will list books in stock, allow the user to make changes and add new book records, and post the changes to the database on the ColdFusion server. It will use Microsoft's Internet Transfer Control to fetch pages from and post changes to the Book Robot, and it will use Allaire's WDDX COM object to deserialize record sets from WDDX Packets, create WDDX-style structure variables, and so on.

The first step is to create the visual interface for the application. Then, in the next section, you add the Visual Basic code that actually makes the application work.

> **N O T E**   If you don't want to go through the steps listed here to create the application, you can open the A2Z `Client.vbp` file from the source code folder on the accompanying CD-ROM for this chapter. You need Visual Basic 5.0 or later to open the file. ▪

To create the visual interface for the A2Z client application, follow these steps:

1. Start Visual Basic. If you already have it open, choose File, New Project from the menu bar.

2. In the New Project dialog box, make sure Standard EXE is selected; click OK.

3. Choose References from the Project menu.

4. In the References dialog box, select the check box for wddx_com 1.0 Type Library in the list of Controls, as shown in Figure 17.4. This allows you to use Allaire's serializer, deserializer, and other WDDX utilities in the application.

   If the control is not in the list, use the Browse button and find the file named wddx_com.dll on your system. Like most DLL files, it is probably in your c:\Windows\System folder if you are using Windows 95 or 98 or in your c:\WinNT\System32 folder if you are using Windows NT. Once you find and select the file, the control should be added to the list so that you can select its check box. If the file is nowhere on your system, reinstall either ColdFusion Application Server 4 or ColdFusion Studio 4.

5. Choose Project, Components from the main menu. On the Controls tab, select the check box for Microsoft Internet Transfer Control. This control allows you to fetch pages from and post form data to Web servers on the Internet. You'll use this capability to communicate with the Book Robot.

   If it is not in the list, add it to the list by browsing for the MSInet.ocx file in your System or System32 folder (see preceding step for instructions). Now close the Components dialog box by clicking OK. If the .ocx file it is not available, reinstall Visual Basic.

6. A new Inet icon should have appeared in the Toolbox. Use your mouse to place two Inet controls on the form. Make sure they are named Inet1 and Inet2. These controls are invisible when your application is actually run, so don't worry about where they are placed on the form.

7. Place a ListBox control at the top of the form, making sure it is named List1.

8. Place a Frame control on the form, underneath the ListBox, and change its Caption property to Details.

9. Place four TextBox controls inside the Frame control (see Figure 17.5) and name them txtISBN, txtTitle, txtAuthorF, and txtAuthorL.

10. Place a command button control on the form, name it btnKeepEdits, and make its caption something like Keep Your Edits To This Record.

11. Place some label controls on the form and arrange all the form elements so that the form looks something like Figure 17.5.

FIGURE 17.4

Adding the wddx_com 1.0 Type Library control to the project allows you to use Allaire's WDDX functions.

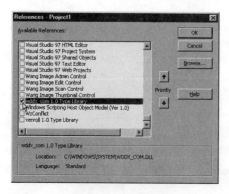

FIGURE 17.5
The ListBox and TextBox controls on this form get populated with data from the Book Robot.

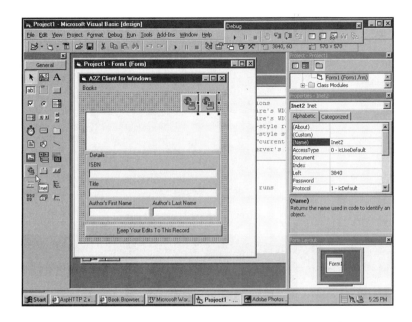

Now you need to add a menu bar to the application so that the user can do things like save records and create new records. Follow these steps to add the menu to your application:

1. Open Visual Basic's Menu Editor by clicking your form and then choosing Menu Editor from the Tools menu.

2. Create a Books menu by typing Books in the Caption blank, MenuBooks in the Name blank. You'll see the Books menu appear in the bottom of the dialog box. Click Next to move on to the new item.

3. Create a New Record item by typing New Record in the Caption blank, MenuNew in the Name blank. Click the right arrow button, which indents the New Record item and makes it part of the Books menu.

4. Create a Get Records From Server item named MenuGet, and a Save Records To Server item named MenuSave, both indented under the Books menu, just like the New Record item.

5. The Menu Editor dialog box should now look something like Figure 17.6. When you're done, close the Menu Editor by clicking OK.

Adding Visual Basic Code to Bring the Application to Life

Now that the visual interface has been put together, you can add the Visual Basic code that makes the application actually work. The code in Listing 17.5 adds several procedures to the project that connect the visual elements on the form (the ListBox and the four TextBoxes). It also declares some global variables that are used throughout the application.

Part
IV

Ch
17

FIGURE 17.6

The menu items added with the Menu Editor use Allaire's WDDX functions to get their work done.

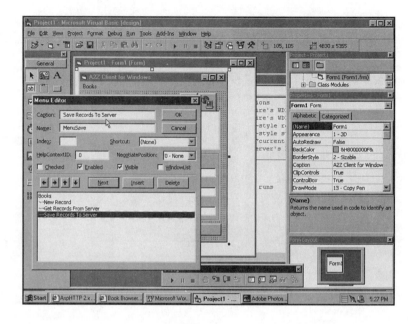

Follow these steps to add the code to your application:

1. Double-click any blank spot on the form. A code editor window opens, with two lines of code already written for you. The two lines of code declare the built-in `Form_Load()` procedure.

2. Since the code in Listing 17.5 provides these two lines of code on its own, delete the two lines of code that Visual Basic wrote for you. The editor window should now be totally blank.

3. Type or copy the code shown in Listing 17.5 into the editor window.

Listing 17.5 `Listing05.txt`—**Visual Basic Code That Initializes the Application's Objects and Populates Form Controls**

```
' Global variables, available to all functions
Private MyDeser As WDDXDeserializer  'Allaire's WDDX deserializer
Private MySer As WDDXSerializer       'Allaire's WDDX serializer
Private MyRS As WDDXRecordset         'WDDX-style recordset object
Private RequestStruct As WDDXStruct   'WDDX-style structure object
Private RowNum As Integer             'The "current" row of recordset
Private RobotServer As String         'Webserver's hostname


' This executes when the application first runs
Private Sub Form_Load()

    ' Create Instances of Allaire objects
```

```
          Set MySer = New WDDXSerializer
          Set MyDeser = New WDDXDeserializer
          Set RequestStruct = New WDDXStruct

          ' Initialize the global MyRS Variable
          ' This holds the book data throughout the app
          Set MyRS = New WDDXRecordset

          ' Add columns we'll be dealing with to recordset
          MyRS.addColumn ("BOOKID")
          MyRS.addColumn ("ISBN")
          MyRS.addColumn ("TITLE")
          MyRS.addColumn ("AUTHORFIRSTNAME")
          MyRS.addColumn ("AUTHORLASTNAME")
          MyRS.addColumn ("WASEDITED")

          ' Webserver to interact with Book Robot at
          RobotServer = "http://127.0.0.1"

End Sub


' This fills form controls with data from recordset
Private Sub InitControls()
  Dim Count, ThisTitle

  ' Clear all current items out of the list box
  List1.Clear

  ' For each row in the recordset, get the title
  ' and then add the title to the list box
  For Count = 1 To MyRS.getRowCount
    ThisTitle = MyRS.getField(Count, "TITLE")
    List1.AddItem (ThisTitle)
  Next Count

End Sub


' This runs when a user selects a book on the form
Private Sub List1_Click()
  ' When user clicks on a book, set global RowNum variable
  ' to the list's index plus one, so all recordset functions
  ' can use RowNum to refer to the current row
  RowNum = List1.ListIndex + 1

  ' Set various data-entry blanks to values from recordset
  txtISBN.Text = MyRS.getField(RowNum, "ISBN")
  txtTitle.Text = MyRS.getField(RowNum, "TITLE")
  txtAuthorF.Text = MyRS.getField(RowNum, "AUTHORFIRSTNAME")
  txtAuthorL.Text = MyRS.getField(RowNum, "AUTHORLASTNAME")

End Sub
```

Part
IV

Ch
17

continues

Listing 17.5   Continued

```
' This executes if user clicks "Keep Edits" button
Private Sub btnKeepEdits_Click()

    ' Update columns in current row of recordset
    MyRS.setField RowNum, "ISBN", txtISBN.Text
    MyRS.setField RowNum, "TITLE", txtTitle.Text
    MyRS.setField RowNum, "AUTHORFIRSTNAME", txtAuthorF.Text
    MyRS.setField RowNum, "AUTHORLASTNAME", txtAuthorL.Text
    MyRS.setField RowNum, "WASEDITED", "Yes"

    ' Update the current item in the list of titles
    List1.List(RowNum - 1) = txtTitle.Text

End Sub
```

The first thing Listing 17.5 does is declare five variables that are used throughout the application. First, a variable named MyDeser is created, of the special type WDDXDeserializer. This tells Visual Basic that whenever you refer to the MyDeser variable, you want to interact with an instance of Allaire's deserializer object class. A serializer object named MySer, a WDDX-style record set object named MyRS, and a WDDX-style structure object named RequestStruct are all created with similar syntax. In addition, a simple integer variable named RowNum is declared; the application uses RowNum to remember which row in the record set is the current row. Finally, a string variable named RobotServer is declared, which is used to store the Internet hostname for the Book Robot. Since these variables are all declared with the Private keyword and appear on their own, outside of any procedure block, they are *global* variables that are available to any procedure in the application. See your Visual Basic documentation for details.

Listing 17.5 declares the Form_Load() procedure, which Visual Basic executes just before the form appears for the first time. In other words, this code runs when your application first starts. It uses Visual Basic's Set statement with the New keyword to create instances of Allaire's four WDDX object classes, binding them to the MySer, MyDeser, and other global variables that were declared at the beginning of the code. It's at this moment that wddx_com.dll file is actually interacted with for the first time. The procedure then uses Allaire's addColumn function to add four columns to the MyRS record set, so that the record set is ready to hold information about books. Finally, it sets the RobotServer variable to http://127.0.0.1 so that the application fetches information from a ColdFusion server on the local machine by default. You need to change this value if you do not have ColdFusion running on the same machine that you will be running the application on.

The next procedure, InitControls(), is in charge of populating the ListBox called List1 with the rows of data in the MyRS record set. Conceptually, this procedure does just about the same thing as the InitControls function in the JavaScript version of the Book Browser from the previous chapter. First, the procedure clears any existing items from the list with the ListBox's Clear method. Then a simple for loop is used to loop through the rows of the record set, advancing the Count variable as it goes. Inside the loop, Allaire's getField function retrieves the title of the current book, which is then added as a new item in the list with the ListBox's AddItem method. The result is that the list box is filled with the titles of all the books in the record set. Of course, there are no rows in the record set when the application first starts, so the code inside the for loop never executes.

 T I P See your Visual Basic documentation for more information about VB-style for loops.

The next procedure, List1_Click(), is in charge of filling the four TextBox controls with the appropriate information when the user clicks an item in the List1 ListBox. First, it sets the RowNum variable with the ListIndex property of the ListBox, plus 1. It's necessary to add 1 because the rows in Allaire's record sets are numbered beginning with 1, whereas the items in the ListBox are numbered beginning with 0. For instance, if the user selects the third book in the list, List1.ListIndex will be 2, so the RowNum variable needs to be set to 3 to reflect the current row in the record set. The procedure then uses Allaire's getField function to retrieve the data from each of the columns in the current row of the record set, feeding each value to the Text property of the corresponding TextBox control. The result is that the text boxes are filled with the appropriate title, author name, and ISBN number when the user clicks a book.

The last procedure, btnKeepEdits_Click(), needs to do the opposite of what the List1_Click() procedure does. It needs to take the information in the TextBox controls and put it into the corresponding columns of the MyRS record set's current row. This is easily done by supplying the Text property of each control to Allaire's setField function. The procedure updates the selected item in the ListBox with the just-typed book title by setting the List1 object's List property to whatever has been typed in the txtTitle control.

Adding the "Get Records From Server" Code   The procedure in Listing 17.6 executes when the user chooses Get Records From Server from the application's Books menu. It's in charge of fetching the book information from the Book Robot and deserializing it into the MyRS record set.

Follow these steps to add the procedure to your application:

1. On the form, click the Books menu and choose the Get Records From Server item, just as a user would with the completed application. The code editor opens with two lines of new code written for you; the MenuGet_Click() procedure is declared for you.

2. Replace the procedure with the code provided in Listing 17.6.

Listing 17.6   `Listing06.txt`—**Fetching Data from the Book Robot and Updating the Form Via WDDX**

```
' This runs when user chooses "Get Records From Server" from menu
Private Sub MenuGet_Click()

    ' If user clicks okay in simple confirmation dialog box...
    If MsgBox("Get book data from server?", vbOKCancel) = vbOK Then
        Dim strURL As String
```

continues

Part

IV

Ch

17

Listing 17.6 Continued

```
' Add a "Columns" element to the request structure
' Then serialize the structure into MyPacket
RequestStruct.setProp "Columns", _
   "BOOKID,ISBN,TITLE,AUTHORFIRSTNAME,AUTHORLASTNAME"
MyPacket = MySer.serialize(RequestStruct)

' Fetch WDDX Packet of data from Book Robot,
' Passing the request packet as a URL Parameter
strURL = RobotServer & "/Robots/BookRobot.cfm?WDDXContent=" & MyPacket
MyXML = Inet1.OpenURL(strURL)

' Deserialize the packet into a recordset
Set MyRS = MyDeser.deserialize(MyXML)
MyRS.addColumn ("WASEDITED")

' Fill various controls on the form with data
InitControls

End If

End Sub
```

Considering that it does most of the application's magic, this code is pretty simple, thanks to Allaire's `serializer` and `structure` objects. First a confirmation message is displayed, allowing the user to click OK or Cancel. Assuming that the user clicks OK, the `setProp` function is used to place a key/value pair in the WDDX-style structure object named `RequestStruct`. The name of the key/value pair is `Columns`, and it is populated with the columns that need to be fetched from the Book Robot.

Next, the `MySer` object's `serialize` function serializes the structure, placing the resulting WDDX Packet into the string variable named `MyPacket`. Then the string variable called `strURL` is put together, which passes the contents of the packet as the URL variable called `WDDXContent`. In other words, the `BookRobot.cfm` template receives the packet as `#URL.WDDXContent#`.

The `Inet1` object's `OpenURL` method is used to fetch the URL from the Web server, placing the received Web page (which you know will be a WDDX Packet full of book information) in the `MyXML` variable. You can find more information about the `OpenURL` method in your Visual Basic documentation, but the basic idea is that it pretends to be a Web browser, behaving as if some user visited that page with Netscape Navigator or some other browser. The `OpenURL` method is comparable to using `METHOD="GET"` with the `CFHTTP` tag in a ColdFusion template.

TIP To get information about the OpenURL method as well as the Internet Transfer Control's other methods and properties, place your cursor on the keyword OpenURL in your code and press F1. You can also look it up in the Visual Basic Books Online, which you can install when you install Visual Basic itself.

Then the `MyDeser` object's `deserialize` function is used to deserialize the received packet into a record set object (which should be full of book information). Visual Basic's `Set` statement replaces the current `MyRS` object with the new record set object. Finally, the `InitControls()` function populates the ListBox with the titles of the just-fetched books.

At this point, you should be able to test the application by choosing Start from Visual Basic's Run menu. Choose Get Records From Server from the menu and click OK in the confirmation message box. After a few moments, the book titles should appear in the ListBox control on the form (see Figure 17.7). If you click a title, you should see the corresponding ISBN and author information in the various TextBox controls; you should be able to edit the information and see that it is being updated in the record set by moving away from and then back to an edited record. All that's left now is allowing the user to enter new records and post the changes to the server!

FIGURE 17.7

The user can browse through records and edit the information about each book.

T I P It is fairly easy to adapt the application so that it provides buttons instead of menus for the user to interact with. See your Visual Basic documentation for details.

Adding the "New Record" Code The procedure in Listing 17.7 executes when the user chooses Get Records From Server from the application's Books menu. It's in charge of fetching the book information from the Book Robot and deserializing it into the `MyRS` record set. Add the code in Listing 17.7 to the New Record menu item the same way that you added the code in Listing 17.6 to the Get Records menu item.

Listing 17.7 `Listing07.txt`**—Allowing the User to Add a New Row to the Record Set**

```
' This runs when user chooses "New Record" from menu
Private Sub MenuNew_Click()
  Dim NewRow As Integer

  ' Add a new row to the recordset
```

continues

Listing 17.7 Continued

```
' Then set NewRow to revised number of rows
MyRS.addRows (1)
NewRow = MyRS.getRowCount

' Put initial values in new row of recordset
MyRS.setField NewRow, "BOOKID", "New"
MyRS.setField NewRow, "TITLE", "(new)"

' Refresh the form controls with new data
InitControls

' "Select" the new row in the list box
List1.ListIndex = NewRow - 1

End Sub
```

First, the procedure uses Allaire's addRows function to add a new, empty row to the record set. The integer variable NewRow is set to the row number of the new row; this is easily obtained by simply using the getRowCount function, which determines the total number of rows. The setField function is used to use the text (new) as the Title for the new book, and to set the new row's BookID column to New, which is used by the ColdFusion page that receives the record set as a flag that this is a new record.

Next, the InitControls() function is called to repopulate the ListBox with the data from the record set (which now includes the new row), and the List1.ListIndex property is used to select the just-added book title in the ListBox. The user is then free to enter the ISBN, title, and author information for the new book.

N O T E This code is remarkably similar to the NewRecord() function from Listing 16.21 in Chapter 16. You might want to check out that listing to see how much this native Windows application is turning out to be like the JavaScript version of the Book Browser. WDDX really does go a long way toward making working with record sets more generic across platforms, languages, and development environments. ▓

Adding the "Save Records To Server" Code Now that the user can retrieve, edit, and add new records, you only need to provide a way for the records to actually be committed to the database. Listing 17.8 provides code that allows the user to do just that. It serializes the MyRS record set—which includes all the changes that the user has made to the data—into a WDDX Packet. It then posts the packet to a ColdFusion template that handles the updates to the database.

Add the code in Listing 17.8 to the Save Records To Server menu item the same way that you added the code in Listing 17.6 to the Get Records menu item.

Listing 17.8 `Listing08.txt`—Serializing the Record Set and Starting It Back to ColdFusion

```
' This runs when user chooses "Save records to server" from menu
Private Sub MenuSave_Click()
  Dim MyPacket
  Dim strURL As String, strFormData As String, strHead As String

  ' Serialize the MyRS recordset into a WDDX packet
  MyPacket = MySer.serialize(MyRS)

  ' Post the packet to the BookRobot.  The packet will
  ' be available to BookRobot.cfm as #Form.WDDXContent#
  strURL = RobotServer & "/Robots/BookRobotCommit.cfm"
  strFormData = "WDDXContent=" & MyPacket
  strHead = "Content-Type: application/x-www-form-urlencoded"

  ' Tell the Inet2 control to start posting the data
  Inet2.Execute URL:=strURL, Operation:="Post", _
    InputData:=strFormData, InputHdrs:=strHead

End Sub
```

The first thing this code does, after declaring some variables, is use the MySer object's serialize function to convert the MyRS record set into a WDDX Packet called MyPacket. This packet is supplied to ColdFusion by posting it as a form parameter to the receiving template. Next, three simple string variables are set in preparation for the actual connection to the ColdFusion server. The strURL variable holds the URL for the BookRobotCommit.cfm template that will receive the packet.

The strFormData variable is set to contain the data that should actually be sent to the server as form data. This needs to contain the same kind of name/value pairs full of information that a browser would normally send when a user submits a form on a Web page. The name/value pairs need to be separated using the = and & characters, just as URL parameters are separated in normal Web page URLs. Here, a single name/value pair is being put together. The name of the pair is WDDXContent, and the pair's value is the contents of the MyPacket variable. This allows the ColdFusion template on the server to refer to the WDDX Packet as #Form.WDDXContent#. Next, the strHead variable is set to a standard Content-Type header, which is sent to the Web server along with the form data. This is the same header that a browser would send to a Web server in most form-submitting situations. It basically tells the Web server how the data is being presented or *encoded*.

N O T E A complete explanation of the need for the Content-Type header—and the reasons = and & are used as separator characters in the form data—is beyond the scope of this chapter. They both are needed for the HTTP submission to work correctly, though. Check your Visual Basic documentation for the Internet Transfer Control for details. You might also want to take a look at the HTTP/1.1 specification at http://www.w3c.org to learn more about these HTTP-related concepts. ▪

Finally, the Inet2 control's `Execute` method is called, which tells the control to start posting the data to the Web server. The `Operation` parameter of the method is set to `Post`, which indicates a form-style submission and is analogous to using `METHOD="POST"` with a `CFHTTP` tag in a ColdFusion template. The URL, form data, and header information are supplied to the method by passing the `strURL` and other variables as parameters. See the Visual Basic documentation about the Internet Transfer Control for more information about the `Execute` method and the parameters you can supply to it.

> **N O T E** The Internet Transfer Control provided in the original version of Visual Basic 5.0—the version that's part of Visual Studio 97—has a bug that causes the `Execute` method in Listing 17.8 to work improperly. Basically, the method doesn't work when its `Operation` parameter is set to `Post`. This was fixed in Service Pack 2 for Visual Studio 97. You need to either obtain Service Pack 2 (or later) or use a later version of Visual Basic, such as Visual Basic 6.0, which was released when this book went to press. ■

Accepting the Posted Packet on the ColdFusion Side   As you can see in Listing 17.8, the edited records are posted to a ColdFusion template named `BookBrowserCommit.cfm`. The code for this template is provided in Listing 17.9. It is almost exactly the same as the `JSBrowserCommit.cfm` template from the previous chapter. Because the WDDX Packet containing the record set has been posted as the form variable called `WDDXContent`, the template can use the `CFWDDX` tag to deserialize `#Form.WDDXContent#` into the CFML-style query record set called `EditedBooks`.

Listing 17.9   BookBrowserCommit.cfm—A ColdFusion Template That Accepts Edited Records and Commits Them to the Database

```
<!--- Eliminate extraneous output from ColdFusion --->
<CFSETTING ENABLECFOUTPUTONLY="YES" SHOWDEBUGOUTPUT="NO">
<!--- Convert the incoming WDDX Packet to "EditedBooks" query --->
<CFWDDX
  INPUT="#WDDXContent#"
  OUTPUT="EditedBooks"
  ACTION="WDDX2CFML">

<!--- We'll increment these counters in the loop --->
<CFSET InsertCount = 0>
<CFSET UpdateCount = 0>

<!--- Loop over each of the records in the query --->
<CFLOOP QUERY="EditedBooks">

  <!--- If it's a new book (the user inserted it) --->
  <CFIF EditedBooks.BookID is "new">
    <CFQUERY DATASOURCE="A2Z">
      INSERT INTO Inventory (ISBN, Title, AuthorFirstName, AuthorLastName)
      VALUES ('#ISBN#', '#Title#', '#AuthorFirstName#', '#AuthorLastName#')
    </CFQUERY>
```

```
    <CFSET InsertCount = InsertCount + 1>

  <!--- It's an existing book (user may have edited) --->
  <CFELSEIF EditedBooks.WasEdited is "Yes">
    <CFQUERY DATASOURCE="A2Z">
      UPDATE Inventory SET
        ISBN = '#ISBN#',
        Title = '#Title#',
        AuthorFirstName = '#AuthorFirstName#',
        AuthorLastName = '#AuthorLastName#'
      WHERE BookID = #BookID#
    </CFQUERY>
    <CFSET UpdateCount = UpdateCount + 1>

  </CFIF>
</CFLOOP>

<!--- Create "Response" Structure to send back as confirmation --->
<CFSCRIPT>
  Response = StructNew();
  Response.Received = EditedBooks.RecordCount;
  Response.Updated  = UpdateCount;
  Response.Inserted = InsertCount;
</CFSCRIPT>

<!--- Convert the Response to WDDX Packet --->
<CFWDDX
  ACTION="CFML2WDDX"
  INPUT="#Response#"
  OUTPUT="ResponseAsWDDX">

<!--- Output WDDX Packet on web page to calling page/application --->
<CFOUTPUT>#ResponseAsWDDX#</CFOUTPUT>
```

Part
IV

Ch

17

For a full explanation of the template's logic, including the CFLOOP block that performs updates or inserts to the database as needed, look at Listing 16.22 in Chapter 16. The only thing that's different about this template is that the InsertCount and UpdateCount variables are placed into a structure named Response instead of being output directly onto the current Web page. The Response structure is then serialized into the WDDX Packet called ResponseAsWDDX, which *is* output to the current Web page. The Visual Basic application receives this packet in the Web server's response to the form submission. The application can then look in the packet to tell the user how many records were inserted and updated to the database.

TIP

If you want to test the template in Listing 17.9, you can go back to the JSBrowser3.cfm template from Chapter 16 and change its form's ACTION parameter to post to this template instead of JSBrowserCommit.cfm. Remember that since this template only outputs a WDDX Packet onto the resulting Web page, you may need to use your browser's View Source command to determine whether the template is behaving correctly.

Receiving the Server's Response   The application is now almost done; only one last bit of code needs to be added. The code in Listing 17.10 creates a procedure called `Inet2_StateChanged()`. Because of the procedure's name, it will be executed each time the state of the Inet2 control changes. The state of the control changes automatically as it goes through the various steps of contacting and communicating with a Web server. For instance, when the control's `Execute` method is first called (see previous listing), the control's state changes to something like connecting, then to something like connected, then to receiving, and then hopefully to something like done.

This code uses Visual Basic's `Select` statement to check the value of the `State` variable. The `Select` statement includes two `Case` statements. The first `Case` statement says that if the `State` variable indicates that an error has been encountered, a `MsgBox` function should be used to inform the user of the problem. The second `Case` says that if the control has finished receiving the Web server's response to the post operation (started in Listing 17.8), then a number of steps should be taken to pull the server's response out of the control's input/output buffer; this is discussed in a moment. If neither `Case` statement fires, the control is presumably still in the middle of connecting to the Web server or receiving its reply, so the procedure does nothing.

N O T E   In practice, it is best to check for all possible values of the `State` variable, not only `icError` and `icResponseCompleted`. See your Visual Basic documentation on the `StateChanged` event for details. ■

Follow these steps to add the procedure to your application:

1. Double-click on the Inet2 control on your form.
2. The code editor has inserted two lines of code for you, defining the `Inet2_StateChanged()` procedure. Replace those two lines with the code provided in Listing 17.10.

Listing 17.10   `Listing10.txt`—**Code That Waits Until the Data Is Posted, Then Displays a Confirmation Message**

```
' This runs whenever "something happens" in the Inet2 control.
' For explanation, click one of the Inet controls on the form
' and press F1.  Then read the example for the StateChanged Event.
Private Sub Inet2_StateChanged(ByVal State As Integer)
    Dim ResponseStruct As WDDXStruct 'WDDX-style structure object
    Dim Received, Updated, Inserted As Integer


    ' What "State" did the control just change to?
    ' (Connected, Receiving, Finished, Error, etc
    Select Case State


    ' If the state of the control is icError (11)
```

```
          Case icError
            MsgBox ("An error occurred while posting data to the webserver.")


          ' If state of control is "Finished Successfully" (12)
          Case icResponseCompleted   ' 12
              Dim Chunk As Variant ' Data variable.
              Dim strData As String: strData = ""
              Dim bDone As Boolean: bDone = False

              ' Pull first "chunk" of data from control's "buffer"
              Chunk = Inet2.GetChunk(1024, icString)
              DoEvents

              ' Until we have extracted all data from control's buffer...
              Do While Not bDone

                  ' Append the Chunk to the strData variable,
                  ' Then pull the next chunk from buffer
                  strData = strData & Chunk
                  Chunk = Inet2.GetChunk(1024, icString)
                  DoEvents

                  ' If the just-pulled chunk is empty, we're done
                  If Len(Chunk) = 0 Then
                      bDone = True
                  End If
              Loop


              ' Extract Response "Structure" from recieved packet
              Set ResponseStruct = MyDeser.deserialize(strData)

              ' Use Structure to set Received, Updated, Inserted vars
              ' Then discard the Response Structure
              Received = ResponseStruct.getProp("RECEIVED")
              Updated = ResponseStruct.getProp("UPDATED")
              Inserted = ResponseStruct.getProp("INSERTED")
              Set ResponseStruct = Nothing


              ' Display "Done" message to user
              MsgBox ("Records sent to server: " & Received & vbCr _
                  & "Records inserted: " & Inserted & vbCr _
                  & "Records updated: " & Updated)


          ' If state of Inet2 control is not "Finished Successfully"
          Case Else
            DoEvents

          End Select

      End Sub
```

Part
IV

Ch

17

As you can see, the bulk of Listing 17.10 is executed only when the State is icResponseCompleted, indicating the end of a successful post operation to the ColdFusion server. The first half of this section—through the Loop line—is very similar to example syntax found in the Visual Basic documentation, and is not discussed here in detail. Basically, the While loop's job is to retrieve the Web server's response from the control and place it, chunk by chunk, into the string variable named strData. By the time the loop finishes executing, the strData variable should hold the complete response from the Web server, which you know holds a WDDX Packet containing information about the number of records inserted and updated.

After the loop, the MyDeser object's deserialize function is used to deserialize the WDDX Packet into a WDDX-style structure object named ResponseStruct. Allaire's getProp function is then used to set the integer variables named Received, Updated, and Inserted to the corresponding values in the structure. Next, the structure variable is set to the reserved word Nothing, which causes Visual Basic to release the structure object. (See your Visual Basic documentation for details about Nothing.) Finally, the MsgBox function is used to display a simple confirmation message to the user, as shown in Figure 17.8.

FIGURE 17.8

The user's changes are processed by the ColdFusion server, and a confirmation message is displayed.

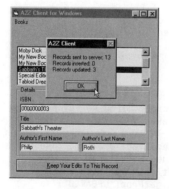

Allowing the User to Choose a Different Store Location The application could provide users with a drop-down list that allows them to choose different store locations from which to get information. It could even communicate with the ASP-based Store Robot that was created earlier in this chapter (see Listing 17.1) to obtain the latest list of store locations for the user to choose from.

Add the Store Locations drop-down list to your application by following these steps:

1. Add a ComboBox control named cboStores to your project, placing it at the top of the form.

2. Add the following line at the top of your project's code, with the other global variables. This defines a record set named StoresRS that is used to hold the list of store locations.

```
Private StoresRS As WDDXRecordset
```

3. Add the following lines of code to the end of your project's `FormLoad()` procedure, placing it immediately before the procedure's `End Sub` statement. This causes the `GetStores` procedure to be run automatically when the application is first run.

```
' Fetch current list of stores from ASP-based Store Robot
GetStores
```

4. Add the code in Listing 17.11 to your project. Place it at the end of your code. It defines two new procedures for your application. Together, they allow your users to browse through and edit the data at any store location on the Store Robot's official list.

Listing 17.11 `Listing11.txt`—**Code to Interact with the Store Robot and Allow Users to Choose Other Store Locations**

```
' This executes when the application first starts up.
' It fetches current list of stores from ASP-based Store Robot.
Private Sub GetStores()
  Dim strURL As String, Count As Integer

  ' Fetch WDDX Packet of data from Store Robot
  MyXML = Inet1.OpenURL("http://127.0.0.1/Robots/StoreRobot.asp")

  ' Deserialize the packet into a recordset
  Set StoresRS = MyDeser.deserialize(MyXML)

  ' Clear the current entries from ListBox
  cboStores.Clear

  ' Loop through the rows of the recordset
  ' For each row, add an item to the ListBox
  For Count = 1 To StoresRS.getRowCount
    cboStores.AddItem (StoresRS.getField(Count, "NAME"))
  Next Count

  ' Select the first item in the ListBox
  cboStores.ListIndex = 0

End Sub


' This executes when the user chooses a new store location.
Private Sub cboStores_Click()
  RowNum = cboStores.ListIndex + 1
  RobotServer = StoresRS.getField(RowNum, "HOST")
End Sub
```

Part

IV

Ch

17

The first procedure is called `GetStores`. Because you added a reference to `GetStores` in the project's `FormLoad()` procedure, this code executes automatically when the form starts. The actual code is just a simplified version of the Get Records From Server code provided in Listing 17.6. The list of stores is fetched from the Active Server Page with the `OpenURL` method. The packet from the Store Robot is then deserialized into the record set called `StoresRS`. The cboStores ComboBox is populated with the rows of the record set's NAME column. Finally, the first item in the ComboBox is selected, which triggers the cboStores_Click() procedure (the second procedure shown in Listing 17.11).

The cboStores_Click() procedure fires whenever the selected store location changes. It simply sets the global RobotServer to the HOST column of the corresponding row in the StoresRS record set. If the user chooses the third store in the ComboBox, RowNum is set to 3, which causes RobotServer to be set to the appropriate hostname.

Since the Get Records From Server and Save Records To Server routines both use the RobotServer variable internally, the user can choose to interact with any of the servers at the bookstore's locations worldwide (see Figure 17.9). ASP, ColdFusion, Visual Basic, HTTP, and WDDX are all working together to produce this slick result.

FIGURE 17.9
The user can select any of the store's locations worldwide.

Integrating with Office Applications

All of the major applications in Microsoft's Office 97 suite—Word 97, Excel 97, and so on—can be automated with a stripped-down version of Visual Basic called Visual Basic for Applications (VBA). Programming in VBA can be very similar to programming in normal Visual Basic or VBScript, except that you have access to various objects, properties, and methods of the actual Office applications. You can use COM objects in VBA code, which means that you can use the WDDX Serializer, WDDX Deserializer, and other WDDX-related goodies from the wddx_com.dll COM object that Allaire supplies.

N O T E The code in this section only works with the Office 97 versions of these applications. Presumably, it also works with future versions as well—such as Microsoft's upcoming Office 2000 release. Previous versions of the applications—Excel 5.0 , Word 6.0, or Word 95—were not scriptable with VBA. Instead, they each provided their own scripting language. For instance, previous versions of Word were scripted with something called WordBasic. It is possible to use the COM objects to get the same effect with these earlier versions of the applications, but the code looks significantly different. Consult each application's documentation for details. ▪

Creating the GetBookInfo Macro

As an example, imagine that you want to create a Word macro that uses the Book Robot to get a list of current books in stock. The macro should then insert all of the book titles into the current document as a nicely-formatted bulleted list. This may sound like a tall order, but it's actually quite simple. A WDDX Packet can be fetched from the Book Robot using the Internet Transfer Control from Microsoft, very similarly to how it was used in the native Visual Basic example earlier in this chapter. Then, using the WDDX COM object from Allaire, you can deserialize the WDDX packet into a record set. All that's needed then is to loop over the record set in VBA, inserting the title for each book as the loop progresses.

 TIP Remember this chapter's big picture: You can probably use WDDX with any program that supports COM objects and provides some kind of programming capability. Although this example deals specifically with Microsoft Word 97, you could do something similar with any other word-processing software—perhaps a current version of Corel's WordPerfect product or WordPro from Lotus—that allows you to script macros that use COM objects.

Part
IV
Ch
17

Listing 17.12 provides the VBA code that does the job. Of course, a complete discussion of VBA is well beyond the scope of this chapter, but the code that creates this macro is fairly simple and easy to understand. The actual code is explained in a moment. Right now, concentrate on getting the code into VBA and making it available as a menu item in Word.

Follow these steps to add the book-listing macro:

1. Open Word.
2. Close all documents. Not even a blank document should be showing.
3. From the Tools menu, choose Macro, Visual Basic Editor. After a moment, Visual Basic for Applications appears.
4. Type or paste the code from Listing 17.12 into the editor window, as shown in Figure 17.10.
5. Choose Close from the File menu and return to Microsoft Word.

Listing 17.12 GetBookInfo.vbs—Using WDDX to Fetch Book Titles from the Web and Insert Them Into Word

```
Public Sub GetBookInfo()
  Dim Count, Retries, MyPacket   ' Local variables

  ' Create instance of Microsoft's Internet Transfer Control
  Set MyInet = CreateObject("InetCtls.Inet")
  ' Create instance of Allaire's WDDXDeserializer object
  Set MyDeser = CreateObject("WDDX.Deserializer.1")

  ' We'll attempt to fetch the packet this many times
  Retries = 10
```

continues

Listing 17.12   Continued

```
' Fetch WDDX packet from webserver and place into MyPacket
' If it's blank, retry, up to our limit
While (MyPacket = "") And (Retries > 0)
  MyPacket = MyInet.OpenURL
➥("http://127.0.0.1/advbook/WDDX/Listings/BookRobot.cfm")
  Retries = Retries - 1
Wend


' Make sure that the "packet" actually has data
If MyPacket = "" Then
  MsgBox ("Couldn't get book list from server. Please try again later.")

' Assuming the WDDX packet contained actual data
Else

  ' Deserialize the packet.  An instance of
  ' Allaire's wddxRecordset object is returned.
  Set MyRS = MyDeser.deserialize(MyPacket)

  ' Insert a line of text in Bold type
  Selection.Font.Bold = True
  Selection.TypeText Text:="Books Currently In Stock"
  Selection.Font.Bold = False
  Selection.TypeParagraph

  ' Start a bulleted list
  Selection.Range.ListFormat.ApplyBulletDefault

  ' Loop through the rows of the recordset
  For Count = 1 To MyRS.getRowCount

    ' Place title of "current" book in Title variable
    ' Insert the title into the current document
    ThisTitle = MyRS.getField(Count, "TITLE")
    Selection.TypeText Text:=ThisTitle
    Selection.TypeParagraph

  Next Count  'Moves on to next book in recordset
End If

' Finished with bulleted list
Selection.Range.ListFormat.RemoveNumbers

' Release the instances of the various objects
Set MyInet = Nothing
Set MyRS = Nothing
Set MyDeser = Nothing

End Sub
```

FIGURE 17.10

Using Allaire's COM object, you can create a macro that performs WDDX actions in Word.

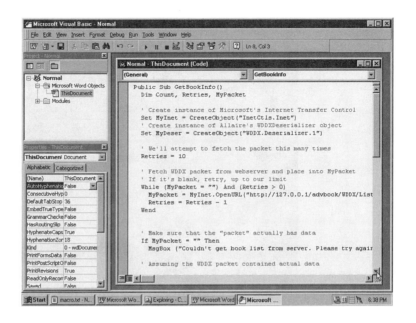

The macro code shown in Listing 17.12 is discussed in the next section.

Now that the macro has been created, add it to Word's menu bar so that the user has a convenient way to use the macro. Follow these steps to create a menu item for the macro:

1. Choose Customize from Word's Tools menu. The Customize dialog box appears.

2. Select the Commands tab at the top of the dialog box.

3. From the Categories list box on the left, click Macros.

4. From the Commands list box on the right, click the macro you just created. It should be labeled something similar to `Normal.ThisDocument.GetBooks`.

5. Drag the new macro over the word Insert on Word's menu bar. The Insert menu drops down. Drag down a bit more and then release the mouse button so that your new macro becomes the first option on the Insert menu (see Figure 17.11).

6. Right-click the menu item you just added. In the pop-up menu that appears, change the name of the menu item to `List Of Books`. Press the Enter key to make the change.

7. Click Close on the Customize dialog box.

The new menu item should be operational. To test it, start a new document by choosing File, New from the menu bar. Choose the new List Of Books item from the Insert menu. The macro should fetch the list of books from the Book Robot and insert the title of each book in the current document, as shown in Figure 17.12.

TIP

If you prefer, you can drag the macro onto a toolbar instead of the menu bar. This creates a button that runs the macro when clicked. You can even choose an icon for the button by right-clicking the button while the Customize dialog box is still open.

Part

IV

Ch

17

FIGURE 17.11

You can put your new macro directly on Word's menu bar.

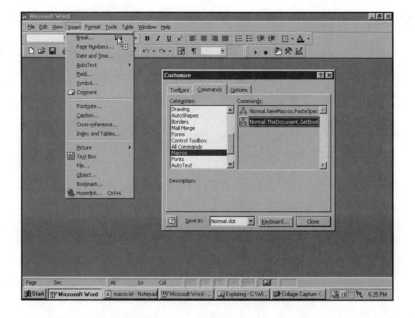

 TIP You can also run the macro by pressing Alt+F8 and then double-clicking the name of the macro (GetBookInfo). Alternatively, you can choose Macro, Macros from Word's Tools menu.

FIGURE 17.12

The macro fetches the current book titles and inserts them into the current document.

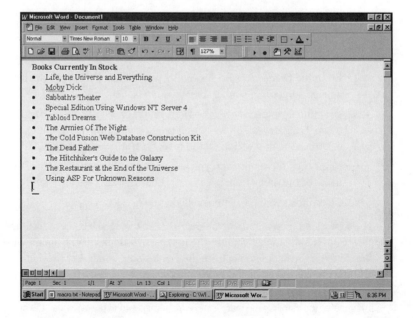

The Macro Code Explained

Now that you've seen the macro in action, you can study the code itself to learn how it works. It's actually quite simple, and looks a lot like the other examples you've seen in this section. The key, of course, is the use of the serialization and record set objects that Allaire provides through COM.

The first line of the macro uses the Dim statement to define four variables—Count, Retries, MyPacket, and ThisTitle—which get used later in the script. This line is actually optional as far as VBA is concerned, but it's conventional to define variable names at the top of a script. It makes the script somewhat easier to read if you know the various variable names right away.

The next line uses the Set and CreateObject keywords to create an instance of Allaire's Deserializer class, which can then be used to deserialize a WDDX Packet. Basically, CreateObject is in charge of talking to Windows and getting an instance of the object for your script. The new object reference is returned to the Set keyword, which creates a local VBA variable called MyDeser, which in turn can be used elsewhere in the script to communicate with the COM object.

Part

IV

Ch

17

 TIP You can use choose Tools, References from the Visual Basic menu bar to add wddx_com 1.0 Type Library to your script's references list. You can then use VBA's New keyword instead of CreateObject to create the instance of the Deserializer object, more like the native Visual Basic code that was shown in Listing 17.5. This also allows the Visual Basic interface to auto-complete your VBA code as you type it. See your VBA or Visual Basic documentation for details.

A similar Set line creates an instance of Microsoft's Internet Transfer Control object called MyInet. The OpenURL method of the MyInet control is then used to fetch a Web page from the Internet. Of course, you know from the URL used that the Web page is going to be a WDDX Packet served up by the Book Robot created in Chapter 16's Listing 16.8. The OpenURL line is placed inside a While loop, which executes the method up to 10 times, in case it fails at first. Basically, the fetched document is returned to the MyPacket variable every time the OpenURL method is executed. If the MyPacket variable actually contains data, the While loop has done its job and code execution proceeds after the Wend keyword. On the other hand, if the MyPacket variable is empty, the Web page was not fetched successfully; the number of available retries is decreased by 1. If the Retries variable reaches 0, the loop stops and the MyPacket variable is still empty, indicating total failure to fetch the page successfully.

A simple If statement is used to make sure that the MyPacket variable has been successfully populated with data. If it is still blank, the page-fetching has failed completely and the script displays an error message to the user with VBA's MsgBox function. As long as the packet is not empty, though, script execution continues into the longer Else block, which does the rest of the actual work.

The first line inside the Else block uses the MyDeser object's deserialize function to take the WDDX Packet stored in the MyPacket variable and deserialize it into an actual record set. Since the `deserialize` function is returning another object (an instance of Allaire's `WDDX.Recordset` class), the `Set` statement is needed to accept the object and give it a name, just as it was needed earlier with the `CreateObject` function. Basically, any function that returns an object needs to return its value to the `Set` statement. The script code can now refer to the record set by the name `MyRS`.

The script now uses the VBA `Selection` object to insert a short heading into the current document. You can read more about the `Selection` object in your Word documentation, but basically it represents the selected spot in the current document (wherever the user placed the cursor before running the macro). The `Bold` subproperty of the selection's `Font` property is set to `True`, which just tells Word to switch to bold type. The `TypeText` method inserts the actual heading into the current document; the `Bold` property is set to `false` to turn off the bold type. Finally, the `TypeParagraph` method starts a new paragraph, and the `ApplyBulletDefault` method turns on Word's bulleting feature.

 TIP   Complete documentation for the Word-specific objects and methods used in Listing 17.12—`Selec-tion`, `TypeText`, and `ApplyBulletDefault`, for example—is available in Word 97's Help files. Select Contents and Index from the Help menu in Word; expand the icon marked Microsoft Word Visual Basic Reference. (If this section is unavailable, you may not have chosen to install the Help files when you installed Word. Try running the Word installation program again.)

Now that all the formatting has been applied, the script is ready to insert the actual book titles. A simple `for` loop gets the job done. You can read more about Visual Basic–style `for` loops in your VBA documentation, but for here knowing that the loop executes once for each row in the record set is sufficient; the `Count` variable always represents the row number of the current row. Note that Allaire's `getRowCount` function is used to obtain the total number of rows in the record set object.

Inside the loop, Allaire's `getField` function is used to retrieve the actual data in the current row of the record set's TITLE column and assign it to the `ThisTitle` variable. The `TypeText` method is used again to insert the title into the current Word document, and `TypeParagraph` is called to start a new line after each title is inserted. Since Word's bulleting feature was turned on before the loop started, a bullet will appear before each title.

After the loop, the `RemoveNumbers` function is used to turn off Word's bulleting feature, and each of the objects used in the script is destroyed one by one. This is done by setting the object variables to the reserved word `Nothing` which Visual Basic defines for releasing object references. See your VBA documentation for details about the `Nothing` keyword.

Fetching WDDX Packets Directly with JavaScript

In Chapter 16 you saw how a JavaScript–based Book Browser could be created and allow the user to browse through and edit records in a WDDX-style record set. The user could even save her changes to her local hard drive; see the `JSBrowser4.cfm` template, which is Listing 16.23 in Chapter 16.

In those examples, the WddxRecordset object referred to in the client-side scripts was generated by querying the database on the server with the CFQUERY tag and then sending the query's results to JavaScript with the help of the CFWDDX tag.

Listing 17.13 shows that it's possible to create a JavaScript–based client that communicates directly with the Book Robot (see Listing 16.8) and Store Robot (see Listing 17.4) that have already been created. The key to making this possible is to figure out a way for the browser to reach out over the Internet to fetch the various WDDX Packets from the robot pages.

One way to do this is to use the AspHTTP COM object (see Listing 17.4 earlier in this chapter) within custom functions that sit on the Book Browser page itself. That's what Listing 17.13 does. It creates two new custom functions, GetURL() and PostURL(), which are in charge of fetching from and posting to remote Web servers, respectively. These functions are created using VBScript syntax rather than JavaScript/JScript syntax, since the COM object was designed to be used with VBScript.

N O T E It's worth noting that Listing 17.13 is a plain HTML page (notice the .htm extension), not a ColdFusion template. This template does not require that ColdFusion be present on the machine that visits it. The file could even be saved on a CD-ROM or floppy disk, although it would still need an Internet connection to retrieve data about stores and books. ▓

Part

IV

Ch

17

Listing 17.13 JSBrowser5.htm—A Version of the Book Browser That Interacts with the Robots Directly

```
<HTML><HEAD>
<TITLE>Book Browser</TITLE>

<!--- Include Microsoft's "Scripting Run-time Library" --->
<!--- Creates FileSystemObject object called MyLocalFS --->
<OBJECT ID="MyLocalFS" WIDTH=0 HEIGHT=0
    CLASSID="CLSID:0D43FE01-F093-11CF-8940-00A0C9054228"
    CODEBASE="http://msdn.microsoft.com/scripting/scrrun/x86/
➥srt31en.cab#version=3,1,0,2230">
</OBJECT>

<!--- Include Allaire's WDDX / JavaScript support --->
<SCRIPT SRC="/cfide/scripts/wddx.js" LANGUAGE="JavaScript"></SCRIPT>
<!--- Include Nate Weiss's wddxDeserializer function --->
<SCRIPT SRC="wddxDes.js" LANGUAGE="JavaScript"></SCRIPT>
<!--- Include the Xparse XML Parser, required by wddxDes.js --->
<SCRIPT SRC="XParse.js" LANGUAGE="JavaScript"></SCRIPT>


<SCRIPT LANGUAGE="JavaScript">

  RobotServer = 'http://127.0.0.1';
```

continues

Listing 17.13   Continued

```
/////////////////////////////////////////////////////
// This function fills the SELECT list with books
function InitControls() {
  with (document.DataForm) {

    // Clear any current OPTIONS from the SELECT
    BookID.options.length = 0;

    // For each book record...
    for (var i = 1; i < Books.getRowCount(); i++) {

      // Create a new OPTION object
      NewOpt = new Option;
      NewOpt.value = Books.bookid[i];
      NewOpt.text = Books.title[i];

      // Add the new object to the SELECT list
      BookID.options[BookID.options.length] = NewOpt;

    }
  }
}


/////////////////////////////////////////////////////
// This function populates other INPUT elements
// when an option in the SELECT box is clicked
function FillControls() {
  with (document.DataForm) {
    // Add one to the OPTION number to get the data row number
    var RowNum = BookID.selectedIndex+1;

    // Populate textboxes with data in that row
    ISBN.value = Books.isbn[RowNum];
    Title.value = Books.title[RowNum];
    AuthorF.value = Books.authorfirstname[RowNum];
    AuthorL.value = Books.authorlastname[RowNum];
  }
}


/////////////////////////////////////////////////////
// This function "saves" data from the various
// text boxes into the wddxRecordset object
function KeepChanges() {
  with (document.DataForm) {
    // Add one to the OPTION number to get the data row number
    var SelectedBook = BookID.selectedIndex;
    var RowNum = SelectedBook + 1;

    // Populate javascript data array with info from textboxes
    Books.isbn[RowNum] = ISBN.value;
    Books.title[RowNum] = Title.value;
    Books.authorfirstname[RowNum] = AuthorF.value;
    Books.authorlastname[RowNum] = AuthorL.value;
```

```
      Books.wasedited[RowNum] = 'Yes';

      // Re-initialize the SELECT list
      InitControls();

      // Re-select the book that was selected before
      BookID.selectedIndex = -1;
      BookID.selectedIndex = SelectedBook;
    }
  }


  ///////////////////////////////////////////////////
  // This function inserts a new row in the
  // wddxRecordset object, ready for editing
  function NewRecord() {
    with (document.DataForm) {
      // Add a new row to the recordset
      Books.addRows(1);
      NewRow = Books.getRowCount()-1;

      Books.setField(NewRow, "bookid", "new");
      Books.setField(NewRow, "title", "(new)");
      Books.setField(NewRow, "isbn", "");
      Books.setField(NewRow, "authorfirstname", "");
      Books.setField(NewRow, "authorlastname", "");

      // Re-initialize the SELECT list
      InitControls();

      // Re-select the book that was selected before
      BookID.selectedIndex = NewRow-1;
      FillControls();
    }
  }


  ///////////////////////////////////////////////////
  // This function inserts a new row in the    // wddxRecordset object, ready for
editing
  function CommitToServer() {
    with (document.DataForm) {
      // Create new WDDX Serializer object (supplied by Allaire)
      MySerializer = new WddxSerializer();

      // Serialize the "Books" recordset into a WDDX packet
      BooksAsWDDX = MySerializer.serialize(Books);

      // Place the packet into the "WDDXContent" hidden field
      WDDXContent.value = BooksAsWDDX;

      // Submit the form
      submit();
    }
  }
```

continues

Part

IV

Ch

17

Listing 17.13 Continued

```
/////////////////////////////////////////////////
// This function saves the Books recordset to
// disk as a WDDX Packet
function LocalFileSave(){
  // Serialize the Books recordset into WDDX Packet
  wddxSerializer = new WddxSerializer();
  BooksAsWDDX = wddxSerializer.serialize(Books);

  // Save the WDDX Packet to disk as c:\BooksAsWDDX.txt
  textstream = MyLocalFS.CreateTextFile("c:\\BooksAsWDDX.txt", true);
  textstream.Write(BooksAsWDDX);
  textstream.Close();

  // Show a message to the user
  window.defaultStatus = Books.getRowCount() + ' Records Saved';
}

/////////////////////////////////////////////////
// This function loads the Books recordset from
// disk (as a WDDX Packet) and deserializes it
function LocalFileOpen(){
  // Load the WDDX Packet from BooksAsWDDX.txt file
  textstream = MyLocalFS.OpenTextFile("c:\\BooksAsWDDX.txt");
  BooksAsWDDX = textstream.ReadAll();
  textstream.Close()

  // Deserialize the packet into the Books recordset
  Books = wddxDeserialize(BooksAsWDDX);
  InitControls();

  // Show a message to the user
  window.defaultStatus = Books.getRowCount() + ' Records Loaded';
}


/////////////////////////////////////////////////////////
// This function fetches the Stores recordset from the
// Store Robot (as a WDDX Packet) and deserializes it
function GetStores() {
  StoreServerURL = 'http://127.0.0.1/Robots/StoreRobot.asp';
  StoresAsWDDX = GetURL(StoreServerURL);

  Stores = wddxDeserialize(StoresAsWDDX);
  InitStores(Stores);
}


/////////////////////////////////////////////////////////
// This function fetches the Stores recordset from the
// Store Robot (as a WDDX Packet) and deserializes it
function InitStores(Stores) {
  with (document.DataForm.StoreDropDown) {
```

```
    // Clear any current OPTIONS from the SELECT
    options.length = 0;

    // Add an option for the local server
    NewOpt = new Option;
    NewOpt.value = 'http://127.0.0.1';
    NewOpt.text = '(local server)';
    options[0] = NewOpt;

    // For each book record, create a new OPTION
    // object and add it to the SELECT list
    for (var i = 1; i < Stores.getRowCount(); i++) {
      NewOpt = new Option;
      NewOpt.value = Stores.host[i];
      NewOpt.text = Stores.name[i];
      options[options.length] = NewOpt;
    }

    // Make the first item in the SELECT be selected
    selectedIndex = 0;
  }
}


//////////////////////////////////////////////////////////
// This function fetches the Stores recordset from the
// Store Robot (as a WDDX Packet) and deserializes it
function GetRecords() {

  // Create a request structure called RequestStructure
  RequestStructure = new Object;
  RequestStructure.Columns =
➥'BookID,ISBN,Title,AuthorFirstName,AuthorLastName';

  // Serialize the structure into the RequestAsWDDX packet
  wddxSerializer = new WddxSerializer();
  RequestAsWDDX = wddxSerializer.serialize(RequestStructure);

  // Post the packet to the BookRobot, using our PostURL function
  RobotServerURL = RobotServer + "/Robots/BookRobot.cfm";
  PostData = "WDDXContent=" + RequestAsWDDX;
  BooksAsWDDX = PostURL(RobotServerURL, PostData);

  // Deserialize the Book Robot's response into Books recordset
  // Add a column called "wasedited" to the recordset
  Books = wddxDeserialize(BooksAsWDDX);
  Books.addColumn("wasedited");

  // When the form is submitted, it should submit to
  // the same server that it got the recordset from
  document.DataForm.action = RobotServer = '/Robots/JSBrowserCommit.cfm';

  // Re-initialize the various form controls with new data
  InitControls();
}
```

Part

IV

Ch

17

continues

Listing 17.13   Continued

```
  </SCRIPT>


  <SCRIPT LANGUAGE="VBScript">
    ' Create an instance of the AspHTTP COM Object
    Dim HttpObj
    Set HttpObj = CreateObject("AspHTTP.Conn")

    ' This function fetches a page from a remote webserver,
    ' Just like a normal web browser "visit"
    Function GetURL(URLToGetFrom)
      HttpObj.Url = URLToGetFrom
      GetURL = HttpObj.GetURL()
    End Function

    ' This function posts data to a page on any webserver,
    ' like a normal web browser form submission
    Function PostURL(URLToPostTo, DataToPost)
      HttpObj.Url = URLToPostTo
      HttpObj.PostData = DataToPost
      HttpObj.RequestMethod = "Post"
      PostURL = HttpObj.GetURL()
    End Function
  </SCRIPT>


  </HEAD>


  <!--- After document loads, run InitControls() function --->
  <BODY onLoad="GetStores();">
  <H2>Offline Book Browser</H2>


  <FORM ACTION="JSBrowserCommit.cfm" METHOD="POST" NAME="DataForm">
    <!--- CommitToServer() function gives this a value --->
    <INPUT TYPE="HIDDEN" NAME="WDDXContent">

  <TABLE BORDER CELLPADDING="10">
  <TR VALIGN="TOP">
  <TD>
    <!--- Allow user to choose store location --->
    <B>Location:</B>
    <SELECT NAME="StoreDropDown" onChange="RobotServer = this.options
  ➥[this.selectedIndex].value"><OPTION>Getting store list...</SELECT>
    <INPUT TYPE="BUTTON" VALUE="Get Books" onClick="GetRecords()"
  ➥ STYLE="width:75px"><BR>

    <!--- SELECT populated by InitControls() function --->
    <!--- When clicked, calls FillControls() function --->
```

```
    <SELECT NAME="BookID" SIZE="10" onChange="FillControls()">
      <OPTION>=======================================
    </SELECT>
  </TD>


  <TD>
    <!--- These controls get populated by FillControls() --->
    <B>ISBN:</B><BR>
    <INPUT NAME="ISBN" SIZE="20" MAXLENGTH="13"><BR>

    <B>Author (first, last):</B><BR>
    <INPUT NAME="AuthorF" SIZE="18" MAXLENGTH="13">
    <INPUT NAME="AuthorL" SIZE="20" MAXLENGTH="13"><BR>

    <B>Title:</B><BR>
    <INPUT NAME="Title" SIZE="40" MAXLENGTH="50"><BR>

    <P>
    <!--- Button to "keep" edits with KeepChanges() function --->
    <INPUT TYPE="BUTTON" VALUE="Keep These Edits" onClick="KeepChanges()">
    <!--- Button to cancel edits with FillChanges() function --->
    <INPUT TYPE="BUTTON" VALUE="Cancel" onClick="FillControls()">
    <!--- Button to insert new book with NewRecord() function --->
    <INPUT TYPE="BUTTON" VALUE="New Record" onClick="NewRecord()"><BR>
  </TD>

  </TR>
  </TABLE>

  <!--- Button to save to server w/ CommitChanges() function --->
  <P><CENTER>
   <INPUT TYPE="BUTTON" VALUE="Commit Changes To Server"
➡ onClick="CommitToServer()"><BR>
   <INPUT TYPE="BUTTON" VALUE="Save To File" onClick="LocalFileSave()">
   <INPUT TYPE="BUTTON" VALUE="Load from File" onClick="LocalFileOpen()"><BR>


  </CENTER>

  </FORM>


  </BODY>
  </HTML>
```

Part

IV

Ch

17

N O T E   This listing is fairly long and contains a number of custom JavaScript functions, but it is really quite simple when you look at each part individually. Most of the functions shown here are unchanged from the previous versions of the Book Browser discussed in Chapter 16. ∎

The first new function introduced in Listing 17.13 is `GetStores()`, which is run automatically when the page loads (because it's in the `BODY` tag's `onLoad` handler). Conceptually, it does about the same thing the `LocalFileOpen()` function that precedes it. Instead of deserializing a WDDX packet from disk, it deserializes a WDDX packet fetched from the ASP-based Store Robot that was created earlier in this chapter. The resulting record set (the list of store locations) ends up in the `Stores` variable, which is passed to the next new function, `InitStores()`.

`InitStores()` is similar conceptually to the `InitControls()` function, which was introduced in Chapter 16 (see Listing 16.19). It simply iterates over the rows in the `Stores` record set and fills the `StoreDropDown` drop-down list with the information about each store location. The user can use this drop-down to choose from which store to grab the current list of books. It also adds an option at the top of the list for the local server (`http://127.0.0.1`); that way you can test the page if the `BookRobot.cfm` page is available locally. Figure 17.13 shows what the drop-down list looks like.

FIGURE 17.13

The user can choose from any of the bookstore's locations around the world.

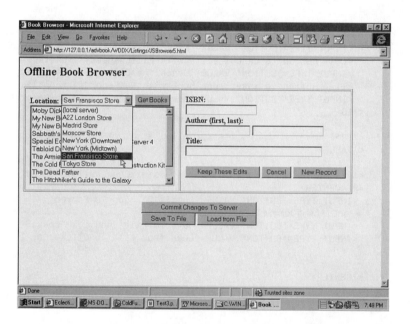

The `GetRecords()` function is what executes when the user clicks the Get Books button shown in Figure 17.13. First, it creates a new object called `RequestStructure`, which becomes the request structure the Book Robot looks for with each request that it receives. A `Columns` property is added to indicate which columns the Book Robot should retrieve from the database. The object is then serialized into a WDDX Packet called `RequestAsWDDX`.

Now the function needs to post the packet to the Book Robot and collect its response. A string variable named `RobotServerURL` is created, which adds the appropriate filename to the currently selected store in the global `RobotServer` variable. A string variable named `PostData` is assembled, consisting of a name/value pair to send as the request's form data (see Listing 17.4 for details).

The request is posted with the custom PostURL() function, and the Book Robot's response is placed into the BooksAsWDDX variable. The packet can then be deserialized into the record set named Books, and the form's controls initialized with the InitControls() function. In addition, the form's action (the location that it submits to) is adjusted to match the server that the books were just fetched from.

> **N O T E** Because Listing 17.13 relies on a COM/ActiveX object to interact with the book and store
> robots, it only works with Microsoft Internet Explorer browsers. If cross-browser compatibility
> is a must, you might consider figuring out a way to get the HTTP functionality that AspHTTP provides by
> using some kind of Java applet. ▪

The big picture here is that the Book Robot and Store Robot have become independent, remote data providers. JavaScript pages and other types of applications can interact directly with them using simple, open standards.

Part
IV

Ch
17

Integrating with Perl

Work is under way to create a Perl module that allows you to use WDDX in Perl scripts. Perl developers will be able to do the same kinds of things that are possible with the ColdFusion, COM, and JavaScript implementations of WDDX. That is, it will be possible to take native Perl variables—such as scalars and arrays—and serialize them into WDDX Packets. Similarly, you'll be able to grab a WDDX Packet from anywhere on the Internet (using HTTP::Request from the libwww-perl package) and deserialize it into the equivalent Perl variables or data structures. You'll also be able to "spit out" JavaScript code dynamically, such as the CFWDDX tag's CFML2JS and WDDX2JS actions.

> **N O T E** When this book went to press, the module had not been fully completed yet. Basically, the
> capability to serialize data was available, but the capability to deserialize it was not. The
> work is being done by David Medinets, president of Eclectic Consulting, Inc. Check http://
> www.codebits.com/wddx/ and http://www.allaire.com/developer/wddx for the latest
> news about the WDDX module for Perl. By the time you read this, it's likely that the fully functional
> version of the module has been completed and is ready for your use. ▪

Getting Started

To get ready to work with WDDX, you need to install two items: the WDDX module for Perl and the XML-Parser for Perl. If these items are not present on your system, the examples in this chapter will not run.

On the CD

To install the WDDX module, simply copy the wddx.pm file from this book's CD-ROM, placing it in a folder in your @INC search path. If you're using ActivePerl, you place the file in the c:\Perl\5.00502\Lib folder. (The 5.00502 part of the folder name will be different if you are using a build of ActivePerl other than Build 502.)

If you're using ActivePerl, the easiest way to install the XML-Parser module is to use the auto-mated package installer provided by the `ppm.pl` script. Go to an MS-DOS prompt and use the CD command to move to your `c:\Perl\5.00502\Bin` folder (or whatever folder name is appro-priate). Type **perl ppm.pl** and press Enter. A special PPM> prompt should appear. Now type **install xml-parser** and press Enter. The package is automatically downloaded from the Internet and installed for you. If the `ppm.pl` utility is not available with your distribution of Perl, the XML-Parser package is freely available at various Perl-resource sites on the Web.

N O T E While it is not required in order to use WDDX with Perl, the examples in this chapter also make use of the `Win32::OBDC` extension for Perl to connect to the A2Z Access database (the `A2z.mdb` file included on this book's CD-ROM). Instructions for downloading, installing, and using `Win32::ODBC` are available from `http://www.roth.net/odbc/`. ■

Serializing Data

Serializing data with the WDDX module is pretty simple. The first thing you need to do is place the following line at the top of your script, which includes the `wddx.pm` file and makes the func-tions that it provides available to you:

```
use wddx;
```

N O T E It's impossible to explain the basics of Perl programming in these pages, so at this point it's assumed that you have at least some familiarity with Perl. Even if you're new to Perl, you'll probably be able to understand most of what you see here. A few hints: Comments are included with the # character, most variables (*scalars*) begin with the $ character, and arrays begin with the @ character. The `->` symbol is used to refer to functions provided by a scalar. ■

Now, serializing data is a simple three-step process. The first step creates a `wddx` object called `$parser`, which provides the actual serialization services needed. Conceptually, this line is similar to the new `WddxSerializer` code that you've seen used in the JavaScript implementa-tion of WDDX (see Listing 17.13):

```
$parser = new wddx();
```

The second step is what actually serializes the packet. Call the `cfwddx` function of the `wddx` object you created in the first step. Specify `perl2wddx` as the function's action and provide the actual data to serialize as the function's input. Note that this is similar to the use of the CFWDDX tag in a ColdFusion template. For instance, the following serializes the string value in `$string`, placing the resulting WDDX Packet into the scalar called `$MyPacket`:

```
$MyPacket = $parser->cfwddx(
  "action" => 'perl2wddx',
  "input" => { "string" => \$string, }
);
```

Finally, call your `wddx` object's `parsestring` function to finish the process:

```
$parser->parsestring($MyPacket);
```

NOTE   Keep in mind that this chapter was written using a pre-release version of the WDDX module. We worked closely with the module's author while preparing this chapter, but some elements of the syntax might have changed since this book went to press. Check `http://www.codebits.com/wddx/` and `http://www.allaire.com/developer/wddx` for the latest news about the WDDX module for Perl.

Re-creating the Store Robot Using Perl

Earlier in this chapter you saw that it is possible to use WDDX to create a Store Robot that serves up the authoritative list of A2Z bookstore locations worldwide. Listing 17.1 created the Store Robot using ASP with the help of Allaire's COM object for WDDX.

The script in Listing 17.14 re-creates the Store Robot in Perl. It does the same thing as the ASP version of the Store Robot; it responds to requests in exactly the same way. The various applications that access the ASP version of the Store Robot could use this version instead (see Listings 17.2, 17.11, and 17.13). The only difference they see is the .pl in the URL.

Part
IV

Ch

17

Listing 17.14   `StoreRobot.pl`—The Store Robot from Listing 17.1, Rewritten in Perl

```
# Include David Medinets' WDDX functionality
# Look for updates at http://www.codebits.com/wddx/
# Or at http://www.allaire.com/developer/wddx/
use wddx;

# Include Dave Roth's ODBC functionality
# ...available at http://www.roth.net/odbc/
use Win32::ODBC;


# Open our connection to the A2Z.mdb database
$db = new Win32::ODBC("A2Z");
die qq(ERROR: Could not open database connection\n) if ! $db;

# Issue SQL Statement to retrieve store info from db
$rc = $db->Sql("SELECT StoreID, Name, Host FROM Stores ORDER BY Name");
die qq(ERROR: SQL statement failed), $db->Error(), qq(\n) if $rc;


# The $RowNum scalar will hold current data row number
$RowNum = 0;

# While there are still rows left to fetch,
# Fetch the next row from ODBC
while ( $db->FetchRow() ) {

  # Place the value from row 1 of StoreID column
  # into @StoreID[1], row 2 into @StoreID[2], etc,
  # and do the same for the Name and Host columns
```

continues

Listing 17.14 Continued

```perl
@StoreID[$RowNum] = $db->Data("StoreID");
@Name[$RowNum]    = $db->Data("Name");
@Host[$RowNum]    = $db->Data("Host");

# Increment the $RowNum variable by one
++$RowNum;
}

# We're done with database connection, so close it
$db->Close();


# Prepare the parser module to deal with WDDX data;
$parser = new wddx();

# Tell parser to generate a WDDX packet, specifically
# a recordset packet with a StoreID column that holds
# the data from the @StoreID array, etc.
$StoresAsWDDX = $parser->cfwddx(
  "action" => 'perl2wddx',
  "goal"   => 'recordset',
  "input" => {
    "StoreID" => \@StoreID,
    "Name"    => \@Name,
    "Host"    => \@Host
  }
);

# Have the parser clean up the packet
$parser->parsestring($StoresAsWDDX);


# Send content-type header to begin HTTP response
print "content-type: text/html\n";
print "\n";

# Output the contents of the packet itself
print $StoresAsWDDX;


# All done!
exit;
```

TIP

If you use ColdFusion Studio 4 to code your Perl scripts, they will be nicely color-coded for you while you type (see Figure 17.14). It's nice that you can do all of your WDDX-related development with one editor. To customize the color-coding, choose Options, Settings, and then click the Color Coding tab.

FIGURE 17.14

ColdFusion Studio 4 provides color-coding for Perl scripts.

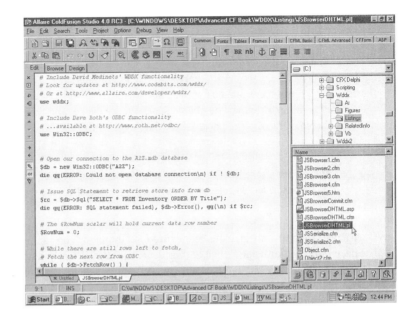

The first thing Listing 17.14 does is include the functionality in the wddx.pm file with the use keyword (see preceding section). The Win32::ODBC extensions are included in the same way.

Next, the new keyword is used to create a new database connection object called $db. Because A2Z is supplied as the ODBC data source name, the script interacts with the same a2z.mdb database file used by various ColdFusion templates throughout this book. A simple SELECT statement is then issued to retrieve all the rows in the Stores table.

 TIP See the Win32::ODBC documentation for more information about the Sql, FetchRow, and Data functions used in Listing 17.14.

Now a simple While loop iterates through all the rows fetched by the SELECT statement. The $db->FetchRow function moves to the next row in the database. The loop continues executing until FetchRow fails, indicating that there are no more rows to fetch. Inside the loop, the $db->Data function is used to get the data in the current row of the StoreID column. The data is placed into the corresponding element of the @StoreID array. For instance, @StoreID[1] has the store ID number from the first data row, and so on. The same thing is done for the @Name and @Host arrays. When the loop is finished, the three arrays have been loaded with all the data fetched from the table. Note that nothing in the loop has anything to do with the WDDX module directly.

Now a new wddx object named $parser is created, and the three arrays are serialized into a WDDX record set packet called $StoresAsWDDX. The parser knows that a record set-style packet is needed because the "goal"=>"recordset" has been specified. You could change the goal to get an array-style packet, for instance.

Notice the way the three arrays are supplied to the input part of the code. The column names for the new record set are provided on the left side of the => symbols. The columns are to be filled with the data in the corresponding arrays to the right of the => symbols.

Once the data has been serialized, there's little left to do but use the print keyword to output the contents of the $StoresAsWDDX packet onto the current Web page. Whatever application is requesting the information will be able to scoop up the packet and deserialize it locally, just as it was able to work with the packet served up by the ASP version of the Store Robot (see Listing 17.1).

N O T E Multiple arrays (one for each column of a record set-to-be) are used here because the WDDX module for Perl does not currently have the notion of a native record set object, per se.

Once again, pause to consider the big picture for a moment. The same remote data server page has been put together using Active Server Pages and Perl. Clearly, it could have been put together with other development packages as well, such as Delphi or ColdFusion itself. The various clients you've seen built in this chapter that interact with the Store Robot don't care what the underlying development environment is—all they care about is getting a WDDX Packet in exchange for their requests. WDDX and HTTP make those kinds of implementation details close to irrelevant. More than ever, you and your company are free to pick the right tool for a particular job, mixing and matching tools from different vendors as your whims—and skill sets—wax and wane.

Using Perl to Output JavaScript On-the-Fly

The various versions of the Book Browser discussed in Chapter 16 all use the CFWDDX tag with ACTION="CFML2JS" to output the contents of a query result set as dynamically produced JavaScript code. The JavaScript code, when interpreted by the browser, created a native WddxRecordset object called Books, which was used by the page to show related information about books in stock (see Listing 16.21).

In addition, a DHTML-enabled version of the Book Browser was created in Listing 16.24 via ColdFusion. It was re-created using ASP earlier in this chapter (see Listing 17.4). Now it will be re-created one last time as a Perl script.

Listing 17.15 shows how to get the job done using the WDDX module for Perl. It's a very simple port to Perl-style syntax; the way the page looks and reacts to the user's actions has not changed (see Figure 17.3).

Listing 17.15 JSBookBrowserDHTML.pl—Re-creating the DHTML Version of the Book Browser Using Perl

```
# Include David Medinets' WDDX functionality
# Look for updates at http://www.codebits.com/wddx/
# Or at http://www.allaire.com/developer/wddx/
use wddx;
```

```perl
# Include Dave Roth's ODBC functionality
# ...available at http://www.roth.net/odbc/
use Win32::ODBC;


# Open our connection to the A2Z.mdb database
$db = new Win32::ODBC("A2Z");
die qq(ERROR: Could not open database connection\n) if ! $db;

# Issue SQL Statement to retrieve store info from db
$rc = $db->Sql("SELECT * FROM Inventory ORDER BY Title");
die qq(ERROR: SQL statement failed), $db->Error(), qq(\n) if $rc;

# The $RowNum scalar will hold current data row number
$RowNum = 0;

# While there are still rows left to fetch,
# Fetch the next row from ODBC
while ( $db->FetchRow() ) {

  # Place the value from row 1 of StoreID column
  # into @S<A HREF="d:\Temp \wddx.pm"></A>toreID[1], row 2 into @StoreID[2],
  ➥etc,
  # and do the same for the Name and Host columns
  @ISBN[$RowNum] = $db->Data("ISBN");
  @Title[$RowNum] = $db->Data("Title");
  @AuthorFirstName[$RowNum] = $db->Data("AuthorFirstName");
  @AuthorLastName[$RowNum] = $db->Data("AuthorLastName");
  @Pages[$RowNum] = $db->Data("Pages");
  @Description[$RowNum] = $db->Data("Description");

  # Increment the $RowNum variable by one
  ++$RowNum;

  # While we're looping through the data rows, concatenate all
  # the DIV elements we'll need later into long $DivsHTML string
  $ThisTitle = $db->Data("Title");
  $DivsHTML = $DivsHTML
  . "    <DIV CLASS=choice "
  . "    onClick=\"this.className = 'choiceSel'; FillControls($RowNum)\"   "
  . "    onMouseOver=\"this.className = 'choiceOver'\"   "
  . "    onMouseOut=\"this.className = 'choice'\">$ThisTitle</DIV>";

}

# We're done with database connection, so close it
$db->Close();


# Prepare the parser module to deal with WDDX data;
$parser = new wddx();

# Tell parser to generate a WDDX packet, specifically
# a recordset packet with a StoreID column that holds
# the data from the @ISBN array, etc.
```

continues

Listing 17.15 Continued

```perl
$BooksAsWDDX = $parser->cfwddx(
  "action" => 'perl2wddx',
  "goal"   => 'recordset',
  "input" => {
    "ISBN"            => \@ISBN,
    "Title"           => \@Title,
    "AuthorFirstName" => \@AuthorFirstName,
    "AuthorLastName"  => \@AuthorLastName,
    "Pages"           => \@Pages,
    "Description"     => \@Description
  }
);

# Have the parser clean up the packet
$parser->parsestring($BooksAsWDDX);

# Send content-type header to begin HTTP response
print "content-type: text/html\n";
print "\n";
print "<HTML><HEAD>";
print "<TITLE>Book Browser</TITLE>";

# Include Allaire's WDDX / Javascript support
print "<SCRIPT SRC=/cfide/scripts/wddx.js LANGUAGE=JavaScript></SCRIPT>";

# Have WDDX module output dynamically produced JavaScript.
# The equivalent of the CFWDDX tag in JSBrowserDHTML.cfm
# This will create the Javascript object named Books,
# which will be a WddxRecordset object full of data
$parser->cfwddx(
  "action" => 'wddx2js',
  "topLevelVariable" => 'Books'
);

# Continue outputting other JavaScript functions...
# This function populates other INPUT elements
# when an option in the SELECT box is clicked
print "<SCRIPT LANGUAGE=JavaScript>";
print "  function FillControls(RowNum) {";
print "    with (document.DataForm) {";
print "      RowNum = RowNum - 1;        ";
print "      ISBN.innerText = Books.isbn[RowNum];";
print "      Title.innerText = Books.title[RowNum];";
print "      Pages.innerText = Books.pages[RowNum];";
print "      Description.innerText = Books.description[RowNum];";
print "      Author.innerText = Books.authorlastname[RowNum] ";
print "                      + ', ' + Books.authorfirstname[RowNum];";
print "    }";
print "  }";
print "</SCRIPT>";
print "</HEAD>";

# Continue outputting the rest of the HTML page
# Define CSS styles to control the "look" of the DIV tags
```

```
print "<BODY>";
print "<STYLE TYPE=text/css>";
print "  Div             {width:350px; padding-left:3px; font:smaller Arial}";
print "  Div.choice      {background:wheat};";
print "  Div.choiceSel   {background:black; color:white; font-weight:bold};";
print "  Div.choiceOver  {background:beige; color:brown};";
print "  Div.bar         {background:brown; color:white; font:bold small
➥Arial};";
print "  H2              {background:black; color:white}";
print "</STYLE>";
print "<H2>Offline Book Browser</H2>";
print "<FORM NAME=DataForm>";
print "<TABLE CELLPADDING=10>";
print "<TR VALIGN=TOP>";

# Books to choose from.  User can click on each Title
# The $DivsHTML scalar holds the HTML for each Div
print "<TD>";
print "  <DIV CLASS=bar>Books</DIV>";
print $DivsHTML;
print "</TD>";

# This info gets updated when user clicks on a Title
# So does the description, underneath
print "<TD>";
print "  <DIV CLASS=bar>ISBN</DIV>";
print "  <DIV CLASS=choice ID=ISBN></DIV><BR>";
print "  <DIV CLASS=bar>Author</DIV>";
print "  <DIV CLASS=choice ID=Author></DIV><BR>";
print "  <DIV CLASS=bar>Title</DIV>";
print "  <DIV CLASS=choice ID=Title></DIV><BR>";
print "  <DIV CLASS=bar>Pages</DIV>";
print "  <DIV CLASS=choice ID=Pages></DIV><BR>";
print "</TD>  ";
print "</TR>  ";
print "<TR><TD COLSPAN=2>";
print "  <DIV CLASS=bar>Description</DIV>";
print "  <DIV CLASS=choice
➥ ID=Description STYLE=height:100px;width=auto> </DIV><BR>";
print "</TD></TR>";
print "</TABLE>";
print "</FORM>";
print "</BODY>";
print "</HTML>";

# All done!
exit;
```

The top portion of the code in Listing 17.15 interacts with the A2Z database to get the data about the books currently in stock. This is the same basic database-access code used in Listing 17.14. The only real difference is that a scalar named $DivsHTML is assembled inside the While loop that iterates over the data rows; the scalar contains all the DIV tags that are needed later in the page to display the book titles. This is the work that was done by the CFOUTPUT block toward the bottom of Listing 16.24 in Chapter 16.

T I P The concatenation operator in Perl is the . (period). Like the & operator in CFML and the + operator in JavaScript, it concatenates two strings. That's nothing new for Perl coders, but if you're looking at this from a ColdFusion background, this may be the first time you're seeing a period used this way.

Other than that, the only thing new here is the syntax used to tell the $parser to insert its dynamically produced JavaScript into the current page. That's accomplished by the line that includes wddx2js in the listing. Note that the function is provided a topLevelVariable, which lets the function know what the WddxRecordset object should be named when it is interpreted by the browser. In other words, the JavaScript that the function writes begins with a line that looks like the following:

```
Books = new WddxRecordset();
```

This is the equivalent of the TOPLEVELVARIABLE attribute of the CFWDDX tag used in Listing 16.24 from Chapter 16. The rest of Listing 17.15 is simply responsible for using the $print keyword to output the remainder of the HTML and JavaScript code that the browser needs to render the page; see Listing 16.24 in Chapter 16 for details. ●

ColdFusion Scripting

Introducing CFScript

ColdFusion 4 includes a new feature called *scripting*, which allows you to write portions of your templates with a new script-style syntax instead of ColdFusion's traditional tag-based syntax. Rather than use a bunch of CFSET, CFIF, CFLOOP, and similar tags, you can mark off a whole portion of your template as a *script block*, where you can deal with variables, loops, conditionals, and expressions a bit more directly.

The result is that the code you write ends up looking a lot like JavaScript instead of like HTML, as most ColdFusion code does. This alternative syntax can often be more concise and straight-forward than the equivalent tag-based code. Also, if you're already familiar with JavaScript—or are coming from a Java or C/C++ background—you might find it more intuitive to write your ColdFusion templates using the script syntax when possible.

CFScript is a new scripting language that has been created especially for use within ColdFusion templates. It uses a simple syntax that will look familiar to you if you've done any JavaScript, JScript, Java, or C++ programming. You can use it as an alternative to traditional, tag-based ColdFusion syntax.

You need to understand that even though the syntax looks similar to these other languages, CFScript is a separate scripting language that can be used only in ColdFusion templates. For instance, as you will soon see, CFScript understands all ColdFusion functions, which JavaScript certainly does not understand. And JavaScript includes many concepts that CFScript doesn't, such as user-defined functions. This means that if a script is very simple, you might be able to cut and paste it back and forth between CFScript and JavaScript without any changes. But as soon as a script gets a bit complex, you will have to do some "conversion" work to move your routine between the two languages.

> **N O T E** This chapter will frequently compare JavaScript and CFScript. CFScript was indeed based on JavaScript, but it's worth noting that JavaScript itself was based originally on the C programming language. Around the same time, Java was also being derived from C, so CFScript syntax looks a lot like Java syntax, too. Also, because two other scripting languages have been derived from JavaScript since it was introduced—specifically, Microsoft's JScript implementation and the ECMAScript language specification—you could say that CFScript is just as related to those languages as it is to JavaScript itself. ■

CFScript Features

CFScript has much to offer to you as a developer. As you will see, its main advantages to you are convenience and freedom to choose the best coding style for a particular job. Because CFScript inherits so much functionality from normal ColdFusion syntax, you are free to use its concise syntax when you want to, without giving up power and flexibility.

CFScript can successfully meld itself seamlessly into CFML because of the following features:

■ CFScript integrates a familiar, JavaScript-like syntax into ColdFusion. The structure of the various CFScript statements that you will learn about in this chapter are all structured the same way as they are in JavaScript. For instance, the use of braces ({}) to indicate a block of code and the use of slashes to provide comments are both borrowed from JavaScript.

■ CFScript supports all ColdFusion functions. You can take advantage of ColdFusion's rich set of string-manipulation, mathematical, list, array, security, and other functions in your CFScript code. This set of functions is far richer than those available to you in JavaScript. In short, you can use any function listed in Appendix B, "ColdFusion Function Reference," in a CFScript.

■ CFScript provides access to all ColdFusion variables and objects. Variables created outside a script are available inside a script, and vice versa. This includes scoped variables, such as the `Client` and `Session` scopes if your application is using ColdFusion's state-management features, the `Caller` and `Attributes` scopes if you're putting together CFML custom tags, and the `Form`, `CGI`, and `URL` scopes that tell you about the current page request. You can also refer to the properties and functions of any object instantiated with the `CFOBJECT` tag.

■ CFScript operates on the server. All CFScript code is executed on the server—not on the client browser, which is the place where JavaScript is traditionally executed. Thus, you don't have to be concerned with which parts of JavaScript are supported by a particular browser. In fact, you don't even need to know whether the browser supports JavaScript at all. If you've used the server-side JavaScript functionality (known at one time as LiveWire) built into current versions of Netscape's Enterprise Server or FastTrack Server Web-server packages, running scripts on the server is a familiar concept to you. Similarly, Web programmers coming from experience with Microsoft's Active Server Pages (ASP) will find this concept familiar.

Part
IV

Ch
18

N O T E You need to understand that although you can make full use of ColdFusion functions such as `DateAdd`, `ArrayNew`, and `ListFind` with CFScript, you can't use ColdFusion tags such as `CFMAIL` or `CFQUERY` within a script. ■

CFScript Limitations

For ColdFusion 4, the CFScript language has been kept pretty simple. So, although it's very useful, easy to write, and easy to learn, it does have its limitations. Given how much CFScript looks like JavaScript, you might expect it to support a number of concepts that it simply does not.

Here's the short list of fundamental CFScript limitations to keep in mind:

■ No user-defined functions—In JavaScript and other languages that look like it, you can use the `function` keyword to create *user-defined functions* (UDFs). A user-defined function can take some parameters, do something with them, and return a value of some kind. The function could be referred to inline as part of an expression, essentially becoming part of the scripting language itself for the duration of the script. This capability isn't supported in CFScript.

■ No locally scoped variables—In JavaScript, you can use the `var` keyword to indicate that a variable should be available only to the currently executing block of script code. A variable declared with `var` goes out of scope when that portion of the script ends, which may allow the memory allocated to the variable to be reclaimed. This capability isn't supported in CFScript. All variables assigned within a CFScript block remain "live" and available for your use until the entire template (CFM file) finishes executing.

■ No access to the Document Object Model—When you think about JavaScript, you generally think about scripting Web pages by referring to the properties and methods of the various objects within the windows, pages, and forms that make up your application. For instance, you might refer to the value property of a text input box to find out what the user typed into the form, or you might use the `open()` method of the window object to open a new "remote-control" window of some kind. None of this "awareness" of the current Web page is available to CFScript. For that to happen, the page would already need to have been "drawn," and ColdFusion would somehow need to understand how the browser has interpreted the page's HTML source code. Given ColdFusion's server-based architecture—as opposed to a client-based or browser-based architecture—this just isn't possible.

■ No JavaScript functions, methods, or operators—Only basic control-of-flow and branching statements such as `if`, `else`, `for`, `while`, `break`, and so on have been brought over from JavaScript to CFScript. None of JavaScript's string-manipulation or other functions such as `escape`, `pos`, and `charAt` are available to you when using CFScript. Instead, you need to use the ColdFusion equivalents to these functions (such as `URLEncodedFormat`, `Find`, and `Mid`, respectively). Similarly, you must use ColdFusion operators for operations such as mathematical comparisons; for instance, you must use the ColdFusion `is` operator to compare two numbers rather than the `==` comparison operator from JavaScript.

T I P If you find that you need more from CFScript than it provides—for instance, if you're imagining writing a set of user-defined functions that call each other in some kind of iterative, nested manner—you might want to consider coding your imagined code as a CFX tag with Visual C++ instead. The syntax will probably look pretty similar, and you'll have all the power that C++ provides, although you won't be able to use ColdFusion functions and expressions inside the tag's code. See Chapter 10, "Writing CFX Tags in Visual C++," for more information.

Simple Scripting

To use ColdFusion scripting syntax in your templates, you put a pair of CFSCRIPT tags in your template. Then, between these tags, you write CFScript code that does whatever you need to get done.

Conceptually, you use two kinds of statements within a CFSCRIPT block:

■ Simple *assignment* statements that assign some value to a variable, using whatever ColdFusion functions and operators you want. Basically, anything that you would normally put in a CFSET tag is allowed, which means that you can be doing math, performing string manipulation, and so on as you set the variable.

- *Control-of-flow* statements, which you use to allow your script code to do the basic decision-making and looping that you generally need to make your scripts make complex calculations. Each statement will be discussed later in this chapter.

First, you need to learn how to incorporate the simple assignment statements into your ColdFusion templates. When you have that process down, the control-of-flow statements covered in the next section will be easy to understand. You'll be up and scripting in no time.

The CFSCRIPT Tag

You first need to place a pair of CFSCRIPT tags into your ColdFusion template. You can put this CFSCRIPT "block" just about anywhere you want; the script code inside it is executed by the ColdFusion server as the CFSCRIPT tag is encountered in your template. If your CFSCRIPT tag is at the top of a template, it is executed first; if it's at the bottom of a template, it is executed last.

In ColdFusion 4, the CFSCRIPT tag itself is very simple; it doesn't take any parameters or attributes. For instance, you might have expected it to accept an optional LANGUAGE attribute, but it does not.

Part
IV
Ch
18

N O T E Of course, because the CFSCRIPT tag is executed as it's encountered in your template, you need to place it in a place that makes contextual sense to ColdFusion. For instance, if you want to be able to refer to the results of a query within a CFSCRIPT block, the query needs to have been run before the script executes, which means that the CFQUERY tag needs to come before the CFSCRIPT block.

T I P Although you probably won't need to do so very often, you can place a CFSCRIPT tag between CFOUTPUT tags, between CFLOOP tags, or even within CFMAIL or CFQUERY tags.

Assigning Values to Variables

Most often in your CFScript code, you assign values to variables, often building your way toward some kind of "result" variable or variables that you want to be able to refer to in your ColdFusion code after the CFSCRIPT block. This work is normally done by the CFSET tag, using ColdFusion's traditional tag-based syntax.

To assign a value to a variable in a script, just provide the variable name, an = sign, and then the actual value that you want to assign to the new variable. If you want, the value can come from an expression made up of any valid combination of ColdFusion operators and functions.

In other words, you can generally take any existing CFSET tag, remove the word CFSET itself, and then drop it unmodified into a CFSCRIPT block. Just as in the CFSET tag, everything after the = sign is evaluated as an expression. The result of the expression is assigned to the variable name before the = sign.

Without Scripting   Consider the traditional ColdFusion code shown in Listing 18.1. This code does some basic variable manipulation without using the new scripting syntax. First, the `Birthday` variable is set to a string value that represents a date. Then the ColdFusion `ParseDateTime` function is used to convert the string into a proper ColdFusion date value. Finally, the `CurrentAge` variable is calculated with the help of ColdFusion's `DateDiff` function.

Listing 18.1   `Variables-NoScript.cfm`—**Setting Variables Without Scripting**

```
<!DOCTYPE HTML PUBLIC "-//W3C//DTD HTML 4 Transitional//EN">

<html>
<head>
    <title>Variable Demonstration</title>
</head>

<body>
<H2>Variable Demonstration</H2>

<!--- Set a few variables, first with a simple
      value, and then using some CF functions   --->

<!--- Setting a simple variable --->
<CFSET Birthday = "March 18, 1969">

<!--- Using functions --->
<CFSET BDayObject = ParseDateTime(Birthday)>
<CFSET CurrentAge = DateDiff("yyyy", BDayObject, Now())>

<!--- Display Age to user --->
<CFOUTPUT>Age: #CurrentAge#</CFOUTPUT>

</body>
</html>
```

The result is that the age of someone who was born on March 18, 1969, is displayed—which at the time of this writing is 29. You can see the results in Figure 18.1. This example, while poignant, doesn't exactly break any new ground, but it's a good way to demonstrate two versions of a piece of real-world logic, "before and after" the introduction of CFScript.

With Scripting   Listing 18.2 performs the same calculations performed by Listing 18.1, except that the expressions in the CFSET tags have been moved into a piece of CFScript code. Everything else about the template is exactly the same. ColdFusion's internal expression "engine" is literally being asked to evaluate the same expressions. And, as you can see, variables set inside the CFSCRIPT block are available for use by the CFOUTPUT tag after the script executes. This fact is proven by the output to the user being exactly the same for both versions of the template (see Figure 18.1).

FIGURE 18.1

This page is displayed by the script or no-script versions of the template.

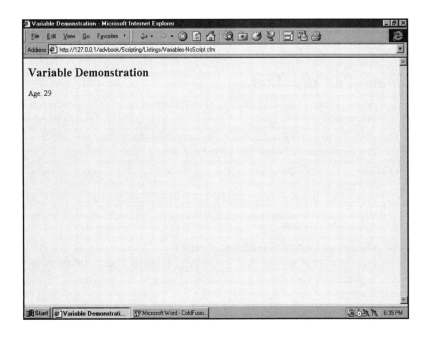

Listing 18.2 `Variables-Script.cfm`—**The Code from Listing 18.1, Rewritten in Script Syntax**

```
<!DOCTYPE HTML PUBLIC "-//W3C//DTD HTML 4 Transitional//EN">

<html>
<head>
    <title>Variable Demonstration</title>
</head>

<body>
<H2>Variable Demonstration</H2>

<CFSCRIPT>
  /* Set a few variables, first with a simple
  value, and then using some CF functions */

  // Setting a simple variable
  Birthday = "March 18, 1969";    // My Birthday

  // Using functions
  BDayObject = ParseDateTime(Birthday);
  CurrentAge = DateDiff("yyyy", BDayObject, Now());
</CFSCRIPT>

<!--- Display Age to user --->
<CFOUTPUT>Age: #CurrentAge#</CFOUTPUT>

</body>
</html>
```

NOTE A semicolon is required at the end of each line of CFScript code. If you forget the semicolon, ColdFusion displays an error message. ■

Commenting Your Code

As you looked at Listing 18.2, you might have noticed that the various comments originally bracketed by the <!--- and ---> symbols in Listing 18.1 were changed a little as they were moved into the CFSCRIPT block. Actually, you can comment out text in CFScript in two ways, just as you can in JavaScript: by using *paired* comment markers and *single-line* comment markers.

You must use one of these two types of commenting styles within a CFSCRIPT tag. You can't use the <!--- and ---> markers within a script block. If you do, ColdFusion displays an error message. ■

The Paired Comment Markers: /* and */   To comment out a text block that might span over more than one line, use the /* marker (a forward slash followed by an asterisk) to mark the beginning of the comment and the */ marker to mark the end of the comment. These symbols work the same way that the <!--- and ---> symbols work in normal ColdFusion code, respectively. Anything between the pair of comment markers is considered a comment by the script parser, which keeps the code from actually being executed when the template is executed.

Use these symbols if you want to include a short paragraph of comments before a block of script code or if you want to keep several lines of script code from executing temporarily. You can see this type of commenting in action at the beginning of the CFSCRIPT block in Listing 18.2.

TIP If you need to comment out all the lines in a script block—leaving no actual script code for ColdFusion to execute—comment out the entire CFSCRIPT block with the <!--- ---> comment style rather than the script code itself with the script-style comments. Use this approach because ColdFusion displays an error message if it encounters an empty CFSCRIPT block, but it doesn't display an error message if the CFSCRIPT block itself is commented out.

Single-Line Comment Markers: //   To comment out a single line of text at a time, you can use the // marker at the beginning of the line to mark it as a comment. This symbol works a little differently than the <!--- and ---> symbols do in normal ColdFusion code because // marks only one line at a time as a comment. If you want to comment out more than one line, you need to place a separate // marker at the beginning of each line. You can see this type of comment used several times within the CFSCRIPT block in Listing 18.2.

Use this method to quickly comment out a single line of code that you think might be giving you trouble or to provide short comments that explain the next line. Anything from the // to the end of the line is considered a comment by the script parser, which keeps the code from actually being executed when the template is brought up in a browser.

TIP You can also use the // marker to put a comment on the same line as a piece of actual code, as shown in Listing 18.2. The line that sets the Birthday variable is conveniently tagged with the comment My Birthday, which keeps the code readable and concise. If you use this technique, make sure that the semicolon comes before the comment marker. Otherwise, the semicolon itself is commented out and causes an error message to appear.

Program-Flow Statements

In many cases, you might want your script code to be able to behave differently at different times, based on some kind of criteria. CFScript provides two program-flow statements that you can use to accomplish this feat: the simple if..else statement and the more complicated switch..case statement.

The following examples make various decisions based on a user's birthday. The code in Listing 18.3 creates a simple form (see Figure 18.2) in which a user types the date of his or her birthday.

Listing 18.3 UsingIfForm.cfm—A Simple Birthday-Entry Form

```
<!DOCTYPE HTML PUBLIC "-//W3C//DTD HTML 4 Transitional//EN">

<html>
<head>
    <title>Is it time to retire yet?</title>
</head>

<body>
<H2>Is it time to retire yet?</H2>

<CFFORM ACTION="UsingIf-NoScript.cfm" METHOD="POST">

  Please enter your birthday (tell the truth!):
  <CFINPUT TYPE="Text"
      NAME="UserBirthday"
      MESSAGE="Please enter a valid birthday to work with."
      VALIDATE="date"
      REQUIRED="No"
      SIZE="12">

  <INPUT TYPE="SUBMIT" VALUE="Go!">

</CFFORM>

</body>
</html>
```

FIGURE 18.2

The script code makes decisions based on the birthday the user submits.

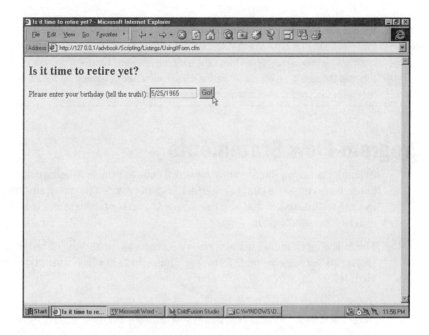

Making Simple Decisions: `if` Statements

If you have some script code that you want to execute only if a certain condition is met, you can include `if` statements in your code. CFScript `if` statements do the same job that `CFIF` tags do in normal ColdFusion code.

Without Scripting   The code in Listing 18.4 is similar to Listing 18.1, except that it displays a message to the user if his or her age is calculated to be above the "retirement age" of 30 (see Figure 18.3). At the beginning of the code, the `Message` variable is set to an empty string (`""`). Then a simple `CFIF` statement is used to test whether the user's age is over the retirement age. If the user is over the retirement age, the `Message` variable is set to a friendly message. Finally, the message (which might be blank) is displayed to the user.

Listing 18.4   `UsingIf-NoScript.cfm`—Making Decisions Without Scripting

```
<!DOCTYPE HTML PUBLIC "-//W3C//DTD HTML 4 Transitional//EN">

<html>
<head>
    <title>Is it time to retire yet?</title>
</head>

<body>
<H2>Is it time to retire yet?</H2>

<!--- When do we consider someone "retired"? --->
<CFSET RetirementAge = 30>
```

```
<!--- Birthday from user's input --->
<CFSET Birthday = Form.UserBirthday>
<!--- Display this after script --->
<CFSET Message = "">

<!--- Calculate user's age based on their birthday --->
<CFSET BDayObject = ParseDateTime(Birthday)>
<CFSET CurrentAge = DateDiff("yyyy", BDayObject, Now())>

<!--- Display message if time to retire --->
<CFIF CurrentAge GTE RetirementAge>
  <CFSET Message = "Time to retire!">
</CFIF>


<!--- Display Age to user --->
<CFOUTPUT>
  Age: #CurrentAge#<BR>
  <P><B>#Message#</B>
</CFOUTPUT>

</body>
</html>
```

FIGURE 18.3

A message is displayed if the user has reached retirement age.

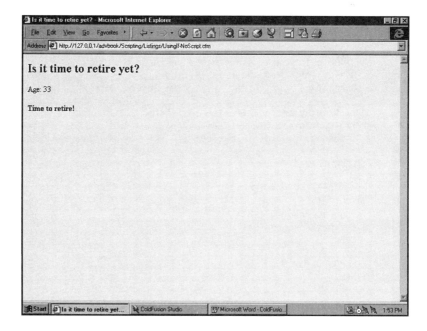

With Scripting   Listing 18.5 converts the code from Listing 18.4 into CFScript code. The decision-making functionality that the CFIF tag originally provided is now being handled by CFScript's if statement.

The syntax for the if statement is the same as it is in JavaScript. First comes the if keyword itself, followed by a condition. The condition—which can be any ColdFusion expression that evaluates to True or False—is enclosed within parentheses. After the condition, a set of braces is used to indicate which script statements should be executed if the condition is met.

Listing 18.5 UsingIf-Script.cfm—Using Script Code Instead of CFIF Tags to Make Decisions

```
<!DOCTYPE HTML PUBLIC "-//W3C//DTD HTML 4 Transitional//EN">

<html>
<head>
    <title>Is it time to retire yet?</title>
</head>

<body>
<H2>Is it time to retire yet?</H2>

<!--- When do we consider someone "retired"? --->
<CFSET RetirementAge = 30>

<CFSCRIPT>
  /* Set simple variables for rest of routine */
  Birthday = Form.UserBirthday; // Birthday from user's input
  Message = "";                 // Display this after script

  // Calculate user's age based on their birthday
  BDayObject = ParseDateTime(Birthday);
  CurrentAge = DateDiff("yyyy", BDayObject, Now());

  // Display message if time to retire
  if (CurrentAge GTE RetirementAge) {
    Message = "Time to retire!";
  }
</CFSCRIPT>

<!--- Display Age to user --->
<CFOUTPUT>
  Age: #CurrentAge#<BR>
  <P><B>#Message#</B>
</CFOUTPUT>

</body>
</html>
```

N O T E If you want to test this code, remember to change the ACTION attribute of the FORM tag in Listing 18.4 from UsingIf-NoScript.cfm to UsingIf-Script.cfm. Then reload the form page in your browser. ■

Making Either/Or Decisions with `if..else` Statements

As you know, in regular ColdFusion templates, you can use the CFELSE tag within a CFIF block to indicate code that should be executed if the CFIF condition isn't met. The net effect is an either/or decision, in which one of two paths is taken, depending on whether the condition evaluates to True or False.

Without Scripting If you need to adapt the tag-based logic from Listing 18.4 to show one message if a user has reached the retirement age and a different message if the user hasn't, adding a CFELSE tag to create the needed either/or logic is a simple matter. Listing 18.6 shows the simple CFIF and CFELSE code that gets this job done.

Listing 18.6 `UsingIfElse-NoScript.cfm`—A `CFIF..CFELSE` **Structure That Can Be Scripted with** `if..else`

```
<!DOCTYPE HTML PUBLIC "-//W3C//DTD HTML 4 Transitional//EN">

<html>
<head>
    <title>Is it time to retire yet?</title>
</head>

<body>
<H2>Is it time to retire yet?</H2>

<!--- When do we consider someone "retired"? --->
<CFSET RetirementAge = 30>


<!--- Birthday from user's input --->
<CFSET Birthday = Form.UserBirthday>
<CFSET MessageColor = "Black">

<!--- Calculate user's age based on their birthday --->
<CFSET BDayObject = ParseDateTime(Birthday)>
<CFSET CurrentAge = DateDiff("yyyy", BDayObject, Now())>

<!--- Display message if time to retire --->
<CFIF CurrentAge GTE RetirementAge>
  <CFSET Message = "Time to retire!">
<CFELSE>
  <CFSET Message = "Not time to retire yet!">
  <CFSET MessageColor = "Red">
</CFIF>


<!--- Display Age to user --->
<CFOUTPUT>
  Age: #CurrentAge#<BR>
  <P><FONT COLOR="#MessageColor#"><B>#Message#</B></FONT></P>
</CFOUTPUT>

</body>
</html>
```

Part

IV

Ch

18

The code in Listing 18.6 also color-codes the message displayed to the user by setting a MessageColor variable along with the Message variable. In the CFOUTPUT section after the script, the MessageColor variable is included as the COLOR attribute of an ordinary FONT tag, which causes the message to displayed in black or red text. So, the page displayed to the user looks just like Figure 18.3, except that the message—and the color of the message—changes depending on the date the user enters as his or her birthday.

With Scripting   As you might expect, adjusting the scripted version of the page to work the same way is now a very simple matter. Just take the code from Listing 18.5 and add CFScript's else keyword right after the braces that now end the if statement. Then, after the else keyword, add a new set of braces and insert the appropriate script statements between them. In other words, the first set of braces encloses the code that will be executed if the if condition is met; the second set of braces holds the statements that will be executed if the condition is *not* met. The resulting code is provided in Listing 18.7.

Listing 18.7   `UsingIfElse-Script.cfm`—**Using the `else` Script Keyword**

```
<!DOCTYPE HTML PUBLIC "-//W3C//DTD HTML 4 Transitional//EN">

<html>
<head>
    <title>Is it time to retire yet?</title>
</head>

<body>
<H2>Is it time to retire yet?</H2>

<!--- When do we consider someone "retired"? --->
<CFSET RetirementAge = 30>

<CFSCRIPT>
  /* Set simple variables for rest of routine */
  Birthday = Form.UserBirthday; // Birthday from user's input

  // Calculate user's age based on their birthday
  BDayObject = ParseDateTime(Birthday);
  CurrentAge = DateDiff("yyyy", BDayObject, Now());

  // Display message if time to retire
  if (CurrentAge GTE RetirementAge) {
    Message = "Time to retire!";
    MessageColor = "Green";
  } else {
    Message = "Not time to retire yet!";
    MessageColor = "Red";
  }
</CFSCRIPT>

<!--- Display Age to user --->
<CFOUTPUT>
  Age: #CurrentAge#<BR>
```

```
   <P><FONT COLOR="#MessageColor#"><B>#Message#</B></FONT>
</CFOUTPUT>

</body>
</html>
```

A Note About Braces

As you've seen in the script examples so far, CFScript uses curly braces to create blocks of script code that should be executed by the `if` or `else` part of an `if..else` statement. Actually, the braces are optional if only one line of code is to be handled by the `if` or the `else` keyword. If you leave out the braces, however, things can get confusing if you need to add additional lines to your code later, so including the braces in your script code is a good habit—even when they aren't explicitly needed.

For example, skip back to Listing 18.5. You could delete the braces in the script code shown there, and the code would execute exactly the same way. In other words, the statement

```
if (CurrentAge GTE RetirementAge) {
  Message = "Time to retire!";
}
```

does the same exact thing as the following statement, which is perfectly legal CFScript code:

```
if (CurrentAge GTE RetirementAge)
  Message = "Time to retire!";
```

You might even want to edit the code so that the whole statement sits on one line:

```
if (CurrentAge GTE RetirementAge) Message = "Time to retire!";
```

This approach would be fine, except that if you return later to change the code to use the `if..else` logic added in Listing 18.7, you might run into problems. For instance, rather than write the code as it appears in the listing, like this:

```
if (CurrentAge GTE RetirementAge) {
  Message = "Time to retire!";
} else {
  Message = "Not time to retire yet!";
  MessageColor = "Red";
}
```

you might get mixed up and forget to add the braces, which leaves you with something like the following, which doesn't work correctly:

```
if (CurrentAge GTE RetirementAge)
  Message = "Time to retire!";
else
  Message = "Not time to retire yet!";
  MessageColor = "Red";
```

Because the braces are optional as far as ColdFusion is concerned, this code doesn't cause any error messages to appear. However, it doesn't perform as expected. Because the `else` part of the statement doesn't have braces around it—which would bind the two last lines to the `else`

Part

IV

Ch

18

keyword—the last line of code isn't actually part of the `if..else` block at all. Therefore, the `MessageColor` variable is *always* set to Red, regardless of whether the condition is met. At the very least, you need to put braces around the `else` part of the statement, like this:

```
if (CurrentAge GTE RetirementAge)
  Message = "Time to retire!";
else {
  Message = "Not time to retire yet!";
  MessageColor = "Red";
}
```

The lesson is that you can leave off the braces if you want, but be careful if you do so. Not using the braces can be a very easy way to introduce bugs into your application because erroneous code often executes without any error messages appearing. In this particular example, no significant damage was done. You can imagine the trouble if this code were calculating interest rates, though; you could very well end up recording the wrong values for quite some time before anyone ever caught on that a problem occurred. Just getting into the habit of always using the braces is probably a good idea so that you don't run into these kinds of issues in your own applications.

Multi-Case Logic Branching: `switch..case`

Sometimes you encounter a situation in which you want your code to be able to choose among a number of possible choices. Because `if..else` statements allow only for choosing between two choices, CFScript allows you to write `switch..case` statements, with which you can easily compare a given expression with any number of possible values.

Without Scripting   Suppose that you want to adapt the birthday-message code from Listing 18.6 so that it displays a number of different messages, depending on how close the user is to retirement. Without scripting, you might put together some message-choosing code that uses the CFSWITCH and CFCASE tags, as shown in Listing 18.8.

> **Listing 18.8** `UsingSwitch-NoScript.cfm`—**Logic Branching Using Conventional Tag-Based Syntax**

```
<!DOCTYPE HTML PUBLIC "-//W3C//DTD HTML 4 Transitional//EN">

<html>
<head>
    <title>Is it time to retire yet?</title>
</head>

<body>
<H2>Is it time to retire yet?</H2>

<!--- When do we consider someone "retired"? --->
<CFSET RetirementAge = 30>


<!--- Birthday from user's input --->
<CFSET Birthday = Form.UserBirthday>
```

```
<CFSET MessageColor = "Black">

<!--- Calculate user's age based on their birthday --->
<CFSET BDayObject = ParseDateTime(Birthday)>
<CFSET CurrentAge = DateDiff("yyyy", BDayObject, Now())>
<CFSET YearsUntilRetirement = RetirementAge - CurrentAge>

<!--- Display message if time to retire --->
<CFSWITCH EXPRESSION="#YearsUntilRetirement#">
  <CFCASE VALUE="0">
    <CFSET Message = "Congratulations, you retire this year!">
    <CFSET MessageColor = "Green">
  </CFCASE>
  <CFCASE VALUE="1">
    <CFSET Message = "Almost there! You retire next year!">
  </CFCASE>
  <CFCASE VALUE="2">
    <CFSET Message = "You retire pretty soon!">
  </CFCASE>
  <CFCASE VALUE="3">
    <CFSET Message = "You've got a while to wait, but don't give up!">
  </CFCASE>
  <CFDEFAULTCASE>
    <CFIF YearsUntilRetirement LT 0>
      <CFSET Message = "You've already retired! Go home!">
    <CFELSE>
      <CFSET Message = "Bad news. Many years of work await you.">
      <CFSET MessageColor = "Red">
    </CFIF>
  </CFDEFAULTCASE>
</CFSWITCH>

<!--- Display Age to user --->
<CFOUTPUT>
  Age: #CurrentAge#<BR>
  <P><FONT COLOR="#MessageColor#"><B>#Message#</B></FONT>
</CFOUTPUT>

</body>
</html>
```

Part
IV

Ch

18

The code in Listing 18.8 creates a variable called YearsUntilRetirement by subtracting the person's age from the retirement age. The result is a positive number if the person hasn't retired yet, zero if the person retires this year, and a negative number if the person's retirement age has already passed. Within the CFSWITCH block, several CFCASE tags test for some possible values of the variable. If none of the CFCASE conditions apply, ColdFusion proceeds to the CFDEFAULTCASE section, inside of which a simple CFIF..CFELSE block is used to display one of two possible "in all other cases" messages.

N O T E The CFSWITCH and CFCASE tags are new for ColdFusion 4. With earlier versions of ColdFusion, you could write this code by placing several CFELSEIF tags within a CFIF block to get the same effect. ▪

The resulting Web page looks similar to the pages that previous examples have generated. The person's age is displayed, along with one of several messages (which appears in one of several colors). Figure 18.4 shows one possible response that might be presented to a user.

FIGURE 18.4

The case-switching code causes one of several color-coded messages to appear.

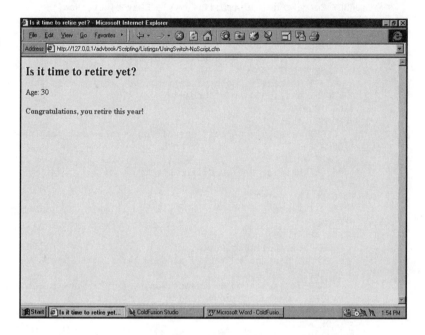

With Scripting To get this kind of effect by using scripting syntax, CFScript supports something called a switch..case statement. You can easily use this kind of statement in a script; as you'll see, the resulting code can be simpler and easier to read than the tag-based version of the same code.

First, type the keyword **switch**, followed by a set of parentheses. Inside the parentheses, put the expression that you want the code to "switch" against—in other words, whatever you would provide for the EXPRESSION parameter of the equivalent CFSWITCH tag. The expression will be evaluated once, at the beginning of the switch statement, and then compared against the possible values that you provide underneath.

After the parentheses, put a pair of braces. Inside the braces, include a case statement for each specific value that you want to test for. You need to construct each case statement by typing the keyword **case**, the value to test for, and then a colon. Now include any statements that you want to execute if the switch expression turns out to be this particular value.

Listing 18.9 shows the switch..case equivalent of the CFSWITCH code in Listing 18.8.

TIP In Listing 18.9, each case statement is testing for numeric values. If you're testing for string values instead of numeric values, you need to put quotation marks around each value. That is, you put quotation marks around whatever you are placing between the case keyword and the colon.

Listing 18.9 `UsingSwitch-NoScript.cfm`**—Constructing Case-Switching Code with Script Syntax**

```
<!DOCTYPE HTML PUBLIC "-//W3C//DTD HTML 4 Transitional//EN">

<html>
<head>
    <title>Is it time to retire yet?</title>
</head>

<body>
<H2>Is it time to retire yet?</H2>

<!--- When do we consider someone "retired"? --->
<CFSET RetirementAge = 30>

<CFSCRIPT>
  /* Set simple variables for rest of routine */
  Birthday = Form.UserBirthday; // Birthday from user's input
  MessageColor = "Black";

  // Calculate user's age based on their birthday
  BDayObject = ParseDateTime(Birthday);
  CurrentAge = DateDiff("yyyy", BDayObject, Now());
  YearsUntilRetirement = RetirementAge - CurrentAge;

  // Display message if time to retire
  switch (YearsUntilRetirement) {
    case 0 :
      Message = "Congratulations, you retire this year!";
      MessageColor = "Green";
    case 1 :
      Message = "Almost there! You retire next year!";
    case 2 :
      Message = "You retire pretty soon!";
    case 3 :
      Message = "You've got a while to wait, but don't give up!";
    default :
      if (YearsUntilRetirement LT 0) {
        Message = "You've already retired! Go home!";
      } else {
        Message = "Bad news. Many years of work await you.";
        MessageColor = "Red";
      }
  }

</CFSCRIPT>

<!--- Display Age to user --->
<CFOUTPUT>
  Age: #CurrentAge#<BR>
  <P><FONT COLOR="#MessageColor#"><B>#Message#</B></FONT>
</CFOUTPUT>

</body>
</html>
```

Part

IV

Ch

18

NOTE One neat feature about the CFCASE tag is that you can provide a comma-separated list of values to its VALUE attribute. For instance, you can change the VALUE="3" attribute found in Listing 18.8 to VALUE="3,4,5,6,7" to make the CASE block handle all five cases. To be consistent with JavaScript, however, CFScript's case statement doesn't allow this change. ■

Looping Statements

Of course, no scripting language would be complete without ways to place a chunk of code into a loop of some kind. Like JavaScript, CFScript provides support for looping by allowing you to include while and for statements in your code. These statements cause the code that follows to be repeated as many times as you want.

Of the two types of loops, while loops are a bit simpler, so the while keyword will be explained first. Then you'll see how to create for loops, which are slightly more complicated (but still reasonably simple).

Repeating Code Until Something Changes with `while`

Often, you need to keep repeating some block of code over and over until something changes. Most scripting and programming languages provide a way to construct some kind of while loop. Such loops keep repeating their code until a variable or an expression reaches some desired value.

You can think of many day-to-day experiences in the physical world in terms of while loops. For instance, imagine a person at a bus stop, reading the newspaper to pass the time until the bus arrives. If you think of this person's plan as a little programming problem, you might imagine a variable called IsBusHere, which is True or False depending on whether the bus has arrived. You could then construct a while loop that represents this thought: "While the IsBusHere variable evaluates to False, read the next paragraph of the newspaper." Thus, the person would keep reading the paper until the bus arrives. Then the loop would end, and code would continue to the next statement in the program (which would probably be something like "Get on the bus!").

Without Scripting In normal ColdFusion code, you use the CFLOOP tag with a CONDITION parameter to create this kind of loop. ColdFusion keeps repeating the code inside the CFLOOP block until the CONDITION becomes true. When the CONDITION becomes true, the loop ends and ColdFusion continues executing the portion of the template after the CFLOOP tag.

Consider the simple form shown in Figure 18.5. This form asks users to provide a date value and choose a day of the week. Suppose that a user inputs **Monday** and **8/25/1998** (August 25, 1998). When the form is submitted, it's the job of your ColdFusion application to find the first Monday in August 1998. Listing 18.10 shows the code for this form.

FIGURE 18.5

The user selects a day of the week and provides a date value.

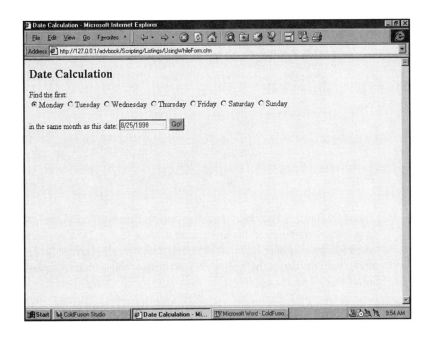

Part

IV

Ch

18

Listing 18.10 UsingWhileForm.cfm—Code to Create the Form Shown in Figure 18.5

```
<!DOCTYPE HTML PUBLIC "-//W3C//DTD HTML 4 Transitional//EN">

<html>
<head>
    <title>Date Calculation</title>
</head>

<body>
<H2>Date Calculation</H2>


<CFFORM ACTION="UsingWhile-Script.cfm" METHOD="POST">

  Find the first:<BR>
  <INPUT TYPE="RADIO" NAME="WhichDayOfWeek" VALUE="2" CHECKED>Monday
  <INPUT TYPE="RADIO" NAME="WhichDayOfWeek" VALUE="3">Tuesday
  <INPUT TYPE="RADIO" NAME="WhichDayOfWeek" VALUE="4">Wednesday
  <INPUT TYPE="RADIO" NAME="WhichDayOfWeek" VALUE="5">Thursday
  <INPUT TYPE="RADIO" NAME="WhichDayOfWeek" VALUE="6">Friday
  <INPUT TYPE="RADIO" NAME="WhichDayOfWeek" VALUE="7">Saturday
  <INPUT TYPE="RADIO" NAME="WhichDayOfWeek" VALUE="1">Sunday<BR>

  <P>in the same month as this date:
  <CFINPUT TYPE="Text"
      NAME="TargetDate"
      VALUE="#DateFormat(Now(), "m/d/yyyy")#"
```

continues

Listing 18.10 Continued

```
        MESSAGE="Please enter a valid date to work with."
        VALIDATE="date"
        REQUIRED="No"
        SIZE="12">

  <INPUT TYPE="SUBMIT" VALUE="Go!">

</CFFORM>

</body>
</html>
```

You might think of a number of ways to approach the problem of calculating the appropriate date. For the purposes of this discussion, assume that you've decided to handle it by finding the first day of the appropriate month, and then continue advancing one day at a time into the month until the day of the week matches the user's selection (Monday). That "advancing one day at a time" part is a perfect time to use CFLOOP in normal ColdFusion code or a while statement in a script. The code in Listing 18.11 shows how you can get your result without scripting, using ColdFusion's traditional CFLOOP tag.

Listing 18.11 UsingWhile-NoScript.cfm—Using CFLOOP to Create a while Loop Without Scripting

```
<!DOCTYPE HTML PUBLIC "-//W3C//DTD HTML 4 Transitional//EN">

<html>
<head>
     <title>Date Calculation</title>
</head>

<body>
<H2>Date Calculation</H2>

<!--- Set datetime var MonthStart to 1st day of selected Month --->
<CFSET DayOfWeekWanted = Form.WhichDayOfWeek>
<CFSET YearStart = CreateDate(Year(Form.TargetDate), 1, 1)>
<CFSET MonthStartOffset = FirstDayOfMonth(Form.TargetDate)>
<CFSET MonthStart = DateAdd("d", MonthStartOffset-1, YearStart)>

<!--- Start at the first day of the month (determined above) --->
<CFSET TryThisDate = MonthStart>

<!--- Keep adding one day to TryThisDate until correct DayOfWeek --->
<CFLOOP CONDITION="DayOfWeek(TryThisDate) is not DayOfWeekWanted">
  <CFSET TryThisDate = DateAdd("d", 1, TryThisDate)>
</CFLOOP>

<!--- Set DayName variable to "Monday", "Tuesday", etc --->
<CFSET DayName = DayOfWeekAsString(Form.WhichDayOfWeek)>
```

```
<!--- Finally, display information to user --->
<CFOUTPUT>
  <I>The first #DayName# in #DateFormat(MonthStart, "mmmm, yyyy")# is:</I>
  <P>#DateFormat(TryThisDate, "dddd, mmmm d, yyyy")#<BR>
</CFOUTPUT>

</body>
</html>
```

The first day of the year is calculated by using CreateDate for January 1 of the year the user entered. Next, the FirstDayOfMonth function is used to populate the MonthStartOffset variable with the day number that indicates the first day of the month that the user entered. Then the DateAdd function is used to return a date/time value for the first day of the appropriate month, by adding MonthStartOffset days to the first day in the year.

Then the CFLOOP tag appears. It's told to compare the value returned by DayOfWeek(TryThisDate) to the DayOfWeekWanted variable. If the two are the same, the loop has completed its work and code execution continues after the CFLOOP. If, on the other hand, the two aren't the same, the DateAdd function is used again to add one more day to the TryThisDate date/time variable. Then the loop repeats itself.

The result is that eventually the TryThisDate variable holds the date the user was looking for. Figure 18.6 shows the results.

N O T E Due to the nature of dates, we, as human beings, know that this loop will execute only six times at the most. However, the CFLOOP really doesn't have that understanding. When you provide a CONDITION for a CFLOOP tag, or when you write a while loop (which will be demonstrated in a moment), make sure that the condition is guaranteed to be met eventually. Otherwise, your template could get caught in an infinite loop.

With Scripting Because the bulk of the code shown in Listing 18.11 is just about setting variables and making calculations, it's a natural piece of code to consider writing as a script instead of using tag-based ColdFusion code. You can create the looping effect that the CFLOOP provided by including a while statement in the script.

The basic syntax for the while statement is the same in CFScript as it is in JavaScript and C/C++. Notice that it also looks quite similar to the syntax for the if statement that you learned about earlier in this chapter.

Follow these simple steps to create a while loop within a script:

1. Type the word **while** at the appropriate spot in the script, followed by a pair of parentheses.
2. Inside the parentheses, type the condition that the while loop should repeatedly test for. The condition is whatever you would have supplied to the CONDITION parameter of a CFLOOP tag and can be any condition that would be valid in the context of a CFIF tag or an if statement.

Part

IV

Ch

18

FIGURE 18.6
When the condition is met, the requested date can be displayed for the user.

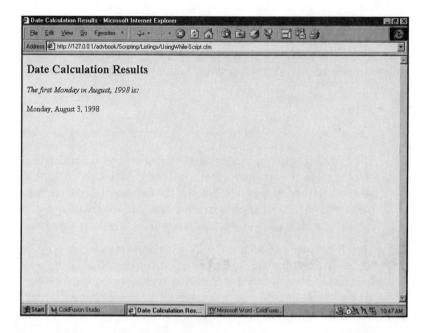

3. Place a pair of braces after the parentheses. Inside the braces, place the code that you want repeated until the `while` condition is met.

Listing 18.12 shows the scripted version of the logic from Listing 18.11. All expressions, decisions, and variables are exactly the same; the only thing that has changed is the syntax. To users, nothing has changed; the application will behave the same way and display the same result when the form is submitted (refer to Figure 18.6).

Listing 18.12 `UsingWhile-Script.cfm`—**Creating a `while` Loop with Script Syntax**

```
<!DOCTYPE HTML PUBLIC "-//W3C//DTD HTML 4 Transitional//EN">

<html>
<head>
    <title>Date Calculation Results</title>
</head>

<body>
<H2>Date Calculation Results</H2>

<!--- Do date-calculation "grunt work" with CFScript --->
<CFSCRIPT>
   // Set datetime var MonthStart to 1st day of selected Month
   DayOfWeekWanted = Form.WhichDayOfWeek;
   MonthStartOffset = FirstDayOfMonth(Form.TargetDate);
   YearStart = CreateDate(Year(Form.TargetDate), 1, 1);
   MonthStart = DateAdd("d", MonthStartOffset-1, YearStart);
```

```
  // Start at the first day of the month (determined above)
  TryThisDate = MonthStart;

  // Keep adding one day to TryThisDate until correct DayOfWeek
  while (DayOfWeek(TryThisDate) is not DayOfWeekWanted) {
    TryThisDate = DateAdd("d", 1, TryThisDate);
  }

  // Set DayName variable to "Monday", "Tuesday", etc
  DayName = DayOfWeekAsString(Form.WhichDayOfWeek);
</CFSCRIPT>

<!--- Finally, display information to user --->
<CFOUTPUT>
  <I>The first #DayName# in #DateFormat(MonthStart, "mmmm, yyyy")# is:</I>
  <P>#DateFormat(TryThisDate, "dddd, mmmm d, yyyy")#<BR>
</CFOUTPUT>

</body>
</html>
```

Guaranteeing That a `while` Loop Executes at Least Once: `do..while`   As you've already seen, the `while` loop in Listing 18.12 will repeat over and over until the condition between the parentheses is met. In most circumstances, this means that the code inside the loop will execute at least once. However, depending on the entries a user makes on the form, the code inside the loop might not execute at all.

For instance, what if the user picks a date during August 1998, and chooses Saturday for the day of the week? August 1, 1998, was a Saturday, which means that when the `while` loop is encountered in the script, the loop's condition has already been met. Therefore, the line that uses `DateAdd` inside the loop will never be executed.

If you want to guarantee that the code inside the loop will be executed at least once, you can use a variation on the `while` loop to get the job done. A `do..while` loop checks to see whether the condition has been met *after* each repetition of the loop rather than *before* each repetition.

 TIP   Sometimes you'll hear people refer to this type of looping construct as an `until` loop or a `do-until` loop.

Follow these simple steps to create a `do..while` loop in your script code:

1. Type **do** at the appropriate spot in your script, followed by a pair of braces.
2. Between the braces, place the script code that you want to be executed over and over by the loop.
3. After the braces, type **while**, followed by a pair of parentheses.
4. Between the parentheses, place the condition that you want the loop to check after each pass through the loop. If the condition is met, the loop has finished its work, and script execution continues directly after the parentheses. If, on the other hand, the condition hasn't been met yet, the script code inside the braces gets executed again.

The code in Listing 18.13 shows how to include a `do..while` loop in your script code. It's almost the same as Listing 18.12. The difference is that the `DateAdd` line inside the loop is guaranteed to "fire" at least once.

Listing 18.13 `UsingDoWhile-Script.cfm`—`do..while` **Loops Always Execute at Least Once**

```
<!DOCTYPE HTML PUBLIC "-//W3C//DTD HTML 4 Transitional//EN">

<html>
<head>
    <title>Date Calculation Results</title>
</head>

<body>
<H2>Date Calculation Results</H2>

<!--- Do date-calculation "grunt work" with CFScript --->
<CFSCRIPT>
  // Set datetime var MonthStart to 1st day of selected Month
  DayOfWeekWanted = Form.WhichDayOfWeek;
  MonthStartOffset = FirstDayOfMonth(Form.TargetDate);
  YearStart = CreateDate(Year(Form.TargetDate), 1, 1);
  MonthStart = DateAdd("d", MonthStartOffset-1, YearStart);

  // Start at the first day of the month (determined above)
  TryThisDate = MonthStart;

  // Keep adding one day to TryThisDate until correct DayOfWeek
  do {
    TryThisDate = DateAdd("d", 1, TryThisDate);
  } while (DayOfWeek(TryThisDate) is not DayOfWeekWanted)

  // Set DayName variable to "Monday", "Tuesday", etc
  DayName = DayOfWeekAsString(Form.WhichDayOfWeek);
</CFSCRIPT>

<!--- Finally, display information to user --->
<CFOUTPUT>
  <I>The first #DayName# in #DateFormat(MonthStart, "mmmm, yyyy")# is:</I>
  <P>#DateFormat(TryThisDate, "dddd, mmmm d, yyyy")#<BR>
</CFOUTPUT>

</body>
</html>
```

Repeating Code a Specific Number of Times: `for`

Another common type of loop commonly found in programming languages is a `for` loop, which is used to repeat a chunk of code for some preset number of times. In normal ColdFusion code, this type of looping is achieved by using TO and FROM parameters in a CFLOOP tag. CFScript allows you to code this type of loop in your scripts by supporting the `for` statement, as found in JavaScript and C/C++.

Without Scripting   Suppose that you need to create a one-dimensional ColdFusion array called `MonthArray` that holds the names of the months of the year. That is, `MonthArray[1]` should hold the string `"January"`, and so on. The easiest way to create this array with tag-based ColdFusion code would be to include a `CFLOOP` block in the template that counts from 1 to 12, appending the appropriate month name to the array as it goes.

The code in Listing 18.14 accomplishes this simple task. First, the array is created, using the `ArrayNew` function. Next, the `CFLOOP` block executes the `ArrayAppend` function 12 times in a row, advancing the value of the `Counter` variable by one for each pass through the loop. As a result, the expression `MonthAsString(Counter)` returns the appropriate month name. The third time through the loop, for instance, the `Counter` variable is 3, which causes the `MonthAsString` variable to return the word `"March"`.

Finally, a second `CFLOOP` is used to display the contents of the array to users to prove that the array was populated properly. Figure 18.7 shows the results.

Listing 18.14   `UsingFor-NoScript.cfm`—**Creating a `for`-Style Loop Without Script Syntax**

```
<!DOCTYPE HTML PUBLIC "-//W3C//DTD HTML 4 Transitional//EN">

<html>
<head>
    <title>Months of the Year</title>
</head>

<body>
<H2>Months of the Year</H2>

<!--- Create new array to hold months of year --->
<CFSET MonthArray = ArrayNew(1)>

<!--- Go from 1-12, populating array with month name --->
<CFLOOP FROM="1" TO="12" INDEX="Counter">
  <CFSET result = ArrayAppend(MonthArray, MonthAsString(Counter))>
</CFLOOP>

<!--- Display the contents of the array --->
<UL>
<CFLOOP FROM="1" TO="#ArrayLen(MonthArray)#" INDEX="ItemNum">
  <CFOUTPUT><LI>#MonthArray[ItemNum]#</CFOUTPUT>
</CFLOOP>
</UL>

</body>
</html>
```

Part
IV

Ch

18

FIGURE 18.7

The loop quickly populates an array with the months of the year.

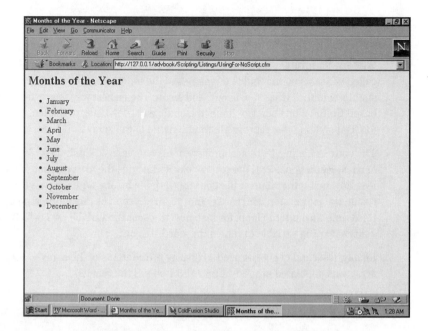

With Scripting   To get the effect of the CFLOOP block in the tag-based code shown in Listing 18.14 in a script, you can use CFScript's for statement. This statement, as implemented in CFScript, is similar to the for statement in JavaScript. Due to differences between the two languages, however, a working for loop looks a bit different in CFScript than it does in JavaScript.

Follow these steps to include a for loop in your CFScript code:

1. Type **for**, followed by a pair of parentheses.

2. Inside the parentheses, insert an expression that initializes the looping variable, followed by a semicolon.

3. After the semicolon, insert a condition that tests the value of the looping variable. The loop will continue executing over and over until the condition becomes true. After the condition, insert another semicolon.

4. After the second semicolon, insert an expression that changes the value of the looping variable, presumably bringing it closer to meeting the condition that you specified in step 3.

5. After the parentheses, place a pair of braces, and insert the script code that you want to be repeated inside the braces.

Listing 18.15 shows a version of the template shown in Listing 18.14, with the first CFLOOP replaced with script syntax. Look at the for loop in the CFSCRIPT block.

When the for statement is first encountered, ColdFusion evaluates the first expression inside the parentheses. In this case, that means setting the Counter variable to 1. Next, ColdFusion checks to see whether the condition (provided as the second item inside the parentheses) is true. Assuming that the condition is true, the code inside the loop itself is executed once. Then ColdFusion evaluates the last expression inside the parentheses, which in this case means that one is added to the current value of the Counter variable. This process repeats over and over again until Counter reaches 12. At that point, the condition fails, which causes the loop to end. Script execution then continues directly after the loop.

Listing 18.15 `UsingFor-Script.cfm`—**Creating a for Loop with Script-Style Syntax**

```
<!DOCTYPE HTML PUBLIC "-//W3C//DTD HTML 4 Transitional//EN">

<html>
<head>
    <title>Months of the Year</title>
</head>

<body>
<H2>Months of the Year</H2>

<CFSCRIPT>
  // Create new array to hold months of year
  MonthArray = ArrayNew(1);

  // Go from 1-12, populating array with month name
  for ( Counter = 1; Counter LTE 12; Counter = Counter + 1 ) {
    ArrayAppend(MonthArray, MonthAsString(Counter));
  }
</CFSCRIPT>

<!--- Display the contents of the array --->
<UL>
<CFLOOP FROM="1" TO="#ArrayLen(MonthArray)#" INDEX="ItemNum">
  <CFOUTPUT><LI>#MonthArray[ItemNum]#</CFOUTPUT>
</CFLOOP>
</UL>

</body>
</html>
```

Part

IV

Ch

18

By providing different expressions to the three items inside the for parentheses, you can gain much control over how the loop behaves. Suppose that you want the loop to count backward from 12 to 1, and that you want it to skip every second and third month. To get this effect, you can change the first expression inside the parentheses to start the Counter variable at 12 instead of 1. Then you can change the second expression to test whether the Counter variable has reached 1 yet. Finally, change the third expression so that it subtracts three from Counter for each pass through the loop rather than adding one to it.

Listing 18.16 shows the revised template, which counts backward and stops at only every third month. Figure 18.8 shows the results.

Listing 18.16 `UsingFor-ScriptReverse.cfm`—**Adapting the Loop to Count Backward and Skip Values**

```
<!DOCTYPE HTML PUBLIC "-//W3C//DTD HTML 4 Transitional//EN">

<html>
<head>
    <title>Months of the Year</title>
</head>

<body>
<H2>Months of the Year</H2>

<CFSCRIPT>
  // Create new array to hold months of year
  MonthArray = ArrayNew(1);

  // Go from 1-12, populating array with month name
  for ( Counter = 12; Counter GTE 1; Counter = Counter - 3 ) {
    ArrayAppend(MonthArray, MonthAsString(Counter));
  }
</CFSCRIPT>

<!--- Display the contents of the array --->
<UL>
<CFLOOP FROM="1" TO="#ArrayLen(MonthArray)#" INDEX="ItemNum">
  <CFOUTPUT><LI>#MonthArray[ItemNum]#</CFOUTPUT>
</CFLOOP>
</UL>

</body>
</html>
```

NOTE If you want to adapt the CFLOOP tag shown in Listing 18.14 so that it steps backward in the same way, you can swap the values of the FROM and TO parameters. Then add a STEP="-3" parameter to make the CFLOOP go back three months at a time. The UsingFor-NoScriptReverse.cfm template included on the CD provides an example. ■

Skipping the Rest of a Loop Iteration: `continue`

Sometimes you might want to abort a particular pass through a loop without aborting the loop itself. Suppose that you need to adapt the template shown in Listing 18.15 so that the script code inside the loop doesn't execute for the month of September. CFScript provides a `continue` statement that you can use for this task. The `continue` statement causes ColdFusion to skip the rest of the current loop iteration. Script execution proceeds immediately to the next iteration of the loop.

For instance, look at Listing 18.17. A simple `if` statement checks to see whether the loop is now processing the month of September. If it is, the `continue` statement is used to abort the current pass through the loop. The loop picks up at the next pass, which in this case means that it picks up at October.

FIGURE 18.8

This loop counts backward, decreasing the `Counter` variable by three with each pass.

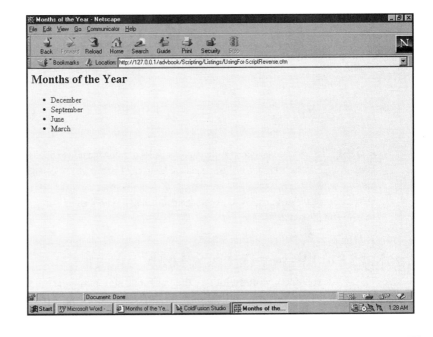

Listing 18.17 `UsingContinue-Script.cfm`—**Using** continue **to Skip Past the Rest of a Loop**

```
<!DOCTYPE HTML PUBLIC "-//W3C//DTD HTML 4 Transitional//EN">

<html>
<head>
    <title>Months of the Year</title>
</head>

<body>
<H2>Months of the Year</H2>

<CFSCRIPT>
  // Create new array to hold months of year
  MonthArray = ArrayNew(1);

  // Go from 1-12, populating array with month name
  for ( Counter = 1; Counter LTE 12; Counter = Counter + 1 ) {
    if (MonthAsString(Counter) is "September") {
      continue;
    }
    ArrayAppend(MonthArray, MonthAsString(Counter));
  }
</CFSCRIPT>

<!--- Display the contents of the array --->
<UL>
<CFLOOP FROM="1" TO="#ArrayLen(MonthArray)#" INDEX="ItemNum">
```

continues

Listing 18.17   Continued

```
  <CFOUTPUT><LI>#MonthArray[ItemNum]#</CFOUTPUT>
</CFLOOP>
</UL>

</body>
</html>
```

N O T E   You can also use `continue` in a `while` loop. When the `continue` is encountered, the
script rechecks the `while` condition. Assuming that the `while` condition hasn't yet been
met, the script starts going through the loop again. If, on the other hand, the `while` condition became
true just before the `continue` was encountered, the loop has finished its work and script execution
continues at the spot right under the loop. ▣

Breaking Completely Out of a Loop: `break`

The `break` statement works a lot like the `continue` statement, except that it causes the entire
loop to stop executing, rather than only the current pass through the loop. For instance, if you
want the code in Listing 18.17 to stop looping when it reaches the month of September (rather
than merely skip it), you can change the word `continue` to `break`. After the condition in the `if`
statement is met, the `break` statement executes, which causes the entire `for` loop to abort
itself. Script execution continues at the spot right after the loop.

TIP   You can also use `break` in a `while` loop. As soon as the `break` is encountered, the loop is "broken out
of." Script execution continues at the spot right under the loop.

Looping over Structures and Variables: `for-in`

In addition to `while` and `for` loops, CFScript also allows you to create `for-in` loops, which
execute once for each element of a ColdFusion structure variable. The structure variable can
be created with the `StructNew` function, or it can be a built-in structure variable that
ColdFusion makes available to you automatically.

For instance, you might have a `Colors` structure variable, filled with color names and each
color's associated hexadecimal value. By looping over the elements of the structure—where an
element might be `Color["Blue"]` or `Color["Red"]`—you can easily output all the available
color names and their values.

Without Scripting   The way to create such a loop using traditional tag-based syntax is to use
the `CFLOOP` tag with a `COLLECTION` attribute. By specifying the structure variable as the collection, you tell ColdFusion that you're interested in processing the code between the `CFLOOP`
blocks for each name/value pair in the structure.

For instance, the code in Listing 18.18 uses this type of looping construct twice. The first
`CFLOOP` loops over the contents of the `Colors` structure variable that has been created by the

StructNew function near the top of the template. Because four key/value pairs have been added to the structure, the code inside the loop executes four times. Each time through the loop, the variable named ThisColor gets set to the "key" value for the current item in the structure. Thus, displaying the color names and values between a pair of CFOUTPUT tags becomes a simple matter.

The second CFLOOP loops over the contents of the built-in Application structure (which ColdFusion automatically makes available when Application Management has been enabled with the CFAPPLICATION tag). The loop executes three times, once for each variable set in the Application scope, setting the ThisVar variable to the current "key" value. All that's needed is to display the variable name and associated value between a pair of CFOUTPUT tags. (This example outputs only the three Application variables set at the top of the template. Of course, if other Application variables had been set in other pages, they would be output by this code as well.) The end result is that the keys and values for the Colors and Application structures are "dumped" onscreen. Figure 18.9 shows the results.

Listing 18.18 UsingForIn-NoScript.cfm—**Looping over the Contents of a Structure**

```
<!--- Enable Application Management --->
<!--- Then set some Application variables --->
<CFAPPLICATION NAME="A2Z">
<CFSET Application.Datasource = "A2Z">
<CFSET Application.AppTitle = "A2Z Books">
<CFSET Application.InfoEmail = "info@a2zbooks.com">

<!--- Create a Structure called Colors --->
<CFSCRIPT>
  Colors = StructNew();
  Colors["Red"]   = "FF0000";
  Colors["White"] = "FFFFFF";
  Colors["Black"] = "000000";
  Colors["Blue"]  = "0000FF";
</CFSCRIPT>


<!DOCTYPE HTML PUBLIC "-//W3C//DTD HTML 4 Transitional//EN">

<html>
<head>
  <title>Looping over Structures</title>
</head>

<body>
<H2>Looping over Structures</H2>


<!--- Loop over the "Colors" Structure --->
<P><I>Listing colors:</I><BR>
<CFLOOP COLLECTION="#Colors#" ITEM="ThisColor">
```

continues

Listing 18.18 Continued

```
<!--- ThisColor is the "index" of "current" Color member --->
<CFOUTPUT>
  <B>#ThisColor#</B> - hex #Colors[ThisColor]#<BR>
</CFOUTPUT>
</CFLOOP>


<!--- Loop over the built-in "Application" Structure --->
<P><I>Listing Application variables:</I><BR>
<CFLOOP COLLECTION="#Application#" ITEM="ThisVar">
  <!--- ThisVar is the "index" of "current" Application member --->
  <CFOUTPUT>
    <B>Variable: #ThisVar# </B><BR>
    Value: #Application[ThisVar]#<BR>
  </CFOUTPUT>
</CFLOOP>


</body>
</html>
```

FIGURE 18.9

The contents of the Colors and Application structures are displayed to the user.

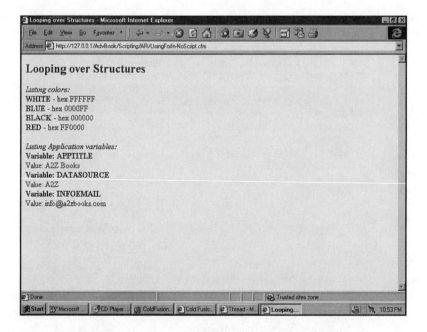

NOTE ColdFusion also provides a built-in structure named Session that works just like the Application structure does, except for Session variables. So, if you need to enumerate the names and values of all currently defined session variables, you can use code similar to the first CFLOOP in Listing 18.18. Just replace the word Application throughout with Session. ■

With Scripting   To get the same effect using script syntax, you can use CFScript's `for-in` statement to create the scripted equivalents of the CFLOOP-style loops that you saw in Listing 18.18. Follow these steps to include a `for-in` loop in your CFScript code:

1. Type **for**, followed by a pair of parentheses.

2. Inside the parentheses, type a variable name, then the word **in**, and then the name of the structure. The loop will execute once for each key/value pair in the structure. Each time through the loop, ColdFusion will populate this variable with the "key" for the current key/value pair.

3. After the parentheses, place the code that you want the loop to repeat, wrapped in a pair of braces.

The code in Listing 18.19 shows how to use `for-in` statements in CFScript code. The result when viewed in a browser will be the same as for Listing 18.18 (shown in Figure 18.9).

N O T E   As you look at Listing 18.19, note that the `WriteOutput` function has been used inside the `for-in` loops to output information onto the current Web page. You can use the `WriteOutput` function anywhere that functions are allowed in ColdFusion templates (such as `CFSET` tags and so on), but it is really designed to be used inside `CFSCRIPT` blocks like you see here. Because you can't use `CFOUTPUT` tags inside scripts, the folks at Allaire wanted to provide some other way of sending text and HTML to the browser from CFScript, so they included the `WriteOutput` function. It's comparable to the `write` and `writeln` functions in JavaScript. ■

Part IV

Ch

18

Listing 18.19 `UsingForIn-Script.cfm`—**Using `for-in` Statements to Loop over Structure Contents**

```
<!--- Enable Application Management --->.i.listings:for-in statements;.i.for-in
loops:CFScript:listing;
<!--- Then set some Application variables --->
<CFAPPLICATION NAME="A2Z">
<CFSET Application.Datasource = "A2Z">
<CFSET Application.AppTitle = "A2Z Books">
<CFSET Application.InfoEmail = "info@a2zbooks.com">

<!--- Create a Structure called Colors --->
<CFSCRIPT>
  Colors = StructNew();
  Colors["Red"]   = "FF0000";
  Colors["White"] = "FFFFFF";
  Colors["Black"] = "000000";
  Colors["Blue"]  = "0000FF";
</CFSCRIPT>


<!DOCTYPE HTML PUBLIC "-//W3C//DTD HTML 4 Transitional//EN">

<html>
<head>
```

continues

Listing 18.19 Continued

```
    <title>Looping over Structures</title>
  </head>

  <body>
  <H2>Looping over Structures</H2>


  <!--- Loop over the "Colors" Structure --->
  <P><I>Listing colors:</I><BR>
  <CFSCRIPT>
    for (ThisColor in Colors) {
      // ThisColor is the "index" of "current" structure element
      WriteOutput("<B>#ThisColor#</B> - hex #Colors[ThisColor]#<BR>");
    }
  </CFSCRIPT>


  <!--- Loop over the built-in "Application" Structure --->
  <P><I>Listing Application variables:</I><BR>
  <CFSCRIPT>
    for (ThisVar in Application) {
      // ThisVar is the "index" of "current" structure element
      WriteOutput("<B>Variable: #ThisVar# </B><BR>");.i.listings:for-in
  statements;.i.for-in loops:CFScript:listing;
      WriteOutput("Value: #Application[ThisVar]#<BR>");
    }
  </CFSCRIPT>


  </body>
  </html>
```

You can also use for-in loops to loop over a "collection" returned by a COM or CORBA object that has been invoked with the CFOBJECT tag. Just put the variable that represents the collection after the in keyword inside the script. You provide this type of loop to the COLLECTION attribute of a CFLOOP tag if you want to loop over the collection using traditional tag-based syntax. See Chapter 12, "Extending ColdFusion with COM/DCOM," and Chapter 13, "Extending ColdFusion with CORBA," for more information about using COM and CORBA objects in your ColdFusion templates.

Structured Error and Retry Handling

Using Standard Error Handling

For most developers, error messages are a fact of life. Many things can happen to cause error messages to be displayed, and most of them fall into one of three categories:

- Invalid code—Illegal code use, invalid attribute values, the use of mutually exclusive attributes, or just simple typos

- Unanticipated conditions—Users going directly to form action pages, alphanumeric data entered into a field when numeric data was expected, referencing URL parameters that a user might not submit, or any other unanticipated condition

- External factors—Databases timing out or running out of connections; mail servers not responding; broken Internet connections causing HTP, FTP, SMTP, POP, and LDAP calls to fail; and any other error beyond your control

Many things can go wrong, and many do.

ColdFusion displays error messages when errors occur, messages such as the one shown in Figure 19.1.

FIGURE 19.1

ColdFusion error message screens provide detailed error information.

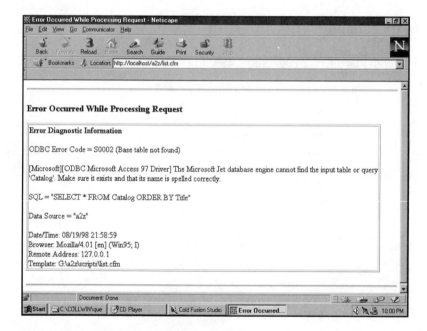

ColdFusion has two built-in error message screens:

- Request error messages are displayed if an error prevents ColdFusion from continuing template processing. These errors include CFML syntax errors, ODBC or database errors, and operating system or file system errors.

■ Validation error messages are displayed if a form submission fails an embedded validation test.

When either error type occurs, the user sees a default ColdFusion error message screen.

Custom Error Messages

Although the default message provides an exact description of what went wrong, that's not always a good thing. You might not want visitors knowing that you passed an incorrect parameter to a ColdFusion function, that you misspelled a variable name, that you constructed an invalid SQL statement, or that your database server ran out of disk space. You also might not want your visitors knowing any details about the underlying databases and architecture within your application, details that the default error messages expose.

For these reasons, and so that you can create more polished-looking applications, ColdFusion allows you to override the standard error messages with messages of your own. To do so, you use the ColdFusion <CFERROR> tag, which lets you specify the name of another ColdFusion file that will be displayed instead of the standard message. <CFERROR> takes three attributes:

■ MAILTO is an optional attribute used to specify the email address of the system administrator. This information isn't displayed automatically, but it's available to you as a variable within the error template.

■ TEMPLATE specifies the name of the template to be displayed if an error occurs. This attribute is required.

■ TYPE is the error type for which the specified template will be displayed. Valid types are REQUEST or VALIDATE. This attribute is required.

TIP The <CFERROR> tag can appear anywhere within your application, but the ideal place for it is actually in the "application template," application.cfm. Putting <CFERROR> in the application template ensures that your entire application will use the custom error messages.

Part
IV
Ch
19

Custom error templates can't use any ColdFusion tags or functions. The only content can be literal text (including HTML or any other client-side technology) and a series of special variables described in this chapter.

N O T E Because ColdFusion tags can't be used within an error template, <CFOUTPUT> isn't needed to be able to refer to the error variables. ColdFusion treats the entire file as though it were enclosed within a <CFOUTPUT> block. ■

Customizing Request Error Messages

Request error messages are a catchall for every error condition other than invalid form field submission. Request error messages are displayed for the following:

■ CFML syntax errors
■ ODBC and database errors

- Low memory or disk space situations
- Request timeouts
- Errors returned by COM/DCOM, CFXs, or interfaces to any other systems
- Any unknown error conditions

The default error message screen (see Figure 19.2) provides detailed information about the error that occurred—sometimes a bit too detailed. This kind of error message is likely to confuse users, create the notion that your site is buggy, and give an all-around unprofessional impression.

FIGURE 19.2

The default request error message screen provides information that's sometimes a bit too detailed.

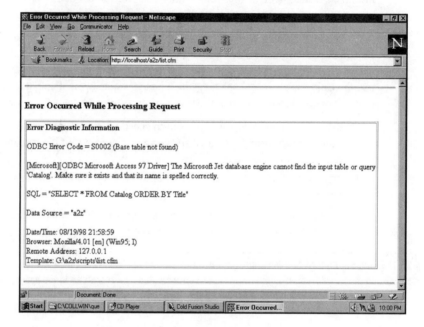

To create a replacement request error message screen, follow these steps:

1. Create a template for ColdFusion to display when an error occurs, using any variables listed in Table 19.1.

2. If no APPLICATION.CFM file exists, create one in the current directory or any directory above it.

3. Insert a <CFERROR> tag in the application.cfm file pointing to the error message template created in step 1, specifying a TYPE of REQUEST.

To understand how to use these variables, look at an example. Listing 19.1 shows code for a request error message screen.

Table 19.1 Request Error Message Variables

Name	Description
Browser	The browser that the client was running, with whatever version and platform information the browser provided
DateTime	The date and time that the error occurred
Diagnostics	Detailed diagnostic error message
HTTPReferer	URL of the page from which the template was accessed
MailTo	System administrator's email address, as specified in the <CFERROR> MAILTO attribute
QueryString	The URL's query string
RemoteAddress	IP address of client
Template	Name of the file being processed when the error occurred

Listing 19.1 error_req.cfm—Sample Request Error Template

```
<HTML>

<HEAD>
<TITLE>Error!</TITLE>
</HEAD>

<BODY>

<CENTER>

<TABLE BORDER=5>
 <TR>
  <TH>
   An error has occurred that prevents us from completing your request.
  </TH>
 </TR>
 <TR>
  <TD>
   We have logged the following information that will help us identify and
   correct the problem:
   <UL>
    <LI>Error occurred at <B>#ERROR.Datetime#</B>
    <LI>Your IP address is <B>#ERROR.RemoteAddress#</B>
    <LI>Your browser is <B>#ERROR.Browser#</B>
    <LI>You were trying to process <B>#ERROR.Template#?#ERROR.QueryString#</B>
   </UL>
   If you can provide us with any additional information that would help us
   fix this problem, please send E-Mail to:
   <A HREF="mailto:#ERROR.MailTo#">#ERROR.MailTo#</A>.
  </TD>
```

Part

IV

Ch

19

continues

Listing 19.1   Continued

```
  </TR>
  </TABLE>

  </CENTER>

  </BODY>

  </HTML>
```

Look closer at the code in Listing 19.1. Most of it is standard HTML; the only non-HTML code references are six ERROR variables from the list in Table 19.1. To use these variables, you must enclose them within pound signs and specify the prefix ERROR, as follows:

```
#ERROR.Browser#
```

Now all you have to do is instruct ColdFusion to use this error message template. To do so, add the following to the application.cfm file:

```
<!--- Custom error message for request errors --->
<CFERROR TYPE="REQUEST" TEMPLATE="error_req.cfm" MAILTO="webmaster@a2zbooks.com">
```

Figure 19.3 shows the new error message that would be displayed for the same error that generated the screen in Figure 19.2. Obviously, the screen shown in Figure 19.3 is more professional, as well as more user-friendly.

TIP   You can use *any* client technologies within error templates, including HTML, DHTML, JavaScript, VBScript, Java, and ActiveX. By using them, you can create even more friendly error screens.

FIGURE 19.3

Custom request error messages allow you to present more professional and user-friendly error screens.

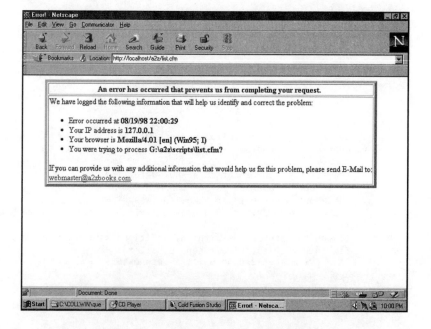

Customizing Form Validation Error Messages

Validation error messages are displayed when embedded hidden form validation rules are used, and form field validation occurs. The default error screen, shown in Figure 19.4, displays a fixed header and footer and an HTML unordered list of the validation errors.

FIGURE 19.4

The default validation error screen uses fixed header and footer text and a simple list of errors.

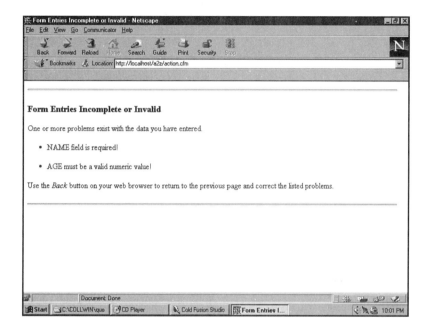

Like the request errors discussed in the preceding section, validation errors can also be overridden if you want. ColdFusion doesn't provide very much flexibility in VALIDATE message files, but you can use HTML elements and other client technologies to make the error screen seem more professional.

To create a replacement validation error message screen, follow these steps:

1. Create a template for ColdFusion to display when an error occurs, using any variables listed in Table 19.2.

2. If no application.cfm file exists, create one in the current directory or any directory above it.

3. Insert a <CFERROR> tag in the application.cfm file pointing to the error message template created in step 1, specifying a TYPE of VALIDATE.

To understand these steps, look at an example. Listing 19.2 contains code for a validation error message screen.

Part
IV

Ch

19

Table 19.2 Validation Error Message Variables

Name	Description
InvalidFields	List of the field form fields
ValidationFooter	Text for footer of error message
ValidationHeader	Text for header of error message

Listing 19.2 `error_val.cfm`—Sample Validation Error Template

```
<HTML>
<HEAD>
<TITLE>Field Validation Error</TITLE>
</HEAD>

<BODY>

<TABLE BORDER="1">
<TR>
 <TH>
  FORM VALIDATION ERROR
 </TH>
</TR>
<TR>
 <TD>
  One or more errors were found in your form submission,
  as shown below. Please click your browser's <B>Back</B>
  button, make any necessary corrections, and then
  resubmit the form.
 </TD>
</TR>
<TR>
 <TD>
  <BR><B>#ERROR.InvalidFields#</B><BR>
 </TD>
</TR>
</TABLE>

</BODY>
</HTML>
```

As before, the code in Listing 19.2 is primarily HTML, with the exception of a reference to #ERROR.InvalidFields#, which returns an unordered HTML list of the validation errors.

Now all you have to do is tell ColdFusion to use this error message template. Add the following to the application.cfm file:

```
<!--- Custom error message for form validation errors --->
<CFERROR TYPE="VALIDATION" TEMPLATE="error_val.cfm">
```

Figure 19.5 shows the new error message that would be displayed for the same error that generated the screen in Figure 19.4.

FIGURE 19.5

Custom validation error messages allow you to present more professional and user-friendly error screens.

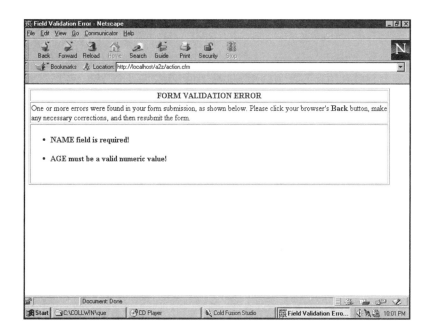

Understanding Structured Error Handling

As useful as <CFERROR> is in creating more visually appealing error messages, it still has one serious limitation: ColdFusion's standard response to an error is aborting further processing, whether or not default or custom error screens are used. <CFERROR> doesn't change how ColdFusion responds to error conditions; all it does is change the display generated after processing is halted.

To completely control error handling, you must use ColdFusion's Structured Error Handling, with which you can write code blocks to execute if an error occurs. When these blocks are defined, ColdFusion transfers code execution to them when an error occurs, rather than continues to process whatever it was that generated the error.

Exception Handling Terminology

Before looking at how ColdFusion supports Structured Error Handling, take a quick look at some terminology used in this technology:

- Exception—An exception is simply an error condition.

- Throw—When an error occurs, an exception is thrown. *Throwing* simply means that program control is thrown (rerouted) to another block of code.

- Raise—Another term for *throw*, you will sometimes see references to exceptions being *raised*.

Part
IV

Ch
19

- Try—Any code to support Structured Error Handling needs to be in a try block. This simply means that the entire code block is enclosed within some identifier that tells the application that exceptions within the block are to be thrown.

- Catch—When an exception is thrown, it's caught by a *catch block*, a block of code that has been designated as the recipient of thrown exceptions.

These terms aren't ColdFusion inventions; *try catch* technology is used by many languages, including C++ and other object-oriented languages. Like those other languages, setting up exception handling involves enclosing your ColdFusion application code within a try block and then creating a series of catch blocks. When an error occurs anywhere within the code in the try block, an exception is thrown, and it's then caught by the catch block. The code flow looks something like this:

```
Start TRY block
 Application goes here
 Start CATCH block
  Error-handling code goes here
 End CATCH block
End TRY block
```

As soon as an error occurs anywhere within the try block, execution is thrown to the catch block.

Creating Try Blocks with <CFTRY>

Creating try blocks in ColdFusion is simple. All you need to do is surround your code with <CFTRY> and </CFTRY> tags. Any code within those tags—your entire application, most likely—will then support Structured Error Handling. If you use the same code flow from the preceding section, your code would look like this:

```
<CFTRY>
 Application goes here
 Start CATCH block
  Error-handling code goes here
 End CATCH block
</CFTRY>
```

 T I P Application.cfm is *not* a good location for the <CFTRY> tag because you have no simple way of ensuring that you would have a matching </CFTRY> tag. As such, your best bet is to have standard include files that you include at the top and bottom of all other templates. The file included at the top starts the try block with a <CFTRY> tag, and the file included at the bottom contains the catch blocks and the </CFTRY> tag.

Now that you've set up a try block, you next need to set up your catch blocks.

Creating Catch Blocks with <CFCATCH>

You set up ColdFusion catch blocks by using the <CFCATCH> and </CFCATCH> tags. Catch blocks have a TYPE associated with them, which specifies the type of error that the catch block should handle. The following types are supported:

- ■ Any handles all exception types, including any unexpected exceptions not explicitly handled by any other exception type.
- ■ Application handles any exceptions explicitly thrown by your application (more details on this issue later in this chapter).
- ■ Database handles ODBC, SQL, and native database driver errors, including any errors generated by <CFQUERY>, <CFINSERT>, <CFUPDATE>, and <CFSTOREDPROC>.
- ■ MissingInclude handles exceptions thrown by the <CFINCLUDE> tag when it can't locate an included template.
- ■ Object handles exceptions thrown by <CFOBJECT> calls to COM/DCOM or CORBA objects.
- ■ Security handles any exceptions thrown by the security tags and functions.
- ■ Template handles application-level exceptions, including all CFML syntax errors.

Every <CFTRY> block needs at least one catch block (one set of <CFCATCH> and </CFCATCH>), but you can specify multiple catch blocks. If you use only one catch block, it should be of type Any so that it can handle all exceptions. Particular exception types can be handled with separate catch blocks.

N O T E Catch blocks are processed sequentially; the first matching block handles the thrown exception. Therefore, if multiple catch blocks are used, the Any block must be the final block in the set. ■

Again, if you use the same code flow as before, your code would look like this:

```
<CFTRY>
 Application goes here
 <CFCATCH TYPE="Any">
  Error-handling code goes here
 </CFCATCH>
</CFTRY>
```

Part

IV

Ch

19

To handle database exceptions separate from any other exceptions, the code flow would look like this:

```
<CFTRY>
 Application goes here
 <CFCATCH TYPE="Database">
  Database error-handling code goes here
 </CFCATCH>
 <CFCATCH TYPE="Any">
  Generic error-handling code goes here
 </CFCATCH>
</CFTRY>
```

Of course, the application can be any application whatsoever, with as many lines of code, queries, and includes as needed. Regardless of the size or complexity of your application, the basic concepts are the same:

1. Create a try block by putting a `<CFTRY>` tag before your application code.
2. After your application code, insert one or more catch blocks using `<CFCATCH>` and `</CFCATCH>`.
3. End your application with a `</CFTRY>` tag to close the try block.

The code between `<CFCATCH>` and `</CFCATCH>` is executed when an exception is thrown. Unlike the error message files used by `<CFERROR>`, the code in a catch block can include *any* ColdFusion tags and functions.

 T I P The default `<CFCATCH>` TYPE is Any. You therefore can specify `<CFCATCH>` instead of `<CFCATCH TYPE="Any">` if you want.

Processing Error Information

To assist you in error processing, ColdFusion passes diagnostic information to your catch blocks. This information is stored in a series of variables as listed in Table 19.3.

Table 19.3 `<CFCATCH>` **Diagnostic Variables**

Variable Name	Description
Detail	A detailed message (generated by ColdFusion itself) describing the error condition. It is essentially the text that would have been displayed in the standard error message pages.
Message	The exception's diagnostic message. It may be empty if no message was provided.
NativeErrorCode	This variable is available only if TYPE is Database, in which case it contains the error code as returned by the database driver. The value is –1 if the database driver doesn't return a value.
SQLState	This variable is available only if TYPE is Database, in which case it contains any diagnostic information returned by the database driver. The value is –1 if the database driver doesn't return any information.
Type	The type of exception thrown.

To display this information, you must refer to the variable by using a fully qualified variable name using the CFCATCH prefix. Consider this example:

```
<CFOUTPUT>
Error message: #CFCATCH.message#
</CFOUTPUT>
```

To better understand how to use these variables, look at Listing 19.3.

Listing 19.3   Sample Application Using Structured Error Handling

```
<!--- Start try block --->
<CFTRY>

<!--- Get inventory --->
<CFQUERY DATASOURCE="A2Z" NAME="books">
SELECT title, last_name, first_name, quantity
FROM Inventory
ORDER BY title, last_name, first_name
</CFQUERY>

<!--- Display books --->
<TABLE BORDER="1">
 <TR>
  <TH>Title</TH>
  <TH>Author</TH>
  <TH>Quantity</TH>
 </TR>
 <CFOUTPUT QUERY="books">
  <TR>
   <TD>#title#</TD>
   <TD>#last_name#, #first_name#</TD>
   <TD>#quantity#</TD>
  </TR>
 </CFOUTPUT>
</TABLE>

<!--- Database catch block --->
<CFCATCH TYPE="Database">

 <!--- Feedback to user --->
 Sorry, we are experiencing database problems at this time.
 Please try your search again later.

 <!--- Send E-Mail to the admin --->
 <CFMAIL TO="webmaster@a2zbooks.com"
         FROM="webmaster@a2zbooks.com"
              SUBJECT="EXCEPTION: #CFCATCH.type#">
 Message:    #CFCATCH.message#
 Error Code: #CFCATCH.nativeerrorcode#
 SQL State:  #CFCATCH.sqlstate#
 Detail:     #CFCATCH.detail#
 </CFMAIL>

</CFCATCH>

<!--- All other errors --->
<CFCATCH TYPE="Any">

 <!--- Send E-Mail to the admin --->
 <CFMAIL TO="webmaster@a2zbooks.com"
         FROM="webmaster@a2zbooks.com"
              SUBJECT="EXCEPTION: #CFCATCH.type#">
```

Part

IV

Ch

19

continues

Listing 19.3 Continued

```
Message:     #CFCATCH.message#
Detail:      #CFCATCH.detail#
</CFMAIL>

<!--- Send the user to a feedback page --->
<CFLOCATION URL="feedback.cfm">

</CFCATCH>

<!--- End try block --->
</CFTRY>
```

Listing 19.3 is a simple ColdFusion template. It retrieves data from a database and displays it within an HTML table. But unlike other templates you've seen before, Listing 19.3 uses Structured Error Handling to trap any thrown exceptions.

To do so, you enclose the entire listing within a try block. The code starts with a <CFTRY> and ends with a </CFTRY>.

At the bottom of the listing are two catch blocks. The first is a Database catch block; it traps any exceptions thrown by the <CFQUERY> tag. If an exception is thrown, the user sees an explanatory error message (and not any database errors), and an email message is sent to the administrator describing the problem in detail.

The second catch block catches all other exceptions. An email message is sent to the administrator, and then the user is rerouted to a feedback screen using the <CFLOCATION> tag.

Throwing Exceptions with <CFTHROW>

The exceptions you've looked at so far are ones generated by ColdFusion itself. In addition to the standard exceptions, ColdFusion allows you to throw exceptions of your own. This capability allows you to

- Abort processing if required variables aren't present
- Trap unauthorized application access
- Stop processing if logical errors occur (for example, no records returned by a query that's valid for a database operation but might not be valid within your application)
- Write your own error-handling system by passing error messages to the catch blocks

Exceptions are explicitly thrown using the <CFTHROW> tag. <CFTHROW> takes one optional attribute, the MESSAGE to be passed to the catch block. Exceptions thrown with <CFTHROW> are handled by a catch block of TYPE Application (and of course by TYPE Any if no explicit Application block was specified).

Your code to throw an exception will look something like this:

```
<CFIF FORM.password IS NOT user.password>
 <CFTHROW MESSAGE="Invalid password, access denied">
</CFIF>
```

Structured Error Handling Dos and Don'ts

ColdFusion's Structured Error Handling is a powerful tool, one that can help you build more professional and user-friendly applications. To help you take advantage of this new capability, here are some dos and don'ts to bear in mind:

- Enclose your entire application within a try block, not just parts of it.
- You can nest try blocks. To debug a specific part of an application, put a try block around it; when an exception is thrown, ColdFusion examines the try stack and passes control to the current try block only.
- Having a generic try block around an entire application and specific try blocks around specific code that needs different handling can often be useful.
- Don't use application.cfm to start a try block.
- Make sure that every try block has a catch block of type Any, and make sure that it's the last catch block in the list.
- For more precise exception handling, create multiple catch blocks, one for each exception TYPE.
- Catch blocks can throw exceptions themselves, allowing you to trap specific exceptions that require special handling.
- You don't need to use catch blocks just for terminating processes gracefully. You can use catch blocks to redirect back to a page so that an operation is retried, or any other operation or function, too.
- Make sure that no code at all appears between the last </CFCATCH> and the closing </CFTRY>.

Part
IV

Ch
19

## CHAPTER 20

Regular Expressions

In this chapter

Introduction to Regular Expressions

Many people have referred to ColdFusion as "Super Perl." This is mainly because, like Perl, ColdFusion can be used for anything and everything. In many places it is actually superior, but in one special case it has been inferior—until now.

One of Perl's best features is a set of capabilities called *regular expressions*, which is basically a small quasi-language used to perform pattern matching and manipulation of text blocks. This allows Perl to do powerful text searches and manipulation with a small amount of code and development time. ColdFusion has supported a subset of this quasi-language since version 2.0, but it never saw much acceptance. With the release of version 4, this subset has been enhanced and now gives most, if not all, of the capabilities of regular expressions. This now promises to be one of the most awaited features.

ColdFusion Support for Regular Expressions

ColdFusion support for regular expressions is done via four functions: REFind, REFindNoCase, REReplace, and REReplaceNoCase. The prefix RE indicates that these are regular expression functions; the rest of the function title is self-explanatory. This chapter first examines the structure of these functions and then gives a full explanation of the regular expression quasi-language, paying special attention to where ColdFusion support may differ from other implementations.

REFind and REFindNoCase

These functions return the position of the regular expression's first occurrence in a text block starting from a specified position in the block. If the regular expression is not found, 0 is returned. REFind is case sensitive, while REFindNoCase is not case sensitive. The REFind/REFindNoCase functions use the following syntax as well as the attributes listed in Table 20.1:

```
REFind(reg_expression, string [, start] [, returnsubexpressions ])
```

Table 20.1   REFind/REFindNoCase **Attributes**

Name	Status	Description
reg_expression	Required	Regular expression used for search.
String	Required	String being searched.
Start	Optional	Starting position for the search.
Returnsubexpressions	Optional	Boolean indicating whether subexpressions are returned. If you set this parameter to TRUE, the function returns a CFML structure with two arrays containing the positions and lengths of the matched subexpressions, if any. You can retrieve from the structure using the keys pos and len. If there are no occurrences of the regular expression, the pos and len arrays each contain 1 (value = 0).

The following examples show you the functions in action. This chapter discusses the actual regular expression syntax later. For now, pay attention to the tag usage.

Find the first case-sensitive occurrence of a followed by c:

```
REFind("ac", "abcaaccdd"): 5
```

Find the first case-sensitive occurrence of one or more as followed by one or more cs:

```
REFind("a+c+", "abcaaccdd"): 4
```

Find the case-sensitive occurrence of the backslash (\), question mark (?), or ampersand (&) followed by the text string rep followed by an equal sign (=):

```
REFind("[\?&]rep=", "report.cfm?rep=1234&u=5"):11
```

Find the first non–case-sensitive occurrence of one or more as followed by one or more cs:

```
REFindNoCase("a+c+", "ABCAACCDD"): 4
```

Find the first non–case-sensitive occurrence of one or more as followed by any number of cs, including none:

```
REFindNoCase("a+c*", "ABCAACCDD"): 1
```

The final example is a little special because it shows ColdFusion's capability to return subexpressions. This is a standard piece of code that finds a word followed by any number of spaces that is, in turn, followed by the same word. The part of the regular expression that is written ([A-Za-z]+) means any series of non-numeric and non-special characters. The [ ]+ part means one or more spaces, and the \1 is a copy of whatever the first character sequence finds (a duplicate, for example).

```
REFind("([A-Za-z]+)[ ]+\1","There is is a cat in in the kitchen",1,"TRUE")
```

The result is not a single number and it fails if placed within a CFOUTPUT. The results include two arrays that contain the length and position of the regular expression searched for. In the earlier case, the results are as follows:

```
subExprs.pos[1] 7 - Start position of the match of the regular expression.
subExprs.len[1]  6 - Total length of the match.
subExprs.pos[2] 7 - Start position of the sub expression match.
subExprs.len[2] 2 - Total length of the sub expression match.
```

REReplace and REReplaceNoCase

These functions return a string with the regular expression replaced with a substring in the specified scope. REReplace is case sensitive, while REReplaceNoCase is not case sensitive. The REReplace/REReplaceNoCase functions use the following syntax as well as the attributes in Table 20.2:

```
REReplace(string, reg_expression, substring [, scope ])
```

Table 20.2 `REFind/REFindNoCase` **Attributes**

Name	Status	Description
String	Required	String being operated on
Reg_expression	Required	Regular expression to be replaced
Substring	Required	String replacing Reg_expression
Scope	Optional	Defines how to complete the replace operation: ONE—Replace only the first occurrence (default) ALL—Replace all occurrences

The following examples show you the functions in action. This chapter discusses the actual regular expression syntax later. For now, pay attention to the tag usage. First there's a short description of what you're trying to do, followed by the code needed to pull it off.

- Replace all occurrences of either C or B with the character G. This is a case-sensitive replace.

  ```
  REReplace("CABARET","C¦B","G","ALL"):GAGARET
  ```

- Replace all occurrences of any letter between A and Z with the character G. This is a case-sensitive replace.

  ```
  REReplace("CABARET","[A-Z]","G","ALL"):GGGGGGG
  ```

- Replace all occurrences of either C or B with the character G. This is a non–case-sensitive replace. Note that while the search is not case sensitive, the replacement is exact.

  ```
  REReplaceNoCase("cabaret","C¦B","G","ALL"):GaGaret
  ```

- Replace the word jell followed by either a y or the characters ies with the work cookies. This is a non–case-sensitive replace.

  ```
  REReplace("I love jellies","jell(y¦ies)","cookies"): I love cookies
  ```

The final example is a little special because it shows the ColdFusion's capability to return and replace subexpressions. This is an expansion of the code you used earlier to find double words. The ([A-Za-z]+) part of the regular expression indicates any series of non-numeric or special characters. The [ ]+ part indicates one or more spaces and the \1 is a copy of whatever the first character sequence is (a duplicate, for example). The replacement \1 is the same as the copy in the expression itself and is used to replace the duplicate. The All option makes this expression deal with every double word, not just the first.

```
REReplace ("There is is a cat in in the kitchen", "([A-Za-z]+)
➥[ ]+\1", "\1", "ALL"): There is a cat in the kitchen
```

The Regular Expression Language

Now that you have a good idea how the function works, examine the regular expression language itself.

Single-Character Matching

The basics of regular expressions are a character-for-character match. What this means is that an a matches an a, the first character of apple and the sixth character of regular. If the case-sensitive version of the RE functions are used (REFind and REReplace), the match is to the case-sensitive character; a will not match A or ,. When searching for a via the caseless versions (REFindNoCase and REReplaceNoCase), either a or A will match. This is true for almost all characters. The exceptions are the special characters used by regular expressions as meta characters. These characters are:

- +
- *
- ?
- .
- [
- ^

- $
- (
-)
- {
- |
- \

Later you examine what each of these characters does. Until then, if you want to search on one of them, you have to escape it. This is done by placing a backslash (\) before the character. This tells the regular expression engine that you're looking for the literal character, not the meta character equivalent.

Single-character matching does not mean you are stuck with a single character. It simply means that the match is a one-for-one match. You could use dog as a regular expression and the engine would interpret that it should look for a lowercase d, followed by a lowercase o, followed by a lowercase g. This exact character pattern has to match for a location to be given.

- REFind: a, ColdFusion: 0
- REFind:(a, This is a test): 9
- REFindNoCase:(a, A quick brown fox): 1
- REFind:(the, This thou they): 11
- REFindNoCase:(col, This is ColdFusion): 9

Now examine one of the meta characters. The first is the period (.). It matches any single character except a new line. This means that .oldFusion matches ColdFusion, coldFusion, BoldFusion, or any other combination as long as it has a single character followed by the text oldFusion. This means that unless modified by additional meta characters, a period must equal one character.

- REFind: .ol, ColdFusion): 1
- REFind: .ol, oldFusion): 0
- REFindNoCase: .ol, This is ColdFusion): 9
- REFind: th., This thou they): 1

Ranges of Characters

As you can see from the last example, the period can be too broad and not exact enough. If you wanted thou or they, you'd have to try something else. Defining a character range is the easiest thing to do, which is done by putting all the potential characters you will search against within brackets ([ ]). The brackets indicate that any single character within them can match. [aeiou] matches any single vowel, while [0123456789] matches any single number. This is also useful when doing a case-sensitive search where you just want a single non–case-sensitive character.

```
REFind('[cC]old[fF]usion', 'Welcome to Coldfusion'): 12
```

The character range capability is used as much for exclusion as inclusion. The preceding example searches for th., which matches thi. What happens if you don't want thi as an answer? Using the following syntax, you could limit your search's definition to exclude thi, but to include other choices:

```
REFind('th[oe]', 'This thou they'): 6
```

This finds the first occurrence of the letter t, followed by the letter h, followed by either the letter o or e. This is much more exact than simply using the period. The same thing can be done by using the OR (|) character. To use this meta character, you place all of the choices within parentheses and then place the OR character between them. The preceding example can then look like this:

```
REFind('th(o¦e)', 'This thou they'): 6
```

You examine parentheses later, but for now all you need to know is that it groups things.

An additional way of doing this is to negate a character range. Placing a caret (^) at the beginning of a character range indicates that any character other than the range is legal. Using this, your example can be written as such:

```
REFind('th[^i]', 'This thou they'): 6
```

The example is looking for the letter t, followed by the letter h, followed by any letter other than i. This does mean that you need to know what you want negated, but allows you to be more exact. If the caret is not the first character, it is treated as a regular character rather than a special one.

When you are searching for a range of characters, you can use a dash between the beginning and end of the range. [0-9] means [0123456789], while [a-d] means [abcd]. This allows you to keep your regular expressions small. In cases where you want to search for a dash (-), you have to have it as the first character. This tells the regular expression engine to find a dash rather than a range.

```
REFind('[0-9]', 'we are in 1st place'): 11
REFind('[-s-z]', 'Cold-Fusion is number 1'): 5
REFindNoCase('[-s-s]', 'Cold-Fusion is number 1'): 1
```

In addition, ColdFusion's regular expression library allows the use of special commands that can take the place of character ranges. These special characters take the place of a single character or character range. A list of all the special commands supported by ColdFusion follows. It should be noted that these are an implementation of the POSIX character classes.

Character Class	Matches
Alpha	Matches any letter. Same as [A-Za-z].
Upper	Matches any uppercase letter. Same as [A-Z].
Lower	Matches any lowercase letter. Same as [a-z].
Digit	Matches any digit. Same as [0-9].
Alnum	Matches any alphanumeric character. Same as [A-Za-z0-9].
Xdigit	Matches any hexadecimal digit. Same as [0-9A-Fa-f].
Space	Matches a tab, new line, vertical tab, form feed, carriage return, or space.
Print	Matches any printable character.
Punct	Matches any punctuation character. (!, ', #, S, %, &, ', (,), *, +, ,, -, ., /, :, ;, <, =, >, ?, @, [, /,], ^, _, {, |, }, ~)
Graph	Matches any of the characters defined as a printable character except those defined as part of the space character class.
Cntrl	Matches any character not part of the character classes [:upper:], [:lower:], [:alpha:], [:digit:], [:punct:], [:graph:], [:print:], or [:xdigit:].

Special commands are accessed using a slightly different syntax than is normal:

```
[[:Special command:]]
```

The only difference between the ColdFusion implementation of these special characters and the standard used by POSIX is the double brackets around the expression. This allows ColdFusion to identify the expression as special and make use of it. If you port any Perl code into ColdFusion, just remember to add the double brackets:

```
REFind('[[:digit:]]', 'we are in 1st place'): 11
REFind('[[:punct:]]', 'we are in 1st place'): 0
REFind('[[:space:]]', 'we are in 1st place'): 3
```

Multi-Character Searches

You've seen that regular expressions can be made of single characters, strings of single characters, and character ranges. What would happen if you wanted to find something such as aaa? You could look for the string aaa or you could use some meta characters to extend what you're searching for. For convenience sake, these meta characters are referred to as *multipliers*.

Before you look at the meta characters, you have to examine the role of the parentheses and define what the meta characters will operate on. You also have to show the positioning of meta characters for effect.

Part
IV

Ch
20

In regular expressions, the parentheses are used to group characters. Earlier you saw the or (|) meta character used within parentheses. Look at an example of that again, with a bit more information:

```
REFind('(and|or)', 'Do you want to be the husband or the wife?'): 27
```

This example uses the parentheses to indicate that the entire string and OR the entire string or should be searched for. Note that you found the and at the end of husband. If you want to specify the words surrounded by a space, you would include that as part of the regular expression searched against:

```
REFind(' (and|or) ', 'Do you want to be the husband or the wife?'): 30
```

Note that you're now finding the space before the word rather than the start of the word itself. You can get more exact by using the Returnsubexpressions part of the REFind commands. You examine that a little later when you deal with back referencing.

The parentheses grouping is needed because of the structure of a regular expression with a multiplier. The expression is either a single character, a range of characters, or a parentheses-defined group followed by a multiplier meta character. The multiplier refers only to that previously defined character or character equivalent.

The most basic of the multiplier meta characters is the asterisk (*); it basically does the last character 0 or more times.

Find the letter c followed by 0 occurrences or more of the letter o:

```
REFind('co*', 'get me a coke'): 10
REFind('co*', 'client variable'): 1
```

Find the 0 or more references to the string hi. Remember to look at case sensitivity:

```
REFind('(hi)*', 'Dee Dee says Hi'): 0
REFind('(hi)*', 'Dexter is hiding '): 11
```

Along the same lines as the asterisk is the plus (+) meta character. It finds one or more of the previous characters.

Find the letter c followed by one or more of the letter o:

```
REFind('co+', 'I''m a cook for a coco'): 7
```

Find the one or more references to the string hi. Remember to look at case sensitivity:

```
REFind('(hi)+', 'Dee Dee says Hi'): 0
REFind('(hi)+', 'Dexter is hiding '): 11
```

The final multiplier is also a limiter. The question mark (?) indicates that the preceding character/character set is to appear 0 or 1 times.

Find the character c either by itself or as the character string chi:

```
REFind('c(hi)?', 'where is the child'): 14
REFind('c(hi)?', 'Dee Dee is in the car'): 19
```

One note is that there are actually two ways of doing all of the multipliers. Besides their normal appearance (*, +, ?), there is a bracket set that mimics the functionality. This bracket set looks like {x,y} and means "at least x but no more than y." In actual usage it looks like {2,4} and means that the preceding character/character set must exist at least two times, but not more than four. To make this bracket set look like the different multipliers is a simple application of logic. An asterisk is {0,}, a plus is {1,}, and a question mark is {0,1}. As you can see, you can have a single value within the brackets before the comma, but never after.

Back Referencing

Back referencing is the capability of regular expressions to remember a section of text and refer to it again later. Say you have a ColdFusion page with the function ParameterExists. You want to change it to IsDefined. The structure of these two functions is basically the same: function name, parenthesis, variable, close parenthesis. The only difference is that the variable in an IsDefined is wrapped in quotation marks. You want to write a line of code using regular expressions that finds all of the text that looks like ParameterExists(*var*) and replace it with IsDefined('*var*'). You use this syntax:

```
ReReplaceNoCase(File, 'ParameterExists\(([[:graph:]]+\)', 'IsDefined
➥(''\1'')', 'ALL')
```

Now examine what you're doing here so you get a handle on back referencing. You're doing a non–case-sensitive replace on the text within a variable called file. In this case, assume it's the contents of a ColdFusion page. Your regular expression reads (in English) as follows: Find the word parameterexists (or the letters that make it up, in order), followed immediately by an open parenthesis, followed by any number of non-space type characters, followed by a close parenthesis.

Note that you define the open and close parenthesis as \(and \). This is to escape them and say you want the actual characters. The next thing to notice is that you use [[:graph:]]+ to define your word. This is done because you know a variable within a parameterexists cannot be a space character and has to be at least one character long. Now this is wrapped within a set of non-escaped parentheses. This defines all of the characters that fit your description as a single group. Refer to this grouping as 1. When you replace the regular expression with IsDefined(''\1''), you're saying that the function should place all of the characters found within the grouping inside the isdefined and you do this by using \1. The backslash says you're looking for a back referenced grouping and the 1 is the grouping in question. If there were three sets of parentheses, you could have three back referencings.

Advanced Regular Expression Example

Listing 20.1 contains a small program example using the regular expression functions. This code reads in a ColdFusion template, sends it to a code optimizer, and then rewrites the template with optimized code. The optimization is based on a number of experiments done with ColdFusion and an understanding of how expressions are processed by the underlying engine.

```
<CFFILE ACTION="READ" FILE="#File#" VARIABLE="Result">
<CF_OptimizePage OptimizePage="#Result#">
<CFFILE ACTION="WRITE" FILE="#File#" OUTPUT="#StripCR(OptimizePage)#">
<CFOUTPUT><XMP>#StripCR(optimizepage)#</XMP></CFOUTPUT>
```

Listing 20.1   Automatic Code Optimization Script

```
<CFSETTING EnableCFOutputOnly="yes">

<CFFILE ACTION="READ" FILE="#File#" VARIABLE="Result">
<!-- Change all ParameterExists to IsDefined -->
<CFSET Result = ReReplaceNoCase(Result, "PARAMETEREXISTS\((([[:graph:]]+)\)
➥", "IsDefined('\1')", "All")>

<!-- Change all Is "" to not Len()-->
<CFSET Result = ReReplaceNoCase(Result, "(CFIF¦AND¦OR) *([[:graph:]]+) *(IS¦EQ)
➥ *['''""]{2,}", "\1 NOT Len( \2)", "All")>

<!-- Change all Is not "" to Len()-->
<CFSET Result = ReReplaceNoCase(Result, "(CFIF¦AND¦OR) *([[:graph:]]+)
➥ *(IS Not¦NEQ) *['''""]{2,}", "\1 Len( \2)", "All")>

<!-- Correct for # in a len()-->
<CFSET Result = ReReplaceNoCase(Result, "Len\(##([[:graph:]]+)##\)", "Len(\1)
➥", "All")>

<!-- Change all primary IF clauses to boolean -->
<CFSET Result = ReReplaceNoCase(Result, "(CFIF¦OR¦AND) *([[:graph:]]+)
➥ *(IS¦EQ¦GT) *['''""]*(yes¦1)['''""]*", "\1 \2", "All")>
<CFSET Result = ReReplaceNoCase(Result, "(CFIF¦AND¦OR) *([[:graph:]]+)
➥ *(IS NOT¦NEQ) *['''""]yes['''""]", "\1 NOT \2", "All")>
<CFSET Result = ReReplaceNoCase(Result, "(CFIF¦AND¦OR) *([[:graph:]]+) *(IS¦EQ)
➥ *['''""]no['''""]", "\1 NOT \2", "All")>
<CFSET Result = ReReplaceNoCase(Result, "(CFIF¦AND¦OR) *([[:graph:]]+) *(IS¦EQ)
➥ *['''""]*0['''""]*", "\1 NOT \2", "All")>
<CFSET Result = ReReplaceNoCase(Result, "(CFIF¦AND¦OR) *([[:graph:]]+)
➥ *(Is Not¦NEQ¦GT) *['''""]*(no¦0)['''""]*", "\1 \2", "All")>

<CFFILE ACTION="WRITE" FILE="#File#" OUTPUT="#StripCR(Result)#">
<CFOUTPUT><XMP>#StripCR(Result)#</XMP></CFOUTPUT>
<CFSETTING EnableCFOutputOnly="No">
```

While regular expression support is not seen as one of the major pieces in the ColdFusion 4 release, developers are likely to receive it very well. ●

Intelligent Agents and Distributed Processing

This chapter deals with two general topics that go hand in hand: transfer protocols, distributed objects, and intelligent agents. These are considered two topics here because the transfer protocols move information, whereas the second two terms are used for operations performed on that information.

Transfer protocols are any standard means used to move data from one place to another. These means include Internet protocols such as HTTP, FTP, LDAP, and others that you have learned about in previous chapters. Transfer protocols are not limited to these techniques, though. Any sort of communications such as ODBC, OLE-DB, and even calls to COM and CORBA objects can fall under this heading. Rather than write a whole book on transfer protocols in ColdFusion, this chapter is limited to the two most common Internet protocols used by ColdFusion: CFHTTP and CFFTP. You can find details on other protocols and other means of transferring information in various chapters of both this and *ColdFusion Web Application Construction Kit*.

Descriptions of distributed objects and intelligent agents make up the other part of this chapter. They are basically ways and means of using information that is transferred using the transfer protocols.

Distributed objects encompass all operations in which you're asking some outside process to perform some calculation and return some data. These operations can be as simple as calling a COM object, calling a stored procedure from a database, or having CFHTTP call another ColdFusion machine to do work for you. The entire focus here is that ColdFusion sends some information or some request to some other machine or process and gets back a final result that can be used without being modified at all.

Intelligent agents, on the other hand, deal more with getting information from somewhere and then parsing through it to get the piece or pieces you want. The most common example is using CFHTTP to retrieve a page with stock values on it and then parsing out only the stock values, leaving the rest of the page unused. In contrast to distributed objects, intelligent agents do most—if not all—of their work locally.

As you go on, you might see a number of overlaps between distributed objects and intelligent agents, and of course, any transfer protocol described in this and other chapters.

CFHTTP

In the following sections you examine the transfer protocols; afterward, you learn about using them for distributed objects and intelligent agents.

The Hypertext Transfer Protocol

Hypertext Transfer Protocol, or HTTP, is a standard means used for transfer of information across the Web from servers (Web servers) to clients (browsers) and back again. Although HTTP is usually associated with Hypertext Markup Language (HTML), it is basically unlimited in the types of files it can transfer. Any file with a defined Multipurpose Internet Mail Extensions (MIME) type can be moved using this protocol.

ColdFusion uses an internal call to this protocol to gain access to data in the same manner as a Web browser. Using the <CFHTTP> tag, you can retrieve any Web page or Web-based file. The tag supports both the retrieval of information using the GET action and the posting of information using the POST action. Basically, anything that can be done through a Web browser can be done through this tag.

The <CFHTTP> tag's attributes offer a large range of options—from simply creating output, resolving embedded links, and even building ColdFusion queries from delimited text files. The standard syntax is as follows:

```
<CFHTTP URL="url" Method="get or post">
```

N O T E POST operations using <CFHTTP> should be terminated with </CFHTTP>. GET operations do not require termination. ▪

The <CFHTTP> tag's behavior can be changed depending on the value of the attributes supplied to it during execution. Table 21.1 explains the attributes and their functions.

Table 21.1 Attributes of the <CFHTTP> Tag

Attribute	Description
URL	Required. Full URL of the host name or IP address of the server on which the specified file resides.
METHOD	Required. GET or POST. Use GET to retrieve a binary or text file or to build a query using the contents of a text file. Use POST to send information to a CGI program or server page for processing. POST operations require use of one or more <CFHTTPPARAM> tags.
USERNAME	Optional. Submitted when a server requires a username for access.
PASSWORD	Optional. Submitted when a server requires a password for access.
NAME	Optional. Name assigned to a query object when a query is to be constructed from a text file.
COLUMNS	Optional. Column names for a query. If no column names are specified, defaults to the columns listed in the first row of the text file.
PATH	Optional. Path to the directory (local) in which a file is to be stored. If a path is not specified in a GET or POST operation, the results are created in the CFHTTP.FileContent variable for output.
FILE	Required in a POST operation if PATH is specified. The filename in which the results of the specified operation are stored. The path to the file is specified in the PATH attribute.
DELIMITER	Required for creating a query. Valid characters are a tab or a comma. The default is a comma (,).

Part

IV

Ch

21

continues

Table 21.1   Continued

Attribute	Description
TEXTQUALIFIER	Required for creating a query. Indicates the start and finish of a column. Must be escaped when embedded in a column. If the qualifier is a quotation mark, it should be escaped as "". If no text qualifier appears in the file, specify a blank space as " ". The default is the double quotation mark (").
RESOLVEURL	Optional. YES or NO. For GET and POST operations. When this attribute is set to YES, any link referenced in the remote page has its internal URL fully resolved and returned to the CFHTTP.FileContent variable so that the links remain intact. The following HTML tags, which may contain links, are resolved: IMG SRC, A HREF, FORM ACTION, APPLET CODE, SCRIPT SRC, EMBED SRC, EMBED PLUGINSPACE, BODY BACKGROUND, FRAME SRC, BGSOUND SRC, OBJECT DATA, OBJECT CLASSID, OBJECT CODEBASE, OBJECT USEMAP.
PROXYSERVER	Optional. Host name or IP address of a proxy server, if required.

Using the <CFHTTPPARAM> Tag

The <CFHTTPPARAM> tag is required when you use <CFHTTP> for a POST operation. The syntax for the <CFHTTPPARAM> tag is as follows:

```
<CFHTTPPARAM NAME="name"
    TYPE="transaction type"
    VALUE="value"
    FILE="filename" >
```

The attributes of this tag are shown in Table 21.2.

Table 21.2   Attributes of the <CFHTTPPARAM> Tag

Attribute	Description
NAME	Required. A variable name for data being passed.
TYPE	Required. The transaction type. Valid entries are URL, FormField, Cookie, CGI, and File.
VALUE	Optional for TYPE="File". Specifies the URL, FormField, Cookie, File, or CGI variable being passed to the server.
FILE	Required for TYPE="File". Fully qualified local filename to be uploaded to the server—for example, c:\temp\amazon.lst.

Now that you have looked at the various attributes and syntax descriptions for the <CFHTTP> and <CFHTTPPARAM> tags, you can write some examples to demonstrate the various facets of the <CFHTTP> tag in operation.

Putting the <CFHTTP> Tag to Use

Using <CFHTTP> with the GET method is a relatively simple one-way transaction. The Web client, whether it is a browser or a ColdFusion application, makes an HTTP request to an HTTP server, and the server returns the requested document. The POST operation is two way, in which the Web client sends specific information to the server or CGI application, and processed data is returned.

Using the GET Method

The first example you create demonstrates a simple GET operation. Listing 21.1 shows the CFML code necessary to use the <CFHTTP> tag in a GET operation. This example fetches the index page from www.excite.com (a large search engine site) and then displays the results.

On the CD

> **Listing 21.1   CFHTTP_1.CFM—Retrieving the Index Page from www.excite.com via the <CFHTTP> Tag**

```
<CFHTTP METHOD="GET" URL="http://www.excite.com" RESOLVEURL="YES">

<CFOUTPUT>
#CFHTTP.FileContent#
</CFOUTPUT>
```

Figure 21.1 shows the output of the example, with the index page from www.excite.com fully displayed, including all its graphics and links.

FIGURE 21.1

Output of the index page from www.excite.com, rendered using the <CFHTTP> tag.

Part
IV
Ch
21

In this example you leave out the FILE and PATH attributes, which forces the result of the <CFHTTP> tag to be stored in the CFHTTP.FileContent variable. You set the RESOLVEURL attribute to YES, indicating that you want the internal links in the page to be turned into absolute versus relative links. Otherwise, when the template is run, any relative link points to the local HTTP server instead.

The next example demonstrates using <CFHTTP> with the GET method to save the results to a file. Here, you modify the preceding example to specify the PATH and FILE attributes. Instead of outputting the CFHTTP.FileContent variable, you use the <CFFILE> tag to read the contents of the download file into a variable and then display the results. The modified template is shown in Listing 21.2.

Listing 21.2   CFHTTP_2.CFM—Using the <CFHTTP> Tag with the GET Method to Download a File

```
<CFHTTP METHOD="GET" URL="http://www.excite.com" FILE="exciteindex.html"
➥ PATH="c:\temp\" RESOLVEURL="YES">

<CFFILE ACTION="READ" VARIABLE="HTTPFILE" FILE="C:\temp\exciteindex.html">
<CFOUTPUT>
#HTTPFILE#
</CFOUTPUT>
```

Figure 21.2 shows the output from the second example. Note that images that were based on relative URLs from the index are not displayed because the RESOLVEURL attribute is ignored when the PATH and FILE attributes are specified. Even though the majority of the hypertext links are displayed, if the page's HTML source were displayed, all the URLs would be relative and would not work on the local server.

The preceding examples used the GET method to display the output of a <CFHTTP> tag. You now build a template that downloads a binary file from a remote Web server using <CFHTTP> and the GET method. An additional variable showing the MimeType of the downloaded file is shown. Listing 21.3 shows the modified example.

On the CD

Listing 21.3   CFHTTP_3.CFM—Using the <CFHTTP> Tag with the GET Method to Download a Binary File

```
<CFHTTP METHOD="GET" URL="http://127.0.0.1/a2z/employee/photos/id02.jpg"
       FILE="id02.jpg" PATH="c:\temp\" RESOLVEURL="YES">

<CFOUTPUT>
MimeType of Downloaded File=#CFHTTP.MimeType#
</CFOUTPUT>
```

Make sure to change the URL in the preceding example to match your installation, if it is different from the example.

FIGURE 21.2

Output of the <CFHTTP> tag using the GET method to save the result to a local file.

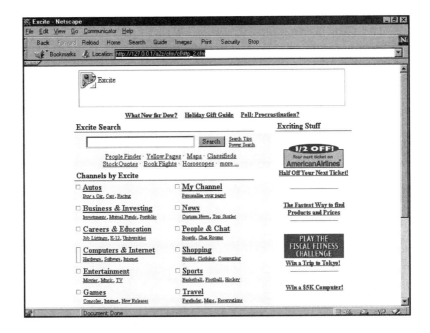

On the CD

The image file used as a sample employee photo (ID02.JPG), which is just a small bitmapped image, is on the CD-ROM that accompanies this book.

This example is a simple modification of the second example, introducing the CFHTTP.MimeType variable, which is displayed after the file is downloaded. In this example, the MimeType of the file is image/jpeg because it is a JPEG file. Figure 21.3 shows the results of this example.

Building a Query from a Text File

The last example, using the GET method, reads a text file and creates a query object from it.

On the CD

Listing 21.4   CFHTTP_4.CFM—Using the <CFHTTP> Tag to Build a Query Using a Text File

```
<HTML>
<HEAD>
<TITLE>CFHTTP QUERY TEST</TITLE>
</HEAD>
<BODY>
<CFHTTP METHOD="GET" URL="http://127.0.0.1/a2z/employee/photolist.txt"
➥ NAME="EMPLOYEES"
        DELIMITER="," TEXTQUALIFIER=""""
➥COLUMNS="LASTNAME,FIRSTNAME,ID,PHOTOFILE">
<TABLE BORDER>
<TR>
<TH ALIGN="LEFT">Last Name</TH>
```

Part
IV

Ch
21

continues

Listing 21.4   Continued

```
<TH ALIGN="LEFT">First Name</TH>
<TH ALIGN="LEFT">Employee ID</TH>
<TH ALIGN="LEFT">Photo File</TH>
</TR>
<CFOUTPUT QUERY="EMPLOYEES">
<TR>
<TD ALIGN="LEFT">#lastname#</TD>
<TD ALIGN="LEFT">#firstname#</TD>
<TD ALIGN="LEFT">#id#</TD>
<TD ALIGN="LEFT"><CFIF #photofile# is ""> 
➥<CFELSE>#photofile#</CFIF></TD>
</TR>
</CFOUTPUT>
</TABLE>
</BODY>
</HTML>
```

FIGURE 21.3

Output from the
<CFHTTP> tag after
downloading a binary
file using the GET
method.

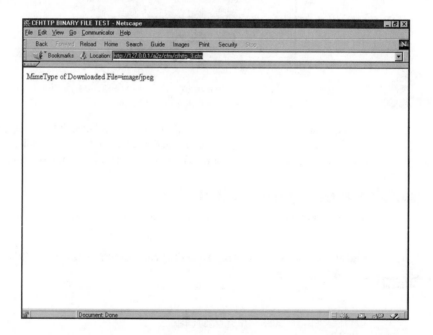

You add a number of attributes to the <CFHTTP> tag to permit it to read an ASCII file and create
a query object. You set the NAME attribute to EMPLOYEES, indicating that you want the query
object to be named EMPLOYEES. Because you know the structure of the file, you can specify the
DELIMITER to , (comma) and the TEXTQUALIFER to " " (quotation marks). In this particular case,
the file does not have a row of column headers in it; you therefore specify the column names
you want in the COLUMNS attribute. You then use normal ColdFusion techniques (<CFOUTPUT>)
to display the data in the query using an HTML table. Figure 21.4 shows the output from this
example.

FIGURE 21.4

Output from query created using the <CFHTTP> tag.

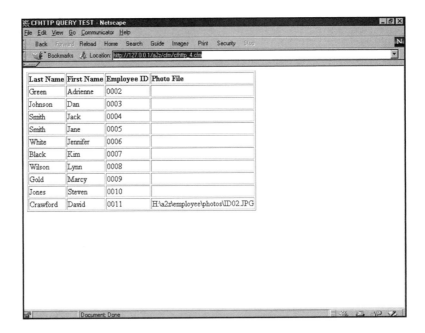

To summarize, text files are processed by the <CFHTTP> tag using the following guidelines:

- The NAME attribute specifies the name of the query object that is created by ColdFusion.
- A delimiter is specified with the DELIMITER attribute. If the delimiter is contained within a field in the file, it must be quoted using the character specified in the TEXTQUALIFIER attribute.
- The first row of the text file is interpreted as the column headers by default. You can override this setting by using the COLUMNS attribute.
- When ColdFusion encounters duplicate column names, it adds an underscore (_) character to the duplicate column name to make it unique.

Using the POST Method

In contrast to the GET method, which is essentially one way, the POST method, when used with <CFHTTP>, provides a two-way transactional environment. To demonstrate this environment, you develop a number of examples that evolve from simple to complex.

The first example demonstrates the capability to transmit multiple variable types to a remote Web server or CGI application. Using a ColdFusion template, you transmit the data to another ColdFusion template using the <CFHTTP> tag and then display the generated output. The code is shown in Listing 21.5.

Part

IV

Ch

21

Listing 21.5 CFHTTP_5.CFM—<CFHTTP> with the POST Method

```
<CFHTTP METHOD="POST" URL="http://127.0.0.1/a2z/cfm/cfhttp_6.cfm">
<CFHTTPPARAM NAME="form_test" TYPE="FormField"
➥VALUE="This is a form variable.">
<CFHTTPPARAM NAME="url_test" TYPE="URL" VALUE="This is a URL variable.">
<CFHTTPPARAM NAME="cgi_test" TYPE="CGI" VALUE="This is a CGI variable.">
<CFHTTPPARAM NAME="cookie_test" TYPE="Cookie" VALUE="This is a cookie.">
</CFHTTP>

<CFOUTPUT>
#CFHTTP.FileContent#
</CFOUTPUT>
```

The code in Listing 21.5 simply posts some information to the template in Listing 21.6. The results are then displayed using a simple CFOUTPUT tag. Figure 21.5 shows the results.

Listing 21.6 CFHTTP_6.CFM—Template That Processes the CFHTTP POST Method Variables

```
<HTML>
<HEAD>
<TITLE>CFHTTP Post Test</TITLE>
</HEAD>
<BODY>
<CFOUTPUT>
The following variables where POSTED here via the CFHTTP_5.CFM template.<P>
Form_Test: #Form.form_test#<BR>
URL_Test: #URL.url_test#<BR>
CGI_Test: #CGI.cgi_test#<BR>
Cookie_Test: #COOKIE.cookie_test#<BR>
</CFOUTPUT>
</BODY>
</HTML>
```

This example shows four of the five variable types that the <CFHTTPPARAM> tag supports. It does not show the FILE type because that type requires additional processing. To demonstrate the FILE variable in a POST operation, modify the preceding example to upload a file to the server. The code for this example is shown in Listing 21.7.

Listing 21.7 CFHTTP_7.CFM—Using the POST Method to Upload a File

```
<CFHTTP METHOD="POST" URL="http://127.0.0.1/a2z/cfm/list25-3.cfm">
<CFHTTPPARAM NAME="filename" TYPE="FILE" FILE="c:\temp\cflogo.gif">
</CFHTTP>
<CFOUTPUT>
#CFHTTP.FileContent#
</CFOUTPUT>
```

FIGURE 21.5

Output from the <CFHTTP> tag using the POST method.

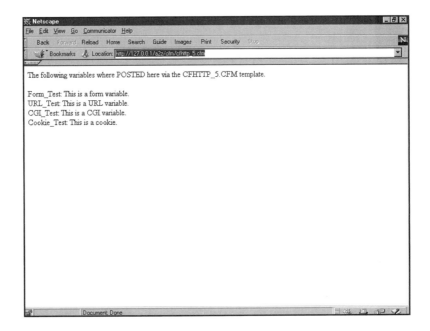

Note that instead of specifying the VALUE attribute, you specify the FILE attribute, which contains the name of the file to be uploaded. The output from the upload operation is then displayed using the CFHTTP.FileContent variable.

Pulling It All Together

The last example of the <CFHTTP> tag you develop in this chapter shows the POST operation passing information from your local server to a book search engine at www.amazon.com and then displaying the results. This example requires a little more work because first you have to identify the fields that the search engine requires and then code your template accordingly. The code in Listing 21.8 shows the fields that must be passed to the search engine. For demonstration purposes, you can simplify the process and search only on an author's name; in this case, use Ben Forta, the lead author of this book.

On the CD

Listing 21.8 CFHTTP_8.CFM—Passing Information to the www.amazon.com Book Search Engine Using <CFHTTP>

```
<CFHTTP METHOD="POST" URL="http://www.amazon.com/exec/obidos/ats-query/
➥6994-1392532-213589" RESOLVEURL="YES">
<CFHTTPPARAM NAME="author-mode" TYPE="formfield" value="full">
<CFHTTPPARAM NAME="author" TYPE="formfield" value="FORTA, BEN">
</CFHTTP>
<CFOUTPUT>
#CFHTTP.FileContent#
</CFOUTPUT>
```

CAUTION

The <CFHTTP> tag to extract HTML from remote Web servers should be used with caution, from an intellectual property perspective. The copyright laws with regard to the Internet are not yet clear, and use of another individual's or corporation's content without permission may open you to liability under copyright or trademark law. Exercise good judgment when you're posting to or downloading from a remote Web server that is not under your exclusive control.

The code in Listing 21.8 is very simple, yet it demonstrates the power of the <CFHTTP> tag. By researching the form fields necessary to drive a search engine, you can add a powerful function to your ColdFusion templates. Only two form fields are required to drive this particular engine. The author-mode field tells the search engine how to search for the data contained in the author field. The full www.amazon.com book search engine provides other functionality, but a more simple approach is needed for this example.

Figure 21.6 shows the output from this example. Note that several images are not displayed properly because, in this example, a client-side map is used; it is not resolved by the URL resolution mechanism of the <CFHTTP> tag. However, the important point is that a remote search engine is manipulated using a ColdFusion template running on a local server.

FIGURE 21.6

Output from the www.amazon.com book search engine, with data provided by the <CFHTTP> tag.

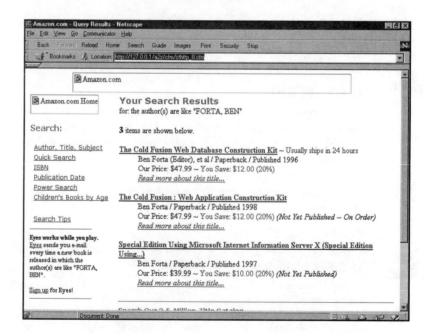

Summarizing the <CFHTTP> Tag

In the preceding examples you learned how you can use the <CFHTTP> tag to interact with remote Web servers and CGI applications. From the simplest request to download a file, to remotely operating a search engine, the <CFHTTP> tag comes with plenty of power. The capability to create queries using text files opens the doors to many different methods of receiving data and processing it using ColdFusion. A new data source becomes available to you; it can accept a delimited file of orders from a customer for processing, as just one example. File uploads, downloads, and interaction with CGI applications such as search engines or other ColdFusion templates provide you with more tools to draw on as they approach application design.

Using the <CFFTP> Tag

Another method provided by ColdFusion to interact with remote servers is the <CFFTP> tag. The <CFFTP> tag operates using the File Transfer Protocol (FTP), which is an Internet standard for transferring files from one computer to another. Both ASCII and binary transfers are supported by the FTP protocol, so it is a common method for distributing software across the Internet.

> **CAUTION**
>
> <CFFTP> is not supported in ColdFusion for Solaris 3.1.

<CFFTP> permits you to implement FTP operations. In its default configuration, the <CFFTP> tag caches connections for reuse within the same template.

Operations using the <CFFTP> tag are divided into two areas:

- Establishing or closing a connection
- File and directory operations

The syntax for the <CFFTP> tag is as follows:

```
<CFFTP ACTION="action"
    USERNAME="username"
    PASSWORD="password"
    SERVER="server"
    TIMEOUT="timeout in seconds"
    PORT="port"
    CONNECTION="name"
    AGENTNAME="name"
    RETRYCOUNT="number"
    STOPONERROR="Yes/No">
```

This form of the <CFFTP> tag is used to establish or close an FTP connection. If you are using a previously cached connection, you do not have to specify the USERNAME, PASSWORD, and SERVER attributes.

The attributes that control the behavior of the <CFFTP> tag during the establishment or closure of a session are shown in Table 21.3.

Part

IV

Ch

21

Table 21.3 `<CFFTP>` **Tag Attributes**

Attribute	Description
ACTION	Required. Determines the FTP operation to perform. Use Open to open an FTP connection. Use Close to close an FTP connection.
USERNAME	Required. Username to pass to the FTP server.
PASSWORD	Required. Password to log on the user specified in USERNAME.
SERVER	Required. The FTP server to connect to, such as `ftp.allaire.com`.
TIMEOUT	Optional. Value in seconds for the timeout of all operations, including individual data request operations. Defaults to 30 seconds.
PORT	Optional. The remote TCP/IP port to connect to. The default is 21 for FTP.
CONNECTION	Optional. Name of the FTP connection. Used to cache the FTP connection information or to reuse a previously opened connection.
AGENTNAME	Optional. Application or entity conducting transfer.
RETRYCOUNT	Optional. Number of retries until failure is reported. Default is 1.
STOPONERROR	Optional. YES or NO. When YES, halts all processing and displays an appropriate error. The default is Yes. When NO, three variables are created and populated: CFFTP.Succeeded—YES or NO. CFFTP.ErrorCode—Error number. (See the FTP error codes in Table 21.7.) CFFTP.ErrorText—Message text explaining error type.

Establishing a Connection

Listing 21.9 shows a simple template that establishes an FTP connection.

On the CD

Listing 21.9 `CFFTP_1.CFM`—**Establishing an FTP Connection**

```
<CFFTP ACTION="Open" USERNAME="anonymous" PASSWORD="info@a2zbooks.com"
➥SERVER="ftp.allaire.com" NAME="ALLAIRE" STOPONERROR="No">

<CFOUTPUT>
Opening the connection.<BR>
FTP Operation Successful: #CFFTP.SUCCEEDED#<BR>
FTP Error Code: #CFFTP.ErrorCode#<BR>
FTP Error Text: #CFFTP.ErrorText#<BR>
</CFOUTPUT>

<CFFTP ACTION="Close" NAME="ALLAIRE" STOPONERROR="No">
<CFOUTPUT>
Closing the Connection.<BR>
```

```
FTP Operation Successful: #CFFTP.SUCCEEDED#<BR>
FTP Error Code: #CFFTP.ErrorCode#<BR>
FTP Error Text: #CFFTP.ErrorText#<BR>
</CFOUTPUT>
```

> **CAUTION**
>
> The <CFFTP> tag is a COM object that runs only on Windows NT 4.0 or Windows 95 with the DCOM update. Before you use the <CFFTP> tag on your site, be sure that your server can use COM objects.

This simple example opens an FTP connection to Allaire's FTP server, checks the status, and then closes the connection. Figure 21.7 shows the results from this code.

FIGURE 21.7
Output after opening and closing an FTP connection to Allaire's FTP server.

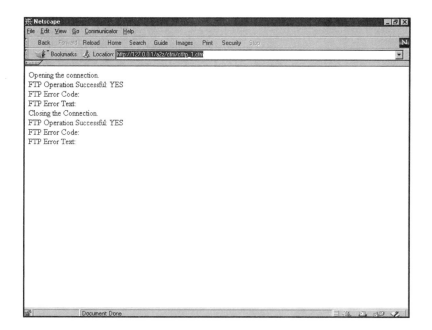

Note that the USERNAME and PASSWORD attributes are required by the <CFFTP> tag. You will be using anonymous FTP in many cases, so you can set the USERNAME attribute to anonymous and the PASSWORD attribute to be the full email address of the user who is making the connection. In the case of a ColdFusion template application, the system administrator's email address is sufficient.

Part
IV

Ch
21

Using File and Directory Operations with <CFFTP>

After you establish an FTP connection, you can perform various file and directory operations to send files to the server or receive files and directory listings from the server.

The attributes of the <CFFTP> tag vary slightly from the attributes required to open or close a connection. The attributes for file and directory operations are shown in the Table 21.4.

Table 21.4   <CFFTP> **File and Directory Operations Attributes**

Attribute	Description
ACTION	Required if connection is not already cached using the CONNECTION attribute. Determines the FTP operation to perform. It can be one of the following: ChangeDir, CreateDir, ListDir, GetFile, PutFile, Rename, Remove, GetCurrentDir, GetCurrentURL, ExistsDir, ExistsFile, or Exists.
USERNAME	Required if the connection is not already cached. See the attributes for establishing an FTP connection in Table 21.3.
PASSWORD	Required if the connection is not already cached. See the attributes for establishing an FTP connection in Table 21.3.
SERVER	Required if the connection is not already cached. See the attributes for establishing an FTP connection in Table 21.3.
TIMEOUT	Optional. Value in seconds for the timeout of all operations, including individual data request operations. Defaults to 30 seconds.
PORT	Optional. The remote TCP/IP port to connect to. The default is 21 for FTP.
CONNECTION	Optional. Name of the FTP connection. Used to cache the FTP connection information or to reuse a previously opened connection.
NAME	Required for ACTION="ListDir". Specifies the query object in which results will be stored.
ASCIIEXTENSIONLIST	Optional. Semicolon-delimited list of file extensions that will force ASCII transfer mode when TRANSERMODE="Autodetect". The default list is txt, htm, html, cfm, cfml, shtm, shtml, css, asp, and asa.
TRANSFERMODE	Optional. The FTP transfer mode. Valid entries are ASCII, Binary, and Autodetect. The default is Autodetect.
AGENTNAME	Optional. Application or entity conducting transfer.
FAILIFEXISTS	Optional. YES or NO. Defaults to YES. Specifies whether a GetFile operation will fail if a local file of the same name exists.
DIRECTORY	Required for ACTION=ChangeDir, CreateDir, ListDir, and ExistsDir. Specifies the directory on which operation will be performed.
LOCALFILE	Required for ACTION=GetFile and PutFile. Specifies a file on the local file system.

Attribute	Description
REMOTEFILE	Required for ACTION=GetFile, PutFile, and ExistsFile. Specifies the filename of the FTP server.
ATTRIBUTES	Optional. Defaults to Normal. A comma-delimited list of attributes. Specifies the file attributes for the local file in a GetFile operation. They can be any combination of the following: ReadOnly, Hidden, System, Archive, Directory, Compressed, Temporary, and Normal. The file attributes vary according to the operating system environment.
ITEM	Required for ACTION=Exists and Remove. Specifies the file, object, or directory for these actions.
EXISTING	Required for ACTION=Rename. Specifies the current name of the file or directory on the remote server.
NEW	Required for ACTION=Rename. Specifies the new name of the file or directory on the remote server.
RETRYCOUNT	Optional. Number of retries until failure is reported. The default is 1.
STOPONERROR	Optional. YES or NO. When YES, halts all processing and displays an appropriate error. The default is YES. When NO, three variables are created and populated: CFFTP.Succeeded—YES or NO. CFFTP.ErrorCode—Error number. (See Table 21.7 for a list of FTP error codes.) CFFTP.ErrorText—Message text explaining error type.

Caching Connections

You can reuse an established FTP connection to perform additional FTP operations. You do so by setting the CONNECTION attribute when the FTP connection is established. Subsequent calls to the <CFFTP> tag in the same template use the same CONNECTION name. Using this name forces <CFFTP> to automatically reuse the connection information, which results in faster connections and improves file transfer performance.

N O T E If you're using a cached connection, you do not have to respecify the USERNAME, PASSWORD, and SERVER attributes. ■

When using frames, you need to make sure that only a single frame refers to a particular cached connection. FTP connections are cached only in the current template. To cache connections across multiple pages, you need to use a session variable for the CONNECTION attribute.

Before establishing a session variable, you need to ensure that you have enabled session variables. See the <CFAPPLICATION> tag reference for further information.

Part
IV

Ch
21

To establish a session variable for the CONNECTION, specify the CONNECTION value to be session.*variablename*, where *variablename* is the name of the connection you want to establish.

N O T E Making changes to cached connections such as changing RETRYCOUNT or TIMEOUT might require you to reestablish the connection. ▇

Table 21.5 shows the attributes required for <CFFTP> actions when a cached connection is used. If a cached connection is not used, the USERNAME, PASSWORD, and SERVER attributes must be set.

Table 21.5 <CFFTP> **Required Attributes Shown by Action**

Action	Attribute	Action	Attribute
Open	None	Rename	EXISTING, NEW
Close	None	Remove	SERVER, ITEM
ChangeDir	DIRECTORY	GetCurrentDir	None
CreateDir	DIRECTORY	GetCurrentURL	None
ListDir	NAME, DIRECTORY	ExistsDir ExistsFile	DIRECTORY REMOTEFILE
GetFile	LOCALFILE REMOTEFILE	Exists	ITEM
PutFile	LOCALFILE REMOTEFILE		

Creating an Example

Building on the first example, you now perform some directory operations using the <CFFTP> tag while connected to Allaire's FTP site. You retrieve a file listing and display the results. You can turn on automatic error checking by setting the STOPONERROR attribute to YES. Connection caching is used so that you can maintain a connection to the server. This code is shown in Listing 21.10.

On the CD

Listing 21.10 CFFTP_2.CFM**—File and Directory Operations Using the** <CFFTP> **Tag**

```
<CFFTP ACTION="Open" USERNAME="anonymous" PASSWORD="info@a2zbooks.com"
SERVER="ftp.allaire.com" CONNECTION="ALLAIRE" STOPONERROR="Yes">

<CFFTP CONNECTION="ALLAIRE" ACTION="GetCurrentDir" STOPONERROR="Yes">

<CFOUTPUT>
FTP Directory Listing of #CFFTP.returnvalue#.<P>
</CFOUTPUT>
```

```
<CFFTP CONNECTION="ALLAIRE" ACTION="ListDir" DIRECTORY="/Evaluations"
➥ NAME="DirList" STOPONERROR="Yes">
<HR>
<TABLE BORDER>
<TR>
<TH>Name</TH>
<TH>Path</TH>
<TH>URL</TH>
<TH>Length</TH>
<TH>LastModified</TH>
<TH>Is Directory</TH>
</TR>
<TR>
<CFOUTPUT QUERY="DirList">
<TD>#name#</TD>
<TD>#path#</TD>
<TD>#url#</TD>
<TD>#length#</TD>
<TD>#DateFormat(lastmodified)#</TD>
<TD>#isdirectory#</TD>
</TR>
</CFOUTPUT>
</TABLE>

<CFFTP ACTION="Close" CONNECTION="ALLAIRE" STOPONERROR="Yes">
```

In this example you establish a connection to the Allaire FTP server (`ftp.allaire.com`). You then execute a directory list of the `Evaluations` directory, which is stored in the query named `DirList`. The results are then output into an HTML table by using `<CFOUTPUT>`. Note the new variable `#CFFTP.returnvalue#`, which is used to display the current directory. Figure 21.8 shows the output from this example.

The `<CFFTP>` tag might return a number of different variables, depending on the setting of its attributes. They are `CFFTP.ReturnValue`, the three variables described for the `STOPONERROR` attribute in Table 21.3, and a query object if the `ACTION="ListDir"`. In the previous example, you used the value of the `CFFTP.ReturnValue` to output the current directory and used the query object `DirList` to display the directory listing. The various values of the `CFFTP.ReturnValue` variable are shown in Table 21.6.

Table 21.6 Values of the `CFFTP.ReturnValue` Variable

`<CFFTP>` Action	Value of `CFFTP.ReturnValue`
GetCurrentDir	String value containing name of the current directory
GetCurrentURL	String value containing the current URL
ExistsDir	YES or NO
ExistsFile	YES or NO
Exists	YES or NO

Part

IV

Ch

21

FIGURE 21.8

The <CFFTP> directory listing.

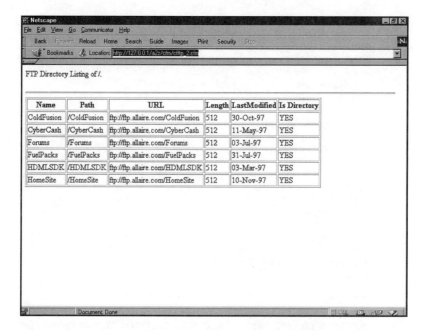

FTP Directory Listing of /.

Name	Path	URL	Length	LastModified	Is Directory
ColdFusion	/ColdFusion	ftp://ftp.allaire.com/ColdFusion	512	30-Oct-97	YES
CyberCash	/CyberCash	ftp://ftp.allaire.com/CyberCash	512	11-May-97	YES
Forums	/Forums	ftp://ftp.allaire.com/Forums	512	03-Jul-97	YES
FuelPacks	/FuelPacks	ftp://ftp.allaire.com/FuelPacks	512	31-Jul-97	YES
HDMLSDK	/HDMLSDK	ftp://ftp.allaire.com/HDMLSDK	512	03-Mar-97	YES
HomeSite	/HomeSite	ftp://ftp.allaire.com/HomeSite	512	10-Nov-97	YES

The variables set when the STOPONERROR attribute is set to NO might contain error codes. Table 21.7 shows the error codes that might be returned and the text explanation of the numeric codes.

Table 21.7 <CFFTP> Error Codes

Error Code	Description
0	Operation succeeded
1	System error (operating system or FTP protocol error)
2	Internet session could not be established
3	FTP session could not be opened
4	File transfer mode not recognized
5	Search connection could not be established
6	Invoked operation valid only during a search
7	Invalid timeout value
8	Invalid port number
9	Not enough memory to allocate system resources
10	Cannot read contents of local file
11	Cannot write to local file
12	Cannot open remote file for reading

Error Code	Description
13	Cannot read remote file
14	Cannot open local file for writing
15	Cannot write to remote file
16	Unknown error
17	Reserved
18	File already exists
19	Reserved
20	Reserved
21	Invalid retry count specified

As shown in the second <CFFTP> example (CFFTP_2.CFM) in Listing 21.10, a query object is created when the ACTION attribute is set to "ListDir". The NAME attribute is then set to the name of the query object that is to be created. After it is created, the query object contains columns that can be referenced using the following form:

`queryname.columnname[row]`

queryname is the value specified in the NAME attribute and columnname is one of the columns defined in the query object, as shown in Table 21.8. row is an integer representing the specific row in the query object returned by the ListDir operation. Information about each file found in the specified directory is stored in a separate row in the query.

Table 21.8   <CFFTP> Query Object Definition

Column	Description
Name	Name of the file or directory
Path	File path (without drive designation)
URL	Complete URL of the file or directory
Length	Number indicating size of the file
LastModified	Date/Time value indicating when the file or directory was last modified
Attributes	String indicating attributes of file or directory
IsDirectory	Boolean value indicating whether the element is a directory

To finish your look at the <CFFTP> tag, you create a template that downloads a specific file from the server. Listing 21.11 shows the code necessary to download a file. In this example you specify a particular file using a cached connection. Set the STOPONERROR attribute to NO so that you can get more detailed error information. You also force the TRANSFERMODE to BINARY.

Part
IV

Ch
21

On the CD

Listing 21.11   `CFFTP_3.CFM`—**Code to Download a Binary File Using** `<CFFTP>`

```
<CFFTP ACTION="Open" USERNAME="anonymous" PASSWORD="info@a2zbooks.com"
SERVER="ftp.allaire.com" CONNECTION="ALLAIRE" STOPONERROR="Yes">


<CFFTP CONNECTION="ALLAIRE" ACTION="GetFile" LOCALFILE="c:\temp\graphlets.zip"
      REMOTEFILE="/Evaluations/FuelPacks/graphlets.zip" STOPONERROR="No"
      TRANSFERMODE="BINARY" FAILIFEXISTS="No">

<CFOUTPUT>
FTP Operation Return Value: #CFFTP.ReturnValue#<BR>
FTP Operation Successful: #CFFTP.Succeeded#<BR>
FTP Operation Error Code: #CFFTP.ErrorCode#<BR>
FTP Operation Error Message: #CFFTP.ErrorText#<BR>
</CFOUTPUT>

<CFFTP ACTION="Close" CONNECTION="ALLAIRE" STOPONERROR="Yes">
```

Figure 21.9 shows the output from this example.

FIGURE 21.9

Output from binary file downloaded using `<CFFTP>`.

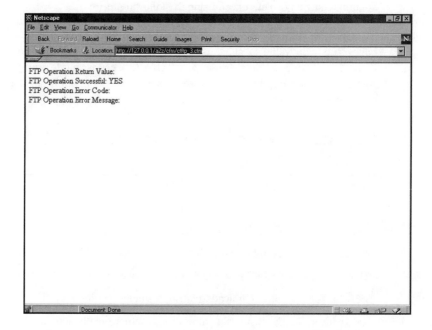

Intelligent Agents

Intelligent agents should really be called intelligent parcers. An *intelligent agent* takes text from some remote location (which can be the result of a distributed process) and parses it for the needed data. Look at the following two examples of a simple parser agent. The first code segment is written using pre-ColdFusion 4 syntax, whereas the second uses more advanced ColdFusion 4 regular expressions. The code is retrieving a page and then getting the meta keywords from the page. This could be part of a spider agent or bookmark application.

```
<!--- Get remote page --->
<cfhttp url="127.0.0.1" method="GET">
<!--- Set text to search for. If this text does not exist, try a different
 approach for the same type of results --->
<CFSET StartText='<META HTTP-EQUIV="Keywords" Content="'>
<CFSET Start = FindNoCase(StartText, Cfhttp.FileContent,1)>
<CFIF Start is 0>
    <CFSET StartText='<META Name="keywords" Content="'>
    <CFSET Start = FindNoCase(StartText, Cfhttp.FileContent,1)>
</CFIF>
<!--- If the text exists, do other operations --->
<CFIF start is not 0>
<!--- Define end text--->
    <CFSET EndText='">'>
      <!--- Define length of start text --->
    <CFSET Length=Len(StartText)>
      <!--- Find end of desired substring --->
    <CFSET End=FindNoCase(EndText, Cfhttp.FileContent, Start)>
      <!--- Get entire substring --->
    <CFSET KeyWords = Mid(Cfhttp.FileContent, Start+length, End-start-length)>
<CFOUTPUT>#KeyWords#</CFOUTPUT>
</CFIF>
```

This second version of the parser performs the same operations but uses regular expressions for the search and comparison operations:

```
<!--- Get remote page --->
<cfhttp url="127.0.0.1" method="GET">
<!--- Set text to search for. Including optional names for meta type--->
<CFSET StartText='<META (HTTP-EQUIV|Name)="KEYWORDS" CONTENT="'>
      <!--- Define end text--->
<CFSET EndText='">'>
<!--- Find location of substring --->
<CFSET Get = ReFindNoCase(StartText&'([^'&EndText&']*)'&EndText,
➥ Cfhttp.FileContent,1,'True')>
<!--- Parse out substring --->
<CFSET Description = Mid(Cfhttp.FileContent, Get.pos[3], Get.len[3])>
<CFOUTPUT>#Description#</CFOUTPUT>
```

If the string you're searching for is the only thing in a document, the parser starts at position 1 and goes to position 48. This position is reflected in Get.Pos[1] and Get.Len[1]. This information is useful when you're looking for a standard start/finish string, but here you're looking for a single piece of the string. Notice that StartText has HTTP-EQUIV and Name in parentheses.

Part
IV

Ch

21

You use parentheses because you know that metatags can use either of these two terms to define the tag type. Placing them in parentheses with a pipe symbol (¦) between them says "either/or." This point is brought up here because the values of Get.Pos[2] and Get.Len[2] actually refer to the text found within these parentheses, which again are not what you need. You finally get to what you need in the body of the ReFindNoCase itself. The regular expression used here is StartText&'([^'&EndText&']*)'&EndText. Notice the parentheses in the middle. This syntax says, "Look for some text that starts with the start text, ends with the end text, and anything within that is not the end text should be within parentheses." This is what you're looking for and it's found in Get.Pos[3] and Get.Len[3]. These elements define the start of the text you want and the length of it, which can easily be used within the Mid function.

Variants of this code are used for modules ranging from stock grabbers to full-fledged UPS shipping interaction. Combining this code with WDDX allows you to save a lot of time on the parsing. ●

## CHAPTER 22

Interacting with the System Registry

Introduction and Warning

There's a famous quote that goes as such: "Abandon all hope all ye who enter here." This quote is doubly true for this chapter. Here you are looking at what is probably the most dangerous of all the ColdFusion tags around: the CFREGISTRY tag. This tag does exactly what its name implies—it gives access to a machine's Registry.

Before reading this chapter, you should brush up on security by reading Chapter 7, "Securing Specific Features and Components." You should also read whatever documentation or books you can find about the Registry. Due to space considerations, the Registry's history and descriptions are kept brief here. More attention is paid to this tag's usage, the location of special keys in the Registry, and examples.

N O T E While the Registry is a Windows-only construct, a simulation is provided on UNIX platforms. This simulation has the same effect as the Windows Registry and the tag reacts the same way to both. ▓

What Is the Registry?

The Registry is a system database that primarily holds information about where things are located in the operating system. Programs, paths, default values, and more are stored within. Because it's a system database, it has very fast access to information. The only problem is that it's not designed for real database work. This is one of the reasons Allaire has allowed an option for client variables to be stored to a database rather than in their current Registry position (see Chapter 7).

> **CAUTION**
>
> If you are not familiar with the Windows Registry, you should not change any of the settings. This cannot be recommended strongly enough! If you decide to explore the Windows Registry, be sure to have a good Registry book on hand, such as *Troubleshooting and Configuring the Windows NT/95 Registry* (Sams Publishing).

One important note is that the Registry is a system database for Windows machines. The structure and job of the Registry only exists for the Windows NT and Windows 95/98 versions of ColdFusion. This does not mean that these tags are of no use on the UNIX platforms. The UNIX versions of ColdFusion ship with a mock Registry that provides all of the storage of ColdFusion information that the Windows NT/95/98 Registry does. This means that all of the code that relates to ColdFusion and the Registry will work on all platforms. This also means that other information—Web server data, program mappings, and other things that are in the Windows Registry—are inaccessible in UNIX.

Terminology

There are certain terms used in conjunction with the Windows Registry that you need to become familiar with to use this chapter:

■ *Key*—This is the same as a directory in a file system. It holds subkeys (subdirectories) and entries (files).

■ *Entry*—A variable within a key that holds a data value. Entries do not change unless they are deleted and re-created. Only their content can be altered.

■ *Value*—The data contained within an entry. ColdFusion does not allow binary data to be set or retrieved from values.

■ *Branch*—A specific path mapping from the root of a Registry tree to a specific subkey.

Common Registry Paths

There are certain Registry paths that are used more than others in ColdFusion. These include the following:

■ Standard ColdFusion path:
`HKEY_LOCAL_MACHINE\SOFTWARE\Allaire\ColdFusion\CurrentVersion\`

■ Forums path (if Forums is installed):
`HKEY_LOCAL_MACHINE\SOFTWARE\Allaire\Forums\CurrentVersion\`

■ ODBC information: `HKEY_LOCAL_MACHINE\SOFTWARE\ODBC\ODBC.INI\`

■ O'Reilly Web site: `HKEY_LOCAL_MACHINE\SOFTWARE\DENNY`
`HKEY_LOCAL_MACHINE\SOFTWARE\EIT`

■ Netscape: `HKEY_LOCAL_MACHINE\SOFTWARE\Netscape\`

CFREGISTRY Basics

The `CFREGISTRY` tags have only two attributes that are shared between them:

`Action`	Required	The type of Registry action you want to perform
`Branch`	Required	The name of the Registry branch containing the keys or values you want to access

While it is possible to dynamically set a tag's action, it is not a good idea. Due to the tight nature of the ColdFusion compiler, any tag that has attributes that do not belong can cause an error in the tag operation. As you see in a moment, all of the tags have different required attributes. If one attribute is added where it does not belong or is missing where it's needed, the tag fails. On the other hand, all tags use the `Branch` attribute and it's usually a good idea to have at least part of the branch dynamic. Later you write some example code and see what is being described.

There are four actions used by the `CFREGISTRY` tag to manipulate the Registry:

■ `Get`
■ `GetAll`
■ `Set`
■ `Delete`

Get Action

The Get action of CFREGISTRY is very similar to the CFSET tag. It sets a variable with a value. Of course, this value comes from the Registry, but that's really the only difference.

ENTRY	Required	The Registry value to be accessed
TYPE	Optional	The type of data you want to access:
		String—Returns a string value (default)
		DWord—Returns a DWord value
		Key—Returns a key's default value
VARIABLE	Required	Variable into which CFREGISTRY places the value

One important note is that this tag will try to set the variable with the entry value no matter what. This means that if the entry does not exist, it will fail. The "GetAll Action" section of this chapter shows a way around this. Listing 22.1 uses CFREGISTRY with the Get action to retrieve the ColdFusion StudioPassword. This is the encrypted password, so don't be surprised with the results.

Listing 22.1 REGISTRY1—Action=Get **Example**

```
<!--- This example uses CFREGISTRY with the Get Action
         to retrieve the ColdFusion StudioPassword --->
<HTML>
<HEAD>
    <TITLE>CFREGISTRY ACTION="Get"</TITLE>
</HEAD>
<BODY>
<!--- Set registryRegistry location for current ColdFusion install --->
<CFSET CFPath = "HKEY_LOCAL_MACHINE\SOFTWARE\Allaire\ColdFusion\CurrentVersion">
<CFREGISTRY
    ACTION="Get"
    BRANCH="#CFPath#\Server"
    ENTRY="StudioPassword"
    TYPE="String"
    Variable="RegValue">
<H1>CFREGISTRY ACTION="Get"</H1>
<cfoutput>
<P>
Value for StudioPassword is #RegValue#
</cfoutput>
</BODY>
</HTML>
```

GetAll Action

The GetAll action is the broadest of the CFREGISTRY actions. It searches and returns all values within a key. This ability covers both Keys and Entry values. The result of this action is a standard ColdFusion query with a name equal to the name attribute.

TYPE	Optional	The type of data you want to access:
		String—Returns string values (default).
		DWord—Returns DWord values.
		Key—Returns keys.
		Any—Returns keys and values.
NAME	Required	The name of the result set to contain returned keys and values.
SORT	Optional	Used to sort query column data returned with ACTION=GETALL. Ignored for all other actions. Sorts on Entry, Type, and Value fields as text. Any combination of columns from query output can be specified in a comma-separated list. ASC (ascending) or DESC (descending) can be specified as qualifiers for column names. ASC is the default.

When run, this tag returns a query with three columns.

Entry	The name of the key or entry
Type	The data type (See TYPE earlier)
Value	If the type is not a key, this holds the value of the entry

Listing 22.2 uses CFREGISTRY with the GetAll action to retrieve ColdFusion server information. Remember that this is returning an entire query.

Listing 22.2 REGISTRY2—CFREGISTRY Action=GetAll

```
<!--- This example uses CFREGISTRY with the GetAll
    Action to retrieve ColdFusion server information --->

<HTML>
<HEAD>
    <TITLE>CFREGISTRY ACTION="GetAll"</TITLE>
</HEAD>
<BODY>
<CFSET CFPath = "HKEY_LOCAL_MACHINE\SOFTWARE\Allaire\ColdFusion\CurrentVersion">
<CFREGISTRY ACTION="GetAll"
    BRANCH="#CFPath#\Server"
    TYPE="Any"
    NAME="RegQuery"
    Sort="value DESC, entry ASC">
<P>
<H1>CFREGISTRY ACTION="GetAll"</H1>
<CFTABLE QUERY="RegQuery" COLHEADERS HTMLTABLE BORDER="Yes">
<CFCOL HEADER="<B>Entry</b>" WIDTH="35" TEXT="#RegQuery.Entry#">
<CFCOL HEADER="<B>Type</b>" WIDTH="10" TEXT="#RegQuery.Type#">
<CFCOL HEADER="<B>Value</b>" WIDTH="35" TEXT="#RegQuery.Value#">
</CFTABLE>
</BODY>
</HTML>
```

Remember that the result of this action is a query object. This means that it can return an empty query. This is very different than the Get action, where it tries to set a variable. If you want to see if a value exists in a key, you must use the GetAll action and loop over the resultant query. The code in Listing 22.3 does a basic Registry value exists-type search. For this example, you determine whether a CFX tag has been installed.

Listing 22.3 checks the Registry to see if a specific CFX tag is installed.

Listing 22.3   Checks Windows Registry to See if a Specific CFX Tag Is Installed

```
<!--- Set registry location for current ColdFusion install --->
<CFSET CFPath = "HKEY_LOCAL_MACHINE\SOFTWARE\Allaire\ColdFusion\CurrentVersion">
<!--- Get all Keys from the CustomTags section of the CFPath. --->
<CFREGISTRY
    ACTION="GetAll"
    BRANCH="#CFPath#\CustomTags"
    TYPE="Key"
    NAME="RegExists">

<!--- Loop over return set to see if the CFX_Spell tag has been installed --->
<CFLOOP QUERY="RegExists">
    <CFIF Entry IS "CFX_Spell">
        CFX_Spell installed
    </CFIF>
</CFLOOP>
```

N O T E   CFREGISTRY does not currently support the Binary type. In one instance of the GetAll action, however, it may seem as though it does: If you use the GetAll action with a type of all, binary types are returned in a special manner. The type shows up as Binary, but no value is shown. This may change in the future. ▩

Set Action

CFREGISTRY's Set action is used for all actual data manipulation for both keys and entries:

ENTRY	Required	The key or value to be set.
TYPE	Optional	The type of data you want to set:
		String—Set a string value (default).
		DWord—Set a DWord value.
		Key—Create a key.
VALUE	Optional	The value data to be set. If you omit this attribute, CFREGISTRY creates default value data, as follows:
		String—Default value is an empty string ("").
		DWord—Default value is 0 (zero).

Creating a new Entry is very straightforward; use all the attributes for this action and the Entry will appear with any value that you want to set. If the Entry already exists, its value will be updated. To create a new key, all you have to do is set the Branch location, the Entry name of the key to create and the Type. This creates an empty key. An error occurs if the branch does not exist. If the Key already exists, nothing happens either to the key or to the data within it.

Listing 22.4 uses CFREGISTRY with the Set action to modify Registry value data.

Listing 22.4 Modifies Registry Value with the Set Action Using CFREGISTRY

```
<!--- This example uses CFREGISTRY with the Set Action to
        modify registry value data --->

<HTML>
<HEAD>
<TITLE>CFREGISTRY ACTION="Set"</TITLE>
</HEAD>
<BODY>
<CFSET Filename = "test">
<CFREGISTRY ACTION="Set"
  BRANCH="HKEY_LOCAL_MACHINE\Software\Allaire"
  ENTRY="LastCFM01" TYPE="String" VALUE="#FileName#">
<H1>CFREGISTRY ACTION="Set"</H1>
</BODY>
</HTML>
```

Delete Action

This action is used to delete Registry keys and entries.

ENTRY   Required   The value to be deleted

Only the branch is needed when deleting a key. This should be done very carefully because all subkeys and values of the specified key will be deleted. This can prove useful in some situations. Listing 22.5 deletes all of the client variables on a machine.

Listing 22.5 uses CFREGISTRY with the Delete action to delete the key you set in the preceding example. If you didn't run the last example, it has nothing to delete. This action is one of the main reasons you're warned not to use this tag without lots of Registry knowledge.

Listing 22.5 Deletes the Key Set in Listing 22.4 Using the Delete Action

```
<CFSET CFPath = "HKEY_LOCAL_MACHINE\SOFTWARE\Allaire\ColdFusion\CurrentVersion">
<CFREGISTRY ACTION="Delete"
  BRANCH="#CFPath#/Clients"
  ENTRY="TempFile01">
```

Multi-Tag Example

To get a good feel for the CFREGISTRY tag and how it can work with other tags, you're going to write some code using it (see Listing 22.6). If you look in the ColdFusion Administration pages, you'll see in the Verity section a list of all the collections by name and with their location. Because these pages are encrypted, you really can't see how it's been done. Let's walk through some code and add a twist. You're going to also see what type of collection you're dealing with.

In order to get directly to the tags in question, this is not explained as a module. Nor are you going to use a ton of tricks to get it tight and fast. You're going to create a query that contains all the data you want to view. To do this you use the standard QueryNew function to create a new query. One additional thing you're going to do at this point is set a variable with the standard CF Registry path. While this path will not change, it's a good idea to see it in use. Just a reminder that you can use variables in parts of the CFREGISTRY tag.

Listing 22.6   Create a New Query with the QueryNew Function

```
<!--- Set the query base --->
<CFSET VerityInfo = QueryNew("Name, Location, Type")>
<CFSET CFRegPath =
 "HKEY_LOCAL_MACHINE\SOFTWARE\Allaire\ColdFusion\CurrentVersion">
```

You add some checker code in Listing 22.7. This is important because the CFREGISTRY tag only exists in ColdFusion 4. You could leave this out if you were sure of the version you were using. This should also work on later versions.

Listing 22.7   Add Checker Code to Listing 22.6

```
<!--- Check if the current version is CF 4 or greater --->
<CFIF Val(server.coldfusion.productversion) LT 4>
    <CFABORT>
</CFIF>
```

Now you get directly into the meat of the example module with Listing 22.8. You're using the CFREGISTRY tag to go to the Collections key in the standard ColdFusion Registry path and retrieve all the subkeys there. These keys are the names of all the collections on the machine; they are also the subkeys that contain the collections' locations. The result of this is a query that you loop through to get all the locations (and then to the collection types). Before you do that, however, you add as many rows to your previously built query as there are collections.

Listing 22.8   Use the CFREGISTRY Tag to Go to the Collections Key and Retrieve All the Subkeys

```
<!--- Get the names of all the collections --->
<CFREGISTRY ACTION="GetAll"
    BRANCH="#CFRegPath#\Collections"
```

```
      NAME="Collections"
      Type="Key">

<!--- Add as many rows to the query as there are collections --->
<CFSET QueryAddRow(VerityInfo, Collections.RecordCount)>
```

At this point, you're going to loop over the query you received from the CFREGISTRY tag in Listing 22.9. With a little change in code, you could use a different loop. There's no specific reason to use an index loop here rather than a query loop. With each iteration of the loop, you set the name of the collection to the query you're building. Additionally, for each loop you'll do another Registry call to the specific collection to get its physical location. This information is in an Entry of TopLevelDirectory. As you see, you're appending the Entry value from the query to the end of the Branch, creating a new branch for each collection.

Listing 22.9   This Code Loops Over the Query Set in Listing 22.8

```
<!--- This should be a query loop but building a caller query within a query
➥loop fails --->
<CFLOOP INDEX="i" FROM="1" TO="#Collections.Recordcount#">
    <CFSET QuerySetCell(verityinfo, "Name", Collections.Entry[i], i)>

    <CFREGISTRY ACTION="Get"
        BRANCH="#CFRegPath#\Collections\#Entry#"
        Entry="TopLevelDirectory"
        Variable="TopLevelDirectory">
```

Once you get the TopLevelDirectory information, you have to see what physical files are on the drive for it. For this you do a standard CFDIRECTORY using the TopLevelDirectory as your root (see Listing 22.10). You can discover whether a collection is from a query or from a file by looking at where the collection information is stored. The Custom directory is used for queries and the File directory for files. Here you're checking the custom directory because there are usually more query-based Verity collections than file-based. You're determining whether the directory search returns more or less than three because every directory automatically has two elements in it. The collection type is revealed by the test results.

Listing 22.10   Use the CFDIRECTORY Command to Perform a File Check Using TopLevelDirectory

```
    <!--- Decide on the collection type --->
    <CFDIRECTORY ACTION="LIST" DIRECTORY=
➥"#TopLevelDirectory#\custom\parts" NAME="Files">
    <CFIF Files.RecordCount LT 3>
        <CFDIRECTORY ACTION="LIST"
➥ DIRECTORY="#TopLevelDirectory#\file\parts" NAME="Files">
        <CFSET IIF
➥(Files.RecordCount GT 3, 'QuerySetCell(VerityInfo, "Location", "File")',
➥ 'QuerySetCell(VerityInfo, "Location", "No Information")')>
```

continues

Listing 22.10 Continued

```
    <CFELSE>
        <CFSET QuerySetCell(VerityInfo,
➥ "Location", "Query")>
    </CFIF>
</CFLOOP>
```

This little program shows an important point. The data returned from the Registry is the same as any other data; it can be used anywhere queries and variables can. ●

Appendixes

ColdFusion Tag Reference

ColdFusion tags are the CFML extensions to HTML. These tags are the instructions to ColdFusion to perform database queries, process results, perform transaction processing, send email, and much more.

The tags are presented here in alphabetical order, and are cross referenced to any related tags wherever appropriate.

<CFABORT>

Description: The <CFABORT> tag is used to immediately halt processing of a ColdFusion template. <CFABORT> attributes are listed in Table A.1.

Syntax:

```
<CFABORT SHOWERROR="Error text">
```

Table A.1   <CFABORT> Attributes

Attribute	Description	Notes
SHOWERROR	Error message	This attribute is optional.

Example: The following example aborts template processing if the user is not in a specific range of valid IP addresses:

```
<CFIF Left(CGI.REMOTE_ADDR, 11) NEQ "208.193.16.">
 <H1>Unauthorized host detected! Access denied!</H1>
 <CFABORT SHOWERROR="You are not authorized to use this function!">
</CFIF>
```

TIP

<CFABORT> can be used to safely terminate the processing of a template if an error condition occurs. For example, if your template were expecting an URL parameter to be passed, you could use the ParameterExists or IsDefined functions to verify its existence and terminate the template with an appropriate error message if it did not exist.

See also: <CFEXIT>

<CFAPPLET>

Description: <CFAPPLET> is used to embed user-supplied Java applets into CFFORM forms. Table A.2 is the complete list of attributes supported by <CFAPPLET>. In addition, you may pass your own attributes as long as they have been registered along with the applet itself.

Before you can use an applet with <CFAPPLET>, it must be registered with the ColdFusion Administrator.

<CFAPPLET> must be used within <CFORM> and </CFORM> tags.

Syntax:

```
<CFAPPLET ALIGN="Alignment" APPLETSOURCE="Regsitered Name" HEIGHT="Height"
HSPACE="Horizontal Spacing" NAME="Field Name"
 NOTSUPPORTED="Text for non Java browsers" VSPACE="Vertical Spacing"
 WIDTH="Width">
```

Table A.2 **<CFAPPLET> Attributes**

Attribute	Description	Notes
ALIGN	Applet alignment	Valid values are: left, right, bottom, top, texttop, middle, absmiddle, baseline, and absbottom. This attribute is optional.
APPLETSOURCE	Name of the registered applet.	This attribute is required.
HEIGHT	Height in pixels.	This attribute is optional.
HSPACE	Horizontal spacing in pixels.	This attribute is optional.
NAME	Form field name.	This attribute is required.
NOTSUPPORTED	Text to display on browsers that do not support Java.	This attribute is optional.
VSPACE	Vertical spacing optional in pixels.	This attribute is optional.
WIDTH	Width in pixels.	This attribute is optional.

Example: The following example embeds a Java spin control applet into a <CFFORM> form, passing the required attributes and two applet-specific attributes:

```
<CFFORM ACTION="process.cfm">
<CFAPPLET APPLETSOURCE="spin" NAME="quantity" MIN="1" MAX="10">
</CFFORM>
```

N O T E   Controls embedded with <CFAPPLET> are accessible only by users with Java-enabled browsers. ▪

See also: <CFFORM>, <CFGRID>, <CFSLIDER>, <CFTEXTINPUT>, <CFTREE>

<CFAPPLICATION>

Description: <CFAPPLICATION> is used to name an application, or part thereof, to restrict the scope of any client, session, and application variables. By default, these variables are visible to all templates. <CFAPPLICATION> allows you to name part of an application so that variables created in other templates are not visible to it, and variables created within it are not visible to other parts of the application. <CFAPPLICATION> attributes are shown in Table A.3.

Syntax:

```
<CFAPPLICATION APPLICATIONTIMEOUT ="Timeout" CLIENTMANAGEMENT ="Yes or No"
 CLIENTSTOREAGE="Storage Type" NAME="Application Name"
 SESSIONMANAGEMENT ="Yes or No" SESSIONTIMEOUT ="Timeout"
 SETCLIENTCOOKIES="Yes or No">
```

Table A.3 <CFAPPLICATION> **Attributes**

Attribute	Description	Notes
APPLICATIONTIMEOUT	Timeout interval for application variables	Application variable timeout; default to value in ColdFusion Administrator.
CLIENTMANAGEMENT	Enable or disable client variables	This optional attribute defaults to No.
CLIENTSTORAGE	Mechanism for storage of client information	This optional attribute defaults to Registry; other values are Cookie and any ODBC data source name.
NAME	Name of application	This attribute is required if you are using application variables; may be up to 64 characters long.
SESSIONMANAGEMENT	Enable or disable session variables	This optional attribute defaults to No.
SESSIONTIMEOUT	Timeout interval for session variables	Session variable timeout; default to value in ColdFusion Administrator.
SETCLIENTCOOKIES	Enable or disable client cookies	This optional attribute defaults to Yes.

Example: The following example names part of an application `Administration` and enables session variables:

```
<CFAPPLICATION NAME="Administration" SESSIONMANAGEMENT="Yes">
```

 TIP The `<CFAPPLICATION>` tag is best used in the `APPLICATION.CFM` template.

For more information about enabling or disabling application and session variables, as well as setting default timeout values, see Chapter 4.

See also: `<CFCOOKIE>`, `<CFSET>`

<CFASSOCIATE>

Description: The `<CFASSOCIATE>` tag is used to associate subtags with base tags. This tag may only be used within custom tags. `<CFASSOCIATE>` attributes are shown in Table A.4.

Syntax:

```
<CFASSOCIATE BASETAG="tag" DATACOLLECTION="collection">
```

Table A.4 `<CFASSOCIATE>` **Attributes**

Attribute	Description	Notes
BASETAG	Name of base tag associated with this subtag.	This attribute is required.
DELETEFILE	Name of the structure in the base tag to store attributes.	This attribute is optional; if not specified, the default structure of `AssocAttribs` is used.

Example: The following example associates a subtag with a base tag:

```
<CFASSOCIATE BASETAG="CF_MENU">
```

See also: `<CFMODULE>`

<CFAUTHENTICATE>

Description: The <CFAUTHENTICATE> tag authenticates a user, setting a security context for the application. The complete list of supported attributes is explained in Table A.5.

Syntax:

```
<CFAUTHENTICATE PASSWORD="password" SECURITYCONTEXT="context" USERNAME="user">
```

Table A.5   **<CFAUTHENTICATE> Attributes**

Attribute	Description	Notes
PASSWORD	User password.	Optional user password.
SECURITYCONTEXT	Context to authenticate against.	This is a required attribute; context must have been defined in the ColdFusion Administrator.
USERNAME	Username.	Required username.

Example: The following example authenticates a user-supplied username and password within an administrator context:

```
<CFAUTHENTICATE SECURITYCONTEXT="administrator" USERNAME="#username#"
 PASSWORD="#password#">
```

<CFCOLLECTION>

Description: The <CFCOLLECTION> tag can be used to programmatically create and administer Verity collections. The complete list of <CFCOLLECTION> attributes is explained in Table A.6.

Syntax:

```
<CFCOLLECTION ACTION="action" COLLECTION="collection" LANGUAGE="language"
 PATH="path">
```

Table A.6   **<CFCOLLECTION> Attributes**

Attribute	Description	Notes
ACTION	Action.	Required attribute; see Table A.7.
COLLECTION	Collection name.	Required; name of the collection to be indexed. If using external collections, this must be a fully qualified path to the collection

Attribute	Description	Notes
LANGUAGE	Collection language.	Optional language; default to English.
PATH	Collection path.	Required if ACTION is CREATE.

Table A.7 **<CFCOLLECTION> Actions**

Action	Description
CREATE	Create a new collection.
DELETE	Delete a collection.
OPTIMIZE	Purge and reorganize a collection.
REPAIR	Fixed a corrupt collection.

Example: The following example fixes a collection named "all":

```
<CFCOLLECTION ACTION="REPAIR" COLLECTION="all">
```

N O T E <CFCOLLECTION> works at the collection level only. To add content to a collection, use <CFINDEX>. ■

See also: <CFINDEX>, <CFSEARCH>

<CFCONTENT>

Description: The <CFCONTENT> tags allows you to send non-HTML documents to a client's browser. <CFCONTENT> lets you specify the MIME type of the file and an optional filename to transmit. The complete list of supported attributes is in Table A.8.

Syntax:

```
<CFCONTENT TYPE="MIME Type" FILE="File Name" DELETEFILE>
```

Table A.8 <CFCONTENT> **Attributes**

Attribute	Description	Notes
TYPE	Content MIME Type	This attribute is required.
FILE	Name of file to send to user	This is an optional attribute that specifies the fully qualified path of a file to be transmitted to the user's browser.
DELETEFILE	Deletes the file once sent	Useful if servingdynamically created graphics. This attribute is optional.

Example: The following example sends data-driven VRML to the user:

```
<CFCONTENT TYPE="x-world/x-vrml">
<CFOUTPUT QUERY="world">
#world#
</CFOUTPUT>
```

This next example sends a Microsoft Word document:

```
<CFCONTENT TYPE="application/msword" FILE="C:\MyDocs\Proposal.DOC">
```

This final example sends a dynamically created map to the user and then deletes it upon completion of the transmission:

```
<CFCONTENT TYPE="image/gif" FILE="C:\Images\Maps\Temp123.gif" DELETEFILE>
```

<CFCOOKIE>

Description: <CFCOOKIE> allows you to set *cookies*, persistent client-side variables, on the client browser. Cookies allow you to set variables on a client's browser, which are then returned every time a page is requested by a browser. Cookies may be sent securely if required.

To access a returned cookie, specify its name and precede it with the COOKIE designator, as in #COOKIE.USER_ID#.

As not all browsers support cookies. You must never make assumptions about the existence of the cookie. Always use the IsDefined function to check for the existence of the cookie before referencing it.

Syntax:

```
<CFCOOKIE NAME="Cookie Name" VALUE="Value" EXPIRES="Expiration" SECURE>
```

Table A.9   <CFCOOKIE> **Attributes**

Attribute	Description	Notes
DOMAIN	The domain for which the cookies are valid	Required only if PATH is used. Separate multiple domains with a ; character.
EXPIRES	Cookie expiration date	The cookie expiration date may be specified as a definite date (as in '10/1/97'), relative days (as in '100'), NOW, or NEVER. This attribute is optional.
NAME	Name of cookie	This attribute is required.
PATH	Subset of the URL to which the cookie applies	This attribute is optional. Separate multiple paths with a ; character.
SECURE	Specify that cookie must be sent securely	This attribute is optional. If it is specified and the browser does not support SSL, the cookie is not sent.
VALUE	Cookie value	This attribute is required.

Example: The following example sends a cookie containing a user ID and sets the expiration date to 60 days from now:

```
<CFCOOKIE NAME="USER_ID" VALUE="100">
```

This next example sets a secure cookie that never expires (until manually deleted):

```
<CFCOOKIR NAME="access" VALUE="admin" SECURE>
```

N O T E   If you use the SECURE attribute to specify that the cookie must be sent securely, it is only sent if the browser supports SSL. If the cookie cannot be sent securely, it is not sent at all. ▪

N O T E   Cookies are domain-specific, meaning they can be set so just the server that set them can retrieve them. ▪

TIP   Setting a cookie expiration date of NOW effectively deletes the cookie from the client's browser.

See also: <CFAPPLICATION>

<CFDIRECTORY>

Description: <CFDIRECTORY> is used for all directory manipulation, including obtaining directory lists and creating or deleting directories.

<CFDIRECTORY> is a flexible and powerful tag, and has many attributes, some of which are mutually exclusive. The values passed to the ACTION attribute dictates what other attributes can be used. The possible ACTION values for <CFDIRECTORY> are listed in Table A.11. LIST is assumed if no ACTION is specified. Table A.12 contains the list of columns returns if ACTION="LIST".

Syntax:

```
<CFDIRECTORY ACTION="Action Type" DIRECTORY="Directory Name"
 FILTER="Search Filter" MODE="Unix Permissions Mode" NAME="Query Name"
 NEWDIRECTORY="New Directory Name" SORT="Sort Order">
```

Table A.10 **<CFDIRECTORY> Attributes**

Attribute	Description	Notes
ACTION	Tag action	This attribute is optional, and will default to LIST if omitted.
DIRECTORY	Directory name	This attribute is required.
FILTER	Filter spec	This attribute is optional and is only valid if ACTION="LIST". Filter may contain wildcard characters.
MODE	Permissions mode	This optional attribute is only valid if ACTION="CREATE". It is used only by the Solaris version of ColdFusion, and is ignored by the Windows versions.
NAME	Query name	Required if ACTION="LIST". Query to hold retrieved directory listing.
NEWDIRECTORY	New directory rename	Required if ACTION="RENAME", ignored by all other actions.

Attribute	Description	Notes
SORT	Sort order	Optional comma -delimited list of columns to sort by; each may use ASC for ascending or DESC for descending. Default is ascending.

Table A.11 <CFDIRECTORY> **Actions**

Action	Description
CREATE	Creates a new directory.
DELETE	Deletes a directory.
LIST	Obtains a list of directory contents.
RENAME	Renames a directory.

Table A.12 <CFDIRECTORY> LIST **Columns**

Action	Description
ATTRIBUTES	File attributes
DATELASTMODIFIED	Last modified date
MODE	Permissions mode (Solaris only)
NAME	File or directory name
SIZE	Size in bytes
TYPE	Type **F** for file or **D** for directory

Example: This first creates a new directory:

```
<CFDIRECTORY ACTION="CREATE"DIRECTORY="C:\STUFF">
```

This next example retrieves a directory list, sorted by filename:

```
<CFDIRECTORY ACTION="LIST"DIRECTORY="C:\STUFF" NAME="Stuff" SORT="Name">
```

See also: <CFFILE>

<CFERROR>

Description: <CFERROR> allows you to override the standard ColdFusion error messages and replace them with templates that you specify. <CFERROR> requires that you specify the type of error message to be overridden and the template containing the error message to be displayed.

There are two different types of error messages in ColdFusion. REQUEST errors occur while processing a template, and VALIDATION errors occur when FORM field validation errors occur. In each scenario, a special set of ColdFusion fields are available for inclusion in your error message template.

Syntax:

```
<CFERROR Type="Error Type" TEMPLATE="Error Message Template
MAILTO="Administrator's email Address">
```

Table A.13 **<CFERROR> Attributes**

Attribute	Description	Notes
MAILTO	The administrator's email address	The email address of the administrator to be notified of any error messages; this value is available with the error message template as #ERROR.MailTo#.
TEMPLATE	Error message template	Name of the template containing the error message to display. This attribute is required.
TYPE	Type of error message	Possible values are "REQUEST" or "VALIDATION". If this attribute is omitted, the default value of "REQUEST" is used.

Table A.14 **ColdFusion Error Message Variables**

Type	Field	Description
REQUEST	#ERROR.RemoteAddress#	Client's IP address.
REQUEST	#ERROR.Browser#	The browser the client was running, with version and platform information if provided by the browser.

Type	Field	Description
REQUEST	#ERROR.DateTime#	The date and time that the error occurred; can be passed to any of the date/time manipulation functions as needed.
REQUEST	#ERROR.Diagnostics#	Detailed diagnostic error message returned by ColdFusion.
REQUEST	#ERROR.HTTPReferer#	URL of the page from which the template was accessed.
REQUEST	#ERROR.MailTo#	Administrator's email address; can be used to send notification of the error.
REQUEST	#ERROR.QueryString#	The URL's query string.
REQUEST	#ERROR.Template#	Template being processed when the error occurred.
VALIDATION	#ERROR.InvalidFields#	List of the invalid form fields.
VALIDATION	#ERROR.ValidationFooter#	Text for footer of error message.
VALIDATION	#ERROR.ValidationHeader#	Text for header of error message.

Example: The following example establishes an error message template for REQUEST errors:

```
<CFERROR TYPE="REQUEST" NAME="ERROR_REQUEST.CFM" MAILTO="admin@a2zbooks.com">
```

Listing A.1   Sample Request Error Template

```
<HTML>

<HEAD>
<TITLE>Application Error!</TITLE>
</HEAD>

<BODY>
<H1>Application Error!</H1>
A critical error has occurred, please try your request later.

</BODY>

</HTML>
```

T I P The <CFERROR> tag is best used in the APPLICATION.CFM template.

<CFEXIT>

Description: <CFEXIT> aborts the processing of a custom tag without aborting processing of the calling template. <CFEXIT> can only be used within custom tags. Unlike <CFABORT>, which terminates caller template processing, <CFEXIT> stops processing the custom tag and returns control to the caller.

Syntax: <CFEXIT>

Example: This example checks to see if any form fields exist and stops processing if there are none:

```
<CFIF IsDefined("FORM.formfields") IS "No">
 <CFEXIT>
</CFIF>
```

See also: <CFABORT>

<CFFILE>

Description: <CFFILE> is used to perform various types of file management, including uploading files from a browser, moving, renaming, copying, and deleting files, and reading and writing of text files.

<CFFILE> is a flexible and powerful tag; it has many attributes, many of which are mutually exclusive. The values passed to the ACTION attribute dictate what other attributes may be used.

<CFFILE> creates a FILE object after every <CFFILE> operation. You can use the variables in this object as you would any other ColdFusion variables, allowing you to check the results of an operation. However, only one FILE object exists, and as soon as you execute a new <CFFILE> tag, the prior FILE object is overwritten with the new one.

Syntax:

```
<CFFILE ACCEPT="Filter" ACTION="Action Type"
 DESTINATION="Destination Directory or File Name" FILE="File Name"
 FILEFIELD="Field Containing File Name" NAMECONFLICT="Conflict Option"
 OUTPUT="Text To Output" SOURCE="Source File Name" VARIABLE="Variable Name">
```

Table A.15   <CFFILE> Attributes

Attribute	Description	Notes
ACCEPT	File type filter	This optional attribute restricts the types of files that may be uploaded, and may only be used if ACTION is UPLOAD. The filter is specified as a MIME type ("image/*", which allows all image types, but nothing else); multiple MIME types may be specified separated by commas.
ACTION	Desired action	This attribute is required.
DESTINATION	Destination file location	This attribute may only be used if ACTION is one the following: APPEND, COPY, MOVE, RENAME, UPLOAD. Destination may be a filename or a fully qualified file path.
FILE	Name of local file to access	This attribute may only be used if ACTION is DELETE, READ, or WRITE, in which case it is required.
FILEFIELD	Name of the form field containing the file	This attribute may only be used if ACTION is UPLOAD, in which case it is required.
NAMECONFLICT	What to do in case of name conflicts	This optional attribute may be used if ACTION is UPLOAD. It specifies the action to be performed if a name conflict arises. If this attribute is omitted, the default value of "ERROR" is used.
OUTPUT	Text to output to file	This attribute may only be used if ACTION is WRITE.
SOURCE	Source filename	Name of the source file to be written to, copied, or moved. May be used only if ACTION is APPEND, COPY, MOVE, or RENAME.
VARIABLE	Variable to store contents of read file	This attribute may only be used if ACTION is READ, in which case it is required.

Table A.16   `<CFFILE>` Actions

Action	Description
APPEND	Appends one text file to the end of another
COPY	Copies a file
DELETE	Deletes a specified file
MOVE	Moves a specified file from one directory to another, or from one filename to another
READ	Reads the contents of a text file
RENAME	Does the same thing as MOVE; see MOVE
UPLOAD	Receives an uploaded file
WRITE	Writes specified text to the end of a text file

Table A.17   File Upload Name Conflict Options

Option	Description
ERROR	The file will not be saved, and ColdFusion will immediately terminate template processing.
SKIP	Neither saves the file nor generates an error message.
OVERWRITE	Overwrites the existing file.
MAKEUNIQUE	Generates a unique filename and saves the file with that new name. To find out what the new name is, inspect the #FILE.ServerFile# field.

Table A.18   `<CFFILE>` FILE Object Fields

Field	Description
#FILE.AttemptedServerFile#	The original attempted filename; will be the same as #FILE.ServerFile# unless the name had to be changed to make it unique.
#FILE.ClientDirectory#	The client directory from where the file was uploaded, as reported by the client browser.
#FILE.ClientFile#	The original filename as reported by the client browser.
#FILE.ClientFileExt#	The original file extension, as reported by the client browser.

Field	Description
#FILE.ClientFileName#	The original filename as reported by the client browser, but without the file extension.
#FILE.ContentSubType#	The MIME subtype of an uploaded file.
#FILE.ContentType#	The primary MIME type of an uploaded file.
#FILE.FileExisted#	Yes if file already existed, No if not.
#FILE.FileWasOverwritten#	Yes if file were overwritten, No if not.
#FILE.FileWasRenamed#	Yes if file were renamed, No if not.
#FILE.FileWasSaved#	Yes is file were saved, No if not.
#FILE.ServerDirectory#	The server directory in which the uploaded file was saved.
#FILE.ServerFile#	The name of the file as saved on the server. (Takes into account updated filename if it was modified to make it unique.)

Example: This first example receives any uploaded files and generates an error message if the specified filename already exists:

```
<CFFILE ACTION="Upload" FORMFIELD="UploadFile" DESTINATION="C:\UPLOADS\FILE.TXT">
```

This next example restricts the upload to Microsoft Word documents and changes the filename to something unique if it already exists:

```
<CFFILE
 ACTION="Upload"
 FORMFIELD="UploadFile"
 DESTINATION="C:\UPLOADS\FILE.TXT"
 ACCEPT="application/msword"
 NAMECONFLICT="MAKEUNIQUE"
>
```

This example appends a log entry to a text file:

```
<CFFILE
 ACTION="WRITE"
 FILE="C:\LOGS\DAILY.LOG"
 OUTPUT="#CGI.REMOTE_ADDR#, #Now()#"
>
```

The following example reads a file called C:\LOGS\DAILY\LOG into a variable called LOG and then displays the results:

```
<CFFILE
 ACTION="READ"
 FILE="C:\LOGS\DAILY.LOG"
 VARIABLE="LOG"
>
```

```
<CFOUTPUT>
<B>Log file:</B><P>#LOG#
</CFOUTPUT>
```

This next example deletes the C:\LOGS\DAILY.LOG file:

```
<CFFILE
 ACTION="DELETE"
 FILE="C:\LOGS\DAILY.LOG"
>
```

See also: <CFDIRECTORY>

<CFFORM>, </CFFORM>

Description: <CFFORM> and </CFFORM> are replacements for the standard HTML <FORM> and </FORM> tags. <CFFORM> itself adds no real value to your forms, but <CFFORM> allows you to embed other tags (<CFGRID>, <CFINPUT>, <CFSELECT>, <CFTEXTINPUT>, <CFTREE>, or any Java applets of your own using <CFAPPLET>). The code generated by <CFFORM> is standard FORM HTML code.

Syntax:

```
<CFFORM ACTION="Action Page" …>
```

Table A.19 **<CFFORM> Attributes**

Attribute	Description	Notes
ACTION	Form action page	This attribute is required.
ENABLECAB	Header value	This optional attribute allows the downloading Java classes in Microsoft cabinet files. If Yes, users are asked upon opening the page if they want to download the CAB file.
NAME	Form name	This attribute is optional. If used, you must ensure that the form name is unique.
ONSUBMIT	JavaScript OnSubmit function	Optional name of function. JavaScript to be executed prior to form submission.
TARGET	Target window	Optional target window.

Example: A simple <CFFORM>:

```
<CFFORM ACTION="process.cfm">
…
</CFFORM>
```

N O T E <CFFORM> automatically embeds METHOD="POST" into your form. ■

See also: <CFAPPLET>, <CFGIRD>, <CFINPUT>, <CFSELECT>, <CFSLIDER>, <CFTEXTINPUT>, <CFTREE>

<CFFTP>

Description: <CFFTP> is the ColdFusion interface to the file transfer protocol. You may interact with remote file systems, retrieve directory lists, and GET and OUT files via <CFFTP>. It is a very powerful and complex tag; Table A.20 lists its attributes. When calls to <CFFTP> are completed, a series of variables is set so you can determine the success or failure of the operation. These variables are listed in Table A.22. An error code is set if an error occurs. Table A.24 lists the complete set of error codes and what they mean. <CFFTP> can be used to retrieve remote directory lists. Lists are returned in ColdFusion query format and Table A.23 lists the query columns.

<CFFTP> is designed to be used two ways: either for single operations or to batch operations together. To use the batch mode (called *cached mode*), you must specify a unique name in the CONNECTION attribute that you can use in future <CFFTP> calls.

Syntax:

```
<CFFTP ACTION="Action" AGENTNAME="Name" ASCIIEXTENSIONLIST="List"
 ATTRIBUTES="Attributes" CONNECTION="Connection Name" DIRECTORY="Directory"
 EXISTING="Name" FAILIFEXISTS="Yes¦No" ITEM="Name" LOCALFILE="Name"
 NAME="Query Name" NEW="Name" PASSWORD="Password" PORT="Port" REMOTEFILE="Name"
 RETRYCOUNT="Count" SERVER="Server Address" STOPONERROR="Yes¦No"
 TIMEOUT="Seconds" TRANSFERMODE="Mode" USERNAME="User Name">
```

Table A.20 **<CFFTP> Attributes**

Attribute	Description	Notes
ACTION	Action	Required attribute.
AGENTNAME	Agent name	Optional attribute; application name.
ASCIIEXTENSIONLIST	ASCII extensions	Optional attribute, semicolon-delimited list of extensions to be treated as ASCII extensions if using TRASNFERMODE of "AutoDetect"; default is "txt;htm;html;cfm; cfml;shtm;shtml;css;asp;asa".
ATTRIBUTES	Attributes list	Comma-delimited list of attributes; specifies the file attributes for the local file; possible values are

continues

Table A.20   Continued

Attribute	Description	Notes
		READONLY, HIDDEN, SYSTEM, ARCHIVE, DIRECTORY, COMPRESSED, TEMPORARY, and NORMAL.
CONNECTION	Connection name	Optional attribute; used to cache connections to perform batches of operations.
DIRECTORY	Directory name	Required if ACTION is CHANGEDIR, CREATEDIR, LISTDIR, or EXISTSDIR; specifies the directory on which to perform the operation.
EXISTING	Existing item name	Required if ACTION is RENAME.
FAILIFEXISTS	Fail if exists	Optional attribute; if Yes, will fail. If the file already exists, default is Yes.
ITEM	Item name	Required if ACTION is EXISTS or REMOVE.
LOCALFILE	Local filename	Required if ACTION is GETFILE or PUTFILE, local filename.
NAME	Query name	Required if ACTION is GETLIST; see Table A.23 for column list.
NEW	New item name	Required if ACTION is RENAME.
PASSWORD	Login password	Required attribute.
PORT	Server port	Optional attribute; defaults to 21.
REMOTEFILE	Remote filename	Required if ACTION is EXISTSFILE, GETFILE, or PUTFILE; local filename.
RETRYCOUNT	Retries	Optional retry count; defaults to 1.
SERVER	Server name	Required attribute; DNS or IP address of FTP server.
STOPONERROR	Error handling	Optional attribute; defaults to Yes.
TIMEOUT	Timeout value	Optional attribute; timeout value in seconds.
TRANSFERMODE	Transfer mode	Optional attribute; values can be ASCII, binary, or AutoDetect; default is AutoDetect.
USERNAME	Login username	Required attribute.

Table A.21   <CFFTP> Actions

Action	Description
CHANGEDIR	Changes directory
CLOSE	Closes a cached connection
CREATEDIR	Creates a directory
EXISTS	Checks to see if an object exists
EXISTSDIR	Checks for a directory's existence
EXISTSFILE	Checks for a file's existence
GETCURRENTDIR	Gets current directory
GETCURRENTURL	Gets current URL
GETFILE	Retrieves a file
LISTDIR	Retrieves directory list
OPEN	Opens a cached connection
PUTFILE	Sends a file
REMOVE	Deletes a file
RENAME	Renames a file

Table A.22   <CFFTP> Status Variables

Variable	Description
#CFFTP.ErrorCode#	Error codes
#CFFTP.ErrorText#	Error text
#CFFTP.Succeeded#	Success; Yes or No

Table A.23   <CFFTP> Query Columns

Column	Description
ATTRIBUTES	Comma-delimited list of attributes
ISDIRECTORY	Yes if directory, No if file
LASTMODIFIED	Date and time last modified
LENGTH	File length

continues

App
A

Table A.23   Continued

Column	Description
NAME	Object name
PATH	Full path to object
URL	Full URL to object

Table A.24   `<CFFTP>` Error Codes

Code	Description
0	Operation succeeded.
1	System error (OS or FTP protocol error).
2	An Internet session could not be established.
3	FTP session could not be opened.
4	File transfer mode not recognized.
5	Search connection could not be established.
6	Invoked operation valid only during a search.
7	Invalid timeout value.
8	Invalid port number.
9	Not enough memory to allocate system resources.
10	Cannot read contents of local file.
11	Cannot write to local file.
12	Cannot open remote file for reading.
13	Cannot read remote file.
14	Cannot open local file for writing.
15	Cannot write to remote file.
16	Unknown error.
18	File already exists.
21	Invalid retry count specified.

Examples:

The following example opens a connection and reads a directory list into a query named `dir`:

```
<CFFTP CONNECTION="FTP" USERNAME="#username#" PASSWORD="#password#"
 SERVER="ftp.a2zbooks.com" ACTION="Open">
<CFFTP CONNECTION="FTP" ACTION="LISTDIR" DIRECTORY="/*." NAME="dir">
<CFFTP CONNECTION="FTP" ACTION="CLOSE">
```

See also: <CFHTTP>

<CFGRID>, <CFGRIDCOLUMN>, <CFGRIDROW>, </CFGRID>

Description: <CFGRID> embeds a Java grid control into your HTML forms. Grids are similar to spreadsheet-style interfaces, and <CFGRID> grids can be used to browse, select, and even edit data. Grids can be populated either by a query or by specifying each row using the <CFGRIDROW> tag. <CFGRIDCOLUMN> can be used to configure the individual columns with a grid.

<CFGRID> must be used between <CFFORM> and </CFFORM> tags.

Syntax:

```
<CFGRID ALIGN="Alignment" APPENDKEY="Yes¦No" BGCOLOR="Color" BOLD="Yes¦No"
 COLHEADERALIGN="Alignment" COLHEADERBOLD="Yes¦No" COLHEADERFONT="Font Face"
 COLHEADERFONTSIZE="Font Size" COLHEADERS="Yes¦No" DELETE="Yes¦No"
 DELETEBUTTON="Button Text" FONT="Font Face" FONTSIZE="Font Size"
 GRIDDATAALIGN="Alignment" GRIDLINES="Yes¦No" HEIGHT="Control Height"
 HIGHLIGHTHREF="Yes¦No" HREF="URL" HREFKEY="Key" HSPACE="Horizontal Spacing"
 INSERT="Yes¦No" INSERTBUTTON="Button Text" ITALIC="Yes¦No" NAME="Field Name"
 NOTSUPPORTED="Non Java Browser Code" ONERROR="Error Function"
 ONVALIDATE="Validation Function" PICTUREBAR="Yes¦No" QUERY="Query"
 ROWHEADER="Yes¦No" Name" ROWHEADERALIGN="Alignment" ROWHEADERBOLD="Yes¦No"
 ROWHEADERFONT="Font Face" ROWHEADERFONTSIZE="Font Size" ROWHEADERWIDTH="Width"
 SELECTCOLOR="Color" SELECTMODE="Mode" SORT="Yes¦No"
 SORTASCENDINGBUTTON="Button Text" SORTDESCENDINGBUTTON="Button Text"
 TARGET="Target Window" VSPACE="Vertical Spacing" WIDTH="Control Width">

<CFGRIDCOLUMN BOLD="Yes¦No" DATAALIGN="Alignment" DISPLAY="Yes¦No"
 FONT="Font Face" FONTSIZE="Font Size" HEADER="Header Text"
 HEADERALIGN="Alignment" HEADERBOLD="Yes¦No" HEADERFONT="Font Face"
 HEADERFONTSIZE="Font Size" HEADERITALIC="Yes¦No" HREF="URL" HREFKEY="Key"
 ITALIC="Yes¦No" NAME="Column Name" NUMBERFORMAT="Format Mask" SELECT="Yes¦No"
 TARGET="Target Window" TYPE="Type" WIDTH="Column Width">
<CFGRIDROW DATA="Data">
```

Table A.25   **<CFGRID> Attributes**

Attribute	Description	Notes
ALIGN	Control alignment	Optional attribute; possible values are top, left, bottom, baseline, texttop, absbottom, middle, absmiddle, right.
APPENDKEY	Append item key to URL	Optional attribute; if Yes, a variable named GRIDKEY is appended to the URL containing the item selected; defaults to Yes.
BGCOLOR	Background color	Optional attribute; possible values are black, cyan, darkgray, gray, lightgray, magenta, orange, pink, white, yellow, or any color specified in RGB form.
BOLD	Bold face text	Optional attribute; must be Yes or No if specified; defaults to No.
COLHEADERALIGN	Column header alignment	Optional attribute; may be left, center, or right; default is left.
COLHEADERBOLD	Column header in bold	Optional; if Yes, column header is displayed in a bold font; default is No.
COLHEADERFONT	Column header font	Optional font to use for column header.
COLHEADERFONTSIZE	Column header font size	Optional font size to use for column header.
COLHEADERITALIC	Column header in italics	Optional; if Yes, row column is displayed in an italic font; default is No.
COLHEADERS	Display column headers	Optional attribute; column headers are displayed if Yes; default is Yes.
DELETE	Allow delete	Optional; if Yes, allows records to be deleted from the grid. Default is No.
DELETEBUTTON	Delete button text	Optional text to use for the Delete button; default is Delete.
FONT	Font face	Optional font face to use.
FONTSIZE	Font Size	Optional font size.
GRIDDATAALIGN	Data alignment	Data alignment; may be left, right, or center; may be overridden at the column level.
GRIDLINES	Display grid lines	Optional grid lines displayed if Yes; default is Yes.

Attribute	Description	Notes
HEIGHT	Control height	Optional height in pixels.
HIGHLIGHTHREF	Highlight links	Optional attribute; if Yes, links are highlighted and underlined; defaults to Yes.
HREF	URL	Optional URL to go to upon item selection; if populated by a query, this may be a query column.
HREFKEY	Primary key column	Optional name of column to be used as the primary key.
HSPACE	Control horizontal spacing	Optional horizontal spacing in pixels.
INSERT	Allow insert	Optional; if Yes, allows records to be added to the grid; default is No.
INSERTBUTTON	Insert button text	Optional text to use for the Insert button; default is Insert.
ITALIC	Italic face text	Optional attribute; must be Yes or No if specified; defaults to No.
NAME	Unique control name	This attribute is required.
NOTSUPPORTED	Text to be used for non Java browsers	Optional text (or HTML code) to be displayed on non–Java-capable browsers.
ONERROR	JavaScript error function	Optional override to your own JavaScript error message function.
ONVALIDATE	JavaScript validation function	Optional override to your own JavaScript validation function.
PICTUREBAR	Display picture bar with icons	Optional attribute; if Yes a button bar with icons is displayed for insert, delete, and sort; default is No.
QUERY	Query to populate grid	Optional name of query to be used to populate the grid.
ROWHEADER	Display row header	Optional attribute displays header if Yes; default is Yes.
ROWHEADERALIGN	Row header alignment	Optional attribute may be left, center, or right; default is left.

continues

Table A.25 Continued

Attribute	Description	Notes
ROWHEADERBOLD	Row header in bold	Optional; if Yes, row header is displayed in a bold font; default is No.
ROWHEADERFONT	Row header font	Optional font to use for row header.
ROWHEADERFONTSIZE	Row header font size	Optional font size to use for row header.
ROWHEADERITALIC	Row header in italics	Optional; if Yes, row header is displayed in an italic font; default is No.
ROWHEADERWIDTH	Row header width	Optional row header width in pixels.
ROWHEIGHT	Row height	Optional height of row in pixels.
SELECTCOLOR	Selection color	Optional attribute; possible values are black, cyan, darkgray, gray, lightgray, magenta, orange, pink, white, yellow, or any color specified in RGB form.
SELECTMODE	Selection mode	Optional attribute, may be EDIT SINGLE ROW COLUMN or BROWSE; default is BROWSE.
SORT	Allow sorting	Optional; if Yes, allows grid data to be sorted; default is No.
SORTASCENDINGBUTTON	Sort ascending button text	Optional text to use for the sort ascending button; default is A -> Z.
SORTDESCENDINGBUTTON	Sort descending button text	Optional text to use for the sort descending button; default is Z -> A.
TARGET	Link target window	Optional name of target window for HREF URL.
VSPACE	Control vertical spacing	Optional vertical spacing in pixels.
WIDTH	Control width	Optional width in pixels.

Table A.26 `<CFGRIDCOLUMN>` Attributes

Attribute	Description	Notes
BOLD	Bold face text	Optional attribute, must be Yes or No if specified; defaults to No.

Attribute	Description	Notes
DATAALIGN	Data alignment	Optional attribute may be left, center, or right; default is left.
DISPLAY	Display column	Optional attribute; if No, column is hidden; default is Yes.
FONT	Font face	Optional font face to use.
FONTSIZE	Font Size	Optional font size.
HEADER	Header text	Optional header text; defaults to column name.
HEADERALIGN	Header alignment	Optional attribute; may be left, center, or right; default is left.
HEADERBOLD	Header in bold	Optional; if Yes, header is displayed in a bold font; default is No.
HEADERFONT	Header font	Optional font to use for header.
HEADERFONTSIZE	Header font size	Optional font size to use for header.
HEADERITALIC	Header in italics	Optional; if Yes, header is displayed in an italic font; default is No.
HREF	URL	URL for selection in this column; may be absolute or relative.
HREFKEY	Primary key	Optional primary key to use for this column.
ITALIC	Italic face text	Optional attribute; must be Yes or No if specified; defaults to No.
NAME	Column name	Required attribute; if using a query to populate the grid, this must be a valid column name.
NUMBERFORMAT	Number formatting	Optional attribute, uses NumberFormat() function masks; see that function for mask details.
SELECT	Allow selection	Optional attribute; if No, selection or editing is not allowed in this column.
TARGET	Target window	Optional target window for HREF.
TYPE	Data type	Optional attribute; may be image or numeric. If image, an appropriate graphic is displayed for the cell value.
WIDTH	Column width	Optional column width in pixels.

Table A.27 `<CFGRIDROW>` **Attributes**

Attribute	Description	Notes
DATA	Row data	Comma-delimited list of data to be displayed; one item for each row in the grid.

Examples: This first example displays the results of a query in a simple browse-only grid:

```
<CFFRORM ACTION="process.cfm">
<CFGRID NAME="Users" QUERY="Users">
</CFGRID>
</CFFORM>
```

This next example specifies the columns to be displayed and allows editing, but prevents the primary key from being edited:

```
<CFFRORM ACTION="process.cfm">
<CFGRID NAME="Users" QUERY="Users" MODE="EDIT">
<CFGRIDITEM NAME="ID" DISPLAY="No">
<CFGRIDITEM NAME="LastName">
<CFGRIDITEM NAME="FirstName">
</CFGRID>
</CFFORM>
```

N O T E The `<CFGRID>` control is only accessible by users with Java-enabled browsers. ▪

See also: `<CFFORM>`, `<CFGRIDUPDATE>`, `<CFINPUT>`, `<CFSELECT>`, `<CFSLIDER>`, `<CFTEXTINPUT>`, `<CFTREE>`

`<CFGRIDUPDATE>`

Description: `<CFGRIDUPDATE>` provides the action back end to support `<CFGRID>` in edit mode. `<CFGRIDUPDATE>` performs all inserts, deletes, and updates in one simple operation. `<CFGRIDUPDATE>` may only be used in an action page to which a form containing a `<CFGRID>` control was submitted. `<CFGRIDUPDATE>` attributes are listed in Table A.28.

Syntax:

```
<CFGRIDUPDATE DATASOURCE="ODBC Data Source Name" DBNAME="database name"
 DBPOOL="pool" DBTYPE="type" DBSERVER="dbms" GRID="Grid Name" KEYONLY="Yes¦No"
 PASSWORD="Password" PROVIDER="provider" PROVIDERDSN="data source"
 TABLENAME="Table Name" TABLEOWNER="Table Owner Name"
 TABLEQUALIFIER="Table Qualifier" USERNAME="User Name">
```

Table A.28   <CFGRIDUPDATE> **Attributes**

Attribute	Description	Notes
DATASOURCE	ODBD data source	This attribute is required.
DBNAME	Sybase database name	Optional attribute; only used if using native Sybase drivers.
DBPOOL	Database connection pool name	Optional database pool name.
DBSERVER	Database server	Optional database server, only used if using native database drives.
DBTYPE	Database type	Optional type; defaults to ODBC; other values are Oracle73, Oracle80, and Sybase11.
GRID	Grid name	This attribute is required; the name of the grid in the submitted form with which to update the table.
KEYONLY	WHERE clause construction	If Yes, the WHERE clause generated by <CFGRID> contains just the primary; default is Yes.
PASSWORD	ODBC login password	Optional ODBC login password.
PROVIDER	OLE-DB COM provider	Optional attribute; only used if using OLE-DB.
PROVIDERDSN	Data source OLE-DB COM provider	Optional attribute; only used if using OLE-DB.
TABLENAME	Table name	This attribute is required.
TABLEOWNER	Table owner	Optional ODBC table owner.
TABLEQUALIFIER	Table qualifier	Optional ODBC table qualifier.
USERNAME	ODBC username	Optional ODBC username.

Examples: The following example updates a table with the data in a editable grid:

```
<CFGRIDUPDATE DATASOURCE="A2Z" TABLE="Employees" GRID="Emp">
```

See also: <CFFORM>, <CFGRID>

<CFHEADER>

Description: <CFHEADER> allows you to control the contents of specific HTTP headers.

Syntax:

```
<CFHEADER NAME="Header Name" VALUE="Value">
```

Table A.29   <CFHEADER> Attributes

Attribute	Description	Notes
NAME	HTTP header to be set	This attribute is required.
VALUE	Header value	This attribute is required.

Example: The following example sets an expiration header to Now() in order to prevent it from being cached:

```
<CFHEADER NAME="Expires" VALUE="#Now()#">
```

> **N O T E**   There is usually little need to use <CFHEADER> because ColdFusion sets the HTTP headers automatically to optimum values. ▪

<CFHTMLHEAD>

Description: <CFHTMLHEAD> writes text into the header section of your Web page.

Syntax:

```
<CFHTMLHEAD TEXT="Text">
```

Table A.30   <CFHTMLHEAD> Attributes

Attribute	Description	Notes
TEXT	Header text	This attribute is required.

Example: This example write a <TITLE> tag into the head section:

```
<CFHTMLHEAD TEXT="<TITLE>A2Z Home Page</TITLE>">
```

<CFHTTP>, <CFHTTPPARAM>, </CFHTTP>

Description: <CFHTTP> allows you to process HTTP GET and POST requests within your ColdFusion code. If using the POST method, parameters may be passed using the <CFHTTPPARAM> tag. <CFHTTPPARAM> can only be used between <CFHTTP> and </CFHTTP> tags.

<CFHTTP attributes are listed in Table A.31, <CFHTTPPARAM> attributes are listed in Table A.32. <CFHTTP> sets special variables upon completion that you can inspect; they are listed in Table A.33.

Syntax:

```
<CFHTTP COLUMNS="Column Names" DELIMITER="Delimiter Character" FILE="File Name"
 METHOD="Get|Post" NAME="Query Name" PASSWORD="Password" PATH="Directory"
 PROXYSERVER="Host Name" RESOLVEURL="Yes|No" TEXTQUALIFIER="Text Qualifier"
 URL="Host Name" USERNAME="User Name">

<CFHTTPPARAM FILE="File Name" NAME="Field Name" TYPE="Type" VALUE="Value">
```

Table A.31 **<CFHTTP> Attributes**

Attribute	Description	Notes
COLUMNS	Query columns	Optional attribute; query columns for retrieved data.
DELIMITER	Column delimiter	Required if NAME is used; default delimiter is a comma.
FILE	Filename	Required only if PATH is used; file to save.
METHOD	Submission method	This attribute is required; must be either GET or POST; use POST to use <CFHTTPPARAM>.
NAME	Query name	Optional attribute; name of query to be constructed with HTTP results.
PASSWORD	User password	Optional attribute; user password if required by server.
PATH	File path	Optional attribute, path to save file if method is POST.
PROXYSERVER	Server name	Optional name of proxy server to use.
RESOLVEURL	Resolve URL	Optional attribute; defaults to No; if Yes, fully resolves embedded URLs.
TEXTQUALIFIER	Text qualifier	Required if NAME is used; delimiter indicating start and end of column.
URL	Host URL	This attribute is required; must be DNS name or IP address of a valid host.
USERNAME	Username	Optional attribute; username if required by server.

Table A.32 `<CFHTTPPARAM>` **Attributes**

Attribute	Description	Notes
FILE	Filename	Required if TYPE is File.
NAME	Field name	This attribute is required.
TYPE	Field type	This attribute is required; must be URL, FORMFIELD, COOKIE, CGI, or FILE.
VALUE	Field value	This attribute is optional unless TYPE is File.

Table A.33 `<CFHTTP>` **Returned Variables**

Field	Description
#FILE.FileContent#	Content returned by HTTP request
#FILE.MimeType#	MIME type of returned data

Examples: This example retrieves the A2Z home page:

```
<CFHTTP URL="www.a2zbooks.com/" METHOD="GET">
```

See also: `<CFFTP>`

`<CFIF>`, `<CFELSEIF>`, `<CFELSE>`, `</CFIF>`

Description: The `<CFIF>` set of tags are what allow you to create conditional CFML code. `<CFIF>` and its supporting tags (`<CFELSEIF>`, `<CFELSE>`, and `</CFIF>`) will likely be the tags your use most in your applications.

Every `<CFIF>` tag must have a matching `</CFIF>` tag. The `<CFELSEIF>` and `<CFELSE>` tags are entirely optional. You may use as many `<CFELSEIF>` tags as needed in a `<CFIF>` statement, but only one `<CFELSE>`. `<CFELSE>` must always be the last compare performed if it is used.

`<CFIF>` uses operators to compare values. Conditions can also be combined to perform more complex comparisons.

You may compare any values, including static text and numbers, ColdFusion fields, database column values, and function results.

Syntax:

```
<CFIF Condition><CFELSEIF Condition><CFELSE></CFIF>
```

Table A.34 ColdFusion Conditional Operators

Operator	Alternate	Description
IS	EQUAL, EQ	Check that the right value is equal to the left value.
IS NOT	NOT EQUAL, NEQ	Check that the right value is not equal to the left value.
CONTAINS		Check that the right value is contained within the left value.
DOES NOT CONTAIN		Check that the right value is not contained within the left value.
GREATER THAN	GT	Check that the left value is greater than the right value.
LESS THAN	LT	Check that the left value is less than the right value.
GREATER THAN OR EQUAL	GTE	Check that the left value is greater than or equal to the right value.
LESS THAN OR EQUAL	LTE	Check that the left value is less than or equal to the right value.

Table A.35 ColdFusion Boolean Operators

Operator	Description
AND	Conjunction; returns TRUE only if both expressions are true.
OR	Disjunction; returns TRUE if either expression is true.
NOT	Negation.

This first example checks to see if a field named LastName exists:

```
<CFIF ParameterExists(LastName)>
```

The following example checks to see if both the FirstName and LastName fields exist:

```
<CFIF (ParameterExists(FirstName)) AND (ParameterExists(LastName))>
```

You could use the following to check for either a first name or a last name:

```
<CFIF (ParameterExists(FirstName)) OR (ParameterExists(LastName))>
```

Often you will want to verify that a field is not empty and that it does not contain blank spaces. The following example demonstrates how this can be accomplished:

```
<CFIF Trim(LastName) IS NOT "">
```

You can use the CONTAINS operator to check if a values is within a range of values. Take a look at both these examples:

```
<CFIF "KY,MI,MN,OH,WI" CONTAINS State>
```

```
<CFIF TaxableStates CONTAINS State>
```

More complex expressions can be created by combining conditions within parentheses. For example, the following condition checks to see whether payment is by check or credit card; if payment is by credit card, it checks to ensure that there is an approval code:

```
<CFIF (PaymentType IS "Check") OR ((PaymentType IS "Credit")
 AND (ApprovalCode IS NOT ""))>
```

The following example is a complete conditional statement that uses <CFELSEIF> to perform additional comparisons, and uses <CFELSE> to specify a default for values that pass none of the compares:

```
<CFIF State IS "MI">
 Code for Michigan only goes here
<CFELSEIF State IS "IN">
 Code for Indiana only goes here
<CFELSEIF (State IS "OH") OR (State IS "KY")>
 Code for Ohio or Kentucky goes here
<CFELSE>
 Code for all other states goes here
</CFIF>
```

See also: <CFSWITCH>

<CFINCLUDE>

Description: <CFINCLUDE> includes the contents of another template into the one being processed.

Syntax:

```
<CFINCLUDE TEMPLATE="Template File Name">
```

Table A.36 <CFINCLUDE> **Attributes**

Attribute	Description	Notes
TEMPLATE	Name of template to include	This attribute is required. Only relative paths are supported.

Example: The following example includes the footer file in the current directory if it exists, a default footer if not:

```
<CFIF FileExists("FOOTER.CFM")>
 <CFINCLUDE TEMPLATE="FOOTER.CFM">
```

```
<CFELSE>
 <CFINCLUDE TEMPLATE="/DEFAULT/FOOTER.CFM">
</CFIF>
```

 TIP <CFINCLUDE> can help you reuse templates. You can use <CFINCLUDE> to break out common components (such as page headers and footers), which enables you to share them among multiple templates.

App

A

See also: <CFLOCATION>

<CFINDEX>

Description: <CFINDEX> is used to populate Verity collections with index data. A collection must be created with the ColdFusion Administrator before it can be populated. <CFINDEX> can be used to index physical files—in which case the filename is returned in searches—or query results—in which case the primary key is returned in searches.

<CFINDEX> attributes are listed in Table A.37.

Syntax:

```
<CFINDEX ACTION="Action" BODY="Text" COLLECTION="Collection Name" CUSTOM1="Data"
 CUSTOM2="Data" EXTENSIONS="File Extensions" EXTERNAL="Yes¦No" KEY="Key"
 QUERY="Query Name" RECURSE="Yes¦No" TITLE="Text" TYPE="Type" URLPATH="Path">
```

Table A.37 <CFINDEX> Attributes

Attribute	Description	Notes
ACTION	Action	Required attribute.
BODY	Body to index	Required if TYPE is Custom; if indexing files, this must be the path to the file to be indexed; if indexing a query, this must be the column to be indexed.
COLLECTION	Collection name	Required; name of the collection to be indexed; if using external collections, this must be a fully qualified path to the collection.
CUSTOM1	Custom data	Optional attribute for storing data during indexing.
CUSTOM2	Custom data	Optional attribute for storing data during indexing.

continues

Table A.37   Continued

Attribute	Description	Notes
EXTENSIONS	File extensions	Optional list of extensions of files to be indexed; list must be comma delimited; only used if TYPE is PATH.
EXTERNAL	External collection	Optional attribute; must be Yes if indexing an external collection.
KEY	Unique key	Optional attribute; used to indicate what makes each record unique, if TYPE is File, this should be the document filename; if TYPE is Path, this should be a full path to the document; if TYPE is Custom, this should be any unique identifier.
QUERY	Query name	Optional attribute.
RECURSE	Recurse directories	Optional attribute; if Yes then all subdirectories are indexed too TITLE Document title Required if TYPE is Custom.
TYPE	Index type	Optional attribute, must be FILE, PATH, or CUSTOM.
URLPATH	URL path	Optional attribute, specifies the URL path for files when TYPE = File or TYPE = Path.

Table A.38   \<CFINDEX> Actions

Action	Description
DELETE	Deletes a key from a collection
OPTIMIZE	Optimizes a collection
PURGE	Clears all data from a collection
REFRESH	Clears all data from a collection and repopulates it
UPDATE	Updates a collection and adds a key if it does not exist

Examples: This examples indexes all HTM and HTML files in all directories beneath the Web server document root:

```
<CFINDEX COLLECTION="Docs" TYPE="Path" KEY="c:\inetpub\wwwroot"
URLPATH="http://127.0.0.1/" EXTENSIONS=".htm, .html" RECURSE="Yes">
```

See also: \<CFCOLLECTION>, \<CFSEARCH>

<CFINPUT>

Description: <CFINPUT> is an enhancement to the standard HTML <INPUT> tag. <CFINPUT> allows you to automatically embed JavaScript client-side validation code in your HTML forms. <CFINPUT> must be used between <CFFORM> and </CFORM> tags; it is not a Java control.

Syntax:

```
<CFINPUT CHECKED MAXLENGTH="Length" MESSAGE="Message Text" NAME="Field Name"
  ONERROR="JavaScipt Error Function" ONVALIDATE="JavaScript Validation Function"
  RANGE="Range Values" REQUIRED="Yes¦No" SIZE="Field Size" TYPE="Type"
  VALIDATE="Validation Type" VALUE="Initial Value">
```

Table A.39 <CFINPUT> **Attributes**

Attribute	Description	Notes
CHECKED	Checked state	Optional; only valid if type is RADIO or CHECKBOX and if present radio button or check box is pre-checked.
MAXLENGTH	Maximum number of characters	Optional attribute.
MESSAGE	Validation failure message	Optional message to display upon validation failure.
NAME	Unique control name	This attribute is required.
ONERROR	JavaScript error	Optional override to function your own JavaScript error message function.
ONVALIDATE	JavaScript validation function	Optional override to your own JavaScript validation function.
RANGE	Range minimum and maximum	Optional range for numeric values only; must be specified as two numbers separated by a comma.
REQUIRED	Field is required	Optional required flag; must be Yes or No if specified; defaults to No.
SIZE	Field size	Optional number of characters to display before needing horizontal scrolling.
TYPE	Input type	Must be TEXT, RADIO, CHECKBOX, or PASSWORD.
VALIDATE	Field validation	Optional field validation.
VALUE	Initial value	Optional initial field value.

Table A.40   `<CFINPUT>` **Validation Types**

Type	Description
Creditcard	Correctly formatted credit card number verified using mod10.
Date	Date in mm/dd/yy format.
Eurodate	European date in dd/mm/yy format.
Float	Number with decimal point.
Integer	Number with no decimal point.
Social_Security_Number	Social Security number formatted as 999-99-9999 (using hyphens or spaces as separators).
Telephone	Phone number in 999-999-9999 format (using hyphens or spaces as separators); area code and exchange must not begin with 0 or 1.
Time	Time in hh:mm or hh:mm:ss format.
Zipcode	U.S. zip code, either 99999 or 99999-9999 format.

Examples: This example creates a simple text field that is flagged as required:

```
<CFFORM ACTION="process.cfm">
<CFINPUT TYPE="text" NAME="name" REQUIRED="Yes" MESSAGE="NAME is required!">
</CFFORM>
```

This next example creates a field that accepts only a valid telephone number:

```
<CFFORM ACTION="process.cfm">
<CFINPUT TYPE="text" NAME="phone" VALIDATE="telephone"
 MESSAGE="You entered an invalid phone number!">
</CFFORM>
```

N O T E   `<CFINPUT>` does not support input fields of type HIDDEN. ■

See also: `<CFFORM>`, `<CFGIRD>`, `<CFSELECT>`, `<CFSLIDER>`, `<CFTEXTINPUT>`, `<CFTREE>`

`<CFINSERT>`

Description: `<CFINSERT>` adds a single row to a database table. `<CFINSERT>` requires that the database and table names be provided. All other attributes are optional.

Syntax:

```
<CFINSERT DATASOURCE="ODBC Data Source" DBNAME="database name" DBPOOL="pool"
 DBTYPE="type" DBSERVER="dbms" FORMFIELDS="List of File to Insert"
```

```
PASSWORD="Password" PROVIDER="provider" PROVIDERDSN="data source"
TABLENAME="Table Name" TABLEOWNER="owner" TABLEQUALIFIER="qualifier"
USERNAME="User Name">
```

Table A.41 **<CFINSERT> Attributes**

Attribute	Description	Notes
DATASOURCE	Name of ODBC data source	The specified data source must already exist. This attribute is required.
DBNAME	Sybase database name	Optional attribute; only used if using native Sybase drivers.
DBPOOL	Database connection pool name	Optional database pool name.
DBSERVER	Database server	Optional database server; only used if using native database drives.
DBTYPE	Database type	Optional type; defaults to ODBC; other values are Oracle73, Oracle80, and Sybase11.
FORMFIELDS	List of fields to insert	This optional attribute specifies which fields are to be inserted if they are present. Any fields present that are not in the list will not be inserted.
PASSWORD	ODBC data source password	This optional attribute is used to override the ODBC login password specified in the ColdFusion Administrator.
PROVIDER	OLE-DB COM provider	Optional attribute; only used if using OLE-DB.
PROVIDERDSN	Data source OLE-DB COM provider	Optional attribute; only used if using OLE-DB.
TABLENAME	Name of table to insert data into	Some ODBC data source require fully qualified table names. This attribute is required.
TABLEOWNER	Table owner name	Optional attribute used by databases that support table ownership.
TABLEQUALIFIER	Table qualifier	Optional attribute used by databases that support full qualifiers.
USERNAME	ODBC data source login name	The optional attribute is used to override the ODBC login name specified in the ColdFusion Administrator.

Your form field names must match the column names in the destination table for <CFINSERT> to work correctly. ▪

 If your form contains fields that are not part of the table into which you are inserting data, use the FORMFIELDS attribute to instruct ColdFusion to ignore those fields.

T I P For more control over the insertion of rows into a database table, you may use the <CFQUERY> tag specifying INSERT as the SQL statement.

Example: The following example inserts a new row into the Employees table in the A2Z data source:

```
<CFINSERT DATASOURCE="A2Z" TABLENAME="Employees">
```

The next example inserts a new row into the same table, but only inserts values into the three specified fields if they exist:

```
<CFINSERT DATASOURCE="A2Z" TABLENAME="Employees"
 FORMFIELD="LastName,FirstName,PhoneExtension">
```

See also: <CFQUERY>, <CFUPDATE>

<CFLDAP>

Description: <CFLDAP> is used to for all interaction with LDAP servers. It can be used to search an LDAP server, as well as to add, change, or delete data. Table A.42 lists the attributes for <CFLDAP>.

Syntax:

```
<CFLDAP ACTION="Action" ATTRIBUTES="Attributes List" DN="Name" FILTER="Filter"
 MAXROWS="Number" NAME="Query Name" PASSWORD="Password" PORT="Port Number"
 SCOPE="Scope" SERVER="Server Address" SORT="Sort Order" START="Start Position"
 STARTROW="Number" TIMEOUT="Timeout" USERNAME="Name">
```

Table A.42 <CFLDAP> **Attributes**

Attribute	Description	Notes
ACTION	Action	Required attribute.
ATTRIBUTES	Desired attributes	Required if ACTION is QUERY; comma-delimited list of desired attributes, query specified in NAME attribute will contain these columns.

Attribute	Description	Notes
DN	Distinguished name	Required if ACTION is ADD MODIFY MODIFYDN or delete.
FILTER	Search filter	Optional search filter used if ACTION is QUERY.
MAXROWS	Maximum rows to retrieve	Optional attribute.
NAME	Query name	Name of query for returned data; required if ACTION is QUERY.
PASSWORD	User password	Optional user password; might be required for update operations.
PORT	Port number	Optional port number; defaults to 389 if not specified.
SCOPE	Search scope	Optional search scope if ACTION is QUERY; valid values are ONELEVEL, BASE and SUBTREE; default is ONELEVEL.
SERVER	Server name	Required DNS name or IP address of LDAP server.
SORT	Sort order	Optional attribute used if ACTION is QUERY; specifies the sort order as a comma-delimited list; may use ASC for ascending and DESC for descending; default is ASC.
START	Start name	Required if ACTION is QUERY; distinguished name to start search at.
STARTROW	Start row	Optional start row; defaults to 1.
TIMEOUT	Timeout value	Optional timeout value.
USERNAME	User login name	Optional user login name; might be required for update operations.

Table A.43   <CFLDAP> Actions

Action	Description
ADD	Adds an entry to an LDAP server
DELETE	Deletes an entry from an LDAP server
MODIFY	Updates an entry on an LDAP server
MODIFYDN	Updates the distinguished name of an entry on an LDAP server
QUERY	Performs a query against an LDAP server

Example: The following example retrieves a list of names from a public directory:

```
<CFLDAP Name="seach" SERVER="ldap.four11.com" ACTION="Query" ATTRIBUTES="cn"
 SCOPE="Subtree" SORT="cn Asc" FILTER="(sn=*)" START="#search#, c=US">
```

<CFLOCATION>

Description: <CFLOCATION> is used to redirect a browser to a different URL.

Syntax:

```
<CFLOCATION ADDTOKEN="Yes or No" URL="URL">
```

Table A.44 <CFLOCATION> **Attributes**

Attribute	Description	Notes
ADDTOKEN	Adds session tokens	Optional attribute; default is Yes.
URL	URL (or relative URL) to redirect to	This attribute is required.

Example: The following example redirects the user to a login page:

```
<CFLOCATION URL="login.cfm">
```

Unlike <CFINCLUDE>, any text or CFML after the <CFLOCATION> tag is ignored by ColdFusion. ■

N O T E   See also: <CFINCLUDE>

<CFLOCK>, </CFLOCK>

Description: <CFLOCK> is used to restrict blocks of code to single threaded access. Once inside a locked block of code, all other threads are queued until the thread with the exclusive lock relinquishes control. Table A.45 lists all the <CFLOCK> attributes.

Syntax:

```
<CFLOCK TIMEOUT="timeout" THROWONTIMEOUT="Yes or No"> … </CFLOCK>
```

Table A.45   <CFLOCK> **Attributes**

Attribute	Description	Notes
TIMEOUT	Timeout interval	This attribute is required.
THROWONTIMEOUT	Timeout handling	This optional attribute specifies how timeouts should be handled; an exception is thrown if Yes, processing continues if No; defaults to Yes.

Example: The following code locks a call to a custom tag:

```
<CFLOCK TIMEOUT="60">
 <CF_MyTag>
</CFLOCK>
```

N O T E   <CFLOCK> is primarily designed for use with custom tags that are not multithreaded. ▪

CAUTION

Avoid unnecessary use of <CFLOCK>. Forcing code to single threaded use only can seriously impact system performance.

See also: <CFCATCH>, <CFTRY>

<CFLOOP>, <CFBREAK>, </CFLOOP>

Description: <CFLOOP> allows you to create loops within your code. *Loops* are blocks of code that are executed repeatedly until a specific condition is met. <CFBREAK> allows you to unconditionally terminate a loop. ColdFusion supports five kinds of loops:

- For loops repeat a specific number of times.
- While loops repeat until a set condition returns FALSE.
- Query loops go through the results of a <CFQUERY> once for each row returned.
- List loops go through the elements of a specified list.
- Collection loops are used to loop over collections.

Syntax:

For loop:

```
<CFLOOP INDEX="Index" FROM="Loop Start" TO="Loop End" STEP="Step Value">
```

While loop:

```
<CFLOOP CONDITION="Expression">
```

Query loop:

```
<CFLOOP QUERY="Query Name" STARTROW="Start Row Value" ENDROW="End Row Value">
```

List loop:

```
<CFLOOP INDEX="Index" LIST="List" DELIMITERS="Delimiters">
```

Collection loop:

```
<CFLOOP COLLECTION="Collection" ITEM="Item">
```

N O T E   The syntax and use of <CFLOOP> varies based on the type of loop being executed. ■

Table A.46   **<CFLOOP> Attributes**

Attribute	Description	Notes
COLLECTION	Collection to loop through	This attribute is required for Collection loops.
CONDITION	While loop condition	This attribute is required for While loops and must be a valid condition.
DELIMITERS	List loop delimiters	This is an optional List loop attribute; if it is omitted, the default delimiter of a comma is used.
ENDROW	Query loop end position	This is an optional Query loop attribute; if it is omitted, all rows are processed.
FROM	For loop start position	This attribute is required for For loops and must be a numeric value.
INDEX	Current element	This attribute is required for For loops and List loops and holds the name of the variable that will contain the current element.
ITEM	Current item	This attribute is required for Collection loops.
LIST	List loop list	This attribute is required for List loops and can be a ColdFusion list field or a static string.
QUERY	Query loop query	This attribute is required for Query loops and must be the name of a previously executed <CFQUERY>.
STARTROW	Query loop start position	Thus is an optional Query loop attribute; if it is omitted, the loop will start at the first row.

Attribute	Description	Notes
STEP	For loop step value	This is an optional For loop attribute; if it is omitted, the default value of 1 is used.
TO	For loop end position	This attribute is required for For loops and must be a numeric value.

Example: The following is a For loop used in a FORM to populate a select field with the years 1901 to 2000. The alternative would have been to enter 100 OPTION values manually:

```
<SELECT NAME="year">
 <CFLOOP INDEX="YearValue" FROM="1901" TO="2000">
 <OPTION><CFOUTPUT>#YearValue#</CFOUTPUT>
</SELECT>
```

The next example does the exact same thing, but presents the list in reverse order. This is done by specifying a STEP value of -1:

```
<SELECT NAME="year">
 <CFLOOP INDEX="YearValue" FROM="2000" TO="1901" STEP="-1">
  <OPTION><CFOUTPUT>#YearValue#</CFOUTPUT>
 </CFLOOP>
</SELECT>
```

This example loops until any random number between 1 and 10, excluding 5, is generated:

```
<CFSET RandomNumber = 0>
<CFLOOP CONDITION= "(#RandomNumber# GT 0) AND (#RandomNumber# NEQ 5)">
 <CFSET RandoNumber = RandRange(1, 10)>
</CFLOOP>
```

This example creates a Query loop that processes an existing <CFQUERY> named Orders, but only processes rows 100 through 150:

```
<CFLOOP QUERY="Orders" STARTROW="100" ENDROW="150">
 <CFOUTPUT>
 #OrderNum# - #DateFormat(OrderDate)# - #DollarFormat(Total)#<BR>
 </CFOUTPUT>
</CFLOOP>
```

This example loops through a user-supplied list of titles, displaying them one at a time:

```
<CFLOOP INDEX="Title" LIST="#FORM.Titles#">
 <CFOUTPUT>
 Title: #Title#<BR>
 </CFOUTPUT>
</CFLOOP>
```

This example uses <CFBREAK> to terminate a loop when a specific row is reached—in this case, an order number greater than 10000:

```
<CFLOOP QUERY="Orders" >
 <CFIF OrderNum GT 10000>
  <CFBREAK>
 </CFIF>
```

```
<CFOUTPUT>
 #OrderNum# - #DateFormat(OrderDate)# - #DollarFormat(Total)#<BR>
</CFOUTPUT>
</CFLOOP>
```

TIP Using <CFLOOP> to process queries is substantially slower than using <CFOUTPUT>. Whenever possible, use <CFOUTPUT> to loop through query results.

N O T E The <CFLOOP> tag may be nested, and there is no limit placed on the number of nested loops allowed. ▪

<CFMAIL>, </CFMAIL>

Description: <CFMAIL> generates SMTP mail from within ColdFusion templates. <CFMAIL> can be used to output query results, just like <CFOUTPUT>, or on its own. The <CFMAIL> tag itself is used to set up the mail message, all text between the <CFMAIL> and </CFMAIL> tags is sent as the message body. <CFMAIL> requires that you specify a sender address, recipient address, and subject. All other attributes are optional.

Syntax:

```
<CFLOCATION CC="Carbon Copy Addresses" FROM="Sender Address" GROUP="Group Name"
 MAXROWS="Maximum Mail Messages" PORT="SMTP TCP/IP Port" QUERY="Query Name"
 SERVER="SMTP Server Address" SUBJECT="Subject" TIMEOUT="SMTP Connection Timeout"
 TO="Recipient Address" TYPE="Message Type" MAILERID="id">
Message
</CFMAIL>
```

Table A.47   <CFMAIL> **Attributes**

Attribute	Description	Notes
CC	Carbon copy addresses	Optional one or more carbon copy addresses separated by commas.
FROM	Sender's address	Required sender's email address.
GROUP	Query column to group on	Optional attribute that specifies column to group on. See <CFOUTPUT> for more information on grouping data.
MAXROWS	Maximum message to send	Optional attribute specifying the maximum number of email messages to generate.
MAILERID	Mailer ID	Optional mailer ID; default is Allaire ColdFusion Application Server.
PORT	TCP/IP SMTP port	Optional TCP/IP SMTP port; overrides the default value of 25 if specified.

Attribute	Description	Notes
QUERY	<CFQUERY> to draw data from	Email can be generated based on the results of a <CFQUERY>; to do this specify the name of the <CFQUERY> here. This is an optional attribute.
SERVER	SMTP mail server	Optional SMTP mail server name; overrides the default setting if specified.
SUBJECT	Message subject	Required message subject.
TIMEOUT	Connection timeout interval	Optional SMTP connection timeout interval; overrides the default setting if specified.
TO	Recipient's address	Required recipient's email address.
TYPE	Message type	Optional message type; currently the only supported type is HTML, indicating that there is HTML code embedded in the message.

Example: The following is a simple email message based on a form submission. It uses form fields in both the attributes and the message body itself:

```
<CFMAIL
 FROM="#FORM.EMail#"
 TO="sales@a2zbooks.com"
 SUBJECT="Customer inquiry"
>
The following customer inquiry was posted to our web site:
Name: #FORM.name#
email: #FORM.EMail#

Message:
#FORM.Message#

</CFMAIL>
```

This next example sends an email message based on <CFQUERY> results. The message is sent once for each row retrieved:

```
<CFMAIL
 QUERY="MailingList"
 FROM="sales@a2zbooks.com"
 TO="#EMailAddress#"
 SUBJECT="Monthly Online Newsletter"
>
Dear #FirstName#,

This email message is to remind you that our new monthly online newsletter
is now on our web site.
```

You can access it at http://www.a2zbooks.com/newsletter

Thanks for you continued interest in our product line.

A2Z Books Sales

</CFMAIL>

 T I P Unlike Web browsers, email programs do not ignore whitespace. Carriage returns are displayed in the email message if you embed carriage returns between the <CFMAIL> and </CFMAIL> tags.

N O T E To use <CFMAIL>, the ColdFusion SMTP interface must be set up and working. If email is not being sent correctly, use the ColdFusion Administrator to verify that ColdFusion can connect to your SMTP mail server. ▪

N O T E The PORT, SERVER, and TIMEOUT attributes will never be used in normal operation. These are primarily used for debugging and troubleshooting email problems. ▪

N O T E Email errors are logged to the \CFUSION\MAIL\LOG directory. Messages that cannot be delivered are stored in the \CFUSION\MAIL\UNDELIVR directory. ▪

See also: <CFPOP>

<CFMODULE>

Description: <CFMODULE> is used to call a custom tag explicitly stating its full or relative path. Table A.48 lists the <CFMODULE> attributes. Your own tag attributes may also be added to this list.

Syntax:

```
<CFMODULE NAME="Path" TEMPLATE="Path" …>
```

Table A.48 **<CFMODULE> Attributes**

Attribute	Description	Notes
NAME	Fixed path to tag file	Either TEMPLATE or NAME must be used, but not both at once; use a period for directory delimiters.
TEMPLATE	Relative path to tag file	Either TEMPLATE or NAME must be used, but not both at once.

Examples: This example calls a custom tag named ShowMenu in the parent directory:

```
<CFMODULE TEMPLATE="../showmenu.cfm">
```

See also: <CFASSOCIATE>

<CFOBJECT>

Description: <CFOBJECT> allows you to use COM, DCOM, and CORBA objects within your ColdFusion applications. You need to know an object's ID or filename in order to use it, as well as its methods and properties. <CFOBJECT> attributes are listed in Table A.49.

To use an object with <CFOBJECT>, that object must be already installed on the server.

Syntax:

```
<CFOBJECT ACTION="Action" CLASS="Class ID" CONTEXT="Context" NAME="Name"
   SERVER="Server Name" TYPE="COM or CORBA">
```

Table A.49   **<CFMODULE> Attributes**

Attribute	Description	Notes
ACTION	Action	Required attribute; must be either CREATE to instantiate an object or CONNECT to connect to a running object; only used when TYPE is COM.
CLASS	Component ProgID	This attribute is required.
CONTEXT	Operation context	Optional attribute, must be InProc, Local, or Remote. Uses Registry setting if not specified.
NAME	Object name	This attribute is required.
SERVER	Valid server name	Server name as UNC, DNS, or IP address; required only if CONTEXT = "remote"; only used if TYPE is COM.
TYPE	Object type	Optional; defaults to COM; valid values are COM and CORBA.

Example: The following example instantiates a COM object named NT.Exec and invokes a method:

```
<CFOBJECT TYPE="COM" CLASS="NT.Exec" ACTION="CREATE" NAME="Exec">
<CFSET Exec.Command = "DIR C:\">
<CFSET temp = Exec.Run()>
```

N O T E   Use of <CFOBJECT> can be disabled in the ColdFusion Administrator program.

`<CFOUTPUT>`, `</CFOUTPUT>`

Description: `<CFOUTPUT>` is used to output the results of a `<CFQUERY>`, or any time text includes variables that are to be expanded. If `<CFQUERY>` is used to process the results of a `<CFQUERY>` tag, any code between `<CFOUTPUT>` and `</CFOUTPUT>` is repeated once for every row. `<CFOUTPUT>` can be used with the GROUP attribute to specify a data group. Data that is grouped together is displayed so that only the first occurrence of each value is output.

Syntax:

```
<CFOUTPUT QUERY="Query Name" MAXROWS="Maximum Rows" STARTROW="Start Row"
 GROUP="Group Column">

Code

</CFOUTPUT>
```

Table A.50   `<CFOUTPUT>` **Attributes**

Attribute	Description	Notes
GROUP	Column to group on	This optional attribute allows you to define output groups.
MAXROWS	Maximum rows to display	This optional attribute specifies the maximum number of rows to display. If omitted, all rows are displayed.
QUERY	Query name	This optional query name refers to the query results within `<CFOUTPUT>` text.
STARTROW	First row to display	The optional attribute specifies the output start row.

Table A.51   `<CFOUTPUT>` **Fields Available When Using the QUERY Attribute**

Field	Description
#ColumnList#	Comma-delimited list of columns with a query
#CurrentRow#	The number of the current row, starting at 1, and incremented each time a row is displayed
#RecordCount#	The total number of records to be output

Example: Any time you use variables or fields within your template, you must enclose them within `<CFOUTPUT>` tags as shown in this example. Otherwise the field name is sent as is and not expanded:

```
<CFOUTPUT>
 Hi #name#, thanks for dropping by again.<P>
```

```
 You have now visited us #NumberFormat(visits)#
 since your first visit on #DateFormat(first_visit)#.
</CFOUTPUT>
```

This example uses <CFOUTPUT> to display the results of a query in an unordered list:

```
<UL>
<CFOUTPUT QUERY="Employees">
 <LI>#LastName#, #FirstName# - Ext: #PhoneExtension#
</CFOUTPUT>
</UL>
```

You can use the GROUP attribute to group output results. This example lists employees within departments:

```
<UL>
 <CFOUTPUT QUERY="Employees" GROUP="Department">
  <LI><B>#Department#</B>
   <UL>
    <CFOUTPUT>
     <LI>#LastName#, #FirstName# - Ext: #PhoneExtension#
    </CFOUTPUT>
   </UL>
  </CFOUTPUT>
</UL>
```

N O T E   There is no limit to the number of nested groups that you may use in a <CFOUTPUT>. However, every column used in a GROUP must be part of the SQL statement ORDER BY clause. ▨

 The STARTROW and MAXROWS attribute can be used to implement a "display next n of n" type display. You should note however, that even though only a subset of the retrieved data is displayed, it has *all* been retrieved by the <CFQUERY> statement. So, while the page might be transmitted to the browser quicker, because it contains less text, the SQL operation itself takes no less time.

See also: <CFLOOP>, <CFMAIL>, <CFQUERY>, <CFTABLE>

<CFPARAM>

Description: <CFPARAM> lets you specify default values for parameters and specify parameters that are required. <CFPARAM> requires that a variable name be passed to it. If a VALUE is passed as well, that value will be used as the default value if the variable is not specified. If VALUE is not specified, <CFPARAM> requires that the named variable be passed; it will generate an error message if it is not.

Syntax:

```
<CFPARAM NAME="Parameter Name" DEFAULT="Default">
```

Table A.52   **<CFPARAM> Attributes**

Attribute	Description	Notes
NAME	Name of variable	Name should be fully qualified with variable type. This attribute is required.
DEFAULT	Default variable value	This attribute is optional. If specified, the value is used as the default value whenever this variable is used.

Example: The following specifies a default value for a field that is to be used in a <CFQUERY> tag, making it unnecessary to write conditional code to build a dynamic SQL statement:

```
<CFPARAM NAME="Minimum" DEFAULT="10">
<CFQUERY NAME="OverDue" DATASOURCE= "A2Z">
 SELECT * FROM Inventory WHERE NumberInStock < #Minimum#
</CFQUERY>
```

This example makes the Minimum field required; an error is generated if you request the template and the Minimum field is not specified:

```
<CFPARAM NAME="Minimum" >
<CFQUERY NAME="OverDue" DATASOURCE= "A2Z">
 SELECT * FROM Inventory WHERE NumberInStock < #Minimum#
</CFQUERY>
```

See also: <CFSET>

<CFPOP>

Description: <CFPOP> retrieves and manipulates mail in a POP3 mailbox. You must know three things in order to access a POP mailbox: the POP server name, the POP login name, and the account password. <CFPOP> has three modes of operation: It can be used to retrieve just mail headers, entire message bodies, and to delete messages. POP messages are not automatically deleted when they are read, and must be deleted explicitly with a DELETE operation. Table A.53 lists the <CFPOP> attributes; Table A.55 lists the columns returned when retrieving mail or mail headers.

Syntax:

```
<CFPOP ACTION="Action" ATTACHMENTSPATH="Path" MAXROWS="Number"
 MESSAGENUMBER="Messages" NAME="Query Name" PASSWORD="Password" PORT="Port
Number"
 SERVER="Mail Server" STARTROW="Number" TIMEOUT="Timeout" USERNAME="User Name">
```

Table A.53 <CFPOP> **Attributes**

Attribute	Description	Notes
ACTION	Action	Optional.
ATTACHMENTSPATH	Attachment path	Optional path to store mail attachments.
MAXROWS	Maximum messages to retrieve	Optional attribute; ignored ID MESSAGENUMBER is used.
MESSAGENUMBER	Message number	Optional message number (or comma-delimited list of message numbers); required if ACTION is DELETE; specifies the messages to be deleted or retrieved.
NAME	Query name	Required if ACTION is GETALL or GETHEADERONLY; name of query to be returned; query columns are listed in Table A.55.
PASSWORD	Password	Optional POP account password; most POP servers require this.
PORT	Mail server port	Optional attribute; defaults to port 110.
SERVER	Mail server	Required; DNS name or IP address of the POP mail server.
STARTROW	Start row	Optional start row; defaults to 1; ignored if MESSAGENUMBER is used.
TIMEOUT	Timeout value	Optional timeout value.
USERNAME	Login name	Optional POP login name; most POP servers require this.

Table A.54 <CFPOP> **Actions**

Action	Description
DELETE	Delete messages from a POP mailbox
GETALL	Gets message headers and body
GETHEADERONLY	Gets just message headers

App

A

Table A.55   `<CFPOP>` **Query Columns**

Column	Description
ATTACHMENTFILES	List of saved attachments; only present if ACTION is GETALL and an ATTACHMENT path was specified.
ATTACHMENTS	List of original attachment names; only present if ACTION is GETALL and an ATTACHMENT path was specified.
CC	List of any carbon copy recipients.
DATE	Message date.
FROM	Sender name.
HEADER	Mail header.
MESSAGENUMBER	Message number for use in calls with future calls.
REPLYTO	Email address to reply to.
SUBJECT	Message subject.
TO	Recipient list.

Examples: This example retrieves a list of waiting mail in a POP mailbox and then displays the message list in an HTML list:

```
<CFPOP SERVER="mail.a2zbooks.com" USERNAME=#username# PASSWORD=#pwd#
 ACTION="GETHEADERONLY" NAME="msg">
<UL>
<CFOUTPUT QUERY="msg">
<LI>From: #from# - Subject: #subject#
</CFOUTPUT>
</UL>
```

N O T E   `<CFPOP>` is used to retrieve mail only. Use the `<CFMAIL>` tag to send mail. ▪

See also: `<CFMAIL>`

`<CFQUERY>`, `</CFQUERY>`

Description: `<CFQUERY>` submits SQL statements to an ODBC driver. SQL statements are not limited to SELECT statements, but can also be INSERT, UPDATE, and DELETE statements, as well as calls to stored procedures. `<CFQUERY>` returns results in a named set if you specify a query name in the NAME attribute. The `<CFQUERY>` attributes set up the query, and any text between the `<CFQUERY>` and `</CFQUERY>` tags becomes the SQL statement that is sent to the ODBC driver. ColdFusion conditional code may be used between the `<CFQUERY>` and `</CFQUERY>` tags, allowing you to create dynamic SQL statements.

Syntax:

```
<CFQUERY NAME="Parameter Name" DATASOURCE="ODBC Data Source"
 DBNAME="database name" DBPOOL="pool" DBTYPE="type" DBSERVER="dbms"
 USERNAME="User Name" PASSWORD="Password" PROVIDER="provider"
 PROVIDERDSN="data source" BLOCKFACTOR="factor" TIMEOUT="timeout value"
 CACHEDAFTER="date" CACHEDWITHIN="time span" DEBUG="Yes or No">
SQL statement
</CFQUERY>
```

Table A.56 `<CFQUERY>` **Attributes**

Attribute	Description	Notes
BLOCKFACTOR	Number of rows to retrieve at once	This optional attribute is available if using ODBC or Oracle drivers; valid values are 1 to 100, default value is 1.
CACHEDAFTER	Cache date	Optional attribute; specifies that query is to be cached and cached copy is to be used after specified date.
CACHEDWITHIN	Cache time span	Optional attribute; specifies that query is to be cached and cached copy is to be used within a relative time span.
DATASOURCE	ODBC data source	This optional attribute is used to override the ODBC data source specified when the report was created.
DBNAME	Sybase database name	Optional attribute; only used if using native Sybase drivers.
DBPOOL	Database connection pool name	Optional database pool name.
DBSERVER	Database server	Optional database server; only used if using native database drives.
DBTYPE	Database type	Optional type; defaults to ODBC; other values are Oracle73, Oracle80, and Sybase11.
DEBUG	Enable query debugging	Optional attribute; turns on query debugging output.

continues

Table A.56 Continued

Attribute	Description	Notes
NAME	Query name	This optional query name is used to refer to the query results in `<CFOUTPUT>`, `<CFMAIL>`, or `<CFTABLE>` tags.
PASSWORD	ODBC data source	This optional attribute password is used to override the ODBC login password specified in the ColdFusion Administrator.
PROVIDER	OLE-DB COM provider	Optional attribute; only used if using OLE-DB.
PROVIDERDSN	Data source OLE-DB COM provider	Optional attribute; only used if using OLE-DB.
TIMEOUT	Timeout value	Optional timeout value in milliseconds.
USERNAME	ODBC data source login name	The optional attribute is used to override the ODBC login name specified in the ColdFusion Administrator.

The following example is a simple data retrieval query:

```
<CFQUERY
 DATASOURCE="A2Z"
 NAME="Employees"
>
 SELECT FirstName, LastName, PhoneExtension FROM Employees
</CFQUERY>
```

This example demonstrates how dynamic SQL statements can be constructed using the ColdFusion conditional tags:

```
<
 CFQUERY
 DATASOURCE="A2Z"
 NAME="Employees"
>
 SELECT FirstName, LastName, PhoneExtension, EmployeeID
      FROM Employees
      WHERE EmployeeID = EmployeeID

<CFIF #FirstName# IS NOT "">
 AND FirstName LIKE '#FirstName#%'
</CFIF>
```

```
<CFIF #LastName# IS NOT "">
 AND LastName LIKE '#LastName#%'
</CFIF>

<CFIF #PhoneExtension# IS NOT "">
 AND PhoneExtension LIKE '#PhoneExtension#%'
</CFIF>

ORDER BY LastName, FirstName

</CFQUERY>
```

<CFOUTPUT> can be used to execute any SQL statement, and the following example demonstrates how <CFOUTPUT> can be used to delete rows from a table:

```
<CFQUERY
 DATASOURCE="A2Z"
>
DELETE FROM Employees WHERE EmployeeID = #EmployeeID#"
</CFQUERY>
```

See also: <CFOUTPUT>, <CFMAIL>, <CFSTOREDPROC>

<CFREGISTRY>

Description: <CFREGISTRY> can be used to directly manipulate the system Registry. The <CFREGISTRY> ACTION attribute specifies the action to be performed, and depending on the action, other attributes may or may not be needed.

<CFREGISTRY> attributes are listed in Table A.57.

Syntax:

```
<CFREGISTRY ACTION="action" BRANCH="branch" ENTRY="entry" NAME="query"
 SORT="sort order" TYPE="type" VALUE="value" VARIABLE="variable">
```

Table A.57   <CFREGISTRY> **Attributes**

Attribute	Description	Notes
ACTION	Action	Required attribute.
BRANCH	Registry branch	Required for all actions.
ENTRY	Branch entry	Required for all actions except GETALL.
NAME	Query name	Required if ACTION is GETALL.
SORT	Sort order	Optional; may be used if ACTION is GETALL.

continues

Table A.57 Continued

Attribute	Description	Notes
TYPE	Value type	Optional; and may be used for all actions except DELETE; valid types are STRING, DWORD, and KEY; default is STRING.
VALUE	Value to set	Required if ACTION is SET.
VARIABLE	Variable to save value in	Required if ACTION is GET.

Table A.58 <CFREGISTRY> Actions

Action	Description
DELETE	Deletes a Registry key
GET	Gets a Registry value
GETALL	Gets all Registry keys in a branch
SET	Sets a Registry value

Example: This example retrieves all the keys beneath the Allaire branch:

```
<CFREGISTRY ACTION="GETALL" NAME="reg"
 BRANCH= "HKEY_LOCAL_MACHINE\SOFTWARE\Allaire">
```

<CFREPORT>, </CFREPORT>

Description: <CFREPORT> is the ColdFusion interface to reports created with the Crystal Reports Professional report writer. <CFREPORT> only requires a single attribute: the name of the report to be processed. The full list of supported attributes is in Table A.59.

Syntax:

```
<CFREPORT REPORT="Report File" ORDERBY="Sort Order" DATASOURCE="ODBC Data Source"
 USERNAME="User Name" PASSWORD="Password" @FORMULANAME="Formula">
Optional filter conditions
</CFREPORT>
```

Table A.59 <CFREPORT> Attributes

Attribute	Description	Notes
DATASOURCE	ODBC data source	This optional attribute is used to override the ODBC data source specified when the report was created.

Attribute	Description	Notes
ORDERBY	Report sort order	This optional attribute overrides the default sort order specified when the report was created.
PASSWORD	ODBC data source password	This optional attribute is used to override the ODBC login password specified in the ColdFusion Administrator.
REPORT	Name of RPT file to process	This attribute is required.
USERNAME	ODBC data source login name	The optional attribute is used to override the ODBC login name specified in the ColdFusion Administrator.
@FORMULANAME	Crystal Reports formula override	This optional parameter allows you to override Crystal Reports formulas with passed formula text. Formula names must begin with an @ character.

Example: The following example processes a report created with Crystal Reports Professional and passes it an optional filter condition:

```
<CFREPORT REPORT="\a2z\scripts\emplist.rpt">
 {Departments.Department} = "Sales"
</CFREPORT>
```

This example processes a report and specifies parameters to override the ODBC data source, user login name and password, and a formula named `title` derived from an HTML form:

```
<CFREPORT REPORT="\a2z\scripts\emplist.rpt" DATASOURCE="A2ZInternal"
 USERNAME="HR" PASSWORD="anarchy" @Title="#FORM.title#">
 {Departments.Department} = "Sales"
</CFREPORT>
```

<CFSCHEDULE>

Description: `<CFSCHEDULE>` allows you to run a specified page at scheduled intervals with the option to write out static HTML pages. This allows you to offer users access to pages that publish data (such as reports) without forcing them to wait while a database transaction that populates the data on the page is performed. ColdFusion scheduled events must be registered using the ColdFusion Administrator before they can be executed. Information supplied by the user includes the scheduled ColdFusion page to execute, the time and frequency for executing the page, and whether the output from the task should be published. A path and file are specified if the output is to be published.

<CFSCHEDULE> attributes are listed in Table A.60.

Syntax:

```
<CFSCHEDULE ACTION="Action" ENDDATE="Date" ENDTIME="Time" FILE="File Name"
 INTERVAL="Interval" LIMITIME="Seconds" OPERATION="HTTPRequest"
 PASSWORD="Password" PATH="Path" PROXYSERVER="Server Name" PUBLISH="Yes¦No"
 RESOLVEURL="Yes¦No" STARTDATE="Date" STARTTIME="Time" TASK="Task Name"
 URL="URL" USERNAME="User Name">
```

Table A.60   `<CFSCHEDULE>` **Attributes**

Attribute	Description	Notes
ACTION	Action (see Table A.61)	Required attribute.
ENDDATE	Event end date	Optional attribute; date the scheduled task should end.
ENDTIME	Event end time	Optional attribute; time the scheduled task should end; enter value in seconds.
FILE	File to create	Required if PUBLISH is Yes.
INTERVAL	Execution interval	Required if ACTION is UPATE; may be specified as number of seconds, as daily, weekly, monthly, or as execute.
LIMITTIME	Maximum execution time	Optional attribute; maximum number of seconds allowed for execution.
OPERATION	Operation	Required if ACTION is UPDATE; currently only HTTPRequest is supported.
PASSWORD	Password	Optional password for protected URLs.
PATH	Path to save published files	Required if PUBLISH is Yes.
PROXYSERVER	Proxy server name	Optional name of proxy server.
PUBLISH	Publish static files	Optional attribute; Yes if the scheduled task should publish files; default is No.
RESOLVEURL	Resolve URLs	Optional attribute; resolve URLs to fully qualified URLs if Yes; default is No.
STARTDATE	Event start date	Optional attribute; date the scheduled task should start.

Attribute	Description	Notes
STARTTIME	Event start time	Optional attribute; time the scheduled task should start; enter value in seconds.
TASK	Task name	Required attribute; the registered task name.
URL	URL	Required if ACTION is UPDATE; the URL to be executed.
USERNAME	Username	Optional username for protected URLs.

Table A.61 **<CFSCHEDULE> Actions**

Action	Description
DELETE	Deletes a task
UPDATE	Updates a task
RUN	Executes a task

Example: This example executes a task and allows it to run for 30 minutes:

```
<CFSCHEDULE TASK="SalesReports" ACTION="RUN" LIMITTIME="1800">
```

N O T E Execution of <CFSCHEDULE> can be disabled in the ColdFusion Administrator.

<CFSCRIPT>, </CFSCRIPT>

Description: <CFSCRIPT> and </CFSCRIPT> are used to mark blocks of ColdFusion script.

Syntax:

```
<CFSCRIPT> script </CFSCRIPT>
```

<CFSEARCH>

Description: <CFSEARCH> performs searches against Verity collections (in much the same way <CFQUERY> performs searches against ODBC data sources). To use <CFSEARCH> you must specify the collection to be searched and the name of the query to be returned. You may search more than one collection at once, and you may also perform searches against Verity collections created with applications other than ColdFusion. Table A.62 lists the <CFSEARCH> attributes.

Syntax:

```
<CFSEARCH COLLECTION="Collection Name" CRITERIA="Search Criteria" CUSTOM1="Data"
 CUSTOM2="Data" EXTERNAL="Yes¦No" MAXROWS="Number" NAME="Name"
 STARTROW="Number" TYPE="Type">
```

Table A.62 <CFSEARCH> **Attributes**

Attribute	Description	Notes
COLLECTION	Collection name	Required attribute; the name of the collection or collections to be searched. Multiple collections must be separated by commas; for external collections specify the full path to the collection.
CRITERIA	Search criteria	Optional attribute; search criteria as shown in Appendix C.
CUSTOM1	Custom data storage	Optional attribute; used to store custom data during an indexing operation.
CUSTOM2	Custom data storage	Optional attribute; used to store custom data during an indexing operation.
EXTERNAL	External collection	Optional attribute; must be Yes if using an external collection; default is No.
MAXROWS	Maximum rows to retrieve	Optional attribute; defaults to all.
NAME	Value column	Optional attribute; column to be used for OPTION VALUE attribute.
STARTROW	Start row	Optional attribute; default is first row.
TYPE	Search type	Optional attribute; may be SIMPLE or EXPLICIT.

Examples: This example performs a search with a user-supplied search criteria:

```
<CFSEARCH NAME="search" COLLECTION="site" TYPE="SIMPLE" CRITERIA="#search#">
```

See also: <CFCOLLECTION>, <CFINDEX>

<CFSELECT>, </CFSELECT>

Description: <CFSELECT> is used to simplify the process of creating data driven SELECT controls. <CFSELECT> is not a Java control. <CFSELECT> requires that you pass it the name of a query for use populating the drop-down list box. <CFSELECT> attributes are listed in Table A.63.

You may add your own options to the SELECT list by adding <OPTION> tags between the <CFSELECT> and </CFSELECT> tags.

Syntax:

```
<CFSELECT DISPLAY="Column Name" MESSAGE="Message Text" MULTIPLE="Yes¦No"
 NAME="Field Name" ONERROR="JavaScript Error Function" QUERY="Query Name"
 REQUIRED="Yes¦No" SELECTED="Value" SIZE="Size" VALUE="Column Name"></CFSELECT>
```

Table A.63   <CFSELECT> **Attributes**

Attribute	Description	Notes
DISPLAY	Column to display	Optional query column to use as the displayed text.
MESSAGE	Validation failure message	Optional message to display upon validation failure.
MULTIPLE	Allow multiple selection	Optional attribute; defaults to No.
NAME	Unique field name	This attribute is required.
ONERROR	JavaScript error function	Optional override to your own JavaScript error message function.
QUERY	Query name	Required attribute; query to be used to populate the SELECT box.
REQUIRED	Field is required	Optional required flag; must be Yes or No if specified; defaults to No.
SELECTED	Selected value	Value of the OPTION to be pre-selected.
SIZE	List size	Required attribute; number of options to display without scrolling.
VALUE	Value column	Optional attribute; column to be used for OPTION VALUE attribute.

Example: This example creates a simple data-driven SELECT control:

```
<CFFORM ACTION="process.cfm">
<CFSELECT QUERY="Users" VALUE="id" DISPLAY="Name" SIZE="1">
</CFSELECT>
</CFFORM>
```

See also: <CFFORM>, <CFGIRD>, <CFINPUT>, <CFSLIDER>, <CFTEXTINPUT>, <CFTREE>

<CFSET>

Description: <CFSET> assigns values to variables. <CFSET> can be used for both client variables (type CLIENT) and standard variables (type VARIABLES). Unlike most other ColdFusion tags, <CFSET> takes no attributes—just the name of the variable being assigned and its value.

Syntax:

```
<CFSET "Variable" = "Value">
```

Example: The following example creates a local variable containing a constant value:

```
<CFSET MaxDisplay = 25>
```

The following example creates a client variable called #BGColor#, which contains a user-specified value and explicitly states the variable type:

```
<CFSET CLIENT.BGColor = FORM.Color>
```

This example stores tomorrow's date in a variable called Tomorrow:

```
<CFSET Tomorrow = Now() + 1>
```

<CFSET> can also be used to concatenate fields:

```
<CFSET VARIABLES.FullName = FORM.FirstName FORM.LastName>
```

Values of different data types also can be concatenated:

```
<CFSET Sentence = FORM.FirstName FORM.LastName & "is" & FORM.age & "years old">
```

TIP   If you ever find yourself performing a calculation or combining strings more than once in a specific template, you're better off doing it once and assigning the results to a variable with <CFSET>; you can then use that variable instead.

See also: <CFAPPLICATION>, <CFCOOKIE>, <CFPARAM>

<CFSETTING>

Description: <CFSETTING> is used to control various aspects of page processing, such as controlling the output of HTML code in your pages or enabling and disabling debug output. One benefit is managing whitespace that can occur in output pages that are served by ColdFusion. <CFSETTING> attributes are listed in Table A.64.

When using <CFSETTING> to disable an option, make sure you have a matching enable option later in the file.

Syntax:

```
<CFSETTING ENABLECFOUTPUTONLY="Yes¦No" SHOWDEBUGOUTPUT="Yes¦No">
```

Table A.64 `<CFSETTING>` Attributes

Attribute	Description	Notes
ENABLECFOUTPUTONLY	Only output text within <CFOUTPUT>	This attribute is optional, and must be blocked. Yes or No is specified.
SHOWDEBUGOUTPUT	Display debug information at bottom of page	This optional attribute overrides the settings in the ColdFusion Administrator.

Examples:

The following demonstrates how `<CFSETTING>` can be used to control generated whitespace:

```
This text will be displayed
<CFSETTING ENABLECFOUTPUTONLY="Yes">
This text will not be displayed as it is not in a <CFOUTOUT> block
<CFOUTPUT>This will be displayed</CFOUTOUT>
<CFSETTING ENABLECFOUTPUTONLY="No">
This text will be displayed even though it is not in a <CFOUTPUT> block
```

`<CFSLIDER>`

Description: `<CFSLIDER>` embeds a Java slider control into your HTML forms. Slider controls are typically used to select one of a range of numbers. `<CFSLIDER>` must be used in between `<CFFORM>` and `</CFFORM>` tags. Table A.65 lists the entire set of `<CFSLIDER>` attributes.

Syntax:

```
<CFSLIDER ALIGN="Alignment" BGCOLOR="Background Color" BOLD="Yes|No"
 FONT="Font Face" FONTSIZE="Font Size" GROOVECOLOR="Groove Color"
 HEIGHT="Control Height" HSPACE="Horizontal Spacing" IMG="Groove Image"
 IMGSTYLE="Groove Image Style" ITALIC="Yes|No" LABEL="Slider Label"
 MESSAGE="Error Message" NAME="Field Name" NOTSUPPORTED="Non Java Browser Code"
 ONERROR="Error Function" ONVALIDATE="Validation Function" RANGE="Numeric Range"
 REFRESHLABEL="Yes|No" SCALE="Increment Value" TEXTCOLOR="Text Color"
 VALUE="Initial Value" VSPACE="Vertical Spacing" WIDTH="Control Width">
```

Table A.65 `<CSLIDER>` Attributes

Attribute	Description	Notes
ALIGN	Control alignment	Optional attribute; possible values are top, left, bottom, baseline, texttop, absbottom, middle, absmiddle, and right.

continues

Table A.65 Continued

Attribute	Description	Notes
BGCOLOR	Background color	Optional attribute; possible values are black, cyan, darkgray, gray, lightgray, magenta, orange, pink, white, yellow, or any color specified in RGB form.
BOLD	Bold face text	Optional attribute; must be Yes or No if specified; defaults to No.
FONT	Font face	Optional font face to use.
FONTSIZE	Font Size	Optional font size.
GROOVECOLOR	Groove color	Optional attribute; possible values are black, cyan, darkgray, gray, lightgray, magenta, orange, pink, white, yellow, or any color specified in RGB form.
HEIGHT	Control height	Optional height in pixels.
HSPACE	Control horizontal spacing	Optional horizontal spacing in pixels.
IMG	Groove image	Optional filename of image to be used for the slider groove.
IMGSTYLE	Grove image style	Optional attribute; may be Centered, Tiled, Scaled, default is Scaled.
ITALIC	Italic face text	Optional attribute; must be Yes or No is specified; defaults to No.
LABEL	Slider label	Optional attribute; may contain the variable %value%, in which case the current value is displayed as the slider is moved.
MESSAGE	Validation failure message	Optional message to display upon validation failure.
NAME	Unique control name	This attribute is required.
NOTSUPPORTED	Text to be used for non Java browsers	Optional text (or HTML code) to be displayed on non–Java-capable browsers.
ONERROR	JavaScript error function	Optional override to your own JavaScript error message function.
ONVALIDATE	JavaScript validation function	Optional override to your own JavaScript validation function.

Attribute	Description	Notes
RANGE	Range minimum and maximum	Optional range for numeric values only; must be specified as two numbers separated by a comma; defaults to "0,100".
REFRESHLABEL	Refresh label as slider is moved	Optional attribute; default is Yes; if you are not using a variable label, this attributeshould be set to No to prevent unnecessary refreshing.
SCALE	Increment scale	Optional increment; defaults to 1.
TEXTCOLOR	Text color	Optional attribute; possible values are black, cyan, darkgray, gray, lightgray, magenta, orange, pink, white, yellow, or any color specified in RGB form.
VALUE	Initial value	Optional initial field value; this value must be within the specified range if range is used.
VSPACE	Control vertical spacing	Optional vertical spacing in pixels.
WIDTH	Control width	Optional width in pixels.

Example: The following example displays a Java slider control that specifies the height, width, font, color, and label:

```
<CFFORM ACTION="process.cfm">
<CFSLIDER NAME="volume" HEIGHT="100" WIDTH="200" FONT="Verdana"
 BGCOLOR="Black" TEXTCOLOR="White" GROOVECOLOR="White" LABEL="Volume %value%">
</CFFORM>
```

N O T E The <CFSLIDER> control is only accessible by users with Java-enabled browsers.

See also: <CFFORM>, <CFGIRD>, <CFINPUT>, <CFSELECT>, <CFTEXTINPUT>, <CFTREE>

<CFSTOREDPROC>, <CFPROCPARAM>, <CFPROCRESULT>, </CFSTOREDPROC>

Description: <CFSTOREDPROC> provides sophisticated support for database stored procedures. Unlike <CFQUERY> (which can also call stored procedures), <CFSTOREDPROC> and its supporting tags can pass and retrieve parameters and access multiple result sets. <CFSTOREDPROC> attributes are listed in Table A.66; <CFPROCPARAM> attributes are listed in Table A.67; <CFPROCRESULT> attributes are listed in Table A.68.

Syntax:

```
<CFSTOREDPROC DATASOURCE="ODBC Data Source" DBNAME="database name" DBPOOL="pool"
 DBTYPE="type" DBSERVER="dbms" USERNAME="User Name" PASSWORD="Password"
 PROCEDURE="Procedure" PROVIDER="provider" PROVIDERDSN="data source"
 BLOCKFACTOR="factor" DEBUG="Yes¦No" RETURNCODE="Yes¦No">
<CFPROCPARAM TYPE="In¦Out¦Inout" VARIABLE="variable" DBVARIABLE="variable"
 VALUE="value" CFSQLTYPE="type" MAXLENGTH="length" SCALE="decimal places">
<CFPROCRESULT NAME="name" RESULTSET="set" MAXROWS="rows">
</CFSTOREDPROC>
```

Table A.66 `<CFSTOREDPROC>` **Attributes**

Attribute	Description	Notes
BLOCKFACTOR	Number of rows to retrieve at once	This optional attribute is available if using ODBC or Oracle drivers; valid values are 1 to 100, default value is 1.
DATASOURCE	ODBC data source	This optional attribute is used to override the ODBC data source specified when the report was created.
DBNAME	Sybase database name	Optional attribute; only used if using native Sybase drivers.
DBPOOL	Database connection pool name	Optional database pool name.
DBSERVER	Database server	Optional database server; only used if using native database drives.
DBTYPE	Database type	Optional type; defaults to ODBC; other values are Oracle73, Oracle80, and Sybase11.
DEBUG	Enable query debugging	Optional attribute; turns on query debugging output.
PASSWORD	ODBC data source password	This optional attribute is used to override the ODBC login password specified in the Cold Fusion Administrator.
PROCEDURE	Stored procedure name	Name of stored procedure to execute.
PROVIDER	OLE-DB COM provider	Optional attribute; only used if using OLE-DB.
PROVIDERDSN	Data source OLE-DB COM provider	Optional attribute; only used if using OLE-DB.

Attribute	Description	Notes
USERNAME	ODBC data source login name	The optional attribute is used to override the ODBC login name specified in the ColdFusion Administrator.

Table A.67 `<CFPROCPARAM>` Attributes

Attribute	Description	Notes
CFSQLTYPE	Variable type	Required; see Table A.69 for list of supported types.
DBVARIABLE	Database variable name	Required if name notation is desired.
MAXLENGTH	Maximum parameter length	Optional attribute.
SCALE	Decimal places	Optional attribute.
TYPE	Parameter type	Optional parameter type; valid values are IN, OUT, or INOUT; defaults to IN.
VALUE	Parameter value	Required for IN and INOUT parameters.
VARIABLE	ColdFusion variable name	Required for OUT or INOUT parameters

Table A.68 `<CFPROCRESULT>` Attributes

Attribute	Description	Notes
MAXROWS	Maximum number of rows	Optional
NAME	Query name	Required
RESULTSET	Result set number	Optional attribute; specifies the desired result set; defaults to 1

Table A.69 `CFSQLTYPE` Types

Type
CF_SQL_BIGINT
CF_SQL_CHAR

continues

Table A.69   Continued

CF_SQL_DATE

CF_SQL_DECIMAL

CF_SQL_DOUBLE

CF_SQL_FLOAT

CF_SQL_IDSTAMP

CF_SQL_INTEGER

CF_SQL_LONGVARCHAR

CF_SQL_MONEY

CF_SQL_MONEY4

CF_SQL_NUMERIC

CF_SQL_REAL

CF_SQL_SMALLINT

CF_SQL_TIME

CF_SQL_TIMESTAMP

CF_SQL_TINYINT

CF_SQL_VARCHAR

See also: <CFQUERY>

<CFSWITCH>, <CFCASE>, </CFCASE>, <CFDEFAULTCASE>, </CFDEFAULTCASE>, </CFSWITCH>

Description: <CFSWITCH> is used to create case statements in ColdFusion. Every <CFSWITCH> must be terminated with a </CFSWITCH>. The individual case statements are specified using the <CFCASE> tag; a default case may be specified using the <CFDEFAULTCASE> tag. <CFSWITCH> attributes are listed in Table A.70; <CFCASE> attributes are listed in Table A.71.

Syntax:

```
<CFSWITCH EXPRESSION="expression"><CFCASE VALUE="value"></CFCASE><CFDEFAULTCASE>
</CFDEFAULTCASE></CFSWITCH>
```

Table A.70   <CFSWITCH> **Attributes**

Attribute	Description	Notes
EXPRESSION	Case expression	This attribute is required.

Table A.71   <CFCASE> **Attributes**

Attribute	Description	Notes
VALUE	Case value	This attribute is required.

Example: The following example checks to see if a state is a known state and displays an appropriate message:

```
<CFSWITCH EXPRESSION="#Ucase(state)#">
 <CFCASE VALUE="CA">California</CFCASE>
 <CFCASE VALUE="FL">Florida</CFCASE>
 <CFCASE VALUE="MI">Michigan</CFCASE>
 <CFCASEDEFAULT>One of the other 47 States</CFCASEDEFAULT>
</CFSWITCH>
```

See also: <CFIF>

<CFTABLE>, <CFCOL>, </CFTABLE>

Description: <CFTABLE> allows you to easily create tables in which to display data. <CFTABLE> can create HTML tables (using the <TABLE> tag) or preformatted text tables that display on all browsers. Using <CFTABLE> involves two tags: <CFTABLE> defines the table itself and one or more <CFCOL> tags define the table columns. The <CFTABLE> attributes are listed in Table A.72; the <CFCOL> attributes are listed in Table A.73.

Syntax:

```
<CFTABLE QUERY="Query Name" MAXROWS="Maximum Rows" COLSPACING="Column Spacing"
 COLHEADERS HEADERLINES ="Header Lines" HTMLTABLE>
<CFCOL HEADER="Header Text" WIDTH ="Width" ALIGN ="Alignment" TEXT="Body Text">
</CFTABLE>
```

Table A.72   <CFTABLE> **Attributes**

Attribute	Description	Notes
COLHEADERS	Display column headers	Column headers are displayed if this optional attribute is present.
COLSPACING	Spaces between columns	This optional attribute overrides the default column spacing of 2 if present.

continues

Table A.72 Continued

Attribute	Description	Notes
HEADERLINES	Number of header lines	The default number of header lines is 2, one for the header and a blank row between the header and the body. You may increase this number if needed.
HTMLTABLE	Create an HTML table	An HTML table is created if this attribute is present. If not, a preformatted text table is created.
MAXROWS	Maximum number of table rows	The optional attribute specifies the maximum number of rows to be displayed in the table.
QUERY	<CFQUERY> name	The name of the query from which to derive the table body text.

Table A.73 <CFCOL> Attributes

Attribute	Description	Notes
ALIGN	Column alignment	Valid values are LEFT, CENTER, or RIGHT.
HEADER	Column header text	
TEXT	Column text	The text attribute is the body of what is displayed in each column. Hypertext jumps can be included, as can any table fields. Expressions cannot be included in the TEXT attribute.
WIDTH	Column width	Optional column width; defaults to 20 if not specified. Any text that fits into the cell is truncated.

Example: The following example creates an HTML table with two columns, Name and Extension.

```
<CFTABLE QUERY="Employees" COLHEADERS HTMLTABLE>
 <CFCOL HEADER="Name" ALIGN=LEFT TEXT ="#LastName#, #FirstName#">
<CFCOL HEADER="Extension" ALIGN=LEFT TEXT ="#PhoneExtension#">
</CFTABLE>
```

TIP The <CFTABLE> tag is an easy and efficient way to create tables for displaying query results. you should create HTML tables manually for greater control over table output, including cell spanning, text and background colors, borders, background images, and nested tables.

See also: <CFOUTPUT>, <CFQUERY>

<CFTEXTINPUT>

Description: <CFTEXTINPUT> embeds a highly configurable Java text input control into your HTML forms. <CFTEXTINPUT> must be used between <CFFORM> and </CFFORM> tags. Unlike the standard HTML INPUT, <CFTEXTINPUT> lets you configure the exact height and width of the edit control, as well as color, font, size, and spacing. <CFTEXTINPUT> can also automatically generate field JavaScript validation code. Table A.74 lists the entire set of <CFTEXTINPUT> attributes.

Syntax:

```
<CFTEXTINPUT ALIGN="Alignment" BGCOLOR="Background Color" BOLD="Yes¦No"
 FONT="Font Face" FONTSIZE="Font Size" HEIGHT="Control Height"
 HSPACE="Horizontal Spacing" ITALIC="Yes¦No" MAXLENGTH="Maximum Length"
 MESSAGE="Error Message" NAME="Field Name" NOTSUPPORTED="Non Java Browser Code"
 ONERROR="Error Function" ONVALIDATE="Validation Function" RANGE="Numeric Range"
 REQUIRED="Yes¦No" SIZE="Field Size" TEXTCOLOR="Text Color"
 VALIDATE="Validation Type" VALUE="Initial Value" VSPACE="Vertical Spacing"
 WIDTH="Control Width">
```

Table A.74   <CFTEXTINPUT> **Attributes**

Attribute	Description	Notes
ALIGN	Control alignment	Optional attribute; possible values are top, left, bottom, baseline, texttop, absbottom, middle, absmiddle, right.
BGCOLOR	Background color	Optional attribute; possible values are black, cyan, darkgray, gray, lightgray, magenta, orange, pink, white, yellow, or any color specified in RGB form.
BOLD	Bold face text	Optional attribute; must be Yes or No if specified; defaults to No.
FONT	Font face	Optional font face to use.
FONTSIZE	Font size	Optional font size.
HEIGHT	Control height	Optional height in pixels.
HSPACE	Control horizontal spacing	Optional horizontal spacing in pixels.
ITALIC	Italic face text	Optional attribute; must be Yes or No if specified; defaults to No.

continues

Table A.74   Continued

Attribute	Description	Notes
MAXLENGTH	Maximum number of characters	Optional attribute.
MESSAGE	Validation failure message	Optional message to display upon validation failure.
NAME	Unique control name	This attribute is required.
NOTSUPPORTED	Text to be used for non Java browsers	Optional text (or HTML code) to be displayed on non–Java-capable browsers.
ONERROR	JavaScript error function	Optional override to your own JavaScript error message function.
ONVALIDATE	JavaScript validation	Optional override to your function own JavaScript validation function.
RANGE	Range minimum and maximum	Optional range for numeric values only; must be specified as two numbers separated by a comma.
REQUIRED	Field is required	Optional required flag; must be Yes or No if specified; defaults to No.
SIZE	Field size	Optional number of characters to display before needing horizontal scrolling.
TEXTCOLOR	Text color	Optional attribute; possible values are black, cyan, darkgray, gray, lightgray, magenta, orange, pink, white, yellow, or any color specified in RGB form.
VALIDATE	Field validation	Optional field validation. If specified, must be any of the validation types listed in Table A.75.
VALUE	Initial value	Optional initial field value.
VSPACE	Control vertical spacing	Optional vertical spacing in pixels.
WIDTH	Control width	Optional width in pixels.

Table A.75 **<CFTEXTINPUT> Validation Types**

Type	Description
Creditcard	Correctly formatted credit card number verified using mod10
Date	Date in mm/dd/yy format
Eurodate	European date in dd/mm/yy format
Float	Number with decimal point
Integer	Number with no decimal point
Social_Security_Number	Social security number formatted as 999-99-9999 (using hyphens or spaces as separators)
Telephone	Phone number in 999-999-9999 format (using hyphens or spaces as separators), area code and exchange must not begin with 0 or 1
Time	Time in hh:mm or hh:mm:ss format
Zipcode	U.S. zip code; either 99999 or 99999-9999 format

Example: The following example displays a simple Java text edit control, specifying the height, width, font, and color:

```
<CFFORM ACTION="process.cfm">
<CFTEXTINPUT NAME="name" HEIGHT="100" WIDTH="200" FONT="Verdana" BGCOLOR="Black"
 TEXTCOLOR="White">
</CFFORM>
```

N O T E   The <CFTEXTINPUT> control is only accessible by users with Java-enabled browsers. ■

See also: <CFFORM>, <CFGIRD>, <CFINPUT>, <CFSELECT>, <CFSLIDER>, <CFTREE>

<CFTHROW>

Description: <CFTHROW> throws an exception. Program control is then handed to the catch code specified in a prior <CFTRY> and <CFCATCH> set. <CFTHROW> can be used to force an error condition, throwing an exception to an application or any catch block. <CFTHROW> attributes are listed in Table A.76.

Syntax:

```
<CFTHROW MESSAGE="message">
```

Table A.76 `<CFTHROW>` **Attributes**

Attribute	Description	Notes
MESSAGE	Error message	This attribute is optional.

Example: This example throws an exception because an invalid password was specified:

```
<CFTHROW MESSAGE="Invalid password specified">
```

See also: `<CFTRY>`

`<CFTRANSACTION>, </CFTRANSACTION>`

Description: `<CFTRANSACTION>` implements transaction and rollback processing. Any `<CFQUERY>` tags placed between `<CFTRANSACTION>` and `</CFTRANSACTION>` tags are automatically rolled back if an error occurs. The `<CFTRANSACTION>` attributes are list in Table A.77.

Syntax:

```
<CFTRANSACTION ISOLATION="Lock Type">
Queries
</CFTRANSACTION>
```

Table A.77 `<CFTRANSACTION>` **Attributes**

Attribute	Description	Notes
ISOLATION	Type of ODBC lock	Optional lock type; possible values are READ_UNCOMMITTED, READ_COMMITTED, REPEATABLE_READ, SERIALIZABLE, and VERSIONING.

Example: The following example shows how `<CFTRANSACTION>` ensures that an operation dependent on two queries does not leave the databases in an inconstant state if one operation fails:

```
<CFTRANSACTION>
 <CFQUERY
  DATASOURCE="Accounts"
 >
  UPDATE Accounts SET Total = Total - #Withdrawal# WHERE AccountNum =
#AccountNum#
 </CFQUERY>
 <CFQUERY
  DATASOURCE="Accounts"
 >
 UPDATE Accounts SET Total = Total + #Withdrawal# WHERE AccountNum = #AccountNum#
 </CFQUERY>
</CFTRANSACTION>
```

N O T E Not all lock types are supported by all ODBC drivers. Consult your database documentation before using the ISOLATION attribute.

<CFTREE>, <CFTREEITEM>, </CFTREE>

Description: <CFTREE> embeds a Java tree control into your HTML forms. The tree control is similar to the Explorer window in Windows 95 and Windows NT. The tree is made up of root entries and branches that can be expanded or closed. Branches can be nested. Each branch has a graphic that is displayed next to it; you can select from any of the supplied graphics or use any of your own.

<CFTREE> trees are constructed using two tags. <CFTREE> creates the tree control and <CFTREEITEM> adds the entries into the tree. Trees may be populated one branch at a time or using query results. <CFTREEITEM> must be used between <CFTREE> and </CFTREE> tags. <CFTREE> attributes are listed in Table A.78; <CFTREEITEM> attributes are listed in Table A.79.

Syntax:

```
<CFTTREE ALIGN="Alignment" APPENDKEY="Yes¦No" BOLD="Yes¦No" BORDER="Yes¦No¦
 COMPLETEPATH="Yes¦No" DELIMITER="Delimiter Character" FONT="Font Face"
 FONTSIZE="Font Size" HEIGHT="Control Height" HIGHLIGHTHREF="Yes¦No"
 HSPACE="Horizontal Spacing" HSCROLL="Yes¦No" ITALIC="Yes¦No"
 MESSAGE="Error Message" NAME="Field Name" NOTSUPPORTED="Non Java Browser Code"
 ONERROR="Error Function" ONVALIDATE="Validation Function" REQUIRED="Yes¦No"
 VSPACE="Vertical Spacing" WIDTH="Control Width">

<CFTREEITEM DISPLAY="Display Text EXPAND="Yes¦No" HREF="URL" IMG="Images"
 IMGOPEN="Images" QUERY="Query Name" QUERYASROOT="Yes¦No" TARGET="Target Name"
 PARENT="Parent Branch" VALUE="Values">
```

Table A.78 **<CFTREE> Attributes**

Attribute	Description	Notes
ALIGN	Control alignment	Optional attribute; possible values are top, left, bottom, baseline, texttop, absbottom, middle, absmiddle, right.
APPENDKEY	Append item key to URL	Optional attribute; if Yes, variable named CFTREEITEMKEY is appended to the URL containing the item selected; defaults to Yes.
BOLD	Bold text	Optional attribute; must be Yes or No if specified; defaults to No.
BORDER	Display border around control	Optional attribute; defaults to Yes.

continues

Table A.78 **Continued**

Attribute	Description	Notes
COMPLETEPATH	Pass complete path	Optional attribute; to selected item the full tree path to the selected item is returned if Yes; defaults to No.
DELIMITER	Path delimiter	Optional attribute; defaults to \.
FONT	Font face	Optional font face to use.
FONTSIZE	Font size	Optional font size.
HEIGHT	Control height	Optional height in pixels.
HIGHLIGHTHREF	Highlight links	Optional attribute; links arehighlighted and underlined if Yes; defaults to Yes.
HSPACE	Control horizontal spacing	Optional horizontal in pixels.
HSCROLL	Display horizontal	Optional attribute; scrollbar default is Yes.
ITALIC	Italic face text	Optional attribute; must be Yes or No if specified, defaults to No.
MESSAGE	Validation failure	Optional message to message display upon validation failure.
NAME	Unique control name	This attribute is required.
NOTSUPPORTED	Text to be used for non-Java browsers	Optional text (or HTML code) to be displayed on non-Java–capable browsers.
ONERROR	JavaScript error function	Optional override to your own JavaScript error message function.
ONVALIDATE	JavaScript validation function	Optional override to your own JavaScript validation function.
REQUIRED	Selection is required	Optional attribute; must be Yes or No; defaults to No.
VSPACE	Control vertical spacing	Optional vertical spacing in pixels.
VSCROLL	Display vertical scrollbar	Optional attribute; default is Yes.
WIDTH	Control width	Optional width in pixels.

Table A.79 `<CFTREEITEM>` **Attributes**

Attribute	Description	Notes
DISPLAY	Display text	Optional attribute, defaults to value is not specified, if populating with a query result set this value should be a comma delimited list of values, one for each tree item.
EXPAND	Open expanded	Optional attribute; branch is initially expanded if Yes; defaults to No.
HREF	Item URL	Optional attribute; URL to go to when an item is selected; if populating with a query result set, this value can be a comma-delimited list of URLs (one for each tree item), or it can be a column name. In that case it is populated dynamically.
IMG	Image	Optional attribute; image to be displayed; if populating with a query result set, this value should be a comma-delimited list of images, one for each tree level; images may be folder, floppy, fixed, CD, document, element, or any image file of your own.
IMGOPEN	Open image	Optional attribute; image to be displayed when branch is open; if populating with a query result set, this value should be a comma-delimited list of images, one for each tree level; images may be folder, floppy, fixed, CD, document, element, or any image file of your own. If omitted, the IMG image is used; if populating with a query result set, this value should be a comma-delimited list of images, one for each tree item.
QUERY	Query name	Optional query name to be used to populate the list.
QUERYASROOT	Use query name as root	Optional attribute; if Yes, query name itself is the tree root branch; defaults to No.
TARGET	Link target window	Optional attribute; the page to open the link in; this value can be a comma-delimited list of targets if populating with a query result set, one for each tree item.
PARENT	Branch parent	Optional attribute; name of parent to attach this branch to.

continues

App

A

Table A.79	Continued	
Attribute	**Description**	**Notes**
VALUE	Value to be returned	Required attribute; this value should be a comma-delimited list of values, one for each tree item, if populating with a query result set.

Examples: This example creates a simple Java tree control with three branches:

```
<CFFORM ACTION="process.cfm">
<CFTREE NAME="states">
<CFTREEITEM VALUE="US">
<CFTREEITEM VALUE="CA" DISPLAY="California" PARENT="US">
<CFTREEITEM VALUE="MI" DISPLAY="Michigan" PARENT="US">
<CFTREEITEM VALUE="NY" DISPLAY="New York" PARENT="US">
</CFTREE>
</CFFORM>
```

This next example populates a tree with a query called Users:

```
<CFFORM ACTION="process.cfm">
<CFTREE NAME="peopletree" HSPACE="20" HSCROLL="no" VSCROLL="Yes" DELIMITER="?"
BORDER="Yes">
<CFTREEITEM VALUE="cn" QUERYASROOT="Yes" QUERY="Users" IMG="folder,document">
</CFTREE>
</CFFORM>
```

N O T E The <CFTREE> control is only accessible by users with Java-enabled browsers. ■

N O T E For examples of using <CFTREE> with browser directories, take a look at the ColdFusion Administrator. ■

See also: <CFFORM>, <CFGIRD>, <CFINPUT>, <CFSELECT>, <CFSLIDER>, <CFTEXTINPUT>

<CFTRY>, <CFCATCH>, </CFCATCH>, </CFTRY>

Description: <CFTRY> is used to catch exceptions thrown by ColdFusion or explicitly with <CFTHROW>. All code between <CFTRY> and </CFTRY> can throw exceptions. Exceptions are caught by <CFCATCH> blocks. Explicit <CFCATCH> blocks may be created for different error types, or one block can catch all errors. <CFCATCH> attributes are listed in Table A.80.

Syntax:

```
<CFTRY> <CFCATCH TYPE="type"> </CFCATCH> </CFTRY>
```

Table A.80 **<CFCATCH> Attributes**

Attribute	Description	Notes
TYPE	Exception type	This attribute is optional.

Table A.81 **<CFCATCH> TYPE values**

Type
Any
Application
Database
MissingInclude
Object
Security
Synchronization
Template

Example: This example throws an exception because an invalid password was specified:

```
<CFTRY>
<CFCATCH TYPE= "Any">some error handling goes here</CFCATCH>
</CFTRY>
```

See also: <CFTHROW>

<CFUPDATE>

Description: <CFUPDATE> updates a single row to a database table; it requires that the database and table names be provided. All other attributes are optional. The full list of <CFUPDATE> attributes is explained in Table A.82.

Syntax:

```
<CFUPDATE DATASOURCE="ODBC Data Source" DBNAME="database name" DBPOOL="pool"
 DBTYPE="type" DBSERVER="dbms" FORMFIELDS="List of File to Update"
 PASSWORD="Password" PROVIDER="provider" PROVIDERDSN="data source"
 TABLENAME="Table Name" TABLEOWNER="owner" TABLEQUALIFIER="qualifier"
 USERNAME="User Name">
```

Table A.82   <CFUPDATE> **Attributes**

Attribute	Description	Notes
DATASOURCE	Name of ODBC data source	The specified data source must already exist. This attribute is required.
DBNAME	Sybase database name	Optional attribute, only used if using native Sybase drivers.
DBPOOL	Database connection pool name	Optional database pool name.
DBSERVER	Database server	Optional database server; only used if using native database drives.
DBTYPE	Database type	Optional type, defaults to ODBC, other values are Oracle73, Oracle80, and Sybase11.
FORMFIELDS	List of fields to insert	This optional attribute specifies which fields are to insert if they are present. Any fields present that are not in the list are not inserted.
PASSWORD	ODBC data source password	This optional attribute is used to override the ODBC login password specified in the ColdFusion Administrator.
PROVIDER	OLE-DB COM provider	Optional attribute; only used if using OLE-DB.
PROVIDERDSN	Data source OLE-DB COM provider	Optional attribute; only used if using OLE-DB.
TABLENAME	Name of table to insert	Some ODBC data source data into.require fully qualified table names. This attribute is required.
TABLEOWNER	Table owner name	Optional attribute used by databases that support table ownership.
TABLEQUALIFIER	Table qualifier	Optional attribute used by databases that support full qualifiers.
USERNAME	ODBC data source login name	The optional attribute is used to override the ODBClogin name specified inthe ColdFusion Administrator.

N O T E For <CFUPDATE> to work correctly, your form field names must match the column names in the destination table, and the primary key value of the row to be updated must be specified.

 T I P If your form contains fields that are not part of the table you are updating, use the FORMFIELDS attribute to instruct ColdFusion to ignore those fields.

T I P For more control over updating rows into a database table, you may use the <CFQUERY> tag specifying UPDATE as the SQL statement.

Example: The following example updates a row in the Employees table in the A2Z data source:

```
<
CFUPDATE
DATASOURCE="A2Z"
TABLENAME="Employees"
>
```

The next example updates a row in the same table, but will only update values into the three specified fields if they exist:

```
<
CFUPDATE
DATASOURCE="A2Z"
TABLENAME="Employees"
FORMFIELD="LastName,FirstName,PhoneExtension"
>
```

See also: <CFINSERT>, <CFQUERY>

<CFWDDX>

Description: <CFWDDX> is used to serialize and deserialize ColdFusion data structures to the XML based WDDX format. The ACTION attribute specifies the action to be performed.

Syntax:

```
<CFWDDX ACTION="action" INPUT="input" OUTPUT="output" TOPLEVELVARIABLE="name">
```

Table A.83	<CFWDDX> **Attributes**	
Attribute	**Description**	**Notes**
ACTION	Action	This attribute is required. Actions are listed in Table A.84.
INPUT	Input value	This attribute is required.

continues

Table A.83   Continued

Attribute	Description	Notes
OUTPUT	Output variable	Required if ACTION is WDDX2CFML.
TOPLEVELVARIABLE	JavaScript top-level variable	Required if ACTION is WDDX2JS or CFML2JS.

Table A.84   <CFWDDX> Actions

Action	Description
CFML2JS	Serializes CFML to JavaScript format
CFML2WDDX	Serializes CFML to WDDX format
WDDX2CFML	Deserializes WDDX to CFML
WDDX2JS	Deserializes WDDX to JavaScript

ColdFusion Function Reference

Using ColdFusion Functions

ColdFusion provides a complete set of data manipulation and formatting functions. Here are some things to remember when using functions:

- Function names are not case sensitive, so NOW() is the same as now(), which is the same as Now().
- When functions are used in body text rather than within a ColdFusion tag, they must be enclosed within <CFOUTPUT> tags.
- Functions can be nested.

To make this function reference easier to use, the functions have been grouped into logical sets. As there are some functions that overlap these groupings, each function has a "see also" list of related functions.

- **String manipulation functions** are a complete set of text parsing, comparison, and conversion functions.
- **Date and time functions** can be used to create, parse, compare, and manipulate date and time values.
- **Data formatting functions** allow you to display data in a variety of formats.
- **Mathematical functions** can be used to perform calculations, conversions, and generate random numbers.
- **International functions** provide localization support for dates, times, and other data types.
- **List manipulation functions** are used to control lists of values.
- **Array manipulation functions** are used to create and manage two- and three-dimensional arrays.
- **Structure manipulation functions** are used to create and manage ColdFusion structures.
- **Query manipulation functions** are used to create and manage ColdFusion queries.
- **Security functions** give you access to security information returned by a <CFAUTHENTICATE> call.
- **System functions** give you access to system directories, temporary files, and path manipulation functions.
- **Client variable manipulation functions** allow you to control client variables.
- **Expression evaluation functions** enable you to create and evaluate expressions on-the-fly.
- **Bit and set manipulation functions** can be used to perform bit-level operations.
- **Miscellaneous functions** are an assortment of functions that you can use to check for the existence of parameters, format URLs, and manipulate lists to be passed to SQL statements.

String Manipulation Functions

The ColdFusion string manipulation functions can be used to perform operations on character data. Strings may be hard-coded constants, table column values, or ColdFusion fields. As with all ColdFusion functions, these string manipulation functions can be nested.

Asc

Description: Asc returns the ASCII value of the leftmost character of a string.

Syntax: Asc(character)

App

B

Example: The following example returns 72, the ASCII value of the character H:

`#Asc("Hello")#`

 T I P The Asc function only processes the leftmost character in a string. To return the ASCII characters of an entire string, you have to loop through the string at process each character individually.

See also: Chr, Val

Chr

Description: Chr converts an ASCII value into a printable character.

Syntax: Chr(number)

Example: The following example returns the letter H, whose ASCII value is 72:

`#Chr(72)#`

See also: Asc, Val

CJustify

Description: CJustify centers a string within a field of a specified length. It does this by padding spaces before and after the specified text. CJustify takes two parameters, the string to process, and the desired string length.

Syntax: CJustify(string, length)

Example: The following example justifies the word Hello so that it is centered within a 20-character–wide field:

`#CJustify("Hello", 20)#`

See also: LJustify, LTrim, RJustify, RTrim, Trim

Compare, CompareNoCase

Description: The Compare and CompareNoCase functions compare two string values. Compare performs a case-sensitive comparison; CompareNoCase performs a non–case-sensitive function.

Both of these functions return a negative number if the first string is less than the second string, a positive number if the first string is greater than the second string, and 0 if the strings are the same.

Syntax:

```
Compare(String1, String2)
```

```
CompareNoCase(String1, String2)
```

Example: This example returns a negative value because the first string is less than the second string:

```
#Compare("Ben", "Bill")#
```

This next example uses the non–case-sensitive comparison function and returns 0 because, aside from case, the strings are the same:

```
#CompareNoCase("Michigan", "MICHIGAN")#
```

NOTE The two comparison functions treat whitespace as characters to be compared. Therefore, if you compare two strings that are identical except for extra spaces at the end of one of them, the compare will not return 0. ■

Find, FindNoCase, REFind, REFindNoCase

Description: ColdFusion provides three functions to search for a specific text within another string. Find performs a case-sensitive search, FindNoCase performs a non–case-sensitive search, REFind performs a case-sensitive search using regular expressions, and REFindNoCase performs a non–case-sensitive search using regular expressions. The parameters for all these functions are the same. The first parameter is the string (or regular expression) to search for, the second parameter is the target string, or string to be searched. An optional third parameter may be provided to specify the position in the target string from which to start the search. All of these functions return the starting position of the first occurrence of the search string within the specified target string. If the search string is not found, 0 is returned.

Syntax:

```
Find(SearchString, TargetString [, StartPosition])
```

```
FindNoCase(SearchString, TargetString [, StartPosition])
```

```
REFind(RegularExpression, TargetString [, StartPosition])
```

```
REFindNoCase(RegularExpression, TargetString [, StartPosition])
```

Example: This first example returns 18, the start position of the word America:

```
#Find("America", "United States of America")#
```

The next example returns 0 because Find performs a case-sensitive search:

```
#Find("AMERICA", "United States of America")#
```

The FindNoCase function performs a non–case-sensitive search, as this example shows:

```
#FindNoCase("AMERICA", "United States of America")#
```

The next example searched for the word of in the string The Flag of the United States of America, and specifies that the search should start from position 15. This example returns 31, the position of the second of. Had the optional start position parameter been omitted, the return value would have been 10, the position of the first of:

```
#Find("of", "The Flag of the United States of America", 15)#
```

See also: FindOneOf, GetToken, Left, Mid, Right

FindOneOf

Description: FindOneOf returns the position of the first target string character that matches any of the characters in a specified set. FindOneOf takes three parameters. The first parameter is a string containing the set of characters to search for, the second parameter is the *target string* (the string to be searched), the third parameter is an optional starting position from which to start the search. These functions return the starting position of the first occurrence of any characters in the search set within the specified target string. If no matching characters are found, 0 is returned.

Syntax:

```
FindOneOf(SearchSet, TargetString, [, StartPosition])
```

Example: The following example returns the position of the first vowel with a ColdFusion field called LastName:

```
The first vowel in your last name is at position #FindOneOf("aeiou", LastName)#
```

 T I P The FindOneOf function is case sensitive, and there is no non–case-sensitive equivalent function. To perform a non–case-sensitive FindOneOf search, you must first convert both the search and target strings to either upper- or lowercase (using the UCase or LCase functions).

See also: Find, FindNoCase

GetToken

Description: *Tokens* are delimited sets of data within a string. The GetToken function allows you to extract a specific token from a string by specifying the *token number* or index. GetToken takes three parameters. The first is the string to search; the second is the index of the token to extract, so 3 will extract the third token and 5 will extract the fifth. The third parameter is an optional set of delimiters that GetToken uses to determine where each token starts and finishes. If the delimiter's parameter is not provided, the default of spaces, tabs, and new line characters is used. The default delimiters effectively allow this function to be used to extract specific words for a string. GetToken returns the token in the specified position, or any empty string if Index is greater than the number of token present.

Syntax:

```
GetToken(String, Index [, Delimiters])
```

Example: The following example uses a hyphen as a delimiter to extract just the area code from a phone number:

```
#GetToken("800-555-1212", 1, "-")#
```

 TIP Use the ColdFusion list functions instead of `GetToken` when working with strings that contain lists of data.

InputBaseN

Description: `InputBaseN` converts a string into a number using the base specified by radix. Valid radix values are 2 through 36.

Syntax:

```
InputBaseN(String, Radix)
```

Example: The following example converts the string containing the binary number `10100010` into its base-10 equivalent of `162`:

```
#InputBaseN("10100010", 2)#
```

 TIP The code `InputBaseN(String, 10)` is functionally equivalent to the code `Val(String)`. If you are converting a number that is base 10, the `Val` function is simpler to use.

See also: FormatBaseN, Val

Insert

Description: `Insert` is used to insert text into a string and takes three parameters. The first parameter, `SourceString`, is the string you want to insert. The second parameter, `TargetString`, is the string into which you are going to insert `SourceString`. The third parameter, `Position`, is a numeric value that specifies the location in the `TargetString` at which to insert the `SourceString`. `Insert` returns the modified string.

Syntax:

```
Insert(SourceString, TargetString, Position)
```

Example: The following example inserts a field called area code in front of a phone number:

```
#Insert(area_code, phone, 0)#
```

 TIP To insert a string at the very beginning of another, use the `Insert` function specifying a `Position` of 0.

See also: RemoveChars, SpanExcluding, SpanIncluding

LCase

Description: LCase converts a string to lowercase. LCase takes a single parameter, the string to be converted, and returns the converted string.

Syntax:

```
LCase(String)
```

Example: The following example converts a user-supplied string to lowercase:

```
#LCase(string_field)#
```

See also: UCase

Left

Description: Left returns the specified leftmost characters from the beginning of a string. Left takes two parameters, the string from which to extract the characters and the number of characters to extract.

Syntax:

```
Left(String, Count)
```

Example: The following example returns the first three characters of a phone number column:

```
#Left(phone_number, 3)#
```

See also: Find, Mid, RemoveChars, Right

Len

Description: Len returns the length of a specified string. Len takes a single parameter, the string whose length you want to determine.

Syntax:

```
Len(String)
```

Example: The following example returns the length of a user-supplied address field after it has been trimmed:

```
#Len(Trim(address))#
```

LJustify

Description: LJustify left-aligns a string within a field of a specified length. It does this by padding spaces after the specified text. LJustify takes two parameters, the string to process and the desired string length.

Syntax:

```
LJustify(String, Length)
```

App
B

Example: The following example left-justifies the string "First Name:" so that it is left-aligned within a 25-character–wide field:

```
#LJustify("First Name:", 25)#
```

See also: CJustify, LTrim, RJustify, RTrim, Trim

LTrim

Description: LTrim trims whitespace (spaces, tabs, and new line characters) from the beginning of a string.

LTrim takes a single parameter, the string to be trimmed.

Syntax:

```
LTrim(String)
```

Example: The following example trims spaces from the beginning of a table note field:

```
#LTrim(notes)#
```

See also: CJustify, LJustify, RJustify, RTrim, Trim, StripCR

Mid

Description: Mid returns a string of characters from any location in a string. Mid takes three parameters, the first is the string from which to extract the characters, the second is the desired characters' starting position, and the third is the number of characters required.

Syntax:

```
Mid(String, StartPosition, Count)
```

Example: The following example extract eight characters from the middle of a table column, starting at position 3:

```
#Mid(order_number, 3, 8)#
```

See also: Find, Left, RemoveChars, Right

RemoveChars

Description: RemoveChars returns a string with specified characters removed from it. This function is the exact opposite of the Mid function. RemoveChars takes three parameters, the first is the string from which to remove the characters, the second is the starting position of the characters to be removed, and the third is the number of characters to be removed.

Syntax:

```
RemoveChars(String, StartPosition, Length)
```

Example: The following example returns a field with characters 10 through 15 removed:

```
#RemoveChars(product_code, 10, 5)#
```

See also: Left, Mid, Right

RepeatString

Description: RepeatString returns a string that is made up of a specified string multiple times. RepeatString takes two parameters, the first is the string to repeat and the second is the number of occurrences.

Syntax:

```
RepeatString(String, Count)
```

Example: The following example creates a horizontal line made up of equal signs:

```
#RepeatString("=", 80)#
```

Replace, REReplace, REReplaceNoCase

Description: Replace, REReplace, and REReplaceNoCase allow you to replace text within strings with alternative text. Replace does a simple text comparison to locate the text to be replaced; REReplace and REReplaceCase perform the same operation but use regular expressions.

All three functions take four parameters. The first parameter is the string to be processed, the second is the text to be replaced, and the third is the text to replace it with. The fourth parameter is optional and specifies the scope of the replacements. Possible scope values are "ONE" to replace the first occurrence only, "ALL" to replace all occurrences, and "RECURSIVE" to replace all occurrences recursively.

Syntax:

```
Replace(String, WhatString, WithString [, Scope])

REReplace(String, WhatString, WithString [, Scope])

REReplaceNoCase(String, WhatString, WithString [, Scope])
```

Example: The following example replaces all occurrences of the text "US" in an address field with the text "USA":

```
#Replace(address, "US", "USA", "ALL")#
```

This next example replaces the area code "(313)" with the area code "(810)", and because no scope is specified, only the first occurrence of "(313)" is replaced:

```
#Replace(phone, "(313)", "(810)")#
```

 T I P The Replace function is case sensitive, and there is no non–case-sensitive equivalent function. In order to perform a non-case-sensitive replacement you must first convert both the search and target strings to either upper- or lowercase (using the UCase or LCase functions).

See also: ReplaceList

ReplaceList

Description: ReplaceList replaces all occurrences of elements in one string with corresponding elements in another. Both sets of elements must be specified as comma-delimited values, and there must be an equal number of values in each set. ReplaceList takes three parameters. The first is the string to be processed, the second is the set of values to be replaced, and the third is the set of values to replace them with.

Syntax:

```
ReplaceList(String, FindWhatList, ReplaceWithList)
```

Example: The following example replaces all occurrences of state names with their appropriate abbreviations:

```
#ReplaceList(address, "CA, IN, MI", "California, Indiana, Michigan")#
```

 TIP The ReplaceList function is case sensitive, and there is no non–case-sensitive equivalent function. To perform a non–case-sensitive replacements you must first convert both the search and target strings to either upper- or lowercase (using the UCase or LCase functions).

N O T E   Unlike other replacement functions, the ReplaceList function takes no scope parameter. ReplaceList replaces all occurrences of matching elements. ▦

See also: Replace

Reverse

Description: Reverse reverses the characters in a string. Reverse takes a single parameter, the string to be reversed.

Syntax:

```
Reverse(String)
```

Example: The following example reverses the contents of a user-supplied field:

```
#Reverse(sequence_id)#
```

Right

Description: Right returns the specified rightmost characters from the end of a string. Right takes two parameters, the string from which to extract the characters and the number of characters to extract.

Syntax:

```
Right(String, Count)
```

Example: The following example returns the last seven characters of a phone number column:

```
#Right(phone_number, 7)#
```

TIP Right does not trim trailing spaces before extracting the specific characters. To ignore whitespace when using Right, you should nest the RTrim within Right, as in #Right(RTrim(String), Count)#.

See also: Find, Left, Mid, RemoveChars

RJustify

Description: RJustify right-aligns a string within a field of a specified length. It does this by padding spaces before the specified text. RJustify takes two parameters, the string to process, and the desired string length. The syntax of the RJustify function is:

Syntax: RJustify(string, length)

Example: The following example right-justifies the contents of a field named Zip so that it is right aligned within a 10-character–wide field:

#RJustify(Zip, 10)#

See also: CJustify, LJustify, LTrim, RTrim, Trim

RTrim

Description: RTrim trims whitespace (spaces, tabs, and new line characters) from the end of a string. RTrim takes a single parameter, the string to be trimmed.

Syntax:

RTrim(String)

Example: The following example trims spaces from the end of a user-supplied field:

#RTrim(first_name)#

See also: CJustify, LJustify, LTrim, RJustify, Trim, StripCR

SpanExcluding

Description: SpanExcluding extracts characters from the beginning of a string until a character that is part of a specified set is reached. SpanExcluding takes two parameters, the string to process and a comma-delimited set of values to compare against.

Syntax:

SpanExcluding(String, Set)

Example: The following example extracts the first word of a sentence by specifying a space as the character to compare against:

#SpanExcluding(sentence, " ")#

TIP The SpanExcluding function is case sensitive, and there is no non–case-sensitive equivalent function. To perform a non–case-sensitive extraction you must first convert both the search and target strings to either upper- or lowercase (using the UCase or LCase functions).

See also: SpanIncluding

SpanIncluding

Description: SpanIncluding extracts characters from the beginning of a string only as long as they match characters in a specified set. SpanIncluding takes two parameters, the string to process and a comma-delimited set of values to compare against.

Syntax:

SpanIncluding(String, Set)

Example: The following example extracts the house number from a street address by specifying a set of values that are digits only:

#SpanIncluding(address, "1,2,3,4,5,6,7,8,9,0")#

TIP The SpanIncluding function is case sensitive, and there is no non–case-sensitive equivalent function. To perform a non–case-sensitive extraction you must first convert both the search and target strings to either upper- or lowercase (using the UCase or LCase functions).

See also: SpanExcluding

StripCR

Description: StripCR removes all carriage return characters from a string. StripCR takes a single parameter, the string to process.

Syntax:

StripCR(String)

Example: The following example removes carriage returns for a field to be displayed in a preformatted text block:

<PRE>#StripCR(comments)#</PRE>

TIP The StripCR function is particularly useful when displaying a string within HTML preformatted text tags (<PRE> and </PRE>) where carriage returns are not ignored.

See also: CJustify, LJustify, LTrim, RJustify, RTrim, Trim

Trim

Description: Trim trims whitespace (spaces, tabs, and new line characters) from both the beginning and the end of a string. Trim takes a single parameter, the string to be trimmed.

Syntax:

```
Trim(String)
```

Example: The following example trims spaces from both the beginning and the end of a user-supplied field:

```
#Trim(notes)#
```

See also: CJustify, LJustify, LTrim, RJustify, RTrim, StripCR

UCase

Description: UCase converts a string to uppercase. UCase takes a single parameter, the string to be converted, and returns the converted string.

Syntax:

```
UCase(String)
```

Example: The following example converts the contents of a table column called States to uppercase:

```
#UCase(State)#
```

See also: LCase

Val

Description: Val converts the beginning of a string to a number. Val takes a single parameter, the string to process. Conversion is only possible if the string begins with numeric characters. If conversion is impossible, 0 is returned.

Syntax:

```
Val(String)
```

Example: The following example extracts the hour portion from a time field:

```
Hour: #Val(time)#
```

 TIP Val converts characters to numbers using a base of 10 only. To convert the string to numbers with a base other than 10, use the InputBaseN function.

See also: Asc, Chr, InputBaseN, IsNumeric

Date and Time Functions

The ColdFusion Date and Time functions allow you to perform date and time manipulation on table columns and user-supplied fields.

Many of these functions work with date/time objects. A *date/time object* is a ColdFusion internal representation of a complete date and time with accuracy to the second. These objects are designed to facilitate the passing of date/time information between different ColdFusion functions and are not designed to be displayed as is. If you need to display a date/time object, you need to use one of the date/time formatting functions.

N O T E   ColdFusion date/time objects are not the same as ODBC date/time fields. Use the CreateODBCDateTime function to convert ColdFusion date/time objects to the ODBC format. ■

Many ColdFusion date and time functions take date and time values as parameters. These parameters must be valid and within a set range; otherwise a ColdFusion syntax error is generated. The range of values allowed for each date and time field is listed in Table B.1.

Table B.1   Valid ColdFusion Date and Time Values

Field	Min	Max
Year	0	9999
Month	1	12
Day	1	31
Hour	0	23
Minute	0	59
Second	0	59

N O T E   Year values of less than 100 are treated as twentieth century values, and 1900 is added automatically to them. ■

Several of the ColdFusion date and time functions allow you to work with parts of the complete date/time object; to add days or weeks to a date, or to find out how many weeks apart two dates are, for example. These functions require that you pass a date/time part specifier that is passed as a string. (They must have quotation marks around them.) The complete list of specifiers is explained in Table B.2.

Table B.2   ColdFusion Date/Time Specifiers

Specifier	Description
D	Day
H	Hour
M	Month
N	Minute
Q	Quarter
S	Second
W	Weekday (day of week)
WW	Week
Y	Day of year
YYYY	Year

CreateDate

Description: The CreateDate function returns a ColdFusion date/time object that can be used with other date manipulation or formatting functions. CreateDate takes three parameters: the date's year, month, and day.

Syntax:

```
CreateDate(Year, Month, Day)
```

Example: The following example creates a date/time object based on three user-supplied fields:

```
#CreateDate(birth_year, birth_month, birth_day)#
```

NOTE Because the CreateDate function takes no time values as parameters, the time portion of the created date/time object is set to all 0s.

See also: CreateDateTime, CreateODBCDate, CreateTime

CreateDateTime

Description: The CreateDateTime function returns a ColdFusion date/time object that can be used with other date- and time-manipulation or formatting functions. CreateDateTime takes six parameters: the date's year, month, and day, and the time's hour, minute, and second.

Syntax:

```
CreateDateTime(Year, Month, Day, Hour, Minute, Second)
```

Example: The following example creates a date/time object for midnight on New Year's Day, 1997:

```
#CreateDateTime(1997, 1, 1, 0, 0, 0)#
```

See also: CreateDate, CreateODBCDateTime, CreateTime, ParseDateTime

CreateODBCDate

Description: The CreateODBCDate function returns an ODBC date/time field that can safely be used in SQL statements. CreateODBCDate takes a single parameter, a ColdFusion date/time object.

Syntax:

```
CreateODBCDate(Date)
```

Example: The following example creates an ODBC date/time field for the current day (retrieved with the Now() function):

```
#CreateODBCDate(Now())#
```

> **N O T E** CreateODBCDate always creates an ODBC date/time field that has the time values set to 0s, even if the passed date/time object had valid time values.

 T I P CreateODBCDate takes a date/time object as a parameter. If you want to pass individual date values as parameters, use the CreateDate as the function parameter and pass it the values.

See also: CreateDate, CreateODBCDateTime, CreateODBCTime

CreateODBCDateTime

Description: The CreateODBCDateTime function returns an ODBC date/time field that can safely be used in SQL statements. CreateODBCDateTime takes a single parameter, a ColdFusion date/time object.

Syntax:

```
CreateODBCDate(Date)
```

Example: The following example creates an ODBC date/time field for the current day (retrieved with the Now() function):

```
#CreateODBCDateTime(Now())#
```

 T I P CreateODBCDateTime takes a date/time object as a parameter. If you want to pass individual date and time values as parameters, use the CreateDateTime as the function parameter and pass it the values.

See also: CreateDate, CreateODBCDate, CreateODBCTime

CreateODBCTime

Description: The CreateODBCTime function returns an ODBC date/time field that can safely be used in SQL statements. CreateODBCTime takes a single parameter, a ColdFusion date/time object.

Syntax:

```
CreateODBCTime(Date)
```

Example: The following example creates an ODBC date/time field for the current day (retrieved with the Now function):

```
#CreateODBCTime(Now())#
```

> **N O T E** CreateODBCTime always creates an ODBC date/time field that has the date values set to 0s, even if the passed date/time object had valid date values.

> **T I P** CreateODBCTime takes a date/time object as a parameter. If you want to pass individual time values as parameters, use the CreateTime as the function parameter and pass it the values.

See also: CreateODBCDate, CreateODBCDateTime, CreateTime

CreateTime

Description: The CreateTime function returns a ColdFusion date/time object that can be used with other time-manipulation or formatting functions. CreateTime takes three parameters: the time's hour, minute, and second.

Syntax:

```
CreateTime(Hour, Minute, Second)
```

Example: The following example creates a date/time object based on three ColdFusion fields:

```
#CreateTime(act_hr, act_mn, act_se)#
```

> **N O T E** Because the CreateTime function takes no date values as parameters, the date portion of the created date/time object is set to all 0s.

See also: CreateDate, CreateDateTime, CreateODBCTime

CreateTimeSpan

Description: CreateTimeSpan creates a date/time object that can be used to rapidly perform date- and time-based calculations. CreateTimeSpan takes four parameters: days, hours, minutes, and seconds. Any of these values can be set to 0 if not needed.

Syntax:

```
CreateTimeSpan(Days, Hours, Minutes, Seconds)
```

Example: The following example creates a date/time object with a time exactly six hours from now:

```
<CFSET #detonation# = #Now()# + #CreateTimeSpan(0, 6, 0, 0)#>
```

T I P The CreateTimeSpan function is designed to speed the process of performing date- and time-based calculations. Creating a date/time object with 30 days—and using standard addition operators to add this to an existing date/time object—is quicker than using the DateAdd function.

See also: DateAdd

DateAdd

Description: DateAdd is used to add or subtract values to a date/time object; to add a week or subtract a year, for example. DateAdd takes three parameters, the first is the date specifier (see Table B.2), the second is the number of units to add or subtract, and the third is the date/time object to be processed. DateAdd returns a modified date/time object.

Syntax:

```
DateAdd( Specifier, Units, Date)
```

Example: The following example returns tomorrow's date (it adds one day to today's date):

```
#DateAdd('D', 1, Now())#
```

The next example returns a date exactly 10 years earlier than the date in a table column:

```
#DateAdd('WW', -10, Now())#
```

T I P To subtract values from a date/time object, use the DateAdd function and pass a negative number of units. For example, -5 subtracts five units of whatever specifier was passed.

DateCompare

Description: DateCompare allows you to compare two dates to see if they are the same or if one is greater than the other. DateCompare takes two parameters, the dates to compare, which may be specified as date/time objects or string representations of dates. DateCompare returns -1 if the first date is less than the second date, 0 if they are the same, and 1 if the first date is greater than the second date.

Syntax:

```
DateCompare(Date1, Date2)
```

Example: The following example verifies that a user-supplied order ship date is valid (not already passed):

```
<CFIF DateCompare(ship_date, Now()) IS -1>
 We can't ship orders yesterday!
</CFIF>
```

See also: DateDiff, DatePart

DateDiff

Description: DateDiff returns the number of units of a passed specifier by which one date is greater than a second date. Unlike DateCompare, which returns the greater date, DateDiff tells you how many days, weeks, or months it is greater by. DateDiff takes three parameters, the first is the date specifier (see Table B.2), and the second and third are the dates to compare.

Syntax:

```
DateDiff(Specifier, Date1, Date2)
```

Example: The following example returns how many weeks are left in this century, by specifying today's date (using the Now() function) and the first date of the next century (using the CreateDate function) as the two dates to compare:

```
There are #DateDiff("WW", Now(), CreateDate(2000, 1, 1))
➥# weeks left in this century!
```

> **N O T E** If the first date passed to DateDiff is greater than the second date, a negative value is returned. Otherwise, a positive value is returned. ▨

See also: DateCompare, DatePart

DatePart

Description: DatePart returns the specified part of a passed date. DatePart takes two parameters, the first is the date specifier (see Table B.2) and the second is the date/time object to process.

Syntax:

```
DatePart(Specifier, Date)
```

Example: The following example returns the day of week that a user was born on (and converts it to a string date using the DayOfWeekAsString function):

```
You were born on a #DayOfWeekAsString(DatePart('W', dob))#
```

See also: DateCompare, DateDiff, Day, DayOfWeek, DayOfYear, Hour, Minute, Month, Quarter, Second, Week, Year

Day

Description: Day returns a date/time object's day of month as a numeric value with possible values of 1–31. Day takes a single parameter, the date/time object to be processed.

Syntax:

```
Day(Date)
```

Example: The following example returns today's day of month:

```
Today is day #Day(Now())# of this month
```

See also: DayOfWeek, DayOfYear, Hour, Minute, Month, Quarter, Second, Week, Year

DayOfWeek

Description: DayOfWeek returns a date/time object's day of week as a numeric value with possible values of 1–7. DayOfWeek takes a single parameter, the date/time object to be processed.

Syntax:

DayOfWeek(Date)

Example: The following example returns today's day of week:

Today is day #DayOfWeek(Now())# of this week

See also: Day, DayOfYear, Hour, Minute, Month, Quarter, Second, Week, Year

DayOfWeekAsString

Description: DayOfWeekAsString returns the English weekday name for a passed day of week number. DayOfWeekAsString takes a single parameter, the day of week to process, with a value of 1–7.

Syntax:

DayOfWeekAsString(DayNumber)

Example: The following example returns today's day of week:

Today is day #DayOfWeekAsString(DayOfWeek(Now()))# of this week

See also: DayOfWeek, MonthAsString

DayOfYear

Description: DayOfYear returns a date/time object's day of year as a numeric value taking into account leap years. DayOfYear takes a single parameter, the date/time object to be processed.

Syntax:

DayOfYear(Date)

Example: The following example returns the today's day of year:

Today is day #DayOfYear(Now())# of year #Year(Now())#

See also: Day, DayOfWeek, Hour, Minute, Month, Quarter, Second, Week, Year

DaysInMonth

Description: DaysInMonth returns the number of days in a specified month, taking into account leap years. DaysInMonth takes a single parameter, the date/time object to evaluate.

Syntax:

DaysInMonth(Date)

Example: The following example returns the number of days in the current month:

```
This month has #DaysInMonth(Now())# days
```

DaysInMonth takes a date/time object as a parameter, and there is no equivalent function that takes a year and month as its parameters. Fortunately, this can easily be accomplished by combining the DaysInMonth and CreateDate functions. For example, to determine how many days are in February 2000, you can create a statement that looks like this: #DaysInMonth(CreateDate(2000, 2, 1))#.

See also: DaysInYear, FirstDayOfMonth

App
B

DaysInYear

Description: DaysInYear returns the number of days in a specified year, taking into account leap years. DaysInYear takes a single parameter, the date/time object to evaluate.

Syntax:

```
DaysInYear(Date)
```

Example: The following example returns the number of days in the current year:

```
This year, #Year(Now())#, has #DaysInYear(Now())# days
```

DaysInYear takes a date/time object as a parameter, and there is no equivalent function that takes just a year as its parameter. Fortunately, this can easily be accomplished by combining the DaysInYear and CreateDate functions. For example, you can create a statement that looks like this to determine how many days are in the year 2000: #DaysInYear(CreateDate(2000, 1, 1))#.

See also: DaysInMonth, FirstDayOfMonth

FirstDayOfMonth

Description: FirstDayOfMonth returns the day of the year on which the specified month starts. FirstDayOfMonth takes a single parameter, the date/time object to evaluate.

Syntax:

```
FirstDayOfMonth(Date)
```

Example: The following example returns the day of the year that the current month starts on:

```
#FirstDayOfMonth(Now())#
```

TIP FirstDayOfMonth takes a date/time object as a parameter, and there is no equivalent function that takes just a month and year as its parameters. Fortunately, this can easily be accomplished by combining the FirstDayOfMonth and CreateDate functions. For example, to determine the day of year that March 1999 starts on, you can create a statement that looks like this: #FirstDayOfMonth(CreateDate(1999, 3, 1))#.

See also: DaysInMonth, DaysInYear

Hour

Description: Hour returns a date/time object's hour as a numeric value with possible values of 0–23. Hour takes a single parameter, the date/time object to be processed.

Syntax:

```
Hour(Date)
```

Example: The following example returns the current hour of day:

```
This is hour #Hour(Now())# of the day
```

See also: Day, DayOfWeek, DayOfYear, Minute, Month, Quarter, Second, Week, Year

IsDate

Description: IsDate checks to see if a string contains a valid date; returns TRUE if it does, FALSE if it does not. IsDate takes a single parameter, the string to be evaluated.

Syntax:

```
IsDate(String)
```

Example: The following example checks to see if a user-supplied date string contains a valid date:

```
<CFIF IsDate(ship_date) IS "No">
 You entered an invalid date!
</CFIF>
```

N O T E IsDate checks U.S.-style dates only. Use the LSIsDate function for international date support. ■

See also: IsLeapYear, LSIsDate, ParseDateTime

IsLeapYear

Description: IsLeapYear checks to see if a specified year is a leap year. IsLeapYear takes a single parameter, the year to check, and returns TRUE if it is a leap year, FALSE if not.

Syntax:

```
IsLeapYear(Year)
```

Example: The following example checks to see if this year is a leap year:

```
<CFIF IsLeapYear(Year(Now()))>
 #Year(Now())# is a leap year
<CFELSE>
#Year(Now())# is a not leap year
</CFIF>
```

 TIP IsLeapYear takes a year as a parameter, not a date/time object. To check if a date stored in a date/time object is a leap year, use the Year function to extract the year and pass that as the parameter to IsLeapYear.

See also: IsDate

IsNumericDate

Description: IsNumericDate checks to see that a value passed as a date in the ColdFusion internal date format is in fact a legitimate date. IsNumericDate takes a single parameter, the date to be checked. This date is a floating point value with precision until the year 9999. IsNumericDate returns TRUE if the passed date value is valid, FALSE if it is not.

Syntax:

```
IsNumericDate(Real)
```

Example: The following example checks to see if a local variable contains a valid date:

```
<CFIF IsNumericDate(var.target_date) IS "Yes">
```

See also: IsDate

Minute

Description: Minute returns a date/time object's hour as a numeric value with possible values of 0–59. Minute takes a single parameter, the date/time object to be processed.

Syntax:

```
Minute(Date)
```

Example: The following example returns the current time's minutes:

```
#Minute(Now())# minutes have elapsed since #Hour(Now())# o'clock
```

See also: Day, DayOfWeek, DayOfYear, Hour, Month, Quarter, Second, Week, Year

Month

Description: Month returns a date/time object's month as a numeric value with possible values of 1–12. Month takes a single parameter, the date/time object to be processed.

Syntax:

```
Month(Date)
```

Example: The following example returns the current month:

```
It is month #Month(Now())# of year #Year(Now())#
```

See also: Day, DayOfWeek, DayOfYear, Hour, Minute, Quarter, Second, Week, Year

MonthAsString

Description: MonthAsString returns the English month name for a passed month number. MonthAsString takes a single parameter, the number of the month to process, with a value of 1–12.

Syntax:

```
MonthAsString(MonthNumber)
```

Example: The following example returns the English name of the current month:

```
It is #MonthAsString(Now())#
```

See also: DayOfWeek, Month

Now

Description: Now returns a date/time object containing the current date and time precise to the second. Now takes no parameters.

Syntax:

```
Now()
```

Example: The following example returns the current date and time formatted for correct display:

```
It is now #DateFormat(Now())# #TimeFormat(Now())#
```

N O T E   The Now function returns the system date and time of the computer running the ColdFusion service, not of the system running the Web browser. ▇

ParseDateTime

Description: ParseDateTime converts a date in string form into a ColdFusion date/time object. ParseDateTime takes a single parameter, the string to be converted.

Syntax:

```
ParseDateTime(String)
```

Example: The following example converts a user-supplied string containing a date into a ColdFusion date/time object:

```
<CFSET ship_date = ParseDateTime(FORM.ship_date)>
```

N O T E ParseDateTime supports U.S.-style dates and times only. Use the LSParseDateTime function for international date and time support. ▪

See also: CreateDateTime, LSParseDateTime

Quarter

Description: Quarter returns a date/time object's quarter as a numeric value with possible values of 1–4. Quarter takes a single parameter, the date/time object to be processed.

Syntax:

Quarter(Date)

Example: The following example returns the current quarter:

We are in quarter #Quarter(Now())# of year #Year(Now())#

See also: Day, DayOfWeek, DayOfYear, Hour, Minute, Month, Second, Week, Year

Second

Description: Second returns a date/time object's hour as a numeric value with possible values of 0–59. Second takes a single parameter, the date/time object to be processed.

Syntax:

Second(Date)

Example: The following example returns the current minute's seconds:

We are now #Second(Now())# seconds into the current minute

See also: Day, DayOfWeek, DayOfYear, Hour, Minute, Month, Quarter, Week, Year

Week

Description: Week returns a date/time object's week in year as a numeric value with possible values of 1–52. Week takes a single parameter, the date/time object to be processed.

Syntax:

Week(Date)

Example: The following example returns the current week in year:

This is week #Week(Now())# of year #Year(Now())#

See also: Day, DayOfWeek, DayOfYear, Hour, Minute, Month, Quarter, Second, Year

Year

Description: Year returns a date/time object's year as a numeric value with possible values of 100–9999. Year takes a single parameter, the date/time object to be processed.

Syntax:

```
Year(Date)
```

Example: The following example returns the current year value:

```
It is year #Year(Now())#
```

See also: Day, DayOfWeek, DayOfYear, Hour, Minute, Month, Quarter, Second, Week

Data Formatting Functions

Powerful data manipulation functions and database interaction capabilities are pretty useless unless there are ways to display data in a clean, readable format. ColdFusion data addresses this need by providing an array of highly capable formatting functions.

Many of these functions take optional format masks as parameters, thereby giving you an even greater level of control over the final output.

DateFormat

Description: DateFormat displays the date portion of a date/time object in a readable format. DateFormat takes two parameters, the first is the date/time object to be displayed and the second is an optional mask value allowing you to control exactly how the data is formatted. If no mask is specified, the default mask of DD-MMM-YY is used. The complete set of date masks is listed in Table B.3.

Syntax:

```
DateFormat(Date [, mask ])
```

Table B.3 DateFormat **Mask Characters**

Mask	Description
D	Day of month in numeric form with no leading 0 for single-digit days.
DD	Day of month in numeric form with a leading 0 for single-digit days.
DDD	Day of week as a three-letter abbreviation (Sun for Sunday is an example).
DDDD	Day of week as its full English name.
M	Month in numeric form with no leading 0 for single-digit months.
MM	Month in numeric form with a leading 0 for single-digit months.
MMM	Month as a three-letter abbreviation (Jan for January is an example).
MMMM	Month as its full English name.
Y	Year as last two digits of year with no leading 0 for years less than 10.

Mask	Description
YY	Year as last two digits of year with a leading 0 for years less than 10.
YYYY	Year as full four digits.

Example: The following example displays today's date with the default formatting options:

```
Today is: #DateFormat(Now())#
```

The next example displays the same date but uses the full names of both the day of week and the month:

```
It is #DateFormat(Now(), "DDDD, MMMM DD, YYYY")#
```

The final example displays today's date in the European format (day/month/year):

```
It is #DateFormat(Now(), "DD/MM/YY")#
```

N O T E Unlike the TimeFormat function mask specifiers, the DateFormat function mask specifiers are non-case-sensitive. ▨

N O T E DateFormat supports U.S.-style dates only. Use the LSDateFormat function for international date support. ▨

See also: LSDateFormat, TimeFormat

DecimalFormat

Description: DecimalFormat is a simplified number formatting function that outputs numbers with two decimal places, commas to separate the thousands, and a minus sign for negative values. DecimalFormat takes a single parameter, the number to display.

Syntax:

```
DecimalFormat(Number)
```

Example: The following example displays a table column in the decimal format:

```
Quantity: #DecimalFormat(quantity)#
```

 T I P For more precise numeric display, use the NumberFormat function instead.

See also: NumberFormat

DollarFormat

Description: DollarFormat is a simplified U.S. currency formatting function that outputs numbers with a dollar sign at the front, two decimal places, commas to separate the thousands, and a minus sign for negative values. DollarFormat takes a single parameter, the number to display.

Syntax:

```
DollarFormat(Number)
```

Example: The following example displays the results of an equation (quantity multiplied by item cost) in the dollar format:

```
Total cost: #DollarFormat(quantity*item_cost)#
```

 TIP For more precise currency display, use the NumberFormat function instead.

NOTE DollarFormat supports U.S. dollars only. Use the LSCurrencyFormat function for international currency support. ▪

See also: LSCurrencyFormat, NumberFormat

FormatBaseN

Description: FormatBaseN converts a number to a string using the base specified. Valid radix values are 2–36.

Syntax:

```
FormatBaseN(Number, Radix)
```

Example: The following example converts a user-supplied number into hexadecimal notation:

```
#FormatBaseN(Number, 16)#
```

To convert a number to its binary format, you can do the following:

```
#FormatBaseN(Number, 2)#
```

See also: InputBaseN

HTMLCodeFormat

Description: HTMLCodeFormat displays text with HTML codes with a preformatted HTML block (using the <PRE> and </PRE> tags). HTMLCodeFormat takes a single parameter, the text to be processed.

Syntax:

```
HTMLCodeFormat(Text)
```

Example: The following example uses preformatted text to display the code used to generate a dynamic Web page:

```
#HTMLEditFormat(page)#
```

 TIP HTMLCodeFormat is very useful for displaying data into FORM TEXTAREA fields.

See also: HTMLCodeFormat, ParagraphFormat

HTMLEditFormat

Description: HTMLEditFormat converts supplied text into a *safe* format, with any HTML control characters converted to their appropriate entity codes. HTMLEditFormat takes a single parameter, the text to convert.

Syntax:

```
HTMLEditFormat(Text)
```

Example: The following example displays the HTML code that is used to render a dynamic Web page inside a bordered box:

```
<TABLE BORDER>
 <TR>
  <TD>#HTMLEditFormat(page)#</TD>
 </TR>
</TABLE>
```

 T I P Use HTMLEditFormat to display HTML code and tags within your page.

See also: HTMLCodeFormat, ParagraphFormat

NumberFormat

Description: NumberFormat allows you to display numeric values in a readable format. NumberFormat takes two parameters, the number to be displayed and an optional mask value. If the mask is not specified, the default mask of ",99999999999999" is used. The complete set of number masks is listed in Table B.4.

Syntax:

```
NumberFormat(Number [, mask ])
```

Table B.4 NumberFormat **Mask Characters**

Mask	Description
_	Optional digit placeholder.
9	Optional digit placeholder (same as _ but shows decimal place more clearly).
.	Location of decimal point.
0	Force padding with 0s.
()	Display parentheses around the number if it is less than 0.
+	Display a plus sign in front of positive numbers, a minus sign in front of negative numbers.

continues

App

B

Table B.4   Continued

Mask	Description
-	Display a minus sign in front of negative numbers, leave a space in front of positive numbers.
,	Separates thousands with commas.
C	Center number within mask width.
L	Left-justify number within mask width.
$	Place a dollar sign in front of the number.
^	Specify the exact location for separating left and right formatting.

Example: To demonstrate how the number masks can be used, Table B.5 lists examples of different masks being used to format the numbers 1453.876 and −1453.876:

Table B.5   Number Formatting Examples

Mask	Result	Notes
NumberFormat(1453.876, "9999")	1454	No decimal point was specified in the mask, so the number is rounded to the nearest integer value.
NumberFormat(-1453.876, "9999")	−1454	
NumberFormat(1453.876, "9999.99")	1453.88	Even though a decimal point is provided, the number of decimal places specified is less than needed; the decimal portion must be rounded to the nearest integer value.
NumberFormat(1453.876, "(9999.99)")	1453.88	The number is a positive number, so the parentheses are ignored.
NumberFormat(-1453.876, "(9999.99)")	(1453.88)	The number is a negative number, so parentheses are displayed around the number.
NumberFormat(1453.876, "-9999.99")	1453.88	The number is a positive number, so the minus is ignored.
NumberFormat(-1453.876, "-9999.99")	−1453.88	The number is a negative number, so the minus is displayed.
NumberFormat(1453.876, "+9999.99")	+1453.88	The number is a positive number, so a plus sign is displayed.

Mask	Result	Notes
NumberFormat(-1453.876, "+9999.99")	−1453.88	The number is a negative number, so a minus is displayed.
NumberFormat(1453.876, "$9999.99")	$1453.88	
NumberFormat(1453.876, "C99999^9999")	1453.876	Position six of the mask is a carat character, so the decimal point is positioned there even though there are less than six digits before the decimal point. This allows you to align columns of numbers at the decimal point.

N O T E Use the LSNumberFormat function for international number support. ▪

See also: DecimalFormat, DollarFormat, LSNumberFormat

TimeFormat

Description: TimeFormat displays the time portion of a date/time object in a readable format. TimeFormat takes two parameters, the first is the date/time object to be displayed and the second is an optional mask value allowing you to control exactly how the data is formatted. If no mask is specified, the default mask of hh:mm:tt is used. The complete set of date masks is listed in Table B.6.

Syntax:

```
TimeFormat(Date [, mask ])
```

Table B.6 TimeFormat **Mask Characters**

Mask	Description
h	Hours in 12-hour clock format with no leading 0 for single-digit hours.
hh	Hours in 12-hour clock format with a leading 0 for single-digit hours.
H	Hours in 24-hour clock format with no leading 0 for single-digit hours.
HH	Hours in 24-hour clock format with a leading 0 for single-digit hours.
m	Minutes with no leading 0 for single-digit minutes.
mm	Minutes with a leading 0 for single-digit minutes.
s	Seconds with no leading 0 for single-digit seconds.
ss	Seconds with a leading 0 for single-digit seconds.

continues

App

B

Table B.6	Continued
Mask	**Description**
t	Single character meridian specifier, either A or P.
tt	Two character meridian specifier, either AM or PM.

Example: The following example displays the current time with the default formatting options:

```
The time is: #TimeFormat(Now())#
```

The next example displays the current time with seconds in 24-hour clock:

```
The time is: #TimeFormat(Now(), "HH:mm:ss")#
```

N O T E   Unlike the DateFormat function mask specifiers, the TimeFormat function mask specifiers are case sensitive. ▨

N O T E   TimeFormat supports U.S.-style times only. Use the LSTimeFormat function for international time support. ▨

See also: DateFormat, LSTimeFormat

ParagraphFormat

Description: ParagraphFormat converts text with embedded carriage returns for correct HTML display. HTML ignores carriage returns in text, so they must be converted to HTML paragraph markers (the <P> tag) in order to be displayed correctly. ParagraphFormat takes a single parameter, the text to be processed.

Syntax:

```
ParagraphFormat(Text)
```

Example: The following example displays a converted text files inside a FORM TEXTAREA field:

```
<TEXTAREA NAME="comments">#ParagraphFormat(comments)#</TEXTAREA>
```

 T I P   ParagraphFormat is very useful for displaying data into FORM TEXTAREA fields.

See also: HTMLCodeFormat, HTMLEditFormat

YesNoFormat

Description: YesNoFormat converts TRUE and FALSE values to Yes and No. YesNoFormat takes a single parameter, the number, string, or expression to evaluate. When evaluating numbers, YesNoFormat treats 0 as FALSE, and any non-zero value as TRUE.

Syntax:

```
YesNoFormat(Value)
```

Example: The following example converts a table Boolean value to a Yes or No string:

```
Member: #YesNoFormat(member)#
```

See also: IsBoolean

Mathematical Functions

To assist you in performing calculations, ColdFusion comes with a complete suite of mathematical and random number generation functions, and arithmetic expressions. As with all ColdFusion functions, these mathematical functions can be nested.

Some of the mathematical functions take one or more numeric values as parameters. You may pass real values, integer values, and ColdFusion fields to these functions.

Table B.7 lists the complete set of ColdFusion mathematical functions. Table B.8 lists the supported arithmetic expressions.

Table B.7   ColdFusion Mathematical Functions

Function	Parameters	Returns
Abs	(number)	Absolute value of passed number.
Atn	(number)	Arc tangent of passed number.
Ceiling	(number)	The closest integer greater than passed number.
Cos	(number)	Cosine of passed number.
DecrementValue	(number)	Number decremented by 1.
Exp	(number)	E to the power of passed number.
Fix	(number)	If passed number is greater than or equal to 0, returns closest integer smaller than the passed number. If not, returns closest integer greater than passed number.
IncrementValue	(number)	Number incremented by 1.
Int	(number)	The closest integer smaller than passed number.
Log	(number)	Natural logarithm of passed number.
Log10	(number)	Base 10 log of passed number.

continues

Table B.7 Continued

Function	Parameters	Returns
Max	(number1, number2)	The greater of the two passed numbers.
Min	(number1, number2)	The smaller of the two passed numbers.
Pi		Value of pi as 3.14159265359.
Rand		A random number between 0 and 1.
Randomize	(number)	Seed the random number generator with the passed number.
RandRange	(number1, number2)	A random integer value between the two passed numbers.
Round	(number)	The integer closest (either greater or smaller) to the passed number.
Sgn	(number)	Sign—either –1, 0, or 1, depending on whether passed number is negative, 0, or positive.
Sin	(number)	Sine of passed number.
Sqr	(number)	Square root of passed number.
Tan	(number)	Tangent of passed number.

Table B.8 ColdFusion Arithmetic Expressions

Expression	Description
+	Addition
–	Subtraction
*	Multiplication
/	Division
MOD	Modular (finds remainder)
\	Integer division (both values must be integers)
^	Power

Example: This first example returns the natural logarithm of the number 10.

```
#Log(10)#
```

This next example returns the value of pi rounded to the nearest integer value, 3.

```
#Round(Pi())#
```

The following example uses the `Min()` and `Max()` functions to determine the greater and smaller of two ColdFusion fields:

```
Of the two numbers #Num1# and #Num2#, Max(#Num1#, #Num2#) is the greater,
➥ and Min(#Num1#, #Num2#) is the smaller
```

To generate random numbers, you can use the `Rand` and `RandRange` functions. The following example generates a random number between 1 and 1,000:

```
#RandRange(1, 1000)#
```

This next example creates a variable that contains a total cost of several items:

```
<CFSET total# = quantity * item_price>
```

NOTE If the `Rand()` or `RandRange()` functions are used prior to issuing a `Randomize()` statement, the random number generator is seeded with a random value. ▨

International Functions

ColdFusion fully supports the display, formatting, and manipulation of international dates, times, numbers, and currencies. In order to use ColdFusion's international support, you must specify the locale. A *locale* is an encapsulation of the set of attributes that govern the display and formatting of international date, time, number, and currency values. The complete list of supported locales is shown in Table B.9.

Table B.9 ColdFusion Locales

Locale
Dutch (Belgian)
Dutch (Standard)
English (Australian)
English (Canadian)
English (New Zealand)
English (U.K.)
English (U.S.)
French (Belgian)
French (Canadian)
French (Standard)

continues

Table B.9   Continued
Locale
French (Swiss)
German (Austrian)
German (Standard)
German (Swiss)
Italian (Standard)
Italian (Swiss)
Norwegian (Bokmal)
Norwegian (Nynorsk)
Portuguese (Brazilian)
Portuguese (Standard)
Spanish (Mexican)
Spanish (Modern)
Spanish (Standard)
Swedish

You must use the SetLocale function to set the locale. You can retrieve the name of the locale currently in use using the GetLocale function.

To utilize ColdFusion's international support, you must use the LS functions listed (later in this chapter). These functions behave much like the standard date, time, and formatting functions, but they honor the current locale setting.

N O T E The ColdFusion server variable Server.ColdFusion.SupportedLocales contains a comma-delimited list of the supported locales. ■

GetLocale

Description: GetLocale returns the name of the locale currently in use.

Syntax:

GetLocale()

Example: The following example saves the current locale to a local variable:

<CFSET current_locale = GetLocale()>

See also: SetLocale

LSCurrencyFormat

Description: LSCurrencyFormat displays currency information formatted for the current locale. LSCurrencyFormat takes two parameters, the number to display and an optional format type. If type is specified, its value must be none, local, international. Type defaults to none.

Syntax:

```
LSCurrencyFormat(Number [, Type])
```

Example: The following example displays the results of an equation (quantity multiplied by item cost) in formatting appropriate for the French locale:

```
<CFSET previous_locale = SetLocale("French (Standard)")>
Total cost: #LSCurrencyFormat(quantity*item_cost)#
```

 TIP For more precise currency display, use the NumberFormat function instead.

N O T E You can use the simpler DollarFormat function for U.S. currency formatting.

See also: DollarFormat, NumberFormat

LSDateFormat

Description: LSDateFormat displays the date portion of a date/time object in a readable format. LSDateFormat is the locale specific version of the DateFormat function. Like DateFormat, LSDateFormat takes two parameters; the first is the date/time object to be displayed and the second is an optional mask value allowing you to control exactly how the data is formatted. If no mask is specified, a format suitable for the current locale is used. The complete set of date masks is listed in Table B.3 in the description of the DateFormat function.

Syntax:

```
LSDateFormat(Date [, mask ])
```

Example: The following example displays today's date with the default formatting options for the current locale:

```
Today is: #LSDateFormat(Now())#
```

The next example displays the same date but uses the current locale's full names of both the day of week and the month:

```
It is #LSDateFormat(Now(), "DDDD, MMMM DD, YYYY")#
```

N O T E You can use the simpler DateFormat function for U.S. dates.

See also: DateFormat, LSNumberFormat, LSTimeFormat

App
B

LSIsCurrency

Description: LSIsCurrency checks to see if a string contains a valid currency for the current locale; returns TRUE if it does, FALSE if it does not. LSIsCurrency takes a single parameter, the string to be evaluated.

Syntax:

LSIsCurrency(String)

Example: The following example checks to see if a user-supplied date string contains a valid German currency value:

```
<CFSET previous_locale = SetLocale("German (Standard)")>
<CFIF LSIsCurrency(total) IS "No">
 You entered an invalid currency amount!
</CFIF>
```

See also: IsNumber, LSIsNumeric

LSIsDate

Description: LSIsDate checks to see if a string contains a valid date for the current locale; returns TRUE if it does, FALSE if it does not. LSIsDate takes a single parameter, the string to be evaluated.

Syntax:

LSIsDate(String)

Example: The following example checks to see if a user-supplied date string contains a valid German date:

```
<CFSET previous_locale = SetLocale("German (Standard)")>
<CFIF LSIsDate(ship_date) IS "No">
 You entered an invalid date!
</CFIF>
```

N O T E   To check U.S. dates, you can use the IsDate function. ■

See also: IsDate, IsLeapYear, LSParseDateTime, ParseDateTime

LSIsNumeric

Description: LSIsNumeric checks to see if a specified value is numeric. LSIsNumeric is the locale-specific version of the IsNumeric function. LSIsNumeric takes a single parameter, the value to be evaluated.

Syntax:

LSIsNumeric(Value)

Example: The following example checks to ensure that a user entered a valid locale-specific age (numeric characters only):

```
<CFIF LSIsNumeric(age) IS "No">
 You entered an invalid age!
</CFIF>
```

N O T E You can use the simpler IsNumeric function for U.S. number support.

See also: InputBaseN, IsNumeric, Val

LSNumberFormat

Description: LSNumberFormat allows you to display numeric values in a locale-specific readable format. LSNumberFormat is the locale-specific version of the NumberFormat function. LSNumberFormat takes two parameters, the number to be displayed and an optional mask value. If the mask is not specified, the default mask of ,99999999999999 is used. The complete set of number masks is listed in Table B.4 in the description of the NumberFormat function.

Syntax:

LSNumberFormat(Number [, mask])

N O T E To display numbers in the any of the U.S. formats, you can use the NumberFormat function.

Example: The following displays a submitted form field in the default format for the current locale:

#LSNumberFormat(FORM.quantity)#

See also: DecimalFormat, DollarFormat, LSCurrencyFormat, LSParseNumber, NumberFormat

LSParseCurrency

Description: LSParseCurrency converts a locale-specific number in string form into a valid number. LSParseCurrency takes two parameters, the string to be converted and an optional type. If type is specified, its value must be none, local, or international. Type defaults to all types if not provided.

Syntax:

LSParseCurrency(String [, Type])

Example: The following example converts a user-supplied currency string into a number:

<CFSET sale_price = LSParseCurrency(FORM.sale_price)>

See also: LSCurrencyFormat, LSParseNumber

LSParseDateTime

Description: LSParseDateTime converts a locale-specific date in string form into a ColdFusion date/time object. LSParseDateTime is the locale-specific version of the ParseDateTime function. LSParseDateTime takes a single parameter, the string to be converted.

Syntax:

LSParseDateTime(String)

Example: The following example converts a user-supplied string containing a date into a ColdFusion date/time object:

<CFSET ship_date = LSParseDateTime(FORM.ship_date)>

N O T E For U.S. date and times you can use the simpler ParseDateTime function. ▇

CAUTION

Unlike the ParseDateTime function, the LSParseDateTime function does not support POP date/time fields. Passing a POP date/time field to LSParseDateTime generates an error.

See also: CreateDateTime, ParseDateTime

LSParseNumber

Description: LSParseNumber converts a locale-specific number in string form into a valid number. LSParseNumber takes a single parameter, the string to be converted.

Syntax:

LSParseNumber(String)

Example: The following example converts a user-supplied numeric string into a number:

<CFSET quantity = LSParseNumber(FORM.quantity)>

See also: LSCurrencyFormat, LSParseCurrency, Val

LSTimeFormat

Description: LSTimeFormat displays the time portion of a date/time object in a locale-specific readable format. LSTimeFormat is the locale-specific version of the TimeFormat function. LSTimeFormat takes two parameters, the first is the date/time object to be displayed and the second is an optional mask value that allows you to control exactly how the data is formatted. If no mask is specified, a mask appropriate for the current locale is used. The complete set of date masks is listed in Table B.6 in the description of the TimeFormat function.

Syntax:

LSTimeFormat(Date [, mask])

Example: The following example displays the current time with the default formatting options for the current locale:

The time is: #LSTimeFormat(Now())#

N O T E You can use the simpler `TimeFormat` function for U.S. times. ▨

See also: `LSDateFormat`, `LSNumberFormat`, `TimeFormat`

SetLocale

Description: `SetLocale` sets the name of the locale to be used by any subsequent calls to the LS functions. `SetLocale` also returns the name of the currently active locale so that it may be saved if needed.

Syntax:

```
SetLocale(locale)
```

Example: The following example sets the locale to British English and saves the current locale to a local variable:

```
<CFSET previous_locale = SetLocale("English (UK)")>
```

See also: `GetLocale`

List Manipulation Functions

ColdFusion lists are an efficient way to manage groups of information. Lists are made up of elements, values separated by delimiting characters. The default delimiter is a comma, but you can change it to any character or string if required. Lists are actually simple two-dimensional arrays. For more complex or multidimensional lists, you should use arrays instead.

This list format is very well suited for ColdFusion applications; it is both the format that HTML forms use to submit fields with multiple values and the format used by SQL to specify lists in SQL statements.

When using the list manipulation functions, remember the following:

▨ List manipulation functions that add to, delete from, or change a list do not alter the original list passed to them. Rather, they return an altered list to you for manipulation. If you do need to update the passed list itself, you must use `<CFSET>` to replace the list with the newly modified list.

▨ All list functions accept as an optional last parameter a string with delimiters to be used in the processing of the list. If this parameter is omitted, the default comma delimiter is used.

N O T E All of the ColdFusion list manipulation functions have names that begin with the word *list*, making them easy to spot in your code. ▨

T I P Lists may be used in conjunction with the `<CFLOOP>` tag for processing.

ListAppend

Description: ListAppend adds an element to a list and returns the new list with the appended element. ListAppend takes two parameters; the first is the current list and the second is the element to be appended.

Syntax:

```
ListAppend(List, Element)
```

Example: The following example appends John to an existing list of users and replaces the old list with the new one:

```
<CFSET Users = ListAppend(Users, "John")>
```

See also: ListInsertAt, ListPrepend, ListSetAt

ListChangeDelims

Description: ListChangeDelims returns a passed list reformatted to use a different delimiter. ListChangeDelims takes two parameters; the first is the list to be reformatted and the second if the new delimiter character.

Syntax:

```
ListChangeDelims(List, Delimiter)
```

Example: The following example creates a new list containing the same elements as the original list, but separated by plus signs:

```
<CFSET URLUsers = ListChangeDelims(Users, "+")>
```

 The default list delimiter, a comma, is the delimiter used by SQL lists. If you are going to pass ColdFusion lists to SQL statements, you should use the default delimiter.

ListContains, ListContainsNoCase

Description: The ListContains and ListContainsNoCase functions search through a list to find the first element that contains the specified search text. If the search text is found, the position of the element containing the text is returned. If no match is found, 0 is returned. ListContains performs a case-sensitive search; ListContainsNoCase performs a non–case-sensitive search. Both functions take two parameters—the first parameter is the list to be searched and the second parameter is the value to search for.

Syntax:

```
ListContains(List, Value)
```

```
ListContainsNoCase(List, Value)
```

Example: The following example returns the position of the first element to contain the text cash (regardless of case):

```
Element #ListContainsNoCase(Payments, "cash")# contains the word "cash"
```

N O T E ListContains and ListContainsNoCase find substrings within elements that match
the specified search text. To perform a search for a matching element, use the ListFind
and ListFindNoCase functions instead. ▪

See also: ListFind, ListFindNoCase

ListDeleteAt

Description: ListDeleteAt deletes a specified element from a list. ListDeleteAt takes two
parameters; the first is the list to be processed and the second is the position of the element to
be deleted. ListDeleteAt returns a modified list with the specified element deleted. The specified element position must exist; an error message is generated if you specify an element that
is beyond the range of the list.

Syntax:

```
ListDeleteAt(List, Position)
```

Example: The following example deletes the second element in a list, but first verifies that it
exists:

```
<CFIF ListLen(Users) GTE 2>
 <CFSET Users = ListDeleteAt(Users, 2)>
</CFIF>
```

See also: ListRest

ListFind, ListFindNoCase

Description: The ListFind and ListFindNoCase functions search through a list to find the
first element that matches the specified search text. If a matching element is found, the position of that element is returned; if no match is found, 0 is returned. ListFind performs a case-
sensitive search; ListFindNoCase performs a non–case-sensitive search. Both functions take
two parameters—the first parameter is the list to be searched and the second parameter is the
element text to search for.

Syntax:

```
ListFind(List, Value)
```

```
ListFindNoCase(List, Value)
```

Example: The following example returns the position of the first element whose value is MI:

```
MI is element #ListFind(States, "MI")#
```

N O T E ListFind and ListFindNoCase only find elements that exactly match the specified
search text. To perform a search for substrings within elements, use the ListContains
and ListContainsNoCase functions. ▪

See also: ListContains, ListContainsNoCase

ListFirst

Description: ListFirst returns the first element in a list. ListFirst takes a single parameter, the list to be processed.

Syntax:

```
ListFirst(List)
```

Example: The following example returns the first selection from a field of book titles submitted by a user:

```
The first title you selected is #ListFirst(titles)#
```

See also: ListGetAt, ListLast, ListRest

ListGetAt

Description: ListGetAt returns the list element at a specified position. ListGetAt takes two parameters: the first is the list to process and the second is the position of the desired element. The value passed as the position parameter must not be greater than the length of the list; otherwise a ColdFusion error message is generated.

Syntax:

```
ListGetAt(List, Position)
```

Example: The following example returns the name of the fourth selection from a field of book titles submitted by a user:

```
The fourth title you selected is #ListGetAt(titles, 4)#
```

See also: ListFirst, ListLast, ListRest

ListInsertAt

Description: ListInsertAt inserts a specified element into a list, shifting all elements after it one position to the right. ListInsertAt takes three parameters; the first is the list to be processed, the second is the desired position for the new element, and the third is the value of the new element. The position parameter must be no greater than the number of elements in the list; a ColdFusion error message is generated if a greater value is provided.

Syntax:

```
ListInsertAt(List, Position, Value)
```

Example: The following example inserts John into the third position of an existing list of users and replaces the old list with the new one:

```
<CFSET Users = ListInsertAt(Users, 3, "John")>
```

See also: ListAppend, ListPrepend, ListSetAt

ListLast

Description: `ListLast` returns the first element in a list. `ListLast` takes a single parameter, the list to be processed.

Syntax:

```
ListLast(List)
```

Example: The following example returns the last selection from a field of book titles submitted by a user:

```
The last title you selected is #ListLast(titles)#
```

See also: `ListFirst, ListGetAt, ListRest`

ListLen

Description: `ListLen` returns the number of elements present in a list. `ListLen` takes a single parameter: the list to be processed.

Syntax:

```
ListLen(List)
```

Example: The following example returns the number of books selected by a user:

```
You selected #ListLen(titles)# titles
```

ListPrepend

Description: `ListPrepend` inserts an element at the beginning of a list, pushing any other elements to the right. `ListPrepend` returns the new list with the prepended element. `ListPrepend` takes two parameters: the first is the current list and the second is the element to be prepended.

Syntax:

```
ListPrepend(List, Element)
```

Example: The following example prepends `John` to an existing list of users and replaces the old list with the new one:

```
<CFSET Users = ListPrepend(Users, "John")>
```

See also: `ListAppend, ListInsertAt, ListSetAt`

ListRest

Description: `ListRest` returns a list containing all the elements after the first element. If the list contains only one element, an empty list (an empty string) is returned. `ListRest` takes a single parameter: the list to be processed.

Syntax: `ListRest(List)`

Example: The following example replaces a list with the list minus the first element:

```
<CFSET Users = ListRest(Users)>
```

See also: `ListDeleteAt`

ListSetAt

Description: `ListSetAt` replaces the value of a specific element in a list with a new value. `ListSetAt` takes three parameters: the first is the list to be processed, the second is the position of the element to be replaced, and the third is the new value. The value passed to the position parameter must be no greater than the number of elements in the list; otherwise a ColdFusion error message is generated.

Syntax: `ListSetAt(List, Position, Value)`

Example: The following searches for an element with the value of `"Ben"` and replaces it with the value `"Benjamin"`:

```
<CFIF ListFindNoCase(Users, "Ben") GT 0>
 <CFSET Users = ListSetAt(Users, ListFindNoCase(Users, "Ben"), "Benjamin")>
</CFIF>
```

See also: `ListAppend, ListInsertAt, ListPrepend`

Array Manipulation Functions

Arrays are special variables made up of collections of data. Array elements are accessed via their index into the array; to access the third element of a simple array you would refer to `array[3]`, for example.

ColdFusion supports arrays with one to three dimensions. A one-dimensional array is very similar to a list. A two-dimensional array is kind of like a grid. (In fact, under the hood, ColdFusion queries are essentially two-dimensional arrays.) Three-dimensional arrays are more like cubes.

Arrays are created using the `ArrayNew` function. To create an array you must specify the number of dimensions needed, between one and three. You do need to specify how many elements will be stored in the array, ColdFusion automatically expands the array as needed.

N O T E   Array elements may be added in any order. If you add an element 10 to an array that has only 5 elements, ColdFusion will automatically create elements 6 to 9 for you. ▪

ArrayAppend

Description: `ArrayAppend` adds an element to the end of an array. `ArrayAppend` takes two parameters: the array to append the element to and the data to be stored in that element. `ArrayAppend` returns `TRUE` if the operation was successful.

Syntax:

```
ArrayAppend(Array, Value)
```

Example: The following example appends an element containing the word January to an array:

```
#ArrayAppend(Month, "January")#
```

This next example appends an element to a three-dimensional array, setting the value of element [10][1]:

```
#ArrayAppend(Users[10][1], "January")#
```

> **NOTE** You can set the values of explicit array elements using the <CFSET> tag. ■

See also: ArrayInsertAt, ArrayPrepend

ArrayAvg

Description: ArrayAvg returns the average numeric value in an array. ArrayAvg takes a single parameter: the array to be checked.

Syntax:

```
ArrayAvg(Array)
```

Example: The following example reports the average cost of items in an array:

```
The average cost of each item in the list is #DollarFormat(ArrayAvg(items))#
```

> **NOTE** ArrayAvg only works with arrays containing numeric data. Do not use this function with arrays that contain text data. ■

See also: ArrayMin, ArrayMax, ArraySum

ArrayClear

Description: ArrayClear deletes all data from an array. ArrayClear takes a single parameter: the array to be deleted. ArrayClear returns TRUE if the operation was successful.

Syntax:

```
ArrayClear(Array)
```

Example: The following example empties an existing array:

```
<CFSET result = ArrayClear(Items)>
```

> **NOTE** ArrayClear does not delete the actual array. Rather, it removes all the contents from it. The array itself remains and may be reused. ■

See also: ArrayDeleteAt, ArrayIsEmpty

ArrayDeleteAt

Description: ArrayDeleteAt deletes an element from an array at a specified position, pulling all remaining elements back one place. ArrayDeleteAt takes two parameters: the array to delete the element from and the position of the element to delete. ArrayDeleteAt returns TRUE if the operation was successful.

Syntax:

```
ArrayDeleteAt(Array, Position)
```

Example: The following example deletes the ninth element from an array:

```
#ArrayDeleteAt(Items, 9)#
```

See also: ArrayClear, ArrayInsertAt

ArrayInsertAt

Description: ArrayInsertAt inserts an element into an array at a specified position, pushing all existing elements over one place. ArrayInsertAt takes three parameters: the array to insert the element into, the position to insert the element at, and the data to be stored in that element. ArrayInsertAt returns TRUE if the operation was successful.

Syntax:

```
ArrayInsertAt(Array, Position, Value)
```

Example: The following example inserts an element containing the word Alaska into the second position of an existing two-dimensional array; it then sets the abbreviation AK into the matching second dimension:

```
<CFSET result = ArrayInsertAt(States[1], 2, "Alaska")>
<CFSET States[2][2] = "AK">
```

See also: ArrayAppend, ArrayDeleteAt, ArrayPrepend

ArrayIsEmpty

Description: ArrayIsEmpty checks to see if an array has data. ArrayIsEmpty takes a single parameter: the array to be checked. ArrayIsEmpty returns TRUE if the array is empty, FALSE if not.

Syntax:

```
ArrayIsEmpty(Array)
```

Example: The following example reports whether an array is empty:

```
<CFOUTPUT>Array empty: #YesNoFormat(ArrayIsEmpty(Users))#</CFOUTPUT>
```

See also: ArrayClear, ArrayLen, IsArray

ArrayLen

Description: `ArrayLen` returns the length of a specified array. `ArrayLen` takes a single parameter: the array to be checked.

Syntax: `ArrayLen(Array)`

Example: The following example reports the size of an array:

```
The items array has #ArrayLen(items)# elements
```

See also: `ArrayIsEmpty`, `ArrayResize`

ArrayMax

Description: `ArrayMax` returns the largest numeric value in an array. `ArrayMax` takes a single parameter, the array to be checked.

Syntax:

```
ArrayMax(Array)
```

Example: The following example reports the cost of the most expensive item in an array:

```
The most expensive item in the list costs #DollarFormat(ArrayMax(items))#
```

N O T E ArrayMax only works with arrays containing numeric data. Do not use this function with arrays that contain text data. ▨

See also: `ArrayAvg`, `ArrayMin`, `ArraySum`

ArrayMin

Description: `ArrayMin` returns the smallest numeric value in an array. `ArrayMin` takes a single parameter: the array to be checked.

Syntax:

```
ArrayMin(Array)
```

Example: The following example reports the cost of the least expensive item in an array:

```
The least expensive item in the list costs #DollarFormat(ArrayMin(items))#
```

N O T E ArrayMin only works with arrays containing numeric data. Do not use this function with arrays that contain text data. ▨

See also: `ArrayAvg`, `ArrayMax`, `ArraySum`

ArrayNew

Description: `ArrayNew` is used to create an array. `ArrayNew` takes a single parameter: the number of dimensions needed. Valid dimensions are one through three. `ArrayNew` returns the array itself.

Syntax:

```
ArrayNew(Dimensions)
```

Example: The following example creates a one-dimensional array:

```
<CFSET Users = ArrayNew(1)>
```

> **N O T E**   Once an array is created, ColdFusion automatically expands it as needed. Use the
> ArrayResize function to manually resize an array. ■

See also: IsArray, ListToArray

ArrayPrepend

Description: ArrayPrepend adds an element to the beginning of an array. ArrayPrepend takes two parameters: the array to insert the element into and the data to be stored in that element. ArrayPrepend returns TRUE if the operation was successful.

Syntax:

```
ArrayPrepend(Array, Value)
```

Example: The following example inserts an element containing the word Alabama into the beginning of an array:

```
#ArrayPrepend(States, "Alabama")#
```

> **N O T E**   You can set the values of explicit array elements using the <CFSET> tag. ■

See also: ArrayAppend, ArrayInsertAt

ArrayResize

Description: ArrayResize changes the size of an array, padding it with empty elements if needed. ArrayResize takes two parameters: the array to be resized and the size at which to resize it. ArrayResize returns TRUE if the operation is successful.

Syntax:

```
ArrayResize(Array, Size)
```

Example: The following example creates an array and immediately resizes it to hold 100 elements:

```
<CFSET Users = ArrayNew(1)>
<CFSET result = ArrayResize(Users, 100)>
```

 TIP   Dynamically expanding arrays is a slow operation. You can dramatically optimize ColdFusion's array processing by resizing the array to the anticipated size immediately after creating it with ArrayNew.

See also: ArrayLen, ArraySet

ArraySet

Description: `ArraySet` initializes one or more elements in an array with a specified value. `ArraySet` takes four parameters, the array itself, the element starting and ending positions, and the value to use. `ArraySet` returns `TRUE` if the operation is successful.

Syntax:

```
ArraySet(Array, Start, End, Value)
```

Example: The following example sets elements 1 through 100 with the value 0:

```
#ArraySet(OrderItems, 1, 100, 0)#
```

See also: `ArrayResize`, `ArraySort`, `ArraySwap`

ArraySort

Description: `ArraySort` sorts the data in an array. `ArraySort` takes three parameters: the array to be sorted, the sort type, and an optional sort order. If the sort order is omitted, the default order of ascending is used. `ArraySort` supports three sort types, as listed in Table B.10.

Table B.10 `ArraySort` **Sort Types**

Type	Description
Numeric	Sorts numerically.
Text	Sorts text alphabetically, uppercase before lowercase
TextNoCase	Sorts text alphabetically; case is ignored

Syntax:

```
ArraySort(Array, Type [, Order])
```

Example: The following example sorts an array alphabetically using a non–case-sensitive sort (also known as a *dictionary sort*):

```
#ArraySort(Users, "textnocase")#
```

N O T E ArraySort sorts the actual passed array, not a copy of it.

See also: `ArraySet`, `ArraySwap`

ArraySum

Description: `ArraySum` returns the sum of all values in an array. `ArraySum` takes a single parameter: the array to be checked.

Syntax:

```
ArraySum(Array)
```

Example: The following example reports the total cost of all items in an array:

```
The total cost of all item in the list is #DollarFormat(ArraySum(items))#
```

N O T E   ArraySum only works with arrays containing numeric data. Do not use this function with arrays that contain text data. ■

See also: ArrayAvg, ArrayMin, ArrayMax

ArraySwap

Description: ArraySwap is used to swap the values in two array elements. ArraySwap takes three parameters: the array itself and the positions of the two elements to be swapped. ArraySwap returns TRUE if the operation is successful.

Syntax:

```
ArraySwap(Array, Position1, Position2)
```

Example: The following example swaps elements 10 and 11 in an array:

```
#ArraySwap(Users, 10, 11)#
```

See also: ArraySet, ArraySort

ArrayToList

Description: ArrayToList converts a one-dimensional ColdFusion array into a list. ArrayToList takes two parameters: the array to be converted and an optional list delimiter. If no delimiter is specified, the default (comma) delimiter is used. ArrayToList creates a new list.

Syntax:

```
ArrayToList (Array [, Delimiter])
```

Example: The following example converts an array of users into a list:

```
<CFSET UserList = ArrayToList(UserArray)>
```

See also: ListToArray

IsArray

Description: IsArray checks to see if a variable is a valid ColdFusion array; it also determines that an array has a specific number of dimensions. IsArray takes two parameters: the variable to be checked and an optional number of dimensions to check for. IsArray returns TRUE if the variable is an array, FALSE if not.

Syntax:

```
IsArray (Array [, Dimension])
```

Example: The following example checks to see if a variable named Users is an array:

```
#IsArray(Users)#
```

This example checks to see if Users is a three-dimensional array:

```
#IsArray(Users, 3)#
```

See also: ArrayIsEmpty

ListToArray

Description: ListToArray converts a ColdFusion list to a one-dimensional array. ListToArray takes two parameters: the list to be converted and an optional list delimiter. If no delimiter is specified, the default (comma) delimiter is used. ListToArray creates a new array.

Syntax:

```
ListToArray(List [, Delimiter])
```

Example: The following example converts a list of users into an array:

```
<CFSET UserArray = ListToArray(UserList)>
```

See also: ArrayToList

Structure Manipulation Functions

ColdFusion *structures* are special data types that contain one or more other variables. Structures are a way to group related variables together.

StructClear

Description: StructClear deletes all data from a structure. StructClear takes a single parameter: the structure to be cleared. StructClear returns TRUE if the operation is successful.

Syntax:

```
StructClear(Structure)
```

Example: The following example empties an existing structure:

```
<CFSET result = StructClear(Items)>
```

NOTE StructClear does not delete the actual structure. Rather, it removes all the contents from it. The structure itself remains and may be reused.

See also: StructDelete, StructIsEmpty

StructCount

Description: StructCount returns the number of items in a specified structure. StructCount takes a single parameter: the structure to be checked.

Syntax:

```
StructCount(Structure)
```

App
B

Example: The following example reports the number of elements in a structure:

```
The items structure has #StructCount(items)# elements
```

See also: StructIsEmpty

StructDelete

Description: StructDelete deletes an item from a structure. StructDelete takes three parameters: the structure, the name of the key to be deleted, and an optional flag that specifies how to handle requests to delete a key that does not exist. StructDelete returns TRUE if the operation was successful, FALSE if not. If an attempt is made to delete a key that does not exist, and the IndicateNotExisting flag is not set to TRUE, the StructDelete returns TRUE.

Syntax:

```
StructDelete(Structure, Key [, IndicateNotExisiting])
```

Example: The following example deletes the name key from a user structure:

```
#StructDelete(user, name)#
```

See also: StructClear, StructKeyExists, StructIsEmpty

StructFind, StructFindNoCase

Description: The StructFind and StructFindNoCase functions search through a structure to find the key that matches the specified search text. If a matching key is found, the value in that key is returned; if no match is found, an empty value is returned. StructFind performs a case-sensitive search and StructFindNoCase performs a non–case-sensitive search. Both functions take two parameters: the first is the structure to be searched and the second is the key to search for.

Syntax:

```
StructFind(Structure, Key)

StructFindNoCase(Structure, Key)
```

Example: The following example returns the username stored in a user structure:

```
User name is #StructFindNoCase(user, first_name)
➥# #StructFindNoCase(user, last_name)#
```

StructInsert

Description: StructInsert inserts an item into a structure. StructInsert takes four parameters: the structure, the name of the key to be inserted, the value, and an optional flag that specifies whether a key may be overwritten or not. StructInsert returns TRUE if the operation was successful, FALSE if not. Values can be overwritten unless AllowOverwrite is set to FALSE.

Syntax:

```
StructInsert(Structure, Key, Value [, AllowOverwrite])
```

Example: The following example inserts a key named `first_name` into a `user` structure:

```
#StructInsert(user, "first_name", "Ben")#
```

See also: `StructDelete`

StructIsEmpty

Description: `StructIsEmpty` checks to see if a structure has data. `StructIsEmpty` takes a single parameter: the structure to be checked. `StructIsEmpty` returns `TRUE` if the array is empty, `FALSE` if not.

Syntax:

```
StructIsEmpty(Structure)
```

Example: The following example reports whether a structure is empty:

```
<CFOUTPUT>Strucure empty: #YesNoFormat(StructIsEmpty(Users))#</CFOUTPUT>
```

See also: `StructClear`, `StructCount`, `StructKeyExists`

StructKeyExists

Description: `StructKeyExists` checks to see if a structure contains a specific key. `StructKeyExists` takes two parameters: the structure to be checked and the key to look for. `StructKeyExists` returns `TRUE` if the key exists, `FALSE` if not.

Syntax:

```
StructKeyExists(Structure, Key)
```

Example: The following checks to see if a key named `first_name` exists:

```
<CFIF StructKeyExists(user, "first_name")>
```

See also: `StructCount`, `StructIsEmpty`

StructNew

Description: `StructNew` creates a new structure. `StructNew` takes no parameters and returns the structure itself.

Syntax:

```
StructNew()
```

Example: The following example creates a simple structure:

```
<CFSET Orders=StructNew()>
```

Query Manipulation Functions

ColdFusion uses queries to return sets of data. Most queries are created with the `<CFQUERY>` tag, but other tags (`<CFPOP>` and `<CFLDAP>`) also return data in queries. ColdFusion also allows you to programmatically create your own queries using the QueryNew function and set query values using QuerySetCell.

> **N O T E** ColdFusion *queries* are essentially arrays with named columns. You may therefore use any of the array functions with queries. ▪

IsQuery

Description: IsQuery checks to see if a variable is a valid ColdFusion query. IsQuery takes a single parameter: the variable to be checked. IsQuery returns TRUE if the variable is a query, FALSE if not.

Syntax:

IsQuery (Query)

Example: The following example checks to see if a variable named Users is a query:

<CFIF IsQuery(Users)>

T I P   IsQuery is particularly useful within custom tags that expect queries as parameters. IsQuery can be used to check that a valid value was passed before any processing occurs.

QueryAddRow

Description: QueryAddRow adds a row to an existing ColdFusion query. QueryAddRow takes two parameters: the query to add a row to and an optional number of rows to add. If the number of rows is omitted, the default number of 1 is used.

Syntax:

QueryAddRow(Query [, Number])

Example: The following example creates a new query called Users and adds 10 rows to it:

<CFSET Users = QueryNew("FirstName, LastName")>
<CFSET temp = QueryAddRow(Users, 10)>

See also: QueryNew, QuerySetCell

QueryNew

Description: QueryNew creates a new ColdFusion query. QueryNew takes a single parameter, a comma-delimited list of columns for the new query. QueryNew returns the newly created query.

Syntax:

QueryNew(Columns)

Example: The following example creates a new query called Users and adds 10 rows to it:

```
<CFSET Users = QueryNew("FirstName, LastName")>
<CFSET temp = QueryAddRow(Users, 10)>
```

See also: QueryAddRow, QuerySetCell

QuerySetCell

Description: QuerySetCell is used to set the values of specific cells in a table. QuerySetCell takes four parameters: the query name, the column name, the value, and an optional row number. If the row number is omitted, the cell in the last query row is set.

Syntax:

```
QuerySetCell(Query, Column, Value [, Row])
```

Example: The following example sets the FirstName column in the third row to the value Ben:

```
<CFSET temp = QuerySetCell(Users, "FirstName", "Ben", 3)>
```

N O T E Query cells can also be set using the <CFSET> tag treating the query as a two-dimensional array.

See also: QueryAddRow, QueryNew

Security Functions

ColdFusion supports advanced security contexts that let you create complete security systems, which secure your applications. Security is managed and maintained using the ColdFusion Administrator. Once security is established, you can make a call to the <CFAUTHENTICATE> tag in order to return security information. Use these security functions to interact with that security information.

IsAuthenticated

Description: IsAuthenticated checks to see if a user has been authenticated with the <CFAUTHENTICATE> tag. IsAuthenticated takes two parameters: the user to be checked and the security context to be checked against. IsAuthenticate returns TRUE if the user has been authenticated, FALSE if not.

Syntax:

```
IsAuthenticated(User, Context)
```

Example: The following example checks to see if a user has been authenticated as an administrator:

```
<CFIF IsAuthenticated("#user#", "administrator")
```

> **N O T E** To use this function, advanced security must be enabled in the ColdFusion Administrator and security contexts must already have been defined. ▪

See also: IsAuthorized

IsAuthorized

Description: IsAuthorized checks to see if a user is authorized to perform specific actions. IsAuthorized takes three parameters: the resource type to be checked, the resource to be checked, and an optional action. IsAuthorized returns TRUE if the action is authorized, FALSE if not. Table B.11 lists the valid resource types.

Syntax:

```
IsAuthorized(ResourceType, ResourceName [, Action])
```

Example: The following example checks to see if a user has been authenticated as an administrator:

Table B.11 Resource Types

Type
Application
CFML
DSN
File
Object

Example: The following example checks to see if a user is authorized to use a specific data source:

```
<CFIF IsAuthorized(DSN, "A2Z")
```

> **N O T E** To use this function, advanced security must be enabled in the ColdFusion Administrator and security contexts must already have been defined. ▪

See also: IsAuthenticated

System Functions

The ColdFusion system functions allow you to perform manipulation of file paths, create temporary files, and verify file existence.

DirectoryExists

Description: DirectoryExists checks for the existence of a specified directory and returns either TRUE or FALSE. DirectoryExists takes a single parameter: the name of the directory to check for. The directory name cannot be a relative path, but must be specified as a fully qualified path.

Syntax:

```
DirectoryExists(Directory)
```

Example: The following example checks for the existence of a directory, creating it if it does not exist:

```
<CFIF DirectoryExists("#directory#") IS "No">
 <CFFILE ACTION="CREATE" DIRECTORY="#directory#">
</CFIF>
```

See also: FileExists

ExpandPath

Description: ExpandPath converts a path relative to the Web server document root into a fully qualified path. ExpandPath takes a single parameter: the path to be converted.

Syntax:

```
ExpandPath(Path)
```

Example: The following example returns the full path of the server's default document:

```
#ExpandPath("index.cfm")#
```

See also: GetTemplatePath

FileExists

Description: FileExists checks for the existence of a specified file and returns either TRUE or FALSE. FileExists takes a single parameter: the name of the file to check for. The filename cannot be a relative path, but must be specified as a fully qualified path.

Syntax:

```
FileExists(File)
```

Example: The following example checks for the existence of an image file before using it in an IMG tag:

```
<CFIF FileExists("C:\root\images\logo.gif")>
 <IMG SRC="/images/logo.gif">
</CFIF>
```

TIP   Use the ExpandPath function so you don't have to hard code the filename passed to the FileExists function; use ExpandPath to convert the relative path to an actual filename.

See also: DirectoryExists

GetDirectoryFromPath

Description: GetDirectoryFromPath extracts the drive and directory (with a trailing backslash) from a fully specified path. GetDirectoryFromPath takes a single parameter: the path to be evaluated.

Syntax:

GetDirectoryFromPath(Path)

Example: The following example returns the directory portion of a current template's full file path:

#GetDirectoryFromPath(GetTemplatePath())#

See also: GetFileFromPath

GetFileFromPath

Description: GetFileFromPath extracts the filename from a fully specified path. GetFileFromPath takes a single parameter: the path to be evaluated.

Syntax:

GetFileFromPath(Path)

Example: The following example returns the filename portion of a temporary file:

#GetFileFromPath(GetTempFile(GetTempDirectory(), "CF"))#

See also: GetDirectoryFromPath

GetTempDirectory

Description: GetTempDirectory returns the full path of the Windows temporary directory with a trailing backslash. GetTempDirectory takes no parameters.

Syntax:

GetTempDirectory()

Example: The following example returns the name of a temporary file beginning with the letters CF in the Windows temporary directory:

#GetTempFile(GetTempDirectory(), "CF")#

See also: GetTempFile

GetTempFile

Description: GetTempFile returns the full path to a temporary file for use by your application. The returned filename is guaranteed to be unique. GetTempFile takes two parameters: the first is the directory where you'd like the temporary file created, and the second is a filename prefix of up to three characters. You cannot omit the prefix, but you may pass an empty string ("").

Syntax:

```
GetTempFile(Directory, Prefix)
```

Example: The following example returns the name of a temporary file beginning with the letters CF in the Windows temporary directory:

```
#GetTempFile(GetTempDirectory(), "CF")#
```

 TIP To create a temporary file in the Windows temporary directory, pass the GetTempDirectory function as the directory parameter.

App

B

See also: GetTempDirectory

GetTemplatePath

Description: GetTemplatePath returns the fully qualified path of the base template being processed. GetTemplatePath takes no parameters.

Syntax:

```
GetTemplatePath()
```

Example: The following example returns the full path of the base template being processed:

```
Processing: #GetTemplatePath()#
```

N O T E GetTemplatePath returns the path of the base template being processed. If you are using GetTemplatePath in a template that is being included in a second template, the path of that second template is returned. ▨

Client Variable Manipulation Functions

Client variables allow you to store client information so that it is available between sessions. Client variables can be accessed just like any other ColdFusion variables; standard variable access tool such as <CFSET> can therefore be used to set variables. In addition, these functions provide special variable manipulation capabilities.

DeleteClientVariable

Description: DeleteClientVariable deletes the client variable whose name is passed as a parameter. Unlike other ColdFusion variables, client variables persist over time and must be deleted with this function. DeleteClientVariable takes a single parameter: the name of the variable to delete. DeleteClientVariable returns TRUE if the variable was deleted, FALSE if it was not.

Syntax:

```
DeleteClientVariable(Variable)
```

Example: The following example deletes a variable named login_name and sets a local variable with the function return value:

```
<CFSET DeleteSuccessful = DeleteClientVariable("login_name")>
```

GetClientVariablesList

Description: GetClientVariablesList returns a comma-delimited list of the read-write client variables available to the template. The standard read-only system client variables, listed in Table B.12, are not returned. GetClientVariablesList takes no parameters.

Syntax:

```
GetClientVariablesList()
```

Table B.12   Read-Only Client Variables

Variable	Description
CFID	Unique ID assigned to this client.
CFToken	Unique security token used to verify the authenticity of a CFID value.
URLToken	Text to append to URLs; contains both CFID and CFToken. (Appended automatically to <CFLOCATION> URLs.)

Example: The following example retrieves the entire list of read-write client variables:

```
#ListLen(GetClientVariablesList())#
➥read-write client variables are currently active
```

TIP

The list of variables returned by the GetClientVariablesList function is comma delimited, which makes it very suitable for processing with the ColdFusion list functions.

Expression Evaluation Functions

ColdFusion allows you to perform *dynamic expression evaluation*. This is an advanced technique that allows you to build and evaluate expressions on-the-fly.

Dynamic expression evaluations are performed on string expressions. A string expression is just that—a string that contains an expression. The string "1+2" contains an expression that, when evaluated, returns 3. String expressions can be as simple or as complex as needed.

DE

Description: DE stands for delay evaluation. This function is designed for use with the IIF and Evaluate functions. It takes a string as a parameter and returns the same string enclosed within quotation marks; all double quotation marks are escaped. This allows you to pass a string to IIf and Evalaute without them being evaluated.

Syntax:

```
DE(String)
```

Example: The following example uses DE to ensure that the string "A" is evaluated, instead of the variable "A".

```
#Evaluate(DE("A"))#
```

Evaluate

Description: Evaluate is used to evaluate string expressions. Evaluate takes one or more string expressions as parameters and evaluates them from left to right.

Syntax:

```
Evaluate(String1, …)
```

Example: The following example evaluates the variable "A":

```
#Evalutate("A")#
```

IIf

Description: IIf evaluates a Boolean condition and evaluates one of two expressions depending on the results of that evaluation. If the Boolean condition returns TRUE, the first expression is evaluated; if the condition returns FALSE, the second expression is evaluated.

Syntax:

```
IIF(Boolean condition, Expression if TRUE, Expression if FALSE)
```

Example: The following example determines if #cnt# has a value of 1; it evaluates "A" if it does, "B" if it does not:

```
#IIf("#cnt# IS 1", "A", "B")#
```

SetVariable

Description: SetVariable sets a specified variable to a passed value.

Syntax:

```
SetVariable(Variable, Value)
```

Example: The following example sets variable #cnt# to the value returned by the passed expression:

```
#SetVariable(#cnt#, "A")#
```

Bit and Set Manipulation Functions

ColdFusion provides a complete set of bit manipulation functions for use by advanced developers only. These functions allow you to manipulate the individual bits within a 32-bit integer.

The complete set of bit manipulation functions is listed in Table B.13. The descriptions for each function are given in the C/C++ syntax.

N O T E Any start, length, or position parameters passed to the bit manipulation functions must be in the range of 0 to 31. ■

Table B.13   ColdFusion Bit and Set Manipulation Functions

Function	Description
BitAnd(x, y)	x and y
BitMaskClear(x, start, length)	x with length bits starting from start cleared
BitMaskRead(x, start, length)	The value of the length bits starting from start
BitMaskSet(x, mask, start, length)	x with mask occupying the length bits starting from start
BitNot(x)	x
BitOr(x, y)	x | y
BitSHLN(x, n)	x << n
BitSHRN(x, n)	x >> n
BitXor(x, y)	x^y

Miscellaneous Functions

These miscellaneous functions are some of the most important ones; are you are likely to find yourself using them repeatedly.

GetBaseTagData

Description: GetBaseTagData is used within subtags. It returns an object containing data from a specified ancestor tag. GetBaseTagData takes two parameters: the name of the tag whose data you want returned and an optional instance number. If no instance is specified, the default value of 1 is used.

Syntax:

```
GetBaseTagData(Tag [, InstanceNumber])
```

Example: The following example retrieves the data in a caller <CFHTTP> tag:

```
#GetBaseTagData(CFHTTP)#
```

Not all tags contain data (for example, the <CFIF> tag). Passing a tag that contains no data to the GetBaseTagData function causes an exception to be thrown. ▪

See also: GetBaseTagList

GetBaseTagList

Description: GetBaseTagList is used within subtags. It returns a comma-delimited list of base tag names. The returned list is in calling order, with the parent tag listed first.

Syntax:

```
GetBaseTagList()
```

Example: The following example displays the top level calling tag:

```
<CFOUTPUT>The top level tag is #ListFirst(GetBaseTagList())#</CFOUTPUT>
```

See also: GetBaseTagData

GetTickCount

Description: GetTickCount performs timing tests with millisecond accuracy. The value that is returned by GetTickCount is of no use other than to compare it to the results of another GetTickCount call to check time spans.

Syntax:

```
GetTickCount()
```

Example: The following example tests how long a code block takes to execute:

```
<CFSET count1=GetTickCount()>
…
<CFSET count2=GetTickCount()>
<CFSET duration=count2-count1>
<CFOUTPUT>Code took #duration# milliseconds to execute</CFOUTPUT>
```

IsBoolean

Description: IsBoolean determines whether a value can be converted to a Boolean value. (Boolean values have two states only, ON and OFF or TRUE and FALSE.) IsBoolean takes a single parameter: the number, string, or expression to evaluate. When evaluating numbers, IsBoolean treats 0 as FALSE, and any non-zero value as TRUE.

Syntax:

```
IsBoolean(Value)
```

Example: The following example checks to see if a value can be safely converted into a Boolean value before passing it to a formatting function:

```
<CFIF IsBoolean(status) IS "Yes">
 #YesNoFormat(status)#
</CFIF>
```

See also: YesNoFormat

IsDebugMode

Description: IsDebugMode checks to see if a page is being sent back to the user in debug mode. IsDebugMode returns TRUE if debug mode is on, FALSE if not. IsDebugMode takes no parameters.

Syntax:

```
IsDebugMode()
```

Example: The following code writes debug data to a log file if in debug mode:

```
<CFIF IsDebugMode()>
 <CFFILE ACTION= APPEND" FILE="log.txt" OUTPUT="#debug_info#">
</CFIF>
```

N O T E IsDebugMode() allows you to leave debugging code when writing your applications; they are not processed at runtime unless debug mode is enabled. ■

IsDefined

Description: IsDefined determines whether a specified variable exists. IsDefined returns TRUE if the specified variable exists, FALSE if not. IsDefined takes a single parameter: the variable to check for. This parameter can be passed as a fully qualified variable, with a preceding variable type designator. The variable name must be enclosed in quotation marks; otherwise ColdFusion checks to see if the contents of the variable exist rather than the variable itself.

Syntax:

```
IsDefined(Parameter)
```

Example: The following example checks to see if a variable of any type named USER_ID exists:

```
<CFIF IsDefined("USER_ID")>
```

The next example checks to see if a CGI variable named USER_ID exists, and ignores variables of other types:

```
<CFIF IsDefined("CGI.USER_ID") >
```

N O T E IsDefined is a little more complicated to use than ParameterExists, but it does allow you to dynamically evaluate and redirect expressions. ■

See also: Evaluate, IsSimpleValue, ParameterExists

IsNumeric

Description: IsNumeric checks to see if a specified value is numeric. IsNumeric takes a single parameter: the value to be evaluated.

Syntax:

```
IsNumeric(Value)
```

Example: The following example checks to ensure that a user entered a valid age (numeric characters only):

```
<CFIF IsNumeric(age) IS "No">
 You entered an invalid age!
</CFIF>
```

N O T E Use the LSIsNumeric function for international number support. ▣

See also: InputBaseN, LSIsNumeric, Val

IsSimpleValue

Description: IsSimpleValue checks to see if a value is a string, number, TRUE/FALSE value, or DATE/TIME value. IsSimpleValue takes a single parameter: the value to be checked. IsSimpleValue returns TRUE if the value is a simple value, FALSE if not.

Syntax:

```
IsSimpleValue(Value)
```

Example: The following example checks to see that a description field is a simple value:

```
<CFIF IsSimpleValue(Description)>
```

See also: Evaluate, IsDefined, ParameterExists

ParameterExists

Description: ParameterExists checks to see if a specified variable exists. ParameterExists returns TRUE if the specified variable exists, FALSE if not. ParameterExists takes a single parameter: the variable to check for. This parameter may be passed as a fully qualified variable, with a preceding variable type designator. Do not enclose the variable name in quotation marks.

Syntax:

```
ParameterExists(Parameter)
```

Example: The following example checks to see if a variable of any type named USER_ID exists:

```
<CFIF ParameterExists(USER_ID) IS "Yes">
```

The next example checks to see if a CGI variable named USER_ID exists, and ignores variables of other types:

```
<CFIF ParameterExists(CGI.USER_ID) IS "Yes">
```

N O T E   One of the most important uses of the ParameterExists function is creating dynamic
SQL statements using the <CFSQL> tag. ■

See also: Evaluate, IsDefined, IsSimpleValue

PreserveSingleQuotes

Description: PreserveSingleQuotes instructs ColdFusion to not escape single quotation marks contained in values derived from dynamic parameters. PreserveSingleQuotes takes a single parameter: the string to be preserved.

Syntax:

```
PreserveSingleQuotes(String)
```

Example: The following example uses PreserveSingleQuotes to ensure that a dynamic parameter in a SQL statement is included correctly:

```
SELECT * FROM Customers
WHERE CustomerName IN ( #PreserveSingleQuotes(CustNames)#)
```

QuotedValueList, ValueList

Description: QuotedValueList and ValueList drive one query with the results of another. Both functions take a single parameter—the name of a query column—and return a list of all the values in that column. QuotedValueList returns a list of values that are each enclosed within quotation marks and separated by commas. ValueList returns the list separated by commas, but not enclosed in quotation marks.

Syntax:

```
QuotedValueList(Column)
```

```
ValueList(Column)
```

Example: The following example ensures that a dynamic parameter in a SQL statement is included correctly:

```
SELECT * FROM Customers
WHERE CustomerName IN ( #PreserveSingleQuotes(CustNames)#)
```

N O T E   The QuotedValueList and ValueList functions are typically only used when
constructing dynamic SQL statements. ■

T I P   The values returned by QuotedValueList and ValueList are both in the standard ColdFusion list
format, and can therefore be manipulated by the list functions.

T I P As a general rule, you should always try to combine both the queries into a single SQL statement unless you need to manipulate the values in the list. The time it takes to process one combined SQL statement is far less than the time it takes to process two simpler statements.

URLEncodedValue

Description: URLEncodedValue encodes a string in a format that can be safely used within URLs. URLs may not contain spaces or any non-alphanumeric characters. The URLEncodedValue function replaces spaces with a plus sign; non-alphanumeric characters are replaced with equivalent hexadecimal escape sequences. URLEncodedValue takes a single parameter—the string to be encoded—and returns the encoded string.

Syntax:

```
URLEncodedValue(String)
```

N O T E ColdFusion automatically decodes all URL parameters that are passed to a template. ▨

Example: The following example creates an URL with a name parameter that can safely include any characters:

```
<A HREF="details.cfm?name=#URLEncodedFormat(name)#">Details</A>
```

App

B

VTML and WIZML Language Reference

VTML and WIZML are XML-based languages used to control and customize the ColdFusion Studio (and HomeSite) environment. Because these languages are XML-based, they both employ the same tag and attribute interface as CFML. In fact, many of the tags in VTML and WIZML closely resemble CFML tags and function in a similar fashion.

Using VTML and WIZML

VTML and WIZML are used primarily for three types of interfaces:

- Tag Editors are used within the ColdFusion Studio environment to display context-specific dialogs for selected tags.
- Tag Lists are trees of tags used to tag selection.
- Wizards are used to simplify or automate recurring or difficult tasks.

You can use each of the tags listed in this appendix in one or more of these interfaces as indicated in the "See also" line in each tag description.

Using Variables

Variables are often used with VTML and WIZML code. Unlike ColdFusion variables, which are delimited by pound signs (the # character), variables in VTML and WIZML code use the following syntax:

`$${field}`

replacing `field` with the name of the variable.

Standard ColdFusion functions can be used within VTML and WIZML code without any special delimiters.

File Locations

ColdFusion Studio extension files have specific locations where they must be saved for Studio to recognize them. All files are saved beneath the ColdFusion Studio root directory, usually `C:\ProgramFiles\Allaire\ColdFusion Studio4`.

Tag Editors   Tag editors are VTM files saved beneath `Extensions\Tag Defs`. You can create your own directories beneath this directory for your own files.

Tag Lists   Tag lists are saved in two files, both stored in the `Extensions` directory beneath the Studio root. `MARKUPTAGS.VTM` contains the Tag Chooser options, and `EXPRESSIONELEMENTS.VTM` contains the Expression Builder options.

Wizards   Wizards are stored in directories beneath the `Extensions` directory beneath the Studio root. A wizard can be named with any name, but it must have a `.VTM` extension.

<ATTRIB>, </ATTRIB>

Description: <ATTRIB> is used with tag editor dialogs to map a tag attribute to a control within the editor dialog. <ATTRIB> takes four attributes, as shown in Table C.1; only NAME is required. The NAME attribute must be the name of an attribute passed to the tag itself. A special attribute named $$TAGBODY can also be used to refer to the body text between start and end tags. <ATTRIB> must be used in between <ATTRIBUTE> and </ATTRIBUTE> tags. The </ATTRIB> end tag is needed only if options are specified with <ATTRIBOPTION>.

Used in: Tag editors

Syntax:

```
<ATTRIB NAME="name" CONTROL="control name" TYPE="type">
```

Table C.1   <ATTRIB> **Attributes**

Name	Description	Notes
CACHEFAMILY	Name of cache family	Optional name of cache family
CONTROL	Name of a control	Optional attribute; if used, must be the name of a control specified in the tag editor; value is used to populate the control
NAME	Name of attribute	The name of the attribute to be read from the editor
TYPE	Attribute type	Optional value; if specified, must be one of the types listed in Table C.2

Table C.2   <ATTRIB> TYPE **Values**

Value	Description
COLOR	Color name or RGB value
DIRECTORY	Directory path
ENUMERATED	List of enumerated values (as specified with the <ATTRIBOPTION> tag)
EXPRESSION	Any valid ColdFusion expression
FILEPATH	Full file path
FLAG	An ON/OFF attribute that contains no value
FONT	Font name
QUERYNAME	Name of a ColdFusion query
RELATIVEPATH	Relative path
TEXT	Freeform text (default)

App

C

Example: The following example reads two attributes (SRC and ALIGN) from a tag and assigns them to two controls within a tag editor:

```
<ATTRIBUTES>
 <ATTRIB NAME="SRC"    CONTROL="txtSource">
 <ATTRIB NAME="ALIGN" CONTROL="dropAlign">
</ATTRIBUTES>
```

See also: <ATTRIBOPTION>, <ATTRIBUTES>

<ATTRIBCATEGORIES>, <ATTRIBGROUP>, </ATTRIBCATEGORIES>

Description: The <ATTRIBCATEGORIES> and <ATTRIBGROUP> tags are used to group attributes together into categories for displaying in the ColdFusion Studio Tag Inspector. <ATTRIBCATEGORIES> takes no attributes, but a pair of <ATTRIBCATEGORIES> and </ATTRIBCATEGORIES> tags must contain one or more <ATTRIBGROUP> tags. Each <ATTRIBGROUP> tag takes two required attributes, as listed in Table C.3.

Used in: Tag editors

Syntax:

```
<ATTRIBCATEGORIES> <ATTRIBGROUP NAME="name" ELEMENTS="elements">
➥ </ATTRIBCATEGORIES>
```

Table C.3	**<ATTRIBGROUP> Attributes**	
Attribute	**Description**	**Notes**
ELEMENTS	Group elements	This required attribute is a comma-delimited list of attributes in this group.
NAME	Group name	This attribute is required.

Example: The following example groups five attributes into two categories for displaying in the Tag Inspector:

```
<ATTRIBCATEGORIES>
 <ATTRIBGROUP NAME="colors" ELEMENTS="BACKGROUND,FOREGROUND,TEXT">
 <ATTRIBGROUP NAME="fonts" ELEMENTS="FONTFACE,FONTSIZE">
</ATTRIBCATEGORIES>
```

See also: <ATTRIB>, <ATTRIBUTES>

<ATTRIBOPTION>

Description: <ATTRIBOPTION> is used to specify a list of valid options for an attribute in a tag editor. <ATTRIBOPTION> is used in between <ATTRIB> and </ATTRIB> tags. <ATTRIBOPTION> takes two attributes, as listed in Table C.4: the CAPTION to display and the VALUE associated with it.

Used in: Tag editors

Syntax:

```
<ATTRIBOPTION CAPTION="caption" VALUE="value">
```

Table C.4 <ATTRIBOPTION> **Attributes**

Attribute	Description	Notes
CAPTION	Option caption	Optional display text (if different from VALUE).
VALUE	Value of option	This attribute is required.

Example: The following example creates an ATTRIBUTES block that checks for an attribute named "state" and accepts only three specified values:

```
<ATTRIBUTES>
 <ATTRIB NAME="state" TYPE="ENUMERATED">
  <ATTRIBOPTION VALUE="CA" CAPTION="California">
  <ATTRIBOPTION VALUE="FL" CAPTION="Florida">
  <ATTRIBOPTION VALUE="MI" CAPTION="Michigan">
 </ATTRIB>
</ATTRIBUTES>
```

See also: <ATTRIB>

<ATTRIBUTES>, </ATTRIBUTES>

Description: <ATTRIBUTES> and </ATTRIBUTES> are used to delimit a block of <ATTRIB> tags within a tag editor. <ATTRIBUTES> takes no attributes.

Used in: Tag editors

Syntax:

```
<ATTRIBUTES> ... </ATTRIBUTES>
```

Example: The following example reads two attributes (SRC and ALIGN) from a tag and assigns them to two controls within a tag editor:

```
<ATTRIBUTES>
 <ATTRIB NAME="SRC"   CONTROL="txtSource">
 <ATTRIB NAME="ALIGN" CONTROL="dropAlign">
</ATTRIBUTES>
```

See also: <ATTRIB>

<CAT>, </CAT>

Description: <CAT> is used to define a category for a list of tags. <CAT> tags must have matching </CAT> tags, and these tags can be nested to create a nested tree control interface. <CAT>

App

C

takes six attributes, as listed in Table C.5, of which only CAPTION is required. To populate the list with elements, use the <E> tag. One or more <E> tags should appear between <CAT> and </CAT> tags.

Used in: Tag lists

Syntax:

```
<CAT CAPTION="caption" DESC="Description" EXPANDED="Yes¦No" HELPFILE="Help file"
➥ ICON="Elements¦Folder¦RelativePath" SHOWSUBELEMENTS="Yes¦No"
➥ VALUE="Value"> ... </CAT>
```

Table C.5   <CAT> **Attributes**

Attribute	Description	Notes
CAPTION	Category caption	The caption of the category. This attribute is required.
DESC	Help text	Optional help text to be displayed for this category.
EXPANDED	Should category be expanded by default	YES to display category expanded; NO not to. The default is NO.
HELPFILE	Name of external help file	Optional external help file to be used for this category (instead of DESC).
ICON	Icon to use for this category	Optional icon to be used for this category; valid values are "Elements" and "Folder". In addition, the relative path of any image can be specified to use that image.
SHOWSUBELEMENTS	Should elements be displayed in right panel	Optional flag specifying whether all the subelements in this category should be displayed in the right panel when the category is selected. The default is NO.

Example: The following example creates a tree category called "File Management" and adds two elements to it—one for the <CFDIRECTORY> tag and one for the <CFFILE> tag:

```
<CAT CAPTION="File Management" ICON="Elements">
 <E CAPTION="CFDIRECTORY" VALUE='<cfdirectory action="" directory="
➥" name="" filter="" sort=""' HELPFILE='Docs/CFMLTags/cfdirectory.htm'>
 <E CAPTION="CFFILE" VALUE='<cffile action="" filefield="" destination="
➥" nameconflict="ERROR" accept=""'     HELPFILE='Docs/CFMLTags/cffile.htm'>
</CAT>
```

See also: <E>

`<CONTAINER>`, `</CONTAINER>`

Description: Tag editors contain controls. Controls are fields (input fields, drop-down list boxes, check boxes, and so on). Controls can be grouped into containers. Although you don't need to use containers, generally each tag editor should contain at least one container, and the controls should be placed into it. The `<CONTAINER>` is used to define containers. Containers can be nested to create different grouping effects. The container contents must be specified in between the `<CONTAINER>` and `</CONTAINER>` tags. `<CONTAINER>` attributes are listed in Table C.6.

Used in: Tag editors

Syntax:

```
<CONTAINER ANCHOR="anchor" CAPTION="caption" CORNER="NW¦NE¦SW¦SE" DOWN="pixels"
➥ HEIGHT="height" LEFT="pixels" NAME="name" RIGHT="pixels" TYPE="type"
➥ UP="pixels" WIDTH="width"> ... </CONTAINER>
```

App

C

Table C.6 `<CONTAINER>` Attributes

Attribute	Description	Notes
ANCHOR	Control to anchor this container to	Optional attribute, specifies the name of another control to which this control is anchored, thus allowing relative control placement.
CAPTION	Container caption	This attribute is optional.
CORNER	Anchor corner	Optional attribute, specifies which corner of the anchor control to place this control relative to. Valid values are NW for left of top, NE for right of top, SW for left of bottom, and SE for right of bottom.
DOWN	Relative position down from anchor	Must be specified in pixels.
HEIGHT	Option height	Optional container height in pixels, or MAXIMUM for maximum height.
LEFT	Relative position left from anchor	Must be specified in pixels.
NAME	Container name	Required unique control name.
RIGHT	Relative position	Must be specified in right from anchor pixels.
TYPE	Container type	Required attribute, must be one of the attributes listed in Table C.7.

continues

Table C.6   Continued

Attribute	Description	Notes
UP	Relative position up from anchor	Must be specified in pixels.
WIDTH	Value of option	Optional container width in pixels, or MAXIMUM available width.

Table C.7   `<CONTAINER>` Types

Type	Description
PANEL	Simple panel; can contain any other control or container except a control of type TABPAGE
TABDIALOG	Tab dialog; can contain one or more tag pages; cannot contain controls
TABPAGE	Tab page; must be used within a tag dialog; can contain any controls or containers

Example: This example creates a tag editor with a two-tabbed dialog:

```
<EDITORLAYOUT HEIGHT=225>
 <CONTAINER  NAME="MainTabDialog" TYPE="TabDialog">
  <CONTAINER  NAME="TabPage1" TYPE="TabPage" CAPTION="MYTAG Tag">
  ... controls go here
  </CONTAINER>
  <CONTAINER  NAME="Advanced" TYPE="TabPage" CAPTION="Advanced">
  ... controls go here
  </CONTAINER>
 </CONTAINER>
</EDITORLAYOUT>
```

See also: `<CONTROL>`, `<EDITORLAYOUT>`

`<CONTROL>`, `</CONTROL>`

Description: Tag editors are made up of controls that are usually placed into one or more containers. Individual controls are created using the `<CONTROL>` tag. Table C.8 lists the `<CONTROL>` tag attributes.

Used in: Tag editors

Syntax:

```
<CONTAINER ALIGN="alignment" ANCHOR="anchor" AUTOSELECT="YES|NO"
➥ AUTORESIZE="YES|NO" CAPTION="caption" CENTER="YES|NO" CHARCASE="case"
➥ CHECKED="YES|NO" CORNER="NW|NE|SW|SE" DIRONLY="YES|NO" DOWN="pixels"
➥ DSNAMECONTROL="name" EDITABLE="YES|NO" FILENAMEONLY="YES|NO"
➥ FILEPATH="path" FILTER="filter" HEIGHT="height" LEFT="pixels"
```

➥ MAXLENGTH="length" NAME="name" PASSWORDCHAR="character" PROGID="id"
➥ RELATIVE="YES¦NO" RIGHT="pixels" QUERYNAMECONTROL="name"
➥ SCROLLBAR="placement" TRANSPARENT="YES¦NO" TYPE="type" UP="pixels"
➥ VALIGN="alignment" VALUE="value" WIDTH="width" WRAP="YES¦NO">
➥ ... </CONTAINER>

Table C.8   <CONTROL> **Attributes**

Attribute	Description	Notes
ALIGN	Control alignment	Optional alignment specifier; valid values are LEFT, CENTER, and RIGHT; valid only if TYPE is LABEL.
ANCHOR	Control to anchor this control to	Optional attribute, specifies the name of another control to which this control is anchored, thus allowing relative control placement.
AUTOSELECT	Initial highlighting flag	Specifies whether a field is initially high-lighted when selected. Valid values are YES and NO; valid only if TYPE is TEXTBOX.
AUTOSIZE	Automatically resize control	Optional flag, specifies that control should be resized automatically; ignored if HEIGHT and WIDTH attributes are used. Valid values are YES and NO; defaults to NO. Valid only if TYPE is IMAGE, LABEL, or TEXTBOX.
CAPTION	Control caption	This attribute is optional.
CENTER	Center image flag	Optional flag, specifies that the image should be displayed centered. Valid values are YES and NO; defaults to NO. Valid only if TYPE is IMAGE.
CHARCASE	Case conversion	Optional case conversion indicator. Valid values are NORMAL, UPPER, and LOWER; defaults to NORMAL. Used only if TYPE is INPUTBOX.
CHECKED	Checked flag	Optional initial state flag for check boxes. Valid values are YES and NO.
CORNER	Anchor corner	Optional attribute, specifies which corner of the anchor control to place this control relative to. Valid values are NW for left of top, NE for right of top, SW for left of bottom, and SE for right of bottom.
DIRONLY	Browse directories only	Optional directory only flag. Valid values are YES and NO; defaults to NO. Used only if TYPE is FILEBROWSER.

continues

Table C.8   Continued

Attribute	Description	Notes
DOWN	Relative position down from anchor	Must be specified in pixels.
DSNAMECONTROL	Data source name control	Optional data source name control; valid only if TYPE is SQLTEXTAREA.
EDITABLE	Editable field flag	Optional flag, specifies that values may be directly typed into a drop-down list box or field. Valid values are YES and NO; defaults to NO. Used only if TYPE is FONTPICKER or TEXTBOX.
FILENAMEONLY	Select files only	Optional files only flag. Valid values are YES and NO; defaults to NO. Used only if TYPE is FILEBROWSER.
FILEPATH	Image file path	Path to a BMP file to display in the dialog. Valid only if TYPE is IMAGE, in which case it is required.
FILTER	File spec filter	Optional file filter spec; can include wildcards. Multiple filters should be separated by commas. Used only if TYPE is FILEBROWSER.
HEIGHT	Option height	Optional control height in pixels, or MAXIMUM for maximum height.
LEFT	Relative position left from anchor	Must be specified in pixels.
MAXLENGTH	Maximum text length	Specifies the maximum number of characters that can be entered into a field. Valid only if TYPE is TEXTBOX.
NAME	Control name	Required unique control name.
PASSWORDCHAR	Password mask character	Optional character to be used as an input mask. Used only if TYPE is INPUTBOX.
PROGID	ActiveX control PROGID	Required if control TYPE is ACTIVEX.
RELATIVE	Relative path flag	Optional relative path flag, specifies that paths should be returned relative instead of physical. Valid values are YES and NO; defaults to NO. Used only if TYPE is FILEBROWSER.
RIGHT	Relative position right from anchor	Must be specified in pixels.

Attribute	Description	Notes
QUERYNAMECONTROL	Query name control	Optional query name control. Valid only if TYPE is SQLTEXTAREA.
SCROLLBAR	Scrollbar placement	Optional scrollbar placement specifier. Valid values are NONE, HORIZONTAL, VERTICAL, and BOTH. Valid only if TYPE is SQLTEXTAREA or TEXTAREA.
TRANSPARENT	Display transparent control flag	Optional flag, specifies that control should be displayed transparently. Valid values are YES and NO; defaults to NO. Valid only if TYPE is IMAGE or LABEL.
TYPE	Control type	Required attribute, must be one of the attributes listed in Table C.9.
UP	Relative position up from anchor	Must be specified in pixels.
VALIGN	Control vertical alignment	Optional vertical alignment specifier. Valid values are TOP, CENTER, and BOTTOM. Valid only if TYPE is LABEL or TEXTBOX.
VALUE	Initial control value	Optional initial control value. Valid only if TYPE is TEXTBOX.
WIDTH	Value of option	Optional control width in pixels, or MAXIMUM available width.
WRAP	Text wrapping flag	Optional text wrapping flag. Valid values are YES and NO. Valid only if TYPE is SQLTEXTAREA or TEXTAREA.

App

C

Table C.9 <CONTROL> Types

Type	Description
ACTIVEX	ActiveX control
CHECKBOX	Check box
COLORPICKER	Color and RGB value picker
DROPDOWN	Drop-down list box
FILEBROWSER	File and directory browser
FONTPICKER	Font selection
IMAGE	Image display

continues

Table C.9 Continued	
Type	**Description**
LABEL	Label (display only)
RADIOGROUP	Group of radio buttons
SQLTEXTAREA	SQL code dialog (with access to SQL Query Builder)
TEXTAREA	Multiline text box
TEXTBOX	Single-line text box

Example: This example creates a label with a text control to the right of it:

```
<CONTROL NAME="lblSource" TYPE="Label" CAPTION="Source:" DOWN=17 RIGHT=10
➥ WIDTH=50/>
<CONTROL NAME="txtSource" TYPE="TextBox" VALUE="Some Value" ANCHOR="lblSource"
➥ CORNER="NE" WIDTH="MAXIMUM" />
```

See also: <CONTAINER>, <EDITORLAYOUT>, <ITEM>

<E>

Description: The <E> tag is used to specify elements within a category in a tag list (chooser). <E> tags must appear in between <CAT> and </CAT> tags. <CAT> takes four attributes, as listed in Table C.10.

Used in: Tag lists

Syntax:

```
<E CAPTION="caption" DESC="Description" HELPFILE="Help file" VALUE="Value">
```

Table C.10 <E> Attributes		
Attribute	**Description**	**Notes**
CAPTION	Element caption	The caption of the element. This attribute is required.
DESC	Help text	Optional help text to be displayed for this element.
HELPFILE	Name of external help file	Optional external help file to be used for this element (instead of DESC).
VALUE	Tag chooser value	Text as passed to the tag's tag editor. If the text contains passed attributes that take quoted strings, then the entire VALUE text should be enclosed within single quotation marks.

Example: The following example creates a tree category called `"File Management"` and adds two elements to it—one for the `<CFDIRECTORY>` tag and one for the `<CFFILE>` tag:

```
<CAT CAPTION="File Management" ICON="Elements">
 <E CAPTION="CFDIRECTORY" VALUE='<cfdirectory action="" directory="" name="
➥" filter="" sort=""' HELPFILE='Docs/CFMLTags/cfdirectory.htm'>
 <E CAPTION="CFFILE" VALUE='<cffile action="" filefield="" destination="
➥" nameconflict="ERROR" accept=""'     HELPFILE='Docs/CFMLTags/cffile.htm'>
</CAT>
```

See also: `<CAT>`

`<EDITORLAYOUT>`, `</EDITORLAYOUT>`

Description: `<EDITORLAYOUT>` is used to define the actual dialog box layout in a tag editor. `<EDITORLAYOUT>` starts the dialog definition, and `</EDITORLAYOUT>` completes it. Place any dialog controls between these two tags. `<EDITORLAYOUT>` must be used in between `<TAG>` and `</TAG>` tags and can contain one or more `<CONTROL>` or `<CONTAINER>` tags. `<EDITORLAYOUT>` takes four optional attributes, as listed in Table C.11.

Used in: Tag editors

Syntax:

```
<EDITORLAYOUT HEIGHT="Height" LFHEIGHT="Height" LFWIDTH="Width" WIDTH="Width">
➥ ... </EDITORLAYOUT>
```

Table C.11 `<EDITORLAYOUT>` **Attributes**

Attribute	Description	Notes
HEIGHT	Dialog height	Optional value in pixels
LFHEIGHT	Font height	Optional font height
LHWIDTH	Font width	Optional font width
WIDTH	Dialog width	Optional value in pixels

Example: The following example creates a dialog 50 pixels high and 200 pixels wide. This dialog contains a single panel with one field.

```
<EDITORLAYOUT HEIGHT=50 WIDTH=200>
 <CONTAINER NAME="Panel1" TYPE="Panel" WIDTH=150 HEIGHT=50>
  <CONTROL NAME="lblCode" TYPE="label" CAPTION="Code" DOWN=20 RIGHT=20
➥ WIDTH=70/>
  <CONTROL NAME="txtCode" TYPE="TextBox" ANCHOR="lblCode" CORNER="NE"
➥ WIDTH="30"/>
 </CONTAINER>
</EDITORLAYOUT>
```

See also: `<CONTAINER>`, `<CONTROL>`, `<TAG>`

App
C

<INPUT>

Description: <INPUT> is used in wizards to prompt for user input. If the name of the <INPUT> control matches that of an underlying parameter on a wizard page, the control is automatically bound to that parameter. Table C.12 lists the <INPUT> tag attributes.

Used in: Wizards

Syntax:

```
<INPUT NAME="name" PARAM="param" DEFAULT="default" REQUIRED="Yes¦No"
➥ VALIDATIONMSG="Message" LISTCONTENTS="list">
```

Table C.12   <INPUT> Attributes

Attribute	Description	Notes
DEFAULT	Default value	Optional attribute.
LISTCONTENTS	List contents	Used only if control is a list box; contains a comma-delimited list of values.
NAME	Control name	Required attribute.
PARAM	Bound parameter	Optional name of parameter to bind field to.
REQUIRED	Field required flag	Optional attribute. Valid values are YES or NO.
VALIDATIONMSG	Validation message	Optional message to display if validation fails.

Example: The following example creates four input fields, only one of which is required:

```
<INPUT name="ddDocType" param="sDocType">
<INPUT name="tbTitle" param="sTitle" required="yes" validationmsg=
➥ "Please enter a document title" or some equivalent message>
<INPUT name="chkMetaDescr" param="bMetaDescr">
<INPUT name="tbMetaDescr" param="sMetaDescr">
```

See also: <WIZARD>

<ITEM>

Description: <ITEM> is used to populate a list of radio buttons in a radio group or options in a drop-down list box. One <ITEM> tag is used for each item. <ITEM> must be used in between <CONTROL> and </CONTROL> tags. <ITEM> takes three attributes, as listed in Table C.13.

Used in: Tag editors

Syntax:

```
<ITEM CAPTION="Caption" VALUE="Value" SELECTED>
```

Table C.13 <ITEM> Attributes

Attribute	Description	Notes
CAPTION	Item caption	The caption of the item. This attribute is required.
SELECTED	Selected flag	Optional selected flag. Valid values are YES and NO; defaults to NO.
VALUE	Item value	The value of this item. This attribute is required.

Example: The following example creates a drop-down list box with three items, the second of which is preselected:

```
<CONTROL NAME="dropTagOptions" TYPE="Size" WIDTH="200">
 <ITEM CAPTION="small" VALUE="Small">
 <ITEM CAPTION="medium" VALUE="Medium" SELECTED>
 <ITEM CAPTION="large" VALUE="Large">
</CONTROL>
```

See also: <CONTROL>

<NEXTPAGE>

Description: <NEXTPAGE> is used to control the next page that is displayed within a wizard. <NEXTPAGE> is used for greater control and complex wizards that programmatically display different pages. <NEXTPAGE> attributes are listed in Table C.14.

Used in: Wizards

Syntax:

```
<NEXTPAGE NAME="Name" CONDITION="Condition">
```

Table C.14 <NEXTPAGE> Attributes

Attribute	Description	Notes
CONDITION	Condition	The condition to be evaluated. If TRUE, the page specified in NAME will be called. This attribute is required.
NAME	Page name	The page to go to if CONDITION is TRUE. This attribute is required.

Example: This example is a line from the ColdFusion Studio DHTML Slide Show Wizard; it specifies a page to be called until the specified number of slides has been reached:

```
<NEXTPAGE name="Page14b_Last" condition="$${ (CurSlide EQ SlideCount) }">
```

See also: <PAGE>, <WIZARD>

App
C

<PAGE>, </PAGE>

Description: <PAGE> is used to define a wizard page. Every page in a wizard must be enclosed within <PAGE> and </PAGE> tags. The <PAGE> tag attributes are listed in Table C.15.

Used in: Wizards

Syntax:

```
<PAGE CAPTION="caption" CONDITION="condition" IMAGE="image" NAME="name"
➥ NEXTPAGE="page" TYPE="type">
```

Table C.15   <PAGE> **Attributes**

Attribute	Description	Notes
CAPTION	Page caption	Optional caption to display at top of page
CONDITION	Condition	Conditional expression that determines whether page should be displayed
IMAGE	Page image	Optional image to display instead of default bitmap
NAME	Page name	Required page name
NEXTPAGE	Next page name	Optional next page; overrides default page
TYPE	Page type	Required only for dynamic pages

Example: The following example defines a dynamic wizard page:

```
<PAGE name="DocAttribs" type="DYNAMIC" caption="HTML Document Attributes"
➥ image="..\\images\\main.bmp">
```

See also: <NEXTPAGE>, <WIZARD>

<PARAM>

Description: <PARAM> is used to define parameters within a page. The parameters are used to generate wizard output. <PARAM> attributes are listed in Table C.16.

Used in: Wizards

Syntax:

```
<PARAM NAME="name" VALUE="value" REQUIRED="Yes¦No">
```

Table C.16 <PARAM> **Attributes**

Attribute	Description	Notes
NAME	Parameter name	Required parameter name.
REQUIRED	Parameter name	Optional required parameter flag. Valid values are TRUE and FALSE.
VALUE	Parameter value	Optional default value.

Example: The following example defines a set of parameters, some required and some not:

```
<PARAM name="sDocType" value="HTML 4.0" required="true">
<PARAM name="sTitle" value="">
<PARAM name="bMetaDescr" value="false">
<PARAM name="sMetaDescr" value="">
<PARAM name="bMetaKeywords" value="false">
<PARAM name="sMetaKeywords" value="">
```

See also: <INPUT>, <PAGE>

App
C

<TAG>, </TAG>

Description: The <TAG> tag is used to create a new tag dialog. All the panels, help, attributes, and any other controls pertaining to the tag must appear between the <TAG> and </TAG> tags. <TAG> takes a single optional attribute, the tag name, as seen in Table C.17.

Used in: Tag editors

Syntax:

```
<TAG NAME="Name" > ... </TAG>
```

Table C.17 <TAG> **Attributes**

Attribute	Description	Notes
NAME	Tag name	Optional tag name

Example: The following code example shows the typical layout for a tag editor definition:

```
<TAG>
 <ATTRIBUTES>
  ... Defines tag attribute properties and behavior
 </ATTRIBUTES>
 <ATTRIBCATEGORIES>
  ... Defines logical grouping for tag attributes
 </ATTRIBCATEGORIES>
 <EDITORLAYOUT>
  ... Defines the layout of a tag editor
 </EDITORLAYOUT>
```

```
<TAGLAYOUT>
 ... Defines the tag generation template
</TAGLAYOUT>
<TAGDESCRIPTION>
 ... HTML-based documentation for the tag
</TAGDESCRIPTION>
</TAG>
```

See also: <ATTRIBUTES>, <EDITORLAYOUT>, <TAGDESCRIPTION>, <TAGLAYOUT>

<TAGDESCRIPTION>, </TAGDESCRIPTION>

Description: <TAGDESCRIPTION> is used to provide context-sensitive help for the tag editor. The help appears in a pop-up window beneath the tag editor dialog or in an optional window. Help text can contain HTML formatting as required. <TAGDESCRIPTION> allows help to be specified in two ways: either typed directly into the tag VTM file or in an external file. If an external file is used, then the name of that file must be passed to the HELPFILE attribute. The complete set of attributes is listed in Table C.18.

Used in: Tag editors

Syntax:

```
<TAGDESCRIPTION HELPFILE="Help file" HEIGHT="Height"> ... </TAGDESCRIPTION>
```

Table C.18   <TAGDESCRIPTION> **Attributes**

Attribute	Description	Notes
HEIGHT	Help panel height	Optional help panel height in pixels
HELPFILE	Help filename	Optional name of external help file

Example: This example demonstrates using <TAGDESCRIPTION> to provide help specified directly within the tag definition file:

```
<TAGDESCRIPTION HEIGHT=100>
 <B>CFAPPLICATION</B>
 <P>Defines scoping for a Cold Fusion application and
 enables or disables storing client variables in the system
 registry. By default, client variables are disabled.
 CFAPPLICATION is typically used in the APPLICATION.CFM
 file to set defaults for a specific Cold Fusion application.
</TAGDESCRIPTION>
```

This next example shows how to use an external help file:

```
<TAGDESCRIPTION HELPFILE="Docs/TagHelpFile.htm">
```

See also: <TAG>

<TAGLAYOUT>, </TAGLAYOUT>

Description: The <TAGLAYOUT> tag is used to define the output generated by the tag editor. Whatever text appears in between <TAGLAYOUT> and </TAGLAYOUT> is pasted into the editor window when the OK button is clicked. Variables can be used within this section, as can conditional processing tags such as <WIZIF>. <TAGLAYOUT> takes no attributes as parameters.

Used in: Tag editors

Syntax:

```
<TAGLAYOUT> ... </TAGLAYOUT>
```

Example: This example generates content for a tag editor for a <CF_MYTAG> tag, which takes a single attribute named COLOR. Whatever color is specified in the $$\{color\} variable is inserted into the editor:

```
<TAGLAYOUT>
<CF_MYTAG COLOR="$${color}">
</TAGLAYOUT>
```

See also: <TAG>

<TEMPLATE>

Description: <TEMPLATE> is used to create the output file within a wizard. <TEMPLATE> must be used in between <WIZARD> and </WIZARD> tags. <TEMPLATE> takes four attributes, as listed in Table C.19.

Used in: Wizards

Syntax:

```
<TEMPLATE NAME="name" OUTPUTFILE="output file" OUTPUTPATH="output path"
➥ DESCRIPTION= description">
```

Table C.19 <WIZARD> **Attributes**

Attribute	Description	Notes
DESCRIPTION	Template description	Optional template description
NAME	Template name	Required template name
OUTPUTFILE	Output file	Required name of file to create
OUTPUTPATH	Output path	Required name of path for output file

Example: The following example is an excerpt from the LDAP Wizard bundled with ColdFusion Studio:

```
<TEMPLATE
  name="Ldap_LdapView.wml"
  outputFile="$${SafeApplicationName}_LdapView.cfm"
  outputPath="$${Location}"
  description="The main page of the LDAP directory viewer. It displays
➡ the entry attributes."
>
```

See also: <WIZARD>

<WIZARD>, </WIZARD>

Description: <WIZARD> is used to create ColdFusion Studio wizards. <WIZARD> takes three attributes, as shown in Table C.20. All the wizard text and tags must be placed between <WIZARD> and </WIZARD> tags.

Used in: Wizards

Syntax:

```
<WIZARD NAME="Name" CAPTION="Caption" IMAGE="image"> ... </WIZARD>
```

Table C.20 <WIZARD> **Attributes**

Attribute	Description	Notes
CAPTION	Wizard caption	Optional wizard caption
IMAGE	Image name	Optional name of image to display in a wizard dialog
NAME	Wizard name	Optional wizard name

Example: The following example is the opening and closing text of the LDAP Wizard bundled with ColdFusion Studio:

```
<WIZARD name="LdapWizard" caption="LDAP Directory Viewer Wizard" image="
➡..\\images\\wizardoutput.bmp">
 ... wizard goes here
</WIZARD>
```

See also: <PAGE>

<WIZIF>, <WIZELSEIF>, <WIZELSE>, </WIZIF>

Description: <WIZIF> and related tags are used to perform conditional processing within a wizard. Every <WIZIF> must be terminated by a </WIZIF> tag. One or more <WIZELSEIF> tags can also be used, as well as a single optional <WIZELSE>.

Used in: Tag editors, wizards

Syntax:

```
<WIZIF condition> ... <WIZELSEIF condition> ... <WIZELSE> ... </WIZIF>
```

Example: The following example is code that is used in most tag editors. If OPTIONLowerCaseTags is TRUE, the first block of code is executed; otherwise, the second block of code is executed.

```
<WIZIF OPTIONLowerCaseTags EQ 'true'>
...
<WIZELSE>
...
</WIZIF>
```

See also: <TAGLAYOUT>, <WIZARD>

<WIZINCLUDE>

Description: <WIZINCLUDE> is used to include one wizard page into another, much like the ColdFusion <CFINCLUDE> tag. <WIZINCLUDE> takes a single attribute, as listed in Table C.21.

Used in: Tag editors, wizards

Syntax:

```
<WIZINCLUDE TEMPLATE="file">
```

Table C.21   **<WIZINCLUDE> Attributes**

Attribute	Description	Notes
TEMPLATE	Template path	Required relative template path

Example: The following example includes a header file into a template:

```
<WIZINCLUDE TEMPLATE="header.vtm">
```

See also: <WIZARD>

<WIZLOOP>, <WIZBREAK>, <WIZCONTINUE>, </WIZLOOP>

Description: <WIZLOOP> and its related tags are used to provide looping capabilities within wizards and tag editors. <WIZLOOP> behaves much like ColdFusion's <CFLOOP> tag and supports multiple list types, as shown in Table C.22. <WIZCONTINUE> and <WIZBREAK> take no attributes. <WIZLOOP> attributes are listed in Table C.23.

Table C.22   `<WIZLOOP>` Types

Type	Description
INDEX	Loop from a number to a number
LIST	Loop over a list of elements
WHILE	Condition-based loop

Used in: Tag editors, wizards

Syntax:

```
<WIZLOOP CONDITION="condition" FROM="value" INDEX="variable" LIST="list"
➥ STEP="value" TO="value"> ... <WIZCONTINUE> ... <WIZBREAK> ... </WIZLOOP>
```

Table C.23   `<WIZLOOP>` Attributes

Attribute	Description	Notes
CONDITION	Loop condition	Condition for while loop
FROM	Base value	Base value for index loop
INDEX	Index variable	Variable to contain value in index loop
LIST	List of values	Values for list loop
STEP	Increment value	Increment value for index loop; defaults to 1
TO	High value	To value for index loop

Example: The following example shows the layout for a simple index loop:

```
<WIZLOOP INDEX="line" FROM="1" TO="10">
 ...
</WIZLOOP>
```

See also: `<TAGLAYOUT>`, `<WIZARD>`

`<WIZSET>`

Description: `<WIZSET>` is used to set variables, much like the ColdFusion `<CFSET>` tag.

Used in: Tag editors, wizards

Syntax:

```
<WIZSET variable=value>
```

Example: The following sample code is used in tag editors to conditionally create variables with attributes in the correct case:

```
<WIZIF OPTIONLowerCaseTags EQ 'true'>
 <WIZSET CFASSOCIATE='cfassociate'>
 <WIZSET BASETAG='basetag'>
 <WIZSET DATACOLLECTION='datacollection'>
<WIZELSE>
 <WIZSET CFASSOCIATE='CFASSOCIATE'>
 <WIZSET BASETAG='BASETAG'>
 <WIZSET DATACOLLECTION='DATACOLLECTION'>
</WIZIF>
```

See also: <TAGLAYOUT>, <WIZARD>

App

C

The WDDX.DTD File

With permission from Allaire, the complete XML DTD (Document Type Definition) for the WDDX data-exchange format is included here for your reference. It describes what elements (*tags*) and attributes can legally appear in a WDDX Packet. It also lays down some ground rules about how certain special values—such as dates, null values, and carriage returns—should be treated. Think of it as the specification for WDDX itself.

Refer to Chapter 16, "Using WDDX to Create Distributed Applications," and Chapter 17, "Advanced WDDX Integration," for an in-depth explanation of WDDX and its use in ColdFusion templates and other applications.

N O T E This appendix contains the latest version, printed here verbatim, of the DTD that was available at the time of this book's writing. It may be revised in the future. You can find the latest version of the DTD on Allaire's Web site at `http://www.allaire.com/developer/wddx`. ▓

The DTD is also provided on this book's CD-ROM. The filename is `wddx_0090.dtd`. You can find it in the folder for Chapter 16.

```
<!-- **************************************************************************
     WDDX DTD:

     Author: Simeon Simeonov (simeons@allaire.com)

     Last modified: 9/28/1998

     Copyright (c) 1998 Allaire Corp. http://www.allaire.com
-->

<!-- **************************************************************************
     Introductory Notes:


     What is WDDX:

     WDDX stands for Web Distributed Data eXchange. WDDX is a mechanism for
     exchanging complex data structures between application environments. It
     has been designed with web applications in mind. WDDX consists of a
     language and platform neutral representation of instantiated data based
     on XML 1.0 (which is defined using this DTD) and a set of serializer/
     deserializer modules for every environment that uses WDDX. The process
     of creating an XML representation of application data is called
     serialization. The process of instantiating application data from a
     WDDX XML representation is called deserialization.

     WDDX packets:

     The WDDX DTD can be used to validate WDDX packets. Packets are
     representations of instantiated data structures in application
     environments. The following is an example of a WDDX packet:
```

```
<?xml version='1.0'?>
<!DOCTYPE wddxPacket SYSTEM 'wddx_0090.dtd'>
<wddxPacket version='0.9'>
    <header/>
    <data>
        <struct>
            <var name='s'>
                <string>a string</string>
            </var>
            <var name='n'>
                <number>-12.456</number>
            </var>
            <var name='d'>
                <dateTime>1998-06-12T04:32:12</dateTime>
            </var>
            <var name='b'>
                <boolean value='true'/>
            </var>
            <var name='a'>
                <array length='2'>
                    <number>10</number>
                    <string>second element</string>
                </array>
            </var>
            <var name='obj'>
                <struct>
                    <var name='s'>
                        <string>a string</string>
                    </var>
                    <var name='n'>
                        <number>-12.456</number>
                    </var>
                </struct>
            </var>
            <var name='r'>
                <recordset rowCount='2' fieldNames='NAME,AGE'>
                    <field name='NAME'>
                        <string>John Doe</string>
                        <string>Jane Doe</string>
                    </field>
                    <field name='AGE'>
                        <number>34</number>
                        <number>31</number>
                    </field>
                </recordset>
            </var>
        </struct>
    </data>
</wddxPacket>
```

It defines a root level object that is a structure (also known as
an associative array) of six properties:

- s which is the string 'a string',
- n which is the number -12.456,
- d which is the date-time value June 12, 1998 4:32:12am,

- b which is the boolean value true,
- a which is an array of two elements (10 and 'second element'),
- obj which is a structure with two properties s and n, and
- r which is a recordset of two rows with fields NAME and AGE.

Basic data types:

WDDX supports the following basic data types: boolean (true/false), number, date-time, and string.

Numbers-
Numbers are internally represented with floating point numbers. Because of differences between WDDX-enabled languages, the range of numbers has been restricted to +/-1.7E+/-308. The precision has been restricted to 15 digits after the decimal point. These requirements are consistent with an 8-byte floating-point representation.

Date-time values-
Date-time values are encoded according to the full form of ISO8601, e.g., 1998-9-15T09:05:32+4:0. Note that single-digit values for months, days, hours, minutes, or seconds do not need to be zero-prefixed. While timezone information is optional, it must be successfully parsed and used to convert to local date-time values. Efforts should me made to ensure that the internal representation of date-time values does not suffer from Y2K problems and covers a sufficient range of dates. In particular, years must always be represented with four digits.

Strings-
Strings can be of arbitrary length and must not contain embedded nulls. To facilitate the inclusion of control characters in strings, the <string> element can contain <char code='??'/> elements. The value of the code attribute is a two-character representation of the UTF-8 hex code for a given control character. For example, <char code='0C'/> represents the form feed character. Control characters are characters in the UTF-8 range 00-1F. Note that tab (09) and newline (0A) characters can be included directly in XML text. The XML 1.0 specification Section 2.11 requires XML processors to not pass carriage return (0D) characters to applications.

Note on end-of-line handling-
End-of-line characters have platform and programming language specific representations. Different application environments may use either a single newline (0A), a single carriage return (0D), or a carriage return and newline combination (0D0A). For the purposes of successful data encoding and translation the elements <char code='0A'/> and <char code='0D'/> must be used to encode newline and carriage return characters when they should be preserved in the deserialized string. Note that Section 2.11 of the XML 1.0 specification requires XML processors to translate all occurrences of carriage returns and the carriage return, newline combination to a single newline character. Therefore, for the purposes of XML, end-of-line is represented by a single newline character.

Complex data types:

WDDX supports the following complex data types: arrays, structures, and recordsets.

Arrays-
Arrays are integer-indexed collections of objects of arbitrary type.
The starting index value is usually 0 with the notable exception of
CFML whose arrays have an initial index value of 1. Because of these
differences working with array indices can lead to non-portable data.

Structures-
Structures are string-indexed collections of objects of arbitrary type.
In many languages they are known as associative arrays. Structures
contain one or more variables. Because some of the languages supported
by WDDX are not case-sensitive, no two variable names can differ only
by their case. Variable names must satisfy the regular expression
[_.0-9A-Za-z]+ where the '.' stands for a period, not 'any character'.

Recordsets-
Recordsets are tabular data encapsulations: a set of named fields with
the same number of rows of data. Only simple data types can be stored in
recordsets. For tabular data storage of complex data types, an array of
structures should be used. Because some of the languages supported by
WDDX are not case-sensitive, no two field names can differ only by
their case. Field names must satisfy the regular expression
[_.0-9A-Za-z]+ where the '.' stands for a period, not 'any character'.

Data type comparisons:

The following table compares the basic WDDX data types with those of
languages/technologies commonly used on the Web.

WDDX Type	COM	Java Type	ECMAScript Type
boolean	boolean	java.lang.Boolean	boolean
number	float?	java.lang.Double	number
dateTime	DATE	java.lang.Date	Date
string	BSTR	java.lang.String	string
array	VARIANT array	java.lang.Vector	Array
struct	IWDDXStruct	java.lang.HashTable	Object
recordset	IWDDXRecordset	java.sql.RecordSet?	WddxRecordset

More on data types:

Null values-
WDDX provides no notion of a null object. Null objects should be
serialized to empty strings. Upon deserialization it is up to the
component performing the operation to determine whether and where
should empty strings be deserialized to null values. Null support
is one area where future extensions are likely.

Serialization model-
WDDX serializes data using a model of pure aggregation. It has no
mechanism for handling object references. Aliased references will
result in multiple object instances being deserialized. WDDX
serialization applied to a data structure that has cyclical references
will most likely result in infinite iteration/recursion, depending on
the serializer implementation. Object references support is another
area of potential future investigation.

Ch
D

```
    DTD verbosity:

    This DTD is purposefully made verbose to aid the readability of WDDX
    packets. If packet size becomes an issue, compressing WDDX packets
    using an HTTP-safe real time compression algorithm is likely to be a
    much more appropriate solution than, for example, a DTD that uses one
    character element and attribute names. Some experiments conducted at
    Allaire suggest that 5 - 15 fold compression rates are achievable.

-->

<!ELEMENT wddxPacket (header, data)>
<!ATTLIST wddxPacket
        version CDATA #FIXED "0.9">

<!ELEMENT header (comment?)>

<!ELEMENT comment (#PCDATA)>

<!ELEMENT data (boolean ¦ number ¦ dateTime ¦ string ¦ array ¦ struct ¦
➥recordset)*>

<!ELEMENT boolean EMPTY>
<!ATTLIST boolean
        value (true ¦ false) #REQUIRED>

<!ELEMENT string (#PCDATA ¦ char)*>

<!ELEMENT char EMPTY>
<!ATTLIST char
        code CDATA #REQUIRED>

<!ELEMENT number (#PCDATA)>

<!ELEMENT dateTime (#PCDATA)>

<!ELEMENT array (boolean ¦ number ¦ dateTime ¦ string ¦ array ¦ struct ¦
➥recordset)*>
<!ATTLIST array
        length CDATA #REQUIRED>

<!ELEMENT struct (var*)>

<!ELEMENT var (boolean ¦ number ¦ dateTime ¦ string ¦ array ¦ struct ¦
➥recordset)>
<!ATTLIST var
        name CDATA #REQUIRED>

<!ELEMENT recordset (field*)>
<!ATTLIST recordset
        rowCount CDATA #REQUIRED
        fieldNames CDATA #REQUIRED>

<!ELEMENT field (boolean ¦ number ¦ dateTime ¦ string)*>
<!ATTLIST field
        name CDATA #REQUIRED>
```

Index

G

Installation Instructions

Windows 95/NT 4

1. Insert the CD-ROM into your CD-ROM drive (see NOTE at bottom).
2. From the Windows desktop, double-click the My Computer icon.
3. Double-click the icon representing your CD-ROM drive.
4. Double-click the START.EXE icon to run the multimedia user interface.

NOTE: If Windows 95/NT 4.0 in installed on your computer and you have the AutoPlay feature enabled, the START.EXE program begins automatically whenever you place the disc in your CD-ROM drive.

Read This Before Opening Software

By opening this package, you are agreeing to be bound by the following:

This software is copyrighted and all rights are reserved by the publisher and its licensers. You are licensed to use this software on a single computer. You may copy the software for backup or archival purposes only. Making copies of the software for any other purpose is a violation of United States copyright laws. THIS SOFTWARE IS SOLD AS IS, WITHOUT WARRANTY OF ANY KIND, EITHER EXPRESSED OR IMPLIED, INCLUDING BUT NOT LIMITED TO THE IMPLIED WARRANTIES OF MERCHANTABILITY AND FITNESS FOR A PARTICULAR PURPOSE. Neither the publisher nor its dealers and distributors nor its licensers assume any liability for any alleged or actual damages arising from the use of this software. (Some states do not allow exclusion of implied warranties, so the exclusion may not apply to you.)

The entire contents of this disc and the compilation of the software are copyrighted and protected by United States copyright laws. The individual programs on the disc are copyrighted by the authors or owners of each program. Each program has its own use permissions and limitations. To use each program, you must follow the individual requirements and restrictions detailed for each. Do not use a program if you do not agree to follow its licensing agreement.